THE ESSENTIAL C
CASEBOOK
SECOND EDITION

Craig A. Smith

Professor of Law
Santa Barbara/Ventura Colleges of Law
Member of the California Bar

Copyright © 2019 by Craig A. Smith

All rights reserved. This book or any portion thereof may not be reproduced or used in any manner whatsoever without the express written permission of the publisher except for the use of brief quotations in a book review or scholarly journal.

No copyright is claimed in government works that appear in this book.

First Publication: 2019
ISBN 978-0-9759876-9-8
(Print Edition)
Also available in digital format.

lawschoolhelp.com
PO Box 90103
Santa Barbara, CA 93190
www.lawschoolhelp.com
www.essentialcivilpro.com

Note on Citations

For two frequently cited treatises that appear in the notes and comments that follow the cases, I have used shortened versions. They are as follows: Friedenthal, Kane and Miller, Civil Procedure (4th ed. 2015), cited as Friedenthal; Wright and Kane, Law of Federal Courts (8th ed. 2016), cited as Wright.

Prepare, Review and Study on the Web

lawschoolhelp.com

Companion Book

www.essentialcivilpro.com

CONTENTS

Chapter 1 — 1

PERSONAL JURISDICTION — 1
  Personal Jurisdiction Based on Presence — 2
    Pennoyer v. Neff — 2
  Personal Jurisdiction Based on Domicile — 10
    Milliken v. Meyer — 10
  Personal Jurisdiction Based on Consent — 12
    Hess v. Palowski — 12
  Personal Jurisdiction Based on Minimum Contacts — 14
    International Shoe Co. v. Washington — 15
    Hanson v. Denckla — 19
  Jurisdiction Over Things and The Absorption of *In Rem* Jurisdiction — 22
    Shaffer v. Heitner — 23
  The Refinement of the Minimum Contacts Analysis — 29
    Asahi Metal Industry Co., Ltd. v. Superior Court — 29
    J. McIntyre Machinery, Ltd. v. Nicastro — 36
    Abdouch v. Lopez — 42
  General In Personam Jurisdiction Over Corporations — 49
    Goodyear Dunlop Tires Operations, S.A. v. Brown — 49
    Daimler AG v. Bauman — 53
  The Continued Viability of Presence — 58
    Burnham vs. Superior Court — 58
  The Constitutional Requirement of Notice — 65
    Mullane v. Central Hanover Bank & Trust — 65
  The Mechanics of Service of Process: Federal and State Court — 72
  Challenge and Waiver of Jurisdiction — 73
Venue — 74
    Thompson v. Greyhound Lines, Inc. — 75
  Transfer of Venue and the Doctrine of *Forum Non Conveniens* — 78
    Piper Aircraft v. Reyno — 78
    Atlantic Marine Construction Co. v. U.S. District Court — 83

Chapter 2 — 89

SUBJECT MATTER JURISDICTION — 89
  Introduction — 89
    Subject Matter Jurisdiction of the Federal Courts — 90

i

Federal Question Jurisdiction — 90
   Boyle v. MTV Networks — 91
Diversity Jurisdiction — 95
   Mas v. Perry — 96
   Hawkins v. Masters Farms, Inc. — 99
   Redner v. Sanders — 102
   Eze v. Yellow Cab Co. of Alexandria, Va., Inc. — 104
Citizenship of Corporations — 105
   Hertz Corp. v. Friend — 105
Amount in Controversy — 108
Aggregation of Claims to Satisfy Amount in Controversy — 108
Supplemental Jurisdiction — 109
   United Mine Workers of America v. Gibbs — 110
   Szendrey-Ramos v. First Bancorp — 115
Removal of Cases From State Court to Federal Court — 119
Restrictions on Removal — 119
   McCurtain County Production Corp. v. Cowett — 120
   Caterpillar Inc. v. Lewis — 122
The Mechanics of Removal — 125
Other Areas of Federal Subject Matter Jurisdiction — 125
Challenging Subject Matter Jurisdiction in the Federal Courts — 126

Chapter 3 — 127

THE *ERIE* DOCTRINE, STATE LAW IN THE FEDERAL COURTS — 127
   Erie Railroad Co. v. Tompkins — 127
   Guaranty Trust Co. v. York — 133
   Byrd v. Blue Ridge Rural Electric Cooperative, Inc. — 134
   Hanna v. Plumer — 136
   Sibbach v. Wilson & Co., Inc. — 141
   Stewart Organization, Inc. v. Ricoh Corp. — 144
Determining State Law Under *Erie* — 148
   McKenna v. Ortho Pharmaceutical Corp. — 148

Chapter 4 — 151

Pleading
   Code Pleading in California — 151
     Semole v. Sansoucie — 152
     Careau & Co. v. Security Pacific Business Credit, Inc. — 155
     The People Ex Rel. Department of Transportation, v. Superior Court — 162

Pleading Under the Federal Rules	**165**
Bell Atlantic Corp. v. Twombly	165
Ashcroft v. Iqbal	169
Heightened Pleading Requirements for Particular Claims	**177**
Stansfield v. Starkey	177
Ethical Constraints on Pleading	**177**
Bridges v. Diesel Service, Inc.	180
Walker v. Norwest Corp.	182
Christian v. Mattel, Inc.	184
Responding to the Complaint	**188**
Default	**188**
King Vision Pay-Per-View Ltd. v. Spice Restaurant & Lounge, Inc.	188
Challenging the Sufficiency of the Complaint	**190**
Pre-Answer Motion	**190**
Northrop v. Hoffman of Simsbury, Inc.	190
More on Rule 12(b)	**194**
Answers	**194**
King Vision Pay Per View v. Dimitri's Restaurant	195
Affirmative Defenses	**196**
Jones v. Bock	197
Amendments to Pleadings	**200**
Beeck v. Aquaslide 'N' Dive Corp.	201
The Relation Back Doctrine	**204**
Smeltzley v. Nicholson Mfg. Co.	205
Moore v. Baker	211
Fictitiously Named "Doe" Defendants	**213**
Streicher v. Tommy's Electric Company	214

Chapter 5

	219
JOINDER OF PARTIES AND CLAIMS	**219**
Joinder of Claims	**219**
Original Claims	**219**
Counterclaims	**220**
Plant v. Blazer Financial Services, Inc.	220
Burlington Northern Railroad Co. v. Strong	224
Crossclaims	**227**
Third Party Claims: Impleading "Strangers" Into the Lawsuit	**227**
Price v. CTB, Inc.	228
Plaintiffs and FRCP 14	**230**
Owen Equipment & Erection Co. v. Kroger	232
Joinder of Parties	**235**
Permissive Joinder of Parties	**235**

Mosley v. General Motors Corp.   235
Baughman v. Lee County, Mississippi   239
Compulsory Joinder of Parties   242
Temple v. Synthes Corp., Ltd.   243
Helzberg's Diamond Shops, Inc. v. Valley West Des Moines Shopping   244
Intervention   249
Natural Resources Defense Council, Inc. v. U.S. Nuclear Regulatory   251
Martin v. Wilks   255
Interpleader   260
State Farm Fire & Casualty Co. v. Tashire   260
    Statutory or Rule Interpleader?   265

Chapter 6   267

CLASS ACTIONS   267
  Hansberry v. Lee   267
  The Problem of Personal Jurisdiction in the Class Action   271
  Phillips Petroleum Co. v. Shutts   271
  Jurisdiction Over Class Actions in Federal Courts   275
  Standard Fire Insurance Co v. Knowles   276
  Rule 23   279
  Chandler v. Southwest Jeep-Eagle, Inc.   282
  Wal-Mart Stores, Inc. v. Dukes   288
  The Requirement of Notice in Class Actions   299
  Settlement of the Class Action   300
  Amchem Products, Inc. v. Windsor   301
  In re: Prudential Ins. Co. America Sales Practice Litigation Agent etc.   308
  Surrendering the Right to Bring a Class Action   316
  American Express Co. v. Italian Colors Restaurant   316

Chapter 7   321

PROVISIONAL REMEDIES   321
  Attachment and Garnishment   321
  Sniadach v. Family Finance Corp.   321
  Fuentes v. Shevin   323
  Mitchell v. W.T. Grant Co.   330
  Preliminary Injunctions and Temporary Restraining Orders   336
  Winter v. Natural Resources Defense Council, Inc.,   336
  Temporary Restraining Orders   342

Chapter 8

DISCOVERY ... 345
DISCOVERY PROCEDURES AND METHODS ... 345
Depositions by Oral Examination ... 345
Interrogatories ... 345
Demands to Inspect or Produce Documents ... 345
Requests for Admission ... 346
Physical and Mental Examinations ... 346
THE SCOPE OF DISCOVERY ... 346
Butler v. Rigsby ... 346
Favale v. Roman Catholic Diocese of Bridgeport ... 347
LIMITATIONS ON DISCOVERY ... 349
DISCOVERY AND PRIVACY ... 352
Morales v. Superior Court ... 352
Renfifo v. Erevos Enterprises, Inc. ... 352
TRIAL PREPARATION MATERIAL ... 357
Hickman v. Taylor ... 359
Nacht & Lewis Architects, Inc., v. Superior Court ... 360
Dowden v. Superior Court ... 364
EXPERT WITNESSES ... 366
Thompson v. The Haskell Co. ... 373
Chiquita International Ltd. v. M/V Bolero Reefer ... 374
ENSURING COMPLIANCE AND CONTROLLING DISCOVERY ABUSES ... 375
SANCTIONS FOR DISCOVERY VIOLATIONS ... 377
ROSALES V. THERMEX-THERMATRON ... 377
SANCTIONS FOR FAILING TO PRESERVE EVIDENCE ... 379
ZUBULAKE V. UBS WARBURG LLP ... 379
NOTES ON DISCOVERY SANCTIONS ... 377

Chapter 9

RESOLUTION WITHOUT TRIAL ... 387
DEFAULT AND DEFAULT JUDGMENTS ... 387
Beeman v. Burling ... 387
Peralta v. Heights Medical Center ... 387
ARBITRATION ... 396
Ferguson v. Countrywide Credit Industries, Inc. ... 397
AT&T Mobility LLC v. Concepcion ... 398
SCOPE OF REVIEW OF THE ARBITRATOR'S DECISION ... 402
Ferguson v. Writers Guild of America, West ... 409

SUMMARY JUDGMENT — 413
- *Celotex Corp. v. Catrett* — 413
- *Aguilar v. Atlantic Richfield Co.* — 416
- *Houchens v. American Home Assurance Co.* — 422
- *Tolan v. Cotton* — 425
- *Bias v. Advantage International, Inc.* — 429
- **TIMING OF THE MOTION FOR SUMMARY JUDGMENT** — 433

Chapter 10 — 435

THE TRIAL — 435
PRETRIAL CONFERENCES AND ORDERS — 435
- *Monfore v. Phillips* — 436
THE JUDGE — 439
THE RIGHT TO A TRIAL BY JURY — 440
- *C & K Engineering Contractors v. Amber Steel Company, Inc.* — 441
MAKING THE DEMAND FOR A JURY TRIAL — 445
CHALLENGING THE JURY'S VERDICT IN THE TRIAL COURT — 445
MOTIONS FOR JUDGMENT AS A MATTER OF LAW — 445
- *Reid v. San Pedro, Los Angeles & Salt Lake Railroad* — 446
- *Pennsylvania Railroad v. Chamberlain* — 448
POST VERDICT MOTIONS FOR JUDGMENT AS A MATTER OF LAW — 452
- *Norton v. Snapper Power Equipment* — 452
- *Lind v. Schenley Industries* — 454
MOTION FOR A NEW TRIAL — 457
- *Peterson v. Wilson* — 457
- *Tribble v. Bruin* — 461
COMBINING THE MOTIONS FOR JUDGMENT AS A MATTER OF LAW AND MOTION FOR A NEW TRIAL — 464

Chapter 11 — 465

APPEAL — 465
WHO CAN APPEAL? — 465
- *Aetna Casualty & Surety Co. v. Cunningham* — 465
THE FINAL ORDER RULE — 466
- *Reise v. Board of Regents of The University of Wisconsin* — 467
EXCEPTIONS TO THE FINAL JUDGMENT RULE — 468
- *Liberty Mutual Insurance Co. v. Wetzel* — 469
PRACTICAL FINALITY — 472
- *Lauro Lines S.R.L. v. Chasser* — 472
OTHER EXCEPTIONS TO THE FINAL JUDGMENT RULE — 475
INJUNCTIONS 28 U.S.C. 1292(A) — 475

Table of Contents vii

INTERLOCUTORY APPEALS UNDER 28 U.S.C. 1292(B)	475
SHORT CIRCUITING THE APPEALS PROCESS THROUGH WRITS	476
Omaha Indemnity Company v. Superior Court	476
SCOPE OF REVIEW	481
LAW AND FACT	481
Anderson v. Bessemer City	481
THE HARMLESS ERROR DOCTRINE	485
Harnden v. Jayco, Inc.	486

Chapter 12

489

FORMER ADJUDICATION	489
TERMINOLOGY	489
IDENTITY OF CLAIMS	490
Ison v. Thomas	490
Sawyer v. First City Financial Corporation, LTD	493
Frier v. City of Vandalia	497
IDENTITY OF PARTIES	500
Taylor v. Sturgell	501
Searle Brothers v. Searle	507
THE REQUIREMENT THAT THE JUDGMENT BE "ON THE MERITS"	510
Gargallo v. Merrill Lynch, Pierce, Fenner & Smith	510
ISSUE PRECLUSION - COLLATERAL ESTOPPEL	513
IDENTITY OF PARTIES AND MUTUALITY OF PRECLUSION	514
Bernhard v. Bank of America	514
Parklane Hosiery Co. v. Shore Kemakdam	522
IDENTITY OF ISSUES	522
Teitelbaum Furs, Inc. v. The Dominion Insurance Company, Ltd.	522
ACTUALLY LITIGATED AND DECIDED	525
Illinois Central Gulf Railroad v. Parks	525
FULL FAITH AND CREDIT	527
Durfee v. Duke	527
OBTAINING RELIEF FROM A JUDGMENT	530
United States v. Beggerly	530

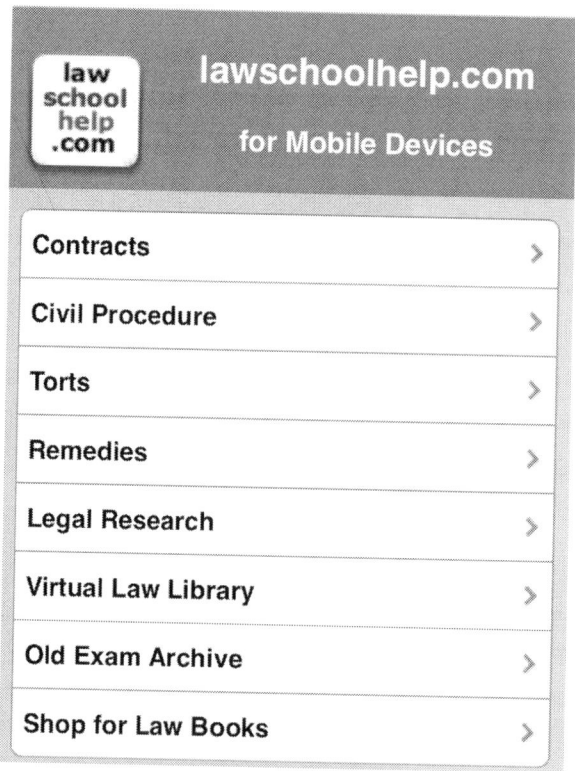

www.lawschoolhelp.com

CHAPTER 1

Personal Jurisdiction

Assume that you have graduated from law school and have passed the bar. A client comes to you with a legal problem, and let's further assume that things have deteriorated to the point where a lawsuit must be filed. The first decision you must make is what court to file the lawsuit in. Can you file in any court? Or is your choice limited? Ideally you would want to file in a court that is in a location that is convenient to both your client and yourself but suppose that court is not convenient to the defendant? Is that something you have to consider in making your choice of where to file? Before you can file, you must determine what court has jurisdiction to hear your particular case. Jurisdiction refers to the power of the court to decide a case. I.e., to render a decision that will be recognized and enforced by authorities and other courts.

There are two types of Jurisdiction: subject matter jurisdiction and jurisdiction over the parties. A court must have both types of jurisdiction before it has jurisdiction to decide the case. This chapter deals with jurisdiction over the parties.

> **Personal Jurisdiction**
>
> Whether someone from another state can be forced to come to the state where the lawsuit was filed to defend.
>
> Depends upon a sufficient connection between the defendant and the forum state.

Jurisdiction over the parties (personal, or *in personam* jurisdiction) relates to the question of whether someone from another state, Alaska, New York, or Nevada can be forced to come to the state where the lawsuit was filed (the "forum state"), for example, California, to defend against the lawsuit. The existence of personal jurisdiction depends upon a sufficient connection between the defendant and the forum state to make it fair to require defense of the action in the forum.

A person may be subject to in personam jurisdiction on any of the following basis: presence, domicile, consent or minimum contacts.

> **A person is subject to in personam jurisdiction on any of the following theories:**
>
> 1. Presence
> 2. Domicile
> 3. Consent
> 4. Minimum Contacts

We start from the premise that the Due Process Clause of the Fourteenth Amendment to the United States Constitution places some limit on the power of state courts to enter binding judgments against persons not served with process within their boundaries. The rules governing the ability of a court to exercise personal jurisdiction, particularly over a defendant who neither resides in, or is found in, the forum state (the state in which the lawsuit was filed) has evolved dramatically over the last 150 years. The cases that follow demonstrate that evolution.

Personal Jurisdiction Based on Presence

Pennoyer v. Neff
95 U.S. 714 (1877)

(Title to RP)

[This was an ejectment action brought in federal court under diversity jurisdiction. Pennoyer, the defendant in that action, held the land under a deed purchased in a sheriff's sale conducted to realize on a judgment for attorney's fees obtained against Neff in a previous action by one Mitchell. At the time of Mitchell's suit in an Oregon State court, Neff was a nonresident of Oregon. An Oregon statute allowed service by publication on nonresidents who had property in the State, and Mitchell had used that procedure to bring Neff before the court. The United States Circuit Court for the District of Oregon, in which Neff brought his ejectment action, refused to recognize the validity of the judgment against Neff in Mitchell's suit, and accordingly awarded the land to Neff. The Supreme Court granted review.]

MR. JUSTICE FIELD delivered the opinion of the court.

This is an action to recover the possession of a tract of land, of the alleged value of

$15,000, situated in the State of Oregon. The plaintiff asserts title to the premises by a patent of the United States issued to him in 1866, under the act of Congress of Sept. 27, 1850, usually known as the Donation Law of Oregon. The defendant claims to have acquired the premises under a sheriff's deed, made upon a sale of the property on execution issued upon a judgment recovered against the plaintiff in one of the circuit courts of the State. The case turns upon the validity of this judgment. (dispositive issue)

It appears from the record that the judgment was rendered in February, 1866, in favor of J. H. Mitchell, for less than $300, including costs, in an action brought by him upon a demand for services as an attorney; that, at the time the action was commenced and the judgment rendered, the defendant therein, the plaintiff here, was a non-resident of the State that he was not personally served with process, and did not appear therein; and that the judgment was entered upon his default in not answering the complaint, upon a constructive service of summons by publication.

The Code of Oregon provides for such service when an action is brought against a non-resident and absent defendant, who has property within the State. It also provides, where the action is for the recovery of money or damages, for the attachment of the property of the non-resident. And it also declares that no natural person is subject to the jurisdiction of a court of the State, 'unless he appear in the court, or be found within the State, or be a resident thereof, or have property therein; and, in the last case, only to the extent of such property at the time the jurisdiction attached.' Construing this latter provision to mean, that, in an action for money or damages where a defendant does not appear in the court, and is not found within the State, and is not a resident thereof, but has property therein, the jurisdiction of the court extends only over such property, the declaration expresses a principle of general, if not universal, law.

The authority of every tribunal is necessarily restricted by the territorial limits of the State in which it is established. Any attempt to exercise authority beyond those limits would be deemed in every other forum, as has been said by this court, in illegitimate assumption of power, and be resisted as mere abuse. D'Arcy v. Ketchum et al., 11 How. 165. In the case against the plaintiff, the property here in controversy sold under the judgment rendered was not attached, nor in any way brought under the jurisdiction of the court. Its first connection with the case was caused by a levy of the execution. It was not, therefore, disposed of pursuant to any adjudication, but only in enforcement of a personal judgment, having no relation to the property, rendered against a non-resident without service of process upon him in the action, or his appearance therein.

The court below did not consider that an attachment of the property was essential to its jurisdiction or to the validity of the sale but held that the judgment was invalid from defects in the affidavit upon which the order of publication was obtained, and in the affidavit by which the publication was proved.

There is some difference of opinion among the members of this court as to the rulings upon these alleged defects. The majority are of opinion that inasmuch as the statute requires, for an order of publication, that certain facts shall appear by affidavit to the satisfaction of the court or judge, defects in such affidavit can only be taken advantage of on appeal, or by some other direct proceeding, and cannot be urged to impeach the judgment collaterally. The majority of the court are also of opinion that the provision of the statute requiring proof of the publication in a newspaper to be made by the 'affidavit of the printer, or his foreman, or his principal clerk,' is satisfied when the affidavit is made by the editor of the paper. The term 'printer,' in their judgment, is there used not to indicate the person who sets up the type,-he does not usually have a foreman or clerks,- it is rather used as synonymous with publisher. ...

If, therefore, we were confined to the rulings of the court below upon the defects in the affidavits mentioned, we should be unable to uphold its decision. But it was also contended in that court, and is insisted upon here, that the judgment in the State court against the plaintiff was void for want of personal service of process on him, or of his appearance in the action in which it was rendered and that the premises in controversy could not be subjected to the payment of the demand of a resident creditor except by a proceeding in rem; that is, by a direct proceeding against the property for that purpose. If these positions are sound, the ruling of the Circuit Court as to the invalidity of that judgment must be sustained, notwithstanding our dissent from the reasons upon which it was made. And that they are sound would seem to follow from two well-established principles of public law respecting the jurisdiction of an independent State over persons and property.

The several States of the Union are not, it is true, in every respect independent, many of the right and powers which originally belonged to them being now vested in the government created by the Constitution. But, except as restrained and limited by that instrument, they possess and exercise the authority of independent States, and the principles of public law to which we have referred are applicable to them. One of these principles is, that every State possesses exclusive jurisdiction and sovereignty over persons and property within its territory. As a consequence, every State has the power to determine for itself the civil status and capacities of its inhabitants; to prescribe the subjects upon which they may contract, the forms and solemnities with which their contracts shall be executed, the rights and obligations arising from them, and the mode in which their validity shall be determined and their obligations enforced; and also the regulate the manner and conditions upon which property situated within such territory, both personal and real, may be acquired, enjoyed, and transferred.

The other principle of public law referred to follows from the one mentioned; that is, that no State can exercise direct jurisdiction and authority over persons or property without its territory. Story, Confl. Laws, c. 2; Wheat. Int. Law, pt. 2, c. 2. The several States are of equal dignity and authority, and the independence of one implies the exclusion of power from all others. And so it is laid down by jurists, as an elementary principle, that the laws of one State have no operation outside of its territory, except so far as is allowed by comity; and that no tribunal established by it can extend its process beyond that territory so as to subject either persons or property to its decisions. 'Any exertion of authority of this sort beyond this limit,' says Story, 'is a mere nullity, and incapable of binding such persons or property in any other tribunals.' Story, Confl. Laws, sect. 539.

But as contracts made in one State may be enforceable only in another State, and property may be held by non-residents, the exercise of the jurisdiction which every State is admitted to possess over persons and property within its own territory will often affect persons and property without it. To any influence exerted in this way by a State affecting persons resident or property situated elsewhere, no objection can be justly taken; whilst any direct exertion of authority upon them, in an attempt to give ex-territorial operation to its laws, or to enforce an ex- territorial jurisdiction by its tribunals, would be deemed an encroachment upon the independence of the State in which the persons are domiciled or the property is situated, and be resisted as usurpation.

Thus the State, through its tribunals, may compel persons domiciled within its limits to execute, in pursuance of their contracts respecting property elsewhere situated, instruments in such form and with such solemnities as to transfer the title, so far as such formalities can be complied with; and the exercise of this jurisdiction in no manner interferes with the supreme control over the property by the State within which it is situated.

So the State, through its tribunals, may subject property situated within its limits owned by non-residents to the payment of the demand of its own citizens against them; and the exercise of this jurisdiction in no respect infringes upon the sovereignty of the State where the owners are domiciled. Every State owes protection to its own citizens; and, when non- residents deal with them, it is a legitimate and just exercise of authority to hold and appropriate any property owned by such non-residents to satisfy the claims of its citizens. It is in virtue of the State's jurisdiction over the property of the non-resident situated within its limits that its tribunals can inquire into that non-resident's obligations to its own citizens, and the inquiry can then be carried only to the extent necessary to control the disposition of the property. If the non- resident have no property in the State, there is nothing upon which the tribunals can adjudicate. . .

. . . If, without personal service, judgments in personam, obtained ex parte against non- residents and absent parties, upon mere publication of process, which, in the great majority of cases, would never be seen by the parties interested, could be upheld and enforced, they would be the constant instruments of fraud and oppression. Judgments for all sorts of claims upon contracts and for torts, real or pretended, would be thus obtained, under which property would be seized, when the evidence of the transactions upon which they were founded, if they ever had any existence, had perished.

Substituted service by publication, or in any other authorized form, may be sufficient to inform parties of the object of proceedings taken where property is once brought under the control of the court by seizure or some equivalent act. The law assumes that property is always in the possession of its owner, in person or by agent; and it proceeds upon the theory that its seizure will inform him, not only that it is taken into the custody of the court, but that he must look to any proceedings authorized by law upon such seizure for its condemnation and sale. Such service may also be sufficient in cases where the object of the action is to reach and dispose of property in the State, or of some interest therein, by enforcing a contract or a lien respecting the same, or to partition it among different owners, or, when the public is a party, to condemn and appropriate it for a public purpose. In other words, such service may answer in all actions which are substantially proceedings in rem. But where the entire object of the action is to determine the personal rights and obligations of the defendants, that is, where the suit is merely in personam, constructive service in this form upon a non-resident is ineffectual for any purpose.

Process from the tribunals of one State cannot run into another State and summon parties there domiciled to leave its territory and respond to proceedings against them. Publication of process or notice within the State where the tribunal sits cannot create any greater obligation upon the non-resident to appear. Process sent to him out of the State, and process published within it, are equally unavailing in proceedings to establish his personal liability.

The want of authority of the tribunals of a State to adjudicate upon the obligations of non-residents, where they have no property within its limits, is not denied by the court below: but the position is assumed, that, where they have property within the State, it is immaterial whether the property is in the first instance brought under the control of the court by attachment or some other equivalent act, and afterwards applied by its judgment to the satisfaction of demands against its owner; or such demands be first established in a personal action, and the property of the non-resident be afterwards seized and sold on execution. But the answer to this position has already been given in the statement, that the jurisdiction of the court to inquire into and determine his obligations at all is only incidental to its jurisdiction over the property. Its jurisdiction in that respect cannot be made to depend upon facts to be ascertained after it has tried the cause and rendered the judgment. If the judgment be previously void, it will not become valid by the subsequent discovery of property of the defendant, or by his subsequent acquisition of it.

The judgment, if void when rendered, will always remain void: it cannot occupy the doubtful position of being valid if property be found, and void if there be none. Even if the position assumed were confined to cases where the non-resident defendant possessed property in the State at the commencement of the action, it would still make the validity of the proceedings and judgment depend upon the question whether, before the levy of the execution, the defendant had or had not disposed of the property. If before the levy the property should be sold, then, according to this position, the judgment would not be binding. This doctrine would introduce a new element of uncertainty in judicial proceedings. The contrary is the law: the validity of every judgment depends upon the jurisdiction of the court before it is rendered, not upon what may occur subsequently...

The force and effect of judgments rendered against non-residents without personal service of process upon them, or their voluntary appearance, have been the subject of frequent consideration in the courts of the United States and of the several States, as attempts have been made to enforce such judgments in States other than those in which they were rendered, under the provision of the Constitution requiring that 'full faith and credit shall be given in each State to the public acts, records, and judicial proceedings of every other State;' and the act of Congress providing for the mode of authenticating such acts, records, and proceedings, and declaring that, when thus authenticated, 'they shall have such faith and credit given to them in every court within the United States as they have by law or usage in the courts of the State from which they are or shall or taken.'

In the earlier cases, it was supposed that the act gave to all judgments the same effect in other States which they had by law in the State where rendered. But this view was afterwards qualified so as to make the act applicable only when the court rendering the judgment had jurisdiction of the parties and of the subject-matter, and not to preclude an inquiry into the jurisdiction of the court in which the judgment was rendered, or the right of the State itself to exercise authority over the person or the subject-matter..... [T]he doctrine of this court is, that the act 'was not designed to displace that principle of natural justice which requires a person to have notice of a suit before he can be conclusively bound by its result, nor those rules of public law which protect persons and property within one State from the exercise of jurisdiction over them by another.' The Lafayette Insurance Co. v. French et al., 18 How. 404.

... In all the cases brought in the State and Federal courts, where attempts have been made under the act of Congress to give effect in one State to personal judgments rendered in another State against non-residents, without service upon them, or upon substituted service by publication, or in some other form, it has been held, without an exception, so far as we are aware, that such judgments were without any binding force, except as to property, or interests in property, within the State, to reach and affect which was the object of the action in which the judgment was rendered, and which property was brought under control of the court in connection with the process against the person. The proceeding in such cases, though in the form of a personal action, has been uniformly treated, where service was not obtained, and the party did not voluntarily appear, as effectual and binding merely as a proceeding in rem, and as having no operation beyond the disposition of the property, or some interest therein. And the reason assigned for this conclusion has been that which we have already stated, that the tribunals of one State have no jurisdiction over persons beyond its limits and can inquire only into their obligations to its citizens when exercising its conceded jurisdiction over their property within its limits....

... In several of the cases, the decision has been accompanied with the observation that a personal judgment thus recovered has no binding force without the State in which it is rendered, implying that in such State it may be valid and binding. But if the court has no jurisdiction over the person of the defendant by reason of his non-residence, and, consequently, no authority to pass upon his personal rights and obligations; if the whole proceeding, without service upon him or his appearance, is coram non judice and void; if to hold a defendant bound by such a judgment is contrary to the first principles of justice,- it is difficult to see how the judgment can legitimately have any force within the State. The language used can be justified only on the ground that there was no mode of directly reviewing such judgment or impeaching its validity within the State where rendered; and that, therefore, it could be called in question only when its enforcement was elsewhere attempted. In later cases, this language is repeated with less frequency than formerly, it beginning to be considered, as it always ought to have been, that a judgment which can be treated in any State of this Union as contrary to the first principles of justice, and as an absolute nullity, because rendered without any jurisdiction of the tribunal over the party, is not entitled to any respect in the State where rendered.

Be that as it may, the courts of the United States are not required to give effect to judgments of this character when any right is claimed under them. Whilst they are not foreign tribunals in their relations to the State courts, they are tribunals of a different sovereignty, exercising a distinct and independent jurisdiction, and are bound to give to the judgments of the State courts only the same faith and credit which the courts of another State are bound to give to them.

Since the adoption of the Fourteenth Amendment to the Federal Constitution, the validity of such judgments may be directly questioned, and their enforcement in the State resisted, on the ground that proceedings in a court of justice to determine the personal rights and obligations of parties over whom that court has no jurisdiction do not constitute due process of law. Whatever difficulty may be experienced in giving to those terms a definition which will embrace every permissible exertion of power affecting private rights, and exclude such as is forbidden, there can be no doubt of their meaning when applied to judicial proceedings. They then mean a course of legal proceedings according to those rules and principles which have been established in our systems of jurisprudence for the protection and enforcement of private rights. To give such proceedings any validity, there must be a tribunal competent by its constitution-that is, by the law of its creation-to pass upon the subject-matter of the suit; and, if that involves merely a determination of the personal liability of the defendant, he must be brought within its jurisdiction by service of process within the State, or his voluntary appearance.

Except in cases affecting the personal *status* of the plaintiff, and cases in which that mode of service may be considered to have been assented to in advance, as hereinafter mentioned, the substituted service of process by publication, allowed by the law of Oregon and by similar laws in other States, where actions are brought against non-residents, is effectual only where, in connection with process against the person for commencing the action, property in the State is brought under the control of the court, and subjected to its disposition by process adapted to that purpose, or where the judgment is sought as a means of reaching such property or affecting some interest therein; in other words, where the action is in the nature of a proceeding *in rem*.

It is true that, in a strict sense, a proceeding *in rem* is one taken directly against property and has for its object the disposition of the property, without reference to the title of individual claimants; but, in a larger and more general sense, the terms are applied to actions between parties, where the direct object is to reach and dispose of property owned by them, or of some interest therein. Such are cases commenced by attachment against the property of debtors, or instituted to partition real estate, foreclose a mortgage, or enforce a lien. So far as they affect property in the State, they are substantially proceedings in rem in the broader sense which we have mentioned. . . .

It follows from the views expressed that the personal judgment recovered in the State court of Oregon against the plaintiff herein, then a non-resident of the State, was without any validity, and did not authorize a sale of the property in controversy.

To prevent any misapplication of the views expressed in this opinion, it is proper to observe that we do not mean to assert, by any thing we have said, that a State may not authorize proceedings to determine the status of one of its citizens towards a non-resident, which would be binding within the State, though made without service of process or personal notice to the non-resident. The jurisdiction which every State possesses to determine the civil status and capacities of all its inhabitants involves authority to prescribe the conditions on which proceedings affecting them may be commenced and carried on within its territory. The State, for example, has absolute right to prescribe the conditions upon which the marriage relation between its own citizens shall be created, and the causes for which it may be dissolved. One of the parties guilty of acts for which, by the law of the State, a dissolution may be granted, may have removed to a State where no dissolution is permitted. The complaining party would, therefore, fail if a divorce were sought in the State of the defendant; and if application could not be made to the tribunals of the complainant's domicile in such case, and proceedings be there instituted without personal service of process or personal notice to the offending party, the injured citizen would be without redress.

Neither do we mean to assert that a State may not require a non- resident entering into a partnership or association within its limits, or making contracts enforceable there, to appoint an agent or representative in the State to receive service of process and notice in legal proceedings instituted with respect to such partnership, association, or contracts, or to designate a place where such service may be made and notice given, and provide, upon their failure, to make such appointment or to designate such place that service may be made upon a public officer designated for that purpose, or in some other prescribed way, and that judgments rendered upon such service may not be binding upon the non-residents both within and without the State. As was said by the Court of Exchequer in Vallee v. Dumergue, 4 Exch. 290, 'It is not contrary to natural justice that a man who has agreed to receive a particular mode of notification of legal proceedings should be bound by a judgment in which that particular mode of notification has been followed, even though he may not have actual notice of them.' See also The Lafayette Insurance Co. v. French et al., 18 How. 404, and Gillespie v. Commercial Mutual Marine Insurance Co., 12 Gray (Mass.), 201. Nor do we doubt that a State, on creating corporations or other institutions for pecuniary or charitable purposes, may provide a mode in which their conduct may be investigated, their obligations enforced, or their charters revoked, which shall require other than personal service upon their officers or members. . .

In the present case, there is no feature of this kind, and, consequently, no consideration of what would be the effect of such legislation in enforcing the contract of a non-resident can arise. The question here respects only the validity of a money judgment rendered in one State, in an action upon a simple contract against the resident of another, without service of process upon him, or his appearance therein.

Judgment affirmed.

Personal Jurisdiction Based on Domicile

Milliken v. Meyer
311 U.S. 457, (1940)

Mr. Justice DOUGLAS delivered the opinion of the Court.

The Colorado Supreme Court held null and void a judgment of the Wyoming court against the claim of Milliken that that judgment was entitled to full faith and credit under the Federal Constitution. 101 Colo. 564, 76 P.2d 420; 105 Colo. 532, 100 P.2d 151. The case is here on a petition for certiorari which we granted, because of the substantial character of the federal question which is raised.

The controversy is over a 1/64th interest in profits from operation of certain Colorado oil properties. Transcontinental on August 31, 1922, contracted to pay Meyer 4/64ths of those profits. Milliken asserted a claim to a two-thirds interest in that 4/64ths share. As a settlement of that dispute Transcontinental on May 3, 1924, contracted to pay Milliken a 2/64ths interest and Milliken assigned to Transcontinental all his claims against Meyer pertaining to the lands in question and to Meyer's 4/64ths interest in the profits.

Later Milliken instituted suit in the Wyoming court alleging a joint adventure with Transcontinental and Meyer and charging a conspiracy on their part to defraud him of his rights. He sought a cancellation of the contracts of May 3, 1924, and an accounting from Transcontinental and Meyer. Meyer, who was asserted to be a resident of Wyoming, was personally served with process in Colorado pursuant to the Wyoming statutes; but he made no appearance in the Wyoming cause. Transcontinental appeared and answered. The court found that there was no joint venture between Milliken and [

Transcontinental; that the contracts of May 3, 1924, were valid; and that the action against Transcontinental should be dismissed with prejudice. It found, however, that there was a joint venture between Milliken and Meyer; that they were entitled to share equally in 6/64ths of the net profits; and that, while Meyer had regularly received 4/64ths, he had refused to account to Milliken for his 1/64th part. The court did not purport to decree the 1/64th interest to Milliken or anyone else but entered an in personam judgment against Meyer for the profits which Meyer had withheld from Milliken, together with interest thereon; and enjoined Transcontinental from paying, and Meyer from receiving, more than 3/64ths of the net profits. This was on July 11, 1931. Thereafter the 1/64th share was withheld from Meyer and paid over to Milliken. In 1935 respondent instituted this suit in the Colorado court praying, inter alia, for a judgment against Milliken for the sums withheld under the Wyoming judgment and paid to Milliken, for an injunction against Milliken attempting to enforce the Wyoming judgment, and for a decree that the Wyoming judgment was a nullity for want of jurisdiction over Meyer or his property. The bill alleged, inter alia, that Meyer at the time of service in the Wyoming court had long ceased to be a resident of Wyoming and was a resident of Colorado; that the service obtained on him did not give the Wyoming court jurisdiction of his person or property; and that such judgment was violative of the due process clause of the Fourteenth Amendment. Milliken's answer alleged, inter alia, that Meyer was a resident of Wyoming at the time of the Wyoming action and that the Wyoming judgment was entitled to full faith and credit in Colorado under the Federal Constitution. Article 4, The Colorado court, on issues joined, found that Meyer was domiciled in Wyoming when the Wyoming suit was commenced, that the Wyoming statutes for substituted service were constitutional, that the affidavit for constructive service on Meyer was filed in good faith, substantially conformed to the Wyoming statute and stated the truth, that Wyoming had jurisdiction over the person of Meyer, that the Wyoming decree was not void, and that the bill should be dismissed.

That judgment was reversed by the Supreme Court of Colorado. . . .

Where a judgment rendered in one state is challenged in another, a want of jurisdiction over either the person or the subject matter is of course open to inquiry. . . .

- [I]t is clear that Wyoming had jurisdiction over Meyer in the 1931 suit. Domicile in the state is alone sufficient to bring an absent defendant within the reach of the state's jurisdiction for purposes of a personal judgment by means of appropriate substituted service. Substituted service in such cases has been quite uniformly upheld where the absent defendant was served at his usual place of abode in the state. . .

As in case of the authority of the United States over its absent citizens (Blackmer v. United States, 284 U.S. 421, 52 S.Ct. 252), the authority of a state over one of its citizens is not terminated by the mere fact of his absence from the state. The state which accords him privileges and affords protection to him and his property by virtue of his domicile may also exact reciprocal duties. 'Enjoyment of the privileges of residence within the state, and the attendant right to invoke the protection of its laws, are inseparable' from the various incidences of state citizenship. . . .

The responsibilities of that citizenship arise out of the relationship to the state which domicile creates. That relationship is not dissolved by mere absence from the state. The attendant duties, like the rights and privileges incident to domicile, are not dependent on continuous presence in the state. One such incidence of domicile is amenability to suit within the state even during sojourns without the state, where the state has provided and employed a reasonable method for apprising such an absent party of the proceedings against him. Here such a reasonable method was so provided and so employed.

Reversed.

Personal Jurisdiction Based on Consent

Hess v. Palowski
274 U.S. 352 (1927)

Mr. Justice BUTLER delivered the opinion of the Court.

This action was brought by defendant in error to recover damages for personal injuries. The declaration alleged that plaintiff in error negligently and wantonly drove a motor vehicle on a public highway in Massachusetts, and that by reason thereof the vehicle struck and injured defendant in error. Plaintiff in error is a resident of Pennsylvania. No personal service was made on him, and no property belonging to him was attached. The service of process was made in compliance with chapter 90, General Laws of Massachusetts, as amended by Stat. 1923, c. 431, 2, the material parts of which follow:

'The acceptance by a nonresident of the rights and privileges conferred by section three or four, as evidence by his operating a motor vehicle thereunder, or the operation by a nonresident of a motor vehicle on a public way in the commonwealth other than under said sections, shall be deemed equivalent to an appointment by such nonresident of the registrar or his successor in office, to be his true and lawful attorney upon whom may be served all lawful processes in any action or proceeding against him, growing out of any accident or collision in which said nonresident may be involved while operating a motor vehicle on such a way, and said acceptance or operation shall be a signification of his agreement that any such process against him which is so served shall be of the same legal force and validity as if served on him personally. Service of such process shall be made by leaving a copy of the process with a fee of two dollars in the hands of the registrar, or in his office, and such service shall be sufficient service upon the said nonresident: Provided, that notice of such service and a copy of the process are forthwith sent by registered mail by the plaintiff to the defendant, and the defendant's return receipt and the plaintiff's affidavit of compliance herewith are appended to the writ and entered with the declaration. The court in which the action is pending may order such continuances as may be necessary to afford the defendant reasonable opportunity to defend the action.'

Plaintiff in error appeared specially for the purpose of contesting jurisdiction and filed an answer in abatement and moved to dismiss on the ground that the service of process, if sustained, would deprive him of his property without due process of law, in violation of the Fourteenth Amendment. The court overruled the answer in abatement and denied the motion. The Supreme Judicial Court held the statute to be a valid exercise of the police power and affirmed the order. At the trial the contention was renewed and again denied. Plaintiff in error excepted. The jury returned a verdict for defendant in error. The exceptions were overruled by the Supreme Judicial Court. Thereupon the superior court entered judgment. The writ of error was allowed by the Chief Justice of that court.

The question is whether the Massachusetts enactment contravenes the due process clause of the Fourteenth Amendment.

The process of a court of one state cannot run into another and summon a party there domiciled to respond to proceedings against him. Notice sent outside the state to a nonresident is unavailing to give jurisdiction in an action against him personally for money recovery. Pennoyer v. Neff, 95 U.S. 741 . There must be actual service within the state of notice upon him or upon someone authorized to accept service for him. A personal judgment rendered against a nonresident, who has neither been served with process nor appeared in the suit, is without validity. McDonald v. Mabee, 243 U.S. 90 , 37 S. Ct. 343, The mere transaction of business in a state by nonresident natural persons does not imply consent to be bound by the process of its courts. The power of a state to exclude foreign corporations, although not absolute, but qualified, is the ground on which such an implication is supported as to them. But a state may not withhold from nonresident individuals the right of doing business therein. The privileges and immunities clause of the Constitution (section 2, art. 4), safeguards to the citizens of one state the right 'to pass through, or to reside in any other state for purposes of trade, agriculture, professional pursuits, or otherwise.' And it prohibits state legislation discriminating against citizens of other states.

Motor vehicles are dangerous machines, and, even when skillfully and carefully operated, their use is attended by serious dangers to persons and property. In the public interest the state may make and enforce regulations reasonable calculated to promote care on the part of all, residents and nonresidents alike, who use its highways. The measure in question operates to require a nonresident to answer for his conduct in the state where arise causes of action alleged against him, as well as to provide for a claimant a convenient method by which he may sue to enforce his rights. Under the statute the implied consent is limited to proceedings growing out of accidents or collisions on a highway in which the nonresident may be involved. It is required that he shall actually receive and receipt for notice of the service and a copy of the process. And it contemplates such continuances as may be found necessary to give reasonable time and opportunity for defense. It makes no hostile discrimination against nonresidents but tends to put them on the same footing as residents. Literal and precise equality in respect of this matter is not attainable; it is not required. The state's power to regulate the use of its highways extends to their use by nonresidents as well as by residents. And, in advance of the operation of a motor vehicle on its highway by a nonresident, the state may require him to appoint one of its officials as his agent on whom process may be served in proceedings growing out of such use. That case recognized power of the state to exclude a nonresident until the formal appointment is made. And, having the power so to exclude, the state may declare that the use of the highway by the nonresident is the equivalent of the appointment of the registrar as agent on whom process may be served. The difference between the formal and implied appointment is not substantial, so far as concerns the application of the due process clause of the Fourteenth Amendment.

Judgment affirmed.

Problem The Szukhents, farmers from Michigan, obtained certain farm equipment from National Equipment Rental under a lease. The lease was on a printed form less than a page and a half in length and consisted of 18 numbered paragraphs. The last numbered paragraph, appearing just above the Szukhent's signatures and printed in the same type used in the remainder of the instrument, provided that "the Lessee hereby designates Florence Weinberg, 4721 Forty-first Street, Long Island City, N. Y., as agent for the purpose of accepting service of any process within the State of New York." The Szukhents were not acquainted with Weinberg. In 1962 National sued the Szukhents in the federal court in New York alleging that the Szukhents had failed to make any of the periodic payments specified by the lease. The Marshal delivered two copies of the summons and complaint to Weinberg. That same day she mailed the summons and complaint to the Szukhents, together with a letter stating that the documents had been served upon her as their agent for the purpose of accepting service of process in New York, in accordance with the agreement contained in the lease. Are the Szukhents subject to personal jurisdiction in New York on the lease agreement with National? (See, *National Equipment Rental v. Szukhent,* 375 U.S. 311 (1964).)

Personal Jurisdiction Based on Minimum Contacts

As we saw in *Pennoyer v. Neff,* the Supreme Court held that a tribunal's jurisdiction over persons reaches no farther than the geographic bounds of the forum. In time, however, that strict territorial approach yielded to a less rigid understanding, spurred by changes in the technology of transportation and communication, and the tremendous growth of interstate business activity.

International Shoe Co. v. Washington
316 U.S. 310 (1945)

Mr. Chief Justice STONE delivered the opinion of the Court.

The questions for decision are (1) whether, within the limitations of the due process clause of the Fourteenth Amendment, appellant, a Delaware corporation, has by its activities in the State of Washington rendered itself amenable to proceedings in the courts of that state to recover unpaid contributions to the state unemployment compensation fund exacted by state statutes, Washington Unemployment Compensation Act, . . . and (2) whether the state can exact those contributions consistently with the due process clause of the Fourteenth Amendment.

The statutes in question set up a comprehensive scheme of unemployment compensation, the costs of which are defrayed by contributions required to be made by employers to a state unemployment compensation fund. The contributions are a specified percentage of the wages payable annually by each employer for his employees' services in the state. The assessment and collection of the contributions and the fund are administered by respondents. Section 14(c) of the Act, Wash.Rev.Stat. 1941 Supp., 9998- 114c, authorizes respondent Commissioner to issue an order and notice of assessment of delinquent contributions upon prescribed personal service of the notice upon the employer if found within the state, or, if not so found, by mailing the notice to the employer by registered mail at his last known address. . . .

In this case, notice of assessment for the years in question was personally served upon a sales solicitor employed by appellant in the State of Washington, and a copy of the notice was mailed by registered mail to appellant at its address in St. Louis, Missouri. Appellant appeared specially before the office of unemployment and moved to set aside the order and notice of assessment on the ground that the service upon appellant's salesman was not proper service upon appellant; that appellant was not a corporation of the State of Washington and was not doing business within the state; that it had no agent within the state upon whom service could be made; and that appellant is not an employer and does not furnish employment within the meaning of the statute. . . .

The facts as found by the appeal tribunal and accepted by the state Superior Court and Supreme Court, are not in dispute. Appellant is a Delaware corporation, having its principal place of business in St. Louis, Missouri, and is engaged in the manufacture and sale of shoes and other footwear. It maintains places of business in several states, other than Washington, at which its manufacturing is carried on and from which its merchandise is distributed interstate through several sales units or branches located outside the State of Washington.

Appellant has no office in Washington and makes no contracts either for sale or purchase of merchandise there. It maintains no stock of merchandise in that state and makes there no deliveries of goods in intrastate commerce. During the years from 1937 to 1940, now in question, appellant employed eleven to thirteen salesmen under direct supervision and control of sales managers located in St. Louis. These salesmen resided in Washington; their principal activities were confined to that state; and they were compensated by commissions based upon the amount of their sales. The commissions for each year totaled more than $31,000. Appellant supplies its salesmen with a line of samples, each consisting of one shoe of a pair, which they display to prospective purchasers. On occasion they rent permanent sample rooms, for exhibiting samples, in business buildings, or rent rooms in hotels or business buildings temporarily for that purpose. The cost of such rentals is reimbursed by appellant.

The authority of the salesmen is limited to exhibiting their samples and soliciting orders from prospective buyers, at prices and on terms fixed by appellant. The salesmen transmit the orders to appellant's office in St. Louis for acceptance or rejection, and when accepted the merchandise for filling the orders is shipped f.o.b. from points outside Washington to the purchasers within the state. All the merchandise shipped into Washington is invoiced at the place of shipment from which collections are made. No salesman has authority to enter into contracts or to make collections. . . .

Appellant . . . insists that its activities within the state were not sufficient to manifest its 'presence' there and that in its absence the state courts were without jurisdiction, that consequently it was a denial of due process for the state to subject appellant to suit. It refers to those cases in which it was said that the mere solicitation of orders for the purchase of goods within a state, to be accepted without the state and filled by shipment of the purchased goods interstate, does not render the corporation seller amenable to suit within the state. . . . And appellant further argues that since it was not present within the state, it is a denial of due process to subject it to taxation or other money exaction. It thus denies the power of the state to lay the tax or to subject appellant to a suit for its collection.

Historically the jurisdiction of courts to render judgment in personam is grounded on their de facto power over the defendant's person. Hence his presence within the territorial jurisdiction of court was prerequisite to its rendition of a judgment personally binding him. Pennoyer v. Neff, 95 U.S. 714 , 733. But now that the capias ad respondendum has given way to personal service of summons or other form of notice, due process requires only that in order to subject a defendant to a judgment in personam, if he be not present within the territory of the forum, he have certain minimum contacts with it such that the maintenance of the suit does not offend 'traditional notions of fair play and substantial justice.' . . .

Since the corporate personality is a fiction, although a fiction intended to be acted upon as though it were a fact, . . . it is clear that unlike an individual its 'presence' without, as well as within, the state of its origin can be manifested only by activities carried on in its behalf by those who are authorized to act for it. To say that the corporation is so far 'present' there as to satisfy due process requirements, for purposes of taxation or the maintenance of suits against it in the courts of the state, is to beg the question to be decided. For the terms 'present' or 'presence' are used merely to symbolize those activities of the corporation's agent within the state which courts will deem to be sufficient to satisfy the demands of due process. L. Hand, J., in Hutchinson v. Chase & Gilbert, 2 Cir., 45 F.2d 139, 141. Those demands may be met by such contacts of the corporation with the state of the forum as make it reasonable, in the context of our federal system of government, to require the corporation to defend the particular suit which is brought there. An 'estimate of the inconveniences' which would result to the corporation from a trial away from its 'home' or principal place of business is relevant in this connection.

'Presence' in the state in this sense has never been doubted when the activities of the corporation there have not only been continuous and systematic, but also give rise to the liabilities sued on, even though no consent to be sued or authorization to an agent to accept service of process has been given. . . . Conversely it has been generally recognized that the casual presence of the corporate agent or even his conduct of single or isolated items of activities in a state in the corporation's behalf are not enough to subject it to suit on causes of action unconnected with the activities there. . . . To require the corporation in such circumstances to defend the suit away from its home or other jurisdiction where it carries on more substantial activities has been thought to lay too great and unreasonable a burden on the corporation to comport with due process. While it has been held in cases on which appellant relies that continuous activity of some sorts within a state is not enough to support the demand that the corporation be amenable to suits unrelated to that activity, . . . there have been instances in which the continuous corporate operations within a state were thought so substantial and of such a nature as to justify suit against it on causes of action arising from dealings entirely distinct from those activities. . . .

Finally, although the commission of some single or occasional acts of the corporate agent in a state sufficient to impose an obligation or liability on the corporation has not been thought to confer upon the state authority to enforce it, other such acts, because of their nature and quality and the circumstances of their commission, may be deemed sufficient to render the corporation liable to suit. . . . True, some of the decisions holding the corporation amenable to suit have been supported by resort to the legal fiction that it has given its consent to service and suit, consent being implied from its presence in the state through the acts of its authorized agents. . . . But more realistically it may be said that those authorized acts were of such a nature as to justify the fiction. . . .

It is evident that the criteria by which we mark the boundary line between those activities which justify the subjection of a corporation to suit, and those which do not, cannot be simply mechanical or quantitative. The test is not merely, as has sometimes been suggested, whether the activity, which the corporation has seen fit to procure through its agents in another state, is a little more or a little less. . . . Whether due process is satisfied must depend rather upon the quality and nature of the activity in relation to the fair and orderly administration of the laws which it was the purpose of the due process clause to insure. That clause does not contemplate that a state may make binding a judgment in personam against an individual or corporate defendant with which the state has no contacts, ties, or relations.

But to the extent that a corporation exercises the privilege of conducting activities within a state, it enjoys the benefits and protection of the laws of that state. The exercise of that privilege may give rise to obligations; and, so far as those obligations arise out of or are connected with the activities within the state, a procedure which requires the corporation to respond to a suit brought to enforce them can, in most instances, hardly be said to be undue. . . .

Rational 2

Applying these standards, the activities carried on in behalf of appellant in the State of Washington were neither irregular nor casual. They were systematic and continuous throughout the years in question. They resulted in a large volume of interstate business, in the course of which appellant received the benefits and protection of the laws of the state, including the right to resort to the courts for the enforcement of its rights. The obligation which is here sued upon arose out of those very activities. It is evident that these operations establish sufficient contacts or ties with the state of the forum to make it reasonable and just according to our traditional conception of fair play and substantial justice to permit the state to enforce the obligations which appellant has incurred there. Hence we cannot say that the maintenance of the present suit in the State of Washington involves an unreasonable or undue procedure.

We are likewise unable to conclude that the service of the process within the state upon an agent whose activities establish appellant's 'presence' there was not sufficient notice of the suit, or that the suit was so unrelated to those activities as to make the agent an inappropriate vehicle for communicating the notice. It is enough that appellant has established such contacts with the state that the particular form of substituted service adopted there gives reasonable assurance that the notice will be actual. . . . Nor can we say that the mailing of the notice of suit to appellant by registered mail at its home office was not reasonably calculated to apprise appellant of the suit. . . .

Appellant having rendered itself amenable to suit upon obligations arising out of the activities of its salesmen in Washington, the state may maintain the present suit in personam to collect the tax laid upon the exercise of the privilege of employing appellant's salesmen within the state. For Washington has made one of those activities, which taken together establish appellant's 'presence' there for purposes of suit, the taxable event by which the state brings appellant within the reach of its taxing power. The state thus has constitutional power to lay the tax and to subject appellant to a suit to recover it. The activities which establish its 'presence' subject it alike to taxation by the state and to suit to recover the tax.

AFFIRMED.

Problem In 1944, Lowell Franklin, a resident of California, purchased a life insurance policy from the Empire Mutual Insurance Company, an Arizona corporation. In 1948 International Life Insurance Co., (International) agreed with Empire Mutual to assume its insurance obligations. International then mailed a reinsurance certificate to Franklin in California offering to insure him in accordance with the terms of the policy he held with Empire Mutual. He accepted this offer, and from that time until his death in 1950, paid premiums by mail from his California home to respondent's Texas office. Franklin's mother was the beneficiary under the policy. She sent proofs of his death to International, but it refused to pay, claiming that he had committed suicide. It appears that neither Empire Mutual nor International has ever had any office or agent in California. And so far as the record shows, International has never solicited or done any insurance business in California apart from the policy involved here. Is International subject to personal jurisdiction in California? (See, *McGee v. International Life Insurance Co.* 355 U.S. 220 (1957))

Hanson v. Denckla
357 U.S. 235 (1958)

[While domiciled in Pennsylvania, a woman executed in Delaware, a revocable deed of trust making a Delaware trust company trustee of certain securities, reserving the income for life and providing that the remainder should be paid to such parties as she should appoint by *inter vivos* or *testamentary* instrument. Later, after becoming domiciled in Florida, where she remained until her death, she executed (1) an inter vivos instrument appointing certain beneficiaries to receive $400,000 of the trust property, and (2) a will containing a residuary clause covering, inter alia, "all property, rights and interest over which I may have power of appointment which prior to my death has not been effectively exercised." In a proceeding in which the Delaware trust company did not appear and was given notice only by mail and publication, a Florida State Court held that the trust and power of appointment were ineffective under Florida law and that the $400,000 passed under the residuary clause of the will. This ruling was sustained by the Supreme Court of Florida, which also held that the Florida court had personal jurisdiction over the nonresident trust company]

The appearing defendants moved to dismiss the suit because the exercise of jurisdiction over indispensable parties, the Delaware trustees, would offend Section 1 of the Fourteenth Amendment....

The issues for our decision are . . . whether Florida erred in holding that it had jurisdiction over the nonresident defendants....

Florida adheres to the general rule that a trustee is an indispensable party to litigation involving the validity of the trust. In the absence of such a party a Florida court may not proceed to adjudicate the controversy. Since state law required the acquisition of jurisdiction over the nonresident trust company before the court was empowered to proceed with the action, any defendant affected by the court's judgment has that "direct and substantial personal interest in the outcome" that is necessary to challenge whether that jurisdiction was in fact acquired.

Appellants charge that this judgment is offensive to the Due Process Clause of the Fourteenth Amendment because the Florida court was without jurisdiction. There is no suggestion that the court failed to employ a means of notice reasonably calculated to inform nonresident defendants of the pending proceedings or denied them an opportunity to be heard in defense of their interests. The alleged defect is the absence of those "affiliating circumstances" without which the courts of a State may not enter a judgment imposing obligations on persons (jurisdiction in personam) . . .

Prior to the Fourteenth Amendment an exercise of jurisdiction over persons or property outside the forum State was thought to be an absolute nullity, but the matter remained a question of state law over which this Court exercised no authority. With the adoption of that Amendment, any judgment purporting to bind the person of a defendant over whom the court had not acquired in personam jurisdiction was void within the State as well as without. Pennoyer v. Neff. Nearly a century has passed without this Court being called upon to apply that principle to an in rem judgment dealing with property outside the forum State. The invalidity of such a judgment within the forum State seems to have been assumed - and with good reason. Since a State is forbidden to enter a judgment attempting to bind a person over whom it has no jurisdiction, it has even less right to enter a judgment purporting to extinguish the interest of such a person in property over which the court has no jurisdiction. Therefore, so far as it purports to rest upon jurisdiction over the trust assets, the judgment of the Florida court cannot be sustained.

In personam jurisdiction. Appellees' stronger argument is for in personam jurisdiction over the Delaware trustee. They urge that the circumstances of this case amount to sufficient affiliation with the State of Florida to empower its courts to exercise personal jurisdiction over this nonresident defendant. Principal reliance is placed upon McGee v. International Life Ins. Co., . In McGee the Court noted the trend of expanding personal jurisdiction over nonresidents. As technological progress has increased the flow of commerce between States, the need for jurisdiction over nonresidents has undergone a similar increase. At the same time, progress in communications and transportation has made the defense of a suit in a foreign tribunal less burdensome. In response to these changes, the requirements for personal jurisdiction over nonresidents have evolved from the rigid rule of Pennoyer v. Neff, to the flexible standard of International Shoe Co. v. Washington. But it is a mistake to assume that this trend heralds the eventual demise of all restrictions on the personal jurisdiction of state courts. Those restrictions are more than a guarantee of immunity from inconvenient or distant litigation. They are a consequence of territorial limitations on the power of the respective States. However minimal the burden of defending in a foreign tribunal, a defendant may not be called upon to do so unless he has had the "minimal contacts" with that State that are a prerequisite to its exercise of power over him. See International Shoe Co. v. Washington.

We fail to find such contacts in the circumstances of this case. The defendant trust company has no office in Florida and transacts no business there. None of the trust assets has ever been held or administered in Florida, and the record discloses no solicitation of business in that State either in person or by mail. Cf. International Shoe Co. v. Washington, McGee v. International Life Ins. Co.

The cause of action in this case is not one that arises out of an act done or transaction consummated in the forum State. In that respect, it differs from McGee v. International Life Ins. Co., and the cases there cited. . . . In contrast, this action involves the validity of an agreement that was entered without any connection with the forum State. The agreement was executed in Delaware by a trust company incorporated in that State and a settlor domiciled in Pennsylvania. The first relationship Florida had to the agreement was years later when the settlor became domiciled there, and the trustee remitted the trust income to her in that State. From Florida Mrs. Donner carried on several bits of trust administration that may be compared to the mailing of premiums in McGee. But the record discloses no instance in which the trustee performed any acts in Florida that bear the same relationship to the agreement as the solicitation in McGee. Consequently, this suit cannot be said to be one to enforce an obligation that arose from a privilege the defendant exercised in Florida. Cf. International Shoe Co. v. Washington. . . .

The execution in Florida of the powers of appointment under which the beneficiaries and appointees claim does not give Florida a substantial connection with the contract on which this suit is based. It is the validity of the trust agreement, not the appointment, that is at issue here. For the purpose of applying its rule that the validity of a trust is determined by the law of the State of its creation, Florida ruled that the appointment amounted to a "republication" of the original trust instrument in Florida. For choice-of-law purposes such a ruling may be justified, but we think it an insubstantial connection with the trust agreement for purposes of determining the question of personal jurisdiction over a nonresident defendant. The unilateral activity of those who claim some relationship with a nonresident defendant cannot satisfy the requirement of contact with the forum State. The application of that rule will vary with the quality and nature of the defendant's activity, but it is essential in each case that there be some act by which the defendant purposefully avails itself of the privilege of conducting activities within the forum State, thus invoking the benefits and protections of its laws. International Shoe Co. v. Washington, The settlor's execution in Florida of her power of appointment cannot remedy the absence of such an act in this case. . .

The issue is personal jurisdiction, . . . It is resolved in this case by considering the acts of the trustee. As we have indicated, they are insufficient to sustain the jurisdiction.

. . . the judgment of the Florida Supreme Court is reversed and the cause is remanded for proceedings not inconsistent with this opinion.

Minimum Contacts - The Four Principles of International Shoe

At this point, it may be useful to review and summarize the four principles that have emerged from *International Shoe* and its progeny. a line of

1) Jurisdiction is permissible when the defendant's activity in the forum is continuous and systematic and the cause of action is related to that activity.

2) Sporadic or casual activity of the defendant in the forum does not justify assertion of jurisdiction on a cause of action unrelated to that forum activity.

3) A court may assert jurisdiction over a defendant whose continuous activities in the forum are unrelated to the cause of action sued upon when the defendant's contacts are sufficiently substantial and of such a nature as to make the state's assertion of jurisdiction reasonable. ("general jurisdiction")

4) Even a defendant whose activity in the forum is sporadic, or consists only of a single act, may be subject to the jurisdiction of the forum's courts when the cause of action arises out of that activity or act. ["specific jurisdiction"] (Friedenthal § 3.10)

Problem Kathy Keeton, a resident of New York, sued Hustler Magazine, Inc., an Ohio corporation, in New Hampshire, claiming she had been libeled. Hustler's contacts with New Hampshire consist of monthly sales of some 10,000 to 15,000 copies of its nationally published magazine. Keeton claims to have been libeled in five separate issues of Hustler published between September 1975 and May 1976. Is Hustler's regular circulation of magazines in New Hampshire sufficient to support an assertion of personal jurisdiction in a libel action based on the contents of the magazine? (See, *Keeton v. Hustler Magazine, Inc.*, 465 U.S. 770 (1984).)

Jurisdiction Over Things and The Absorption of *In Rem* Jurisdiction

So far, we have only considered jurisdiction over persons or corporations. A court may also take jurisdiction over a thing as opposed to a person. *In rem* jurisdiction is the power of a court to deal with a thing (e.g. a parcel of land, an automobile, a ship) and to determine its status in relation to the legal rights of all persons known and unknown. I.e., in a proceeding *in rem*, the court exercises its power to determine the status of property and the determination of the court is binding with respect to all possible interest holders in that property. The potential liability of a defendant in an *in rem* action is limited by the value of the property.

"A judgment *in rem* affects the interests of all persons in designated property. A judgment *quasi in rem* affects the interests of particular persons in designated property. The latter is of two types. In one, the plaintiff is seeking to secure a pre-existing claim in the subject property and to extinguish or establish the nonexistence of similar interests of particular persons. In the other, the plaintiff seeks to apply what he concedes to be the property of the defendant to the satisfaction of a claim against him. Restatement, Judgments, 5-9." *Hanson v. Denckla*, 357 U. S. 235, 246 n. 12 (1958).

The basis of the jurisdiction, whether it be *in rem* or *quasi in rem,* is the presence of the subject property within the territorial jurisdiction of the forum State. Tangible property poses no problem for the application of this rule, but the situs of intangibles is often a matter of controversy. (*Hanson v. Denckla* 357 U.S. 235, 246.) Must the assertion of *in rem* jurisdiction satisfy the same constitutional standards as the assertion of *in personam* jurisdiction?

Shaffer v. Heitner
433 U.S. 186 (1977)

MR. JUSTICE MARSHALL delivered the opinion of the Court.

The controversy in this case concerns the constitutionality of a Delaware statute that allows a court of that State to take jurisdiction of a lawsuit by sequestering any property of the defendant that happens to be located in Delaware. Appellants contend that the sequestration statute as applied in this case violates the Due Process Clause of the Fourteenth Amendment, both because it permits the state courts to exercise jurisdiction despite the absence of sufficient contacts among the defendants, the litigation, and the State of Delaware, and because it authorizes the deprivation of defendants' property without providing adequate procedural safeguards. We find it necessary to consider only the first of these contentions.

I

Appellee Heitner, a nonresident of Delaware, is the owner of one share of stock in the Greyhound Corp., a business incorporated under the laws of Delaware with its principal place of business in Phoenix, Ariz. On May 22, 1974, he filed a shareholder's derivative suit in the Court of Chancery for New Castle County, Del., in which he named as defendants Greyhound, its wholly owned subsidiary Greyhound Lines, Inc., and 28 present or former officers or directors of one or both of the corporations. In essence, Heitner alleged that the individual defendants had violated their duties to Greyhound by causing it and its subsidiary to engage in actions that resulted in the corporations being held liable for substantial damages in a private antitrust suit and a large fine in a criminal contempt action. The activities which led to these penalties took place in Oregon.

Simultaneously with his complaint, Heitner filed a motion for an order of sequestration of the Delaware property of the individual defendants pursuant to Del. Code Ann., Tit. 10, 366 (1975). This motion was accompanied by a supporting affidavit of counsel which stated that the individual defendants were nonresidents of Delaware. The affidavit identified the property to be sequestered as "common stock, 3% Second

Cumulative Preferred Stock and stock unit credits of the Defendant Greyhound Corporation, a Delaware corporation, as well as all options and all warrants to purchase said stock issued to said individual Defendants and all contractual [sic] obligations, all rights, debts or credits due or accrued to or for the benefit of any of the said Defendants under any type of written agreement, contract or other legal instrument of any kind whatever between any of the individual Defendants and said corporation."

The requested sequestration order was signed the day the motion was filed. Pursuant to that order, the sequestrator "seized" approximately 82,000 shares of Greyhound common stock belonging to 19 of the defendants, and options belonging to another 2 defendants. These seizures were accomplished by placing "stop transfer" orders or their equivalents on the books of the Greyhound Corp. So far as the record shows, none of the certificates representing the seized property was physically present in Delaware. The stock was considered to be in Delaware, and so subject to seizure, by virtue of Del. Code Ann., Tit. 8, 169 (1975), which makes Delaware the situs of ownership of all stock in Delaware corporations.

All 28 defendants were notified of the initiation of the suit by certified mail directed to their last known addresses and by publication in a New Castle County newspaper. The 21 defendants whose property was seized (hereafter referred to as appellants) responded by entering a special appearance for the purpose of moving to quash service of process and to vacate the sequestration order. They contended that the ex parte sequestration procedure did not accord them due process of law and that the property seized was not capable of attachment in Delaware. In addition, appellants asserted that under the rule of International Shoe Co. v. Washington, (1945), they did not have sufficient contacts with Delaware to sustain the jurisdiction of that State's courts. . . .

II

The Delaware courts rejected appellants' jurisdictional challenge by noting that this suit was brought as a quasi in rem proceeding. Since quasi in rem jurisdiction is traditionally based on attachment or seizure of property present in the jurisdiction, not on contacts between the defendant and the State, the courts considered appellants' claimed lack of contacts with Delaware to be unimportant. This categorical analysis assumes the continued soundness of the conceptual structure founded on the century-old case of Pennoyer v. Neff. . .

Pennoyer sharply limited the availability of in personam jurisdiction over defendants not resident in the forum State. If a nonresident defendant could not be found in a State, he could not be sued there. On the other hand, since the State in which property was located was considered to have exclusive sovereignty over that property, in rem actions could proceed regardless of the owner's location. Indeed, since a State's process could not reach beyond its borders, this Court held after Pennoyer that due process did not require any effort to give a property owner personal notice that his property was involved in an in rem proceeding.

The Pennoyer rules generally favored nonresident defendants by making them harder to sue. This advantage was reduced, however, by the ability of a resident plaintiff to satisfy a claim against a nonresident defendant by bringing into court any property of the defendant located in the plaintiff's State. See, e. g., Zammit, Quasi-In-Rem Jurisdiction: Outmoded and Unconstitutional?, 49 St. John's L. Rev. 668, 670 (1975). For example, in the well-known case of Harris v. Balk, 198 U.S. 215 (1905), Epstein, a resident of Maryland, had a claim against Balk, a resident of North Carolina. Harris, another North Carolina resident, owed money to Balk. When Harris happened to visit Maryland, Epstein garnished his debt to Balk. Harris did not contest the debt to Balk and paid it to Epstein's North Carolina attorney. When Balk later sued Harris in North Carolina, this Court held that the Full Faith and Credit Clause, U.S. Const., Art. IV, 1, required that Harris' payment to Epstein be treated as a discharge of his debt to Balk. This Court reasoned that the debt Harris owed Balk was an intangible form of property belonging to Balk, and that the location of that property traveled with the debtor. By obtaining personal jurisdiction over Harris, of a Maryland tribunal. . .

Although this Court has not addressed this argument directly, we have held that property cannot be subjected to a court's judgment unless reasonable and appropriate efforts have been made to give the property owners actual notice of the action. Mullane v. Central Hanover Bank & Trust Co., 339 U.S. 306 (1950). This conclusion recognizes, contrary to Pennoyer, that an adverse judgment in rem directly affects the property owner by divesting him of his rights in the property before the court.

It is clear, therefore, that the law of state-court jurisdiction no longer stands securely on the foundation established in Pennoyer. We think that the time is ripe to consider whether the standard of fairness and substantial justice set forth in International Shoe should be held to govern actions in rem as well as in personam.

III

The case for applying to jurisdiction in rem the same test of "fair play and substantial justice" as governs assertions of jurisdiction in personam is simple and straightforward. It is premised on recognition that "[t]he phrase, 'judicial jurisdiction over a thing,' is a customary elliptical way of referring to jurisdiction over the interests of persons in a thing." Restatement (Second) of Conflict of Laws 56, Introductory Note (1971) (hereafter Restatement). This recognition leads to the conclusion that in order to justify an exercise of jurisdiction in rem, the basis for jurisdiction must be sufficient to justify exercising "jurisdiction over the interests of persons in a thing." The standard for determining whether an exercise of jurisdiction over the interests of persons is consistent with the Due Process Clause is the minimum-contacts standard elucidated in International Shoe.

This argument, of course, does not ignore the fact that the presence of property in a State may bear on the existence of jurisdiction by providing contacts among the forum State, the defendant, and the litigation. For example, when claims to the property itself are the source of the underlying controversy between the plaintiff and the defendant, it would be unusual for the State where the property is located not to have jurisdiction. In such cases, the defendant's claim to property located in the State would normally indicate that he expected to benefit from the State's protection of his interest. The State's strong interests in assuring the marketability of property within its borders and in providing a procedure for peaceful resolution of disputes about the possession of that property would also support jurisdiction, as would the likelihood that important records and witnesses will be found in the State. The presence of property may also favor jurisdiction in cases, such as suits for injury suffered on the land of an absentee owner, where the defendant's ownership of the property is conceded but the cause of action is otherwise related to rights and duties growing out of that ownership.

It appears, therefore, that jurisdiction over many types of actions which now are or might be brought in rem would not be affected by a holding that any assertion of state-court jurisdiction must satisfy the International Shoe standard. For the type of quasi in rem action typified by Harris v. Balk and the present case, however, accepting the proposed analysis would result in significant change. These are cases where the property which now serves as the basis for state-court jurisdiction is completely unrelated to the plaintiff's cause of action. Thus, although the presence of the defendant's property in a State might suggest the existence of other ties among the defendant, the State, and the litigation, the presence of the property alone would not support the State's jurisdiction. If those other ties did not exist, cases over which the State is now thought to have jurisdiction could not be brought in that forum.

Since acceptance of the International Shoe test would most affect this class of cases, we examine the arguments against adopting that standard as they relate to this category of litigation. Before doing so, however, we note that this type of case also presents the clearest illustration of the argument in favor of assessing assertions of jurisdiction by a single standard. For in cases such as Harris and this one, the only role played by the property is to provide the basis for bringing the defendant into court. Indeed, the express purpose of the Delaware sequestration procedure is to compel the defendant to enter a personal appearance. In such cases, if a direct assertion of personal jurisdiction over the defendant would violate the Constitution, it would seem that an indirect assertion of that jurisdiction should be equally impermissible.

The primary rationale for treating the presence of property as a sufficient basis for jurisdiction to adjudicate claims over which the State would not have jurisdiction if International Shoe applied is that a wrongdoer "should not be able to avoid payment of his obligations by the expedient of removing his assets to a place where he is not subject to an in personam suit." Restatement 66, Comment a. This justification, however, does not explain why jurisdiction should be recognized without regard to whether the property is present in the State because of an effort to avoid the owner's obligations. Nor does it support jurisdiction to adjudicate the underlying claim. . . .

It might also be suggested that allowing in rem jurisdiction avoids the uncertainty inherent in the International Shoe standard and assures a plaintiff of a forum. We believe, however, that the fairness standard of International Shoe can be easily applied in the vast majority of cases. Moreover, when the existence of jurisdiction in a particular forum under International Shoe is unclear, the cost of simplifying the litigation by avoiding the jurisdictional question may be the sacrifice of "fair play and substantial justice." That cost is too high.

We are left, then, to consider the significance of the long history of jurisdiction based solely on the presence of property in a State. Although the theory that territorial power is both essential to and sufficient for jurisdiction has been undermined, we have never held that the presence of property in a State does not automatically confer jurisdiction over the owner's interest in that property. This history must be considered as supporting the proposition that jurisdiction based solely on the presence of property satisfies the demands of due process, but it is not decisive. "[T]raditional notions of fair play and substantial justice" can be as readily offended by the perpetuation of ancient forms that are no longer justified as by the adoption of new procedures that are inconsistent with the basic values of our constitutional heritage. Cf. Sniadach v. Family Finance Corp., 395 U.S., at 340 ; Wolf v. Colorado, 338 U.S. 25, 27 (1949). The fiction that an assertion of jurisdiction over property is anything but an assertion of jurisdiction over the owner of the property supports an ancient form without substantial modern justification. Its continued acceptance would serve only to allow state-court jurisdiction that is fundamentally unfair to the defendant.

We therefore conclude that all assertions of state-court jurisdiction must be evaluated according to the standards set forth in International Shoe and its progeny.

IV

The Delaware courts based their assertion of jurisdiction in this case solely on the statutory presence of appellants' property in Delaware. Yet that property is not the subject matter of this litigation, nor is the underlying cause of action related to the property. Appellants' holdings in Greyhound do not, therefore, provide contacts with Delaware sufficient to support the jurisdiction of that State's courts over appellants. If it exists, that jurisdiction must have some other foundation.

Appellee Heitner did not allege and does not now claim that appellants have ever set foot in Delaware. Nor does he identify any act related to his cause of action as having taken place in Delaware. Nevertheless, he contends that appellants' positions as directors and officers of a corporation chartered in Delaware provide sufficient "contacts, ties, or relations," International Shoe Co. v. Washington, 326 U.S., at 319, with that State to give its court's jurisdiction over appellants in this stockholder's derivative action. This argument is based primarily on what Heitner asserts to be the strong interest of Delaware in supervising the management of a Delaware corporation. That interest is said to derive from the role of Delaware law in establishing the corporation and defining the obligations owed to it by its officers and directors. In order to protect this interest, appellee concludes, Delaware's courts must have jurisdiction over corporate fiduciaries such as appellants.

This argument is undercut by the failure of the Delaware Legislature to assert the state interest appellee finds so compelling. Delaware law bases jurisdiction, not on appellants' status as corporate fiduciaries, but rather on the presence of their property in the State. Although the sequestration procedure used here may be most frequently used in derivative suits against officers and directors, Hughes Tool Co. v. Fawcett Publications, Inc., 290 A. 2d 693, 695 (Del. Ch. 1972), the authorizing statute evinces no specific concern with such actions. Sequestration can be used in any suit against a nonresident, see, e. g., U.S. Industries, Inc. v. Gregg, 540 F.2d 142 (CA3 1976), cert. pending, No. 76-359 (breach of contract); Hughes Tool Co. v. Fawcett Publications, Inc., supra (same), and reaches corporate fiduciaries only if they happen to own interests in a Delaware corporation, or other property in the State. But as Heitner's failure to secure jurisdiction over seven of the defendants named in his complaint demonstrates, there is no necessary relationship between holding a position as a corporate fiduciary and owning stock or other interests in the corporation. If Delaware perceived its interest in securing jurisdiction over corporate fiduciaries to be as great as Heitner suggests, we would expect it to have enacted a statute more clearly designed to protect that interest. . . .

Appellee suggests that by accepting positions as officers or directors of a Delaware corporation, appellants performed the acts required by Hanson v. Denckla. He notes that Delaware law provides substantial benefits to corporate officers and directors, and that these benefits were at least in part the incentive for appellants to assume their positions. It is, he says, "only fair and just" to require appellants, in return for these benefits, to respond in the State of Delaware when they are accused of misusing their power. Brief for Appellee 15.

But like Heitner's first argument, this line of reasoning establishes only that it is appropriate for Delaware law to govern the obligations of appellants to Greyhound and its stockholders. It does not demonstrate that appellants have "purposefully avail[ed themselves] of the privilege of conducting activities within the forum State," Hanson v. Denckla, supra, at 253, in a way that would justify bringing them before a Delaware tribunal. Appellants have simply had nothing to do with the State of Delaware. Moreover, appellants had no reason to expect to be haled before a Delaware court. Delaware, unlike some States, has not enacted a statute that treats acceptance of a directorship as consent to jurisdiction in the State. And "[i]t strains reason . . . to suggest that anyone buying securities in a corporation formed in Delaware 'impliedly consents' to subject himself to Delaware's . . . jurisdiction on any cause of action." Folk & Moyer, supra, n. 10, at 785. Appellants, who were not required to acquire interests in Greyhound in order to hold their positions, did not by acquiring those interests surrender their right to be brought to judgment only in States with which they had had "minimum contacts."

The Due Process Clause "does not contemplate that a state may make binding a judgment . . . against an individual or corporate defendant with which the state has no contacts, ties, or relations." International Shoe Co. v. Washington, 326 U.S., at 319.

Delaware's assertion of jurisdiction over appellants in this case is inconsistent with that constitutional limitation on state power. The judgment of the Delaware Supreme Court must, therefore, be reversed.

It is so ordered.

The Refinement of the Minimum Contacts Analysis

Many states have statutes that base personal jurisdiction over nonresidents on the doing of acts or on other contacts within the State, and permit notice to be given to the defendant outside the State. As you read the next case, and many of the cases that follow it, keep in mind that in order to take advantage of the minimum contacts test, the forum state must have such a statute which authorizes the assertion of personal jurisdiction over absentee defendants. Because these statutes reach beyond the borders of the state, they have come to be known by the colorful name of "long-arm" statutes.

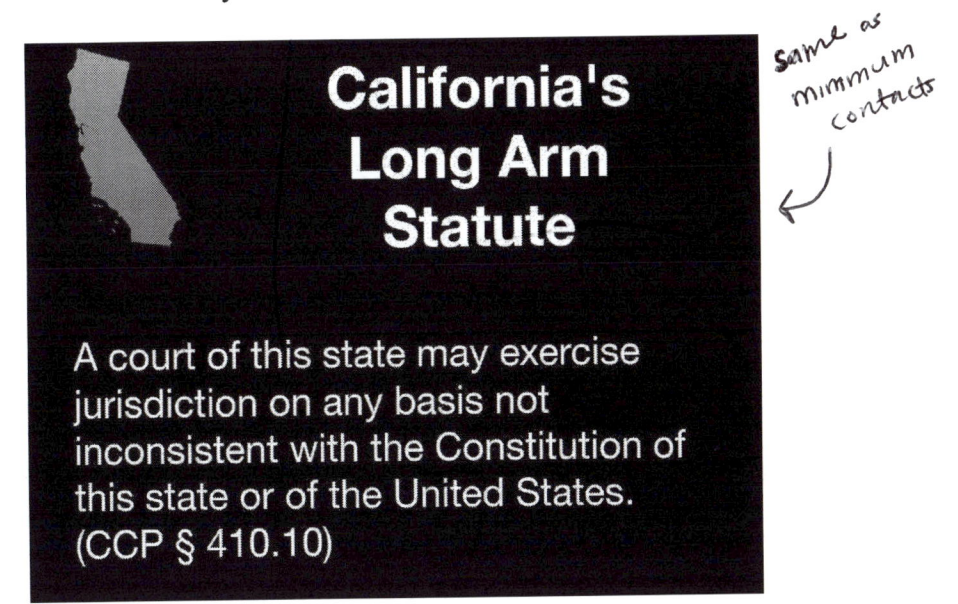

California's Long Arm Statute

A court of this state may exercise jurisdiction on any basis not inconsistent with the Constitution of this state or of the United States. (CCP § 410.10)

[handwritten annotation: same as minimum contacts]

Asahi Metal Industry Co., Ltd. v. Superior Court
480 U.S. 102 (1987)

JUSTICE O'CONNOR announced the judgment of the Court and delivered the unanimous opinion of the Court with respect to Part I, the opinion of the Court with respect to Part II-B, in which THE CHIEF JUSTICE, JUSTICE BRENNAN, JUSTICE WHITE, JUSTICE MARSHALL, JUSTICE BLACKMUN, JUSTICE POWELL, and JUSTICE STEVENS join, and an opinion with respect to Parts II-A and III, in which THE CHIEF JUSTICE, JUSTICE POWELL, and JUSTICE SCALIA join.

This case presents the question whether the mere awareness on the part of a foreign defendant that the components it manufactured, sold, and delivered outside the United

States would reach the forum State in the stream of commerce constitutes "minimum contacts" between the defendant and the forum State such that the exercise of jurisdiction "does not offend 'traditional notions of fair play and substantial justice.'" International Shoe Co. v. Washington, 326 U.S. 310, 316 (1945), quoting Milliken v. Meyer, 311 U.S. 457, 463 (1940).

I

On September 23, 1978, on Interstate Highway 80 in Solano County, California, Gary Zurcher lost control of his Honda motorcycle and collided with a tractor. Zurcher was severely injured, and his passenger and wife, Ruth Ann Moreno, was killed. In September 1979, Zurcher filed a product liability action in the Superior Court of the State of California in and for the County of Solano. Zurcher alleged that the 1978 accident was caused by a sudden loss of air and an explosion in the rear tire of the motorcycle, and alleged that the motorcycle tire, tube, and sealant were defective. Zurcher's complaint named, inter alia, Cheng Shin Rubber Industrial Co., Ltd. (Cheng Shin), the Taiwanese manufacturer of the tube. Cheng Shin in turn filed a cross-complaint seeking indemnification from its codefendants and from petitioner, Asahi Metal Industry Co., Ltd. (Asahi), the manufacturer of the tube's valve assembly. Zurcher's claims against Cheng Shin and the other defendants were eventually settled and dismissed, leaving only Cheng Shin's indemnity action against Asahi.

California's long-arm statute authorizes the exercise of jurisdiction "on any basis not inconsistent with the Constitution of this state or of the United States." Cal. Civ. Proc. Code Ann. 410.10 (West 1973). Asahi moved to quash Cheng Shin's service of summons, arguing the State could not exert jurisdiction over it consistent with the Due Process Clause of the Fourteenth Amendment.

In relation to the motion, the following information was submitted by Asahi and Cheng Shin. Asahi is a Japanese corporation. It manufactures tire valve assemblies in Japan and sells the assemblies to Cheng Shin, and to several other tire manufacturers, for use as components in finished tire tubes. Asahi's sales to Cheng Shin took place in Taiwan. The shipments from Asahi to Cheng Shin were sent from Japan to Taiwan. Cheng Shin bought and incorporated into its tire tubes 150,000 Asahi valve assemblies in 1978; 500,000 in 1979; 500,000 in 1980; 100,000 in 1981; and 100,000 in 1982. Sales to Cheng Shin accounted for 1.24 percent of Asahi's income in 1981 and 0.44 percent in 1982. Cheng Shin alleged that approximately 20 percent of its sales in the United States are in California. Cheng Shin purchases valve assemblies from other suppliers as well and sells finished tubes throughout the world.

In 1983 an attorney for Cheng Shin conducted an informal examination of the valve stems of the tire tubes sold in one cycle store in Solano County. The attorney declared that of the approximately 115 tire tubes in the store, 97 were purportedly manufactured in Japan or Taiwan, and of those 97, 21 valve stems were marked with the circled letter "A", apparently Asahi's trademark. Of the 21 Asahi valve stems, 12 were incorporated into Cheng Shin tire tubes. The store contained 41 other Cheng Shin tubes that incorporated the valve assemblies of other manufacturers. Declaration of Kenneth B. Shepard in Opposition to Motion to Quash Subpoena, App. to Brief for Respondent 5-6. An affidavit of a manager of Cheng Shin whose duties included the purchasing of component parts stated: "'In discussions with Asahi regarding the purchase of valve stem assemblies the fact that my Company sells tubes throughout the world and specifically the United States has been discussed. I am informed and believe that Asahi was fully aware that valve stem assemblies sold to my Company and to others would end up throughout the United States and in California.'" 39 Cal. 3d 35, 48, n. 4, 702 P.2d 543, 549-550, n. 4 (1985). An affidavit of the president of Asahi, on the other hand, declared that Asahi "'has never contemplated that its limited sales of tire valves to Cheng Shin in Taiwan would subject it to lawsuits in California.'" Ibid. The record does not include any contract between Cheng Shin and Asahi.

Primarily on the basis of the above information, the Superior Court denied the motion to quash summons, stating: "Asahi obviously does business on an international scale. It is not unreasonable that they defend claims of defect in their product on an international scale." Order Denying Motion to Quash Summons, Zurcher v. Dunlop Tire & Rubber Co., No. 76180 (Super. Ct., Solano County, Cal., Apr. 20, 1983).

The Court of Appeal of the State of California issued a peremptory writ of mandate commanding the Superior Court to quash service of summons. The court concluded that "it would be unreasonable to require Asahi to respond in California solely on the basis of ultimately realized foreseeability that the product into which its component was embodied would be sold all over the world including California."

The Supreme Court of the State of California reversed and discharged the writ issued by the Court of Appeal. 39 Cal. 3d 35, 702 P.2d 543 (1985). The court observed: "Asahi has no offices, property or agents in California. It solicits no business in California and has made no direct sales [in California]." Id., at 48, 702 P.2d, at 549. Moreover, "Asahi did not design or control the system of distribution that carried its valve assemblies into California." Id., at 49, 702 P.2d, at 549. Nevertheless, the court found the exercise of jurisdiction over Asahi to be consistent with the Due Process Clause. It concluded that Asahi knew that some of the valve assemblies sold to Cheng Shin would be incorporated into tire tubes sold in California, and that Asahi benefited indirectly from the sale in California of products incorporating its components. The court considered Asahi's intentional act of placing its components into the stream of commerce - that is, by delivering the components to Cheng Shin in Taiwan - coupled with Asahi's awareness that some of the components would eventually find their way into California, sufficient to form the basis for state court jurisdiction under the Due Process Clause.

We granted certiorari, 475 U.S. 1044 (1986), and now reverse.

II-A

The Due Process Clause of the Fourteenth Amendment limits the power of a state court to exert personal jurisdiction over a nonresident defendant. "[T]he constitutional touchstone" of the determination whether an exercise of personal jurisdiction comports with due process "remains whether the defendant purposefully established 'minimum contacts' in the forum State." Burger King Corp. v. Rudzewicz, 471 U.S. 462, 474 (1985), quoting International Shoe Co. v. Washington, 326 U.S., at 316. Most recently we have reaffirmed the oft-quoted reasoning of Hanson v. Denckla, 357 U.S. 235, 253 (1958), that minimum contacts must have a basis in "some act by which the defendant purposefully avails itself of the privilege of conducting activities within the forum State, thus invoking the benefits and protections of its laws." Burger King, 471 U.S., at 475 . "Jurisdiction is proper . . . where the contacts proximately result from actions by the defendant himself that create a 'substantial connection' with the forum State." Ibid., quoting McGee v. International Life Insurance Co., 355 U.S. 220, 223 (1957) (emphasis in original).

Applying the principle that minimum contacts must be based on an act of the defendant, the Court in World-Wide Volkswagen Corp. v. Woodson, 444 U.S. 286 (1980), rejected the assertion that a consumer's unilateral act of bringing the defendant's product into the forum State was a sufficient constitutional basis for personal jurisdiction over the defendant. It had been argued in World-Wide Volkswagen that because an automobile retailer and its wholesale distributor sold a product mobile by design and purpose, they could foresee being haled into court in the distant States into which their customers might drive. The Court rejected this concept of foreseeability as an insufficient basis for jurisdiction under the Due Process Clause. Id., at 295-296. The Court disclaimed, however, the idea that "foreseeability is wholly irrelevant" to personal jurisdiction, concluding that "[t]he forum State does not exceed its powers under the Due Process Clause if it asserts personal jurisdiction over a corporation that delivers its products into the stream of commerce with the expectation that they will be purchased by consumers in the forum State." . . .

In World-Wide Volkswagen itself, the state court sought to base jurisdiction not on any act of the defendant, but on the foreseeable unilateral actions of the consumer. Since World-Wide Volkswagen, lower courts have been confronted with cases in which the defendant acted by placing a product in the stream of commerce, and the stream eventually swept defendant's product into the forum State, but the defendant did nothing else to purposefully avail itself of the market in the forum State. Some courts have understood the Due Process Clause, as interpreted in World-Wide Volkswagen, to allow an exercise of personal jurisdiction to be based on no more than the defendant's act of placing the product in the stream of commerce. Other courts have understood the Due Process Clause and the above-quoted language in World-Wide Volkswagen to require the action of the defendant to be more purposefully directed at the forum State than the mere act of placing a product in the stream of commerce.

The reasoning of the Supreme Court of California in the present case illustrates the former interpretation of World-Wide Volkswagen. The Supreme Court of California held that, because the stream of commerce eventually brought some valves Asahi sold Cheng Shin into California, Asahi's awareness that its valves would be sold in California was sufficient to permit California to exercise jurisdiction over Asahi consistent with the requirements of the Due Process Clause. The Supreme Court of California's position was consistent with those courts that have held that mere foreseeability or awareness was a constitutionally sufficient basis for personal jurisdiction if the defendant's product made its way into the forum State while still in the stream of commerce. See Bean Dredging Corp. v. Dredge Technology Corp., 744 F.2d 1081 (CA5 1984); Hedrick v. Daiko Shoji Co., 715 F.2d 1355 (CA9 1983).

Other courts, however, have understood the Due Process Clause to require something more than that the defendant was aware of its product's entry into the forum State through the stream of commerce in order for the State to exert jurisdiction over the defendant. In the present case, for example, the State Court of Appeal did not read the Due Process Clause, as interpreted by World-Wide Volkswagen, to allow "mere foreseeability that the product will enter the forum state [to] be enough by itself to establish jurisdiction over the distributor and retailer." App. to Pet. for Cert. B5. In Humble v. Toyota Motor Co., 727 F.2d 709 (CA8 1984), an injured car passenger brought suit against Arakawa Auto Body Company, a Japanese corporation that manufactured car seats for Toyota. Arakawa did no business in the United States; it had no office, affiliate, subsidiary, or agent in the United States; it manufactured its component parts outside the United States and delivered them to Toyota Motor Company in Japan. The Court of Appeals, adopting the reasoning of the District Court in that case, noted that although it "does not doubt that Arakawa could have foreseen that its product would find its way into the United States," it would be "manifestly unjust" to require Arakawa to defend itself in the United States. Id., at 710-711, quoting 578 F. Supp. 530, 533 (ND Iowa 1982). See also Hutson v. Fehr Bros., Inc., 584 F.2d 833 (CA8 1978); see generally Max Daetwyler Corp. v. R. Meyer, 762 F.2d 290, 299 (CA3 1985) (collecting "stream of commerce" cases in which the "manufacturers involved had made deliberate decisions to market their products in the forum state").

We now find this latter position to be consonant with the requirements of due process. The "substantial connection," Burger King, 471 U.S., at 475 ; McGee, 355 U.S., at 223_, between the defendant and the forum State necessary for a finding of minimum contacts must come about by an action of the defendant purposefully directed toward the forum State. Burger King, supra, at 476; Keeton v. Hustler Magazine, Inc., 465 U.S. 770, 774 (1984). The placement of a product into the stream of commerce, without more, is not an act of the defendant purposefully directed toward the forum State. Additional conduct of the defendant may indicate an intent or purpose to serve the market in the forum State, for example, designing the product for the market in the forum State, advertising in the forum State, establishing channels for providing regular advice to customers in the forum State, or marketing the product through a distributor who has agreed to serve as the sales agent in the forum State. But a defendant's awareness that the stream of commerce may or will sweep the product into the forum State does not convert the mere act of placing the product into the stream into an act purposefully directed toward the forum State.

Assuming, arguendo, that respondents have established Asahi's awareness that some of the valves sold to Cheng Shin would be incorporated into tire tubes sold in California, respondents have not demonstrated any action by Asahi to purposefully avail itself of the California market. Asahi does not do business in California. It has no office, agents, employees, or property in California. It does not advertise or otherwise solicit business in California. It did not create, control, or employ the distribution system that brought its valves to California. There is no evidence that Asahi designed its product in anticipation of sales in California. Cf. Rockwell International Corp. v. Costruzioni Aeronautiche Giovanni Agusta, 553 F. Supp. 328 (ED Pa. 1982). On the basis of these facts, the exertion of personal jurisdiction over Asahi by the Superior Court of California exceeds the limits of due process.

III

Because the facts of this case do not establish minimum contacts such that the exercise of personal jurisdiction is consistent with fair play and substantial justice, the judgment of the Supreme Court of California is reversed, and the case is remanded for further proceedings not inconsistent with this opinion.

It is so ordered.

Problem Lloyd Hull knew he had a serious drinking problem. Ever since his retirement from the Navy two years before, it seemed as though he needed to get a little high, or better, every day. After getting off work on September 21, 1977, in Berryville, Arkansas, Lloyd was on his way to visit his older sister in Okarche, Oklahoma. Next to the bottle of Jim Beam on the front seat was a loaded .22 Magnum pistol for shooting jack rabbits on his sister's farm. Lloyd was driving a 1971 Ford Torino he had bought just the week before, paying $500 down. It had a large V-8 engine, good tires and brakes, and was in perfect working condition. As he drove along, Lloyd took shots from the bottle of bourbon. After passing through Tulsa around nightfall, he relaxed as he got on the Turner Turnpike that runs to Oklahoma City. He was not in any particular hurry to get to his sister's place, and he was not paying attention to his speed. Later he assumed he must have been driving too fast on account of the liquor. Lloyd did not notice the small car ahead of him until he was nearly on top of it. By the time he managed to hit his brakes, it was too late to avoid the car. His Torino slammed into the other car, a little off center on the driver's side. In the other car were Harry and Kay Robinson. They had purchased the new Audi they were traveling in from Seaway Volkswagen in Massena, N.Y., in 1976. The following year, the Robinsons left their residence in New York for a new home in Arizona. As they passed through Oklahoma, Hull's car struck their Audi in the rear, causing a fire which severely burned Kay Robinson and her two children. Hull was an obvious defendant, but he had no liability insurance, and consequently any judgment the Robinsons could obtain against him would be uncollectible. To obtain an enforceable judgment, the Robinsons would have to sue the manufacturer of the Audi on a products liability claim.

The Robinsons brought a products-liability action in Oklahoma., claiming that their injuries resulted from defective design and placement of the Audi's gas tank and fuel system. They joined as defendants the automobile's manufacturer, Audi; its importer, Volkswagen of America, Inc.; its regional distributor, World-Wide Volkswagen Corp. ; and its retail dealer, Seaway. Seaway and World-Wide are both incorporated and do business in New York. There is no evidence that either World-Wide or Seaway does any business in Oklahoma, ships or sells any products to or in that State, has an agent to receive process there, or purchases advertisements in any media calculated to reach Oklahoma. In fact, there is no showing that any automobile sold by World-Wide or Seaway has ever entered Oklahoma with the single exception of the vehicle involved in the present case. Seaway and World-Wide entered special appearances, claiming that Oklahoma's exercise of jurisdiction over them would offend the limitations on the State's jurisdiction imposed by the Due Process Clause of the Fourteenth Amendment.

Does Oklahoma have personal jurisdiction over World-Wide or Seaway? (See, *World-Wide Volkswagen Corp. v. Woodson* 444 U.S. 286 (1980) and World-Wide Volkswagen v. Woodson -- *The Rest of the Story*, 72 Neb. L. Rev. 1122 (1993).)

Summing Up the So-Called "Stream of Commerce Cases" *Asahi Metal Industry*: Specific jurisdiction may lie over a foreign defendant that places a product into the "stream of commerce" while also "designing the product for the market in the forum State, advertising in the forum State, establishing channels for providing regular advice to customers in the forum State, or marketing the product through a distributor who has agreed to serve as the sales agent in the forum State"; *World-Wide Volkswagen*: "[I]f the sale of a product of a manufacturer or distributor such as Audi or Volkswagen is not simply an isolated occurrence, but arises from the efforts of the manufacturer or distributor to serve, directly or indirectly, the market for its product in other States, it is not unreasonable to subject it to suit in one of those States if its allegedly defective merchandise has there been the source of injury to its owner or to others."; *Calder v. Jones*: California court had specific jurisdiction to hear suit brought by California plaintiff where Florida-based publisher of a newspaper having its largest circulation in California published an article allegedly defaming the complaining Californian; under those circumstances, defendants "must `reasonably anticipate being haled into [a California] court'"; *Keeton v. Hustler Magazine*: New York resident may maintain suit for libel in New Hampshire state court against California-based magazine that sold 10,000 to 15,000 copies in New Hampshire each month; as long as the defendant "continuously and deliberately exploited the New Hampshire market," it could reasonably be expected to answer a libel suit there.

J. McIntyre Machinery, Ltd. v. Nicastro
564 US 873 (2011)

[A three-ton metal shearing machine severed four fingers on Robert Nicastro's right hand. Alleging that the machine was a dangerous product defectively made, Nicastro sought compensation from the machine's manufacturer, J. McIntyre Machinery Ltd. (McIntyre UK). Established in 1872 as a United Kingdom corporation, and headquartered in Nottingham, England. The Supreme Court of New Jersey, held that New Jersey's courts could exercise personal jurisdiction over the British manufacturer. The U.S. Supreme Court granted review.]

Justice KENNEDY announced the judgment of the Court and delivered an opinion, in which THE CHIEF JUSTICE, Justice SCALIA, and Justice THOMAS join.

Whether a person or entity is subject to the jurisdiction of a state court despite not having been present in the State either at the time of suit or at the time of the alleged injury, and despite not having consented to the exercise of jurisdiction, is a question that arises with great frequency in the routine course of litigation. The rules and standards for determining when a State does or does not have jurisdiction over an absent party have been unclear because of decades-old questions left open in *Asahi Metal Industry Co. v. Superior Court of Cal., Solano Cty.,* 480 U.S. 102, 107 S.Ct. 1026, 94 L.Ed.2d 92 (1987).

Here, the Supreme Court of New Jersey, relying in part on *Asahi,* held that New Jersey's courts can exercise jurisdiction over a foreign manufacturer of a product so long as the manufacturer "knows or reasonably should know that its products are distributed through a nationwide distribution system that might lead to those products being sold in any of the fifty states." *Nicastro v. McIntyre Machinery America, Ltd.,* 201 N.J. 48, 76, 77, 987 A.2d 575, 591, 592 (2010). Applying that test, the court concluded that a British manufacturer of scrap metal machines was subject to jurisdiction in New Jersey, even though at no time had it advertised in, sent goods to, or in any relevant sense targeted the State.

That decision cannot be sustained. Although the New Jersey Supreme Court issued an extensive opinion with careful attention to this Court's cases and to its own precedent, the "stream of commerce" metaphor carried the decision far afield. Due process protects the defendant's right not to be coerced except by lawful judicial power. As a general rule, the exercise of judicial power is not lawful unless the defendant "purposefully avails itself of the privilege of conducting activities within the forum State, thus invoking the benefits and protections of its laws." *Hanson v. Denckla,* 357 U.S. 235, 253, 78 S.Ct. 1228, 2 L.Ed.2d 1283 (1958). There may be exceptions, say, for instance, in cases involving an intentional tort. But the general rule is applicable in this products-liability case, and the so-called "stream-of-commerce" doctrine cannot displace it.

I

This case arises from a products-liability suit filed in New Jersey state court. Robert Nicastro seriously injured his hand while using a metal-shearing machine manufactured by J. McIntyre Machinery, Ltd. (J. McIntyre). The accident occurred in New Jersey, but the machine was manufactured in England, where J. McIntyre is incorporated and operates. The question here is whether the New Jersey courts have jurisdiction over J. McIntyre, notwithstanding the fact that the company at no time either marketed goods in the State or shipped them there. Nicastro was a plaintiff in the New Jersey trial court and is the respondent here; J. McIntyre was a defendant and is now the petitioner.

At oral argument in this Court, Nicastro's counsel stressed three primary facts in defense of New Jersey's assertion of jurisdiction over J. McIntyre.

First, an independent company agreed to sell J. McIntyre's machines in the United States. J. McIntyre itself did not sell its machines to buyers in this country beyond the U.S. distributor, and there is no allegation that the distributor was under J. McIntyre's control.

Second, J. McIntyre officials attended annual conventions for the scrap recycling industry to advertise J. McIntyre's machines alongside the distributor. The conventions took place in various States, but never in New Jersey.

Third, no more than four machines (the record suggests only one, see App. to Pet. for Cert. 130a), including the machine that caused the injuries that are the basis for this suit, ended up in New Jersey

In addition to these facts emphasized by petitioner, the New Jersey Supreme Court noted that J. McIntyre held both United States and European patents on its recycling technology. 201 N.J., at 55, 987 A.2d, at 579. It also noted that the U.S. distributor "structured [its] advertising and sales efforts in accordance with" J. McIntyre's "direction and guidance whenever possible," and that "at least some of the machines were sold on consignment to" the distributor.

In light of these facts, the New Jersey Supreme Court concluded that New Jersey courts could exercise jurisdiction over petitioner without contravention of the Due Process Clause. Jurisdiction was proper, in that court's view, because the injury occurred in New Jersey; because petitioner knew or reasonably should have known "that its products are distributed through a nationwide distribution system that might lead to those products being sold in any of the fifty states"; and because petitioner failed to "take some reasonable step to prevent the distribution of its products in this State." *Id.*, at 77, 987 A.2d, at 592.

Both the New Jersey Supreme Court's holding and its account of what it called "[t]he stream-of-commerce doctrine of jurisdiction," *id.*, at 80, 987 A.2d, at 594, were incorrect, however. This Court's *Asahi* decision may be responsible in part for that court's error regarding the stream of commerce, and this case presents an opportunity to provide greater clarity.

II

. . . A court may subject a defendant to judgment only when the defendant has sufficient contacts with the sovereign "such that the maintenance of the suit does not offend 'traditional notions of fair play and substantial justice.'" International Shoe Co. v. Washington, 326 U.S. 310, 316, 66 S.Ct. 154, 90 L.Ed. 95 (1945) (quoting Milliken v. Meyer, 311 U.S. 457, 463, 61 S.Ct. 339, 85 L.Ed. 278 (1940)). Freeform notions of fundamental fairness divorced from traditional practice cannot transform a judgment rendered in the absence of authority into law. As a general rule, the sovereign's exercise of power requires some act by which the defendant "purposefully avails itself of the privilege of conducting activities within the forum State, thus invoking the benefits and protections of its laws," Hanson, 357 U.S., at 253, 78 S.Ct. 1228, though in some cases, as with an intentional tort, the defendant might well fall within the State's authority by reason of his attempt to obstruct its laws. In products-liability cases like this one, it is the defendant's purposeful availment that makes jurisdiction consistent with "traditional notions of fair play and substantial justice."

A person may submit to a State's authority in a number of ways. There is, of course, explicit consent. *E.g., Insurance Corp. of Ireland v. Compagnie des Bauxites de Guinee*, 456 U.S. 694, 703, 102 S.Ct. 2099, 72 L.Ed.2d 492 (1982). Presence within a State at the time suit commences through service of process is another example. See *Burnham, supra*. Citizenship or domicile—or, by analogy, incorporation or principal place of business for corporations—also indicates general submission to a State's powers. *Goodyear Dunlop Tires Operations, S.A. v. Brown, post*, p. 2854. Each of these examples reveals circumstances, or a course of conduct, from which it is proper to infer an intention to benefit from and thus an intention to submit to the laws of the forum State. Cf. *Burger King Corp. v. Rudzewicz*, 471 U.S. 462, 476, 105 S.Ct. 2174, 85 L.Ed.2d 528 (1985). These examples support exercise of the general jurisdiction of the State's courts and allow the State to resolve both matters that originate within the State and those based on activities and events elsewhere. *Helicopteros Nacionales de Colombia, S.A. v. Hall*, 466 U.S. 408, 414, and n. 9, 104 S.Ct. 1868, 80 L.Ed.2d 404 (1984). By contrast, those who live or operate primarily outside a State have a due process right not to be subjected to judgment in its courts as a general matter.

There is also a more limited form of submission to a State's authority for disputes that "arise out of or are connected with the activities within the state." *International Shoe Co., supra*, at 319, 66 S.Ct. 154. Where a defendant "purposefully avails itself of the privilege of conducting activities within the forum State, thus invoking the benefits and protections of its [2788] laws," *Hanson, supra*, at 253, 78 S.Ct. 1228, it submits to the judicial power of an otherwise foreign sovereign to the extent that power is exercised in connection with the defendant's activities touching on the State. In other words, submission through contact with and activity directed at a sovereign may justify specific jurisdiction "in a suit arising out of or related to the defendant's contacts with the forum."

The imprecision arising from *Asahi,* for the most part, results from its statement of the relation between jurisdiction and the "stream of commerce." The stream of commerce, like other metaphors, has its deficiencies as well as its utility. It refers to the movement of goods from manufacturers through distributors to consumers, yet beyond that descriptive purpose its meaning is far from exact. This Court has stated that a defendant's placing goods into the stream of commerce "with the expectation that they will be purchased by consumers within the forum State" may indicate purposeful availment. *World-Wide Volkswagen Corp. v. Woodson,* 444 U.S. 286, 298, 100 S.Ct. 559, 62 L.Ed.2d 490 (1980) (finding that expectation lacking). But that statement does not amend the general rule of personal jurisdiction. It merely observes that a defendant may in an appropriate case be subject to jurisdiction without entering the forum—itself an unexceptional proposition—as where manufacturers or distributors "seek to serve" a given State's market. *Id.,* at 295, 100 S.Ct. 559. The principal inquiry in cases of this sort is whether the defendant's activities manifest an intention to submit to the power of a sovereign. In other words, the defendant must "purposefully avai[l] itself of the privilege of conducting activities within the forum State, thus invoking the benefits and protections of its laws." *Hanson, supra,* at 253, 78 S.Ct. 1228; *Insurance Corp., supra,* at 704-705, 102 S.Ct. 2099 ("[A]ctions of the defendant may amount to a legal submission to the jurisdiction of the court"). Sometimes a defendant does so by sending its goods rather than its agents. The defendant's transmission of goods permits the exercise of jurisdiction only where the defendant can be said to have targeted the forum; as a general rule, it is not enough that the defendant might have predicted that its goods will reach the forum State.

In *Asahi,* an opinion by Justice Brennan for four Justices outlined a different approach. It discarded the central concept of sovereign authority in favor of considerations of fairness and foreseeability. As that concurrence contended, "jurisdiction premised on the placement of a product into the stream of commerce [without more] is consistent with the Due Process Clause," for "[a]s long as a participant in this process is aware that the final product is being marketed in the forum State, the possibility of a lawsuit there cannot come as a surprise." 480 U.S., at 117, 107 S.Ct. 1026 (opinion concurring in part and concurring in judgment). It was the premise of the concurring opinion that the defendant's ability to anticipate suit renders the assertion of jurisdiction fair. In this way, the opinion made foreseeability the touchstone of jurisdiction.

The standard set forth in Justice Brennan's concurrence was rejected in an opinion written by Justice O'Connor; but the relevant part of that opinion, too, commanded the assent of only four Justices, not a majority of the Court. That opinion stated: "The `substantial connection' between the defendant and the forum State necessary for a finding of minimum contacts must come about by an action of the defendant purposefully directed toward the forum State. The placement of a product into the stream of commerce, without more, is not an act of the defendant purposefully directed toward the forum State." *Id.,* at 112, 107 S.Ct. 1026 (emphasis deleted; citations omitted).

Since *Asahi* was decided, the courts have sought to reconcile the competing opinions. But Justice Brennan's concurrence, advocating a rule based on general notions of fairness and foreseeability, is inconsistent with the premises of lawful judicial power. This Court's precedents make clear that it is the defendant's actions, not his expectations, that empower a State's courts to subject him to judgment. . . .

Two principles are implicit in the foregoing. First, personal jurisdiction requires a forum-by-forum, or sovereign-by-sovereign, analysis. The question is whether a defendant has followed a course of conduct directed at the society or economy existing within the jurisdiction of a given sovereign, so that the sovereign has the power to subject the defendant to judgment concerning that conduct. Personal jurisdiction, of course, restricts "judicial power not as a matter of sovereignty, but as a matter of individual liberty," for due process protects the individual's right to be subject only to lawful power. *Insurance Corp.,* 456 U.S., at 702, 102 S.Ct. 2099. But whether a judicial judgment is lawful depends on whether the sovereign has authority to render it.

The second principle is a corollary of the first. Because the United States is a distinct sovereign, a defendant may in principle be subject to the jurisdiction of the courts of the United States but not of any particular State. This is consistent with the premises and unique genius of our Constitution. Ours is "a legal system unprecedented in form and design, establishing two orders of government, each with its own direct relationship, its own privity, its own set of mutual rights and obligations to the people who sustain it and are governed by it." *U.S. Term Limits, Inc. v. Thornton,* 514 U.S. 779, 838, 115 S.Ct. 1842, 131 L.Ed.2d 881 (1995) (KENNEDY, J., concurring). For jurisdiction, a litigant may have the requisite relationship with the United States Government but not with the government of any individual State. That would be an exceptional case, however. If the defendant is a domestic domiciliary, the courts of its home State are available and can exercise general jurisdiction. And if another State were to assert jurisdiction in an inappropriate case, it would upset the federal balance, which posits that each State has a sovereignty that is not subject to unlawful intrusion by other States. Furthermore, foreign corporations will often target or concentrate on particular States, subjecting them to specific jurisdiction in those forums.

It must be remembered, however, that although this case and *Asahi* both involve foreign manufacturers, the undesirable consequences of Justice Brennan's approach are no less significant for domestic producers. The owner of a small Florida farm might sell crops to a large nearby distributor, for example, who might then distribute them to grocers across the country. If foreseeability were the controlling criterion, the farmer could be sued in Alaska or any number of other States' courts without ever leaving town. And the issue of foreseeability may itself be contested so that significant expenses are incurred just on the preliminary issue of jurisdiction. Jurisdictional rules should avoid these costs whenever possible.

The conclusion that the authority to subject a defendant to judgment depends on purposeful availment, consistent with Justice O'Connor's opinion in *Asahi,* does not by itself resolve many difficult questions of jurisdiction that will arise in particular cases. The defendant's conduct and the economic realities of the market the defendant seeks to serve will differ across cases, and judicial exposition will, in common-law fashion, clarify the contours of that principle.

III

In this case, petitioner directed marketing and sales efforts at the United States. It may be that, assuming it were otherwise empowered to legislate on the subject, the Congress could authorize the exercise of jurisdiction in appropriate courts. That circumstance is not presented in this case, however, and it is neither necessary nor appropriate to address here any constitutional concerns that might be attendant to that exercise of power. See *Asahi,* 480 U.S., at 113, 107 S.Ct. 1026, n. Nor is it necessary to determine what substantive law might apply were Congress to authorize jurisdiction in a federal court in New Jersey. See *Hanson,* 357 U.S., at 254, 78 S.Ct. 1228 ("The issue is personal jurisdiction, not choice of law"). A sovereign's legislative authority to regulate conduct may present considerations different from those presented by its authority to subject a defendant to judgment in its courts. Here the question concerns the authority of a New Jersey state court to exercise jurisdiction, so it is petitioner's purposeful contacts with New Jersey, not with the United States, that alone are relevant.

Respondent has not established that J. McIntyre engaged in conduct purposefully directed at New Jersey. Recall that respondent's claim of jurisdiction centers on three facts: The distributor agreed to sell J. McIntyre's machines in the United States; J. McIntyre officials attended trade shows in several States but not in New Jersey; and up to four machines ended up in New Jersey. The British manufacturer had no office in New Jersey; it neither paid taxes nor owned property there; and it neither advertised in, nor sent any employees to, the State. Indeed, after discovery the trial court found that the "defendant does not have a single contact with New Jersey short of the machine in question ending up in this state." These facts may reveal an intent to serve the U.S. market, but they do not show that J. McIntyre purposefully availed itself of the New Jersey market. . . .

Due process protects petitioner's right to be subject only to lawful authority. At no time did petitioner engage in any activities in New Jersey that reveal an intent to invoke or benefit from the protection of its laws. New Jersey is without power to adjudge the rights and liabilities of J. McIntyre, and its exercise of jurisdiction would violate due process. The contrary judgment of the New Jersey Supreme Court is

Reversed.

Abdouch v. Lopez
285 Neb. 718 (2013)

I. NATURE OF CASE

Helen Abdouch filed suit against an out-of-state defendant, Ken Lopez, individually and as owner and operator of his company, Ken Lopez Bookseller (KLB), under Neb. Rev.Stat. § 20-202 (Reissue 2012) for violating her privacy rights by using an inscription in Abdouch's stolen copy of a book entitled "Revolutionary Road" to advertise on the KLB rare books website. Although not reflected in the case title, the parties and the lower court refer to Lopez and KLB as separate defendants, and so we will treat them as such in this opinion. Lopez and KLB filed, and the district court sustained, a motion to dismiss for lack of personal jurisdiction. Abdouch now appeals.

II. BACKGROUND

Abdouch is a resident of Omaha, Nebraska. In 1960, Abdouch was the executive secretary of the Nebraska presidential campaign of John F. Kennedy. In 1963, Abdouch received a copy of the book, which was inscribed to her by the late author Richard Yates. The inscription stated: "For Helen Abdouch — with admiration and best wishes. Dick Yates. 8/19/1963."

At some time not specified by the record, Abdouch's inscribed copy of the book was stolen. Lopez and his company, KLB, bought the book in 2009 from a seller in Georgia and sold it that same year to a customer not in Nebraska. In 2011, Abdouch, who does not own a computer, learned from a friend that Lopez had used the inscription in the book for advertising purposes on his Web site, http://www.lopezbooks.com. The commercial advertisement had been used with the word "SOLD" on the Web site for more than 3 years after the book was sold. The advertisement associated with a picture of the inscription stated in relevant part:

> This copy is inscribed by Yates: For Helen Abdouch — with admiration and best wishes. Dick Yates. 8/19/63. Yates had worked as a speech writer for Robert Kennedy when Kennedy served as Attorney General; Abdouch was the executive secretary of the Nebraska (John F.) Kennedy organization when Robert Kennedy was campaign manager. The book is cocked; the boards are stained; the text is clean. A very good copy in a near fine, spine-tanned dust jacket. A scarce book, and it is extremely uncommon to find this advance issue of it signed. Given the date of the inscription — that is, during JFK's Presidency — and the connection between writer and recipient, it's reasonable to suppose this was an author's copy, presented to Abdouch by Yates. [# 028096] SOLD

Lopez is the owner and sole proprietor of KLB, which is a rare book business based in Hadley, Massachusetts. KLB buys and sells rare books and manuscripts. KLB sells these books and manuscripts through published catalogs and through the Web site.

Generally, the website contains KLB's inventory of rare books and manuscripts. Individuals that visit the Website can browse and search the inventory. If individuals or entities choose to, they can purchase through the Web site.

In addition to selling books through catalogs and online, KLB attends and has exhibits at various antiquarian bookfairs. Over the past 25 years, Lopez and/or KLB have attended and exhibited at an estimated 300 to 400 bookfairs in various locations within the United States, as well as overseas. Lopez and KLB have never exhibited at or attended a book fair in Nebraska.

KLB has an active mailing list for its catalogs of approximately 1,000 individuals and entities. Among that list, only two are located in Nebraska. According to Lopez' affidavit, KLB did not solicit the two Nebraska members; rather, the two individuals solicited contact with KLB and requested to be placed on the mailing list. Neither of these two individuals has any connection to the claims at issue in this lawsuit.

Neither Lopez nor KLB is registered to do business in Nebraska in any capacity. Lopez and KLB do not own or lease real estate in Nebraska, do not maintain an office in Nebraska, and have never conducted or attended meetings in Nebraska. Neither Lopez nor KLB has paid any Nebraska sales tax.

Lopez and KLB do not advertise in any publication that is published in or that otherwise originates from Nebraska. Lopez and KLB do not advertise in any publication that specifically targets potential customers in Nebraska. Beyond the two customers on the mailing list, Lopez and KLB do not target or reach out to customers or potential customers in Nebraska in any way.

The amount of contact with Nebraska and Nebraska residents is also demonstrated by KLB's sales. KLB's total sales for 2009 through 2011 were approximately $3.9 million. In 2009, KLB sold three books to a single Nebraska customer, earning a total of $76. In 2010, KLB sold three books to two Nebraska customers for $239.87. In 2011, two books were sold to a Nebraska customer for $299. All of these sales were initiated by the customers through the Web site.

Abdouch alleges that Lopez knew she was a resident of Nebraska when he violated her privacy. Lopez avers in his affidavit that he did not know that Abdouch was a resident of Nebraska until in or around June 2011, at which time he was contacted by someone and told that Abdouch lived in Nebraska. In Abdouch's affidavit, she counters that she has been informed that she can be easily found and identified as a Nebraska resident on the Internet and that there are only two people named "Helen Abdouch" in the entire United States.

After discovering Lopez and KLB's use of the inscribed book as an advertisement, Abdouch brought suit pursuant to § 20-202 against Lopez and KLB for violating her vigilantly protected right of privacy. In a relevant part of the complaint, she alleged:

5. That ... Lopez did an internet search for Helen Abdouch and found a brief reference to her as executive secretary of the Nebraska (John F.) Kennedy campaign in an October 10, 1960, Time Magazine article entitled: DEMOCRATS: Little Brother is Watching based on an interview with Robert F. Kennedy, campaign manager of his brother's John F. Kennedy's presidential campaign.

6. That based on this article, ... Lopez wrote an ad for the sale of Abdouch's book on his online catalogue linking [Abdouch] to Yates through the Kennedy connection ... and placed on [the KLB Web site] at www.lopezbooks.com and which was broadcast or sent out over the world wide web.

7. That by his own admission, ... Lopez did not search the internet to determine whether ... Abdouch was still alive and assumed she was dead so he made no further effort to get her permission.

Lopez and KLB filed a motion to dismiss for lack of personal jurisdiction, alleging that they do not have sufficient contacts with Nebraska for purposes of personal jurisdiction and have not purposefully availed themselves of the benefits and protections of the forum state. The district court granted the motion and dismissed the case. . . .

V. ANALYSIS

Abdouch argues that the district court erred in finding that the State lacked personal jurisdiction over Lopez and KLB. Abdouch argues that Lopez and KLB's active website deliberately targeted Abdouch with tortious conduct. She alleges these contacts are sufficient to create the necessary minimum contacts for specific jurisdiction.

Personal jurisdiction is the power of a tribunal to subject and bind a particular entity to its decisions. Before a court can exercise personal jurisdiction over a nonresident defendant, the court must determine, first, whether the long-arm statute is satisfied and, if the long-arm statute is satisfied, second, whether minimum contacts exist between the defendant and the forum state for personal jurisdiction over the defendant without offending due process.

1. LONG-ARM STATUTE

Nebraska's long-arm statute, Neb.Rev.Stat. § 25-536 (Reissue 2008), provides: "A court may exercise personal jurisdiction over a person ... [w]ho has any other contact with or maintains any other relation to this state to afford a basis for the exercise of personal jurisdiction consistent with the Constitution of the United States." It was the intention of the Legislature to provide for the broadest allowable jurisdiction over nonresidents under Nebraska's long-arm statute.8 Nebraska's long-arm statute, therefore, extends Nebraska's jurisdiction over nonresidents having any contact with or maintaining any relation to this state as far as the U.S. Constitution permits. "[W]hen a state construes its long-arm statute to confer jurisdiction to the fullest extent permitted by the due process clause, ... the inquiry collapses into the single question of whether exercise of personal jurisdiction comports with due process." Therefore, the issue is whether Lopez and KLB had sufficient contacts with Nebraska so that the exercise of personal jurisdiction would not offend federal principles of due process. . . .

(a) "Sliding Scale" Test

The Internet and its interaction with personal jurisdiction over a nonresident is an issue of first impression for this court. Although other courts will help guide our decision, we take note that technological advances do not render impotent our longstanding principles on personal jurisdiction. The U.S. Supreme Court explained:

> As technological progress has increased the flow of commerce between States, the need for jurisdiction over nonresidents has undergone a similar increase. At the same time, progress in communications and transportation has made the defense of a suit in a foreign tribunal less burdensome. In response to these changes, the requirements for personal jurisdiction over nonresidents have evolved from the rigid rule of Pennoyer v. Neff, 95 U.S. 714 [24 L.Ed. 565] [(1877)], to the flexible standard of International Shoe Co. v. Washington, 326 U.S. 310 [66 S.Ct. 154, 90 L.Ed. 95] [(1945)]. But it is a mistake to assume that this trend heralds the eventual demise of all restrictions on the personal jurisdiction of state courts.... Those restrictions are more than a guarantee of immunity from inconvenient or distant litigation. They are a consequence of territorial limitations on the power of the respective States.

With this in mind, the Eighth Circuit, as well as the majority of circuits, has adopted the analytical framework set forth in *Zippo Mfg. Co. v. Zippo Dot Com., Inc.,* for internet jurisdiction cases. In that case, Zippo Manufacturing Company filed a complaint in Pennsylvania against nonresident Zippo Dot Com, Inc., alleging causes of action under the federal Trademark Act of 1946. Zippo Dot Com's contact with Pennsylvania consisted of over 3,000 Pennsylvania residents subscribing to its Web site. The district court in *Zippo Mfg. Co.* famously created a "sliding scale" test that considers a Web site's interactivity and the nature of the commercial activities conducted over the Internet to determine whether the courts have personal jurisdiction over nonresident defendants. The court in *Zippo Mfg. Co.* explained the "sliding scale" as follows:

> At one end of the spectrum are situations where a defendant clearly does business over the Internet. If the defendant enters into contracts with residents of a foreign jurisdiction that involve the knowing and repeated transmission of computer files over the Internet, personal jurisdiction is proper.... At the opposite end are situations where a defendant has simply posted information on an Internet Web site which is accessible to users in foreign jurisdictions. A passive website that does little more than make information available to those who are interested in it is not grounds for the exercise [of] personal jurisdiction.... The

middle ground is occupied by interactive Web sites where a user can exchange information with the host computer. In these cases, the exercise of jurisdiction is determined by examining the level of interactivity and commercial nature of the exchange of information that occurs on the Web site.

The district court held that Pennsylvania had personal jurisdiction over Zippo Dot Com and the causes of action. In doing so, the district court made two important findings. First, the district court found that the Zippo Dot Com Web site was a highly interactive commercial Web site. Second, and more important, the district court found that the trademark infringement causes of action were related to the business contacts with customers in Pennsylvania.

- Although widely recognized and accepted, most circuits use the *Zippo Mfg. Co.* sliding scale of interactivity test only as a starting point. As the Second Circuit noted, "'it does not amount to a separate framework for analyzing internet-based jurisdiction'"; instead, "'traditional statutory and constitutional principles remain the touchstone of the inquiry.'"

The Seventh Circuit has noted that "'[c]ourts should be careful in resolving questions about personal jurisdiction involving online contacts to ensure that a defendant is not haled into court simply because the defendant owns or operates a website that is accessible in the forum state, even if that site is "interactive."'" Many courts have held that even if the defendant operates a "'highly interactive'" Web site which is accessible from, but does not target, the forum state, then the defendant may not be haled into court in that state without offending the Constitution.

Our precedent states that for there to be specific personal jurisdiction, the cause of action must arise out of or be related to the defendant's contacts with the forum state. This is consistent with the U.S. Supreme Court's precedent which has stated "mere purchases, even if occurring at regular intervals, are not enough to warrant a State's assertion of *in personam* jurisdiction over a nonresident corporation in a cause of action not related to those purchase transactions."

In the case at hand, it is evident that the Web site is interactive under the *Zippo Mfg. Co.* sliding scale test. In his affidavit, Lopez admits that customers can browse and purchase books from the online inventory. Lopez admits that he has two customers in Nebraska who are on the mailing list for KLB's catalogs. He admits that from 2009 through 2011, a total of $614.87 in sales from the Web site was made to Nebraska residents out of an estimated $3.9 million in total sales.

But, beyond the minimal Web site sales to Nebraska residents and mailing catalogs to two Nebraska residents, Lopez' and KLB's contacts with Nebraska are nonexistent. Lopez and KLB do not own, lease, or rent land in Nebraska. They have never advertised directly in Nebraska, participated in bookfairs in Nebraska, or attended meetings in Nebraska, and neither has paid sales tax in Nebraska.

Furthermore, the Seventh Circuit has recently stated that when "the plaintiff's claims are for intentional torts, the inquiry focuses on whether the conduct underlying the claims was purposely directed at the forum state." The reason for requiring purposeful direction is to "`ensure that an out-of-state defendant is not bound to appear to account for merely "random, fortuitous, or attenuated contacts" with the forum state.'" Here, Abdouch's cause of action is an intentional tort based on Nebraska's privacy statute. There is no evidence, as discussed in greater detail later in the opinion, that Lopez and KLB purposefully directed the advertisement at Nebraska. Further, there is no evidence that Lopez and KLB intended to invade Abdouch's privacy in the State of Nebraska. Rather, the limited Internet sales appear to be random, fortuitous, and attenuated contacts with Nebraska.

Therefore, although Lopez and KLB's Web site is highly interactive, all of the contacts created by the Web site with the State of Nebraska are unrelated to Abdouch's cause of action.

(b) *Calder* Effects Test

Abdouch argues that the effects test formulated by the U.S. Supreme Court in *Calder v. Jones* creates personal jurisdiction over Lopez and KLB, because Lopez and KLB aimed their tortious conduct at Abdouch and the State of Nebraska. In *Calder*, two Florida residents participated in the publication of an article about a California resident who brought a libel action in California against the Florida residents. Both defendants asserted that as Florida residents, they were not subject to the jurisdiction of the California court in which the libel action was filed. The Supreme Court rejected the defendants' argument and noted that the defendants were not charged with mere untargeted negligence. Rather, their intentional, and allegedly tortious, actions were expressly aimed at California. Petitioner[s] wrote and ... edited an article that they knew would have a potentially devastating impact upon respondent. And they knew that the brunt of that injury would be felt by respondent in the State in which she lives and works and in which the National Enquirer has its largest circulation. Under the circumstances, petitioners must reasonably anticipate being haled into court there to answer for the truth of the statements made in their article.

In coming to its holding, the U.S. Supreme Court created a test, now known as the *Calder* effects test, which has been explained by the Eighth Circuit:

> [A] defendant's tortious acts can serve as a source of personal jurisdiction only where the plaintiff makes a prima facie showing that the defendant's acts (1) were intentional, (2) were uniquely or expressly aimed at the forum state, and (3) caused harm, the brunt of which was suffered — and which the defendant knew was likely to be suffered — [in the forum state].

The Third Circuit has noted that the effects test "can only be satisfied if the plaintiff can point to contacts which demonstrate that the defendant *expressly aimed* its tortious conduct at the forum, and thereby made the forum the focal point of the tortious activity." Stated another way by the Third Circuit, "the effects test asks whether the plaintiff felt the brunt of the harm in the forum state, but it also asks whether defendants *knew* that the plaintiff would suffer the harm there and whether they *aimed* their tortious conduct at that state." Similarly, the Eighth Circuit has stated that the *Calder* effects test "allows the assertion of personal jurisdiction over non-resident defendants whose acts 'are performed for the very purpose of having their consequences felt in the forum state.'"

. . . Lopez and KLB's placement of the advertisement online was directed at the entire world, without expressly aiming the posting at the State of Nebraska. Abdouch pleaded in her complaint that the advertisement was "'broadcast' or sent out over the world wide web," but Abdouch failed to plead facts that demonstrate that Nebraska residents were targeted with the advertisement. Although the advertisement does mention that "Abdouch was the executive secretary of the Nebraska (John F.) Kennedy organization," the advertisement does not expressly direct its offer of sale to Nebraska. As in *Johnson*, the mention of Nebraska here is incidental and was not included for the purposes of having the consequences felt in Nebraska. As in *Revell*, Lopez did not know that Abdouch was a resident of Nebraska. He assumed that she had passed away and thus had no way of knowing that the brunt of harm would be suffered in Nebraska. Abdouch's complaint fails to demonstrate that Lopez and KLB had an intent to target and focus on Nebraska residents. . . .

VI. CONCLUSION

We conclude that Abdouch's complaint fails to plead facts to demonstrate that Lopez and KLB have sufficient minimum contacts with the State of Nebraska. Although the Web site used to post the advertisement is interactive, the contacts created by the Web site are unrelated to Abdouch's cause of action. Furthermore, under the *Calder* effects test, the pleadings fail to establish that Lopez and KLB expressly aimed their tortious conduct at the State of Nebraska. For these reasons, Lopez and KLB could not have anticipated being haled into a Nebraska court for their online advertisement.

AFFIRMED.

> **How to Analyze a Personal Jurisdiction Issue**
>
> (1) Is there a statute which authorizes the assumption of personal jurisdiction,
>
> if so
>
> (2) does the statute comport with the minimum contacts analysis of *Int'l Shoe*?

General *In Personam* Jurisdiction Over Corporations

General jurisdiction requires affiliations "so 'continuous and systematic' as to render [the foreign corporation] essentially at home in the forum State." i.e., comparable to a domestic enterprise in that State.

Goodyear Dunlop Tires Operations, S.A. v. Brown
564 US 915 (2011)

Justice GINSBURG delivered the opinion of the Court.

This case concerns the jurisdiction of state courts over corporations organized and operating abroad. We address, in particular, this question: Are foreign subsidiaries of a United States parent corporation amenable to suit in state court on claims unrelated to any activity of the subsidiaries in the forum State?

A bus accident outside Paris that took the lives of two 13-year-old boys from North Carolina gave rise to the litigation we here consider. Attributing the accident to a defective tire manufactured in Turkey at the plant of a foreign subsidiary of The Goodyear Tire and Rubber Company (Goodyear USA), the boys' parents commenced an action for damages in a North Carolina state court; they named as defendants Goodyear USA, an Ohio corporation, and three of its subsidiaries, organized and operating, respectively, in Turkey, France, and Luxembourg. Goodyear USA, which had plants in North Carolina and regularly engaged in commercial activity there, did not contest the North Carolina court's jurisdiction over it; Goodyear USA's foreign subsidiaries, however, maintained that North Carolina lacked adjudicatory authority over them.

A state court's assertion of jurisdiction exposes defendants to the State's coercive power and is therefore subject to review for compatibility with the Fourteenth Amendment's Due Process Clause. *International Shoe Co. v. Washington,* 326 U.S. 310, 316, 66 S.Ct. 154, 90 L.Ed. 95 (1945) (assertion of jurisdiction over out-of-state corporation must comply with "'traditional [2851] notions of fair play and substantial justice'" (quoting *Milliken v. Meyer,* 311 U.S. 457, 463, 61 S.Ct. 339, 85 L.Ed. 278 (1940))). Opinions in the wake of the path marking *International Shoe* decision have differentiated between general or all-purpose jurisdiction, and specific or case-linked jurisdiction. *Helicopteros Nacionales de Colombia, S.A. v. Hall,* 466 U.S. 408, 414, nn. 8, 9, 104 S.Ct. 1868, 80 L.Ed.2d 404 (1984).

A court may assert general jurisdiction over foreign (sister-state or foreign-country) corporations to hear any and all claims against them when their affiliations with the State are so "continuous and systematic" as to render them essentially at home in the forum State. See *International Shoe,* 326 U.S., at 317, 66 S.Ct. 154. Specific jurisdiction, on the other hand, depends on an "affiliatio[n] between the forum and the underlying controversy," principally, activity or an occurrence that takes place in the forum State and is therefore subject to the State's regulation. von Mehren & Trautman, Jurisdiction to Adjudicate: A Suggested Analysis, 79 Harv. L.Rev. 1121, 1136 (1966) (hereinafter von Mehren & Trautman); see Brilmayer et al., A General Look at General Jurisdiction, 66 Texas L.Rev. 721, 782 (1988) (hereinafter Brilmayer). In contrast to general, all-purpose jurisdiction, specific jurisdiction is confined to adjudication of "issues deriving from, or connected with, the very controversy that establishes jurisdiction."

Because the episode-in-suit, the bus accident, occurred in France, and the tire alleged to have caused the accident was manufactured and sold abroad, North Carolina courts lacked specific jurisdiction to adjudicate the controversy. The North Carolina Court of Appeals so acknowledged. *Brown v. Meter,* 199 N.C.App. 50, 57-58, 681 S.E.2d 382, 388 (2009). Were the foreign subsidiaries nonetheless amenable to general jurisdiction in North Carolina courts? Confusing or blending general and specific jurisdictional inquiries, the North Carolina courts answered yes. Some of the tires made abroad by Goodyear's foreign subsidiaries, the North Carolina Court of Appeals stressed, had reached North Carolina through "the stream of commerce"; that connection, the Court of Appeals believed, gave North Carolina courts the handle needed for the exercise of general jurisdiction over the foreign corporations. *Id.,* at 67-68, 681 S.E.2d, at 394-395.

A connection so limited between the forum and the foreign corporation, we hold, is an inadequate basis for the exercise of general jurisdiction. Such a connection does not establish the "continuous and systematic" affiliation necessary to empower North Carolina courts to entertain claims unrelated to the foreign corporation's contacts with the State. . . .

Endeavoring to give specific content to the "fair play and substantial justice" concept, the Court in *International Shoe* classified cases involving out-of-state corporate defendants. First, as in *International Shoe* itself, jurisdiction unquestionably could be asserted where the corporation's in-state activity is "continuous and systematic" and *that activity gave rise to the episode-in-suit.* 326 U.S., at 317, 66 S.Ct. 154. Further, the Court observed, the commission of certain "single or occasional acts" in a State may be sufficient to render a corporation answerable in that State with respect to those acts, though not with respect to matters unrelated to the forum connections. *Id.,* at 318, 66 S.Ct. 154. The heading courts today use to encompass these two *International Shoe* categories is "specific jurisdiction." See von Mehren & Trautman 1144-1163. Adjudicatory authority is "specific" when the suit "aris[es] out of or relate[s] to the defendant's contacts with the forum." . . .

In only two decisions postdating *International Shoe* has this Court considered whether an out-of-state corporate defendant's in-state contacts were sufficiently "continuous and systematic" to justify the exercise of general jurisdiction over claims unrelated to those contacts: *Perkins v. Benguet Consol. Mining Co.,* 342 U.S. 437, 72 S.Ct. 413, 96 L.Ed. 485 (1952) (general jurisdiction appropriately exercised over Philippine corporation sued in Ohio, where the company's affairs were overseen during World War II); and *Helicopteros,* 466 U.S. 408, 104 S.Ct. 1868, 80 L.Ed.2d 404 (helicopter owned by Colombian corporation crashed in Peru; survivors of U.S. citizens who died in the crash, the Court held, could not maintain wrongful-death actions against the Colombian corporation in Texas, for the corporation's helicopter purchases and purchase-linked activity in Texas were insufficient to subject it to Texas court's general jurisdiction).

B

To justify the exercise of general jurisdiction over petitioners, the North Carolina courts relied on the petitioners' placement of their tires in the "stream of commerce." See *supra,* at 2852. The [2855] stream-of-commerce metaphor has been invoked frequently in lower court decisions permitting "jurisdiction in products liability cases in which the product has traveled through an extensive chain of distribution before reaching the ultimate consumer." 18 W. Fletcher, Cyclopedia of the Law of Corporations § 8640.40, p. 133 (rev. ed.2007). Typically, in such cases, a nonresident defendant, acting *outside* the forum, places in the stream of commerce a product that ultimately causes harm *inside* the forum. See generally Dayton, Personal Jurisdiction and the Stream of Commerce, 7 Rev. Litigation 239, 262-268 (1988) (discussing origins and evolution of the stream-of-commerce doctrine).

Many States have enacted long-arm statutes authorizing courts to exercise specific jurisdiction over manufacturers when the events in suit, or some of them, occurred within the forum state. For example, the "Local Injury; Foreign Act" subsection of North Carolina's long-arm statute authorizes North Carolina courts to exercise personal jurisdiction in "any action claiming injury to person or property within this State arising out of [the defendant's] act or omission outside this State," if, "in addition[,] at or about the time of the injury," "[p]roducts ... manufactured by the defendant were used or consumed, within this State in the ordinary course of trade." N.C. Gen.Stat. Ann. § 1-75.4(4)(b) As the North Carolina Court of Appeals recognized, this provision of the State's long-arm statute "does not apply to this case," for both the act alleged to have caused injury (the fabrication of the allegedly defective tire) and its impact (the accident) occurred outside the forum.

The North Carolina court's stream-of-commerce analysis elided the essential difference between case-specific and all-purpose (general) jurisdiction. Flow of a manufacturer's products into the forum, we have explained, may bolster an affiliation germane to *specific* jurisdiction. See, *e.g., World-Wide Volkswagen*, 444 U.S., at 297, 100 S.Ct. 559 (where "the sale of a product ... is not simply an isolated occurrence but arises from the efforts of the manufacturer or distributor to serve... the market for its product in [several] States, it is not unreasonable to subject it to suit in one of those States if its allegedly defective merchandise *has there been the source of injury to its owner or to others*" (emphasis added)). But ties serving to bolster the exercise of specific jurisdiction do not warrant a determination that, based on those ties, the forum has *general* jurisdiction over a defendant. . . .

A corporation's "continuous activity of some sorts within a state," *International Shoe* instructed, "is not enough to support the demand that the corporation be amenable to suits unrelated to that activity." Our 1952 decision in *Perkins v. Benguet Consol. Mining Co.* remains "[t]he textbook case of general jurisdiction appropriately exercised over a foreign corporation that has not consented to suit in the forum." *Donahue v. Far Eastern Air Transport Corp.,* 652 F.2d 1032, 1037 (C.A.D.C.1981).

Sued in Ohio, the defendant in *Perkins* was a Philippine mining corporation that had ceased activities in the Philippines during World War II. To the extent that the company was conducting any business during and immediately after the Japanese occupation of the Philippines, it was doing so in Ohio: the corporation's president maintained his office there, kept the company files in that office, and supervised from the Ohio office "the necessarily limited wartime activities of the company." *Perkins,* 342 U.S., at 447-448, 72 S.Ct. 413. Although the claim-in-suit did not arise in Ohio, this Court ruled that it would not violate due process for Ohio to adjudicate the controversy. . . .

Measured against *Helicopteros* and *Perkins,* North Carolina is not a forum in which it would be permissible to subject petitioners to general jurisdiction. Unlike the defendant in *Perkins,* whose sole wartime business activity was conducted in Ohio, petitioners are in no sense at home in North Carolina. Their attenuated connections to the State, see *supra,* at 2852, fall far short of the "the continuous and systematic general business contacts" necessary to empower North Carolina to entertain suit against them on claims unrelated to anything that connects them to the State. *Helicopteros,* 466 U.S., at 416, 104 S.Ct. 1868. . . .

For the reasons stated, the judgment of the North Carolina Court of Appeals is

Reversed.

Daimler AG v. Bauman
571 US 117 (2014)

Justice Ginsburg delivered the opinion of the Court.

This case concerns the authority of a court in the United States to entertain a claim brought by foreign plaintiffs against a foreign defendant based on events occurring entirely outside the United States. The litigation commenced in 2004, when twenty-two Argentinian residents filed a complaint in the United States District Court for the Northern District of California against DaimlerChrysler Aktiengesellschaft (Daimler), a German public stock company, headquartered in Stuttgart, that manufactures Mercedes-Benz vehicles in Germany. The complaint alleged that during Argentina's 1976–1983 "Dirty War," Daimler's Argentinian subsidiary, Mercedes-Benz Argentina (MB Argentina) collaborated with state security forces to kidnap, detain, torture, and kill certain MB Argentina workers, among them, plaintiffs or persons closely related to plaintiffs. Damages for the alleged human-rights violations were sought from Daimler under the laws of the United States, California, and Argentina. Jurisdiction over the lawsuit was predicated on the California contacts of Mercedes-Benz USA, LLC (MBUSA), a subsidiary of Daimler incorporated in Delaware with its principal place of business in New Jersey. MBUSA distributes Daimler-manufactured vehicles to independent dealerships throughout the United States, including California.

The question presented is whether the Due Process Clause of the Fourteenth Amendment precludes the District Court from exercising jurisdiction over Daimler in this case, given the absence of any California connection to the atrocities, perpetrators, or victims described in the complaint. Plaintiffs invoked the court's general or all-purpose jurisdiction. California, they urge, is a place where Daimler may be sued on any and all claims against it, wherever in the world the claims may arise. For example, as plaintiffs' counsel affirmed, under the proffered jurisdictional theory, if a Daimler-manufactured vehicle overturned in Poland, injuring a Polish driver and passenger, the injured parties could maintain a design defect suit in California. Exercises of personal jurisdiction so exorbitant, we hold, are barred by due process constraints on the assertion of adjudicatory authority.

In Goodyear Dunlop Tires Operations, S. A. v. Brown, 564 U. S. ___ (2011), we addressed the distinction between general or all-purpose jurisdiction, and specific or conduct-linked jurisdiction. As to the former, we held that a court may assert jurisdiction over a foreign corporation "to hear any and all claims against [it]" only when the corporation's affiliations with the State in which suit is brought are so constant and pervasive "as to render [it] essentially at home in the forum State." Instructed by

Goodyear, we conclude Daimler is not "at home" in California and cannot be sued there for injuries plaintiffs attribute to MB Argentina's conduct in Argentina.

I

In 2004, plaintiffs (respondents here) filed suit in the United States District Court for the Northern District of California, alleging that MB Argentina collaborated with Argentinian state security forces to kidnap, detain, torture, and kill plaintiffs and their relatives during the military dictatorship in place there from 1976 through 1983, a period known as Argentina's "Dirty War." Based on those allegations, plaintiffs asserted claims under the Alien Tort Statute, 28 U. S. C. §1350, and the Torture Victim Protection Act of 1991, 106 Stat. 73, note following 28 U. S. C. §1350, as well as claims for wrongful death and intentional infliction of emotional distress under the laws of California and Argentina. The incidents recounted in the complaint center on MB Argentina's plant in Gonzalez Catan, Argentina; no part of MB Argentina's alleged collaboration with Argentinian authorities took place in California or anywhere else in the United States.

Plaintiffs' operative complaint names only one corporate defendant: Daimler, the petitioner here. Plaintiffs seek to hold Daimler vicariously liable for MB Argentina's alleged malfeasance. Daimler is a German Aktiengesellschaft (public stock company) that manufactures Mercedes-Benz vehicles in Germany and has its headquarters in Stuttgart. At times relevant to this case, MB Argentina was a subsidiary wholly owned by Daimler's predecessor in interest.

Daimler moved to dismiss the action for want of personal jurisdiction. Opposing the motion, plaintiffs submitted declarations and exhibits purporting to demonstrate the presence of Daimler itself in California. Alternatively, plaintiffs maintained that jurisdiction over Daimler could be founded on the California contacts of MBUSA, a distinct corporate entity that, according to plaintiffs, should be treated as Daimler's agent for jurisdictional purposes.

MBUSA, an indirect subsidiary of Daimler, is a Delaware limited liability corporation. MBUSA serves as Daimler's exclusive importer and distributor in the United States, purchasing Mercedes-Benz automobiles from Daimler in Germany, then importing those vehicles, and ultimately distributing them to independent dealerships located throughout the Nation. Although MBUSA's principal place of business is in New Jersey, MBUSA has multiple California-based facilities, including a regional office in Costa Mesa, a Vehicle Preparation Center in Carson, and a Classic Center in Irvine. According to the record developed below, MBUSA is the largest supplier of luxury vehicles to the California market. In particular, over 10% of all sales of new vehicles in the United States take place in California, and MBUSA's California sales account for 2.4% of Daimler's worldwide sales.

• The relationship between Daimler and MBUSA is delineated in a General Distributor Agreement, which sets forth requirements for MBUSA's distribution of Mercedes-Benz vehicles in the United States. That agreement established MBUSA as an "independent contracto[r]" that "buy[s] and sell[s] [vehicles] . . . as an independent business for [its] own account." App. 179a. The agreement "does not make [MBUSA] . . . a general or special agent, partner, joint venturer or employee of DAIMLERCHRYSLER or any DaimlerChrysler Group Company"; MBUSA "ha[s] no authority to make binding obligations for or act on behalf of DAIMLERCHRYSLER or any DaimlerChrysler Group Company." Ibid.

After allowing jurisdictional discovery on plaintiffs' agency allegations, the District Court granted Daimler's motion to dismiss. Daimler's own affiliations with California, the court first determined, were insufficient to support the exercise of all-purpose jurisdiction over the corporation. Next, the court declined to attribute MBUSA's California contacts to Daimler on an agency theory, concluding that plaintiffs failed to demonstrate that MBUSA acted as Daimler's agent. . . .

We granted certiorari to decide whether, consistent with the Due Process Clause of the Fourteenth Amendment, Daimler is amenable to suit in California courts for claims involving only foreign plaintiffs and conduct occurring entirely abroad. . . .

Since International Shoe, "specific jurisdiction has become the centerpiece of modern jurisdiction theory, while general jurisdiction [has played] a reduced role." Goodyear, 564 U. S., at ___ (slip op., at 8) (quoting Twitchell, The Myth of General Jurisdiction, 101 Harv. L. Rev. 610, 628 (1988)). International Shoe's momentous departure from Pennoyer's rigidly territorial focus, we have noted, unleashed a rapid expansion of tribunals' ability to hear claims against out-of-state defendants when the episode-in-suit occurred in the forum or the defendant purposefully availed itself of the forum. Our subsequent decisions have continued to bear out the prediction that "specific jurisdiction will come into sharper relief and form a considerably more significant part of the scene." . . .

Most recently, in Goodyear, we answered the question: "Are foreign subsidiaries of a United States parent corporation amenable to suit in state court on claims unrelated to any activity of the subsidiaries in the forum State? . . .

As is evident from Perkins, Helicopteros, and Goodyear, general and specific jurisdiction have followed markedly different trajectories post-International Shoe. Specific jurisdiction has been cut loose from Pennoyer's sway, but we have declined to stretch general jurisdiction beyond limits traditionally recognized. As this Court has increasingly trained on the "relationship among the defendant, the forum, and the litigation," Shaffer, 433 U. S., at 204, i.e., specific jurisdiction, general jurisdiction has come to occupy a less dominant place in the contemporary scheme.

IV

With this background, we turn directly to the question whether Daimler's affiliations with California are sufficient to subject it to the general (all-purpose) personal jurisdiction of that State's courts. In the proceedings below, the parties agreed on, or failed to contest, certain points we now take as given. Plaintiffs have never attempted to fit this case into the specific jurisdiction category. Nor did plaintiffs challenge on appeal the District Court's holding that Daimler's own contacts with California were, by themselves, too sporadic to justify the exercise of general jurisdiction. While plaintiffs ultimately persuaded the Ninth Circuit to impute MBUSA's California contacts to Daimler on an agency theory, at no point have they maintained that MBUSA is an alter ego of Daimler.

Daimler, on the other hand, failed to object below to plaintiffs' assertion that the California courts could exercise all-purpose jurisdiction over MBUSA We will assume then, for purposes of this decision only, that MBUSA qualifies as at home in California.

B

Even if we were to assume that MBUSA is at home in California, and further to assume MBUSA's contacts are imputable to Daimler, there would still be no basis to subject Daimler to general jurisdiction in California, for Daimler's slim contacts with the State hardly render it at home there.

Goodyear made clear that only a limited set of affiliations with a forum will render a defendant amenable to all-purpose jurisdiction there. "For an individual, the paradigm forum for the exercise of general jurisdiction is the individual's domicile; for a corporation, it is an equivalent place, one in which the corporation is fairly regarded as at home." 564 U. S., at ___ (slip op., at 7) (citing Brilmayer et al., A General Look at General Jurisdiction, 66 Texas L. Rev. 721, 728 (1988)). With respect to a corporation, the place of incorporation and principal place of business are "paradigm[m] . . . bases for general jurisdiction.". Those affiliations have the virtue of being unique—that is, each ordinarily indicates only one place—as well as easily ascertainable. Cf. Hertz Corp. v. Friend, 559 U. S. 77, 94 (2010) ("Simple jurisdictional rules . . . promote greater predictability."). These bases afford plaintiffs recourse to at least one clear and certain forum in which a corporate defendant may be sued on any and all claims.

Goodyear did not hold that a corporation may be subject to general jurisdiction only in a forum where it is incorporated or has its principal place of business; it simply typed those places paradigm all-purpose forums. Plaintiffs would have us look beyond the exemplar bases Goodyear identified, and approve the exercise of general jurisdiction in every State in which a corporation "engages in a substantial, continuous, and systematic course of business." That formulation, we hold, is unacceptably grasping. . . .

Accordingly, the inquiry under Goodyear is not whether a foreign corporation's in-forum contacts can be said to be in some sense "continuous and systematic," it is whether that corporation's "affiliations with the State are so 'continuous and systematic' as to render [it] essentially at home in the forum State.

Here, neither Daimler nor MBUSA is incorporated in California, nor does either entity have its principal place of business there. If Daimler's California activities sufficed to allow adjudication of this Argentina-rooted case in California, the same global reach would presumably be available in every other State in which MBUSA's sales are sizable. Such exorbitant exercises of all-purpose jurisdiction would scarcely permit out-of-state defendants "to structure their primary conduct with some minimum assurance as to where that conduct will and will not render them liable to suit." Burger King Corp., 471 U. S., at 472 (internal quotation marks omitted).

It was therefore error for the Ninth Circuit to conclude that Daimler, even with MBUSA's contacts attributed to it, was at home in California, and hence subject to suit there on claims by foreign plaintiffs having nothing to do with anything that occurred or had its principal impact in California.

C

Finally, the transnational context of this dispute bears attention. The Court of Appeals emphasized, as supportive of the exercise of general jurisdiction, plaintiffs' assertion of claims under the Alien Tort Statute (ATS), 28 U. S. C. §1350, and the Torture Victim Protection Act of 1991 (TVPA), 106Stat. 73, note following 28 U. S. C. §1350. See 644 F. 3d, at 927 ("American federal courts, be they in California or any other state, have a strong interest in adjudicating and redressing international human rights abuses."). Recent decisions of this Court, however, have rendered plaintiffs' ATS and TVPA claims infirm. See Kibble v. Royal Dutch Petroleum Co., 569 U. S. ___, ___ (2013) (slip op., at 14) (presumption against extra-territorial application controls claims under the ATS); Mohamad v. Palestinian Authority, 566 U. S. ___, ___ (2012) (slip op., at 1) (only natural persons are subject to liability under the TVPA).

The Ninth Circuit, moreover, paid little heed to the risks to international comity its expansive view of general jurisdiction posed. Other nations do not share the uninhibited approach to personal jurisdiction advanced by the Court of Appeals in this case. In the European Union, for example, a corporation may generally be sued in the nation in which it is "domiciled," a term defined to refer only to the location of the corporation's "statutory seat," "central administration," or "principal place of business." European Parliament and Council Reg. 1215/2012, Arts. 4(1), and 63(1), 2012 O. J. (L. 351) 7, 18. See also id., Art. 7(5), 2012 O. J. 7 (as to "a dispute arising out of the operations of a branch, agency or other establishment," a corporation may be sued "in the courts for the place where the branch, agency or other establishment is situated" (emphasis added)). The Solicitor General informs us, in this regard, that "foreign governments' objections to some domestic courts' expansive views of general jurisdiction have in the past impeded negotiations of international agreements on the reciprocal recognition and enforcement of judgments." Considerations of international rapport thus reinforce our determination that subjecting Daimler to the general jurisdiction of courts in California would not accord with the "fair play and substantial justice" due process demands.

For the reasons stated, the judgment of the United States Court of Appeals for the Ninth Circuit is

Reversed.

The Continued Viability of "Presence"

Burnham vs. Superior Court
495 U.S. 604 (1990)

JUSTICE SCALIA announced the judgment of the Court and delivered an opinion in which THE CHIEF JUSTICE and JUSTICE KENNEDY join, and in which JUSTICE WHITE joins with respect to Parts I, II-A, II-B, and II-C.

The question presented is whether the Due Process Clause of the Fourteenth Amendment denies California courts jurisdiction over a nonresident, who was personally served with process while temporarily in that State, in a suit unrelated to his activities in the State.

I

Petitioner Dennis Burnham married Francie Burnham in 1976 in West Virginia. In 1977 the couple moved to New Jersey, where their two children were born. In July 1987 the Burnhams decided to separate. They agreed that Mrs. Burnham, who intended to move to California, would take custody of the children. Shortly before Mrs. Burnham departed for California that same month, she and petitioner agreed that she would file for divorce on grounds of "irreconcilable differences."

In October 1987, petitioner filed for divorce in New Jersey state court on grounds of "desertion." Petitioner did not, however, obtain an issuance of summons against his wife and did not attempt to serve her with process. Mrs. Burnham, after unsuccessfully demanding that petitioner adhere to their prior agreement to submit to an "irreconcilable differences" divorce, brought suit for divorce in California state court in early January 1988.

In late January, petitioner visited southern California on business, after which he went north to visit his children in the San Francisco Bay area, where his wife resided. He took the older child to San Francisco for the weekend. Upon returning the child to Mrs. Burnham's home on January 24, 1988, petitioner was served with a California court summons and a copy of Mrs. Burnham's divorce petition. He then returned to New Jersey.

Later that year, petitioner made a special appearance in the California Superior Court, moving to quash the service of process on the ground that the court lacked personal jurisdiction over him because his only contacts with California were a few short visits to the State for the purposes of conducting business and visiting his children. The Superior Court denied the motion, and the California Court of Appeal denied mandamus relief, rejecting petitioner's contention that the Due Process Clause prohibited California courts from asserting jurisdiction over him because he lacked "minimum contacts" with the State. The court held it to be "a valid jurisdictional predicate for in personam jurisdiction" that the "defendant [was] present in the forum state and personally served with process." We granted certiorari.

II

A

To determine whether the assertion of personal jurisdiction is consistent with due process, we have long relied on the principles traditionally followed by American courts in marking out the territorial limits of each State's authority. That criterion was first announced in Pennoyer v. Neff, supra, in which we stated that due process "mean[s] a course of legal proceedings according to those rules and principles which have been established in our systems of jurisprudence for the protection and enforcement of private rights," id., at 733, including the "well-established principles of public law respecting the jurisdiction of an independent State over persons and property," In what has become the classic expression of the criterion, we said in International Shoe Co. v. Washington, 326 U.S. 310 (1945), that a state court's assertion of personal jurisdiction satisfies the Due Process Clause if it does not violate "'traditional notions of fair play and substantial justice.'" Id., at 316, quoting Milliken v. Meyer, 311 U.S. 457, 463 (1940). See also Insurance Corp. of Ireland v. Compagnie des Bauxites de Guinee, 456 U.S. 694, 703 (1982). Since International Shoe, we have only been called upon to decide whether these "traditional notions" permit States to exercise jurisdiction over absent defendants in a manner that deviates from the rules of jurisdiction applied in the 19th century. We have held such deviations permissible, but only with respect to suits arising out of the absent defendant's contacts with the State. See, e. g., Helicopteros Nacionales de Colombia v. Hall, 466 U.S. 408, 414 (1984). The question we must decide today is whether due process requires a similar connection between the litigation and the defendant's contacts with the State in cases where the defendant is physically present in the State at the time process is served upon him.

B

Among the most firmly established principles of personal jurisdiction in American tradition is that the courts of a State have jurisdiction over nonresidents who are physically present in the State. The view developed early that each State had the power to hale before its courts any individual who could be found within its borders, and that once having acquired jurisdiction over such a person by properly serving him with process, the State could retain jurisdiction to enter judgment against him, no matter how fleeting his visit. That view had antecedents in English common-law practice, which sometimes allowed "transitory" actions, arising out of events outside the country, to be maintained against seemingly nonresident defendants who were present in England. See, e. g., Mostyn v. Fabrigas, 98 Eng. Rep. 1021 (K. B. 1774); Cartwright v. Pettus, 22 Eng. Rep. 916 (Ch. 1675). Justice Story believed the principle, which he traced to Roman origins, to be firmly grounded in English tradition: "[B]y the common law[,] personal actions, being transitory, may be brought in any place, where the party defendant may be found," for "every nation may . . . rightfully exercise jurisdiction over all persons within its domains." J. Story, Commentaries on the Conflict of Laws 554, 543 (1846). See also id., 530-538; Picquet v. Swan, supra, at 611-612 (Story, J.) ("Where a party is within a territory, he may justly be subjected to its process, and bound personally by the judgment pronounced, on such process, against him").

Recent scholarship has suggested that English tradition was not as clear as Story thought, see Hazard, A General Theory of State-Court Jurisdiction, 1965 S. Ct. Rev. 241, 253-260; Ehrenzweig, The Transient Rule of Personal Jurisdiction: The "Power" Myth and Forum Conveniens, 65 Yale L. J. 289 (1956). Accurate or not, however, judging by the evidence of contemporaneous or near-contemporaneous decisions, one must conclude that Story's understanding was shared by American courts at the crucial time for present purposes: 1868, when the Fourteenth Amendment was adopted.

C

Despite this formidable body of precedent, petitioner contends, in reliance on our decisions applying the International Shoe standard, that in the absence of "continuous and systematic" contacts with the forum, a nonresident defendant can be subjected to judgment only as to matters that arise out of or relate to his contacts with the forum. This argument rests on a thorough misunderstanding of our cases. . . .

Nothing in International Shoe or the cases that have followed it, however, offers support for the very different proposition petitioner seeks to establish today: that a defendant's presence in the forum is not only unnecessary to validate novel, nontraditional assertions of jurisdiction, but is itself no longer sufficient to establish jurisdiction. . . .

The short of the matter is that jurisdiction based on physical presence alone constitutes due process because it is one of the continuing traditions of our legal system that define the due process standard of "traditional notions of fair play and substantial justice." That standard was developed by analogy to "physical presence," and it would be perverse to say it could now be turned against that touchstone of jurisdiction.

D

Petitioner's strongest argument, though we ultimately reject it, relies upon our decision in Shaffer v. Heitner, 433 U.S. 186 (1977). In that case, a Delaware court hearing a shareholder's derivative suit against a corporation's directors secured jurisdiction quasi in rem by sequestering the out-of-state defendant's stock in the company, the situs of which was Delaware under Delaware law. Reasoning that Delaware's sequestration procedure was simply a mechanism to compel the absent defendants to appear in a suit to determine their personal rights and obligations, we concluded that the normal rules we had developed under International Shoe for jurisdiction over suits against absent defendants should apply - viz., Delaware could not hear the suit because the defendants' sole contact with the State (ownership of property there) was unrelated to the lawsuit. 433 U.S., at 213 -215.

It goes too far to say, as petitioner contends, that Shaffer compels the conclusion that a State lacks jurisdiction over an individual unless the litigation arises out of his activities in the State. Shaffer, like International Shoe, involved jurisdiction over an absent defendant, and it stands for nothing more than the proposition that when the "minimum contact" that is a substitute for physical presence consists of property ownership it must, like other minimum contacts, be related to the litigation. Petitioner wrenches out of its context our statement in Shaffer that "all assertions of state-court jurisdiction must be evaluated according to the standards set forth in International Shoe and its progeny." When read together with the two sentences that preceded it, the meaning of this statement becomes clear:

> "The fiction that an assertion of jurisdiction over property is anything but an assertion of jurisdiction over the owner of the property supports an ancient form without substantial modern justification. Its continued acceptance would serve only to allow state-court jurisdiction that is fundamentally unfair to the defendant.
>
> "We therefore conclude that all assertions of state-court jurisdiction must be evaluated according to the standards set forth in International Shoe and its progeny." Ibid. (emphasis added).

Shaffer was saying, in other words, not that all bases for the assertion of in personam jurisdiction (including, presumably, in-state service) must be treated alike and subjected to the "minimum contacts" analysis of International Shoe; but rather that quasi in rem jurisdiction, that fictional "ancient form," and in personam jurisdiction, are really one and the same and must be treated alike - leading to the conclusion that quasi in rem jurisdiction, i. e., that form of in personam jurisdiction based upon a "property ownership" contact and by definition unaccompanied by personal, in-state service, must satisfy the litigation-relatedness requirement of International Shoe. The logic of Shaffer's holding - which places all suits against absent nonresidents on the same constitutional footing, regardless of whether a separate Latin label is attached to one particular basis of contact - does not compel the conclusion that physically present defendants must be treated identically to absent ones. As we have demonstrated at length, our tradition has treated the two classes of defendants quite differently, and it is unreasonable to read Shaffer as casually obliterating that distinction. International Shoe confined its "minimum contacts" requirement to situations in which the defendant "be not present within the territory of the forum," and nothing in Shaffer expands that requirement beyond that.

It is fair to say, however, that while our holding today does not contradict Shaffer, our basic approach to the due process question is different. We have conducted no independent inquiry into the desirability or fairness of the prevailing in-state service rule, leaving that judgment to the legislatures that are free to amend it; for our purposes, its validation is its pedigree, as the phrase "traditional notions of fair play and substantial justice" makes clear. Shaffer did conduct such an independent inquiry, asserting that "'traditional notions of fair play and substantial justice' can be as readily offended by the perpetuation of ancient forms that are no longer justified as by the adoption of new procedures that are inconsistent with the basic values of our constitutional heritage." Perhaps that assertion can be sustained when the "perpetuation of ancient forms" is engaged in by only a very small minority of the States. Where, however, as in the present case, a jurisdictional principle is both firmly approved by tradition and still favored, it is impossible to imagine what standard we could appeal to for the judgment that it is "no longer justified." While in no way receding from or casting doubt upon the holding of Shaffer or any other case, we reaffirm today our time-honored approach, see, e. g., Ownbey v. Morgan, 256 U.S. 94, 110 -112 (1921); Hurtado v. California, 110 U.S., at 528-529; Murray's Lessee v. Hoboken Land & Improvement Co., 59 U.S. 272, 276 -277 (1856). For new procedures, hitherto unknown, the Due Process clause requires analysis to determine whether "traditional notions of fair play and substantial justice" have been offended. International Shoe, 326 U.S., at 316 . But a doctrine of personal jurisdiction that dates back to the adoption of the Fourteenth Amendment and is still generally observed unquestionably meets that standard. . . .

III

A few words in response to JUSTICE BRENNAN's opinion concurring in the judgment: It insists that we apply "contemporary notions of due process" to determine the constitutionality of California's assertion of jurisdiction. Post, at 632. But our analysis today comports with that prescription, at least if we give it the only sense allowed by our precedents. The "contemporary notions of due process" applicable to personal jurisdiction are the enduring "traditional notions of fair play and substantial justice" established as the test by International Shoe. By its very language, that test is satisfied if a state court adheres to jurisdictional rules that are generally applied and have always been applied in the United States.

But the concurrence's proposed standard of "contemporary notions of due process" requires more: It measures state-court jurisdiction not only against traditional doctrines in this country, including current state-court practice, but also against each Justice's subjective assessment of what is fair and just. Authority for that seductive standard is not to be found in any of our personal jurisdiction cases. It is, indeed, an outright break with the test of "traditional notions of fair play and substantial justice," which would have to be reformulated "our notions of fair play and substantial justice."

The subjectivity, and hence inadequacy, of this approach becomes apparent when the concurrence tries to explain why the assertion of jurisdiction in the present case meets its standard of continuing-American-tradition-plus-innate-fairness. JUSTICE BRENNAN lists the "benefits" Mr. Burnham derived from the State of California - the fact that, during the few days he was there, "[h]is health and safety [were] guaranteed by the State's police, fire, and emergency medical services; he [was] free to travel on the State's roads and waterways; he likely enjoy[ed] the fruits of the State's economy." Three days' worth of these benefits strike us as powerfully inadequate to establish, as an abstract matter, that it is "fair" for California to decree the ownership of all Mr. Burnham's worldly goods acquired during the 10 years of his marriage, and the custody over his children. We daresay a contractual exchange swapping those benefits for that power would not survive the "unconscionability" provision of the Uniform Commercial Code. . . .

Suppose, for example, that a defendant in Mr. Burnham's situation enjoys not three days' worth of California's "benefits," but 15 minutes' worth. Or suppose we remove one of those "benefits" - "enjoy[ment of] the fruits of the State's economy" - by positing that Mr. Burnham had not come to California on business, but only to visit his children. . . .

What if, for example, Mr. Burnham were visiting a sick child? Or a dying child? Cf. Kulko v. Superior Court of California, City and County of San Francisco, 436 U.S. 84, 93 (1978) (finding the exercise of long-arm jurisdiction over an absent parent unreasonable because it would "discourage parents from entering into reasonable visitation agreements"). . . .

The difference between us and JUSTICE BRENNAN has nothing to do with whether "further progress [is] to be made" in the "evolution of our legal system." It has to do with whether changes are to be adopted as progressive by the American people or decreed as progressive by the Justices of this Court. Nothing we say today prevents individual States from limiting or entirely abandoning the in-state-service basis of jurisdiction. And nothing prevents an overwhelming majority of them from doing so, with the consequence that the "traditional notions of fairness" that this Court applies may change. But the States have overwhelmingly declined to adopt such limitation or abandonment, evidently not considering it to be progress. The question is whether, armed with no authority other than individual Justices' perceptions of fairness that conflict with both past and current practice, this Court can compel the States to make such a change on the ground that "due process" requires it. We hold that it cannot.

Two Service of Process Problems:

Serving the defendant with a copy of the summons and complaint while the defendant is temporarily present in the forum state has been described as "tag" jurisdiction (as in "tag you're it"). Consider the following examples of "tag" jurisdiction.

The Mile High Club Preston and Charlotte Grace, citizens of Arkansas, brought suit in Arkansas against Ronnie Smith, a citizen of Tennessee, and others for breach of a written contract. Smith was served with a copy of the summons and complaint by a U.S. Marshal "by personally delivering to him a copy on the Braniff Airplane, Flight No. 337, non-stop flight from Memphis, Tenn. to Dallas, Texas, said copy being delivered to him at 5:16 P.M. at which time the said airplane was in the Eastern District of Arkansas and directly above Pine Bluff, Arkansas, in said District." Assuming the contract was entered into, and was to be performed, in Illinois, and Smith has no other contacts with Arkansas, is Smith subject to personal jurisdiction in Arkansas? (See, *Grace v. MacArthur* 170 F. Supp. 442 (1959).)

Secret Lovers Appellant and appellee were both married, but not to each other. They had known each other for some years and had engaged in meretricious relations. He was a resident of New York and never lived in Florida. On October 25, 1935, while appellee was in Salt Lake City, Utah, he received a telegram from the appellant, which read: "Account illness home planning leaving. Please come on way back. Must see you." Upon appellee's return to New York he received a letter from appellant stating that her mother was dying in Ireland; that she was leaving the United States for good to go to her mother; that she could not go without seeing the appellee once more; and that she wanted to discuss her affairs with him before she left. Shortly after the receipt of this letter, they spoke to each other on the telephone, whereupon the appellant repeated, in a hysterical and distressed voice, the substance of her letter. Appellee promised to go to Florida in a week or ten days and agreed to notify her when he would arrive. This he did, but before leaving New York by plane he received a letter couched in endearing terms and expressing love and affection for him, as well as her delight at his coming. Before leaving New York, appellee telegraphed appellant, suggesting arrangements for their accommodations together while in Miami, Fla. She telegraphed him at a hotel in Washington, D. C., where he was to stop en route, advising him that the arrangements requested had been made. Appellee arrived at 6 o'clock in the morning at the Miami Airport and saw the appellant standing with her sister some 75 feet distant. He was met by a deputy sheriff who, upon identifying appellee, served him with process in a suit for $500,000. Thereupon a stranger introduced himself and offered to take appellee to his home, stating that he knew a lawyer who was acquainted with the appellant's attorney. The attorney whom appellee was advised to consult came to the stranger's home and seemed to know about the case. The attorney invited appellee to his office, and upon his arrival he found one of the lawyers for the appellant there. Appellee did not retain the Florida attorney to represent him. He returned to New York by plane that evening and consulted his New York counsel, who advised him to ignore the summons served in Florida. He did so, and judgment was entered by default. Did the Florida court acquire good personal jurisdiction over the appellant? (See, *Wyman v. Newhouse*) 93 F. 2d 313 (1937)

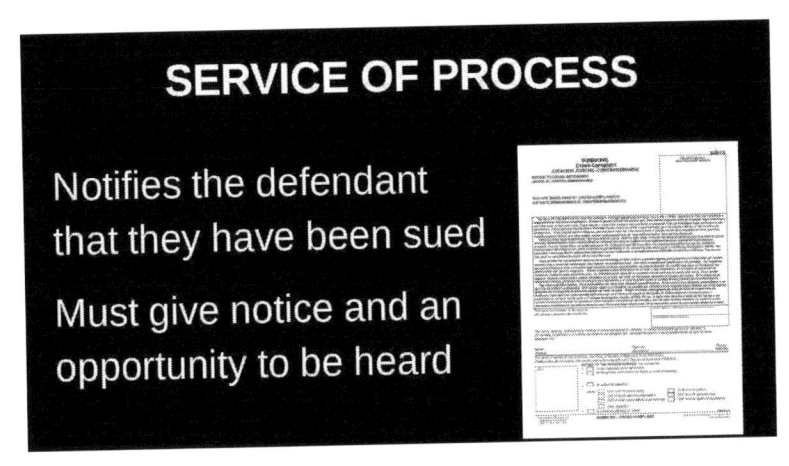

SERVICE OF PROCESS

Notifies the defendant that they have been sued

Must give notice and an opportunity to be heard

The Constitutional Requirement of Notice

You have now learned that the existence of personal jurisdiction depends upon a sufficient connection between the defendant and the forum state to make it fair to require defense of the action in the forum. However, there is a second requirement that must be satisfied in order for a court to have personal jurisdiction over a defendant; the giving of reasonable notice to the defendant that an action has been brought. If the defendant has not received proper notice, the court's power to adjudicate is imperfect. Notice is usually given by serving the defendant with the "process" (e.g. a copy of the summons and the complaint) of the court. Up to now, our analysis of personal jurisdiction have always assumed the existence of proper notice. What kind of notice is necessary?

Mullane v. Central Hanover Bank & Trust
339 U.S. 306, (1950)

MR. JUSTICE JACKSON delivered the opinion of the Court.

This controversy questions the constitutional sufficiency of notice to notice to beneficiaries on judicial settlement of accounts by the trustee of a common trust fund established under the New York Banking Law. . . .

Common trust fund legislation is addressed to a problem appropriate for state action. Mounting overheads have made administration of small trusts undesirable to corporate trustees. In order that donors and testators of moderately sized trusts may not be denied the service of corporate fiduciaries, the District of Columbia and some thirty states other than New York have permitted pooling small trust estates into one fund for investment administration. The income, capital gains, losses and expenses of the collective trust are shared by the constituent trusts in proportion to their contribution. By this plan, diversification of risk and economy of management can be extended to those whose capital standing alone would not obtain such advantage.

Statutory authorization for the establishment of such common trust funds is provided in the New York Banking Law, Under this Act a trust company may, with approval of the State Banking Board, establish a common fund and, within prescribed limits, invest therein the assets of an unlimited number of estates, trusts or other funds of which it is trustee. Each participating trust shares ratably in the common fund, but exclusive management and control is in the trust company as trustee, and neither a fiduciary nor any beneficiary of a participating trust is deemed to have ownership in any particular asset or investment of this common fund. The trust company must keep fund assets separate from its own, and in its fiduciary capacity may not deal with itself or any affiliate. Provisions are made for accounting twelve to fifteen months after the establishment of a fund and triennially thereafter. The decree in each such judicial settlement of accounts is made binding and conclusive as to any matter set forth in the account upon everyone having any interest in the common fund or in any participating estate, trust or fund.

In January 1946, Central Hanover Bank and Trust Company established a common trust fund in accordance with these provisions, and in March 1947, it petitioned the Surrogate's Court for settlement of its first account as common trustee. During the accounting period a total of 113 trusts, approximately half inter vivos and half testamentary, participated in the common trust fund, the gross capital of which was nearly three million dollars. The record does not show the number or residence of the beneficiaries, but they were many and it is clear that some of them were not residents of the State of New York.

The only notice given beneficiaries of this specific application was by publication in a local newspaper in strict compliance with the minimum requirements of N. Y. Banking Law 100-c (12): "After filing such petition [for judicial settlement of its account] the petitioner shall cause to be issued by the court in which the petition is filed and shall publish not less than once in each week for four successive weeks in a newspaper to be designated by the court a notice or citation addressed generally without naming them to all parties interested in such common trust fund and in such estates, trusts or funds mentioned in the petition, all of which may be described in the notice or citation only in the manner set forth in said petition and without setting forth the residence of any such decedent or donor of any such estate, trust or fund." Thus the only notice required, and the only one given, was by newspaper publication setting forth merely the name and address of the trust company, the name and the date of establishment of the common trust fund, and a list of all participating estates, trusts or funds.

At the time the first investment in the common fund was made on behalf of each participating estate, however, the trust company, pursuant to the requirements of 100-c

(9), had notified by mail each person of full age and sound mind whose name and address were then known to it and who was "entitled to share in the income therefrom . . . [or] . . . who would be entitled to share in the principal if the event upon which such estate, trust or fund will become distributable should have occurred at the time of sending such notice." Included in the notice was a copy of those provisions of the Act relating to the sending of the notice itself and to the judicial settlement of common trust fund accounts.

Upon the filing of the petition for the settlement of accounts, appellant was, by order of the court, appointed special guardian and attorney for all persons known or unknown not otherwise appearing who had or might thereafter have any interest in the income of the common trust fund; and appellee Vaughan was appointed to represent those similarly interested in the principal. There were no other appearances on behalf of anyone interested in either interest or principal.

Appellant appeared specially, objecting that notice and the statutory provisions for notice to beneficiaries were inadequate to afford due process under the Fourteenth Amendment, and therefore that the court was without jurisdiction to render a final and binding decree. Appellant's objections were entertained and overruled, the Surrogate holding that the notice required and given was sufficient. A final decree accepting the accounts has been entered, affirmed by the Appellate Division of the Supreme Court, and by the Court of Appeals of the State of New York.

The effect of this decree, as held below, is to settle "all questions respecting the management of the common fund." We understand that every right which beneficiaries would otherwise have against the trust company, either as trustee of the common fund or as trustee of any individual trust, for improper management of the common trust fund during the period covered by the accounting is sealed and wholly terminated by the decree.

We are met at the outset with a challenge to the power of the State - the right of its courts to adjudicate at all as against those beneficiaries who reside without the State of New York. It is contended that the proceeding is one in personam in that the decree affects neither title to nor possession of any res but adjudges only personal rights of the beneficiaries to surcharge their trustee for negligence or breach of trust. Accordingly, it is said, under the strict doctrine of Pennoyer v. Neff, the Surrogate is without jurisdiction as to nonresidents upon whom personal service of process was not made.

Distinctions between actions in rem and those in personam are ancient and originally expressed in procedural terms what seems really to have been a distinction in the substantive law of property under a system quite unlike our own. Buckland and McNair, Roman Law and Common Law, 66; Burdick, Principles of Roman Law and Their Relation to Modern Law, 298. The legal recognition and rise in economic importance of incorporeal or intangible forms of property have upset the ancient simplicity of property law and the clarity of its distinctions, while new forms of proceedings have confused the old procedural classification. American courts have sometimes classed certain actions as in rem because personal service of process was not required, and at other times have held personal service of process not required because the action was in rem.

Judicial proceedings to settle fiduciary accounts have been sometimes termed in rem, or more indefinitely quasi in rem, or more vaguely still, "in the nature of a proceeding in rem." It is not readily apparent how the courts of New York did or would classify the present proceeding, which has some characteristics and is wanting in some features of proceedings both in rem and in personam. But in any event we think that the requirements of the Fourteenth Amendment to the Federal Constitution do not depend upon a classification for which the standards are so elusive and confused generally and which, being primarily for state courts to define, may and do vary from state to state. Without disparaging the usefulness of distinctions between actions in rem and those in personam in many branches of law, or on other issues, or the reasoning which underlies them, we do not rest the power of the State to resort to constructive service in this proceeding upon how its courts or this Court may regard this historic antithesis. It is sufficient to observe that, whatever the technical definition of its chosen procedure, the interest of each state in providing means to close trusts that exist by the grace of its laws and are administered under the supervision of its courts is so insistent and rooted in custom as to establish beyond doubt the right of its courts to determine the interests of all claimants, resident or nonresident, provided its procedure accords full opportunity to appear and be heard.

Quite different from the question of a state's power to discharge trustees is that of the opportunity it must give beneficiaries to contest. Many controversies have raged about the cryptic and abstract words of the Due Process Clause but there can be no doubt that at a minimum they require that deprivation of life, liberty or property by adjudication be preceded by notice and opportunity for hearing appropriate to the nature of the case.

In two ways this proceeding does or may deprive beneficiaries of property. It may cut off their rights to have the trustee answer for negligent or illegal impairments of their interests. Also, their interests are presumably subject to diminution in the proceeding by allowance of fees and expenses to one who, in their names but without their knowledge, may conduct a fruitless or un-compensatory contest. Certainly the proceeding is one in which they may be deprived of property rights and hence notice and hearing must measure up to the standards of due process.

Personal service of written notice within the jurisdiction is the classic form of notice always adequate in any type of proceeding. But the vital interest of the State in bringing any issues as to its fiduciaries to a final settlement can be served only if interests or claims of individuals who are outside of the State can somehow be determined. A construction of the Due Process Clause which would place impossible or impractical obstacles in the way could not be justified.

Against this interest of the State we must balance the individual interest sought to be protected by the Fourteenth Amendment. This is defined by our holding that "The fundamental requisite of due process of law is the opportunity to be heard." This right to be heard has little reality or worth unless one is informed that the matter is pending and can choose for himself whether to appear or default, acquiesce or contest.

The Court has not committed itself to any formula achieving a balance between these interests in a particular proceeding or determining when constructive notice may be utilized or what test it must meet. Personal service has not in all circumstances been regarded as indispensable to the process due to residents, and it has more often been held unnecessary as to nonresidents. We disturb none of the established rules on these subjects. No decision constitutes a controlling or even a very illuminating precedent for the case before us. But a few general principles stand out in the books.

An elementary and fundamental requirement of due process in any proceeding which is to be accorded finality is notice reasonably calculated, under all the circumstances, to apprise interested parties of the pendency of the action and afford them an opportunity to present their objections. The notice must be of such nature as reasonably to convey the required information, Grannis v. Ordean, supra, and it must afford a reasonable time for those interested to make their appearance. But if with due regard for the practicalities and peculiarities of the case these conditions are reasonably met, the constitutional requirements are satisfied. . . .

But when notice is a person's due, process which is a mere gesture is not due process. The means employed must be such as one desirous of actually informing the absentee might reasonably adopt to accomplish it. The reasonableness and hence the constitutional validity of any chosen method may be defended on the ground that it is in itself reasonably certain, or, where conditions do not reasonably permit such notice, that the form chosen is not substantially less likely to bring home notice than other of the feasible and customary substitutes.

It would be idle to pretend that publication alone, as prescribed here, is a reliable means of acquainting interested parties of the fact that their rights are before the courts. It is not an accident that the greater number of cases reaching this Court on the question of adequacy of notice have been concerned with actions founded on process constructively served through local newspapers. Chance alone brings to the attention of even a local resident an advertisement in small type inserted in the back pages of a newspaper, and if he makes his home outside the area of the newspaper's normal circulation the odds that the information will never reach him are large indeed. The chance of actual notice is further reduced when, as here, the notice required does not even name those whose attention it is supposed to attract and does not inform acquaintances who might call it to attention. In weighing its sufficiency on the basis of equivalence with actual notice, we are unable to regard this as more than a feint.

Nor is publication here reinforced by steps likely to attract the parties' attention to the proceeding. It is true that publication traditionally has been acceptable as notification supplemental to other action which in itself may reasonably be expected to convey a warning. The ways of an owner with tangible property are such that he usually arranges means to learn of any direct attack upon his possessory or proprietary rights. Hence, libel of a ship, attachment of a chattel or entry upon real estate in the name of law may reasonably be expected to come promptly to the owner's attention. When the state within which the owner has located such property seizes it for some reason, publication or posting affords an additional measure of notification. A state may indulge the assumption that one who has left tangible property in the state either has abandoned it, in which case proceedings against it deprive him of nothing, or that he has left some caretaker under a duty to let him know that it is being jeopardized. . . .

In the case before us there is, of course, no abandonment. On the other hand these beneficiaries do have a resident fiduciary as caretaker of their interest in this property. But it is their caretaker who in the accounting becomes their adversary. Their trustee is released from giving notice of jeopardy, and no one else is expected to do so. Not even the special guardian is required or apparently expected to communicate with his ward and client, and, of course, if such a duty were merely transferred from the trustee to the guardian, economy would not be served and more likely the cost would be increased.

This Court has not hesitated to approve of resort to publication as a customary substitute in another class of cases where it is not reasonably possible or practicable to give more adequate warning. Thus it has been recognized that, in the case of persons missing or unknown, employment of an indirect and even a probably futile means of notification is all that the situation permits and creates no constitutional bar to a final decree foreclosing their rights.

Those beneficiaries represented by appellant whose interests or whereabouts could not with due diligence be ascertained come clearly within this category. As to them the statutory notice is sufficient. However great the odds that publication will never reach the eyes of such unknown parties, it is not in the typical case much more likely to fail than any of the choices open to legislators endeavoring to prescribe the best notice practicable.

Nor do we consider it unreasonable for the State to dispense with more certain notice to those beneficiaries whose interests are either conjectural or future or, although they could be discovered upon investigation, do not in due course of business come to knowledge of the common trustee. Whatever searches might be required in another situation under ordinary standards of diligence, in view of the character of the proceedings and the nature of the interests here involved we think them unnecessary. We recognize the practical difficulties and costs that would be attendant on frequent investigations into the status of great numbers of beneficiaries, many of whose interests in the common fund are so remote as to be ephemeral; and we have no doubt that such impracticable and extended searches are not required in the name of due process. The expense of keeping informed from day to day of substitutions among even current income beneficiaries and presumptive remaindermen, to say nothing of the far greater number of contingent beneficiaries, would impose a severe burden on the plan, and would likely dissipate its advantages. These are practical matters in which we should be reluctant to disturb the judgment of the state authorities.

Accordingly, we overrule appellant's constitutional objections to published notice insofar as they are urged on behalf of any beneficiaries whose interests or addresses are unknown to the trustee.

As to known present beneficiaries of known place of residence, however, notice by publication stands on a different footing. Exceptions in the name of necessity do not sweep away the rule that within the limits of practicability notice must be such as is reasonably calculated to reach interested parties. Where the names and post office addresses of those affected by a proceeding are at hand, the reasons disappear for resort to means less likely than the mails to apprise them of its pendency.

The trustee has on its books the names and addresses of the income beneficiaries represented by appellant, and we find no tenable ground for dispensing with a serious effort to inform them personally of the accounting, at least by ordinary mail to the record addresses. Certainly sending them a copy of the statute months and perhaps years in advance does not answer this purpose. The trustee periodically remits their income to them, and we think that they might reasonably expect that with or apart from their remittances word might come to them personally that steps were being taken affecting their interests.

We need not weigh contentions that a requirement of personal service of citation on even the large number of known resident or nonresident beneficiaries would, by reasons of delay if not of expense, seriously interfere with the proper administration of the fund. Of course personal service even without the jurisdiction of the issuing authority serves the end of actual and personal notice, whatever power of compulsion it might lack. However, no such service is required under the circumstances. This type of trust presupposes a large number of small interests. The individual interest does not stand alone but is identical with that of a class. The rights of each in the integrity of the fund and the fidelity of the trustee are shared by many other beneficiaries. Therefore notice reasonably certain to reach most of those interested in objecting is likely to safeguard the interests of all, since any objection sustained would inure to the benefit of all. We think that under such circumstances reasonable risks that notice might not actually reach every beneficiary are justifiable. "Now and then an extraordinary case may turn up, but constitutional law like other mortal contrivances has to take some chances, and in the great majority of instances no doubt justice will be done."

The statutory notice to known beneficiaries is inadequate, not because in fact it fails to reach everyone, but because under the circumstances it is not reasonably calculated to reach those who could easily be informed by other means at hand. However it may have been in former times, the mails today are recognized as an efficient and inexpensive means of communication. Moreover, the fact that the trust company has been able to give mailed notice to known beneficiaries at the time the common trust fund was established is persuasive that postal notification at the time of accounting would not seriously burden the plan.

In some situations the law requires greater precautions in its proceedings than the business world accepts for its own purposes. In few, if any, will it be satisfied with less. Certainly it is instructive, in determining the reasonableness of the impersonal broadcast notification here used, to ask whether it would satisfy a prudent man of business, counting his pennies but finding it in his interest to convey information to many persons whose names and addresses are in his files. We are not satisfied that it would. Publication may theoretically be available for all the world to see, but it is too much in our day to suppose that each or any individual beneficiary does or could examine all that is published to see if something may be tucked away in it that affects his property interests. We have before indicated in reference to notice by publication that, "Great caution should be used not to let fiction deny the fair play that can be secured only by a pretty close adhesion to fact." McDonald v. Mabee, 243 U.S. 90, 91.

We hold that the notice of judicial settlement of accounts required by the New York Banking Law 100-c (12) is incompatible with the requirements of the Fourteenth Amendment as a basis for adjudication depriving known persons whose whereabouts are also known of substantial property rights. Accordingly the judgment is reversed and the cause remanded for further proceedings not inconsistent with this opinion.

Reversed.

Problem The actor Charlie Chaplin was the defendant in a paternity suit. It was alleged that he evaded service of process. The plaintiff argued that notwithstanding her inability to serve him with process, because of publicity through press and radio and receipt of private letters and telegrams concerning the pendency of the action, Chaplin actually knew of the suit. Was this proper notice? (See, *Chaplin v. Superior Court* (1927) 81 CA 367).

The Mechanics of Service of Process

Federal Court

In federal court, service of process is governed by Federal Rule of Civil Procedure 4. (The Federal Rules of Civil Procedure [hereinafter FRCP] set forth the procedures to be followed in civil actions and proceedings in United States district courts.) The three methods of serving process are personal service, substituted service, and constructive service. FRCP 4(e)(1) also authorizes service of process under the law of the state in which the district court sits upon most defendants. In other words, FRCP 4(e)(1) expressly allows resort in Federal district courts to the procedures provided by State law for effecting service on nonresident parties (as well as on domiciliaries not found within the State). For example, if state law authorizes service by mail of a summons and complaint upon an individual or organization, then subsection (3)(1) authorizes service by mail for United States district courts in that state. FRCP 4(e)(1) authorizes the use of any means of service provided by the law not only of the forum state, but also of the state in which a defendant is served, unless the defendant is a minor or incompetent.

Due process does not require that the defendant be served personally however, as *Mullane* dictates, notice must be reasonably calculated under all the circumstances to apprise the defendant of the pendency of the action.

State Court

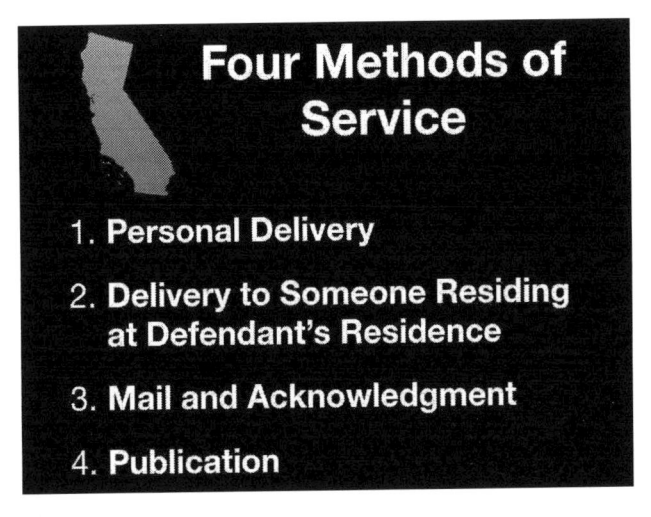

Four Methods of Service

1. Personal Delivery
2. Delivery to Someone Residing at Defendant's Residence
3. Mail and Acknowledgment
4. Publication

In California, the basic statutes governing service of process can be found at Cal.Code.Civ. Proc. § 413.10 et. seq.

Challenge and Waiver of Jurisdiction

By making an "appearance" in response to a lawsuit, a defendant is in effect submitting to the jurisdiction of the court and waiving any defects, if any, in personal jurisdiction. In most states a defendant who wishes to challenge personal jurisdiction may do so by making a special appearance which is limited to the issue of jurisdiction. (See, e.g., Cal.Code.Civ.Proc. § 418.10) If he or she raises any other issues or claims, he has made a general appearance and waives any defects in jurisdiction. In federal courts no special appearance is necessary. Personal jurisdiction may be challenged in a FRCP 12(b)(2) motion or included as a defense in the answer.

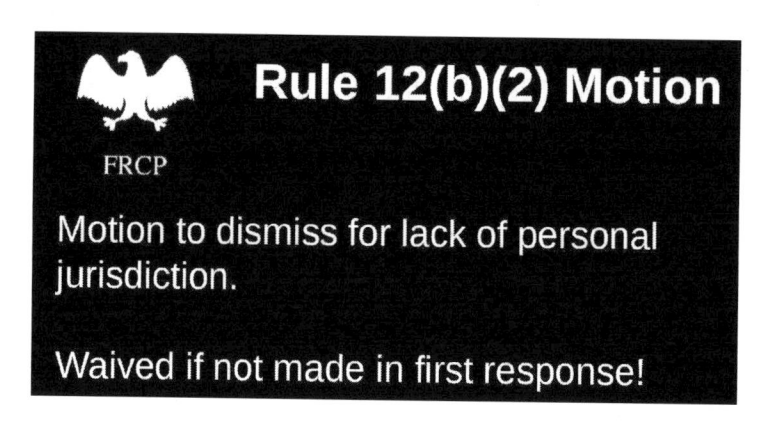

> **Rule 12(b)(2) Motion** — FRCP
>
> Motion to dismiss for lack of personal jurisdiction.
>
> Waived if not made in first response!

Defective service of process can be challenged by a FRCP 12(b)(5) motion to dismiss, or the objection can be made in the answer. Defective service of process goes to lack of notice.

Venue

If personal jurisdiction determines what state a suit can be brought in, venue determines what county or judicial district in that state the lawsuit may be brought in. The purpose of venue rules is to limit the plaintiff's choice of forum in order to ensure that the locality of the lawsuit has some logical relationship to the litigants or the subject matter of the dispute. In federal courts, the simplified rule is that venue is proper in the district where all defendants reside if all the defendants reside in the same state, or in the district in which the claim arose, or, alternatively, where any of the defendants may be found.

Improper venue, like lack of personal jurisdiction, may be waived.

California has a number of overlapping statutory provisions on venue. They all have one fundamental premise, as stated in Code of Civil Procedure § 395: A defendant is entitled to have an action tried in the county of his/her residence unless the action falls within some statutory exception to this general venue rule. When there are multiple defendants, venue is generally proper in any county where at least one of them resides.

> # Venue
> ## (28 U.S.C. § 1391)
>
> 1. a judicial district where any defendant resides, if all defendants reside in the same State, — *in which the district is located*
> 2. a judicial district in which a substantial part of the events or omissions giving rise to the claim occurred, or a substantial part of property that is the subject of the action is situated,
> 3. a judicial district in which any defendant may be found, if there is no district in which the action may otherwise be brought.

Section 1391 governs "venue generally," that is, in cases where a more specific venue provision does not apply. Cf., e.g., § 1400 (identifying proper venue for copyright and patent suits).

Thompson v. Greyhound Lines, Inc.
United States District Court, S.D. Alabama, Southern Division.

WILLIAM H. STEELE, District Judge.

This matter is before the Court on the motion of defendant Greyhound Lines, Inc. ("Greyhound") to dismiss. (Doc. 7). The appearing parties have filed briefs in support of their respective positions, (Docs. 7, 15, 16), and the motion is ripe for resolution.

BACKGROUND

According to the complaint, (Doc. 1), on March 14, 2011, the plaintiff purchased from Greyhound in Pensacola a one-way ticket to Tunica, Mississippi, to arrive at 5:05 p.m. on March 15. A Greyhound bus delivered the plaintiff from Pensacola to Mobile just after midnight on March 15. Seven hours later, Greyhound personnel directed the plaintiff to board a Colonial Trailways bus. The driver, defendant Terry Reeves, announced that the bus was traveling only to Jackson, Mississippi and would thereafter return to Mobile. Reeves also announced that his bus was scheduled to arrive in Jackson at 12:05 p.m. and that a bus would depart Jackson at 12:30 p.m., arriving in Tunica at 5:05 p.m. The plaintiff, upon hearing this, decided it was time for a nap.

So far, so good. But when the plaintiff awakened, he realized it was almost 2:30 p.m. and that the bus was now headed back to Mobile. He and Reeves exchanged words, but the bus continued to Mobile, where the plaintiff remained for over nine hours before his brother sent him a pre-paid ticket back to Pensacola. Because of these events, the plaintiff "missed his court-date and was found guilty in absentia." The plaintiff sues Greyhound, Colonial Trailways and Reeves on several state law causes of action. Subject matter jurisdiction is based on diversity of citizenship.

DISCUSSION

Greyhound argues that the action should be dismissed for improper venue or, in the alternative, for failure to state a claim. It is well established that a court should address challenges to subject matter jurisdiction under Rule 12(b)(1) and challenges to personal jurisdiction under Rule 12(b)(2) before considering a Rule 12(b)(6) motion based on failure to state a claim. *E.g., Republic of Panama v. BCCI Holdings (Luxembourg) S.A.,* 119 F.3d 935, 940 (11th Cir. 1997); *Jones v. State of Georgia,* 725 F.2d 622, 623 (11th Cir. 1984). For similar reasons, the Court concludes that it should resolve Greyhound's challenge to venue under Rule 12(b)(3) before addressing its Rule 12(b)(6) motion. *See Arrowsmith v. United Press International,* 320 F.2d 219, 221 (2nd Cir. 1963) (venue should be resolved before addressing failure to state a claim).

Although unnoted by the parties, "[t]he plaintiff has the burden of showing that venue in the forum is proper." *Pinson v. Rumsfeld,* 192 Fed. Appx. 811, 817 (11th Cir. 2006). However, "[w]hen a complaint is dismissed on the basis of improper venue without an evidentiary hearing, 'the plaintiff must present only a prima facie showing of venue.' . . . "Further, '[t]he facts as alleged in the complaint are taken as true to the extent they are uncontroverted by defendants' affidavits.'" *Home Insurance Co. v. Thomas Industries, Inc.,* 896 F.3d 1352, 1355 (11th Cir. 1990) (quoting *Delong Equipment Co. v. Washington Mills Abrasive Co.,* 840 F.2d 843, 845 (11th Cir. 1988)). Greyhound did not request an evidentiary hearing, so the plaintiff need present only a prima facie showing of venue. Neither side presented affidavits or other evidence, so the Court's review is limited to the complaint. As discussed below, that document does not suffice to meet the plaintiff's burden of making a prima facie showing of proper venue.

The propriety of venue in this case is to be measured by 28 U.S.C. § 1391(b). This statute provides two means of establishing proper venue, with a third means available if proper venue cannot be established under either of the first two.

Venue is proper in "a judicial district in which any defendant resides, if all defendants are residents of the State in which the district is located." 28 U.S.C. § 1391(b)(1). For purposes of this provision, an individual resides "in the United States district in which that person is domiciled." *Id.* § 1391(c)(1). According to the complaint, Reeves "is a citizen of Florida with his domicile residence in the State of Florida." (Doc. 1 at 2). Because Reeves does not reside in Alabama, venue is not proper under Section 1391(b)(1).

Venue is also proper in "a judicial district in which a substantial part of the events or omissions giving rise to the claim occurred." 28 U.S.C. § 1391(b)(2). Under this provision, "[o]nly the events that directly give rise to a claim are relevant." Jenkins Brick Co. v. Bremer, 321 F.3d 1366, 1371 (11th Cir. 2003). The only event that occurred in this District was that the plaintiff changed buses here, and that event did not "directly give rise to a claim." The plaintiff does not allege that the transfer constituted a breach of contract, only that Greyhound had not told him, when he purchased the ticket to Tunica the previous day, that he would be transferring to a Colonial Trailways bus. Greyhound's alleged negligence and breach of contract, according to the complaint, derive from its failure to safely and successfully transport the plaintiff to Tunica, and nothing that occurred in Alabama caused or contributed to such failure. According to the complaint, Greyhound contracted to get him to Tunica at 5:05 p.m. on March 15 and taking the Colonial Trailways bus to Jackson would have (but for his sleeping through the transfer) gotten him to Tunica at precisely that time. The mere fact that the plaintiff passed through this District and changed buses here is not a "part of the events or omissions giving rise to the claim," much less a "substantial" part Accordingly, venue is not proper under Section 1391(b)(2).

However, a substantial part of the events or omissions giving rise to the plaintiff's claims certainly occurred in the Southern District of Mississippi. Greyhound explicitly concedes the propriety of venue in that District. Because proper venue can be established under Section 1391(b)(2) (only not in this District), the plaintiff cannot rely on Section 1391(b)(3) to establish venue.

"The district court of a district in which is filed a case laying venue in the wrong division or district shall dismiss, or if it be in the interest of justice, transfer such case to any district or division in which it could have been brought." 28 U.S.C. § 1406(a). To the extent the phrase "in which it could have been brought" requires that personal jurisdiction over the defendants exist in the transferee district, specific personal jurisdiction exists in the Southern District of Mississippi, as the plaintiff's claims arise from and relate to the defendant's' contacts with that District — Reeves' driving of the plaintiff there (and not waking him up in Jackson), Colonial Trailways' operation of the bus there, and Greyhound's sale of a ticket to transport the plaintiff through there. The parties make no argument to the contrary.

Greyhound requests the Court to dismiss rather than transfer, but it offers no explanation why this route should be preferred. As this Court has noted, "[g]enerally, the interests of justice [favor] transferring a case to the appropriate judicial district rather than dismissing it." For the reasons set forth in that decision, and in light of Greyhound's inability to articulate any reason why the action should be dismissed, the Court exercises its discretion in favor of transfer.

CONCLUSION

For the reasons set forth above, Greyhound's motion to dismiss for improper venue is denied. This action is transferred to the Southern District of Mississippi. . . .

DONE and ORDERED.

Transfer of Venue and the Doctrine of *Forum Non Conveniens*

The doctrine of *forum non conveniens* permits a court having jurisdiction over an action to refuse to exercise its jurisdiction when the litigation could be brought more appropriately in another forum.

Piper Aircraft v. Reyno
454 U.S. 235 (1981)

JUSTICE MARSHALL delivered the opinion of the Court. . . .

I

A

In July 1976, a small commercial aircraft crashed in the Scottish highlands during the course of a charter flight from Blackpool to Perth. The pilot and five passengers were killed instantly. The decedents were all Scottish subjects and residents, as are their heirs and next of kin. There were no eyewitnesses to the accident. At the time of the crash the plane was subject to Scottish air traffic control.

The aircraft, a twin-engine Piper Aztec, was manufactured in Pennsylvania by petitioner Piper Aircraft Co. (Piper). The propellers were manufactured in Ohio by petitioner Hartzell Propeller, Inc. (Hartzell). At the time of the crash the aircraft was registered in Great Britain and was owned and maintained by Air Navigation and Trading Co., Ltd. (Air Navigation). It was operated by McDonald Aviation, Ltd. (McDonald), a Scottish air taxi service. Both Air Navigation and McDonald were organized in the United Kingdom. The wreckage of the plane is now in a hangar in Farnsborough, England.

The British Department of Trade investigated the accident shortly after it occurred. A preliminary report found that the plane crashed after developing a spin and suggested that mechanical failure in the plane or the propeller was responsible. At Hartzell's request, this report was reviewed by a three-member Review Board, which held a 9-day adversary hearing attended by all interested parties. The Review Board found no evidence of defective equipment and indicated that pilot error may have contributed to the accident. The pilot, who had obtained his commercial pilot's license only three months earlier, was flying over high ground at an altitude considerably lower than the minimum height required by his company's operations manual.

In July 1977, a California probate court appointed respondent Gaynell Reyno administratrix of the estates of the five passengers. Reyno is not related to and does not know any of the decedents or their survivors; she was a legal secretary to the attorney who filed this lawsuit. Several days after her appointment, Reyno commenced separate wrongful-death actions against Piper and Hartzell in the Superior Court of California, claiming negligence and strict liability. Air Navigation, McDonald, and the estate of the pilot are not parties to this litigation. The survivors of the five passengers whose estates are represented by Reyno filed a separate action in the United Kingdom against Air Navigation, McDonald, and the pilot's estate. Reyno candidly admits that the action against Piper and Hartzell was filed in the United States because its laws regarding liability, capacity to sue, and damages are more favorable to her position than are those of Scotland. Scottish law does not recognize strict liability in tort. Moreover, it permits wrongful-death actions only when brought by a decedent's relatives. The relatives may sue only for "loss of support and society."

On petitioner's' motion, the suit was removed to the United States District Court for the Central District of California. Piper then moved for transfer to the United States District Court for the Middle District of Pennsylvania, pursuant to 28 U.S.C. 1404(a). Hartzell moved to dismiss for lack of personal jurisdiction, or in the alternative, to transfer. In December 1977, the District Court quashed service on Hartzell and transferred the case to the Middle District of Pennsylvania. Respondent then properly served process on Hartzell.

B

In May 1978, after the suit had been transferred, both Hartzell and Piper moved to dismiss the action on the ground of forum non conveniens. The District Court granted these motions in October 1979. It relied on the balancing test set forth by this Court in Gulf Oil Corp. v. Gilbert, 330 U.S. 501 (1947), and its companion case, Koster v. Lumbermens Mut. Cas. Co., 330 U.S. 518 (1947). In those decisions, the Court stated that a plaintiff's choice of forum should rarely be disturbed. However, when an alternative forum has jurisdiction to hear the case, and when trial in the chosen forum would "establish . . . oppressiveness and vexation to a defendant . . . out of all proportion to plaintiff's convenience," or when the "chosen forum [is] inappropriate because of considerations affecting the court's own administrative and legal problems," the court may, in the exercise of its sound discretion, dismiss the case. To guide trial court discretion, the Court provided a list of "private interest factors" affecting the convenience of the litigants, and a list of "public interest factors" affecting the convenience of the forum.

[The Third Circuit reversed, on the ground that dismissal for forum non conveniens is never appropriate where the law of the alternative forum is less favorable to the plaintiff.]

II

The Court of Appeals erred in holding that plaintiffs may defeat a motion to dismiss on the ground of forum non conveniens merely by showing that the substantive law that would be applied in the alternative forum is less favorable to the plaintiffs than that of the present forum. The possibility of a change in substantive law should ordinarily not be given conclusive or even substantial weight in the forum non conveniens inquiry.

We expressly rejected the position adopted by the Court of Appeals in our decision in Canada Malting Co. v. Paterson Steamships, Ltd., 285 U.S. 413 (1932)....

The Court of Appeals' decision is inconsistent with this Court's earlier forum non conveniens decisions in another respect. Those decisions have repeatedly emphasized the need to retain flexibility....

In fact, if conclusive or substantial weight were given to the possibility of a change in law, the forum non conveniens doctrine would become virtually useless. Jurisdiction and venue requirements are often easily satisfied. As a result, many plaintiffs are able to choose from among several forums. Ordinarily, these plaintiffs will select that forum whose choice-of-law rules are most advantageous. Thus, if the possibility of an unfavorable change in substantive law is given substantial weight in the forum non conveniens inquiry, dismissal would rarely be proper....

Upholding the decision of the Court of Appeals would result in other practical problems. At least where the foreign plaintiff named an American manufacturer as defendant, a court could not dismiss the case on grounds of forum non conveniens where dismissal might lead to an unfavorable change in law. The American courts, which are already extremely attractive to foreign plaintiffs, would become even more attractive. The flow of litigation into the United States would increase and further congest already crowded courts....

We do not hold that the possibility of an unfavorable change in law should never be a relevant consideration in a forum non conveniens inquiry. Of course, if the remedy provided by the alternative forum is so clearly inadequate or unsatisfactory that it is no remedy at all, the unfavorable change in law may be given substantial weight; the district court may conclude that dismissal would not be in the interests of justice. In these cases, however, the remedies that would be provided by the Scottish courts do not fall within this category. Although the relatives of the decedents may not be able to rely on a strict liability theory, and although their potential damages award may be smaller, there is no danger that they will be deprived of any remedy or treated unfairly.

III

The Court of Appeals also erred in rejecting the District Court's Gilbert analysis....

A

The District Court acknowledged that there is ordinarily a strong presumption in favor of the plaintiff's choice of forum, which may be overcome only when the private and public interest factors clearly point towards trial in the alternative forum. It held, however, that the presumption applies with less force when the plaintiff or real parties in interest are foreign.

The District Court's distinction between resident or citizen plaintiffs and foreign plaintiffs is fully justified. In Koster, the Court indicated that a plaintiff's choice of forum is entitled to greater deference when the plaintiff has chosen the home forum. When the home forum has been chosen, it is reasonable to assume that this choice is convenient. When the plaintiff is foreign, however, this assumption is much less reasonable. Because the central purpose of any forum non conveniens inquiry is to ensure that the trial is convenient, a foreign plaintiff's choice deserves less deference.

B

The forum non conveniens determination is committed to the sound discretion of the trial court. It may be reversed only when there has been a clear abuse of discretion. . . .

(1)

In analyzing the private interest factors, the District Court stated that the connections with Scotland are "overwhelming." This characterization may be somewhat exaggerated. Particularly with respect to the question of relative ease of access to sources of proof, the private interests point in both directions. As respondent emphasizes, records concerning the design, manufacture, and testing of the propeller and plane are located in the United States. She would have greater access to sources of proof relevant to her strict liability and negligence theories if trial were held here. However, the District Court did not act unreasonably in concluding that fewer evidentiary problems would be posed if the trial were held in Scotland. A large proportion of the relevant evidence is located in Great Britain. . . .

The District Court correctly concluded that the problems posed by the inability to implead potential third-party defendants clearly supported holding the trial in Scotland. Joinder of the pilot's estate, Air Navigation, and McDonald is crucial to the presentation of petitioners' defense. If Piper and Hartzell can show that the accident was caused not by a design defect, but rather by the negligence of the pilot, the plane's owners, or the charter company, they will be relieved of all liability. . . .

(2)

The District Court's review of the factors relating to the public interest was also reasonable. On the basis of its choice-of-law analysis, it concluded that if the case were tried in the Middle District of Pennsylvania, Pennsylvania law would apply to Piper and

Scottish law to Hartzell. It stated that a trial involving two sets of laws would be confusing to the jury. It also noted its own lack of familiarity with Scottish law. Consideration of these problems was clearly appropriate under *Gilbert*. . . .

Scotland has a very strong interest in this litigation. The accident occurred in its airspace. All of the decedents were Scottish. Apart from Piper and Hartzell, all potential plaintiffs and defendants are either Scottish or English. As we stated in Gilbert, there is "a local interest in having localized controversies decided at home. "Respondent argues that American citizens have an interest in ensuring that American manufacturers are deterred from producing defective products, and that additional deterrence might be obtained if Piper and Hartzell were tried in the United States, where they could be sued on the basis of both negligence and strict liability. However, the incremental deterrence that would be gained if this trial were held in an American court is likely to be insignificant. The American interest in this accident is simply not sufficient to justify the enormous commitment of judicial time and resources that would inevitably be required if the case were to be tried here.

IV

The Court of Appeals erred in holding that the possibility of an unfavorable change in law bars dismissal on the ground of forum non conveniens. It also erred in rejecting the District Court's Gilbert analysis. The District Court properly decided that the presumption in favor of the respondent's forum choice applied with less than maximum force because the real parties in interest are foreign. It did not act unreasonably in deciding that the private interests pointed towards trial in Scotland. Nor did it act unreasonably in deciding that the public interests favored trial in Scotland. Thus, the judgment of the Court of Appeals is

Reversed.

Transfer of Venue

If a civil action is commenced in the wrong district or division, the court may transfer the case to any district or division in which it could have been brought.

Atlantic Marine Construction Co. v. U.S. District Court
571 U.S. 49 (2013)

Justice ALITO delivered the opinion of the Court.

The question in this case concerns the procedure that is available for a defendant in a civil case who seeks to enforce a forum-selection clause. We reject petitioner's argument that such a clause may be enforced by a motion to dismiss under 28 U.S.C. § 1406(a) or Rule 12(b)(3) of the Federal Rules of Civil Procedure. Instead, a forum-selection clause may be enforced by a motion to transfer under § 1404(a) (2006 ed., Supp. V), which provides that "[f]or the convenience of parties and witnesses, in the interest of justice, a district court may transfer any civil action to any other district or division where it might have been brought or to any district or division to which all parties have consented." When a defendant files such a motion, we conclude, a district court should transfer the case unless extraordinary circumstances unrelated to the convenience of the parties clearly disfavor a transfer. In the present case, both the District Court and the Court of Appeals misunderstood the standards to be applied in adjudicating a § 1404(a) motion in a case involving a forum-selection clause, and we therefore reverse the decision below.

I

Petitioner Atlantic Marine Construction Co., a Virginia corporation with its principal place of business in Virginia, entered into a contract with the United States Army Corps of Engineers to construct a child-development center at Fort Hood in the Western District of Texas. Atlantic Marine then entered into a subcontract with respondent J-Crew Management, Inc., a Texas corporation, for work on the project. This subcontract included a forum-selection clause, which stated that all disputes between the parties "'shall be litigated in the Circuit Court for the City of Norfolk, Virginia, or the United States District Court for the Eastern District of Virginia, Norfolk Division.'". . .

When a dispute about payment under the subcontract arose, however, J-Crew sued Atlantic Marine in the Western District of Texas, invoking that court's diversity jurisdiction. Atlantic Marine moved to dismiss the suit, arguing that the forum-selection clause rendered venue in the Western District of Texas "wrong" under § 1406(a) and "improper" under Federal Rule of Civil Procedure 12(b)(3). In the alternative, Atlantic Marine moved to transfer the case to the Eastern District of Virginia under § 1404(a). J-Crew opposed these motions.

The District Court denied both motions [and the Fifth Circuit affirmed] . . . .

Relying on Stewart Organization, Inc. v. Ricoh Corp., 487 U.S. 22, 108 S.Ct. 2239, 101 L.Ed.2d 22 (1988), the Court of Appeals agreed with the District Court that § 1404(a) is the exclusive mechanism for enforcing a forum-selection clause that points to another federal forum when venue is otherwise proper in the district where the case was brought. The court stated, however, that if a forum-selection clause points to a nonfederal forum, dismissal under Rule 12(b)(3) would be the correct mechanism to enforce the clause because § 1404(a) by its terms does not permit transfer to any tribunal other than another federal court. The Court of Appeals then concluded that the District Court had not clearly abused its discretion in refusing to transfer the case after conducting the balance-of-interests analysis required by § 1404(a). That was so even though there was no dispute that the forum-selection clause was valid. We granted certiorari. . . .

II

Atlantic Marine contends that a party may enforce a forum-selection clause by seeking dismissal of the suit under § 1406(a) and Rule 12(b)(3). We disagree. Section 1406(a) and Rule 12(b)(3) allow dismissal only when venue is "wrong" or "improper." Whether venue is "wrong" or "improper" depends exclusively on whether the court in which the case was brought satisfies the requirements of federal venue laws, and those provisions say nothing about a forum-selection clause.

A

Section 1406(a) provides that "[t]he district court of a district in which is filed a case laying venue in the wrong division or district shall dismiss, or if it be in the interest of justice, transfer such case to any district or division in which it could have been brought." Rule 12(b)(3) states that a party may move to dismiss a case for "improper venue." These provisions therefore authorize dismissal only when venue is "wrong" or "improper" in the forum in which it was brought.

This question — whether venue is "wrong" or "improper" — is generally governed by 28 U.S.C. § 1391 That provision states that "[e]xcept as otherwise provided by law ... this section shall govern the venue of all civil actions brought in district courts of the United States." § 1391(a)(1) (emphasis added). It further provides that "[a] civil action may be brought in — (1) a judicial district in which any defendant resides, if all defendants are residents of the State in which the district is located; (2) a judicial district in which a substantial part of the events or omissions giving rise to the claim occurred, or a substantial part of property that is the subject of the action is situated; or (3) if there is no district in which an action may otherwise be brought as provided in this section, any judicial district in which any defendant is subject to the court's personal jurisdiction with respect to such action." § 1391(b) When venue is challenged, the court must determine whether the case falls within one of the three categories set out in § 1391(b). If it does, venue is proper; if it does not, venue is improper, and the case must be dismissed or transferred under § 1406(a). Whether the parties entered into a contract containing a forum-selection clause has no bearing on whether a case falls into one of the categories of cases listed in § 1391(b). As a result, a case filed in a district that falls within § 1391 may not be dismissed under § 1406(a) or Rule 12(b)(3).

Petitioner's contrary view improperly conflates the special statutory term "venue" and the word "forum." It is certainly true that, in some contexts, the word "venue" is used synonymously with the term "forum," but § 1391 makes clear that venue in "all civil actions" must be determined in accordance with the criteria outlined in that section. That language cannot reasonably be read to allow judicial consideration of other, extra-statutory limitations on the forum in which a case may be brought.

The structure of the federal venue provisions confirms that they alone define whether venue exists in a given forum. In particular, the venue statutes reflect Congress' intent that venue should always lie in some federal court whenever federal courts have personal jurisdiction over the defendant. . . . As we have previously noted, "Congress does not in general intend to create venue gaps, which take away with one hand what Congress has given by way of jurisdictional grant with the other." . . .

B

Although a forum-selection clause does not render venue in a court "wrong" or "improper" within the meaning of § 1406(a) or Rule 12(b)(3), the clause may be enforced through a motion to transfer under § 1404(a). That provision states that "[f]or the convenience of parties and witnesses, in the interest of justice, a district court may transfer any civil action to any other district or division where it might have been brought or to any district or division to which all parties have consented." Unlike § 1406(a), § 1404(a) does not condition transfer on the initial forum's being "wrong." And it permits transfer to any district where venue is also proper (i.e., "where [the case] might have been brought") or to any other district to which the parties have agreed by contract or stipulation.

Section 1404(a) therefore provides a mechanism for enforcement of forum-selection clauses that point to a particular federal district. And for the reasons we address in Part III, infra, a proper application of § 1404(a) requires that a forum-selection clause be "given controlling weight in all but the most exceptional cases." Stewart, supra, at 33, 108 S.Ct. 2239 (KENNEDY, J., concurring).

Atlantic Marine argues that § 1404(a) is not a suitable mechanism to enforce forum-selection clauses because that provision cannot provide for transfer when a forum-selection clause specifies a state or foreign tribunal and we agree with Atlantic Marine that the Court of Appeals failed to provide a sound answer to this problem. The Court of Appeals opined that a forum-selection clause pointing to a nonfederal forum should be enforced through Rule 12(b)(3), which permits a party to move for dismissal of a case based on "improper venue." 701 F.3d, at 740. As Atlantic Marine persuasively argues, however, that conclusion cannot be reconciled with our construction of the term "improper venue" in § 1406 to refer only to a forum that does not satisfy federal venue laws. If venue is proper under federal venue rules, it does not matter for the purpose of Rule 12(b)(3) whether the forum-selection clause points to a federal or a nonfederal forum.

Instead, the appropriate way to enforce a forum-selection clause pointing to a state or foreign forum is through the doctrine of forum non conveniens. Section 1404(a) is merely a codification of the doctrine of forum non conveniens for the subset of cases in which the transferee forum is within the federal court system; in such cases, Congress has replaced the traditional remedy of outright dismissal with transfer. See Sinochem Int'l Co. v. Malaysia Int'l Shipping Corp., 549 U.S. 422, 430, 127 S.Ct. 1184, 167 L.Ed.2d 15 (2007) ("For the federal court system, Congress has codified the doctrine ..."); see also notes following § 1404 (Historical and Revision Notes) (Section 1404(a) "was drafted in accordance with the doctrine of forum non conveniens, permitting transfer to a more convenient forum, even though the venue is proper"). For the remaining set of cases calling for a nonfederal forum, § 1404(a) has no application, but the residual doctrine of forum non conveniens "has continuing application in federal courts." Sinochem, 549 U.S., at 430, 127 S.Ct. 1184 (internal quotation marks and brackets omitted); see also ibid. (noting that federal courts invoke forum non conveniens "in cases where the alternative forum is abroad, and perhaps in rare instances where a state or territorial court serves litigational convenience best" (internal quotation marks and citation omitted)). And because both § 1404(a) and the forum non conveniens doctrine from which it derives entail the same balancing-of-interests standard, courts should evaluate a forum-selection clause pointing to a nonfederal forum in the same way that they evaluate a forum-selection clause pointing to a federal forum. . . .

III

Although the Court of Appeals correctly identified § 1404(a) as the appropriate provision to enforce the forum-selection clause in this case, the Court of Appeals erred in failing to make the adjustments required in a § 1404(a) analysis when the transfer motion is premised on a forum-selection clause. When the parties have agreed to a valid forum-selection clause, a district court should ordinarily transfer the case to the forum specified in that clause. Only under extraordinary circumstances unrelated to the convenience of the parties should a § 1404(a) motion be denied. And no such exceptional factors appear to be present in this case. . . .

When parties have contracted in advance to litigate disputes in a particular forum, courts should not unnecessarily disrupt the parties' settled expectations. A forum-selection clause, after all, may have figured centrally in the parties' negotiations and may have affected how they set monetary and other contractual terms; it may, in fact, have been a critical factor in their agreement to do business together in the first place. In all but the most unusual cases, therefore, "the interest of justice" is served by holding parties to their bargain. . . .

We reverse the judgment of the Court of Appeals for the Fifth Circuit. Although no public-interest factors that might support the denial of Atlantic Marine's motion to transfer are apparent on the record before us, we remand the case for the courts below to decide that question.

It is so ordered.

Forum Non Conveniens Compared to Motion to Transfer to Proper Venue A defendant invoking forum non conveniens ordinarily bears a heavy burden in opposing the plaintiff's chosen forum.). That is because of the "hars[h] result" of that doctrine: Unlike a § 1404(a) motion, a successful motion under forum non conveniens requires dismissal of the case. *Norwood*, 349 U.S., at 32, 75 S.Ct. 544. That inconveniences plaintiffs in several respects and even "makes it possible for [plaintiffs] to lose out completely, through the running of the statute of limitations in the forum finally deemed appropriate." (*Atlantic Marine, supra* fn. 8)

CHAPTER 2

SUBJECT MATTER JURISDICTION

Introduction

In Chapter 1, we explored where a plaintiff, in terms of place and location, may choose to bring a lawsuit against a defendant. As we learned, the options are limited by the Due Process clause of the U.S. Constitution. In other words, a defendant cannot be sued in a particular state or forum unless the defendant has contacts, ties or relations with the forum that make it reasonable to compel the defendant to appear and defend in the forum. Once we have determined the place or location where a defendant may be sued, the plaintiff has another decision to make; which court system, state or federal, to bring the lawsuit in. All courts, do not have the power to decide all types of cases. The issue of which court system is the appropriate court system is one of subject matter jurisdiction.

> **Subject Matter Jurisdiction**
>
> Refers to the question of whether a particular court has the power or competence to decide the kind of controversy that is involved.

Subject matter jurisdiction (as opposed to personal jurisdiction) refers to the question of whether a particular court has the power or competence to decide the kind of controversy that is involved. (Friedenthal § 2.1) Note that subject matter jurisdiction is not an alternative to personal jurisdiction (the court's authority to enter a judgment binding on the particular defendant involved) but rather, is an additional hurdle to be cleared.

The federal government and each of the 50 states has its own system of trial courts and appellate courts. Since lawsuits always start at the trial court level we will begin there. In California, the trial court is the Superior Court. In the federal court system the trial courts are the United States District Courts.

Subject Matter Jurisdiction of the Federal Courts

Federal Courts Are Courts of Limited Jurisdiction

Unlike state courts which are typically courts of general jurisdiction (such as the Superior Court in California) which have jurisdiction over the subject matter of a wide variety of lawsuits, federal jurisdiction is limited in nature. Federal courts only exercise the limited subject matter jurisdiction bestowed by the Constitution and Congress. (See U.S. Const. Art. III, sec. 2) There is a presumption against federal jurisdiction. The existence of subject matter jurisdiction generally must be demonstrated at the outset by the party seeking to invoke it. (See FRCP 8) It cannot be conferred by consent of the parties, nor can its absence be waived. (Friedenthal § 2.2)

Although there are a number of areas where Congress has bestowed subject matter jurisdiction in the federal courts, admiralty, bankruptcy, anti-trust, we will focus on the two principal areas of federal subject matter jurisdiction, federal question jurisdiction and diversity of citizenship.

Federal Question Jurisdiction

> **Federal Question Jurisdiction**
>
> Cases or controversies arising under the Constitution and laws of the United States

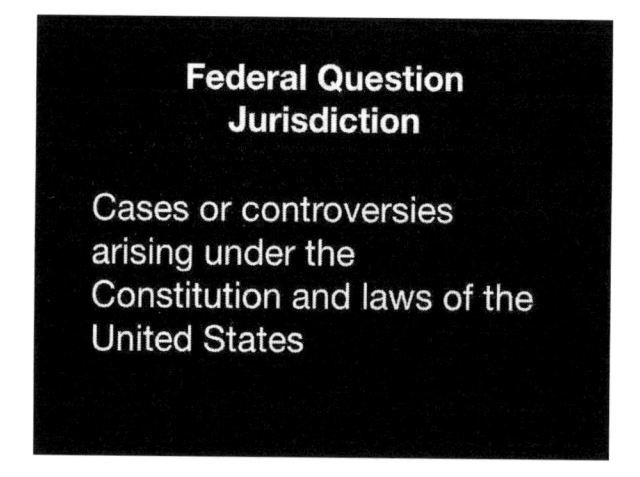

Congress has conferred upon federal courts jurisdiction to decide *federal questions* i.e., cases or controversies arising under the Constitution and laws of the United States (28 U.S.C. § 1331) The rule that a suit arises under the Constitution and laws of the United States only when the plaintiff's statement of his own cause of action so demonstrates is called the "well pleaded complaint rule."

Boyle v. MTV Networks
766 F.Supp. 809 (1991)

FERN M. SMITH, District Judge.

This matter is before the Court on Plaintiff's motion for remand. Plaintiff filed suit in state court seeking relief based on California law. Defendants removed to this Court, claiming that federal law preempts Plaintiff's state law causes of action and that Plaintiff had "artfully pleaded" around her true federal basis for relief. For the reasons discussed in this Order, Defendants' removal was inappropriate because this Court lacks subject matter jurisdiction; Plaintiff's motion to remand is therefore GRANTED.

FACTS

On August 23, 1990, Plaintiff filed her first amended complaint in San Mateo Superior Court. She purports to bring her action on behalf of the general public and seeks injunctive relief and restitution for violation of California Business and Professions Code section 17200. The named Defendants are MTV Networks, Inc., a Delaware corporation ("MTV"); AT & T, Inc., a New York corporation ("AT&T"); and Pacific Bell, Inc., a California corporation ("PACBELL").

On September 19, 1990, Defendants timely removed the action to this Court. On October 3, 1990, Plaintiff filed her motion for remand.

The gravamen of the complaint is that Defendants have participated in games of chance, which are allegedly illegal under California Penal Code sections 319, 320, and 322. Specifically, Plaintiff alleges that defendant MTV has conducted lotteries on two nationwide television channels, and that defendant AT & T has provided 900 phone service for call-in entries to these lotteries. Fees earned from "900" calls are divided between defendants MTV and AT & T. Plaintiff alleges that Defendants AT & T, PACBELL, and various Does bill for these calls.

Plaintiff seeks restitution to callers billed for calls from California. In addition, she asks the Court to enjoin MTV from continuing its practice unless the following requirements are satisfied: (1) MTV must give equal publicity about the free mail-in method of entry to the games of chance when advertising the paid phone-in method; (2) Defendants must provide something of value for phone-in (paid) entries; and (3) Defendants must provide publicity about the minimum age requirement when advertising the game. Finally, Plaintiff seeks costs and attorney's fees, under California Code of Civil Procedure section 1021.5. . . .

I. SUBJECT MATTER JURISDICTION.

The United States Code confers subject matter jurisdiction on federal district court only in limited circumstances. The two provisions pertinent to this case are federal question and diversity of citizenship. 28 U.S.C.A. §§ 1331, 1332. The requirements for jurisdiction under diversity of citizenship are not satisfied because the parties are not completely diverse—both Plaintiff and Defendant PACBELL are citizens of California. 28 U.S.C.A. § 1332(a)(1), (c)(1). Additionally the amount in controversy is not satisfied. Id.

The federal question statute, section 1331, provides, on the other hand, that "district courts shall have original jurisdiction of all civil actions arising under the ... laws ... of the United States." 28 U.S.C.A. § 1331 (emphasis added). The pertinent inquiry, therefore, is whether Plaintiff's state law action is one "arising under" federal law. To determine whether a case meets this criterion, the federal courts examine the face of the complaint. The "well-pleaded" complaint rule "provides that federal jurisdiction exists only when a federal question is presented on the face of the plaintiff's properly pleaded complaint." This rule applies equally "to the original jurisdiction of the district courts as well as to their removal jurisdiction."

Plaintiff's complaint does not state a claim "arising under" federal law for three separate and independent reasons: (1) the "well-pleaded" complaint does not allege a federal claim; (2) Plaintiff does not have standing to sue in federal court; and (3) federal law does not "completely pre-empt" state law in this area. This Court does not, therefore, have subject matter jurisdiction and must remand this case to the state court under 28 U.S.C.A. section 1447(c).

A. The "Well-Pleaded" Complaint Rule.

The underlying premise of the "well-pleaded" complaint rule is that a plaintiff is the master of his or her case and has the right to choose whether to rely on state or federal law. If a plaintiff "can maintain his claim on both state and federal grounds, he may ignore the federal question and assert only a state law claim and defeat removal."

Moreover, the Supreme Court has repeatedly stated that "'whether a case is one arising under ... a law ... of the United States, in the sense of the jurisdictional statute, ... must be determined from what necessarily appears in the plaintiff's ... [complaint], unaided by anything alleged in anticipation of avoidance of defenses which it is thought the defendant may interpose.' ... For better or worse, ... a defendant may not remove a case to federal court unless the plaintiff's complaint establishes that the case 'arises under' federal law." Franchise Tax Bd., 463 U.S. at 10, 103 S.Ct. at 2846-47 (emphasis in original), Furthermore, it is "settled law that a case may not be removed to federal court on the basis of a federal defense, including the defense of pre-emption...."

In Franchise Tax Board, the Supreme Court applied these principles to a state law suit to enforce a levy. The defendant removed to the federal district court, claiming that ERISA pre-empted the State's power to levy under the state statute. In a unanimous decision, the Supreme Court held that "a straightforward application of the well-pleaded complaint rule precludes original federal-court jurisdiction. California law establishes a set of conditions, without reference to federal law, under which a tax levy may be enforced; federal law becomes relevant only by way of a defense to an obligation created entirely by state law, and then only if appellant has made out a valid claim for relief under state law." Id. at 13, 103 S.Ct. at 2848.

The Franchise Tax Board Court went on, however, to state that "[e]ven though state law creates appellant's causes of action, its case might still `arise under' the laws of the United States if a well-pleaded complaint established that its right to relief under state law requires resolution of substantial question of federal law in dispute between the parties." The Court applied this reasoning to a declaratory judgment action brought to establish the rights and duties of the parties. Since the only questions in that claim concerned the parties' legal rights and duties under ERISA, the question of federal pre-emption was a necessary element of the declaratory judgment claim; therefore, it had to be part of the well-pleaded complaint, which thereby raised a question of federal law. This is not the case here, however, because Plaintiff does not seek a declaration of rights under federal law. Indeed, she has scrupulously avoided federal claims.

The California statutes under which Plaintiff sues establish a set of conditions, without reference to federal law, under which liability attaches. Defendants claim that if they are forced to comply with these state laws, they will violate federal law prohibiting discrimination under the Federal Communications Act ("FCA") section 202, 47 U.S.C. § 202. Defendants argue that federal law therefore pre-empts Plaintiff's state law causes of action. This argument is asserted only as a defense to Plaintiff's state law cause of action; as a defense, it becomes relevant only after Plaintiff has made out a valid claim under state law. This defense is insufficient to support removal. Id. Under the "well-pleaded" complaint rule, Plaintiff's claim does not "arise under" federal law. This Court does not have subject matter jurisdiction and remand is therefore appropriate. . . .

CONCLUSION

The Court lacks subject matter jurisdiction . . . the "well-pleaded" complaint does not on its face state a claim "arising under" federal law. . . Accordingly, Plaintiff's motion for remand is GRANTED.

"Well Pleaded Complaint Rule"

A suit arises under the Constitution and laws of the United States only when the plaintiff's statement of his own cause of action so demonstrates.

Note So what does a "well-pleaded complaint look like? Note FRCP 8's requirement that: "A pleading that states a claim for relief must contain: (1) a short and plain statement of the grounds for the court's jurisdiction . . ." Here is an example:

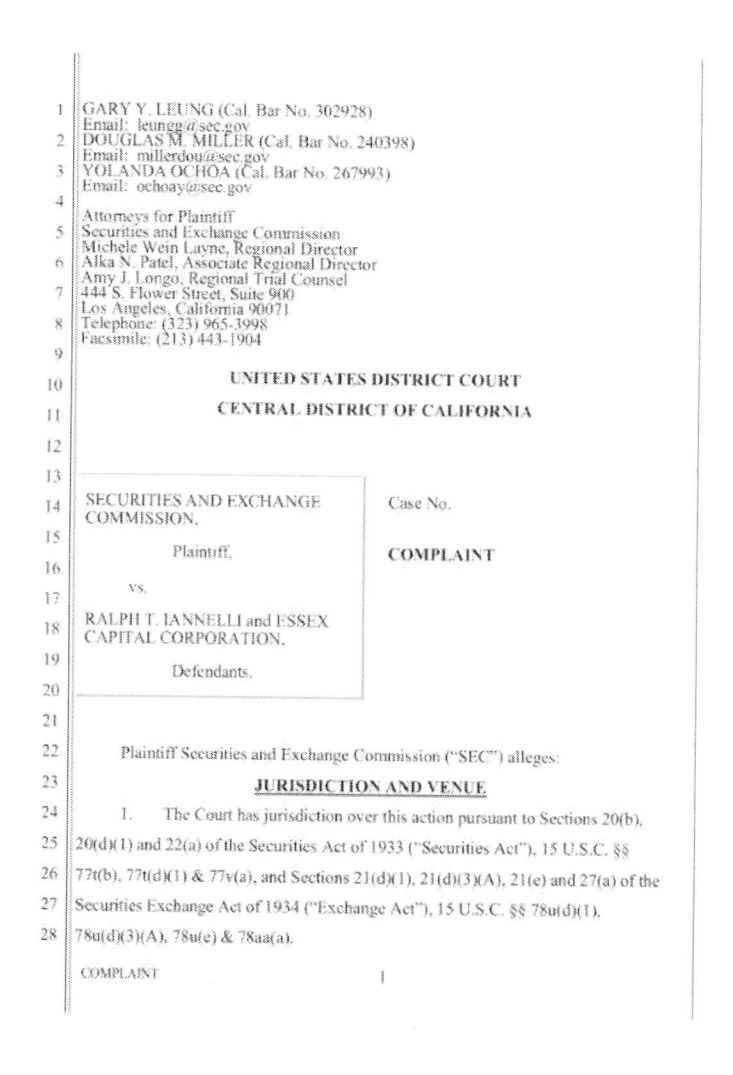

```
GARY Y. LEUNG (Cal. Bar No. 302928)
Email: leungg@sec.gov
DOUGLAS M. MILLER (Cal. Bar No. 240398)
Email: millerdou@sec.gov
YOLANDA OCHOA (Cal. Bar No. 267993)
Email: ochoay@sec.gov

Attorneys for Plaintiff
Securities and Exchange Commission
Michele Wein Layne, Regional Director
Alka N. Patel, Associate Regional Director
Amy J. Longo, Regional Trial Counsel
444 S. Flower Street, Suite 900
Los Angeles, California 90071
Telephone: (323) 965-3998
Facsimile: (213) 443-1904
```

UNITED STATES DISTRICT COURT
CENTRAL DISTRICT OF CALIFORNIA

SECURITIES AND EXCHANGE COMMISSION,	Case No.
Plaintiff,	COMPLAINT
vs.	
RALPH T. IANNELLI and ESSEX CAPITAL CORPORATION,	
Defendants.	

Plaintiff Securities and Exchange Commission ("SEC") alleges:

JURISDICTION AND VENUE

1. The Court has jurisdiction over this action pursuant to Sections 20(b), 20(d)(1) and 22(a) of the Securities Act of 1933 ("Securities Act"), 15 U.S.C. §§ 77t(b), 77t(d)(1) & 77v(a), and Sections 21(d)(1), 21(d)(3)(A), 21(e) and 27(a) of the Securities Exchange Act of 1934 ("Exchange Act"), 15 U.S.C. §§ 78u(d)(1), 78u(d)(3)(A), 78u(e) & 78aa(a).

Problem The Mottleys had been injured in a railway accident, and the railroad, as part of a settlement of their claims against it, had agreed to give them free passes for the rest of their lives. The railroad issued the passes for 29 years, but, after the enactment in 1907 of a federal statute making it unlawful for railroads to give free passes, it refused to renew the Mottley's pass. The Mottleys brought suit in federal court for specific performance. Their complaint alleged that they anticipated that the railroad would raise the 1907 statute as a defense and their response to that defense would be that the statute did not apply to them, and that, if it did apply to them, it was an unconstitutional taking of their property. Does federal question jurisdiction apply to their claim? (See, *Louisville and Nashville Railroad Company v. Mottley*, 211 U.S. 149 (1908))

Diversity Jurisdiction

> **Diversity Jurisdiction**
>
> Citizenship of Plaintiffs ≠ Citizenship of Defendants
>
> and
>
> Amount in Controversy > $75,000

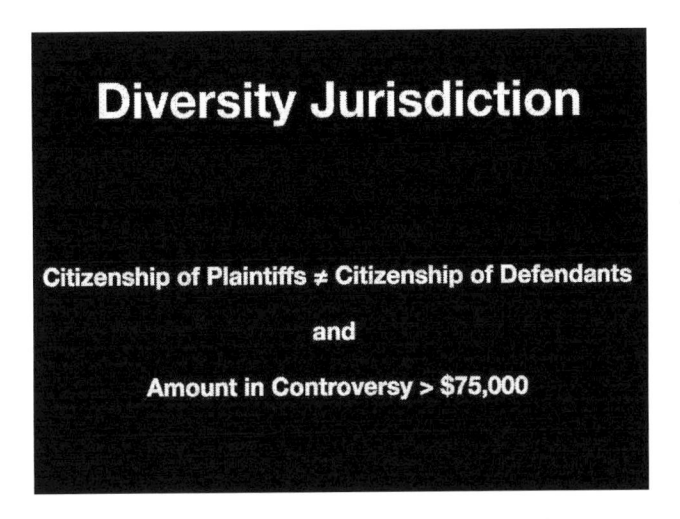

In diversity cases the subject matter jurisdiction of the federal courts is defined by who the parties to the lawsuit are rather than the subject matter of the underlying dispute. Federal subject matter jurisdiction exists in cases where the opposing parties are citizens of different states and the amount in controversy exceeds $75,000 exclusive of interests and costs. (28 U.S.C. § 1332) "Citizenship" is synonymous with "domicile", and "domicile" means physical presence in the state coupled with the intent to reside there indefinitely. There must be complete diversity of citizenship between the parties on each side, i.e., all plaintiffs must be citizens of different states than all defendants.

The Rule of "Complete Diversity" The "rule of complete diversity" holds that there is no diversity jurisdiction when any party on one side of the dispute is a citizen of the same state as any party on the other side. If any plaintiff shares a common citizenship with any defendant, then diversity is destroyed and along with it federal jurisdiction. (*Strawbridge v. Curtis*, 7 U.S. (3 Cranch) 267, 2 L.Ed. 435 (1806).)

This "complete diversity" interpretation of the general-diversity provision is a matter of statutory construction. "Article III poses no obstacle to the legislative extension of federal jurisdiction, founded on diversity, so long as any two adverse parties are not co-citizens." *State Farm Fire & Casualty Co. v. Tashire*, 386 U. S. 523, 531 (1967). So, Congress could, and in a few situations has, provided for federal jurisdiction in non-federal question cases where there is less than complete diversity among all parties.

Mas v. Perry
489 F.2d 1396 (1974)

AINSWORTH, Circuit Judge:

This case presents questions pertaining to federal diversity jurisdiction under 28 U.S.C. § 1332, which, pursuant to article III, section II of the Constitution, provides for original jurisdiction in federal district courts of all civil actions that are between, inter alia, citizens of different States or citizens of a State and citizens of foreign states and in which the amount in controversy is more than $10,000.

Appellees Jean Paul Mas, a citizen of France, and Judy Mas were married at her home in Jackson, Mississippi. Prior to their marriage, Mr. and Mrs. Mas were graduate assistants, pursuing coursework as well as performing teaching duties, for approximately nine months and one year, respectively, at Louisiana State University in Baton Rouge, Louisiana. Shortly after their marriage, they returned to Baton Rouge to resume their duties as graduate assistants at LSU. They remained in Baton Rouge for approximately two more years, after which they moved to Park Ridge, Illinois. At the time of the trial in this case, it was their intention to return to Baton Rouge while Mr. Mas finished his studies for the degree of Doctor of Philosophy. Mr. and Mrs. Mas were undecided as to where they would reside after that.

Upon their return to Baton Rouge after their marriage, appellees rented an apartment from appellant Oliver H. Perry, a citizen of Louisiana. This appeal arises from a final judgment entered on a jury verdict awarding $5,000 to Mr. Mas and $15,000 to Mrs. Mas for damages incurred by them as a result of the discovery that their bedroom and bathroom contained "two-way" mirrors and that they had been watched through them by the appellant during three of the first four months of their marriage.

At the close of the appellees' case at trial, appellant made an oral motion to dismiss for lack of jurisdiction. The motion was denied by the district court. Before this Court, appellant challenges the final judgment below solely on jurisdictional grounds, contending that appellees failed to prove diversity of citizenship among the parties and that the requisite jurisdictional amount is lacking with respect to Mr. Mas. Finding no merit to these contentions, we affirm. Under section 1332(a) (2), the federal judicial power extends to the claim of Mr. Mas, a citizen of France, against the appellant, a citizen of Louisiana. Since we conclude that Mrs. Mas is a citizen of Mississippi for diversity purposes, the district court also properly had jurisdiction under section 1332(a)(1) of her claim.

It has long been the general rule that complete diversity of parties is required in order that diversity jurisdiction obtain; that is, no party on one side may be a citizen of the same State as any party on the other side. Strawbridge v. Curtiss, 7 U.S. (3 Cranch) 267, 2 L.Ed. 435 (1806); see cases cited in 1 W. Barron & A. Holtzoff, Federal Practice and Procedure § 26, at 145 n. 95 (Wright ed. 1960). This determination of one's State citizenship for diversity purposes is controlled by federal law, not by the law of any State. 1 J. Moore, Moore's Federal Practice ¶ 0.74 [1], at 707.1 (1972). As is the case in other areas of federal jurisdiction, the diverse citizenship among adverse parties must be present at the time the complaint is filed. Jurisdiction is unaffected by subsequent changes in the citizenship of the parties. The burden of pleading the diverse citizenship is upon the party invoking federal jurisdiction, and if the diversity jurisdiction is properly challenged, that party also bears the burden of proof.

To be a citizen of a State within the meaning of section 1332, a natural person must be both a citizen of the United States, and a domiciliary of that State. For diversity purposes, citizenship means domicile; mere residence in the State is not sufficient.

A person's domicile is the place of "his true, fixed, and permanent home and principal establishment, and to which he has the intention of returning whenever he is absent therefrom . . . ." A change of domicile may be effected only by a combination of two elements: (a) taking up residence in a different domicile with (b) the intention to remain there.

It is clear that at the time of her marriage, Mrs. Mas was a domiciliary of the State of Mississippi. While it is generally the case that the domicile of the wife—and, consequently, her State citizenship for purposes of diversity jurisdiction—is deemed to be that of her husband, we find no precedent for extending this concept to the situation here, in which the husband is a citizen of a foreign state but resides in the United States. Indeed, such a fiction would work absurd results on the facts before us. If Mr. Mas were considered a domiciliary of France—as he would be since he had lived in Louisiana as a student-teaching assistant prior to filing this suit, —then Mrs. Mas would also be deemed a domiciliary, and thus, fictionally at least, a citizen of France. She would not be a citizen of any State and could not sue in a federal court on that basis; nor could she invoke the alienage jurisdiction to bring her claim in federal court, since she is not an alien. See C. Wright, Federal Courts 80 (1970). On the other hand, if Mrs. Mas's domicile were Louisiana, she would become a Louisiana citizen for diversity purposes and could not bring suit with her husband against appellant, also a Louisiana citizen, on the basis of diversity jurisdiction. These are curious results under a rule arising from the theoretical identity of person and interest of the married couple. SAn American woman is not deemed to have lost her United States citizenship solely by reason of her marriage to an alien. 8 U.S.C. § 1489. Similarly, we conclude that for diversity purposes a woman does not have her domicile or State citizenship changed solely by reason of her marriage to an alien.

Mrs. Mas's Mississippi domicile was disturbed neither by her year in Louisiana prior to her marriage nor as a result of the time she and her husband spent at LSU after their marriage, since for both periods she was a graduate assistant at LSU. Though she testified that after her marriage she had no intention of returning to her parents' home in Mississippi, Mrs. Mas did not effect a change of domicile since she and Mr. Mas were in Louisiana only as students and lacked the requisite intention to remain there. Until she acquires a new domicile, she remains a domiciliary, and thus a citizen, of Mississippi.

Appellant also contends that Mr. Mas's claim should have been dismissed for failure to establish the requisite jurisdictional amount for diversity cases of more than $10,000. In their complaint Mr. and Mrs. Mas alleged that they had each been damaged in the amount of $100,000. As we have noted, Mr. Mas ultimately recovered $5,000.

It is well settled that the amount in controversy is determined by the amount claimed by the plaintiff in good faith. Federal jurisdiction is not lost because a judgment of less than the jurisdictional amount is awarded. That Mr. Mas recovered only $5,000 is, therefore, not compelling. As the Supreme Court stated in St. Paul Mercury Indemnity Co. v. Red Cab Co., 303 U.S. 283, 288-290, 58 S.Ct. 586, 590-591, 82 L.Ed. 845:

[T]he sum claimed by the plaintiff controls if the claim is apparently made in good faith.

It must appear to a legal certainty that the claim is really for less than the jurisdictional amount to justify dismissal. The inability of the plaintiff to recover an amount adequate to give the court jurisdiction does not show his bad faith or oust the jurisdiction. . . .

. . . His good faith in choosing the federal forum is open to challenge not only by resort to the face of his complaint, but by the facts disclosed at trial, and if from either source it is clear that his claim never could have amounted to the sum necessary to give jurisdiction there is no injustice in dismissing the suit.

Having heard the evidence presented at the trial, the district court concluded that the appellees properly met the requirements of section 1332 with respect to jurisdictional amount. Upon examination of the record in this case, we are also satisfied that the requisite amount was in controversy.

Thus the power of the federal district court to entertain the claims of appellees in this case stands on two separate legs of diversity jurisdiction: a claim by an alien against a State citizen; and an action between citizens of different States. We also note, however, the propriety of having the federal district court entertain a spouse's action against a defendant, where the district court already has jurisdiction over a claim, arising from the same transaction, by the other spouse against the same defendant. See ALI Study of the Division of Jurisdiction Between State and Federal Courts, pt. I, at 9-10. (Official Draft 1965.) In the case before us, such a result is particularly desirable. The claims of Mr. and Mrs. Mas arise from the same operative facts, and there was almost complete interdependence between their claims with respect to the proof required and the issues raised at trial. Thus, since the district court had jurisdiction of Mr. Mas's action, sound judicial administration militates strongly in favor of federal jurisdiction of Mrs. Mas's claim.

Affirmed.

Hawkins v. Masters Farms, Inc.
CIVIL ACTION No. 02-2595-GTV. (D. Kan. Jul. 7, 2003)

G. THOMAS VANBEBBER, Senior District Judge

Plaintiffs, Mary Ann Hawkins, as Personal Representative to the Estate of James Patrick Creal, and Rachel Baldwin, as heir of Mr. Creal, bring this action pursuant to K.S.A. §§ 60-1901 and 1902 against Defendants, Masters Farms, Inc., Harhge Farms, Inc., and Jack E. Masters. Plaintiffs' claims arise from a December 8, 2000 traffic accident in which a tractor driven by Defendant Masters collided with Mr. Creal's automobile, resulting in the death of Mr. Creal. Plaintiffs filed this action in federal court alleging the existence of diversity jurisdiction under 28 U.S.C. § 1332. Defendants dispute that there is complete diversity among the parties, and the matter is before the court on Defendants' motion to dismiss (Doc. 9) for lack of subject matter jurisdiction. For the reasons set forth below, Defendants' motion is granted. . . .

Here, Defendants mount a factual attack on Plaintiffs' allegations of diversity subject matter jurisdiction. In addition to Plaintiffs' complaint itself, deposition testimony and other documents have been submitted for the court's review. As the party seeking to invoke federal jurisdiction, Plaintiffs bear the burden of proving that jurisdiction is proper. Because federal courts are courts of limited jurisdiction, the presumption is against federal jurisdiction.

II. FACTUAL BACKGROUND

On December 8, 2000, Mr. Creal was killed in an automobile accident on Mineral Point Road, just south of Troy, Kansas, when his 1988 Chevrolet van collided with a

New Holland tractor driven by Defendant Masters. At the time of his death, Mr. Creal was living in Troy with his wife, Elizabeth Creal, and her children. He was approximately forty-four years old when he died.

James and Elizabeth Creal first met in St. Joseph, Missouri in November 1999. Mr. Creal had lived in St. Joseph for most of his life, while Mrs. Creal resided in Troy for the majority of her life. When the couple first met, Mr. Creal was living at his mother's home in St. Joseph, where he had been residing since obtaining a divorce from his previous wife.

Beginning in January 2000, Mr. Creal began spending the night at the apartment Mrs. Creal shared with her children on South Park Street in Troy. Initially, Mr. Creal would return to his mother's house every evening after work, shower, gather some clothes, and proceed to the apartment to retire for the evening. Mrs. Creal paid the rent for the apartment on South Park Street, while Mr. Creal contributed by buying the groceries for himself, Mrs. Creal, and her two children. Mr. and Mrs. Creal split the cost of utilities for the apartment.

When Mrs. Creal and her children moved into an apartment on 1st Street in Troy in March 2000, Mr. Creal brought his clothes, some furniture, pictures, photo albums, and other memorabilia to the new apartment. Mr. and Mrs. Creal also purchased a bedroom set for the apartment. When they moved into the apartment, Mr. Creal stopped going to his mother's house in St. Joseph to shower and change after work, and instead came directly back to Troy to spend the night. Also at that time, Mr. and Mrs. Creal opened a joint checking account into which Mr. Creal began depositing his paychecks to help pay the household bills. Mr. and Mrs. Creal were married in July 2000.

In November 2000, Mr. and Mrs. Creal moved into a house on Streeter Creek Road in Troy. Mr. Creal died approximately two weeks later. His death certificate lists Kansas as his residence.

From the time Mr. and Mrs. Creal first met until Mr. Creal's death in December 2000, Mr. Creal retained certain connections with the State of Missouri. In November 1999, he applied for a Missouri title and license for his Chevrolet van using his mother's St. Joseph address. In December 1999, he applied for automobile insurance on the van using the same address. In March 2000, he listed the address when he took out a loan and applied for a new Missouri title on the van to name a new lien holder. In April 2000, he renewed his Missouri driver's license for three more years under the address. In May 2000, he filled out a form for life insurance listing the address. Mr. Creal also received mail and his paycheck stubs at his mother's house, where he stopped by every week to visit. After his death, an estate was opened for Mr. Creal in Buchanan County, Missouri alleging that he resided at his mother's address at the time of his death.

Finally, although Mr. and Mrs. Creal left open the possibility of leaving Troy to move to a location closer to Kansas City, Missouri, such as Platte City or Faucett, Missouri, they never looked for houses elsewhere and never made any specific plans to leave. Mrs. Creal testified in deposition that she was, for the most part, satisfied living in Troy.

III. DISCUSSION

Defendants move to dismiss Plaintiffs' claims pursuant to Fed.R.Civ.P. 12(b)(1), arguing that the complete diversity of citizenship required by 28 U.S.C. § 1332 is lacking among the parties. The parties do not dispute that all Defendants are citizens of the State of Kansas and that Plaintiff Baldwin is a citizen of the State of Missouri. Although Plaintiff Hawkins, as an individual, is also a citizen of the State of Missouri, her role in this case as Personal Representative of the Estate of Mr. Creal mandates that the court focus on the citizenship of Mr. Creal at the time of his death, not the citizenship of Plaintiff Hawkins herself. 28 U.S.C. § 1332(c)(2) ("[T]he legal representative of the estate of a decedent shall be deemed to be a citizen only of the same State as the decedent. . . ."). Whether Mr. Creal was a citizen of the State of Kansas or the State of Missouri at the time of his death is the central dispute currently before the court.

For purposes of determining whether diversity jurisdiction exists, a person is a "citizen" of the state in which he or she is "domiciled." Crowley v. Glaze, 710 F.2d 676, 678 (10th Cir. 1983). "For adults, domicile is established by physical presence in a place in connection with a certain state of mind concerning one's intent to remain there. "Miss. Band of Choctaw Indians v. Holyfield, 490 U.S. 30, 48 (1989) (citation omitted).

Here, the court concludes that at the time of his death, Mr. Creal had not only established a physical presence in the State of Kansas, but also displayed an intent to remain there. Although Mr. Creal lived the majority of his life in St. Joseph, Missouri, he had been living in Troy, Kansas with his wife of five months for nearly one year at the time he died. Among other things, he had moved his clothes, some furniture, pictures, photo albums, and other memorabilia into the home he shared with Mrs. Creal and her children; he contributed to household costs; and he purchased a new bedroom set with his wife. Although Mr. Creal retained some connections with the State of Missouri, the court does not find these connections sufficient to overcome the evidence that his actions from January 2000 until the time of his death demonstrated an intent to remain with his wife in the State of Kansas. In fact, the only evidence presented by Plaintiffs that directly calls Mr. Creal's intent into question is the deposition testimony of Mrs. Creal that the couple left open the possibility of leaving Troy to move to a location like Platte City or Faucett, Missouri, but that they never looked for houses there or made any specific plans to leave. At most, Mrs. Creal's testimony evidences a "floating intention" of Mr. Creal to return to his former domicile, which is insufficient to overcome the evidence that he was domiciled in the State of Kansas at the time of his death. Crowley, 710 F.2d at 678 (holding that a plaintiff's "floating intention" to return to the State of Colorado failed to overcome the evidence that his residence in the State of Minnesota for the previous year established his domicile there).

In conclusion, the court has considered all of the evidence and arguments presented by the parties and holds that Mr. Creal was a citizen of the State of Kansas at the time of his death. Because Plaintiffs have failed to carry their burden of showing that complete diversity exists among the parties, the court grants Defendants' motion to dismiss for lack of subject matter jurisdiction.

IT IS, THEREFORE, BY THE COURT ORDERED that Defendants' motion to dismiss is granted.

Redner v. Sanders
(S.D.N.Y. Aug. 16, 2000)

THOMAS P. GRIESA, United States District Judge.

Plaintiff in this action asserts that federal jurisdiction is based on diversity of citizenship. Defendants move under Fed.R.Civ.P. 12(b)(1) to dismiss for lack of jurisdiction. The motion is granted.

The complaint alleges that plaintiff "is, and at all times herein mentioned was, a citizen of the United States residing in France," and that two individual defendants are residents of the State of New York and the corporate defendant has its principal place of business in New York. The complaint avers that diversity jurisdiction exists because plaintiff "is a resident of a foreign state, while defendants are residents of the State of New York."

The applicable statute is 28 U.S.C. § 1332, which provides in pertinent part:

(a) The district courts shall have original jurisdiction of all civil actions where the matter in controversy exceeds the sum or value of $75,000, exclusive of interest and costs, and is between —
(1) citizens of different States;
(2) citizens of a State and citizens or subjects of a foreign state; . . .

Plaintiff apparently seeks to invoke subsection (a)(2) as a basis for jurisdiction. However, plaintiff's complaint speaks of residence whereas the statute speaks of citizenship. The two are not synonymous.

It appears in fact that defendants are citizens of the State of New York. But for jurisdiction to exist under (a)(2) plaintiff would need to be a citizen of a foreign state, not merely a resident, and the complaint itself alleges that plaintiff is a citizen of the United States. Thus the case does not involve an action between citizens of the United States and a citizen of a foreign state. There is no jurisdiction under § 1332(a)(2).

In responding to the motion, plaintiff does not really defend the idea of jurisdiction based upon his location in France but shifts the ground to a discussion of his connection with California. Plaintiff has filed an affidavit stating that he was raised and educated in California commencing in 1948, and that while he has resided in France for the last several years (his attorney's brief says since 1990), he has maintained certain contacts with California, including a license to practice law, and a law office there which he states he has visited at least four times a year since living abroad. He has a California driver's' license. He recently solicited two San Francisco law offices for possible employment, although there is no indication of any affirmative response. Plaintiff's affidavit states that he has "not given up the idea of returning to California" and that he considers California as his domicile.

To the extent that plaintiff now argues for a California domicile, it would appear that he might be attempting to lay a basis for jurisdiction under § 1332(a)(1). This subsection would, of course, allow a citizen of California to invoke diversity jurisdiction in a suit against citizens of New York. A person is a citizen of a state of the United States within the meaning of 28 U.S.C. § 1332 if he is a citizen of the United States and is domiciled within the state in question. Newman-Green Inc. v. Alfonzo-Larrain, 490 U.S. 826, 828 (1989).

However, plaintiff's factual submission is not sufficient to demonstrate a California domicile. See Kavowras v. Pinkerton, Inc., 1998 WL 209617 (S.D.N.Y. 1998). Plaintiff's affidavit is entirely lacking in details about what his living in France has involved. Plaintiff provides no information about exactly where he lives, what kind of a residence he has, whether he has any family in France, or what professional activities he carries out in France.

Moreover, despite the discussion of domicile to some extent, neither plaintiff's affidavit nor his attorney's brief actually asserts the claim that there is jurisdiction on the basis of a California domicile or makes a request to amend the complaint to assert such a claim.

The action is dismissed for lack of subject matter jurisdiction. This dismissal is without prejudice.

SO ORDERED.

Eze v. Yellow Cab Co. of Alexandria, Va., Inc.
782 F.2d 1064 (1986)

PER CURIAM:

Plaintiffs are citizens of Nigeria. They commenced a personal injury action based on an automobile accident alleged to have occurred in the District of Columbia. Their complaint names two defendants: Yellow Cab Company of Alexandria, Va., Inc.; and Godwin Sam Okakpa (correct name: Akakpo), the alleged driver of the Yellow Cab vehicle in which plaintiffs were passengers at the time of the accident. Plaintiffs invoked federal court jurisdiction on the basis of "alienage."

Defendant Yellow Cab moved to dismiss for lack of jurisdiction over the subject matter, contending that the requisite diversity of citizenship had not been asserted. Yellow Cab emphasized that plaintiffs had not alleged the citizenship of the defendant taxicab driver but had simply stated that Akakpo "has a residence which is presently unknown to the Plaintiffs."

Plaintiffs failed to answer the motion to dismiss within the 10 days prescribed by D.D.C. Rule 1-9(d). Nor did plaintiffs request a time extension. The district court therefore treated the motion as conceded and dismissed the complaint. In its dismissal order, the court observed that plaintiffs "ha[d] failed to allege the citizenship of the defendant Godwin Sam [Akakpo] such that 28 U.S.C. § 1332 could be applied to afford jurisdiction."

We affirm, as indeed we must in view of the representation at oral argument made by counsel for plaintiff-appellants that Akakpo is an alien, a citizen of Ghana.

Federal jurisdiction is authorized where there is a suit between a citizen of a state and citizens or subjects of a foreign state. 28 U.S.C. § 1332(a)(2) (1982). Congress has also authorized federal jurisdiction in suits between citizens of different states in which citizens of foreign countries are additional parties. Id. at § 1332(a)(3). But under long-held precedent, diversity must be "complete." Strawbridge v. Curtiss, 7 U.S. (3 Cranch) 267, 2 L.Ed. 435 (1806). A diversity suit, in line with the Strawbridge rule, may not be maintained in federal court by an alien against a citizen of a state and a citizen of some other foreign country. See Ed & Fred, Inc. v. Puritan Marine Ins. Underwriters Corp., 506 F.2d 757, 758 (5th Cir.1975) (requisite complete diversity is absent in suit by citizen of Netherlands Antilles against two defendants, one a citizen of Bermuda, the other, a citizen of Massachusetts); Fosen v. United Technologies Corp., 484 F.Supp. 490, 495 (S.D.N.Y.), aff'd, 633 F.2d 203 (2d Cir.1980) (no diversity jurisdiction in suit by Norwegian plaintiffs against Japanese and United States defendants).

Plaintiffs here had abundant notice of the jurisdictional defect urged in support of the motion to dismiss. They now acknowledge that their two-defendant lawsuit does not meet the complete diversity requirement. They did not move in the district court to drop the individual defendant as a party. Instead, they did nothing to overcome the impediment to federal court adjudication of their case. Under these circumstances, the district court's order was entirely proper and is accordingly

Affirmed.

Citizenship of Corporations

For diversity purposes, corporations have dual citizenship. The state of incorporation and where they have their chief place of business. For example, If Stooge Corporation, incorporated in Delaware, and with its principal place of business in California, is a party to the suit, diversity is lacking if any adverse party is a citizen of either Delaware or of California. (Wright, § 27) It is generally accepted that a corporation can have only one principal place of business for purposes of diversity jurisdiction.

Hertz Corp. v. Friend
559 U.S. 77 (2010)

The federal diversity jurisdiction statute provides that "a corporation shall be deemed to be a citizen of any State by which it has been incorporated and of the State where it has its principal place of business." 28 U.S.C. § 1332(c)(1) (emphasis added). We seek here to resolve different interpretations that the Circuits have given this phrase. In doing so, we place primary weight upon the need for judicial administration of a jurisdictional statute to remain as simple as possible. And we conclude that the phrase "principal place of business" refers to the place where the corporation's high-level officers direct, control, and coordinate the corporation's activities. Lower federal courts have often metaphorically called that place the corporation's "nerve center." We believe that the "nerve center" will typically be found at a corporation's headquarters.

In September 2007, respondents Melinda Friend and John Nhieu, two California citizens, sued petitioner, the Hertz Corporation, . . . They sought damages for what they claimed were violations of California's wage and hour laws. And they requested relief on behalf of a potential class composed of California citizens who had allegedly suffered similar harms.

. . .Hertz claimed that the plaintiffs and the defendant were citizens of different States. §§ 1332(a)(1), (c)(1). Hence, the federal court possessed diversity-of-citizenship jurisdiction. Friend and Nhieu, however, claimed that the Hertz Corporation was a California citizen, like themselves, and that, hence, diversity jurisdiction was lacking.

To support its position, Hertz submitted a declaration by an employee relations manager that sought to show that Hertz's "principal place of business" was in New Jersey, not in California. The declaration stated, among other things, that Hertz operated facilities in 44 States; and that California—which had about 12% of the Nation's population, Pet. for Cert. 8—accounted for 273 of Hertz's 1,606 car rental locations; about 2,300 of its 11,230 full=time employees; about $811 million of its $4.371 billion in annual revenue; and about 3.8 million of its approximately 21 million annual transactions, i.e., rentals. The declaration also stated that the "leadership of Hertz and its domestic subsidiaries" is located at Hertz's "corporate headquarters" in Park Ridge, New Jersey; that its "core executive and administrative functions . . . are carried out" there and "to a lesser extent" in Oklahoma City, Oklahoma; and that its "major administrative operations. . . are found" at those two locations. App. to Pet. for Cert. 26a-30a.

The District Court of the Northern District of California accepted Hertz's statement of the facts as undisputed. But it concluded that, given those facts, Hertz was a citizen of California. In reaching this conclusion, the court applied Ninth Circuit precedent, which instructs courts to identify a corporation's "principal place of business" by first determining the amount of a corporation's business activity State by State. If the amount of activity is "significantly larger" or "substantially predominates" in one State, then that State is the corporation's "principal place of business." If there is no such State, then the "principal place of business" is the corporation's "'nerve center,'" i.e., the place where "'the majority of its executive and administrative functions are performed.'"

Applying this test, the District Court found that the "plurality of each of the relevant business activities" was in California, and that "the differential between the amount of those activities" in California and the amount in "the next closest state" was "significant." Order 4. Hence, Hertz's "principal place of business" was California, and diversity jurisdiction was thus lacking. The District Court consequently remanded the case to the state courts.

Hertz appealed the District Court's remand order. 28 U.S.C. § 1453(c). The Ninth Circuit affirmed in a brief memorandum opinion. Hertz filed a petition for certiorari. And, in light of differences among the Circuits in the application of the test for corporate citizenship, we granted the writ.

In an effort to find a single, more uniform interpretation of the statutory phrase, we have reviewed the Courts of Appeals' divergent and increasingly complex interpretations. Having done so, we now return to, and expand, Judge Weinfeld's approach, as applied in the Seventh Circuit.. We conclude that "principal place of business" is best read as referring to the place where a corporation's officers direct, control, and coordinate the corporation's activities. It is the place that Courts of Appeals have called the corporation's "nerve center." And in practice it should normally be the place where the corporation maintains its headquarters—provided that the headquarters is the actual center of direction, control, and coordination, i.e., the "nerve center," and not simply an office where the corporation holds its board meetings (for example, attended by directors and officers who have traveled there for the occasion).

Three sets of considerations, taken together, convince us that this approach, while imperfect, is superior to other possibilities. First, the statute's language supports the approach. The statute's text deems a corporation a citizen of the "State where it has its principal place of business." 28 U.S.C. § 1332(c)(1). The word "place" is in the singular, not the plural.. . . .

Second, administrative simplicity is a major virtue in a jurisdictional statute. Complex jurisdictional tests complicate a case, eating up time and money as the parties litigate, not the merits of their claims, but which court is the right court to decide those claims. Complex tests produce appeals and reversals, encourage gamesmanship, and, again, diminish the likelihood that results and settlements will reflect a claim's legal and factual merits. Judicial resources too are at stake. Courts have an independent obligation to determine whether subject-matter jurisdiction exists, even when no party challenges it. So courts benefit from straightforward rules under which they can readily assure themselves of their power to hear a case.

We recognize that there may be no perfect test that satisfies all administrative and purposive criteria. We recognize as well that, under the "nerve center" test we adopt today, there will be hard cases. For example, in this era of telecommuting, some corporations may divide their command and coordinating functions among officers who work at several different locations, perhaps communicating over the Internet. That said, our test nonetheless points courts in a single direction, towards the center of overall direction, control, and coordination. Courts do not have to try to weigh corporate functions, assets, or revenues different in kind, one from the other. Our approach provides a sensible test that is relatively easier to apply, not a test that will, in all instances, automatically generate a result.

We also recognize that the use of a "nerve center" test may in some cases produce results that seem to cut against the basic rationale for 28 U.S.C. § 1332, see supra, at 1188. For example, if the bulk of a company's business activities visible to the public take place in New Jersey, while its top officers direct those activities just across the river in New York, the "principal place of business" is New York. One could argue that members of the public in New Jersey would be less likely to be prejudiced against the corporation than persons in New York—yet the corporation will still be entitled to remove a New Jersey state case to federal court. And note too that the same corporation would be unable to remove a New York state case to federal court, despite the New York public's presumed prejudice against the corporation.

We understand that such seeming anomalies will arise. However, in view of the necessity of having a clearer rule, we must accept them. Accepting occasionally counterintuitive results is the price the legal system must pay to avoid overly complex jurisdictional administration while producing the benefits that accompany a more uniform legal system. . . .

Amount in Controversy

Diversity jurisdiction can be invoked only if the amount in controversy (i.e., the amount of money the plaintiff is seeking from the defendant) exceeds the sum of $75,000 exclusive of interest and costs. (See 28 U.S.C. § 1332) The words are interpreted literally. If the matter in controversy is precisely $75,000 or less, there is no jurisdiction. (Friedenthal § 2.8) Note, there is no amount in controversy requirement for federal question cases. In determining whether the amount in controversy requirement has been met, the court looks to the sum demanded by the plaintiff in his complaint. (Wright, § 33)

Aggregation of Claims to Satisfy Amount in Controversy

> **Amount in Controversy**
> - Single plaintiff may assert two or more claims against single defendant and amounts may be added together.
> - Single plaintiff cannot aggregate amounts sought from different defendants.

If a single plaintiff has two entirely unrelated claims against a single defendant, for example, each for $40,000, he/she may sue in federal court since the aggregate of the claims exceeds $75,000.

> **Amount in Controversy**
>
> - Multiple plaintiffs may not add their claims together.
> - As long as one plaintiff alleges a sufficient amount in controversy other plaintiffs seeking less may join.

If two plaintiffs each have a $40,000 claim against a single defendant, they may not aggregate their claims, and may not sue in federal court, no matter how similar the claims may be. If a single plaintiff is suing a single defendant, FRCP 18 permits the plaintiff to join as many claims as he may have against the defendant regardless of their nature, and the value of all the claims is added together in determining whether the jurisdictional amount is met. (Wright, § 36) Multiple plaintiffs with separate and distinct claims must each satisfy the jurisdictional amount requirement. (*Id.*)

Supplemental Jurisdiction

As we have seen, subject matter jurisdiction in the federal courts is limited to that which is specifically conferred by the Constitution and which Congress has empowered the courts to exercise. However, federal jurisdiction may be exercised over claims which fall outside these categories when those claims are joined in a single suit with a jurisdictionally sufficient claim.

> **Supplemental Jurisdiction**
>
> If plaintiff brings a proper federal question or diversity claim, court may hear all other claims that are part of "same case or controversy."

Supplemental jurisdiction allows a federal court to assert jurisdiction over claims that are sufficiently related or subordinated to an action properly within the court's subject matter jurisdiction. Usually, it is invoked to permit a federal court to adjudicate claims that technically are jurisdictionally defective because they involve non-diverse parties or are less than the requisite jurisdictional amount. Under the unified umbrella of "supplemental jurisdiction," as long as there is one federal claim against one defendant, related state law claims against additional parties (whether added by plaintiff or defendant) may be adjudicated in federal court. 28 U.S.C. §1367 provides that in any action in which the federal court has jurisdiction over a federal claim, the federal court also has supplemental jurisdiction over state claims "that are so related to claims in the action within such original jurisdiction that they form part of the same case or controversy under Article III of the Constitution."

United Mine Workers of America v. Gibbs
383 U.S. 715 (1966)

MR. JUSTICE BRENNAN delivered the opinion of the Court.

Respondent Paul Gibbs was awarded compensatory and punitive damages in this action against petitioner United Mine Workers of America (UMW) for alleged violations of § 303 of the Labor Management Relations Act, 1947, 61 Stat. 158, as amended, and of the common law of 718*718 Tennessee. The case grew out of the rivalry between the United Mine Workers and the Southern Labor Union over representation of workers in the southern Appalachian coal fields. Tennessee Consolidated Coal Company, not a party here, laid off 100 miners of the UMW's Local 5881 when it closed one of its mines in southern Tennessee during the spring of 1960. Late that summer, Grundy Company, a wholly owned subsidiary of Consolidated, hired respondent as mine superintendent to attempt to open a new mine on Consolidated's property at nearby Gray's Creek through use of members of the Southern Labor Union. As part of the arrangement, Grundy also gave respondent a contract to haul the mine's coal to the nearest railroad loading point.

On August 15 and 16, 1960, armed members of Local 5881 forcibly prevented the opening of the mine, threatening respondent and beating an organizer for the rival union. The members of the local believed Consolidated had promised them the jobs at the new mine; they insisted that if anyone would do the work, they would. At this time, no representative of the UMW, their international union, was present. George Gilbert, the UMW's field representative for the area including Local 5881, was away at Middlesboro, Kentucky, attending an Executive Board meeting when the members of the local discovered Grundy's plan; he did not return to the area until late in the day of August 16. There was uncontradicted testimony that he first learned of the violence while at the meeting and returned with explicit instructions from his international union superiors to establish a limited picket line, to prevent any further violence, and to see to it that the strike did not spread to neighboring mines. There was no further violence at the mine site; a picket line was maintained there for nine months; and no further attempts were made to open the mine during that period.

Respondent lost his job as superintendent, and never entered into performance of his haulage contract. He testified that he soon began to lose other trucking contracts and mine leases he held in nearby areas. Claiming these effects to be the result of a concerted union plan against him, he sought recovery not against Local 5881 or its members, but only against petitioner, the international union. The suit was brought in the United States District Court for the Eastern District of Tennessee, and jurisdiction was premised on allegations of secondary boycotts under § 303. The state law claim, for which jurisdiction was based upon the doctrine of pendent jurisdiction, asserted "an unlawful conspiracy and an unlawful boycott aimed at him and [Grundy] to maliciously, wantonly and willfully interfere with his contract of employment and with his contract of haulage."

The trial judge refused to submit to the jury the claims of pressure intended to cause mining firms other than Grundy to cease doing business with Gibbs; he found those claims unsupported by the evidence. The jury's verdict was that the UMW had violated both § 303 and state law. Gibbs was awarded $60,000 as damages under the employment contract and $14,500 under the haulage contract; he was also awarded $100,000 punitive damages. On motion, the trial court set aside the award of damages with respect to the haulage contract on the ground that damage was unproved. It also held that union pressure on Grundy to discharge respondent as supervisor would constitute only a primary dispute with Grundy, as respondent's employer, and hence was not cognizable as a claim under § 303. Interference with the employment relationship was cognizable as a state claim, however, and a remitted award was sustained on the state law claim. The Court of Appeals for the Sixth Circuit affirmed. We granted certiorari. We reverse.

A threshold question is whether the District Court properly entertained jurisdiction of the claim based on Tennessee law. . . .

The fact that state remedies were not entirely pre-empted does not, however, answer the question whether the state claim was properly adjudicated in the District Court absent diversity jurisdiction. The Court held in Hurn v. Oursler, 289 U. S. 238, that state law claims are appropriate for federal court determination if they form a separate but parallel ground for relief also sought in a substantial claim based on federal law. The Court distinguished permissible from nonpermissible exercises of federal judicial power over state law claims by contrasting "a case where two distinct grounds in support of a single cause of action are alleged, one only of which presents a federal question, and a case where two separate and distinct causes of action are alleged, one only of which is federal in character. In the former, where the federal question averred is not plainly wanting in substance, the federal court, even though the federal ground be not established, may nevertheless retain and dispose of the case upon the non-federal ground; in the latter it may not do so upon the non-federal cause of action." The question is into which category the present action fell.

Hurn was decided in 1933, before the unification of law and equity by the Federal Rules of Civil Procedure. At the time, the meaning of "cause of action" was a subject of serious dispute; the phrase might "mean one thing for one purpose and something different for another." The Court in Hurn identified what it meant by the term by citation of Baltimore S. S. Co. v. Phillips, 274 U. S. 316, a case in which "cause of action" had been used to identify the operative scope of the doctrine of res judicata. In that case the Court had noted that " `the whole tendency of our decisions is to require a plaintiff to try his whole cause of action and his whole case at one time.' " . . . . Had the Court found a jurisdictional bar to reaching the state claim in Hurn, we assume that the doctrine of res judicata would not have been applicable in any subsequent state suit. But the citation of Baltimore S. S. Co. shows that the Court found that the weighty policies of judicial economy and fairness to parties reflected in res judicata doctrine were in themselves strong counsel for the adoption of a rule which would permit federal courts to dispose of the state as well as the federal claims.

With the adoption of the Federal Rules of Civil Procedure and the unified form of action, Fed. Rule Civ. Proc. 2, much of the controversy over "cause of action" abated. The phrase remained as the keystone of the Hurn test, however, and, as commentators have noted, has been the source of considerable confusion. Under the Rules, the impulse is toward entertaining the broadest possible scope of action consistent with fairness to the parties; joinder of claims, parties and remedies is strongly encouraged. Yet because the Hurn question involves issues of jurisdiction as well as convenience, there has been some tendency to limit its application to cases in which the state and federal claims are, as in Hurn, "little more than the equivalent of different epithets to characterize the same group of circumstances."

This limited approach is unnecessarily grudging Pendent jurisdiction, in the sense of judicial power, exists whenever there is a claim "arising under [the] Constitution, the Laws of the United States, and Treaties made, or which shall be made, under their Authority . . . ," U. S. Const., Art. III, § 2, and the relationship between that claim and the state claim permits the conclusion that the entire action before the court comprises but one constitutional "case." The federal claim must have substance sufficient to confer subject matter jurisdiction on the court. The state and federal claims must derive from a common nucleus of operative fact. But if, considered without regard to their federal or state character, a plaintiff's claims are such that he would ordinarily be expected to try them all in one judicial proceeding, then, assuming substantiality of the federal issues, there is power in federal courts to hear the whole.

That power need not be exercised in every case in which it is found to exist. It has consistently been recognized that pendent jurisdiction is a doctrine of discretion, not of plaintiff's right. Its justification lies in considerations of judicial economy, convenience and fairness to litigants; if these are not present a federal court should hesitate to exercise jurisdiction over state claims, even though bound to apply state law to them, Erie R. Co. v. Tompkins, 304 U. S. 64. Needless decisions of state law should be avoided both as a matter of comity and to promote justice between the parties, by procuring for them a surer-footed reading of applicable law. Certainly, if the federal claims are dismissed before trial, even though not insubstantial in a jurisdictional sense, the state claims should be dismissed as well. Similarly, if it appears that the state issues substantially predominate, whether in terms of proof, of the scope of the issues raised, or of the comprehensiveness of the remedy sought, the state claims may be dismissed without prejudice and left for resolution to state tribunals. There may, on the other hand, be situations in which the state claim is so closely tied to questions of federal policy that the argument for exercise of pendent jurisdiction is particularly strong. In the present case, for example, the allowable scope of the state claim implicates the federal doctrine of pre-emption; while this interrelationship does not create statutory federal question jurisdiction, Louisville & N. R. Co. v. Mottley, 211 U. S. 149, its existence is relevant to the exercise of discretion. Finally, there may be reasons independent of jurisdictional considerations, such as the likelihood of jury confusion in treating divergent legal theories of relief, that would justify separating state and federal claims for trial, Fed. Rule Civ. Proc. 42 (b). If so, jurisdiction should ordinarily be refused.

The question of power will ordinarily be resolved on the pleadings. But the issue whether pendent jurisdiction has been properly assumed is one which remains open throughout the litigation. Pretrial procedures or even the trial itself may reveal a substantial hegemony of state law claims, or likelihood of jury confusion, which could not have been anticipated at the pleading stage. Although it will of course be appropriate to take account in this circumstance of the already completed course of the litigation, dismissal of the state claim might even then be merited. For example, it may appear that the plaintiff was well aware of the nature of his proofs and the relative importance of his claims; recognition of a federal court's wide latitude to decide ancillary questions of state law does not imply that it must tolerate a litigant's effort to impose upon it what is in effect only a state law case. Once it appears that a state claim constitutes the real body of a case, to which the federal claim is only an appendage, the state claim may fairly be dismissed.

We are not prepared to say that in the present case the District Court exceeded its discretion in proceeding to judgment on the state claim. We may assume for purposes of decision that the District Court was correct in its holding that the claim of pressure on Grundy to terminate the employment contract was outside the purview of § 303. Even so, the § 303 claims based on secondary pressures on Grundy relative to the haulage contract and on other coal operators generally were substantial. Although § 303 limited recovery to compensatory damages based on secondary pressures, and state law allowed both compensatory and punitive damages, and allowed such damages as to both secondary and primary activity, the state and federal claims arose from the same nucleus of operative fact and reflected alternative remedies. Indeed, the verdict sheet sent in to the jury authorized only one award of damages, so that recovery could not be given separately on the federal and state claims.

It is true that the § 303 claims ultimately failed and that the only recovery allowed respondent was on the state claim. We cannot confidently say, however, that the federal issues were so remote or played such a minor role at the trial that in effect the state claim only was tried. Although the District Court dismissed as unproved the § 303 claims that petitioner's secondary activities included attempts to induce coal operators other than Grundy to cease doing business with respondent, the court submitted the § 303 claims relating to Grundy to the jury. The jury returned verdicts against petitioner on those § 303 claims, and it was only on petitioner's motion for a directed verdict and a judgment n. o. v. that the verdicts on those claims were set aside. The District Judge considered the claim as to the haulage contract proved as to liability, and held it failed only for lack of proof of damages. Although there was some risk of confusing the jury in joining the state and federal claims—especially since, as will be developed, differing standards of proof of UMW involvement applied— the possibility of confusion could be lessened by employing a special verdict form, as the District Court did. Moreover, the question whether the permissible scope of the state claim was limited by the doctrine of pre-emption afforded a special reason for the exercise of pendent jurisdiction; the federal courts are particularly appropriate bodies for the application of pre-emption principles. We thus conclude that although it may be that the District Court might, in its sound discretion, have dismissed the state claim, the circumstances show no error in refusing to do so....

Since the record establishes only peaceful activities in this regard on the part of petitioner, respondent was limited to his § 303 remedy. Although our result would undoubtedly be firmer if the petitioner had assured respondent that, having assumed control of the strike, it would prevent further violence, in the circumstances of this case the crucial fact of petitioner's participation in or ratification of the violence that occurred was not proved to the degree of certainty required by § 6.

Reversed

Problem James Kroger was electrocuted when the boom of a steel crane next to which he was walking came too close to a high-tension electric power line. The plaintiff (his widow, who is the administratrix of his estate) filed a wrongful-death action in the United States District Court for the District of Nebraska against the Omaha Public Power District (OPPD). Her complaint alleged that OPPD's negligent construction, maintenance, and operation of the power line had caused Kroger's death. Federal jurisdiction was based on diversity of citizenship, since the plaintiff was a citizen of Iowa and OPPD was a Nebraska corporation.

OPPD then filed a third-party complaint pursuant to FRCP 14(a) against Owen Equipment and Erection Co. (Owen), alleging that the crane was owned and operated by

Owen, and that Owen's negligence had been the proximate cause of Kroger's death. OPPD later moved for summary judgment on the plaintiff's complaint against it. While this motion was pending, the plaintiff was granted leave to file an amended complaint naming Owen as an additional defendant. Thereafter, the District Court granted OPPD's motion for summary judgment. The case thus went to trial between the plaintiff and Owen alone.

The plaintiff's amended complaint alleged that Owen was "a Nebraska corporation with its principal place of business in Nebraska." Owen's answer admitted that it was "a corporation organized and existing under the laws of the State of Nebraska," and denied every other allegation of the complaint. On the third day of trial, however, it was disclosed that the petitioner's principal place of business was in Iowa, not Nebraska, and that the petitioner and Owen were thus both citizens of Iowa. Owen then moved to plaintiff the complaint for lack of jurisdiction.

Notwithstanding the fact there was lack of diversity between plaintiff and Owen, was there nevertheless supplementary jurisdiction over plaintiff's claim against Owen? (See, *Owen Equipment & Erection Co. v. Kroger*, 437 U.S. 365 (1978) and 28 U.S.C. 1367(b).)

Szendrey-Ramos v. First Bancorp
512 F.Supp.2d 81 (2007)

CASELLAS, Senior District Judge

In March 2005, Szendrey (the defendant bank's general counsel) received a report from an external law firm that included information about possible ethical and/or legal violations committed by bank officials in relation to the accounting for the bulk purchase of mortgage loans from other financial institutions. Szendrey conducted an investigation into this issue, focusing on the possibility of whether the bank officials' conduct amounted to a violation of law or the bank's Code of Ethics. Upon conclusion of such investigation, Szendrey concluded that there had been irregularities and violations of the Code of Ethics and reported such findings to outside counsel for the bank as well as bank officials. She also divulged her findings to the Board of Directors at a meeting in which she was present. . . . (Ultimately Szendrey was terminated from her employment and brought suit alleging violations of federal employment law (title VII) and also stating a number of claims under the laws of Puerto Rico for wrongful discharge, defamation and tortious interference with contractual relations.)

Upon careful consideration of the issues presented by this case, and the law governing such issues, we decline to exercise supplemental jurisdiction over the P.R. law claims. Accordingly, these claims will be dismissed without prejudice, and Defendants' arguments for dismissal on the merits of such claims are thus moot. As for the Title VII discrimination and retaliation claims, they survive the motion to dismiss. This case thus goes forward solely under Title VII. We explain our reasoning below.

I. Supplemental Jurisdiction

28 U.S.C.A. § 1367, in part provides:

(a) Except as provided in subsections (b) and (c) or as expressly provided otherwise by Federal statute, in any civil action of which the district courts have original jurisdiction, the district courts shall have" supplemental jurisdiction over all other claims that are so related to claims in the action within such original jurisdiction that they form part of the same case or controversy under Article III of the United States Constitution. Such supplemental jurisdiction shall include claims that involve the joinder or intervention of additional parties.

This statute codifies the principles of pendent and ancillary jurisdiction set forth by the Supreme Court, to wit, that a "federal court's original jurisdiction over federal questions carries with it jurisdiction over state law claims that 'derive from a common nucleus of operative fact,' such that the relationship between [the federal] claim and the state claim permits the conclusion that the entire action before the court comprises but one constitutional case.'" City of Chicago v. Int'l Coll. of Surgeons, 522 U.S. 156, 164-165, 118 S.Ct. 523, 139 L.Ed.2d 525 (1997) (quoting, Mine Workers v. Gibbs, 383 U.S. 715, 725, 86 S.Ct. 1130, 16 L.Ed.2d 218 (1966)).

Supplemental jurisdiction, however, is subject to exceptions, also codified at § 1367:

(c) The district courts may decline to exercise supplemental jurisdiction over a claim under subsection (a) if
(1) the claim raises a novel or complex issue of State law,
(2) the claim substantially predominates over the claim or claims over which the district court has original jurisdiction,
(3) the district court has dismissed all claims over which it has original jurisdiction, or
(4) in exceptional circumstances, there are other compelling reasons for declining jurisdiction.

In including these exceptions, Congress was also recognizing long-standing Supreme Court precedent that "pendent jurisdiction 'is a doctrine of discretion not of plaintiff's right,' and that district courts can decline to exercise jurisdiction over pendent claims for a number of valid reasons." City of Chicago, 522 U.S. at 172, 118 S.Ct. 523 (quoting, Gibbs, 383 U.S. at 726-727, 86 S.Ct. 1130). The Supreme Court, in City of Chicago, explained that:

Depending on a host of factors, then including the circumstances of the particular case, the nature of the state law claims, the character of the governing state law, and the relationship between the state and federal claims — district courts may decline to exercise jurisdiction over supplemental state law claims. The statute thereby reflects the understanding that, when deciding whether to exercise supplemental jurisdiction, "a federal court should consider and weigh in each case, and at every stage of the litigation, the values of judicial economy, convenience, fairness, and comity."

The Court finds that two of § 1367(c)'s subsections are at issue here: (1) that the state law claims raise complex or novel issues and (2) that the state-law claims substantially predominate over the federal claim. We start with the latter and work our way back to the former.

Plaintiffs' complaint includes two lonesome claims under Title VII, for discrimination and retaliation thereunder. The remaining claims all arise, out of P.R. law: Act 100, 29 P.R. Laws Ann. § 146 et seq. (for gender discrimination); Act 115, 29 P.R. Laws Ann. § 194 et sew. (for retaliation); Act 80, 29 P.R. Laws Ann. § 185a et seq. (for wrongful discharge); §§ 1, 8 and 16 of the P.R. Constitution (for violations to Plaintiffs' dignity, honor, and personal integrity); and under Art. 1802 of the P.R. Civil Code, 31 P.R. Laws Ann. § 5141 (both for tortious interference with contracts and for defamation). Not only do the P.R. law claims far outnumber the federal claims, but their scope also exceeds that of the federal claims. On that point we note that although some of the P.R. law claims mimic the federal claims (i.e., the Act 100 and Act 115 claims), the remaining P.R. law claims (wrongful discharge, tortious actions infringing Plaintiffs constitutional rights, tortious interference with contracts, and defamation) are distinct and each has its own elements of proof; proof that is not necessary to establish the Title VII claims. That the state-law claims predominate over the federal claims is, in and of itself, reason enough to decline to exercise supplemental jurisdiction. . . .

Moreover, we note that the P,R. law claims require a much fuller incursion into the performance of Szendrey as General Counsel and any shortcomings she may have had as such. This, in turn, leads us to the other reason for declining to exercise supplemental jurisdiction: the presence of complex or novel issues of state law. The main issue raised by Defendants in their motion to dismiss, that Plaintiffs' prosecution of their claims would run afoul of Canon 21 of the Puerto Rico Code of Professional Ethics, 4 P.R. Laws Ann. Ap. IX C. 21, is at its apex in the P.R. law claims. For example, in order to prove that Defendants defamed her, Szendrey would have to establish that what was said about her (i.e., that she participated in wrongful acts) was false. In order to prove such falsity, Szendrey would have to reveal the extent of her participation regarding such wrongful acts, including what information she became aware of as General Counsel, what actions she took after learning such information, and what advice she offered her client with regards to such information.

Canon 21 indisputably belongs to an exclusively Puerto Rican body of law, and one that deals with the highly sensitive matter of lawyers' conduct, and its relation to society's interest in a fully functioning legal system. The interpretation of the canons is normally the province of the Puerto Rico Supreme Court, which is entrusted with the regulation and supervision of the legal profession. See, In re Godinez Morales, 2004 TSPR 17, 2004 WL 324471, at *3 (P.R. Feb. 3, 2004) (the authority to regulate the legal profession in Puerto Rico belongs exclusively to the P.R. Supreme Court as part of its inherent powers). We note, moreover, that Canon 21 is decidedly different to the corresponding Model Rule of the American Bar Association. Unlike this Court and several U.S. jurisdictions, Puerto Rico has not adopted the latest version of the American Bar Association's Model, Rules.

Canon 21 is decidedly silent on the issue of a lawyer's claim — whether in-house or not — against his former client, and the possibility of divulging confidential information in order to pursue such a claim. While the parties have pointed us to decisions by several courts ruling one way or the other as to the viability of those claims, it is important to underscore that such decisions are based on the ethical provisions that governed the attorney claimants in those cases. Helpful though those decisions may be to understand the viability of a claim by an attorney against a former client when that attorney is bound by the New York Code of Ethics or by the ABA Model Rules, they do not conclusively establish whether a Puerto Rican attorney, bound by the P.R. Code of Ethics, may bring suit against his former client when such a suit would entail the disclosure of information subject to the attorney-client privilege. This is an issue of Puerto Rico law that has yet to be addressed by the Puerto Rico courts and which is imbued with important considerations of public policy. This is particularly so as to Szendrey's constitutional claims; even if Canon 21 were, for example, held to bar an Act 80 claim, there would still be a question of whether an attorney's action to redress the violation of her constitutional rights must succumb under the heavy duty of silence imposed by Canon 21. Considerations of comity counsel against the Court assuming jurisdiction over such delicate and as of yet unresolved Puerto Rico law issues.

Because the Puerto Rico law claims substantially predominate over the federal claims in this case, and because they posit novel and complex issues of state law, the Court declines to exercise supplemental jurisdiction. Accordingly, the Puerto Rico law claims will be dismissed without prejudice, so that Plaintiffs may re-file them in the Puerto Rico courts.

Removal of Cases From State Court to Federal Court

> **REMOVAL**
>
> Permits a defendant to second-guess the plaintiff's choice of a state court and force the plaintiff to litigate in federal court.

"Removal jurisdiction permits a defendant to force the plaintiff to litigate certain actions in federal court, rather than in the state forum, originally selected." (Friedenthal § 2.11) Although, removal permits a defendant to second-guess the plaintiff's choice of state court, it does not permit a defendant to second-guess the choice of state. A case can only be removed "to the district court of the United States for the district and division embracing the place where such action is pending" (28 U. S. C. § 1441(a)) As federal districts are drawn as to not cross state lines, that means the federal court, to which the action is removed will always be in the same state as the court in which the action originated.

Restrictions on Removal

Only a defendant may remove a case. (28 U.S.C. § 1441(a))

All defendants must join in the petition for removal.

> **REMOVAL**
>
> **Federal question cases =** removable without regard to the citizenship or residence of the parties.
>
> **Diversity cases =** removable only if ≠ defendants is a citizen of the State in which such action is brought.

Diversity cases are removable only if none of the defendants is a citizen of the state in which the action is brought. (28 U.S.C. § 1441(b).) For example, if a citizen of Utah sues a citizen of Texas in the state court in Texas, defendant cannot remove if diversity is the only basis for federal jurisdiction. The defendant could remove if suit were brought in any other state. However, if jurisdiction is based on a federal question, even a resident defendant may remove.

McCurtain County Production Corp. v. Cowett
482 F.Supp. 809 (E.D. Okla. 1978)

DAUGHERTY, Chief Judge.

Plaintiff commenced this action in the District Court of McCurtain County, Oklahoma seeking to recover on a promissory note. Contending that the federal court has original jurisdiction of the action by reason of diversity of citizenship and amount in controversy, Defendant John Deere Company (John Deere) removed the case to this Court.

In its Petition and Amended Petition (hereinafter referred to as "complaint") filed in the state court, Plaintiff alleges that Defendants R. B. Cowett and Shelba Cowett executed a promissory note to the Plaintiff in the amount of $15,215.59 and secured the note by giving Plaintiff a security interest in a two-thirds share of 130 acres of soybeans in McCurtain County and in a 1972 John Deere combine. Plaintiff asserts that the Cowetts have defaulted on the note and that the aforementioned soybeans were sold to Defendant Clarksville Grain and Elevator Co., Inc. (Clarksville Grain) for the sum of $10,948.27. Plaintiff alleges that Clarksville Grain issued three checks in payment for the soybeans. One of the checks was issued to Lester Boden, the owner of a one-third share in the soybeans, and the other two checks were issued to R. B. Cowett. Cowett endorsed one of the checks, in the amount of $4,394.90, to B & B Automotive, and converted the other check, in the amount of $2,903.94, into a money order and gave the same to John Deere. Plaintiff seeks a judgment in the amount of $15,215.59 against the Cowetts on the promissory note. It further seeks a judgment in the amount of $7,298.84 against Clarksville Grain for that portion of the proceeds from the sale of the soybeans which Clarksville Grain conveyed to R. B. Cowett. In the alternative, Plaintiff seeks a judgment against Defendant Willie John Blair, d/b/a B & B Automotive Company, for $4,394.90, and against John Deere for $2,903.94.

In its Motion to Remand, Plaintiff asserts that the removal of this case to federal court was improvident as all Defendants herein did not join in the removal petition filed by John Deere and as Plaintiff's claim against John Deere was for an amount less than the jurisdictional amount required for a federal court to have diversity jurisdiction.

In opposition to Plaintiff's Motion to Remand, John Deere asserts that the Court lacks jurisdiction over any of the Defendants except John Deere, and that by reason of such a lack of jurisdiction, John Deere is entitled to remove the action without the consent of the remaining Defendants. John Deere maintains that although the other Defendants have been served, there has been no determination that the state court has jurisdiction over those Defendants and that they apparently do not want to risk submitting themselves to the jurisdiction of the court by joining in the removal petition. With regard to Plaintiff's contention that there is an insufficient amount in controversy, John Deere takes the position that the total amount of the soybeans sold to Clarksville Grain is the true amount in controversy and that such value exceeds the jurisdictional amount required....

The right to remove a case from a local forum into federal court is solely one conferred by statute, rather than one which is constitutionally derived. Inasmuch as the removal statutes represent Congressionally-authorized encroachments by the federal courts into the various states' sovereignties, those provisions must be strictly construed, and their established procedures rigidly adhered to. In the instant case, the cause has been improperly removed both by reason of a defect in the removal procedure employed by John Deere and by the cause's failure to meet the criteria of the invoked removal statute....

[Section] 1446(a) has been interpreted to mean that all defendants in multi-defendant cases must join in the petition for removal or consent to such action within the 30-day time limitation applicable to removal procedures. On petition to remove a case to federal court, the defendants are to be treated collectively, and as a general rule, all defendants who may properly join in the removal petition must do so.

There are exceptions to this requirement. When a separate and independent claim that is removable under 28 U.S.C. § 1441(c) is joined with other nonremovable claims, only the defendant or defendants to the separate and independent claim need seek removal. Nominal or formal parties may be disregarded. An improperly joined party is not required to join in the removal petition.

In the instant case, the failure of all Defendants to join in the petition for removal filed herein by John Deere or to consent to such action within the 30-day time limitation makes the removal of this case improper. From an examination of the record herein, the Court is unable to apply any of the aforementioned exceptions to this case. There is not a separate and independent claim stated against John Deere. The Defendants who have not joined in the removal petition are not nominal or formal parties, nor is there any indication that they have been improvidently joined in this action. As John Deere has stated in its removal petition that the other Defendants have been served, they were required to join in the removal. Under modern pleading rules, the technical distinctions between a special appearance and a general appearance have vanished and a defendant waives nothing by removing the case and may move to dismiss for lack of personal jurisdiction after the removal. The fact that a defendant has removed does not act as a general consent to jurisdiction to defeat the motion. Id. Accordingly, all Defendants in this case could properly have joined in the removal petition of John Deere. Their failure to so join constitutes a defect in the removal procedure employed by John Deere and warrants the remand of the case to the state court from which it was removed. . . .

Moreover, the case should also be remanded on the basis that the cause was improperly removed as the amount in controversy therein fails to meet the statutory criteria for the removal of a diversity case. . . .

Upon consideration of the Plaintiff's complaint, the Court concludes that although Plaintiff's claim against the Cowetts amounts to more than the jurisdictional minimum, the Court is without jurisdiction over the claims involving the remaining Defendants which amount to less than the jurisdictional minimum. The right of Defendants Clarksville Grain, John Deere and Blair to aggregate the claims against them with the claim against the Cowetts for the purposes of removal is not available in this case. The alleged liability of the Cowetts is separate and distinct from the liabilities of the remaining Defendants. Accordingly, each claim, standing alone, must satisfy the jurisdictional amount requirement, and aggregation is not permissible. . . .

In view of the foregoing, the Court concludes that it is without jurisdiction of this action; that removal of the action to this Court was improvident; and that the case should be remanded to the state court from which it was removed. 28 U.S.C. § 1447(c).

Plaintiff's Motion to Remand is sustained and the Court remands this case to the District Court of McCurtain County, Oklahoma.

Caterpillar Inc. v. Lewis
519 U.S. 61 (1996)

Justice Ginsburg, delivered the opinion of the Court.

The question presented is whether the absence of complete diversity at the time of removal is fatal to federal-court adjudication. We hold that a district court's error in failing to remand a case improperly removed is not fatal to the ensuing adjudication if federal jurisdictional requirements are met at the time judgment is entered.

Respondent James David Lewis, a resident of Kentucky, filed this lawsuit in Kentucky state court on June 22, 1989, after sustaining injuries while operating a bulldozer. Asserting state-law claims based on defective manufacture, negligent maintenance, failure to warn, and breach of warranty, Lewis named as defendants both the manufacturer of the bulldozer—petitioner Caterpillar Inc., a Delaware corporation with its principal place of business in Illinois—and the company that serviced the bulldozer—Whayne Supply Company, a Kentucky corporation with its principal place of business in Kentucky.

Several months later, Liberty Mutual Insurance Group, the insurance carrier for

Lewis' employer, intervened in the lawsuit as a plaintiff. A Massachusetts corporation with its principal place of business in that State, Liberty Mutual asserted subrogation claims against both Caterpillar and Whayne Supply for workers' compensation benefits Liberty Mutual had paid to Lewis on behalf of his employer.

Lewis entered into a settlement agreement with defendant Whayne Supply less than a year after filing his complaint. Shortly after learning of this agreement, Caterpillar filed a notice of removal, on June 21, 1990, in the United States District Court for the Eastern District of Kentucky. Grounding federal jurisdiction on diversity of citizenship, see 28 U. S. C. § 1332, Caterpillar satisfied with only a day to spare the statutory requirement that a diversity-based removal take place within one year of a lawsuit's commencement, see 28 U. S. C. § 1446(b). Caterpillar's notice of removal explained that the case was nonremovable at the lawsuit's start: Complete diversity was absent then because plaintiff Lewis and defendant Whayne Supply shared Kentucky citizenship. App. 31. Proceeding on the understanding that the settlement agreement between these two Kentucky parties would result in the dismissal of Whayne Supply from the lawsuit, Caterpillar stated that the settlement rendered the case removable.

Lewis objected to the removal and moved to remand the case to state court. Lewis acknowledged that he had settled his own claims against Whayne Supply. But Liberty Mutual had not yet settled its subrogation claim against Whayne Supply, Lewis asserted. Whayne Supply's presence as a defendant in the lawsuit, Lewis urged, defeated diversity of citizenship. Without addressing this argument, the District Court denied Lewis' motion to remand on September 24, 1990, treating as dispositive Lewis' admission that he had settled his own claims against Whayne Supply. . . .

In June 1993, plaintiff Liberty Mutual and defendant Whayne Supply entered into a settlement of Liberty Mutual's subrogation claim, and the District Court dismissed Whayne Supply from the lawsuit. With Caterpillar as the sole defendant adverse to Lewis, the case proceeded to a six-day jury trial in November 1993, ending in a unanimous verdict for Caterpillar. . . .

We note, initially, two "givens" in this case as we have accepted it for review. First, the District Court, in its decision denying Lewis' timely motion to remand, incorrectly treated Whayne Supply, the nondiverse defendant, as effectively dropped from the case prior to removal. Second, the Sixth Circuit correctly determined that the complete diversity requirement was not satisfied at the time of removal. We accordingly home in on this question: Does the District Court's initial misjudgment still burden and run with the case, or is it overcome by the eventual dismissal of the nondiverse defendant? . . .

Having preserved his objection to an improper removal, Lewis urges that an "all's well that ends well" approach is inappropriate here. He maintains that ultimate satisfaction of the subject-matter jurisdiction requirement ought not swallow up antecedent statutory violations. The course Caterpillar advocates, Lewis observes, would disfavor diligent plaintiffs who timely, but unsuccessfully, move to check improper removals in district court. Further, that course would allow improperly removing defendants to profit from their disregard of Congress' instructions, and their ability to lead district judges into error.

Concretely, in this very case, Lewis emphasizes, adherence to the rules Congress prescribed for removal would have kept the case in state court. Only by removing prematurely was Caterpillar able to get to federal court inside the one-year limitation set in § 1446(b) Had Caterpillar waited until the case was ripe for removal, i. E., until Whayne Supply was dismissed as a defendant, the one-year limitation would have barred the way and plaintiff's choice of forum would have been preserved.

These arguments are hardly meritless, but they run up against an overriding consideration. Once a diversity case has been tried in federal court, with rules of decision supplied by state law under the regime of Erie R. Co. v. Tompkins, 304 U. S. 64 (1938), considerations of finality, efficiency, and economy become overwhelming...

Our view is in harmony with a main theme of the removal scheme Congress devised. Congress ordered a procedure calling for expeditious superintendence by district courts. The lawmakers specified a short time, 30 days, for motions to remand for defects in removal procedure, 28 U. S. C. § 1447(c), and district court orders remanding cases to state courts generally are "not reviewable on appeal or otherwise," § 1447(d). Congress did not similarly exclude appellate review of refusals to remand. But an evident concern that may explain the lack of symmetry relates to the federal courts' subject-matter jurisdiction. Despite a federal trial court's threshold denial of a motion to remand, if, at the end of the day and case, a jurisdictional defect remains uncured, the judgment must be vacated. See Fed. Rule Civ. Proc. 12(h)(3) ("Whenever it appears by suggestion of the parties or otherwise that the court lacks jurisdiction of the subject matter, the court shall dismiss the action."); In this case, however, no jurisdictional defect lingered through judgment in the District Court. To wipe out the adjudication post judgment and return to state court a case now satisfying all federal jurisdictional requirements, would impose an exorbitant cost on our dual court system, a cost incompatible with the fair and unprotracted administration of justice.

Lewis ultimately argues that, if the final judgment against him is allowed to stand, "all of the various procedural requirements for removal will become unenforceable"; therefore, "defendants will have an enormous incentive to attempt wrongful removals." In particular, Lewis suggests that defendants will remove prematurely "in the hope that some subsequent developments, such as the eventual dismissal of nondiverse defendants, will permit th[e] case to be kept in federal court." We do not anticipate the dire consequences Lewis forecasts.

The procedural requirements for removal remain enforceable by the federal trial court judges to whom those requirements are directly addressed. Lewis' prediction that rejection of his petition will "encourag[e] state court defendants to remove cases improperly," rests on an assumption we do not indulge—that district courts generally will not comprehend, or will balk at applying, the rules on removal Congress has prescribed. The prediction furthermore assumes defendants' readiness to gamble that any jurisdictional defect, for example, the absence of complete diversity, will first escape detection, then disappear prior to judgment. The well-advised defendant, we are satisfied, will foresee the likely outcome of an unwarranted removal— a swift and nonreviewable remand order, see 28 U. S. C. §§ 1447(c), (d), attended by the displeasure of a district court whose authority has been improperly invoked. The odds against any gain from a wrongful removal, in sum, render improbable Lewis' projection of increased resort to the maneuver.

For the reasons stated, the judgment of the Court of Appeals is reversed, and the case is remanded for proceedings consistent with this opinion.

It is so ordered.

The Mechanics of Removal Notice of removal must be filed within thirty days after the receipt by the defendant of the initial pleading setting forth the claim for relief upon which such action or proceeding is based. If the case stated by the initial pleading is not removable, a notice of removal may be filed within thirty days after receipt by the defendant of an amended pleading, motion, order or other paper from which it may first be ascertained that the case is one which is or has become removable. (28 U. S. C. § 1446(b))

A motion to remand the case to the state court on the basis of any defect in removal procedure must be made within 30 days after the filing of the notice of removal. If at any time before final judgment it appears that the district court lacks subject matter jurisdiction, the case shall be remanded. 28 U. S. C. § 1447(c)

In cases removed on the basis of diversity, there is a one-year limitation in order to reduce the opportunity for removal after substantial progress has been made in state court.

Other Areas of Federal Subject Matter Jurisdiction

Federal question and diversity are not the only areas within the subject matter jurisdiction of the federal courts, they are just the two major ones. Other areas of federal jurisdiction include, among others, admiralty, antitrust and bankruptcy. However, these areas are so specialized that they merit their own dedicated courses in the law school curriculum. (For a complete listing of the matters that fall within federal subject matter jurisdiction see, 28 U.S.C. §§ 1330 to 1369). Other than the occasional odd case that may be found later in this book, this will be the only mention of them.

Challenging Subject Matter Jurisdiction in the Federal Courts

Since federal courts are courts of limited jurisdiction, the opportunities to challenge the plaintiff's choice of federal court as a forum arise far more frequently than when a plaintiff elects to file suit in state court. A defendant who wishes to challenge subject matter jurisdiction in federal court does so by making a motion to dismiss pursuant to FRCP 12(b)(1).

"FRCP 12(b)(1) motions for lack of subject matter jurisdiction generally take one of two forms: (1) a facial attack on the sufficiency of the complaint's allegations as to subject matter jurisdiction; or (2) a challenge to the actual facts upon which subject matter jurisdiction is based. A court reviewing a facial challenge must accept the plaintiff's factual allegations regarding jurisdiction as true. In contrast, a court reviewing a factual attack may not presume that the plaintiff's allegations are true. Rather, "[a] court has wide discretion to allow affidavits, other documents, and a limited evidentiary hearing to resolve disputed jurisdictional facts under Rule 12(b)(1)." (*Hawkins v. Masters Farms, supra* p.97.)

Lack of subject matter jurisdiction is never waived and can be raised as an objection at any point in the litigation. It can even be raised for the first time on appeal! The parties cannot consent to federal subject matter jurisdiction where it is lacking and the court itself can dismiss for lack of subject matter jurisdiction *sua sponte* (on its own motion).

CHAPTER 3

THE *ERIE* DOCTRINE, STATE LAW IN THE FEDERAL COURTS

Nature of the Problem

Once you have determined which court or courts have the proper jurisdiction to decide a case, the next question one is faced with is what law should the court apply? State courts apply state law. In federal question cases both federal and state courts apply federal law. But in diversity cases, a case that could have been brought in a state court but is being brought in federal court due solely to the citizenship of the parties, what law will a federal court apply? Federal or state? And what is meant by "law"? As you know by now, not only do legislatures enact statutes, but judges have the power to establish common law in areas where the legislature has not acted. Are federal courts sitting in diversity cases bound to follow the common law as made by the state court judges of the states in which they sit? Prior to 1938, the U.S. Supreme Court in the case of *Swift v. Tyson* , 41 U.S. (16 Pet.) 1, 10 L.Ed. 865 (1842) held that federal court judges were free to apply the law so as to reach a result they thought was just regardless of state common law. However that changed with the decision in *Erie R.R. v. Tompkins*.

Erie Railroad Co. v. Tompkins
304 U.S. 64 (1938)

MR. JUSTICE BRANDEIS delivered the opinion of the Court.

The question for decision is whether the oft-challenged doctrine of Swift v. Tyson shall now be disapproved.

Tompkins, a citizen of Pennsylvania, was injured on a dark night by a passing freight train of the Erie Railroad Company while walking along its right of way at Hughestown in that State. He claimed that the accident occurred through negligence in the operation, or maintenance, of the train; that he was rightfully on the premises as licensee because on a commonly used beaten footpath which ran for a short distance alongside the tracks; and that he was struck by something which looked like a door projecting from one of the moving cars. To enforce that claim he brought an action in the federal court for southern New York, which had jurisdiction because the company is a corporation of that State. It denied liability; and the case was tried by a jury.

The Erie insisted that its duty to Tompkins was no greater than that owed to a trespasser. It contended, among other things, that its duty to Tompkins, and hence its liability, should be determined in accordance with the Pennsylvania law; that under the law of Pennsylvania, as declared by its highest court, persons who use pathways along the railroad right of way — that is a longitudinal pathway as distinguished from a crossing — are to be deemed trespassers; and that the railroad is not liable for injuries to undiscovered trespassers resulting from its negligence, unless it be wanton or willful. Tompkins denied that any such rule had been established by the decisions of the Pennsylvania courts; and contended that, since there was no statute of the State on the subject, the railroad's duty and liability is to be determined in federal courts as a matter of general law.

The trial judge refused to rule that the applicable law precluded recovery. The jury brought in a verdict of $30,000; and the judgment entered thereon was affirmed by the Circuit Court of Appeals, which held, that it was unnecessary to consider whether the law of Pennsylvania was as contended, because the question was one not of local, but of general, law and that "upon questions of general law the federal courts are free, in the absence of a local statute, to exercise their independent judgment as to what the law is; and it is well settled that the question of the responsibility of a railroad for injuries caused by its servants is one of general law. . . .

The Erie had contended that application of the Pennsylvania rule was required, among other things, by § 34 of the Federal Judiciary Act of September 24, 1789, c. 20, 28 U.S.C. § 725, which provides:

"The laws of the several States, except where the Constitution, treaties, or statutes of the United States otherwise require or provide, shall be regarded as rules of decision in trials at common law, in the courts of the United States, in cases where they apply."

Because of the importance of the question whether the federal court was free to disregard the alleged rule of the Pennsylvania common law, we granted certiorari.

First. Swift v. Tyson, 16 Pet. 1, 18, held that federal courts exercising jurisdiction on the ground of diversity of citizenship need not, in matters of general jurisprudence, apply the unwritten law of the State as declared by its highest court; that they are free to exercise an independent judgment as to what the common law of the State is — or should be; and that, as there stated by Mr. Justice Story:

"the true interpretation of the thirty-fourth section limited its application to state laws strictly local, that is to say, to the positive statutes of the state, and the construction thereof adopted by the local tribunals, and to rights and titles to things having a permanent locality, such as the rights and titles to real estate, and other matters immovable and intra-territorial in their nature and character. It never has been supposed by us, that the section did apply, or was intended to apply, to questions of a more general nature, not at all dependent upon local statutes or local usages of a fixed and permanent operation, as, for example, to the construction of ordinary contracts or other written instruments, and especially to questions of general commercial law, where the state tribunals are called upon to perform the like functions as ourselves, that is, to ascertain upon general reasoning and legal analogies, what is the true exposition of the contract or instrument, or what is the just rule furnished by the principles of commercial law to govern the case."

The federal courts assumed, in the broad field of "general law," the power to declare rules of decision which Congress was confessedly without power to enact as statutes. Doubt was repeatedly expressed as to the correctness of the construction given § 34, and as to the soundness of the rule which it introduced. But it was the more recent research of a competent scholar, who examined the original document, which established that the construction given to it by the Court was erroneous; and that the purpose of the section was merely to make certain that, in all matters except those in which some federal law is controlling, the federal courts exercising jurisdiction in diversity of citizenship cases would apply as their rules of decision the law of the State, unwritten as well as written.

Criticism of the doctrine became widespread after the decision of Black & White Taxicab Co. v. Brown & Yellow Taxicab Co., 276 U.S. 518. There, Brown and Yellow, a Kentucky corporation owned by Kentuckians, and the Louisville and Nashville Railroad, also a Kentucky corporation, wished that the former should have the exclusive privilege of soliciting passenger and baggage transportation at the Bowling Green, Kentucky, railroad station; and that the Black and White, a competing Kentucky corporation, should be prevented from interfering with that privilege. Knowing that such a contract would be void under the common law of Kentucky, it was arranged that the Brown and Yellow reincorporate under the law of Tennessee, and that the contract with the railroad should be executed there. The suit was then brought by the Tennessee corporation in the federal court for western Kentucky to enjoin competition by the Black and White; an injunction issued by the District Court was sustained by the Court of Appeals; and this Court, citing many decisions in which the doctrine of Swift v. Tyson had been applied, affirmed the decree.

Second. Experience in applying the doctrine of Swift v. Tyson, had revealed its defects, political and social; and the benefits expected to flow from the rule did not accrue. Persistence of state courts in their own opinions on questions of common law prevented uniformity; and the impossibility of discovering a satisfactory line of demarcation between the province of general law and that of local law developed a new well of uncertainties.

On the other hand, the mischievous results of the doctrine had become apparent. Diversity of citizenship jurisdiction was conferred in order to prevent apprehended discrimination in state courts against those not citizens of the State. Swift v. Tyson introduced grave discrimination by non-citizens against citizens. It made rights enjoyed under the unwritten "general law" vary according to whether enforcement was sought in the state or in the federal court; and the privilege of selecting the court in which the right should be determined was conferred upon the non-citizen. Thus, the doctrine rendered impossible equal protection of the law. In attempting to promote uniformity of law throughout the United States, the doctrine had prevented uniformity in the administration of the law of the State.

The discrimination resulting became in practice far-reaching. This resulted in part from the broad province accorded to the so-called "general law" as to which federal courts exercised an independent judgment. In addition to questions of purely commercial law, "general law" was held to include the obligations under contracts entered into and to be performed within the State, the extent to which a carrier operating within a State may stipulate for exemption from liability for his own negligence or that of his employee; the liability for torts committed within the State upon persons resident or property located there, even where the question of liability depended upon the scope of a property right conferred by the State; and the right to exemplary or punitive damages .Furthermore, state decisions construing local deed-,mineral conveyances, and even devises of real estate were disregarded.

In part the discrimination resulted from the wide range of persons held entitled to avail themselves of the federal rule by resort to the diversity of citizenship jurisdiction. Through this jurisdiction individual citizens willing to remove from their own State and become citizens of another might avail themselves of the federal rule. And, without even change of residence, a corporate citizen of the State could avail itself of the federal rule by re-incorporating under the laws of another State, as was done in the Taxicab case.

The injustice and confusion incident to the doctrine of Swift v. Tyson have been repeatedly urged as reasons for abolishing or limiting diversity of citizenship jurisdiction. Other legislative relief has been proposed. If only a question of statutory construction were involved, we should not be prepared to abandon a doctrine so widely applied throughout nearly a century. But the unconstitutionality of the course pursued has now been made clear and compels us to do so.

Third. Except in matters governed by the Federal Constitution or by Acts of Congress, the law to be applied in any case is the law of the State. And whether the law of the State shall be declared by its Legislature in a statute or by its highest court in a decision is not a matter of federal concern. There is no federal general common law. Congress has no power to declare substantive rules of common law applicable in a State whether they be local in their nature or "general," be they commercial law or a part of the law of torts. And no clause in the Constitution purports to confer such a power upon the federal courts. As stated by Mr. Justice Field when protesting in Baltimore & Ohio R. Co. v. Baugh, 149 U.S. 368, 401, against ignoring the Ohio common law of fellow servant liability:

"I am aware that what has been termed the general law of the country — which is often little less than what the judge advancing the doctrine thinks at the time should be the general law on a particular subject — has been often advanced in judicial opinions of this court to control a conflicting law of a State. I admit that learned judges have fallen into the habit of repeating this doctrine as a convenient mode of brushing aside the law of a State in conflict with their views. And I confess that, moved and governed by the authority of the great names of those judges, I have, myself, in many instances, unhesitatingly and confidently, but I think now erroneously, repeated the same doctrine. But, notwithstanding the great names which may be cited in favor of the doctrine, and notwithstanding the frequency with which the doctrine has been reiterated, there stands, as a perpetual protest against its repetition, the Constitution of the United States, which recognizes and preserves the autonomy and independence of the States — independence in their legislative and independence in their judicial departments. Supervision over either the legislative or the judicial action of the States is in no case permissible except as to matters by the Constitution specifically authorized or delegated to the United States. Any interference with either, except as thus permitted, is an invasion of the authority of the State and, to that extent, a denial of its independence."

The fallacy underlying the rule declared in Swift v. Tyson is made clear by Mr. Justice Holmes. The doctrine rests upon the assumption that there is "a transcendental body of law outside of any particular State but obligatory within it unless and until changed by statute," that federal courts have the power to use their judgment as to what the rules of common law are; and that in the federal courts "the parties are entitled to an independent judgment on matters of general law":

> "but law in the sense in which courts speak of it today does not exist without some definite authority behind it. The common law so far as it is enforced in a State, whether called common law or not, is not the common law generally but the law of that State existing by the authority of that State without regard to what it may have been in England or anywhere else. . . . "the authority and only authority is the State, and if that be so, the voice adopted by the State as its own [whether it be of its Legislature or of its Supreme Court] should utter the last word."

Thus the doctrine of Swift v. Tyson, is, as Mr. Justice Holmes said, "an unconstitutional assumption of powers by courts of the United States which no lapse of time or respectable array of opinion should make us hesitate to correct." In disapproving that doctrine we do not hold unconstitutional § 34 of the Federal Judiciary Act of 1789 or any other Act of Congress. We merely declare that in applying the doctrine this Court and the lower courts have invaded rights which in our opinion are reserved by the Constitution to the several States.

Fourth. The defendant contended that by the common law of Pennsylvania as declared by its highest court in Falchetti v. Pennsylvania R. Co., 307 Pa. 203; 160 A. 859, the only duty owed to the plaintiff was to refrain from willful or wanton injury. The plaintiff denied that such is the Pennsylvania law. In support of their respective contentions the parties discussed and cited many decisions of the Supreme Court of the State. The Circuit Court of Appeals ruled that the question of liability is one of general law; and on that ground declined to decide the issue of state law. As we hold this was error, the judgment is reversed and the case remanded to it for further proceedings in conformity with our opinion.

Reversed.

Summing Up *Erie*

The *Erie* Court expressly intended that federal courts were to be governed by the law of each state, whether it be declared by its legislature, or by its highest court in a decision.

> ***Erie* Doctrine**
>
> Federal courts sitting in diversity cases apply the substantive law of the state in which they sit and federal procedural rules.

"*Erie* was something more than an opinion which worried about "forum-shopping and avoidance of inequitable administration of the laws," although to be sure these were important elements of the decision. I have always regarded that decision as one of the modern cornerstones of our federalism, expressing policies that profoundly touch the allocation of judicial power between the state and federal systems. *Erie* recognized that there should not be two conflicting systems of law controlling the primary activity of citizens, for such alternative governing authority must necessarily give rise to a debilitating uncertainty in the planning of everyday affairs. And it recognized that the scheme of our Constitution envisions an allocation of law-making functions between state and federal legislative processes which is undercut if the federal judiciary can make substantive law affecting state affairs beyond the bounds of congressional legislative powers in this regard. Thus, in diversity cases *Erie* commands that it be the state law governing primary private activity which prevails." (Justice Harlan, concurring in *Hanna v. Plumer,* 380 U.S. 460, 1965)

Guaranty Trust Co. v. York
326 U.S. 99 (1945)

MR. JUSTICE FRANKFURTER delivered the opinion of the Court.

Our starting point must be the policy of federal jurisdiction which Erie R. Co. v.Tompkins, 304 U.S. 64, embodies. In overruling Swift v. Tyson, 16 Pet. 1, Erie R. Co.v. Tompkins did not merely overrule a venerable case. It overruled a particular way of looking at law which dominated the judicial process long after its inadequacies had been laid bare. Law was conceived as a "brooding omnipresence" of Reason, of which decisions were merely evidence and not themselves the controlling formulations. Accordingly, federal courts deemed themselves free to ascertain what Reason, and therefore Law, required wholly independent of authoritatively declared State law, even in cases where a legal right as the basis for relief was created by State authority and could not be created by federal authority and the case got into a federal court merely because it was "between Citizens of different States" under Art. III, § 2 of the Constitution of the United States. . . .

And so this case reduces itself to the narrow question whether, when no recovery could be had in a State court because the action is barred by the statute of limitations, a federal court in equity can take cognizance of the suit because there is diversity of citizenship between the parties. . . .

And so the question is not whether a statute of limitations is deemed a matter of "procedure" in some sense. The question is whether such a statute concerns merely the manner and the means by which a right to recover, as recognized by the State, is enforced, or whether such statutory limitation is a matter of substance in the aspect that alone is relevant to our problem, namely, does it significantly affect the result of a litigation for a federal court to disregard a law of a State that would be controlling in an action upon the same claim by the same parties in a State court?

It is therefore immaterial whether statutes of limitation are characterized either as "substantive" or "procedural" in State court opinions in any use of those terms unrelated to the specific issue before us. Erie R. Co. v. Tompkins was not an endeavor to formulate scientific legal terminology. It expressed a policy that touches vitally the proper distribution of judicial power between State and federal courts. In essence, the intent of that decision was to ensure that, in all cases where a federal court is exercising jurisdiction solely because of the diversity of citizenship of the parties, the outcome of the litigation in the federal court should be substantially the same, so far as legal rules determine the outcome of a litigation, as it would be if tried in a State court. The nub of the policy that underlies Erie R. Co. v. Tompkins is that for the same transaction the accident of a suit by a non-resident litigant in a federal court instead of in a State court a block away should not lead to a substantially different result. . . .

The judgment is reversed and the case is remanded for proceedings not inconsistent with this opinion.

Problems 1. A Kansas statute of limitations provides that an action is deemed commenced when service is made on the defendant. FRCP 3 provides that an action commences with the filing of the complaint. In a diversity case, should a federal court apply the Kansas statute or FRCP 3? (See, *Ragan v. Merchants Transfer Co.*, 337 U. S. 530 (1949))

2. A state statute requires a small stockholder in a stockholder derivative suit to post a bond securing payment of defense costs as a condition to prosecuting an action. FRCP 23.1 does not so require. In a diversity case, should a federal court apply the state statute or FRCP 23.1? (See, *Cohen v. Beneficial Loan Corp.*, 337 U. S. 541 (1949))

3. A Mississippi statute bars out-of-state corporations not paying Mississippi taxes from suing in state courts. Should a federal court sitting in Mississippi allow an out-of-state corporation that has not paid taxes to sue in a case invoking diversity jurisdiction? (*Woods v. Interstate Realty Co.*, 337 U. S. 535 (1949))

4. Vermont bars arbitration of employment practices. A federal statute requires arbitration. Should a federal court sitting in Vermont require arbitration is a suit brought under diversity jurisdiction? (See, *Bernhardt v. Polygraphic Co.*, 350 U. S. 198 (1956))

Byrd v. Blue Ridge Rural Electric Cooperative, Inc.
356 U.S. 525 (1958)

MR. JUSTICE BRENNAN delivered the opinion of the Court.

A question is also presented as to whether on remand the factual issue is to be decided by the judge or by the jury. The respondent argues on the basis of the decision of the Supreme Court of South Carolina in Adams v. Davison-Paxon Co., 230 S. C. 532, 96 S. E. 2d 566, that the issue of immunity should be decided by the judge and not by the jury. . . .

The respondent argues that this state-court decision governs the present diversity case and "divests the jury of its normal function" to decide the disputed fact question of the respondent's immunity under § 72-111. This is to contend that the federal court is bound under Erie R. Co. v. Tompkins, 304 U. S. 64, to follow the state court's holding to secure uniform enforcement of the immunity created by the State.

First. It was decided in Erie R. Co. v. Tompkins that the federal courts in diversity cases must respect the definition of state-created rights and obligations by the state courts. We must, therefore, first examine the rule in Adams v. Davison-Paxon Co. to determine whether it is bound up with these rights and obligations in such a way that its application in the federal court is required.

The Workmen's Compensation Act is administered in South Carolina by its Industrial

Commission. The South Carolina courts hold that, on judicial review of actions of the Commission under § 72-111, the question whether the claim of an injured workman is within the Commission's jurisdiction is a matter of law for decision by the court, which makes its own findings of fact relating to that jurisdiction. The South Carolina Supreme Court states no reasons in Adams v. Davison-Paxon Co. why, although the jury decides all other factual issues raised by the cause of action and defenses, the jury is displaced as to the factual issue raised by the affirmative defense under § 72-111. . . . We find nothing to suggest that this rule was announced as an integral part of the special relationship created by the statute. Thus the requirement appears to be merely a form and mode of enforcing the immunity, Guaranty Trust Co. v. York, 326 U. S. 99, 108, and not a rule intended to be bound up with the definition of the rights and obligations of the parties. . . .

Second. But cases following Erie have evinced a broader policy to the effect that the federal courts should conform as near as may be—in the absence of other considerations—to state rules even of form and mode where the state rules may bear substantially on the question whether the litigation would come out one way in the federal court and another way in the state court if the federal court failed to apply a particular local rule. E. g., Guaranty Trust Co. v. York, supra; Concededly the nature of the tribunal which tries issues may be important in the enforcement of the parcel of rights making up a cause of action or defense and bear significantly upon achievement of uniform enforcement of the right. It may well be that in the instant personal-injury case the outcome would be substantially affected by whether the issue of immunity is decided by a judge or a jury. Therefore, were "outcome" the only consideration, a strong case might appear for saying that the federal court should follow the state practice.

But there are affirmative countervailing considerations at work here. The federal system is an independent system for administering justice to litigants who properly invoke its jurisdiction. An essential characteristic of that system is the manner in which, in civil common-law actions, it distributes trial functions between judge and jury and, under the influence—if not the command—of the Seventh Amendment, assigns the decisions of disputed questions of fact to the jury. The policy of uniform enforcement of state-created rights and obligations, see, e. g., Guaranty Trust Co. v. York, supra, cannot in every case exact compliance with a state rule—not bound up with rights and obligations— which disrupts the federal system of allocating functions between judge and jury. Thus the inquiry here is whether the federal policy favoring jury decisions of disputed fact questions should yield to the state rule in the interest of furthering the objective that the litigation should not come out one way in the federal court and another way in the state court.

We think that in the circumstances of this case the federal court should not follow the state rule. It cannot be gainsaid that there is a strong federal policy against allowing state rules to disrupt the judge-jury relationship in the federal courts. . . . Perhaps even more clearly in light of the influence of the Seventh Amendment, the function assigned to the jury "is an essential factor in the process for which the Federal Constitution provides." . . .

Third. We have discussed the problem upon the assumption that the outcome of the litigation may be substantially affected by whether the issue of immunity is decided by a judge or a jury. But clearly there is not present here the certainty that a different result would follow, cf. Guaranty Trust Co. v. York, supra, or even the strong possibility that this would be the case, cf. There are factors present here which might reduce that possibility. The trial judge in the federal system has powers denied the judges of many States to comment on the weight of evidence and credibility of witnesses, and discretion to grant a new trial if the verdict appears to him to be against the weight of the evidence. We do not think the likelihood of a different result is so strong as to require the federal practice of jury determination of disputed factual issues to yield to the state rule in the interest of uniformity of outcome.

Reversed and remanded.

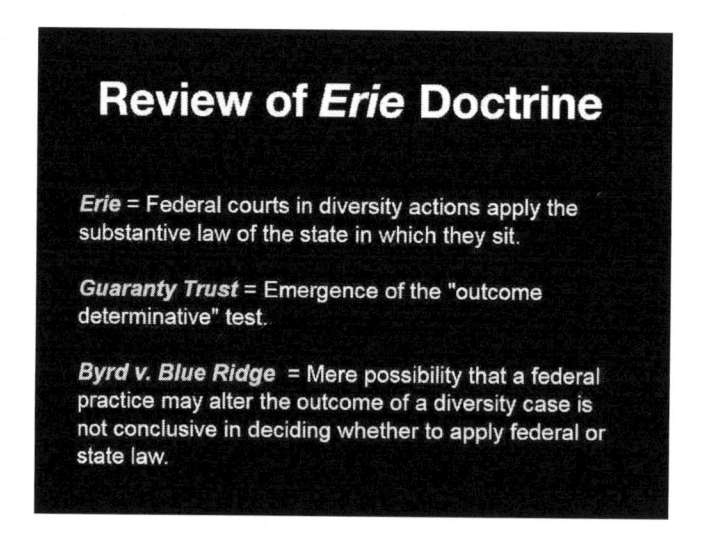

Review of *Erie* Doctrine

Erie = Federal courts in diversity actions apply the substantive law of the state in which they sit.

Guaranty Trust = Emergence of the "outcome determinative" test.

Byrd v. Blue Ridge = Mere possibility that a federal practice may alter the outcome of a diversity case is not conclusive in deciding whether to apply federal or state law.

Hanna v. Plumer
380 U.S. 460 (1965)

MR. CHIEF JUSTICE WARREN delivered the opinion of the Court.

The question to be decided is whether, in a civil action where the jurisdiction of the United States district court is based upon diversity of citizenship between the parties, service of process shall be made in the manner prescribed by state law or that set forth in Rule 4 (d) (1) of the Federal Rules of Civil Procedure.

On February 6, 1963, petitioner, a citizen of Ohio, filed her complaint in the District Court for the District of Massachusetts, claiming damages in excess of $10,000 for personal injuries resulting from an automobile accident in South Carolina, allegedly caused by the negligence of one Louise Plumer Osgood, a Massachusetts citizen deceased at the time of the filing of the complaint. Respondent, Mrs. Osgood's executor and also a Massachusetts citizen, was named as defendant. On February 8, service was made by leaving copies of the summons and the complaint with respondent's wife at his residence, concededly in compliance with Rule 4 (d) (1), which provides:

"The summons and complaint shall be served together. The plaintiff shall furnish the person making service with such copies as are necessary. Service shall be made as follows:

"(1) Upon an individual other than an infant or an incompetent person, by delivering a copy of the summons and of the complaint to him personally or by leaving copies thereof at his dwelling house or usual place of abode with some person of suitable age and discretion then residing therein . . . ."

Respondent filed his answer on February 26, alleging, inter alia, that the action could not be maintained because it had been brought "contrary to and in violation of the provisions of Massachusetts General Laws (Ter. Ed.) Chapter 197, Section 9." That section provides:

"Except as provided in this chapter, an executor or administrator shall not be held to answer to an action by a creditor of the deceased which is not commenced within one year from the time of his giving bond for the performance of his trust, or to such an action which is commenced within said year unless before the expiration thereof the writ in such action has been served by delivery in hand upon such executor or administrator . . .

We conclude that the adoption of Rule 4 (d) (1), designed to control service of process in diversity actions, neither exceeded the congressional mandate embodied in the Rules Enabling Act nor transgressed constitutional bounds, and that the Rule is therefore the standard against which the District Court should have measured the adequacy of the service. Accordingly, we reverse the decision of the Court of Appeals.

The Rules Enabling Act, 28 U. S. C. § 2072 (1958 ed.), provides, in pertinent part:

"The Supreme Court shall have the power to prescribe, by general rules, the forms of process, writs, pleadings, and motions, and the practice and procedure of the district courts of the United States in civil actions."

"Such rules shall not abridge, enlarge or modify any substantive right and shall preserve the right of trial by jury . . . ."

Under the cases construing the scope of the Enabling Act, Rule 4 (d) (1) clearly passes muster. Prescribing the manner in which a defendant is to be notified that a suit has been instituted against him, it relates to the "practice and procedure of the district courts."

"The test must be whether a rule really regulates procedure, —the judicial process for enforcing rights and duties recognized by substantive law and for justly administering remedy and redress for disregard or infraction of them." Sibbach v. Wilson & Co., 312 U. S. 1, 14 . . .

Thus were there no conflicting state procedure, Rule 4 (d) (1) would clearly control. National Rental v. Szukhent, 375 U. S. 311, 316. However, respondent, focusing on the contrary Massachusetts rule, calls to the Court's attention another line of cases, a line which—like the Federal Rules—had its birth in 1938. Erie R. Co. v. Tompkins, 304 U. S. 64, overruling Swift v. Tyson, 16 Pet. 1, held that federal courts sitting in diversity cases, when deciding questions of "substantive" law, are bound by state court decisions as well as state statutes. The broad command of Erie was therefore identical to that of the Enabling Act: federal courts are to apply state substantive law and federal procedural law. However, as subsequent cases sharpened the distinction between substance and procedure, the line of cases following Erie diverged markedly from the line construing the Enabling Act. . . .

Respondent, by placing primary reliance on York and Ragan, suggests that the Erie doctrine acts as a check on the Federal Rules of Civil Procedure, that despite the clear command of Rule 4 (d) (1), Erie and its progeny demand the application of the Massachusetts rule. . . .

In the first place, it is doubtful that, even if there were no Federal Rule making it clear that in-hand service is not required in diversity actions, the Erie rule would have obligated the District Court to follow the Massachusetts procedure. "Outcome-determination" analysis was never intended to serve as a talisman. Byrd v. Blue Ridge Cooperative, 356 U. S. 525, 537. Indeed, the message of York itself is that choices between state and federal law are to be made not by application of any automatic, "litmus paper" criterion, but rather by reference to the policies underlying the Erie rule.

The Erie rule is rooted in part in a realization that it would be unfair for the character or result of a litigation materially to differ because the suit had been brought in a federal court. . . The decision was also in part a reaction to the practice of "forum-shopping" which had grown up in response to the rule of Swift v. Tyson. That the York test was an attempt to effectuate these policies is demonstrated by the fact that the opinion framed the inquiry in terms of "substantial" variations between state and federal litigation. Not only are non-substantial, or trivial, variations not likely to raise the sort of equal protection problems which troubled the Court in Erie; they are also unlikely to influence the choice of a forum. The "outcome-determination" test therefore cannot be read without reference to the twin aims of the Erie rule: discouragement of forum-shopping, and avoidance of inequitable administration of the laws.

The difference between the conclusion that the Massachusetts rule is applicable, and the conclusion that it is not, is of course at this point "outcome-determinative" in the sense that if we hold the state rule to apply, respondent prevails, whereas if we hold that Rule 4 (d) (1) governs, the litigation will continue. But in this sense every procedural variation is "outcome-determinative." For example, having brought suit in a federal court, a plaintiff cannot then insist on the right to file subsequent pleadings in accord with the time limits applicable in the state courts, even though enforcement of the federal timetable will, if he continues to insist that he must meet only the state time limit, result in determination of the controversy against him. So it is here. Though choice of the federal or state rule will at this point have a marked effect upon the outcome of the litigation, the difference between the two rules would be of scant, if any, relevance to the choice of a forum. Petitioner, in choosing her forum, was not presented with a situation where application of the state rule would wholly bar recovery; rather, adherence to the state rule would have resulted only in altering the way in which process was served. Moreover, it is difficult to argue that permitting service of defendant's wife to take the place of in-hand service of defendant himself alters the mode of enforcement of state-created rights in a fashion sufficiently "substantial" to raise the sort of equal protection problems to which the Erie opinion alluded.

There is, however, a more fundamental flaw in respondent's syllogism: the incorrect assumption that the rule of Erie R. Co. v. Tompkins constitutes the appropriate test of the validity and therefore the applicability of a Federal Rule of Civil Procedure. The Erie rule has never been invoked to void a Federal Rule. It is true that there have been cases where this Court has held applicable a state rule in the face of an argument that the situation was governed by one of the Federal Rules. But the holding of each such case was not that Erie commanded displacement of a Federal Rule by an inconsistent state rule, but rather that the scope of the Federal Rule was not as broad as the losing party urged, and therefore, there being no Federal Rule which covered the point in dispute, Erie commanded the enforcement of state law. . . . (Here, of course, the clash is unavoidable; Rule 4 (d) (1) says—implicitly, but with unmistakable clarity—that in-hand service is not required in federal courts.) At the same time, in cases adjudicating the validity of Federal Rules, we have not applied the York rule or other refinements of Erie but have to this day continued to decide questions concerning the scope of the Enabling Act and the constitutionality of specific Federal Rules in light of the distinction set forth in Sibbach.

Nor has the development of two separate lines of cases been inadvertent. The line between "substance" and "procedure" shifts as the legal context changes. "Each implies different variables depending upon the particular problem for which it is used." Guaranty Trust Co. v. York, supra, at 108; It is true that both the Enabling Act and the Erie rule say, roughly, that federal courts are to apply state "substantive" law and federal "procedural" law, but from that it need not follow that the tests are identical. For they were designed to control very different sorts of decisions. When a situation is covered by one of the Federal Rules, the question facing the court is a far cry from the typical, relatively unguided Erie choice: the court has been instructed to apply the Federal Rule and can refuse to do so only if the Advisory Committee, this Court, and Congress erred in their prima facie judgment that the Rule in question transgresses neither the terms of the Enabling Act nor constitutional restrictions. . . .

Erie and its offspring cast no doubt on the long-recognized power of Congress to prescribe housekeeping rules for federal courts even though some of those rules will inevitably differ from comparable state rules. "When, because the plaintiff happens to be a non-resident, such a right is enforceable in a federal as well as in a State court, the forms and mode of enforcing the right may at times, naturally enough, vary because the two judicial systems are not identical." Guaranty Trust Co. v. York, supra, at 108; Cohen v. Beneficial Loan Corp., 337 U. S. 541, 555. Thus, though a court, in measuring a Federal Rule against the standards contained in the Enabling Act and the Constitution, need not wholly blind itself to the degree to which the Rule makes the character and result of the federal litigation stray from the course it would follow in state courts, Sibbach v. Wilson & Co., supra, at 13-14, it cannot be forgotten that the Erie rule, and the guidelines suggested in York, were created to serve another purpose altogether. To hold that a Federal Rule of Civil Procedure must cease to function whenever it alters the mode of enforcing state-created rights would be to disembowel either the Constitution's grant of power over federal procedure or Congress' attempt to exercise that power in the Enabling Act Rule 4 (d)(1) is valid and controls the instant case.

Reversed.

Making Sense of Hanna

Hanna announces a two-part test. First, when a litigant asserts that state law conflicts with a federal procedural statute or formal rule of procedure, a court's first task is to determine whether the disputed point in question in fact falls within the scope of the federal statute or rule. If the answer is yes, then the court must determine whether a conflict between the federal rule and state law exists, or whether the federal rule is "narrower" in its coverage (i.e., does not cover the issue in question) than the state statute. In other words, does the federal rule or statute leave no room for the operation of state law? To put it yet another way, is there a "direct collision" between state and federal law? This language is not meant to mandate that federal law and state law be perfectly coextensive and equally applicable to the issue at hand; rather, the "direct collision" language, at least where the applicability of a federal statute is at issue, expresses the requirement that the federal statute be sufficiently broad to cover the point in dispute. See *Hanna v. Plumer, supra,*. It would make no sense for the supremacy of federal law to wane precisely because there is no state law directly on point. (*Stewart Organization v. Ricoh, infra,* fn. 4)

If there is a direct conflict between state practice and a federal rule, then the court must determine whether the federal rule is a valid exercise of the rule making power granted to the Supreme Court by Congress. (Friedenthal § 4.4) (To date, no federal rule of civil procedure has ever been found to be an invalid exercise of the rule making power.)

> **Hanna Two-Part Test Simplified**
>
> (1) If there is a valid Federal Rule on the subject, the rule is to be applied.
>
> (2) In the absence of a federal rule the court is to consider the problem in light of the twin aims of the *Erie* rule.

If no federal statute or Rule covers the point in dispute, the district court then proceeds to evaluate whether application of federal judge-made law would disserve the so-called "twin aims of the *Erie* rule: discouragement of forum-shopping and avoidance of inequitable administration of the laws." *Hanna v. Plumer, supra,* If application of federal judge-made law would disserve these two policies, the district court should apply state law. (See *Walker v. Armco Steel Corp.*, 446 U.S. 740 (1980), at 752-753.)

The next two cases will hopefully shed light on how that process works.

Sibbach v. Wilson & Co., Inc.
312 U.S. 1 (1941)

MR. JUSTICE ROBERTS delivered the opinion of the Court.

This case calls for decision as to the validity of Rules 35 and 37 of the Rules of Civil Procedure for District Courts of the United States.

In an action brought by the petitioner in the District Court for Northern Illinois to recover damages for bodily injuries, inflicted in Indiana, respondent answered denying the allegations of the complaint, and moved for an order requiring the petitioner to submit to a physical examination by one or more physicians appointed by the court to determine the nature and extent of her injuries. The court ordered that the petitioner submit to such an examination by a physician so appointed.

Compliance having been refused, the respondent obtained an order to show cause why the petitioner should not be punished for contempt. In response the petitioner challenged the authority of the court to order her to submit to the examination, asserting that the order was void. It appeared that the courts of Indiana, the state where the cause of action arose, hold such an order proper, whereas the courts of Illinois, the state in which the trial court sat, hold that such an order cannot be made Neither state has any statute governing the matter.

The court adjudged the petitioner guilty of contempt and directed that she be committed until she should obey the order for examination or otherwise should be legally discharged from custody. The petitioner appealed.

The Circuit Court of Appeals decided that Rule 35, which authorizes an order for a physical examination in such a case, is valid, and affirmed the judgment. The writ of certiorari was granted because of the importance of the question involved.

The contention of the petitioner, in final analysis, is that Rules 35 and 37 are not within the mandate of Congress to this court. This is the limit of permissible debate, since argument touching the broader questions of Congressional power and of the obligation of federal courts to apply the substantive law of a state is foreclosed.

Congress has undoubted power to regulate the practice and procedure of federal courts, and may exercise that power by delegating to this or other federal courts authority to make rules not inconsistent with the statutes or constitution of the United States; but it has never essayed to declare the substantive state law, or to abolish or nullify a right recognized by the substantive law of the state where the cause of action arose, save where a right or duty is imposed in a field committed to Congress by the Constitution. On the contrary it has enacted that the state law shall be the rule of decision in the federal courts.

Hence we conclude that the Act of June 19, 1934, was purposely restricted in its operation to matters of pleading and court practice and procedure. Its two provisos or caveats emphasize this restriction. The first is that the court shall not "abridge, enlarge, nor modify substantive rights," in the guise of regulating procedure. The second is that if the rules are to prescribe a single form of action for cases at law and suits in equity, the constitutional right to jury trial inherent in the former must be preserved. There are other limitations upon the authority to prescribe rules which might have been but were not mentioned in the Act; for instance, the inability of a court, by rule, to extend or restrict the jurisdiction conferred by a statute.

Whatever may be said as to the effect of the Conformity Act while it remained in force, the rules, if they are within the authority granted by Congress, repeal that statute, and the District Court was not bound to follow the Illinois practice respecting an order for physical examination. On the other hand if the right to be exempt from such an order is one of substantive law, the Rules of Decision Act required the District Court, though sitting in Illinois, to apply the law of Indiana, the state where the cause of action arose, and to order the examination. To avoid this dilemma the petitioner admits, and, we think, correctly, that Rules 35 and 37 are rules of procedure. She insists, nevertheless, that by the prohibition against abridging substantive rights, Congress has banned the rules here challenged. In order to reach this result she translates "substantive" into "important" or "substantial" rights. And she urges that if a rule affects such a right, albeit the rule is one of procedure merely, its prescription is not within the statutory grant of power embodied in the Act of June 19, 1934. She contends that our decisions and recognized principles require us so to hold. . . .

We are thrown back, then, to the arguments drawn from the language of the Act of June 19, 1934. Is the phrase "substantive rights" confined to rights conferred by law to be protected and enforced in accordance with the adjective law of judicial procedure? It certainly embraces such rights. One of them is the right not to be injured in one's person by another's negligence, to redress infraction of which the present action was brought. The petitioner says the phrase connotes more; that by its use Congress intended that in regulating procedure this court should not deal with important and substantial rights theretofore recognized. Recognized where and by whom? The state courts are divided as to the power in the absence of statute to order a physical examination In a number such an order is authorized by statute or rule. The rules in question accord with the procedure now in force in Canada and England.

The asserted right, moreover, is no more important than many others enjoyed by litigants in District Courts sitting in the several states, before the Federal Rules of Civil Procedure altered and abolished old rights or privileges and created new ones in connection with the conduct of litigation. The suggestion that the rule offends the important right to freedom from invasion of the person ignores the fact that, as we hold, no invasion of freedom from personal restraint attaches to refusal so to comply with its provisions. If we were to adopt the suggested criterion of the importance of the alleged right we should invite endless litigation and confusion worse confounded. The test must be whether a rule really regulates procedure, — the judicial process for enforcing rights and duties recognized by substantive law and for justly administering remedy and redress for disregard or infraction of them. That the rules in question are such is admitted.

Finally, it is urged that Rules 35 and 37 work a major change of policy and that this was not intended by Congress. Apart from the fact already stated, that the policy of the states in this respect has not been uniform, it is to be noted that the authorization of a comprehensive system of court rules was a departure in policy, and that the new policy envisaged in the enabling act of 1934 was that the whole field of court procedure be regulated in the interest of speedy, fair and exact determination of the truth. The challenged rules comport with this policy. Moreover, in accordance with the Act, the rules were submitted to the Congress so that that body might examine them and veto their going into effect if contrary to the policy of the legislature. . . .

The District Court treated the refusal to comply with its order as a contempt and committed the petitioner therefor. Neither in the Circuit Court of Appeals nor here was this action assigned as error. We think, however, that in the light of the provisions of Rule 37 it was plain error of such a fundamental nature that we should notice it. Section (b) (2) (iv) of Rule 37 exempts from punishment as for contempt the refusal to obey an order that a party submit to a physical or mental examination. The District Court was in error in going counter to this express exemption. The remedies available under the rule in such a case are those enumerated in § (b) (2) (i) (ii) and (iii). For this error we reverse the judgment and remand the cause to the District Court for further proceedings in conformity to this opinion.

Reversed.

Stewart Organization, Inc. v. Ricoh Corp.
487 U.S. 22 (1988)

JUSTICE MARSHALL delivered the opinion of the Court.

This case presents the issue whether a federal court sitting in diversity should apply state or federal law in adjudicating a motion to transfer a case to a venue provided in a contractual forum-selection clause.

The dispute underlying this case grew out of a dealership agreement that obligated petitioner company, an Alabama corporation, to market copier products of respondent, a nationwide manufacturer with its principal place of business in New Jersey. The agreement contained a forum-selection clause providing that any dispute arising out of the contract could be brought only in a court located in Manhattan. Business relations between the parties soured under circumstances that are not relevant here. In September 1984, petitioner brought a complaint in the United States District Court for the Northern District of Alabama. The core of the complaint was an allegation that respondent had breached the dealership agreement, but petitioner also included claims for breach of warranty, fraud, and antitrust violations.

Relying on the contractual forum-selection clause, respondent moved the District Court either to transfer the case to the Southern District of New York under 28 U. S. C. § 1404(a) or to dismiss the case for improper venue under 28 U. S. C. § 1406. The District Court denied the motion. It reasoned that the transfer motion was controlled by Alabama law and that Alabama looks unfavorably upon contractual forum-selection clauses. The court certified its ruling for interlocutory appeal, and the Court of Appeals for the Eleventh Circuit accepted jurisdiction.

On appeal, a divided panel of the Eleventh Circuit reversed the District Court. The panel concluded that questions of venue in diversity actions are governed by federal law, and that the parties' forum-selection clause was enforceable as a matter of federal law. 779 F. 2d 643 (1986). The panel therefore reversed the order of the District Court and remanded with instructions to transfer the case to a Manhattan court. After petitioner successfully moved for rehearing en banc, 785 F. 2d 896 (1986), the full Court of Appeals proceeded to adopt the result, and much of the reasoning, of the panel opinion. 810 F. 2d 1066 (1987). The en banc court, citing Congress' enactment or approval of several rules to govern venue determinations in diversity actions, first determined that "[v]enue is a matter of federal procedure." Id., at 1068. The Court of Appeals then applied the standards articulated in the admiralty case of The Bremen v. Zapata Off-Shore Co., 407 U. S. 1 (1972), to conclude that "the choice of forum clause in this contract is in all respects enforceable generally as a matter of federal law . . . ." 810 F. 2d, at 1071. We now affirm under somewhat different reasoning.

. . . Our cases indicate that when the federal law sought to be applied is a congressional statute, the first and chief question for the district court's determination is whether the statute is "sufficiently broad to control the issue before the Court." Walker v. Armco Steel Corp., 446 U. S. 740, 749-750 (1980); Burlington Northern R. Co. v. Woods, 480 U. S. 1, 4-5 (1987). This question involves a straightforward exercise in statutory interpretation to determine if the statute covers the point in dispute.

If the district court determines that a federal statute covers the point in dispute, it proceeds to inquire whether the statute represents a valid exercise of Congress' authority under the Constitution. See Hanna v. Plumer, supra, at 471 (citing Erie R. Co. v. Tompkins, supra, at 77-79). If Congress intended to reach the issue before the district court, and if it enacted its intention into law in a manner that abides with the Constitution, that is the end of the matter; "[f]ederal courts are bound to apply rules enacted by Congress with respect to matters . . . over which it has legislative power." Prima Paint Corp. v. Flood & Conklin Mfg. Co., 388 U. S. 395, 406 (1967); cf. Hanna v. Plumer, supra, at 471 ("When a situation is covered by one of the Federal Rules . . . the court has been instructed to apply the Federal Rule and can refuse to do so only if the Advisory Committee, this Court, and Congress erred in their prima facie judgment that the Rule in question transgresses neither the terms of the Enabling Act nor constitutional restrictions"). Thus, a district court sitting in diversity must apply a federal statute that controls the issue before the court and that represents a valid exercise of Congress' constitutional powers.

Applying the above analysis to this case persuades us that federal law, specifically 28 U. S. C. § 1404(a), governs the parties' venue dispute.

At the outset we underscore a methodological difference in our approach to the question from that taken by the Court of Appeals. The en banc court determined that federal law controlled the issue based on a survey of different statutes and judicial decisions that together revealed a significant federal interest in questions of venue in general, and in choice-of-forum clauses in particular. The Court of Appeals then proceeded to apply the standards announced in our opinion in The Bremen v. Zapata Off-Shore Co., 407 U. S. 1 (1972), to determine that the forum-selection clause in this case was enforceable. But the immediate issue before the District Court was whether to grant respondent's motion to transfer the action under § 1404(a), and as Judge Tjoflat properly noted in his special concurrence below, the immediate issue before the Court of Appeals was whether the District Court's denial of the § 1404(a) motion constituted an abuse of discretion. Although we agree with the Court of Appeals that the Bremen case may prove "instructive" in resolving the parties' dispute, 810 F. 2d, at 1069; but cf.

Texas Industries, Inc. v. Radcliff Materials, Inc., 451 U. S. 630, 641-642 (1981) (federal common law developed under admiralty jurisdiction not freely transferable to diversity setting), we disagree with the court's articulation of the relevant inquiry as "whether the forum selection clause in this case is unenforceable under the standards set forth in The Bremen." 810 F. 2d, at 1069. Rather, the first question for consideration should have been whether § 1404(a) itself controls respondent's request to give effect to the parties' contractual choice of venue and transfer this case to a Manhattan court. For the reasons that follow, we hold that it does.

Section 1404(a) provides: "For the convenience of parties and witnesses, in the interest of justice, a district court may transfer any civil action to any other district or division where it might have been brought." Under the analysis outlined above, we first consider whether this provision is sufficiently broad to control the issue before the court. That issue is whether to transfer the case to a court in Manhattan in accordance with the forum-selection clause. We believe that the statute, fairly construed, does cover the point in dispute.

Section 1404(a) is intended to place discretion in the district court to adjudicate motions for transfer according to an "individualized, case-by-case consideration of convenience and fairness." Van Dusen v. Barrack, 376 U. S. 612, 622 (1964). A motion to transfer under § 1404(a) thus calls on the district court to weigh in the balance a number of case-specific factors. The presence of a forum-selection clause such as the parties entered into in this case will be a significant factor that figures centrally in the district court's calculus. In its resolution of the § 1404(a) motion in this case, for example, the District Court will be called on to address such issues as the convenience of a Manhattan forum given the parties' expressed preference for that venue, and the fairness of transfer in light of the forum-selection clause and the parties' relative bargaining power. The flexible and individualized analysis Congress prescribed in § 1404(a) thus encompasses consideration of the parties' private expression of their venue preferences.

Section 1404(a) may not be the only potential source of guidance for the District Court to consult in weighing the parties' private designation of a suitable forum. The premise of the dispute between the parties is that Alabama law may refuse to enforce forum-selection clauses providing for out-of-state venues as a matter of state public policy. If that is so, the District Court will have either to integrate the factor of the forum-selection clause into its weighing of considerations as prescribed by Congress, or else to apply, as it did in this case, Alabama's categorical policy disfavoring forum-selection clauses. Our cases make clear that, as between these two choices in a single "field of operation," Burlington Northern R. Co. v. Woods, 480 U. S., at 7, the instructions of Congress are supreme. Cf. ibid. (where federal law's "discretionary mode of operation" conflicts with the nondiscretionary provision of Alabama law, federal law applies in diversity).

It is true that § 1404(a) and Alabama's putative policy regarding forum-selection clauses are not perfectly coextensive. Section 1404(a) directs a district court to take account of factors other than those that bear solely on the parties' private ordering of their affairs. The district court also must weigh in the balance the convenience of the witnesses and those public-interest factors of systemic integrity and fairness that, in addition to private concerns, come under the heading of "the interest of justice." It is conceivable in a particular case, for example, that because of these factors a district court acting under § 1404(a) would refuse to transfer a case notwithstanding the counterweight of a forum-selection clause, whereas the coordinate state rule might dictate the opposite result. See 15 C. Wright, A. Miller, & E. Cooper, Federal Practice and Procedure § 3847, p. 371 (2d ed. 1986). But this potential conflict in fact frames an additional argument for the supremacy of federal law. Congress has directed that multiple considerations govern transfer within the federal court system, and a state policy focusing on a single concern or a subset of the factors identified in § 1404(a) would defeat that command. Its application would impoverish the flexible and multifaceted analysis that Congress intended to govern motions to transfer within the federal system. The forum-selection clause, which represents the parties' agreement as to the most proper forum, should receive neither dispositive consideration (as respondent might have it) nor no consideration (as Alabama law might have it), but rather the consideration for which Congress provided in § 1404(a). Cf. Norwood v. Kirkpatrick, 349 U. S. 29, 32 (1955) (§ 1404(a) accords broad discretion to district court, and plaintiff's choice of forum is only one relevant factor for its consideration). This is thus not a case in which state and federal rules "can exist side by side . . . each controlling its own intended sphere of coverage without conflict." Walker v. Armco Steel Corp., 446 U. S., at 752.

Because § 1404(a) controls the issue before the District Court, it must be applied if it represents a valid exercise of Congress' authority under the Constitution. The constitutional authority of Congress to enact § 1404(a) is not subject to serious question. As the Court made plain in Hanna, "the constitutional provision for a federal court system . . . carries with it congressional power to make rules governing the practice and pleading in those courts, which in turn includes a power to regulate matters which, though falling within the uncertain area between substance and procedure, are rationally capable of classification as either." 380 U. S., at 472. See also id., at 473 ("Erie and its offspring cast no doubt on the long-recognized power of Congress to prescribe housekeeping rules for federal courts"). Section 1404(a) is doubtless capable of classification as a procedural rule, and indeed, we have so classified it in holding that a transfer pursuant to § 1404(a) does not carry with it a change in the applicable law. See Van Dusen v. Barrack, 376 U. S., at 636-637 ("[B]oth the history and purposes of § 1404(a) indicate that it should be regarded as a federal judicial housekeeping measure"). It therefore falls comfortably within Congress' powers under Article III as augmented by the Necessary and Proper Clause.

We hold that federal law, specifically 28 U. S. C. § 1404(a), governs the District Court's decision whether to give effect to the parties' forum-selection clause and transfer this case to a court in Manhattan. We therefore affirm the Eleventh Circuit order reversing the District Court's application of Alabama law. The case is remanded so that the District Court may determine in the first instance the appropriate effect under federal law of the parties' forum-selection clause on respondent's § 1404(a) motion.

It is so ordered.

Determining State Law Under *Erie*

Under the *Erie* doctrine, a federal court exercising diversity jurisdiction must apply state rather than federal decisional law to questions of a "substantive" character. In order to determine which state's law applies, a federal court must ascertain the substantive law that would be applied to the question by a court of the state in which it is located, (*Klaxon Co. v. Stanton Elec. Mfg. Co.*, 313 U.S. 487, 61 S.Ct. 1020, 85 L.Ed. 1477 (1943)) However, state law, particularly the judge-made common law of a state, is not always settled. As pointed out in *McKenna*, below, this is a problem of "ascertainment." Consider the oft-quoted comment of Circuit Judge Friendly: "Our principal task, in this diversity of citizenship case, is to determine what the New York courts would think the California courts would think on an issue about which neither has thought." (*Nolan v. Transocean Air Lines*, 276 F.2d 280 (1960).)

McKenna v. Ortho Pharmaceutical Corp.
622 F.2d 657 (1980)

ADAMS, Circuit Judge.

After trial, but prior to the presentation of the case to the jury, the district court in this diversity case granted defendants' motion for a directed verdict on the ground that Ohio law barred recovery. Because we are persuaded by a careful review of the Ohio decisional law, as well as other relevant sources, that the Supreme Court of Ohio would not construe its statute of limitations so as to preclude recovery in this case, we reverse.

James and Sondra McKenna brought this suit for negligence, misrepresentation, and products liability against Ortho Pharmaceutical Corporation (Ortho). The plaintiffs charged that Mrs. McKenna suffered severe personal injury and permanent disability as a result of ingesting Ortho-Novum, an oral contraceptive manufactured and marketed by Ortho. Following the birth of the McKenna's second child, Mrs. McKenna began using Ortho-Novum in January 1965, after receiving assurances both from Ortho's published brochure and from her personal physician, that the drug was safe and posed no serious risks. In 1967, Mrs. McKenna developed severe headaches and also experienced two attacks of transient ischemia. While hospitalized in 1969 for a stomach ailment involving vessel wall damage, Mrs. McKenna was told that she had high blood pressure, which was characterized as hypertension. In June 1969, Mrs. McKenna ceased using the oral contraceptives. Three years later, in March 1972, she suffered a catastrophic cerebrovascular stroke that left her severely and permanently paralyzed.

One year and nine months thereafter, in November 1973, the McKennas commenced this action in a Pennsylvania state court by a praecipe for a writ of trespass. On Ortho's motion, the suit was removed to the federal district court in Pittsburgh, where it was ultimately tried. The plaintiffs claimed that Mrs. McKenna's injuries were caused by her ingestion of Ortho-Novum; that Mrs. McKenna relied on Ortho's false assurances about the product's safety in deciding to use Ortho-Novum; that Ortho knew or should have known that these statements were false; and that Ortho-Novum posed a risk of serious harm to its users. . . .

Accordingly, because the McKenna's' cause of action arose in Ohio, we must look to Ohio law to determine when Ohio's statute of limitations commenced to run. And the question for decision, then, is whether Ohio's statute of limitations commenced to run prior to the date Mrs. McKenna knew, or reasonably should have discovered, that her injuries were caused by Ortho-Novum.

Given that Ohio law governs the question for decision, the task remains to determine what the pertinent Ohio law is and then to apply it to this controversy. The question of how a federal court is to ascertain and apply state decisional law to a particular case has provoked considerable comment from courts and commentators alike. As some have noted, the concept that a federal court must determine state law is somewhat misleading inasmuch as it implies the existence of a readily accessible and easily understood body of state law. On the contrary, the law of a state is frequently "dynamic rather than static," and consists of a working body of rules, which find expression in a number of sources. It is this working body of rules to which a federal court must look in order to ascertain the state law that governs in a particular case.

In those few instances in which the highest state court has recently spoken to the precise question at issue in a particular setting, the duty of the federal court to determine and apply state law is easily met. After all, "[t]he State's highest court is the best authority on its own law." The problem of ascertainment arises when, as here, the highest state court has not yet authoritatively addressed the critical issue. Recent opinions of this Court make clear that our disposition of such cases must be governed by a prediction of how the state's highest court would decide were it confronted with the problem. Although some have characterized this assignment as speculative or crystal-ball gazing, nonetheless it is a task which we may not decline.

An accurate forecast of Ohio's law, as it would be expressed by its highest court, requires an examination of all relevant sources of that state's law in order to isolate those factors that would inform its decision. The primary source that must be analyzed of course, is the decisional law of the Ohio Supreme Court. In the absence of authority directly on point, decisions by that court in analogous cases provide useful indications of the court's probable disposition of a particular question of law. It is important to note, however, that our prediction "cannot be the product of a mere recitation of previously decided cases." In determining state law, a federal tribunal should be careful to avoid the "danger" of giving "a state court decision a more binding effect than would a court of that state under similar circumstances. "Rather, relevant state precedents must be scrutinized with an eye toward the broad policies that informed those adjudications, and to the doctrinal trends which they evince.

Considered dicta by the state's highest court may also provide a federal court with reliable indicia of how the state tribunal might rule on a particular question. Because the highest state court "enjoys some latitude of decision in ascertaining the law applicable to a particular dispute even where there may be dicta in point," however, a federal court should be circumspect in surrendering its own judgment concerning what the state law is on account of dicta. As Professor Charles Alan Wright has written, "much depends on the character of the dictum." Of somewhat less importance to a prognostication of what the highest state court will do are decisions of lower state courts and other federal courts. Such decisions should be accorded "proper regard" of course, but not conclusive effect. Thus, the Supreme Court has held that although the decision of a lower state court "should be `attributed some weight . . . the decision [is] not controlling . . .' where the highest court of the State has not spoken on the point. . . . Thus, under some conditions, federal authority may not be bound even by an intermediate state appellate court ruling." Additionally, federal courts may consider scholarly treatises, the Restatement of Law, and germane law review articles—particularly, it seems, of schools within the state whose law is to be predicted.

In sum, a federal court attempting to forecast state law must consider relevant state precedents, analogous decisions, considered dicta, scholarly works, and any other reliable data tending convincingly to show how the highest court in the state would decide the issue at hand. The rule of Erie calls on us to apply state law and not, as the dissent notes, "to participate in an effort to change it" merely because we doubt its soundness. At the same time, however, blind adherence to state precedents "without evaluating the decision[s] in the light of other relevant data as to what the state law is, will result in injustice and a perversion of the state law which the federal court sets out to apply." As this Court has declared:

> A diversity litigant should not be drawn to the federal forum by the prospect of a more favorable outcome than he could expect in the state courts. But neither should he be penalized for his choice of the federal court by being deprived of the flexibility that a state court could reasonably be expected to show.

. . . Accordingly, we reverse the judgment of the district court, and remand for further proceedings consistent with this opinion.

CHAPTER 4

PLEADING

The first stage in any lawsuit is the pleading stage. Plaintiff initiates the lawsuit by filing a pleading, usually called a "complaint." Defendant then may respond by filing one of the responsive pleadings. Usually this is a pleading called the "answer."

At common law there were very strict rules regarding pleading. The pleadings could continue indefinitely until they had produced a single issue of law or fact that would then be decided. Thus, there were rigid stages of denial, avoidance, or demurrer, eventually to reach a single issue of law or fact upon which the case would be tried.

The common law recognized very specific forms of action such as trespass, case, ejectment, covenant, debt and assumpsit, etc. The pleader had to fit his facts into one of these forms of action. If he was unable to do so, the lawsuit was thrown out at the pleading stage without there ever being a trial on the merits. Furthermore, law and equity were separate systems. To be entitled to equitable relief one had to show that any available legal remedies would be inadequate.

Historically Pleadings Have Had Four Functions:

1. Giving notice of the nature of a claim or defense.

2. Set forth the facts each party believes to exist.

3. Narrow the issues.

4. Provide a means for speedy disposition of sham claims and insubstantial defenses.

Code Pleading in California

Common law pleading eventually gave way to code pleading. The two most prominent features of which were the abolition of the common law forms of action and the merger of law and equity. The important emphasis under the codes was on developing the facts by pleadings.

In code pleading states, such as California, a pleader is required to plead "ultimate facts." Cal.Code.Civ.Proc. § 425.10(a) provides that the complaint must contain "a statement of the facts constituting the cause of action in ordinary and concise language"

Semole v. Sansoucie
28 Cal.App.3d 714 (1972)

HERNDON, Acting P.J.

Plaintiffs (appellants) appeal from the order dismissing this action brought against respondent to recover damages for wrongful death. The dismissal was entered after respondent's demurrer to appellants' second amended complaint had been sustained without leave to amend on the ground that no cause of action had been stated.

The original complaint, filed on July 11, 1966, alleges that on May 9, 1966, appellants' son, John Semole, was fatally injured while loading piggyback trailers onto railroad flatcars. It named as defendants the decedent's employer, Pacific Motor Trucking Company, and a fellow employee, Robert J. Sansoucie, respondent herein, and 10 Does.

On December 11, 1970, the court below granted the motion of the defendant corporation for summary judgment and dismissed the action as to that defendant on the ground that the action against decedent's employer was barred by Labor Code section 3601 which, with inapplicable exceptions, limits the remedy to the recovery of workmen's compensation. Appellants took no appeal from that judgment but have sought to maintain the action against respondent, decedent's fellow employee, by invoking Labor Code section 3601, subdivision (a)(3) which read at that time as follows: "(a) Where the conditions of compensation exist, the right to recover such compensation, pursuant to the provisions of this division is, except as provided in Section 3706, the exclusive remedy for injury or death of an employee against the employer or against any other employee of the employer acting within the scope of his employment, except that an employee, or his dependents in the event of his death, shall, in addition to the right to compensation against the employer, have a right to bring an action at law for damages against such other employee, as if this division did not apply, in the following cases: ...

"(3) When the injury or death is proximately caused by an act of such other employee which evinces a reckless disregard for the safety of the employee injured, and a calculated and conscious willingness to permit injury or death to such employee."

Respondent filed a general demurrer to the complaint and sought a dismissal of the action on the grounds: (1) that summons was not served upon him within the three-year period as provided in Code of Civil Procedure section 581a; and (2) that the action was barred by Labor Code section 3601.

The trial court refused to dismiss the action under section 581a holding that the filing of respondent's answers to interrogatories on March 2, 1970, had constituted a general appearance. . . . Respondent's demurrer was sustained with leave to amend on the ground that facts sufficient to state a cause of action under Labor Code section 3601, subdivision (a)(3) had not been alleged.

Respondent demurred to appellant's first and second amended complaints on the grounds that a cause of action under Labor Code section 3601, subdivision (a)(3) had still not been stated and that the action was barred by the statute of limitations. (Code Civ. Proc., § 340.) The court sustained the demurrers, the latter without leave to amend, "pursuant to points and authorities filed." Thus, the first issue presented is whether or not the second amended complaint alleges facts sufficient to state a cause of action.

The Complaint Does Set Forth Facts Sufficient to State a Cause of Action.

The earlier versions of the complaint charged respondent with negligence and reckless disregard for the safety of others. Since this action is subject to the provisions of Labor Code section 3601, above quoted, they were manifestly insufficient to state a claim, for they failed to allege the "calculated and conscious willingness to permit injury or death" required by the statute.

In an effort to remedy the indicated deficiency, the second amended complaint, the charging allegations of which are set forth in full in the margin, included an allegation cast in the words of the statute. Citing the rule that allegations of "willful misconduct" require that the facts must be stated more fully than in ordinary negligence cases (Snider v. Whitson, 184 Cal. App.2d 211 [7 Cal. Rptr. 353]), respondent contends that the complaint must be held inadequate.

No cases dealing precisely with the question before the court have been cited, nor has our independent investigation uncovered any, and so our inquiry must necessarily be rooted in general principles.

It is well settled that "[i]n considering the sufficiency of a pleading, we are bound by the rule that on appeal from a judgment entered on demurrer, the allegations of the complaint must be liberally construed with a view to attaining substantial justice among the parties. (Code Civ. Proc., § 452.)" Obviously, the complaint must be read as a whole and each part must be given the meaning it derives from the total context wherein it appears.

The Supreme Court has consistently stated the guideline that "a plaintiff is required only to set forth the essential facts of his case with reasonable precision and with particularity sufficient to acquaint a defendant with the nature, source and extent of his cause of action." It has also been stated that "[t]he particularity required in pleading facts depends on the extent to which the defendant in fairness needs detailed information that can be conveniently provided by the plaintiff; less particularity is required where the defendant may be assumed to have knowledge of the facts equal to that possessed by the plaintiff.".) This seems particularly applicable to a wrongful death action where none of the plaintiff-heirs was present at the site of the fatal injury.

Finally, it must be noted that the modern discovery procedures necessarily affect the amount of detail that should be required in a pleading.

Applying these principles to the case at bar, we hold that the complaint, though hardly a model of pleading, stated a cause of action. The statutory requirement is that the death be caused by a fellow-employee's act "which evinces a reckless disregard for the safety of the employee injured, and a calculated and conscious willingness to permit injury or death to such employee." (Lab. Code, § 3601, subd. (a)(3).) In substance, the complaint alleges that respondent failed to inspect the area into which he was backing and that he acted with the state of mind required by the statute.

Respondent contends that paragraph X of the complaint is only a characterization — a conclusion of law — with no additional factual support. "The distinction between conclusions of law and ultimate facts is not at all clear and involves at most a matter of degree. For example, the courts have permitted allegations which obviously included conclusions of law and have termed them 'ultimate facts' or 'conclusions of fact.'"

In Smith v. Kern County Land Co., supra, 51 Cal.2d 205, the issue was whether an allegation that defendant "desired and wished" that plaintiff come onto his land to remove tree stumps and roots was a sufficient averment of plaintiff's status as an invitee, not a licensee. The Supreme Court ruled, . . . "This allegation is not, as defendant contends, a mere conclusion of law. The cases it relies on are readily distinguishable. Wheeler v. Oppenheimer, 140 Cal. App.2d 497 [295 P.2d 128], held only that the technical term 'bad faith' was a conclusion of law. Faulkner v. California Toll Bridge Authority, 40 Cal.2d 317 [253 P.2d 659], held to be legal conclusions the allegations that an investigation was 'insufficient' and that acts were 'arbitrary, capricious, fraudulent, wrongful and unlawful.' The applicability of each of these words depends on more than, as in the case at bar, the mere presence of a state of mind."

The pleading in the case at bar is not as clearly susceptible to that distinction as the pleading in Smith. But we do feel that the allegation here possesses enough of a factual thrust that we cannot agree with respondent's contention that it is only a characterization that adds no additional factual support.

In Jones v. Oxnard School Dist., 270 Cal. App.2d 587, 593 [75 Cal. Rptr. 836], the court stated: "The applicable principle is that the 'conclusion of law — ultimate fact' dichotomy is not an absolute but that the fair import of language used in the pleading must be received to determine whether the adversary has been fairly apprised of the factual basis of the claim against him." That, we think, places the dichotomy in its proper perspective. . . .

Careau & Co. v. Security Pacific Business Credit, Inc.
222 Cal.App.3d 1371 (1990)

CROSKEY, J.

. . .Plaintiffs appeal from a judgment which was based upon an order sustaining demurrers without leave to amend. . .

. . .At the heart of these consolidated actions is the effort to finance the purchase of an egg production facility in Moorpark, California, known as Julius Goldman's Egg City (Egg City). Plaintiffs, or at least one of the plaintiffs, sought to purchase Egg City and sought funding of $13 million from defendants. This financing never materialized and plaintiffs were allegedly unable to make the purchase until a new lender was found. They eventually obtained the necessary funding elsewhere, but on less desirable terms. Plaintiffs filed these actions, contending, . . .that defendants breached oral and written contracts. . . .

[T]he defendants filed demurrers to the first amended complaints. . . all the demurrers were sustained without leave to amend. . . .

3. Whether the Complaints Plead Sufficient Facts to State a Cause of Action on Any Theory
a. Claims Based on Contract
(1) Written or Oral Contract

In their first two counts plaintiffs have attempted to plead the breach of both the written and an oral contract. However, they rely upon the same allegations for each and we see no need to distinguish between them.

A cause of action for damages for breach of contract is comprised of the following elements: (1) the contract, (2) plaintiff's performance or excuse for nonperformance, (3) defendant's breach, and (4) the resulting damages to plaintiff. What plaintiffs have failed to do here is adequately allege the due satisfaction of several conditions precedent to the formation of a binding contract.

Plaintiffs assert that the letter of August 25 sets forth the terms of a contractual commitment to provide financing. While they acknowledge that the letter contains some conditions, they argue that they have alleged sufficient facts to demonstrate, at least for pleading purposes, that each of such conditions has been satisfied, waived or excused. Defendants, on the other hand, argue that the letter is tentative and nothing more than an expression of intent subject to many conditions, the satisfaction of which plaintiffs have not alleged.

On its face, the August 25 letter is a conditional agreement to provide financing if certain "conditions precedent" are met. The conditions listed are both specific and substantial. In addition, the letter refers to financial, legal and collateral investigations which remain to be completed and expressly anticipates the possibility that a loan will not be made; and, as already discussed, the letter expressly cautions that since it is subject to so many conditions which obviously had not been satisfied as of August 25, "it should not be relied upon by any third party as a final commitment to make a loan." As the court noted in Kruse v. Bank of America (1988) 202 Cal. App.3d 38 [248 Cal. Rptr. 217], "Preliminary negotiations or an agreement for future negotiations are not the functional equivalent of a valid, subsisting agreement. `A manifestation of willingness to enter into a bargain is not an offer if the person to whom it is addressed knows or has reason to know that the person making it does not intend to conclude a bargain until he has made a further manifestation of assent.' [Citation.]" (Id., at p. 59.)

Where contractual liability depends upon the satisfaction or performance of one or more conditions precedent, the allegation of such satisfaction or performance is an essential part of the cause of action. This requirement can be satisfied by allegations in general terms. It is sufficient for a plaintiff to simply allege that he has "duly performed all the conditions on his part." (Code Civ. Proc., § 457.) However, this rule is subject to two important caveats, both of which are applicable here.

First, where the condition is an event, as distinguished from an act to be performed by the plaintiff, a specific allegation of the happening of the condition is a necessary part of pleading the defendant's breach. Second, general pleadings are controlled by specific allegations. Thus, a general allegation of due performance will not suffice if the plaintiff also sets forth what has actually occurred and such specific facts do not constitute due performance.

For example, where plaintiff alleges a permissible conclusion of law such as the due performance of a condition precedent but also avers specific additional facts which either do not support such conclusion, or are inconsistent therewith, such specific allegations will control "and a complaint which might have been sufficient with general allegations alone may be rendered defective...."

When we apply these rules to plaintiffs' pleadings we are forced to conclude that they have failed to state a cause of action for breach of contract. There are no specific allegations of the performance of any of the conditions. Although this is their third pleading effort, all plaintiffs have alleged is that conditions "had been met and satisfied" and "defendants were fully satisfied that the conditions had been met" and "all conditions precedent ... had either been met and satisfied or waived or excused...." These are simply general conclusions. However, since at least six of the eight conditions were events which had to exist or occur, and not simply acts to be performed by plaintiffs, such general allegations are not adequate.

Nor are plaintiffs' contract claims saved by the allegations of the oral statements attributed to Torres, the officer of SPBC with whom they were dealing. Plaintiffs rely on Torres's statements as a sufficient specific allegation of due performance but unfortunately all that plaintiffs have done is beg the question.

While those statements may be some evidence that one or more conditions were satisfied, they do not constitute the direct, specific allegation of performance which is required. A complaint must allege the ultimate facts necessary to the statement of an actionable claim. It is both improper and insufficient for a plaintiff to simply plead the evidence by which he hopes to prove such ultimate facts. Here, plaintiffs rely heavily on their allegations that Torres had stated to Carrott and others that "the loan commitment had been approved by SPBC" (and other conclusionary statements as to the satisfaction of one or more conditions). These allegations do not demonstrate due performance. If at trial a jury were to find that Torres had indeed made such statements, that would not be the equivalent of a finding that any of the conditions in the August 25 letter had been satisfied, excused or waived. It would only mean that it was true that Torres had said certain things about them.

This is obviously more than a quibble. If plaintiffs, after four years of substantial discovery and three separate pleadings, can allege nothing more than they have, then we have serious doubts that they can truthfully allege that any of the conditions were satisfied. All they have done is allege that Torres made certain statements which they contend constitute an excuse or waiver of performance. However, such conclusory allegations are not sufficient. The pleading of excuse or waiver of performance of conditions precedent requires specific not general allegations. Thus, plaintiffs have failed to adequately allege a cause of action for the breach of either a written or an oral agreement. Their failure to sufficiently allege the satisfaction of several significant, if not critical, conditions precedent to any obligation on the part of SPBC to provide financing is fatal to their contract claims.

These pleading defects are at once matters of both form and substance. However, we cannot conclude, without effectively resolving a factual issue, that there is no reasonable possibility of plaintiffs making the direct allegations necessary to demonstrate the existence of a binding contract. On appeal, it is not our task to be concerned with the possible difficulty or inability of proving such allegations. Therefore, it is appropriate that plaintiffs be given the opportunity to correct the specific pleading errors we have described. It was therefore error to sustain a demurrer to these contract counts without leave to amend.

Summarizing Semole and Careau

So what do the previous two cases teach us about pleading in California? We know that to be sufficient as a complaint, the complaint must allege "ultimate" facts as opposed to legal conclusions. On the other hand, "evidentiary" facts are not sufficient. What are the distinctions between "ultimate" facts, conclusions of law and "evidentiary" facts?

In California, the state's Judicial Council has approved Official Form Pleadings (complaints, cross-complaints and answers) for optional use for several of the basic causes of action. (Code Civ.Proc., §425.12.). (An example appears beginning on the following pages.)

Chapter 4 PLEADING

PLD-PI-001

ATTORNEY OR PARTY WITHOUT ATTORNEY (Name, State Bar number, and address):	FOR COURT USE ONLY
TELEPHONE NO: FAX NO. (Optional): E-MAIL ADDRESS (Optional): ATTORNEY FOR (Name):	
SUPERIOR COURT OF CALIFORNIA, COUNTY OF STREET ADDRESS: MAILING ADDRESS: CITY AND ZIP CODE: BRANCH NAME:	
PLAINTIFF: DEFENDANT: ☐ DOES 1 TO _____	

COMPLAINT—Personal Injury, Property Damage, Wrongful Death
 ☐ **AMENDED** *(Number):*
 Type *(check all that apply):*
 ☐ **MOTOR VEHICLE**   ☐ **OTHER** *(specify):*
     ☐ **Property Damage**   ☐ **Wrongful Death**
     ☐ **Personal Injury**   ☐ **Other Damages** *(specify):*
	CASE NUMBER:

Jurisdiction *(check all that apply):*
 ☐ **ACTION IS A LIMITED CIVIL CASE**
    Amount demanded   ☐ does not exceed $10,000
                           ☐ exceeds $10,000, but does not exceed $25,000
 ☐ **ACTION IS AN UNLIMITED CIVIL CASE (exceeds $25,000)**
 ☐ **ACTION IS RECLASSIFIED** by this amended complaint
     ☐ from limited to unlimited
     ☐ from unlimited to limited	

1. **Plaintiff** *(name or names):*

   alleges causes of action against **defendant** *(name or names):*

2. This pleading, including attachments and exhibits, consists of the following number of pages:
3. Each plaintiff named above is a competent adult
   a. ☐ **except** plaintiff *(name):*
      - (1) ☐ a corporation qualified to do business in California
      - (2) ☐ an unincorporated entity *(describe):*
      - (3) ☐ a public entity *(describe):*
      - (4) ☐ a minor   ☐ an adult
        - (a) ☐ for whom a guardian or conservator of the estate or a guardian ad litem has been appointed
        - (b) ☐ other *(specify):*
      - (5) ☐ other *(specify):*
   b. ☐ **except** plaintiff *(name):*
      - (1) ☐ a corporation qualified to do business in California
      - (2) ☐ an unincorporated entity *(describe):*
      - (3) ☐ a public entity *(describe):*
      - (4) ☐ a minor   ☐ an adult
        - (a) ☐ for whom a guardian or conservator of the estate or a guardian ad litem has been appointed
        - (b) ☐ other *(specify):*
      - (5) ☐ other *(specify):*

   ☐ Information about additional plaintiffs who are not competent adults is shown in Attachment 3.

Page 1 of 3

Form Approved for Optional Use
 Judicial Council of California
 PLD-PI-001 [Rev. January 1, 2007]

COMPLAINT—Personal Injury, Property Damage, Wrongful Death

Code of Civil Procedure, § 425.12 <br> www.courtinfo.ca.gov

SHORT TITLE:	CASE NUMBER:

PLD-PI-001

4. ☐ Plaintiff *(name):*
   is doing business under the fictitious name *(specify):*

   and has complied with the fictitious business name laws.
5. Each defendant named above is a natural person
   a. ☐ **except** defendant *(name):*
      (1) ☐ a business organization, form unknown
      (2) ☐ a corporation
      (3) ☐ an unincorporated entity *(describe):*

      (4) ☐ a public entity *(describe):*

      (5) ☐ other *(specify):*

   c. ☐ **except** defendant *(name):*
      (1) ☐ a business organization, form unknown
      (2) ☐ a corporation
      (3) ☐ an unincorporated entity *(describe):*

      (4) ☐ a public entity *(describe):*

      (5) ☐ other *(specify):*

   b. ☐ **except** defendant *(name):*
      (1) ☐ a business organization, form unknown
      (2) ☐ a corporation
      (3) ☐ an unincorporated entity *(describe):*

      (4) ☐ a public entity *(describe):*

      (5) ☐ other *(specify):*

   d. ☐ **except** defendant *(name):*
      (1) ☐ a business organization, form unknown
      (2) ☐ a corporation
      (3) ☐ an unincorporated entity *(describe):*

      (4) ☐ a public entity *(describe):*

      (5) ☐ other *(specify):*

   ☐ Information about additional defendants who are not natural persons is contained in Attachment 5.
6. The true names of defendants sued as Does are unknown to plaintiff.
   a. ☐ Doe defendants *(specify Doe numbers):* _____ were the agents or employees of other named defendants and acted within the scope of that agency or employment.
   b. ☐ Doe defendants *(specify Doe numbers):* _____ are persons whose capacities are unknown to plaintiff.
7. ☐ Defendants who are joined under Code of Civil Procedure section 382 are *(names):*

8. This court is the proper court because
   a. ☐ at least one defendant now resides in its jurisdictional area.
   b. ☐ the principal place of business of a defendant corporation or unincorporated association is in its jurisdictional area.
   c. ☐ injury to person or damage to personal property occurred in its jurisdictional area.
   d. ☐ other *(specify):*

9. ☐ Plaintiff is required to comply with a claims statute, **and**
   a. ☐ has complied with applicable claims statutes, **or**
   b. ☐ is excused from complying because *(specify):*

COMPLAINT—Personal Injury, Property Damage, Wrongful Death

                                                                              PLD-PI-001

SHORT TITLE: CASE NUMBER:

10. The following causes of action are attached and the statements above apply to each *(each complaint must have one or more causes of action attached)*:
    a. ☐ Motor Vehicle
    b. ☐ General Negligence
    c. ☐ Intentional Tort
    d. ☐ Products Liability
    e. ☐ Premises Liability
    f. ☐ Other *(specify)*:

11. Plaintiff has suffered
    a. ☐ wage loss
    b. ☐ loss of use of property
    c. ☐ hospital and medical expenses
    d. ☐ general damage
    e. ☐ property damage
    f. ☐ loss of earning capacity
    g. ☐ other damage *(specify)*:

12. ☐ The damages claimed for wrongful death and the relationships of plaintiff to the deceased are
    a. ☐ listed in Attachment 12.
    b. ☐ as follows:

13. The relief sought in this complaint is within the jurisdiction of this court.

14. **Plaintiff prays** for judgment for costs of suit; for such relief as is fair, just, and equitable; and for
    a. (1) ☐ compensatory damages
       (2) ☐ punitive damages
       The amount of damages is *(in cases for personal injury or wrongful death, you must check (1))*:
       (1) ☐ according to proof
       (2) ☐ in the amount of: $

15. ☐ The paragraphs of this complaint alleged on information and belief are as follows *(specify paragraph numbers)*:

Date:

▶

_____   _____
(TYPE OR PRINT NAME)   (SIGNATURE OF PLAINTIFF OR ATTORNEY)

PLD-PI-001 [Rev. January 1, 2007]   **COMPLAINT—Personal Injury, Property Damage, Wrongful Death**   Page 3 of 3

But does using the official form pleadings guarantee that the causes of action alleged can't be demurred to? For the answer to that question, read the next case.

The People Ex Rel. Department of Transportation, v. Superior Court
5 Cal.App.4th 1480 (1992)

GILBERT, J.

Are Judicial Council form complaints invulnerable to a demurrer? No.

Real parties in interest used a form complaint to state a cause of action against a governmental entity. The governmental entity demurred. The trial court overruled the demurrer on the ground that a Judicial Council form complaint is immune from attack by way of demurrer. We conclude otherwise. A Judicial Council form complaint may be subject to demurrer. We therefore grant a writ of mandate.

FACTS

Petitioner, State of California, Department of Transportation (CalTrans) is a defendant in this lawsuit. Real parties are the plaintiffs. They filed their complaint on a form prepared by the Judicial Council. In their complaint, they alleged that CalTrans maintained public property in a dangerous condition. They also alleged that on January 12, 1990, a traffic collision occurred on Highway 101, and that real parties have suffered personal injuries as a result of the collision.

A section of the form complaint with the heading "Prem.L-1." provides space for a plaintiff to fulfill the requirement to supply a "description of premises and circumstances of injury."

Real parties describe the circumstances of the injury as follows: "U.S. Highway 101 approximately 1,652 feet north of the Arroyo Hondo Bridge in the County of Santa Barbara, State of California. Plaintiff Ernesto Verdeja was driving his 1979 Datsun northbound at said time and place. Plaintiffs Elizabeth Hernandez and Luis Fabian Hernandez were passengers in his car. Another vehicle driven by defendant Seth R. Wood traveling southbound crossed over the dirt center divider and struck plaintiff's vehicle head-on."

On October 17, 1991, CalTrans filed a demurrer to the first amended complaint. It claimed that the complaint did not set forth adequate "`circumstances of injury'" and "`reasons for liability'" as required in a suit for dangerous condition of public property. (See Code Civ. Proc., § 425.10; Gov. Code, § 835.)

On November 6, 1991, the superior court judge overruled the demurrer. In making his ruling, the judge said, "I will make it easy. Regardless of its deficiencies and by whatever else the Code of Civil Procedure or prior Supreme Court or Court of Appeal rules have given us as to the sufficiency of pleadings, all this aside, if you use a Judicial Council form, it is nondemurrable. Okay. That is my order and take it up, please."

CalTrans followed this advice and seeks a writ of mandate. . . .

CalTrans points out that claims for damages against governmental entities must be pled with specificity. Its position is that the adoption of official forms has not relieved the parties from alleging the ultimate facts that are essential to state a cause of action.. . . Therefore, the demurrer should have been sustained without leave to amend.

DISCUSSION

Government Code section 68511 provides that "[t]he Judicial Council may prescribe by rule the form and content of forms used in the courts of this state." (See also Code Civ. Proc., § 425.12.) The Judicial Council has adopted a pleading form for a complaint for personal injury. (Cal. Rules of Court, rule 982.1.)

The Judicial Council pleading forms have simplified the art of pleading and have made the task of drafting much easier. Nevertheless, in some cases more is required than merely placing an "X" in a box. "Adoption of Official Forms for the most common civil actions has not changed the statutory requirement that the complaint contain `facts constituting the cause of action.'" Thus, in order to be demurrer-proof, a form "complaint must contain whatever ultimate facts are essential to state a cause of action under existing statutes or case law."

A cause of action for dangerous condition of public property must allege:
1. a dangerous condition of public property;
2. a proximate causal connection between the condition and the injury sustained;
3. a reasonably foreseeable risk that the kind of injury that occurred would result from the dangerous condition; and
4. the entity either created the condition or had actual notice or constructive notice of its existence, and there was sufficient time before the injury for it to have taken remedial action.

Real parties have merely alleged that a motorist crossed a dirt median of Highway 101 and struck their vehicle.

Real parties argue that the "inescapable conclusion from the allegations of paragraph Prem.L-1 is `but for' the failure by CalTrans to properly isolate the north and southbound lanes of Highway 101 in the vicinity of the accident, the head-on collision would not have occurred." They believe that the existence of a median barrier would have prevented the accident.

It is true that the allegations in a complaint must be liberally construed. (Code Civ. Proc., § 452.) It is also true that "`... the essence is fairness in pleading in order to give the defendant sufficient notice of the cause of action stated against him so that he will be able to prepare his case Therefore, we must not so liberally construe the allegations of the complaint so as to deny the defendant adequate notice to defend the case.

A while ago, Justice Field lamented, "in numerous instances before us, pleadings [are] filled with recitals, digressions and stories, which only tend to prolixity and obscurity." The Judicial Council went a long way in answering Justice Field's lament. Brevity is the soul of a well-pled complaint. Providing too many details obscures rather than enlightens. On the other hand, too little information confounds and obfuscates. In either case the environment is cloudy and justice cannot shine.

The problem with the allegations in Prem.L-1 is that they do not tell enough. Real parties argue that the allegations necessarily indicate the absence of a barrier contributed to the accident. Although that may be a possible inference to draw from the allegations, it is not the only one. The median may have had nothing to do with the accident. For example, other factors, such as a wet or slick highway, could have contributed to the accident.

Real parties have an obligation to give CalTrans more information. The complaint fails to tell CalTrans in what manner the existence of the dirt median was hazardous. It fails to state whether a proper median barrier was lacking, and it fails to inform CalTrans about the nature of the relationship between the condition of the median and the injuries suffered by real parties.

Relief against a public entity is limited to those theories set forth in the complaint. Here, the inadequate pleadings prevent CalTrans from determining under what theory real parties are seeking relief. This deprives CalTrans of certain possible defenses. It also prevents CalTrans from determining whether real parties' basis for recovery is at variance with their Board of Control claim.

In some cases, merely checking a box on a Judicial Council form complaint will be sufficient. In other cases, such as this one, where specific allegations need be alleged, the form complaint is like a partially completed painting. It is up to the pleader to add the details that complete the picture. The form complaint here, standing alone, is no more immune to demurrer than any other complaint that fails to meet essential pleading requirements to state a cause of action.

CONCLUSION

Let a writ of mandate issue commanding respondent superior court to set aside its order overruling the demurrer and to enter a new order sustaining the demurrer with leave to amend.

PLEADING UNDER THE FEDERAL RULES

Rather than adopt the often-byzantine system of code pleading, federal courts use notice pleading which under FRCP 8 requires only a "short and plain statement showing that the pleader is entitled to relief." Stated another way, a complaint was sufficient and would survive a motion to dismiss pursuant to FRCP 12(b)(6) as long as it gave defendant "fair notice of what the plaintiff's claim is and the grounds upon which it rests. (*Conley v. Gibson*, 355 U.S. 41, 47.) However, notice pleading has recently fallen into disfavor with the U.S. Supreme Court. Consider the following two cases.

Bell Atlantic Corp. v. Twombly
550 U.S. 544 (2007)

Justice SOUTER delivered the opinion of the Court.

Liability under § 1 of the Sherman Act, 15 U.S.C. § 1, requires a "contract, combination ..., or conspiracy, in restraint of trade or commerce." The question in this putative class action is whether a § 1 complaint can survive a motion to dismiss when it alleges that major telecommunications providers engaged in certain parallel conduct unfavorable to competition, absent some factual context suggesting agreement, as distinct from identical, independent action. We hold that such a complaint should be dismissed...

Respondents William Twombly and Lawrence Marcus (hereinafter plaintiffs) represent a putative class consisting of all "subscribers of local telephone and/or high-speed internet services ... from February 8, 1996 to present." In this action against petitioners, a group of "Incumbent Local Exchange Carriers" (ILECs) plaintiffs seek treble damages and declaratory and injunctive relief for claimed violations of § 1 of the Sherman Act, ch. 647, 26 Stat. 209, as amended, 15 U.S.C. § 1, which prohibits "[e]very contract, combination in the form of trust or otherwise, or conspiracy, in restraint of trade or commerce among the several States, or with foreign nations."

The complaint alleges that the ILECs conspired to restrain trade in two ways, each supposedly inflating charges for local telephone and high-speed Internet services. Plaintiffs say, first, that the ILECs "engaged in parallel conduct" in their respective service areas to inhibit the growth of upstart "competitive local exchange carriers"

(CLECs.) Their actions allegedly included making unfair agreements with the CLECs for access to ILEC networks, providing inferior connections to the networks, overcharging, and billing in ways designed to sabotage the CLECs' relations with their own customers. According to the complaint, the ILECs' "compelling common motivatio[n]" to thwart the CLECs' competitive efforts naturally led them to form a conspiracy; "[h]ad any one [ILEC] not sought to prevent CLECs ... from competing effectively..., the resulting greater competitive inroads into that [ILEC's] territory would have revealed the degree to which competitive entry by CLECs would have been successful in the other territories in the absence of such conduct."

Second, the complaint charges agreements by the ILECs to refrain from competing against one another. These are to be inferred from the ILECs' common failure "meaningfully [to] pursu[e]" "attractive business opportunit[ies]" in contiguous markets where they possessed "substantial competitive advantages," id., ¶¶ 40-41, App. 21-22, and from a statement of Richard Notebaert, chief executive officer (CEO) of the ILEC Qwest, that competing in the territory of another ILEC "`might be a good way to turn a quick dollar but that doesn't make it right,'" id., ¶ 42, App. 22.

The complaint couches its ultimate allegations this way:

"In the absence of any meaningful competition between the [ILECs] in one another's markets, and in light of the parallel course of conduct that each engaged in to prevent competition from CLECs within their respective local telephone and/or high speed internet services markets and the other facts and market circumstances alleged above, Plaintiffs allege upon information and belief that [the ILECs] have entered into a contract, combination or conspiracy to prevent competitive entry in their respective local telephone and/or high speed internet services markets and have agreed not to compete with one another and otherwise allocated customers and markets to one another."

The United States District Court for the Southern District of New York dismissed the complaint for failure to state a claim upon which relief can be granted. The District Court acknowledged that "plaintiffs may allege a conspiracy by citing instances of parallel business behavior that suggest an agreement," but emphasized that "while `[c]ircumstantial evidence of consciously parallel behavior may have made heavy inroads into the traditional judicial attitude toward conspiracy[,...] "conscious parallelism" has not yet read conspiracy out of the Sherman Act entirely.'" 313 F.Supp.2d 174, 179 (2003) (quoting Theatre Enterprises, Inc. v. Paramount Film Distributing Corp., 346 U.S. 537, 541, 74 S.Ct. 257, 98 L.Ed. 273 (1954); alterations in original). Thus, the District Court understood that allegations of parallel business conduct, taken alone, do not state a claim under § 1; plaintiffs must allege additional facts that "ten[d] to exclude independent self-interested conduct as an explanation for defendants' parallel behavior." 313 F.Supp.2d, at 179. The District Court found plaintiffs' allegations of parallel ILEC actions to discourage competition inadequate because "the behavior of each ILEC in resisting the incursion of CLECs is fully explained by the ILEC's own interests in defending its individual territory." . . .

The Court of Appeals for the Second Circuit reversed, holding that the District Court tested the complaint by the wrong standard. It held that "plus factors are not required to be pleaded to permit an antitrust claim based on parallel conduct to survive dismissal." Although the Court of Appeals took the view that plaintiffs must plead facts that "include conspiracy among the realm of 'plausible' possibilities in order to survive a motion to dismiss," it then said that "to rule that allegations of parallel anticompetitive conduct fail to support a plausible conspiracy claim, a court would have to conclude that there is no set of facts that would permit a plaintiff to demonstrate that the particular parallelism asserted was the product of collusion rather than coincidence."

We granted certiorari to address the proper standard for pleading an antitrust conspiracy through allegations of parallel conduct and now reverse. . . .

This case presents the antecedent question of what a plaintiff must plead in order to state a claim under § 1 of the Sherman Act. Federal Rule of Civil Procedure 8(a)(2) requires only "a short and plain statement of the claim showing that the pleader is entitled to relief," in order to "give the defendant fair notice of what the ... claim is and the grounds upon which it rests," Conley v. Gibson, 355 U.S. 41, 47, 78 S.Ct. 99, 2 L.Ed.2d 80 (1957). While a complaint attacked by a Rule 12(b)(6) motion to dismiss does not need detailed factual allegations, a plaintiffs obligation to provide the "grounds" of his "entitle[ment] to relief" requires more than labels and conclusions, and a formulaic recitation of the elements of a cause of action will not do, Factual allegations must be enough to raise a right to relief above the speculative level, ("[T]he pleading must contain something more ... than ... a statement of facts that merely creates a suspicion [of] a legally cognizable right of action"), on the assumption that all the allegations in the complaint are true (even if doubtful in fact), ("Rule 12(b)(6) does not countenance ... dismissals based on a judge's disbelief of a complaint's factual allegations"); Scheuer v. Rhodes, 416 U.S. 232, 236, 94 S.Ct. 1683, 40 L.Ed.2d 90 (1974) (a well-pleaded complaint may proceed even if it appears "that a recovery is very remote and unlikely").

In applying these general standards to a § 1 claim, we hold that stating such a claim requires a complaint with enough factual matter (taken as true) to suggest that an agreement was made. Asking for plausible grounds to infer an agreement does not impose a probability requirement at the pleading stage; it simply calls for enough fact to raise a reasonable expectation that discovery will reveal evidence of illegal agreement. And, of course, a well-pleaded complaint may proceed even if it strikes a savvy judge that actual proof of those facts is improbable, and "that a recovery is very remote and unlikely." Ibid. In identifying facts that are suggestive enough to render a § 1 conspiracy plausible, we have the benefit of the prior rulings and considered views of leading commentators, already quoted, that lawful parallel conduct fails to be-speak unlawful agreement. It makes sense to say, therefore, that an allegation of parallel conduct and a bare assertion of conspiracy will not suffice. Without more, parallel conduct does not suggest conspiracy, and a conclusory allegation of agreement at some unidentified point does not supply facts adequate to show illegality. Hence, when allegations of parallel conduct are set out in order to make a § 1 claim, they must be placed in a context that raises a suggestion of a preceding agreement, not merely parallel conduct that could just as well be independent action.

The need at the pleading stage for allegations plausibly suggesting (not merely consistent with) agreement reflects the threshold requirement of Rule 8(a)(2) that the "plain statement" possess enough heft to "sho[w] that the pleader is entitled to relief." A statement of parallel conduct, even conduct consciously undertaken, needs some setting suggesting the agreement necessary to make out a § 1 claim; without that further circumstance pointing toward a meeting of the minds, an account of a defendant's commercial efforts stays in neutral territory. An allegation of parallel conduct is thus much like a naked assertion of conspiracy in a § 1 complaint: it gets the complaint close to stating a claim, but without some further factual enhancement it stops short of the line between possibility and plausibility of "entitle[ment] to relief." ("[T]erms like `conspiracy,' or even `agreement,' are border-line: they might well be sufficient in conjunction with a more specific allegation — for example, identifying a written agreement or even a basis for inferring a tacit agreement, ... but a court is not required to accept such terms as a sufficient basis for a complaint"). . . .

[A] good many judges and commentators have balked at taking the literal terms of the Conley passage as a pleading standard.). . .

. . . Conley's "no set of facts" language has been questioned, criticized, and explained away long enough. To be fair to the Conley Court, the passage should be understood in light of the opinion's preceding summary of the complaint's concrete allegations, which the Court quite reasonably understood as amply stating a claim for relief. But the passage so often quoted fails to mention this understanding on the part of the Court, and after puzzling the profession for 50 years, this famous observation has earned its retirement. The phrase is best forgotten as an incomplete, negative gloss on an accepted pleading standard: once a claim has been stated adequately, it may be supported by showing any set of facts consistent with the allegations in the complaint. Conley, then, described the breadth of opportunity to prove what an adequate complaint claims, not the minimum standard of adequate pleading to govern a complaint's survival.

When we look for plausibility in this complaint, we agree with the District Court that plaintiffs' claim of conspiracy in restraint of trade comes up short. To begin with, the complaint leaves no doubt that plaintiffs rest their § 1 claim on descriptions of parallel conduct and not on any independent allegation of actual agreement among the ILECs. Supra, at 1962-1963. Although in form a few stray statements speak directly of agreement, on fair reading these are merely legal conclusions resting on the prior allegations. Thus, the complaint first takes account of the alleged "absence of any meaningful competition between [the ILECs] in one another's markets," "the parallel course of conduct that each [ILEC] engaged in to prevent competition from CLECs," "and the other facts and market circumstances alleged [earlier]"; "in light of" these, the complaint concludes "that [the ILECs] have entered into a contract, combination or conspiracy to prevent competitive entry into their ... markets and have agreed not to compete with one another." The nub of the complaint, then, is the ILECs' parallel behavior, consisting of steps to keep the CLECs out and manifest disinterest in becoming CLECs themselves, and its sufficiency turns on the suggestions raised by this conduct when viewed in light of common economic experience . . .

Because the plaintiffs here have not nudged their claims across the line from conceivable to plausible, their complaint must be dismissed.

The judgment of the Court of Appeals for the Second Circuit is reversed, and the case is remanded for further proceedings consistent with this opinion.

Ashcroft v. Iqbal
556 U.S. 662 (2009)

Justice KENNEDY delivered the opinion of the Court.

Javaid Iqbal (hereinafter respondent) is a citizen of Pakistan and a Muslim. In the wake of the September 11, 2001, terrorist attacks he was arrested in the United States on criminal charges and detained by federal officials. Respondent claims he was deprived of various constitutional protections while in federal custody. To redress the alleged deprivations, respondent filed a complaint against numerous federal officials, including John Ashcroft, the former Attorney General of the United States, and Robert Mueller, the Director of the Federal Bureau of Investigation (FBI). Ashcroft and Mueller are the petitioners in the case now before us. As to these two petitioners, the complaint alleges that they adopted an unconstitutional policy that subjected respondent to harsh conditions of confinement on account of his race, religion, or national origin.

In the District Court petitioners raised the defense of qualified immunity and moved to dismiss the suit, contending the complaint was not sufficient to state a claim against them. The District Court denied the motion to dismiss, concluding the complaint was sufficient to state a claim despite petitioners' official status at the times in question. Petitioners brought an interlocutory appeal in the Court of Appeals for the Second Circuit. The court, without discussion, assumed it had jurisdiction over the order denying the motion to dismiss; and it affirmed the District Court's decision.

Respondent's account of his prison ordeal could, if proved, demonstrate unconstitutional misconduct by some governmental actors. But the allegations and pleadings with respect to these actors are not before us here. This case instead turns on a narrower question: Did respondent, as the plaintiff in the District Court, plead factual matter that, if taken as true, states a claim that petitioners deprived him of his clearly established constitutional rights. We hold respondent's pleadings are insufficient. . . .

The 21-cause-of-action complaint does not challenge respondent's arrest or his confinement in the MDC's general prison population. Rather, it concentrates on his treatment while confined to the ADMAX SHU. The complaint sets forth various claims against defendants who are not before us. For instance, the complaint alleges that respondent's jailors "kicked him in the stomach, punched him in the face, and dragged him across" his cell without justification, subjected him to serial strip and body-cavity searches when he posed no safety risk to himself or others and refused to let him and other Muslims pray because there would be "[n]o prayers for terrorists,"

The allegations against petitioners are the only ones relevant here. The complaint contends that petitioners designated respondent a person of high interest on account of his race, religion, or national origin, in contravention of the First and Fifth Amendments to the Constitution. The complaint alleges that "the [FBI], under the direction of Defendant MUELLER, arrested and detained thousands of Arab Muslim men ... as part of its investigation of the events of September 11." It further alleges that "[t]he policy of holding post-September-11th detainees in highly restrictive conditions of confinement until they were 'cleared' by the FBI was approved by Defendants ASHCROFT and MUELLER in discussions in the weeks after September 11, 2001." Lastly, the complaint posits that petitioners "each knew of, condoned, and willfully and maliciously agreed to subject" respondent to harsh conditions of confinement "as a matter of policy, solely on account of [his] religion, race, and/or national origin and for no legitimate penological interest." The pleading names Ashcroft as the "principal architect" of the policy,, and identifies Mueller as "instrumental in [its] adoption, promulgation, and implementation,"

Petitioners moved to dismiss the complaint for failure to state sufficient allegations to show their own involvement in clearly established unconstitutional conduct. The District Court denied their motion. Accepting all of the allegations in respondent's complaint as true, the court held that "it cannot be said that there [is] no set of facts on which [respondent] would be entitled to relief as against" petitioners. (relying on Conley v. Gibson, 355 U.S. 41, 78 S.Ct. 99, 2 L.Ed.2d 80 (1957)). Invoking the collateral-order doctrine petitioners filed an interlocutory appeal in the United States Court of Appeals for the Second Circuit. While that appeal was pending, this Court decided Bell Atlantic Corp. v. Twombly, 550 U.S. 544, 127 S.Ct. 1955, 167 L.Ed.2d 929 (2007), which discussed the standard for evaluating whether a complaint is sufficient to survive a motion to dismiss.

The Court of Appeals considered Twombly's applicability to this case. Acknowledging that Twombly retired the Conley no-set-of-facts test relied upon by the District Court, the Court of Appeals' opinion discussed at length how to apply this Court's "standard for assessing the adequacy of pleadings." It concluded that Twombly called for a "flexible 'plausibility standard,' which obliges a pleader to amplify a claim with some factual allegations in those contexts where such amplification is needed to render the claim plausible." Id., at 157-158. The court found that petitioners' appeal did not present one of "those contexts" requiring amplification. As a consequence, it held respondent's pleading adequate to allege petitioners' personal involvement in discriminatory decisions which, if true, violated clearly established constitutional law. . . .

We turn to respondent's complaint. Under Federal Rule of Civil Procedure 8(a)(2), a pleading must contain a "short and plain statement of the claim showing that the pleader is entitled to relief." As the Court held in Twombly, 550 U.S. 544, 127 S.Ct. 1955, 167 L.Ed.2d 929, the pleading standard Rule 8 announces does not require "detailed factual allegations," but it demands more than an unadorned, the-defendant-unlawfully-harmed-me accusation. A pleading that offers "labels and conclusions" or "a formulaic recitation of the elements of a cause of action will not do. "Nor does a complaint suffice if it tenders "naked assertion[s]" devoid of "further factual enhancement."

To survive a motion to dismiss, a complaint must contain sufficient factual matter, accepted as true, to "state a claim to relief that is plausible on its face." A claim has facial plausibility when the plaintiff pleads factual content that allows the court to draw the reasonable inference that the defendant is liable for the misconduct alleged. The plausibility standard is not akin to a "probability requirement," but it asks for more than a sheer possibility that a defendant has acted unlawfully. Ibid. Where a complaint pleads facts that are "merely consistent with" a defendant's liability, it "stops short of the line between possibility and plausibility of 'entitlement to relief.'"

Two working principles underlie our decision in Twombly. First, the tenet that a court must accept as true all of the allegations contained in a complaint is inapplicable to legal conclusions. Threadbare recitals of the elements of a cause of action, supported by mere conclusory statements, do not suffice. (Although for the purposes of a motion to dismiss we must take all of the factual allegations in the complaint as true, we "are not bound to accept as true a legal conclusion couched as a factual allegation" (internal quotation marks omitted)). Rule 8 marks a notable and generous departure from the hyper technical, code-pleading regime of a prior era, but it does not unlock the doors of discovery for a plaintiff armed with nothing more than conclusions. Second, only a complaint that states a plausible claim for relief survives a motion to dismiss. Determining whether a complaint states a plausible claim for relief will, as the Court of

Appeals observed, be a context-specific task that requires the reviewing court to draw on its judicial experience and common sense. But where the well-pleaded facts do not permit the court to infer more than the mere possibility of misconduct, the complaint has alleged — but it has not "show[n]" — "that the pleader is entitled to relief." Fed. Rule Civ. Proc. 8(a)(2).

In keeping with these principles a court considering a motion to dismiss can choose to begin by identifying pleadings that, because they are no more than conclusions, are not entitled to the assumption of truth. While legal conclusions can provide the framework of a complaint, they must be supported by factual allegations. When there are well-pleaded factual allegations, a court should assume their veracity and then determine whether they plausibly give rise to an entitlement to relief.

Our decision in Twombly illustrates the two-pronged approach. There, we considered the sufficiency of a complaint alleging that incumbent telecommunications providers had entered an agreement not to compete and to forestall competitive entry, in violation of the Sherman Act, 15 U.S.C. § 1. Recognizing that § 1 enjoins only anticompetitive conduct "effected by a contract, combination, or conspiracy," the plaintiffs in Twombly flatly pleaded that the defendants "ha[d] entered into a contract, combination or conspiracy to prevent competitive entry... and ha[d] agreed not to compete with one another." The complaint also alleged that the defendants' "parallel course of conduct ... to prevent competition" and inflate prices was indicative of the unlawful agreement alleged.

The Court held the plaintiffs' complaint deficient under Rule 8. In doing so it first noted that the plaintiffs' assertion of an unlawful agreement was a "'legal conclusion'" and, as such, was not entitled to the assumption of truth. Had the Court simply credited the allegation of a conspiracy, the plaintiffs would have stated a claim for relief and been entitled to proceed perforce. The Court next addressed the "nub" of the plaintiffs' complaint — the well-pleaded, nonconclusory factual allegation of parallel behavior — to determine whether it gave rise to a "plausible suggestion of conspiracy." Acknowledging that parallel conduct was consistent with an unlawful agreement, the Court nevertheless concluded that it did not plausibly suggest an illicit accord because it was not only compatible with, but indeed was more likely explained by, lawful, unchoreographed free-market behavior. Because the well-pleaded fact of parallel conduct, accepted as true, did not plausibly suggest an unlawful agreement, the Court held the plaintiffs' complaint must be dismissed.

Under Twombly's construction of Rule 8, we conclude that respondent's complaint has not "nudged [his] claims" of invidious discrimination "across the line from conceivable to plausible."

We begin our analysis by identifying the allegations in the complaint that are not entitled to the assumption of truth. Respondent pleads that petitioners "knew of, condoned, and willfully and maliciously agreed to subject [him]" to harsh conditions of confinement "as a matter of policy, solely on account of [his] religion, race, and/or national origin and for no legitimate penological interest." Complaint ¶ 96, App. to Pet. for Cert. 173a-174a. The complaint alleges that Ashcroft was the "principal architect" of this invidious policy, and that Mueller was "instrumental" in adopting and executing it, These bare assertions, much like the pleading of conspiracy in Twombly, amount to nothing more than a "formulaic recitation of the elements" of a constitutional discrimination claim, namely, that petitioners adopted a policy "`because of,' not merely `in spite of,' its adverse effects upon an identifiable group,". As such, the allegations are conclusory and not entitled to be assumed true. To be clear, we do not reject these bald allegations on the ground that they are unrealistic or nonsensical. We do not so characterize them any more than the Court in Twombly rejected the plaintiffs' express allegation of a "`contract, combination or conspiracy to prevent competitive entry,'" because it thought that claim too chimerical to be maintained. It is the conclusory nature of respondent's allegations, rather than their extravagantly fanciful nature, that disentitles them to the presumption of truth.

We next consider the factual allegations in respondent's complaint to determine if they plausibly suggest an entitlement to relief. The complaint alleges that "the [FBI], under the direction of Defendant MUELLER, arrested and detained thousands of Arab Muslim men ... as part of its investigation of the events of September 11.". It further claims that "[t]he policy of holding post-September-11th detainees in highly restrictive conditions of confinement until they were `cleared' by the FBI was approved by Defendants ASHCROFT and MUELLER in discussions in the weeks after September 11, 2001." Taken as true, these allegations are consistent with petitioners' purposefully designating detainees "of high interest" because of their race, religion, or national origin. But given more likely explanations, they do not plausibly establish this purpose.

The September 11 attacks were perpetrated by 19 Arab Muslim hijackers who counted themselves members in good standing of al Qaeda, an Islamic fundamentalist group. Al Qaeda was headed by another Arab Muslim — Osama bin Laden — and composed in large part of his Arab Muslim disciples. It should come as no surprise that a legitimate policy directing law enforcement to arrest and detain individuals because of their suspected link to the attacks would produce a disparate, incidental impact on Arab Muslims, even though the purpose of the policy was to target neither Arabs nor Muslims. On the facts respondent alleges the arrests Mueller oversaw were likely lawful and justified by his nondiscriminatory intent to detain aliens who were illegally present in the United States and who had potential connections to those who committed terrorist acts. As between that "obvious alternative explanation" for the arrests, and the purposeful, invidious discrimination respondent asks us to infer, discrimination is not a plausible conclusion.

But even if the complaint's well-pleaded facts give rise to a plausible inference that respondent's arrest was the result of unconstitutional discrimination, that inference alone would not entitle respondent to relief. It is important to recall that respondent's complaint challenges neither the constitutionality of his arrest nor his initial detention in the MDC. Respondent's constitutional claims against petitioners rest solely on their ostensible "policy of holding post-September-11th detainees" in the ADMAX SHU once they were categorized as "of high interest. "To prevail on that theory, the complaint must contain facts plausibly showing that petitioners purposefully adopted a policy of classifying post-September-11 detainees as "of high interest" because of their race, religion, or national origin.

This the complaint fails to do. Though respondent alleges that various other defendants, who are not before us, may have labeled him a person "of high interest" for impermissible reasons, his only factual allegation against petitioners accuses them of adopting a policy approving "restrictive conditions of confinement" for post-September-11 detainees until they were "`cleared' by the FBI." Ibid. Accepting the truth of that allegation, the complaint does not show, or even intimate, that petitioners purposefully housed detainees in the ADMAX SHU due to their race, religion, or national origin. All it plausibly suggests is that the Nation's top law enforcement officers, in the aftermath of a devastating terrorist attack, sought to keep suspected terrorists in the most secure conditions available until the suspects could be cleared of terrorist activity. Respondent does not argue, nor can he, that such a motive would violate petitioners' constitutional obligations. He would need to allege more by way of factual content to "nudg[e]" his claim of purposeful discrimination "across the line from conceivable to plausible." Twombly, 550 U.S., at 570, 127 S.Ct. 1955.

To be sure, respondent can attempt to draw certain contrasts between the pleadings the Court considered in Twombly and the pleadings at issue here. In Twombly, the complaint alleged general wrongdoing that extended over a period of years, whereas here the complaint alleges discrete wrongs — for instance, beatings — by lower level Government actors. The allegations here, if true, and if condoned by petitioners, could be the basis for some inference of wrongful intent on petitioners' part. Despite these distinctions, respondent's pleadings do not suffice to state a claim. Unlike in Twombly, where the doctrine of respondeat superior could bind the corporate defendant, here, as we have noted, petitioners cannot be held liable unless they themselves acted on account of a constitutionally protected characteristic. Yet respondent's complaint does not contain any factual allegation sufficient to plausibly suggest petitioners' discriminatory state of mind. His pleadings thus do not meet the standard necessary to comply with Rule 8.

It is important to note, however, that we express no opinion concerning the sufficiency of respondent's complaint against the defendants who are not before us.

Respondent's account of his prison ordeal alleges serious official misconduct that we need not address here. Our decision is limited to the determination that respondent's complaint does not entitle him to relief from petitioners.

Respondent offers three arguments that bear on our disposition of his case, but none is persuasive.

Respondent first says that our decision in Twombly should be limited to pleadings made in the context of an antitrust dispute. Iqbal Brief 37-38. This argument is not supported by Twombly and is incompatible with the Federal Rules of Civil Procedure. Though Twombly determined the sufficiency of a complaint sounding in antitrust, the decision was based on our interpretation and application of Rule 8. That Rule in turn governs the pleading standard "in all civil actions and proceedings in the United States district courts." Fed. Rule Civ. Proc. 1. Our decision in Twombly expounded the pleading standard for "all civil actions," ibid., and it applies to antitrust and discrimination suits alike.

Respondent next implies that our construction of Rule 8 should be tempered where, as here, the Court of Appeals has "instructed the district court to cabin discovery in such a way as to preserve" petitioners' defense of qualified immunity "as much as possible in anticipation of a summary judgment motion." We have held, however, that the question presented by a motion to dismiss a complaint for insufficient pleadings does not turn on the controls placed upon the discovery process. . . .

Our rejection of the careful-case-management approach is especially important in suits where Government-official defendants are entitled to assert the defense of qualified immunity. The basic thrust of the qualified-immunity doctrine is to free officials from the concerns of litigation, including "avoidance of disruptive discovery." There are serious and legitimate reasons for this. If a Government official is to devote time to his or her duties, and to the formulation of sound and responsible policies, it is counterproductive to require the substantial diversion that is attendant to participating in litigation and making informed decisions as to how it should proceed. Litigation, though necessary to ensure that officials comply with the law, exacts heavy costs in terms of efficiency and expenditure of valuable time and resources that might otherwise be directed to the proper execution of the work of the Government. . . .

It is no answer to these concerns to say that discovery for petitioners can be deferred while pretrial proceedings continue for other defendants. It is quite likely that, when discovery as to the other parties proceeds, it would prove necessary for petitioners and their counsel to participate in the process to ensure the case does not develop in a misleading or slanted way that causes prejudice to their position. Even if petitioners are not yet themselves subject to discovery orders, then, they would not be free from the burdens of discovery. . . .

Respondent finally maintains that the Federal Rules expressly allow him to allege petitioners' discriminatory intent "generally," which he equates with a conclusory allegation. It follows, respondent says, that his complaint is sufficiently well pleaded because it claims that petitioners discriminated against him "on account of [his] religion, race, and/or national origin and for no legitimate penological interest." Were we required to accept this allegation as true, respondent's complaint would survive petitioners' motion to dismiss. But the Federal Rules do not require courts to credit a complaint's conclusory statements without reference to its factual context.

It is true that Rule 9(b) requires particularity when pleading "fraud or mistake," while allowing "[m]alice, intent, knowledge, and other conditions of a person's mind [to] be alleged generally." But "generally" is a relative term. In the context of Rule 9, it is to be compared to the particularity requirement applicable to fraud or mistake. Rule 9 merely excuses a party from pleading discriminatory intent under an elevated pleading standard. It does not give him license to evade the less rigid — though still operative — strictures of Rule 8. . . .

We hold that respondent's complaint fails to plead sufficient facts to state a claim for purposeful and unlawful discrimination against petitioners. The Court of Appeals should decide in the first instance whether to remand to the District Court so that respondent can seek leave to amend his deficient complaint.

The judgment of the Court of Appeals is reversed, and the case is remanded for further proceedings consistent with this opinion.

It is so ordered.

Notes The holdings in *Twombly* and *Ashcroft* have been described as marking a shift from "minimal notice pleading to a robust gatekeeping regime." One that has "destabilized the entire system of civil litigation." (Inventing Tests, Destabilizing Systems, 95 Iowa L. Rev. 821 (2009-2010).)

Heightened Pleading Requirements for Particular Claims

> **Rule 9(b)**
> FRCP
>
> In alleging fraud or mistake, a party must state with particularity the circumstances constituting fraud or mistake.
>
> Malice, intent, knowledge, and other conditions of a person's mind may be alleged generally.

Stansfield v. Starkey
220 Cal.App.3d 59 (1990)

WOODS (Fred), J.

The trial court sustained without leave to amend demurrers to appellants' fifth amended complaint and dismissed actions against respondents Author Services, Inc., and Church of Spiritual Technology. . . .

[A]ppellants (six individuals, one nonprofit organization, and a present class of approximately four hundred persons who could number several thousand) filed their original complaint. Named as defendants were fourteen individuals, one estate, six nonprofit organizations, one for profit corporation, one nonprofit religious corporation, five undesignated entities, and one hundred Does. Three causes of action were alleged: (1) fraud, (2) breach of a fiduciary relationship or duty, and (3) injunctive relief and constructive trust.

The complaint alleged that appellants were or had been members of the Church of Scientology, that they had been induced to join the church by defendants' misrepresentations, that defendants had breached a fiduciary duty by disclosing confidential confessional information, and that defendants had diverted church property to themselves.

Appellants alleged a fraud cause of action in each of their first three pleadings. Demurrers to the first and second fraud pleadings were sustained with leave to amend. But the demurrers to the third fraud pleading were sustained without leave to amend.

We therefore consider whether or not this sustainment order was within the court's discretion.

The elements of fraud or deceit (see Civ. Code, §§ 1709, 1710) are: a representation, usually of fact, which is false, knowledge of its falsity, intent to defraud, justifiable reliance upon the misrepresentation, and damage resulting from that justifiable reliance.

"Every element of the cause of action for fraud must be alleged in the proper manner and the facts constituting the fraud must be alleged with sufficient specificity to allow defendant to understand fully the nature of the charge made."

But the rationale for this "'strict requirement of pleading'" is not merely notice to the defendant. "'The idea seems to be that allegations of fraud involve a serious attack on character, and fairness to the defendant demands that he should receive the fullest possible details of the charge in order to prepare his defense.'" (Ibid.) Thus "'the policy of liberal construction of the pleadings ... will not ordinarily be invoked to sustain a pleading defective in any material respect.'" (Ibid.)

This particularity requirement necessitates pleading facts which "show how, when, where, to whom, and by what means the representations were tendered." ...

Appellants alleged the following misrepresentations: the Church of Scientology was tax exempt; it had a charitable nature; its founder, L. Ron Hubbard, received no funds paid by members; L. Ron Hubbard received low level compensation for his work; L. Ron Hubbard was a nuclear physicist, highly decorated war veteran who had been wounded during four years of combat; L. Ron Hubbard was twice pronounced medically dead but cured himself with dianetics; and L. Ron Hubbard, by applying the principles of dianetics and scientology, was in perfect health. Appellants also alleged justifiable reliance. As to the "how, when, where, to whom, and by what means the representations were tendered" (Hills Trans. Co. v. Southwest, supra, 266 Cal. App.3d at p. 707) the following allegation is representative.

"Valerie Stanfield, a member from 1961 to 1983, paid in excess of $10,000 to the church and labored for said church in excess of ten (10) years. The representations made in paragraph 31 above were made to Valerie Stansfield by a staff member of the church — Harold Deford. The representations were also made in tapes of L. Ron Hubbard and certain publications of Scientology. These representations were made in 1961 in Washington, DC."

It was alleged that each named appellant upon hearing or reading the representations joined the church. Some joined as early as 1957, some as late as 1974. They also left at different times. Some in 1982, some in 1983, some in 1984.

The trial court found these allegations inadequate. We conclude it was within its discretion to so find.

As the trial court noted appellants did not allege "who acted as the agent of what principal." In appellant Valerie Stanfield's circumstance it was alleged that in 1961 a Harold Deford made the misrepresentations. But it was not alleged that Harold Deford, in 1961, was an agent of either respondent ASI or CST, nor even that ASI or CST had a corporate existence in 1961. . . .

It also was not clearly alleged that each representation was false when made. E.g., the complaint alleges that all representations were made to each of the six named appellants. But the complaint does not allege that the tax-exempt representation was false in each of the six years (1957, 1961, 1962, 1965, 1968, and 1974) individual appellants relied upon it to join the church.

Similarly vague was the alleged causal connection between the misrepresentations and the harm to appellants. Appellants did not allege, e.g., that in reliance upon the tax-exempt representation they claimed and had been denied charitable tax deductions. Nor did appellants allege a representation they would be compensated for their labor.

Less than explicit and material were the allegations of inducement, viz., that appellants joined a church because it was tax exempt, its founder underpaid and a wounded war hero. Conversely, the representation that L. Ron Hubbard twice rose from the dead appears to implicate religious beliefs and thus is not justiciable.

Additionally, allegations purporting to explain delayed discovery of the falsity of the representations were cloudy and inconsistent. Although it was alleged that the representations were made as early as 1957 it was not until 1987 that appellants allegedly discovered their falsity. Yet it was simultaneously alleged, without explanation, that appellants left the church in 1982, 1983, and 1984 and that much of the true information was in the public domain by July 1984.

Equally general and imprecise was the allegation of intent to defraud. Appellants alleged that respondents (and all defendants) acted "with the intent to deceive the plaintiffs and cause them to form an alliance with the defendant 'church.' The extent and degree of the fraudulent misrepresentations varied depending upon the immediate goal of these defendants."

The trial court, in sustaining the demurrers without leave to amend, acted within its discretion.

Note Consider FRCP 9(b) which states: "In alleging fraud or mistake, a party must state with particularity the circumstances constituting fraud or mistake." The primary purpose of the Rule 9(b) is to afford a litigant accused of fraud "fair notice of the claim and the factual ground upon which it is based." (*Stradford v. Zurich Insurance Co.* 2002 WL 31027517 (S.D.N.Y. 2002)

Ethical Constraints on Pleading

FRCP 11 places a great emphasis on the duty of lawyers to avoid abuse of litigation by requiring an attorney to investigate both the legal and factual basis of a claim before filing suit, and by authorizing the use of sanctions for violation of the obligations imposed by the rule.

Rule 11 provides for the striking of pleadings and the imposition of disciplinary sanctions to check abuses in the signing of pleadings. The rule permits the court to award expenses, including attorney's fees, to a litigant whose opponent acts in bad faith in instituting or conducting litigation.

Bridges v. Diesel Service, Inc.
United States District Court for the Eastern District of Pennsylvania, 1994

HUYETT, J.

I. BACKGROUND

James Bridges ("Plaintiff") commenced this action against Diesel Service, Inc. ("Defendant") under the Americans with Disabilities Act ("ADA") . . . By Order dated June 29, 1994, the Court dismissed Plaintiff's Complaint without prejudice for failure to exhaust administrative remedies. In particular, Plaintiff did not file a charge with the Equal Employment Opportunity Commission ("EEOC") until after commencement of this action. Defendant now moves for sanctions pursuant to Fed. R. Civ. P. 11. For the following reasons, Defendant's motion is DENIED.

II. DISCUSSION

. . .[A]s explained in this Court's June 29 Order, the filing of a charge with the EEOC is still a condition precedent to maintenance of a discrimination suit under the ADA. . . . The parties do not dispute that administrative remedies must be exhausted before commencement of an action under the ADA.

Rule 11 "imposes an obligation on counsel and client analogous to the railroad crossing sign, 'Stop, Look and Listen'. It may be rephrased, 'Stop, Think, Investigate and

Research' before filing papers either to initiate the suit or to conduct the litigation." Gaiardo v. Ethyl Corp. . . .; Project 74 Allentown, Inc. v. Frost. . . . Rule 11 is violated only if, at the time of signing, the signing of the document filed was objectively unreasonable under the circumstances. Ford Motor Co. v. Summit Motor Products, Inc. . . . "The Rule does not permit the use of the 'pure heart and an empty head' defense.". . . Rather, counsel's signature certifies the pleading is supported by a reasonable factual investigation and "a normally competent level of legal research."

The Court is not convinced that Plaintiff's counsel displayed a competent level of legal research. A brief review of case law would have revealed the EEOC filing requirement. Further, an award of sanctions for failure to exhaust administrative remedies is not unprecedented. . . .

Notwithstanding, the Court will not grant sanctions. Rule 11 is not intended as a general fee shifting device. . . . The prime goal of Rule 11 sanctions is deterrence of improper conduct. Waltz v. County of Lycoming . . . ; Doering v. Union County Bd. of Chosen Freeholders. . . . In this case, monetary sanctions are not necessary to deter future misconduct. Plaintiff's counsel immediately acknowledged its error and attempted to rectify the situation by filing a charge with the EEOC and moving to place this action in civil suspense. In fact, the Complaint has been dismissed without prejudice. The Court expects that Plaintiff's counsel has learned its lesson and will demonstrate greater diligence in future.

Further, Rule 11 sanctions should be reserved for those exceptional circumstances where the claim asserted is patently unmeritorious or frivolous. Doering, 857 F.2d at 194. The mistake in the present case was procedural rather than substantive. It is also possible that Plaintiff's counsel was confused by the different interpretations of the Supreme Court's holding in Zipes. Finally, the Court is aware of the need to avoid "chilling" Title VII litigation.

III. CONCLUSION

For the above stated reasons, Defendant's motion pursuant to Fed. R. Civ. P. 11, is DENIED. However, this Opinion should not be read as condoning the conduct of Plaintiff's counsel. As stated above, the standard of pre-filing research was below that required of competent counsel. Plaintiff's case has been dismissed without prejudice. If the action is refiled, the Court fully expects to see a high standard of legal product from Plaintiff's counsel - in particular attorney London, who signed the Complaint.

Walker v. Norwest Corp.
108 F.3d 158 (1997)

JOHN R. GIBSON, Circuit Judge.

Jimmy Lee Walker, III, his guardian, Cynthia Walker, and their attorney, James Harrison Massey, appeal from the district court's award of sanctions against Massey for filing a diversity case in which he failed to plead complete diversity of citizenship, and indeed, pleaded facts which tended to show there was not complete diversity. The Walkers and Massey contend that the district court erred in awarding sanctions at all, in determining the amount of sanctions, and in not allowing the Walkers to amend their complaint. We affirm.

Massey filed a complaint in the district court for the District of South Dakota on behalf of the Walkers, alleging breach of fiduciary duty and other state law causes of action in connection with the administration of a trust fund held for Jimmy Lee Walker at Norwest Bank South Dakota, N.A. The complaint stated that jurisdiction was based on diversity, since "the Plaintiff and some of the Defendants are citizens of different states." (Emphasis added). The Walkers are both South Dakotans. The complaint averred that one of the defendants, Norwest Corporation, was a Minnesota corporation. The complaint did not allege the other defendants' citizenship precisely but stated that many of them were South Dakota "residents." The individual defendants included employees of Norwest or its subsidiary corporations and a South Dakota lawyer who represented Norwest. The corporate defendants were Norwest subsidiaries. The Walkers also joined a South Dakota law firm that represented Norwest. All the individuals were named in their individual, as well as official, capacities.

Upon receiving the complaint, the attorney for Norwest Corporation and its subsidiaries and officers wrote Mr. Massey informing him that his complaint showed on its face that there was no diversity jurisdiction. The letter asked Massey to dismiss the complaint, and warned that if he did not, Norwest would seek sanctions, including attorneys' fees. Massey's only answer was a letter that acknowledged Norwest's correspondence, but made no substantive response to the deficiency counsel had pointed out.

After Massey failed to offer any explanation for his defective complaint or to move to amend or dismiss it, Norwest moved to dismiss and for an award of sanctions, as it had promised to do. . . .

The district court granted the Fed.R.Civ.P. 12(b)(1) motion to dismiss for lack of jurisdiction and sanctioned attorney Massey under Fed.R.Civ.P. 11. . . .

[Appellants] contend that Rule 11 does not require the kind of "complicated, in-depth, and possibly impossible inquiry" that would have been necessary to determine the defendants' citizenship before filing a complaint based on diversity of citizenship.

We review the district court's decision in a Rule 11 proceeding for abuse of discretion. Cooter & Gell v. Hartmarx Corp., 496 U.S. 384, 399-405, 110 S.Ct. 2447, 2457-61, 110 L.Ed.2d 359 (1990). A district court necessarily abuses its discretion if it bases its ruling on an erroneous view of the law.

It was the Walkers' burden to plead the citizenship of the parties in attempting to invoke diversity jurisdiction.

Furthermore, even though it is the Walkers' burden to plead, and if necessary, prove diversity, they did not allege that all of the defendants are domiciled in a state other than South Dakota. Instead, they argue that finding out the defendants' citizenship would be more trouble than they should be expected to take. This is a burden that plaintiffs desiring to invoke diversity jurisdiction have assumed since the days of Chief Justice Marshall. See Strawbridge v. Curtiss, 7 U.S. at 267. The fact that the Walkers did not allege the citizenship of the defendants convinces us that the district court did not abuse its discretion in determining that Rule 11 sanctions were appropriate.

The Walkers and Massey next contend that the district court abused its discretion in awarding monetary sanctions, since dismissal of the complaint would have been adequate. They argue that the award of monetary sanctions in this case would discourage "novel legal arguments." Their legal argument in the district court was contrary to the established statutory requirements for diversity. See 28 U.S.C. § 1332(a)(1) (1994). They also argue that the district court should have inquired into Massey's financial circumstances, and that if it had done so, it would have found that he "is presently experiencing financial hardships and is unable to pay this sanction." Not only did Massey fail to argue this point to the district court, but there is no record evidence to support the argument before this court. Finally, they argue that the defendants have no need for compensation for their fees and expenses, since they are "multi-billion/million-dollar defendants." There is no record evidence of the defendants' financial condition, but there is evidence that they incurred fees and expenses because of the Walkers' lawsuit. We see no abuse of discretion in awarding monetary sanctions.

The Walkers and Massey contend that the district court abused its discretion in denying their request to amend their complaint. Although the Walkers did ask for leave to amend their complaint in their response to the motion to dismiss, they did not comply with the local rule requiring them to file a copy of the proposed pleading. Nor did they give any hint of how they wished to change their complaint. They did not indicate a desire to dismiss any of the defendants before the district court dismissed their complaint. The district court has no obligation to dismiss non-diverse defendants sua sponte. After the dismissal and denial of the motion to reconsider, the district court held a hearing on the amount of attorneys' fees to be awarded. At that hearing, Massey began to reargue the merits of the dismissal. The court stated that some of the individual defendants were South Dakota residents. Mr. Massey replied: "I think an appropriate step for the Court to have taken would have been to dismiss those individuals that the Court considered that it could not bring into the diversity statute through pendent jurisdiction which is within the discretion of the Court." Massey still had not alleged a citizenship for many of the defendants and did not identify which defendants should be dismissed to create diversity jurisdiction. The district court is not obliged to do Massey's research for him, especially at such a late date. There was no abuse of discretion.

We affirm the district court's entry of Rule 11 sanctions in the amounts provided.

Christian v. Mattel, Inc.
286 F.3d 1118 (2002)

McKEOWN, Circuit Judge.

It is difficult to imagine that the Barbie doll, so perfect in her sculpture and presentation, and so comfortable in every setting, from "California girl" to "Chief Executive Officer Barbie," could spawn such acrimonious litigation and such egregious conduct on the part of her challenger. In her wildest dreams, Barbie could not have imagined herself in the middle of Rule 11 proceedings. But the intersection of copyrights on Barbie sculptures and the scope of Rule 11 is precisely what defines this case.

James Hicks appeals from a district court order requiring him, pursuant to Federal Rule of Civil Procedure 11, to pay Mattel, Inc. $501,565 in attorneys' fees that it incurred in defending against what the district court determined to be a frivolous action. . . .

Mattel is a toy company that is perhaps best recognized as the manufacturer of the world-famous Barbie doll. Since Barbie's creation in 1959, Mattel has outfitted her in fashions and accessories that have evolved over time. In perhaps the most classic embodiment, Barbie is depicted as a slender-figured doll with long blonde hair and blue eyes. Mattel has sought to protect its intellectual property by registering various Barbie-related copyrights, including copyrights protecting the doll's head sculpture. Mattel has vigorously litigated against putative infringers.

In 1990, Claudene Christian, then an undergraduate student at the University of Southern California ("USC"), decided to create and market a collegiate cheerleader doll. The doll, which the parties refer to throughout their papers as "Claudene," had blonde hair and blue eyes and was outfitted to resemble a USC cheerleader. . .

In the complaint, which Hicks signed, Christian alleged that Mattel obtained a copy of the copyrighted Claudene doll in 1996, the year of its creation, and then infringed its overall appearance, including its face paint, by developing a new Barbie line called "Cool Blue" that was substantially similar to Claudene. Christian sought damages in the amount of $2.4 billion and various forms of injunctive relief. . . .

Two months after the complaint was filed, Mattel moved for summary judgment. In support of its motion, Mattel proffered evidence that the Cool Blue Barbie doll contained a 1991 copyright notice on the back of its head, indicating that it predated Claudene's head sculpture copyright by approximately six years Mattel therefore argued that Cool Blue Barbie could not as a matter of law infringe Claudene's head sculpture copyright.

At a follow-up counsel meeting required by a local rule, Mattel's counsel attempted to convince Hicks that his complaint was frivolous. During the videotaped meeting, they presented Hicks with copies of various Barbie dolls that not only had been created prior to 1996 (the date of Claudene's creation), but also had copyright designations on their heads that pre-dated Claudene's creation. Additionally, Mattel's counsel noted that the face paint on some of the earlier-created Barbie dolls was virtually identical to that used on Claudene. Hicks declined Mattel's invitation to inspect the dolls and, later during the meeting, hurled them in disgust from a conference table.

Having been unsuccessful in convincing Hicks to dismiss Christian's action voluntarily, Mattel served Hicks with a motion for Rule 11 sanctions. In its motion papers, Mattel argued, among other things, that Hicks had signed and filed a frivolous complaint based on a legally meritless theory that Mattel's prior-created head sculptures infringed Claudene's 1997 copyright. Hicks declined to withdraw the complaint during the 21-day safe harbor period provided by Rule 11, and Mattel filed its motion. . . .

The district court granted Mattel's motions for summary judgment and Rule 11 sanctions. The court ruled that Mattel did not infringe the 1997 Claudene copyright because it could not possibly have accessed the Claudene doll at the time it created the head sculptures of the Cool Blue (copyrighted in 1991) and Virginia Tech (copyrighted in 1976) Barbies. . . .

As for Mattel's Rule 11 motion, the district court found that Hicks had "filed a meritless claim against defendant Mattel. A reasonable investigation by Mr. Hicks would have revealed that there was no factual foundation for [Christian's] copyright claim." Indeed, the district court noted that Hicks needed to do little more than examine "the back of the heads of the Barbie dolls he claims were infringing," because such a perfunctory inquiry would have revealed "the pre-1996 copyright notices on the Cool Blue and [Virginia Tech] Barbie doll heads."

Additionally, the district court made other findings regarding Hicks' misconduct in litigating against Mattel, all of which demonstrated that his conduct fell "below the standards of attorneys practicing in the Central District of California." The district court singled out the following conduct:

- Sanctions imposed by the district court against Hicks in a related action against Mattel for failing, among other things, to file a memorandum of law in support of papers styled as a motion to dismiss and failing to appear at oral argument;

- Hicks' behavior during the Early Meeting of Counsel, in which he "toss[ed] Barbie dolls off a table";

- Hicks' interruption of Christian's deposition after Christian made a "damaging admission ... that a pre-1996 Barbie doll allegedly infringed the later created Claudene doll head...." When asked whether the prior-created Pioneer Barbie doll infringed Claudene, Christian stated, "I think so ... [b]ecause it's got the look...." At that juncture, Hicks requested an immediate recess, during which he lambasted his client in plain view of Mattel's attorneys and the video camera.

- Hicks' misrepresentations during oral argument on Mattel's summary judgment motion about the number of dolls alleged in the complaint to be infringing and whether he had ever reviewed a particular Barbie catalogue (when a videotape presented to the district court by Mattel demonstrated that Hicks had reviewed it during a deposition);

- Hicks' misstatement of law in a summary judgment opposition brief about the circuit's holdings regarding joint authorship of copyrightable works.

After Mattel submitted a general description of the fees that it incurred in defending against Christian's action, the court requested Mattel to submit a more specific itemization and description of work performed by its attorneys. Mattel complied.

The district court awarded Mattel $501,565 in attorneys' fees. . . .

The district court did not abuse its discretion in concluding that Hicks' failure to investigate fell below the requisite standard established by Rule 11. . . .

Hicks argues that even if the district court were justified in sanctioning him under Rule 11 based on Christian's complaint and the follow-on motions, its conclusion was tainted because it impermissibly considered other misconduct that cannot be sanctioned under Rule 11, such as discovery abuses, misstatements made during oral argument, and conduct in other litigation.

Hicks' argument has merit. While Rule 11 permits the district court to sanction an attorney for conduct regarding "pleading[s], written motion[s], and other paper[s]" that have been signed and filed in a given case, Fed.R.Civ.P. 11(a), it does not authorize sanctions for, among other things, discovery abuses or misstatements made to the court during an oral presentation. . . .

The orders clearly demonstrate that the district court decided, at least in part, to sanction Hicks because he signed and filed a factually and legally meritless complaint and for misrepresentations in subsequent briefing. But the orders, coupled with the supporting examples, also strongly suggest that the court considered extra-pleadings conduct as a basis for Rule 11 sanctions. . . .

The laundry list of Hicks' outlandish conduct is a long one and raises serious questions as to his respect for the judicial process. Nonetheless, Rule 11 sanctions are limited to "paper[s]" signed in violation of the rule. Conduct in depositions, discovery meetings of counsel, oral representations at hearings, and behavior in prior proceedings do not fall within the ambit of Rule 11. Because we do not know for certain whether the district court granted Mattel's Rule 11 motion as a result of an impermissible intertwining of its conclusion about the complaint's frivolity and Hicks' extrinsic misconduct, we must vacate the district court's Rule 11 orders.

We decline Mattel's suggestion that the district court's sanctions orders could be supported in their entirety under the court's inherent authority. To impose sanctions under its inherent authority, the district court must "make an explicit finding [which it did not do here] that counsel's conduct constituted or was tantamount to bad faith." Primus Auto. Fin. Serv., Inc. v. Batarse, 115 F.3d 644, 648 (9th Cir.1997) (internal quotation marks omitted). We acknowledge that the district court has a broad array of sanctions options at its disposal: Rule 11, 28 U.S.C. § 1927, and the court's inherent authority. Each of these sanctions alternatives has its own particular requirements, and it is important that the grounds be separately articulated to assure that the conduct at issue falls within the scope of the sanctions remedy. See, e.g., B.K.B. v. Maui Police Dep't., 276 F.3d 1091, 1107 (9th Cir.2002) (holding that misconduct committed "in an unreasonable and vexatious manner" that "multiplies the proceedings" violates § 1927); Fink v. Gomez, 239 F.3d 989, 991-992 (9th Cir.2001) (holding that sanctions may be imposed under the court's inherent authority for "bad faith" actions by counsel, "which includes a broad range of willful improper conduct"). On remand, the district court will have an opportunity to delineate the factual and legal basis for its sanctions orders. . . .

Notes Filing a complaint in federal court is no trifling undertaking. An attorney's signature on a complaint is tantamount to a warranty that the complaint is well grounded in fact and "existing law" (or proposes a good faith extension of the existing law) and that it is not filed for an improper purpose.

Language added by the 1983 amendment to FRCP 11 stressed the need for some prefiling inquiry into both the facts and the law to satisfy the affirmative duty imposed by the rule. The standard is one of reasonableness under the circumstances. This standard is more stringent than the original good-faith formula and thus it is expected that a greater range of circumstances will trigger its violation. (Advisory Committee Notes, 1983 Amendment)

The rule is not intended to chill an attorney's enthusiasm or creativity in pursuing factual or legal theories. The court is expected to avoid using the wisdom of hindsight and should test the signer's conduct by inquiring what was reasonable to believe at the time the pleading, motion, or other paper was submitted. Thus, what constitutes a reasonable inquiry may depend on such factors as how much time for investigation was available to the signer; whether he had to rely on a client for information as to the facts underlying the pleading, motion, or other paper; whether the pleading, motion, or other paper was based on a plausible view of the law; or whether he depended on forwarding counsel or another member of the bar. (*Id.*)

You should also take a look at California Code of Civil Procedure section 128.7, which is patterned directly on FRCP 11.

An "appropriate sanction" under Rule 11 may include paying the other party's expenses. (*Cooter & Gell v. Hartmarx Corp.,* 496 U.S. 384, 110 S.Ct. 2447 (1990)) Under both FRCP 11 and CCP § 128.7, sanctions are discretionary with the court, not mandatory and there is a "safe harbor" provision. In other words, a party served with a motion for sanctions has 21 days to withdraw or correct the challenged paper before the sanction motion may be filed.

Responding to the Complaint

A defendant who is served with a complaint has three options. 1) Do nothing and risk a default judgment; 2) File a pre-answer motion to dismiss (or if in state court, demurrer); 3) Address the merits of the complaint by filing an answer.

Default

King Vision Pay-Per-View Ltd. v. Spice Restaurant & Lounge, Inc.
244 F.Supp.2d 1173 (2003)

MURGUIA, District Judge.

This case arises out of defendants' allegedly willful and illegal interception and misappropriation of a closed-circuit exhibition of the November 13, 1999 boxing match between Evander Holyfield and Lennox Lewis. Plaintiff asserts that it possessed the proprietary rights to exhibit and sublicense the right to exhibit the closed-circuit telecast of the November 13, 1999 event. Plaintiff contends that defendants unlawfully intercepted the transmission of this event and made it available to patrons of defendants' establishment, all in violation of 47 U.S.C. §§ 553 and 605.

Pending before the court is plaintiff King Vision Pay Per View, Ltd.'s motion for default judgment. Plaintiff asks the court to enter default judgment against defendants Joe Robinson and Bobby Carpenter. . . .

Plaintiff filed this case on April 23, 2001, naming Spice Restaurant & Lounge, Inc., Joe Robinson, and Bobby Carpenter as defendants. On May 30, 2001, the court issued summonses for all three defendants. On June 28, 2001, defendant Carpenter was served with the summons and complaint. Similarly, on July 1, 2001, defendant Robinson was served. . . .

[P]laintiff asked the Clerk of the Court to enter default against defendants Robinson and Carpenter based upon their failure to respond to the complaint. On October 18, 2001, the Clerk of the Court entered default as requested.

Because the court has determined that defendants Carpenter and Robinson are in default, "the factual allegations of plaintiffs complaint, except those relating to the amount of damages, will be taken as true." Accordingly, the following facts are established by the record.

[The court listed the allegations of the complaint that were established as fact.]

Plaintiff now asks this court to enter default judgment against defendants Carpenter and Robinson. Federal Rule of Civil Procedure 55 provides for entry of default and subsequent judgment of default where the opposing party has failed to plead or otherwise defend. Fed. R.Civ.P. 55; The rule requires that a party respond to a complaint with some action to defend pursuant to the Federal Rules of Civil Procedure. Fed. R.Civ.P. 55; see also Brooks v. Graber, No. 00-2262-DES, 2000 WL 1679420, (D.Kan. Nov.6, 2000) (the rule "contemplates a complete failure of a party to address or confront a pending complaint"). Upon the entry of default on the record, a party is entitled to move for judgment by default. Fed.R.Civ.P. 55 . . .

When considering a motion for default judgment, the court must first determine that plaintiff has made a prima facie showing of the court's personal jurisdiction over the defaulting party. While the court may hold a hearing to make this determination, it is not necessary to do so if the plaintiffs entitlement to relief is evident from the record.

After prima facie evidence of the court's personal jurisdiction is determined, the court must turn its attention to the plaintiffs entitlement to the relief it seeks. Fed.R.Civ.P. 55(b)....

Plaintiff has established this court's personal jurisdiction over defendants Carpenter and Robinson because the evidence in the record establishes that these two defendants had sufficient minimum contacts with the State of Kansas to confer jurisdiction upon Kansas courts....

Plaintiffs complaint presents two claims for relief. The first is a claim of theft of satellite communications under 47 U.S.C. § 605. Plaintiffs second claim is for theft of cable communications under 47 U.S.C. § 553. The evidentiary record establishes plaintiffs entitlement to relief on its claims....

IT IS THEREFORE ORDERED that plaintiffs motion for default judgment is granted in part. Judgment shall be entered in favor of plaintiff and against defendant Carpenter and Robinson collectively on Counts I and II of plaintiffs complaint in the total amount of $10,000 in statutory damages....

Note The opinion makes reference to two motions the plaintiff made, a motion for entry of default and a motion for default judgment. What is the distinction between the two motions?

Challenging the Sufficiency of the Complaint

Pre-Answer Motion

In state court, a challenge to the sufficiency of a complaint is called a "general demurrer." Under the Federal Rules, demurrers have been abolished. Instead, we have the motion to dismiss for failure to state a claim (FRCP 12(b)(6)) and a motion to strike an insufficient answer. (FRCP 12(f)) These motions serve the same purpose as general demurrers. Each asks, assuming all of the allegations of the complaint are true, whether the complaint has stated a valid claim for relief.

Northrop v. Hoffman of Simsbury, Inc.
134 F.3d 41 (1997)

JOSÉ A. CABRANES, Circuit Judge:

Plaintiff-appellant Deborah Northrop appeals from a ruling of the United States District Court for the District of Connecticut (Alfred V. Covello, Judge), dismissing her complaint for failure to state a claim for relief under the Fair Credit Reporting Act, 15 U.S.C. § 1681 et seq. (1994) ("FCRA" or the "Act"). For the reasons set forth below, we vacate the ruling of the district court and remand the case for further proceedings.

In reviewing the dismissal of a complaint under Rule 12(b)(6) of the Federal Rules of Civil Procedure for failure to state a claim upon which relief can be granted, we must accept as true the facts alleged in the complaint and draw all reasonable inferences in the plaintiff's favor. The facts alleged in plaintiff-appellant Northrop's Second Amended Complaint are as follows.

On or about September 25, 1995, Northrop was in the process of obtaining a mortgage to refinance her home through a company called Mortgage Master. As part of that process, Mortgage Master requested and received plaintiff's consumer credit report from United Data Services. That report indicated that on July 3, 1995, defendant-appellee Hoffman of Simsbury, Inc., d/b/a Hoffman Honda of Avon ("Hoffman"), had made an inquiry and received Northrop's consumer credit report. At the time that Hoffman requested plaintiff's credit report, Northrop was conducting no business with Hoffman of any kind.

As a result of Hoffman's request for Northrop's consumer credit report, Mortgage Master demanded that Northrop explain the basis for the inquiry by Hoffman. On or about October 3, 1995, Northrop contacted Hoffman to find out who had requested her consumer credit report and the reason for that request but was given no answer. On or about October 5, 1995, Northrop was told by a Hoffman employee that Hoffman's computerized records had been destroyed. Northrop's subsequent telephone calls to Hoffman have not been returned.

Plaintiff claims that these actions interfered with her efforts to obtain a mortgage and inflicted emotional distress. She brings this action based on alleged violations of the FCRA and the Connecticut Unfair Trade Practices Act, Conn.Gen.Stat. § 42-110a et seq., seeking actual and punitive damages, costs, and attorney's fees as well as equitable relief in the form of an injunction, enjoining all defendants from using or disclosing the contents of her credit report. The district court granted defendants' motion to dismiss in a ruling dated February 3, 1997, holding that plaintiff had not stated a claim upon which relief could be granted under the FCRA, and declining to exercise jurisdiction over the remaining state law claim. Plaintiff now appeals.

We review de novo the grant of a motion to dismiss under Rule 12(b)(6) for failure to state a claim upon which relief can be granted. The complaint may be dismissed only where "'it appears beyond doubt that the plaintiff can prove no set of facts in support of his claim which would entitle him to relief.'"

Plaintiff-appellant's Second Amended Complaint claimed that defendants violated 15 U.S.C. §§ 1681b, c, and/or e, all of which are sections of the FCRA that impose obligations solely upon "consumer reporting agencies." Based on the defendants' alleged violations of the FCRA, appellant sought relief under § 1681n, which provides for a cause of action against "[a]ny consumer reporting agency or user of information which willfully fails to comply with any requirement imposed under [the FCRA]." (emphasis supplied).

The district court, in dismissing plaintiff-appellant's complaint, found that the defendants were not "consumer reporting agencies." Although the only sections specifically alleged in plaintiff-appellant's Second Amended Complaint to have been violated were sections relating to "consumer reporting agencies," the district court recognized that the FCRA also imposes liability upon "users of information." It found, however, that the only obligations placed upon "users" by the FCRA, and therefore the only basis for liability against them under § 1681n, are the disclosure obligations imposed by § 1681m "[w]henever credit ... is denied or the charge for such credit ... is increased." 15 U.S.C. § 1681m. Inasmuch as Northrop did not allege that defendants denied her credit or increased the charge for credit — the requirements necessary to trigger § 1681m — the court found that plaintiff failed to state a claim under the FCRA.

On appeal, appellant does not contest the conclusion that defendants are not "consumer reporting agencies," nor does she contest the fact that defendants did not deny her credit or increase the charge for credit. Rather, she argues that defendants can be held liable under § 1681n because they willfully violated the "requirement" imposed by § 1681q, a criminal provision of the FCRA that imposes penalties upon "[a]ny person who knowingly and willfully obtains information on a consumer from a consumer reporting agency under false pretenses." (emphasis supplied). While the district court indicated that users of information can be held liable under § 1681n solely for violating the disclosure obligations of § 1681m, which apply only when "credit ... is denied or the charge for such credit ... is increased," appellant argues that users of information may also be held civilly liable under § 1681n for violating § 1681q, which is incorporated into § 1681n. That is, appellant argues that § 1681q, prohibiting "any person" from procuring credit information under false pretenses, is among the FCRA "requirements" whose willful violation by users of information supports civil liability under § 1681n. We agree.

As a preliminary matter, we must decide whether appellant is foreclosed from seeking relief under § 1681n pursuant to a violation of § 1681q by her failure to cite § 1681q in her Second Amended Complaint. We recognize that appellant's failure to cite § 1681q as a potential basis for liability under § 1681n gave the district court little or no reason or opportunity to address this theory of liability. Nevertheless, appellant's failure to cite the correct section of the FCRA does not require us to affirm the dismissal of her complaint so long as she has alleged facts sufficient to support a meritorious legal claim.

Under the liberal pleading principles established by Rule 8 of the Federal Rules of Civil Procedure, in ruling on a 12(b)(6) motion "[t]he failure in a complaint to cite a statute, or to cite the correct one, in no way affects the merits of a claim. Factual allegations alone are what matters." Albert v. Carovano, 851 F.2d 561, 571 n. 3 (2d Cir.1988) (in banc) (citing Newman v. Silver, 713 F.2d 14, 15 n. 1 (2d Cir.1983)); see also Flickinger v. Harold C. Brown & Co., 947 F.2d 595, 600 (2d Cir.1991) ("[Defendant] ... point[s] out that [plaintiff] failed to plead the third-party beneficiary theory in his complaint. To this, we simply respond that federal pleading is by statement of claim, not by legal theory.").

Northrop's Second Amended Complaint did allege that defendants received her consumer credit report from a credit reporting agency while they were conducting no business with her of any kind, the natural implication of which is that they did so "under false pretenses." Indeed, the memorandum of law offered in support of one of the defendants' motions to dismiss evidences clear awareness of the substance of plaintiff's claim — even if the statutory basis of her complaint remained opaque — stating that "[t]he essence of Plaintiff's Second Amended Complaint" is "that Hoffman and Mr. Katzke improperly requested [her] consumer credit report from a consumer credit reporting agency." See Kelly v. Schmidberger, 806 F.2d 44, 46 (2d Cir.1986)("The test of a complaint's sufficiency is whether it is detailed and informative enough to enable defendant to respond....") (internal quotation marks omitted). Accordingly, plaintiff's Second Amended Complaint is sufficient to survive a motion to dismiss so long as (1) § 1681n can, as a matter of law, support liability against users of information who violate § 1681q by procuring credit reports under false pretenses, and (2) defendants are "users of information" under § 1681n. . . .

We join the other Courts of Appeals that have ruled on the question in holding that § 1681n incorporates § 1681q. The plain language of § 1681n, imposing liability upon "user[s] of information which willfully fail[] to comply with any requirement imposed under [the FCRA]," appears on its face to encompass the "requirement" imposed by § 1681q not to obtain credit information under false pretenses. "Phrasing the 'requirement' as a thing prohibited or required not to be done rather than as an affirmative obligation does not deprive Section 1681q of its status as a requirement. Nor does imposition of criminal penalties for violation of Section 1681q rob it of its enforceability through Section 1681n."

Accordingly, assuming that defendants are "users of information" under § 1681n, Northrop's Second Amended Complaint, which suggests that defendants obtained her consumer credit report under false pretenses, does allege facts sufficient to state a claim upon which relief can be granted — namely, a claim for relief under § 1681n based on an alleged violation of § 1681q.

More on Rule 12(b)

Additional grounds for dismissing claims are listed in FRCP 12(b). The Rule 12(b) motions include all the threshold motions to dismiss for lack of jurisdiction, insufficiency of service of process, failure to state a claim, or failure to join an indispensable party. All Rule 12(b) motions must be brought at one time and must be made before the filing of a substantive pleading such as an answer.

Waiver of Preservation of Certain Defenses The defenses of lack of jurisdiction over the person, improper venue, insufficiency of process and insufficiency of service of process are waived if not included in a Rule 12 motion, or, if no such motion is made, if they are not included in the responsive pleading or an amendment as of right to that pleading. The defenses of failure to state a claim upon which relief can be granted; failure to join an indispensable party under FRCP 19, and failure to state a legal defense to a claim may be made in any pleading permitted under FRCP 7, or by a motion for judgment on the pleadings, or at the trial on the merits. Most courts consider the defense of failure to join an indispensable party jurisdictional and therefore never waived. The defense of lack of subject matter jurisdiction is never waived.

Answers

The answer is the pleading that directly responds to the allegations made in the plaintiff's complaint. An answer constitutes a "general appearance." In other words, it waives any defects in personal jurisdiction which traditionally was challenged by making a limited or "special appearance." Furthermore, it prevents a default from being taken against the defendant and it requires the plaintiff to prove all of the material allegations of the complaint that have been denied in the answer.

THE ANSWER

- Constitutes a "general appearance."
- Prevents default judgment
- Requires plaintiff to prove all material allegations of complaint that are denied in answer

An answer may generally deny all of the allegations of the complaint, or it may admit or deny specific allegations.

A general denial consists of one sentence simply stating that "defendant denies each and every allegation of plaintiff's complaint." A specific denial involves a sentence-by-sentence or paragraph-by-paragraph analysis of the complaint, denying only those allegations that defendant intends to contest. Typically, the general denial is used when defendant contests the basic sum and substance of the complaint even though a few of the allegations are true. Federal courts limit the use of general denials to those cases in which defendant actually intends to controvert each and every one of plaintiff's allegations. (See FRCP 8(b)) This virtually eliminates use of the general denial since it will be an exceedingly rare complaint in which none of the facts alleged is true. (Friedenthal § 5.19) In California, if a complaint is verified (signed by the pleader under penalty of perjury) the answer not only must be verified but it cannot contain a general denial. (Cal.Code.Civ.Proc. § 431.30(d).)

The effect of a denial is to require the plaintiff to prove the fact that has been denied at trial.

King Vision Pay Per View v. Dimitri's Restaurant
180 F.R.D. 332 (N.D. Ill. 1998)

[The owner of the "pay-per-view" rights to a heavyweight boxing match filed a complaint against a restaurant basically alleging that the restaurant "stole" the closed-circuit broadcast signal. The restaurant then filed a response where 30 of the response's 35 paragraphs contained nonresponsive language to the effect that the restaurant neither admitted nor denied the allegations of a paragraph, but demanded strict proof thereof. This response triggered the following opinion by the judge of the trial court.]

OPINION BY: Milton I. Shadur.

J.C. Dimitri's Restaurant, Inc. ("Dimitri's") and James Chelios ("Chelios") have filed what purports to be a Response to Complaint that addresses the Complaint filed against them by King Vision Pay Per View, Ltd. This sua sponte opinion is triggered by the Response's pervasive and impermissible flouting of the crystal-clear directive of Fed. R. Civ. P. ("Rule") 8(b) as to how any responsive pleading to a federal complaint must be drafted.

This is it. For too many years and in too many hundreds of cases this Court has been reading, and has been compelled to order the correction of, allegedly responsive pleadings that are written by lawyers who are either unaware of or who choose to depart from Rule 8(b)'s plain roadmap. It identifies only three alternatives as available for use in an answer to the allegations of a complaint: to admit those allegations, to deny them or to state a disclaimer (if it can be made in the objective and subjective good faith demanded by Rule 11) in the express terms of the second sentence of Rule 8(b), which then entitles the pleader to the benefit of a deemed denial.

Here Dimitri's' and Chelios' counsel has engaged in a particularly vexatious violation of that most fundamental aspect of federal pleading. It is hard to imagine, but fully 30 of the Response's 35 paragraphs contain this nonresponse, in direct violation of Rule 8(b)'s express teaching: Neither admit nor deny the allegations of said Paragraph -- but demand strict proof thereof.

Gilbert and a host of this Court's unpublished opinions since then speak not only of the unacceptability of any such Rule 8(b) violation but also to the equally unacceptable "demand" for "strict proof," a concept that to this Court's knowledge is unknown to the federal practice or to any other system of modern pleading.

This Court's efforts at lawyer education through the issuance of repeated brief opinions or oral rulings, or through faculty participation in seminars and symposia on federal pleading and practice, have proved unavailing. It is time for this Court to follow the Rules itself, in this instance Rule 8(d): Averments in a pleading to which a responsive pleading is required, other than those as to the amount of damage, are admitted when not denied in the responsive pleading.

Accordingly all of the allegations of Complaint PP6-12, 17, 25-26 and 33-34 are held to have been admitted by Dimitri's and Chelios, and this action will proceed on that basis. And although the same phenomenon referred to [above] probably makes it quite unlikely that the lawyers who are most prone to commit the same offense will be lawyers who are regular (or even sporadic) readers of F. Supp. or F.R.D., this opinion is being sent to West Publishing Company for publication. Future Rule 8(b) violators are hereby placed on constructive notice that their similarly defective pleadings will encounter like treatment.

Question So what would have been a proper response to the allegations of the complaint that would not have drawn the wrath of the trial judge? Read FRCP 8(b)(1)-(6) and articulate what the defendant in this case should have done in order to properly respond to the allegations of the complaint.

Affirmative Defenses

Even if all plaintiff's allegations are true, defendant may be able to present additional facts establishing a defense. In such a case, the defense is called an affirmative defense and defendant must plead it in the answer in order that plaintiff is aware of the allegations and has an opportunity to prepare to meet them. Unless an affirmative defense is plead, it cannot be proved at trial, although the court in its discretion, may give defendant leave to amend the answer to add the defense at any time. One can distinguish an affirmative defense from one that can be raised by denial merely by determining whether the particular fact controverts one of plaintiff's allegations or whether it deals with an entirely new matter having nothing to do with whether plaintiff's claims are true or not. (Friedenthal § 5.20)

FRCP 8(c) lists 19 affirmative defenses that must be raised specifically. However, this list is not exhaustive. In determining whether a particular defense must be affirmatively raised, courts look to statutes in the case of federal questions and to state practice in diversity cases. In general, defendants must raise affirmatively defenses that do not flow logically from the plaintiff's complaint.

Jones v. Bock
549 U.S. 199 (2007)

[The Prison Litigation Reform Act of 1995 (PLRA), in order to address the large number of prisoner complaints filed in federal court, mandates early judicial screening of prisoner complaints and requires prisoners to exhaust prison grievance procedures before filing suit. 42 U.S.C. § 1997e(a). Petitioners, inmates in Michigan prisons, filed grievances using the Michigan Department of Corrections (MDOC) grievance process. After unsuccessfully seeking redress through that process, petitioner Jones filed a § 1983 suit against six prison officials. The District Court dismissed on the merits as to four of them and as to two others found that Jones had failed to adequately plead exhaustion in his complaint. Petitioner Williams also filed a § 1983 suit after his two MDOC grievances were denied. The District Court found that he had not exhausted his administrative remedies with regard to one of the grievances because he had not identified any of the respondents named in the lawsuit during the grievance process. While the court found Williams's other claim properly exhausted, it dismissed the entire suit under the Sixth Circuit's total exhaustion rule for PLRA cases. Petitioner Walton's § 1983 lawsuit also was dismissed under the total exhaustion rule because his MDOC grievance named only one of the six defendants in his lawsuit. The Sixth Circuit affirmed in each case, relying on its procedural rules that require a prisoner to allege and demonstrate exhaustion in his complaint.]

Chief Justice ROBERTS delivered the opinion of the Court.

Prisoner litigation continues to "account for an outsized share of filings" in federal district courts. In 2005, nearly 10 percent of all civil cases filed in federal courts nationwide were prisoner complaints challenging prison conditions or claiming civil rights violations. Most of these cases have no merit; many are frivolous. Our legal system, however, remains committed to guaranteeing that prisoner claims of illegal conduct by their custodians are fairly handled according to law. The challenge lies in ensuring that the flood of nonmeritorious claims does not submerge and effectively preclude consideration of the allegations with merit.

Congress addressed that challenge in the PLRA. What this country needs, Congress decided, is fewer and better prisoner suits. To that end, Congress enacted a variety of reforms designed to filter out the bad claims and facilitate consideration of the good. Key among these was the requirement that inmates complaining about prison conditions exhaust prison grievance remedies before initiating a lawsuit.

The exhaustion provision of the PLRA states:

"No action shall be brought with respect to prison conditions under [42 U.S.C. § 1983], or any other Federal law, by a prisoner confined in any jail, prison, or other correctional facility until such administrative remedies as are available are exhausted."

Requiring exhaustion allows prison officials an opportunity to resolve disputes concerning the exercise of their responsibilities before being hauled into court. This has the potential to reduce the number of inmate suits, and also to improve the quality of suits that are filed by producing a useful administrative record. In an attempt to implement the exhaustion requirement, some lower courts have imposed procedural rules that have become the subject of varying levels of disagreement among the federal courts of appeals.

The first question presented centers on a conflict over whether exhaustion under the PLRA a pleading requirement is the prisoner must satisfy in his complaint or an affirmative defense the defendant must plead and prove. . . .

There is no question that exhaustion is mandatory under the PLRA and that unexhausted claims cannot be brought in court. What is less clear is whether it falls to the prisoner to plead and demonstrate exhaustion in the complaint, or to the defendant to raise lack of exhaustion as an affirmative defense. The minority rule, adopted by the Sixth Circuit, places the burden of pleading exhaustion in a case covered by the PLRA on the prisoner; most courts view failure to exhaust as an affirmative defense.

We think petitioners, and the majority of courts to consider the question, have the better of the argument. Federal Rule of Civil Procedure 8(a) requires simply a "short and plain statement of the claim" in a complaint, while Rule 8(c) identifies a nonexhaustive list of affirmative defenses that must be pleaded in response. The PLRA itself is not a source of a prisoner's claim; claims covered by the PLRA are typically brought under 42 U.S.C. § 1983, which does not require exhaustion at all, Petitioners assert that courts typically regard exhaustion as an affirmative defense in other contexts, see Brief for Petitioners 34-36, and nn. 12-13 (citing cases), and respondents do not seriously dispute the general proposition. We have referred to exhaustion in these terms, see, e.g., Wright v. Universal Maritime Service Corp., 525 U.S. 70, 75, 119 S.Ct. 391,

142 L.Ed.2d 361 (1998) (referring to "failure to exhaust" as an "affirmative defens[e]"), including in the similar statutory scheme governing habeas corpus, Day v. McDonough, 547 U.S. 198, 208, 126 S.Ct. 1675 (2006) (referring to exhaustion as a "defense"). The PLRA dealt extensively with the subject of exhaustion, see 42 U.S.C. §§ 1997e(a), (c)(2), but is silent on the issue whether exhaustion must be pleaded by the plaintiff or is an affirmative defense. This is strong evidence that the usual practice should be followed, and the usual practice under the Federal Rules is to regard exhaustion as an affirmative defense.

In a series of recent cases, we have explained that courts should generally not depart from the usual practice under the Federal Rules on the basis of perceived policy concerns. Thus, in Leatherman v. Tarrant County Narcotics Intelligence and Coordination Unit, 507 U.S. 163, 113 S.Ct. 1160, 122 L.Ed.2d 517 (1993), we unanimously reversed the Court of Appeals for imposing a heightened pleading standard in § 1983 suits against municipalities. We explained that "[p]erhaps if [the] Rules ... were rewritten today, claims against municipalities under § 1983 might be subjected to the added specificity requirement.... But that is a result which must be obtained by the process of amending the Federal Rules, and not by judicial interpretation."

In Swierkiewicz v. Sorema N.A., 534 U.S. 506, 122 S.Ct. 992, 152 L.Ed.2d 1 (2002), we unanimously reversed the Court of Appeals for requiring employment discrimination plaintiffs to specifically allege the elements of a prima facie case of discrimination. We explained that "the Federal Rules do not contain a heightened pleading standard for employment discrimination suits," and a "requirement of greater specificity for particular claims" must be obtained by amending the Federal Rules. Id., at 515, 122 S.Ct. 992 (citing Leatherman). And just last Term, in Hill v. McDonough, 547 U.S. 573, 126 S.Ct. 2096, 165 L.Ed.2d 44 (2006), we unanimously rejected a proposal that § 1983 suits challenging a method of execution must identify an acceptable alternative: "Specific pleading requirements are mandated by the Federal Rules of Civil Procedure, and not, as a general rule, through case-by-case determinations of the federal courts."

The argument that screening would be more effective if exhaustion had to be shown in the complaint proves too much; the same could be said with respect to any affirmative defense. . . .

We conclude that failure to exhaust is an affirmative defense under the PLRA, and that inmates are not required to specially plead or demonstrate exhaustion in their complaints. We understand the reasons behind the decisions of some lower courts to impose a pleading requirement on plaintiffs in this context, but that effort cannot fairly be viewed as an interpretation of the PLRA. "Whatever temptations the statesmanship of policy-making might wisely suggest," the judge's job is to construe the statute — not to make it better. Frankfurter, Some Reflections on the Reading of Statutes, 47 Colum. L.Rev. 527, 533 (1947). The judge "must not read in by way of creation," but instead abide by the "duty of restraint, th[e] humility of function as merely the translator of another's command." Id., at 533-534. See United States v. Goldenberg, 168 U.S. 95, 103, 18 S.Ct. 3, 42 L.Ed. 394 (1897) ("No mere omission ... which it may seem wise to have specifically provided for, justif[ies] any judicial addition to the language of the statute"). Given that the PLRA does not itself require plaintiffs to plead exhaustion, such a result "must be obtained by the process of amending the Federal Rules, and not by judicial interpretation." ...

We are not insensitive to the challenges faced by the lower federal courts in managing their dockets and attempting to separate, when it comes to prisoner suits, not so much wheat from chaff as needles from haystacks. We once again reiterate, however — as we did unanimously in Leatherman, Swierkiewicz, and Hill — that adopting different and more onerous pleading rules to deal with particular categories of cases should be done through established rulemaking procedures, and not on a case-by-case basis by the courts.

Amendments to Pleadings

Suppose the plaintiff after filing the complaint wants to make changes to it. For example, they want to add an additional defendant or cause of action. Or perhaps they want to ask for additional relief. May they do so? FRCP 15(a) allows a party to amend its pleading once as a matter of course, meaning they do not have to make a motion to amend.

> **Amendment Rule 15(a)** (FRCP)
> - Allows a party to amend its pleading once as a matter of course within 21 days of serving it.
> - The grant or denial of an opportunity to amend is within the discretion of the trial court.

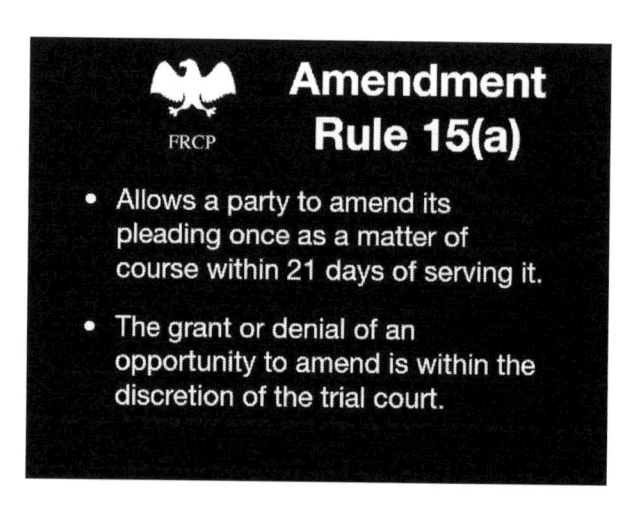

"The right to amend once as a matter of course terminates 21 days after service of a motion to dismiss under FRCP 12(b), (e), or (f). This forces the pleader to consider carefully and promptly the wisdom of amending to meet the arguments in the motion. A responsive amendment may avoid the need to decide the motion or reduce the number of issues to be decided and will expedite determination of issues that otherwise might be raised seriatim. It also should advance other pretrial proceedings. (Comment to Rule 15)

FRCP 15(a), further provides that "leave shall be freely given when justice so requires." In other words, courts are to be liberal in allowing parties to amend their pleadings. In practice, the only constraint on the right to amend should be whether the opposing party will be unduly prejudiced by the amendment. As a general rule, the later in the litigation process the amendment is sought to be made, the more likely it is to be deemed prejudicial to the other party. The rational is that if parties have spent time and gone to the effort of preparing to defend against one claim, it is prejudicial to require them to start the preparation process over again to defend against a new claim.

Beeck v. Aquaslide `N' Dive Corp.
562 F.2d 537 (1977)

BENSON, District Judge.

This case is an appeal from the trial court's exercise of discretion on procedural matters in a diversity personal injury action.

Jerry A. Beeck was severely injured on July 15, 1972, while using a water slide. He and his wife, Judy A. Beeck, sued Aquaslide `N' Dive Corporation (Aquaslide), a Texas corporation, alleging it manufactured the slide involved in the accident, and sought to recover substantial damages on theories of negligence, strict liability and breach of implied warranty.

Aquaslide initially admitted manufacture of the slide, but later moved to amend its answer to deny manufacture; the motion was resisted. The district court granted leave to amend. On motion of the defendant, a separate trial was held on the issue of "whether the defendant designed, manufactured or sold the slide in question." This motion was also resisted by the plaintiffs. The issue was tried to a jury, which returned a verdict for the defendant, after which the trial court entered summary judgment of dismissal of the case. Plaintiffs took this appeal, and stated the issues presented for review to be:

1. Where the manufacturer of the product, a water slide, admitted in its Answer and later in its Answer to Interrogatories both filed prior to the running of the statute of limitations that it designed, manufactured and sold the water slide in question, was it an abuse of the trial court's discretion to grant leave to amend to the manufacturer in order to deny these admissions after the running of the statute of limitations?

2. After granting the manufacturer's Motion for Leave to Amend in order to deny the prior admissions of design, manufacture and sale of the water slide in question, was it an

abuse of the trial court's discretion to further grant the manufacturer's Motion for a Separate Trial on the issue of manufacture?

I. Facts.

A brief review of the facts found by the trial court in its order granting leave to amend, and which do not appear to have been in dispute, is essential to a full understanding of appellants' claims.

In 1971 Kimberly Village Home Association of Davenport, Iowa, ordered an Aquaslide product from one George Boldt, who was a local distributor handling defendant's products. The order was forwarded by Boldt to Sentry Pool and Chemical Supply Co. in Rock Island, Illinois, and Sentry forwarded the order to Purity Swimming Pool Supply in Hammond, Indiana. A slide was delivered from a Purity warehouse to Kimberly Village, and was installed by Kimberly employees. On July 15, 1972, Jerry A. Beeck was injured while using the slide at a social gathering sponsored at Kimberly Village by his employer, Harker Wholesale Meats, Inc. Soon after the accident investigations were undertaken by representatives of the separate insurers of Harker and Kimberly Village. On October 31, 1972, Aquaslide first learned of the accident through a letter sent by a representative of Kimberly's insurer to Aquaslide, advising that "one of your Queen Model # Q-3D slides" was involved in the accident. Aquaslide forwarded this notification to its insurer. Aquaslide's insurance adjuster made an on-site investigation of the slide in May 1973, and also interviewed persons connected with the ordering and assembly of the slide. An inter-office letter dated September 23, 1973, indicates that Aquaslide's insurer was of the opinion the "Aquaslide in question was definitely manufactured by our insured." The complaint was filed October 15, 1973. Investigators for three different insurance companies, representing Harker, Kimberly and the defendant, had concluded that the slide had been manufactured by Aquaslide, and the defendant, with no information to the contrary, answered the complaint on December 12, 1973, and admitted that it "designed, manufactured, assembled and sold" the slide in question.

The statute of limitations on plaintiff's personal injury claim expired on July 15, 1974. About six and one-half months later Carl Meyer, president and owner of Aquaslide, visited the site of the accident prior to the taking of his deposition by the plaintiff. From his on-site inspection of the slide, he determined it was not a product of the defendant. Thereafter, Aquaslide moved the court for leave to amend its answer to deny manufacture of the slide.

II. Leave to Amend.

Amendment of pleadings in civil actions is governed by Rule 15(a), F.R.Civ.P., which provides in part that once issue is joined in a lawsuit, a party may amend his pleading "only by leave of court or by written consent of the adverse party; and leave shall be freely given when justice so requires."

In Foman v. Davis, 371 U.S. 178, 83 S.Ct. 227, 9 L.Ed.2d 222 (1962), the Supreme Court had occasion to construe that portion of Rule 15(a) set out above:

> Rule 15(a) declares that leave to amend "shall be freely given when justice so requires," this mandate is to be heeded. . . . If the underlying facts or circumstances relied upon by a plaintiff may be a proper subject of relief, he ought to be afforded an opportunity to test his claim on the merits. In the absence of any apparent or declared reason—such as undue delay, bad faith or dilatory motive on the part of the movant, repeated failure to cure deficiencies by amendments previously allowed, undue prejudice to the opposing party by virtue of allowance of the amendment, futility of amendment, etc.—the leave sought should, as the rules require, be "freely given." Of course, the grant or denial of an opportunity to amend is within the discretion of the District Court, . . .

This Court in Hanson v. Hunt Oil Co., 398 F.2d 578, 582 (8th Cir. 1968), held that "[p]rejudice must be shown." (Emphasis added). The burden is on the party opposing the amendment to show such prejudice. In ruling on a motion for leave to amend, the trial court must inquire into the issue of prejudice to the opposing party, in light of the particular facts of the case.

Certain principles apply to appellate review of a trial court's grant or denial of a motion to amend pleadings. First, as noted in Foman v. Davis, allowance or denial of leave to amend lies within the sound discretion of the trial court and is reviewable only for an abuse of discretion. The appellate court must view the case in the posture in which the trial court acted in ruling on the motion to amend.

It is evident from the order of the district court that in the exercise of its discretion in ruling on defendant's motion for leave to amend, it searched the record for evidence of bad faith, prejudice and undue delay which might be sufficient to overbalance the mandate of Rule 15(a), F.R.Civ.P., and Foman v. Davis, that leave to amend should be "freely given." Plaintiffs had not at any time conceded that the slide in question had not been manufactured by the defendant, and at the time the motion for leave to amend was at issue, the court had to decide whether the defendant should be permitted to litigate a material factual issue on its merits.

In inquiring into the issue of bad faith, the court noted the fact that the defendant, in initially concluding that it had manufactured the slide, relied upon the conclusions of three different insurance companies, each of which had conducted an investigation into the circumstances surrounding the accident. This reliance upon investigations of three insurance companies, and the fact that "no contention has been made by anyone that the defendant influenced this possibly erroneous conclusion," persuaded the court that "defendant has not acted in such bad faith as to be precluded from contesting the issue of manufacture at trial." The court further found "[t]o the extent that 'blame' is to be spread regarding the original identification, the record indicates that it should be shared equally."

In considering the issue of prejudice that might result to the plaintiffs from the granting of the motion for leave to amend, the trial court held that the facts presented to it did not support plaintiffs' assertion that, because of the running of the two-year Iowa statute of limitations on personal injury claims, the allowance of the amendment would sound the "death knell" of the litigation. In order to accept plaintiffs' argument, the court would have had to assume that the defendant would prevail at trial on the factual issue of manufacture of the slide, and further that plaintiffs would be foreclosed, should the amendment be allowed, from proceeding against other parties if they were unsuccessful in pressing their claim against Aquaslide. On the state of the record before it, the trial court was unwilling to make such assumptions, and concluded "[u]nder these circumstances, the Court deems that the possible prejudice to the plaintiffs is an insufficient basis on which to deny the proposed amendment." The court reasoned that the amendment would merely allow the defendant to contest a disputed factual issue at trial, and further that it would be prejudicial to the defendant to deny the amendment.

The court also held that defendant and its insurance carrier, in investigating the circumstances surrounding the accident, had not been so lacking in diligence as to dictate a denial of the right to litigate the factual issue of manufacture of the slide.

On this record we hold that the trial court did not abuse its discretion in allowing the defendant to amend its answer. . . .

The judgment of the district court is affirmed.

The Relation Back Doctrine

A civil action is commenced by filing a complaint with the court. (FRCP 3) However, plaintiffs do not have unlimited time within which to file a complaint. Deadlines for filing complaints are dictated by the applicable statute of limitations. Different claims or causes of action, will have different statutes of limitation. For example, the statute of limitations for a breach of a written contract will typically be longer than the statute of limitations for a claim of personal injury. In some jurisdictions the mere filing of the complaint stops the running of the statute, while in other jurisdictions service of the summons and complaint is required to stop the statute from running. What if a plaintiff seeks to amend a complaint after the time the statute of limitations would have run but for the filing of the original complaint? FRCP 15(c) provides that whenever "the claim or defense asserted in the amended pleading arose out of the conduct, transaction, or occurrence set forth or attempted to be set forth in the original pleading, the amendment relates back to the date of the original pleading."

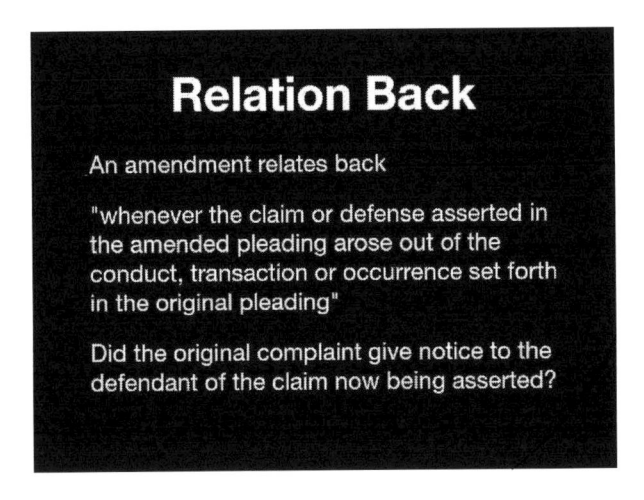

> **Relation Back**
>
> An amendment relates back
>
> "whenever the claim or defense asserted in the amended pleading arose out of the conduct, transaction or occurrence set forth in the original pleading"
>
> Did the original complaint give notice to the defendant of the claim now being asserted?

Smeltzley v. Nicholson Mfg. Co.
18 Cal.3d 932 (1977)

TOBRINER, Acting C.J.

Plaintiff's original complaint alleged injuries caused by his employers' failure to provide him a safe place to work; his amended complaint, filed after the statute of limitations had run, added a cause of action alleging that his injuries resulted from a defective machine manufactured by defendant Nicholson Manufacturing Company (hereinafter Nicholson). The trial court sustained Nicholson's demurrer without leave to amend and entered judgment for Nicholson.

We reverse that judgment. In Austin v. Massachusetts Bonding & Insurance Co.(1961) 56 Cal.2d 596 [15 Cal. Rptr. 817, 364 P.2d 681] and subsequent cases the California courts have established the rule that an amended complaint relates back to the filing of the original complaint, and thus avoids the bar of the statute of limitations, so long as recovery is sought in both pleadings on the same general set of facts. As we shall explain, since plaintiff's amended complaint seeks recovery for the same accident and injuries as the original complaint, it falls within the purview of the foregoing rule, and thus relates back to the date of filing of the original complaint. The trial court therefore erred in holding that plaintiff's cause of action against Nicholson was barred by the statute of limitations.

Plaintiff's leg was amputated as a result of injuries he sustained on March 24, 1971, while operating a debarking machine manufactured by defendant Nicholson. On March 24, 1972, he filed a complaint for personal injuries against his employers and several fictitiously named defendants. His first cause of action alleged that defendants were in control of the Sierra Mountain Mill, and owed plaintiff a duty to provide a safe place to work. Plaintiff asserts that "the place of employment was unsafe, dangerous and defective, all of which was either known or should have been known to the defendants. Nonetheless defendants ... directed the plaintiff to work at a place of employment which was dangerous, and through the negligence and carelessness of defendants ... in failing to provide a safe place to work, caused the plaintiff's leg to be amputated." Plaintiff's second cause of action added allegations that defendants recklessly disregarded plaintiff's safety, thus stating a cause of action under Labor Code section 3601. Both causes of action included a standard paragraph alleging that the true names and capacities of the fictitious defendants were unknown to plaintiff, but that each such defendant "is responsible in some manner for the events and happenings herein referred to, and caused injuries and damages proximately brought to the plaintiff as herein alleged."

On November 6, 1973, two and one-half years after the accident, plaintiff filed a first amended complaint. Substituting defendant Nicholson for Doe I, plaintiff alleged in his first cause of action that Nicholson manufactured the debarking machine which injured plaintiff, that the machine was "defective, dangerous and unsafe for its intended use," and that plaintiff's injury was the proximate result of the defective machine. The second and third causes of action of the first amended complaint restated the causes of action against plaintiff's employers which appeared in the original complaint.

Nicholson demurred to the first amended complaint, asserting that plaintiff's cause of action against Nicholson was barred by the one-year limitation of Code of Civil Procedure section 340, subdivision 3. The trial court sustained the demurrer without leave to amend and entered judgment for Nicholson. Plaintiff appeals from that judgment.

Plaintiff contends that his amended complaint relates back to the date of filing of the original complaint, and thus avoids the bar of the statute of limitations. The decision of this court in Austin v. Massachusetts Bonding & Insurance Co., supra, 56 Cal.2d 596 and subsequent decisions of the Courts of Appeal support that contention.

In Austin, plaintiff's original complaint charged that Pacific States Securities Corporation, its officers, and defendants sued under fictitious names refused to deliver securities and money received on behalf of plaintiff. The complaint alleged that defendants filed a "'surety bond in the sum of $5,000 for the faithful performance of its duties as a licensed broker. 'Plaintiff did not allege that defendants were surety on the bond or that plaintiff sought indemnification from the surety. The amended complaint, filed two years after the running of the statute of limitations, nevertheless substituted

Massachusetts Bonding for one of the fictitiously named defendants, and asserted the liability of Massachusetts Bonding under its surety bond for the defalcations of Pacific's officers.

In a unanimous opinion by Chief Justice Gibson, we reversed the trial court's judgment in favor of Massachusetts Bonding. Reviewing the California cases, we rejected both the older cases which decided that any amendment that changed the legal theory of the complaint could not relate back, and the more recent cases which held that an amendment would not relate back if it set forth a wholly different cause of action. "The modern rule," we explained, "is that ... where an amendment is sought after the statute of limitations has run, the amended complaint will be deemed filed as of the date of the original complaint provided recovery is sought in both pleadings on the same general set of facts."

The court then stated the rational foundation for its view in these words: "This rule is the result of a development which, in furtherance of the policy that cases should be decided on their merits, gradually broadened the right of a party to amend a pleading without incurring the bar of the statute of limitations."

Applying the foregoing rule to that case, the court found that both complaints alleged the same misconduct by Pacific and its officers, which misconduct constituted the grounds for the action on the bond added by the amended complaint. We concluded that "both pleadings are thus based on the same general set of facts.... Had Massachusetts Bonding been sued by its true name in the original complaint, the amendment changing the character of its obligation from that of a principal to that of a surety would have related back for purposes of the statute of limitations. The fact that it was initially designated by a fictitious name does not warrant a different result."

Seven years later, in Garrett v. Crown Coach Corp. (1968) 259 Cal. App.2d 647 [66 Cal. Rptr. 590], the Court of Appeal applied the principles established by Austin to a factual setting indistinguishable from the present case. Plaintiff Garrett's original complaint asserted that the named defendants and Does one through five negligently maintained and operated a school bus, causing the bus to strike plaintiff's vehicle and injure plaintiff. Garrett's second amended complaint, filed after the running of the statute of limitations, substituted Crown Coach Corporation for Doe I, and alleged that Crown negligently designed and manufactured the bus. The trial court sustained Crown's demurrer without leave to amend.

Relying on Austin, the Court of Appeal reversed the court below. Justice Files wrote that "plaintiff is seeking to hold Crown legally responsible for the same accident and the same injuries referred to in the original complaint. The amendment changes the alleged obligation of 'Doe One' from that of an operator to that of a manufacturer. This is no more drastic than the change of theory reflected by the amendment in Austin."

Garrett and the instant case present a striking parallel. In Garrett the original complaint charged the named and fictitious defendants with liability based upon their operation and maintenance of a bus; in the present case plaintiff charged the named and fictitious defendants with liability based upon their control and operation of a lumber mill. In both cases the original complaint did not state any facts upon which defendants' liability as a manufacturer could be predicated; the amended complaints, however, sought to change the obligation of "Doe One" from that of an operator to that of a manufacturer. Finally, in both cases the amended complaint sought recovery for the same accident and the same injuries as the original complaint. Rarely is a precedent so closely on point.

Nicholson does not assert that Garrett was wrongly decided, but unsuccessfully attempts to distinguish that precedent. Nicholson argues that in Garrett the original complaint referred to the bus as the cause of the accident, but that plaintiff's original complaint in the present case did not mention a debarking machine. But plaintiff's reference in the original complaint to defendants' control over the lumber mill necessarily includes defendants' control over machinery at that site; plaintiff's assertion of unsafe, dangerous and defective conditions at the mill is sufficiently general to comprehend any danger arising from defective mill machinery.

The crucial fact, moreover, is not whether the original complaint mentioned the debarking machine as the reason the mill premises were dangerous, but that, in the language of Garrett, the amended complaint refers to "the same accident and the same injuries referred to in the original complaint." Thus under the reasoning of Garrett, since the amended complaint in the present case rests upon the same general set of facts as the original complaint, it relates back to the filing of the original complaint.

The Garrett case found unanimous and express confirmation in a recent decision of this court: Grudt v. City of Los Angeles (1970) 2 Cal.3d 575 [86 Cal. Rptr. 465, 468 P.2d 825]. In that case plaintiff's initial complaint alleged that city police officers had intentionally killed her husband; the complaint predicated liability of the city upon respondeat superior. The amended complaint charged that "the City was liable for its own negligence in retaining the services of officers known to be dangerous." Although Grudt thus factually differs from the instant case in that it did not, as here, involve the addition of a new party defendant after the lapse of a period of limitation, it did embrace the addition of a new theory of action after such a lapse. This court, relying upon Austin and Garrett upheld the addition, holding that the counts against the officers and the city "recite the same acts ... as the gravamen of the action, and the recovery is sought in both counts to compensate plaintiff for the loss of her husband."

Finally, the recent Court of Appeal decision in Barnes v. Wilson (1974) 40 Cal. App.3d 199 [114 Cal. Rptr. 839] further extends the principles expounded in Austin,

Garrett and Grudt. Plaintiffs in a wrongful death action alleged that defendants, the owners of the Golden Gloves Tavern, negligently failed to warn the decedent of the danger created by his assailant's presence and negligently failed to protect decedent from the assailant. The fourth amended complaint, filed long after the statute of limitations had run, substituted defendants Theodore and Phyllis Noyd for Does II and III, and alleged that the Noyds, owners of the neighboring Copper Door Tavern, negligently served liquor to the already intoxicated assailant. The trial court sustained the Noyds' demurrer without leave to amend.

In reversing the trial court, the Court of Appeal relied upon the test established by Austin, inquiring whether recovery is sought on the same general set of facts. The court concluded that "In the case at bench, just as in Grudt v. City of Los Angeles, supra, 2 Cal.3d 575, and Garrett v. Crown Coach Corp., supra, 259 Cal. App.2d 647, plaintiffs' fourth amended complaint seeks to hold the Noyds responsible for the same occurrence and damage alleged in the original complaint. The amendment alleging a cause of action against the Noyds for negligently contributing to the dangerous behavior of the assailant is no more drastic than the amendment in Grudt alleging a cause of action against the city for allegedly retaining the officers with known propensities for violence, or the amendment in Garrett alleging a cause of action against the bus company for negligent design and manufacture."

Nicholson does not argue that Barnes was incorrectly decided or attempt to distinguish the pleadings in that case from the present case. Nicholson, instead, notes that in Barnes the court observed that the plaintiffs cannot be said to have "slept on their rights" and insinuates that the contrary is true in the present case. Defendant's demurrer, however, tests only the sufficiency of the pleadings. (3) (See fn. 1.) Nothing in the pleadings suggests that plaintiff, after learning of his cause of action against defendant, was dilatory in amending his complaint, or that defendant suffered prejudice from any such delay.

The foregoing precedents rest on the fundamental philosophy that "cases should be decided on their merits." In conformity with that policy, we conclude in the present case that plaintiff's amended complaint relates back to the filing of the original complaint. Both complaints issue from the same injuries and the same accident. The original complaint asserts that the injuries were caused by a dangerous condition of the employers' premises; the amended complaint identifies that condition as a defective machine manufactured by Nicholson. Thus, within the rule of Austin v. Massachusetts Bonding & Insurance Co., supra, 56 Cal.2d 596, the two complaints relate to the "same general set of facts."

In arguing to the contrary Nicholson contends that the facts necessary to establish a right to relief on a theory of failure to provide a safe place to work are different from those required to prove a product liability case; that the two causes of action rest upon different theories and invoke different legal duties. If plaintiff proved only the facts alleged in the original complaint, Nicholson observes, he would not be entitled to relief from Nicholson; if plaintiff proved only those in the first cause of action of the amended complaint, he would not be entitled to recover from the mill operators.

Nicholson's arguments, however, do not demonstrate that the original and amended complaint here do not relate to the same general set of facts within the Austin rule; they merely betray a misunderstanding of Austin and subsequent cases. In all of the cases discussed, supra, the original and amended complaints rested upon different theories and invoked different legal duties; consequently in each of those cases the facts necessary to prove liability under the amended complaint differed significantly from those required to prove liability under the original complaint. Thus in every such case proof of the facts alleged in the original complaint would not suffice to establish plaintiff's right to relief against the substituted defendant — otherwise plaintiff would have had no reason to amend the original complaint. In two cases, Garrett and Barnes, proof of the facts alleged in the amended complaint would not have established a right to relief against the original defendants. Nicholson's argument thus fails to offer any basis for distinguishing the present case from Austin and subsequent precedents.

Nicholson's argument not only totally fails to distinguish Austin and its progeny but relies upon principles clearly repudiated in those decisions. As Austin noted, it has long been held that a change in legal theory will not prevent an amendment from relating back. And Chief Justice Gibson warned that any attempt to determine whether an amendment related back by inquiring whether it stated a "'wholly different cause of action' ... results in confusion and undue restrictions of the right to amend." (P. 601.) Thus the fact that plaintiff's amended complaint in the instant case rests upon a different legal theory and may state a different cause of action than his original complaint is irrelevant under Austin; the test is whether the two complaints relate to the same general set of facts. And as we have explained, plaintiff's amended complaint, by seeking recovery for the same accident and injuries as the original complaint, complies with that test.

The judgment dismissing plaintiff's action as to defendant Nicholson Manufacturing Company is reversed.

Problem Sidney was involved in a traffic accident. In April 1986, five months after the accident, Sidney sued the other party and sought relief for property damage. In April 1987 Sidney, filed an amended complaint for personal injury. Assume that the statute of limitations is one year. Does the amended complaint for personal injury relate back to the original April 1986 complaint for property damage? (See, *Sidney v. Superior Court*, (1988) 198 Cal. App. 3d 710, 717, n4 and *Barrington v. A.H. Robins Co.*, (1985) 39 Cal.3d 146, 151)

Moore v. Baker
989 F.2d 1129 (1993)

MORGAN, Senior Circuit Judge:

. . . Appellant, Judith Moore, was suffering from a partial blockage of her left common carotid artery, which impeded the flow of oxygen to her brain and caused her to feel dizzy and tired. In April of 1989, she consulted with appellee Dr. Roy Baker, an employee of the Neurological Institute of Savannah, P.C. (NIS), about her symptoms. Dr. Baker diagnosed a blockage of her left carotid artery due to atherosclerotic plaque and recommended that she undergo a neurosurgical procedure . . . to correct her medical problem.

Dr. Baker discussed the proposed procedure with Moore and advised her of the risks of undergoing the surgery. He did not advise her, however, of an alternative treatment known as EDTA therapy. Moore signed a written consent allowing Dr. Baker to perform the carotid endarterectomy on April 7, 1989. Following surgery, she appeared to recover well, but soon the hospital staff discovered that Moore was weak on one side. Dr. Baker reopened the operative wound and removed a blood clot that had formed in the artery. Although the clot was removed and the area repaired, Moore suffered permanent brain damage. As a result, Moore is permanently and severely disabled.

On April 8, 1991, the last day permitted by the statute of limitations, Moore filed a complaint alleging that Dr. Baker committed medical malpractice by failing to inform her of the availability of EDTA therapy as an alternative to surgery in violation of Georgia's informed consent law, According to Moore's complaint, EDTA therapy is as effective as carotid endarterectomy in treating coronary blockages, but it does not entail those risks that accompany invasive surgery.

On August 6, 1991 Dr. Baker filed a motion for summary judgment on the issue of informed consent. On August 26, 1991, Moore moved to amend her complaint to assert allegations of negligence by Dr. Baker in the performance of the surgery and in his post-operative care of Moore. Originally, on September 3, 1991, the district court granted Moore's motion to amend her complaint. Shortly thereafter, the district court granted Dr. Baker's motion for summary judgment on the informed consent issue, finding that EDTA therapy is not a "generally recognized or accepted" alternative treatment for coronary surgery. One month later, the district court vacated its September 3rd order and denied Moore's motion to amend her complaint, thus terminating all of Moore's outstanding claims. Moore now appeals the denial of her motion to amend her complaint as well as the grant of summary judgment in favor of Dr. Baker and NIS.

Moore claims that the district court abused its discretion by vacating its earlier order and denying Moore's motion to amend her complaint. Leave to amend a complaint "shall be freely given when justice so requires." Fed.R.Civ.P. 15(a). While a decision whether to grant leave to amend is clearly within the discretion of the district court, a justifying reason must be apparent for denial of a motion to amend. In the instant case, the lower court denied leave to amend on the ground that the newly-asserted claim was barred by the applicable statute of limitations and that allowing the amendment would, therefore, be futile. If correct, the district court's rationale would be sufficient to support a denial of leave to amend the complaint. See Middle Atl. Util. Co. v. S.M.W. Dev. Corp., 392 F.2d 380, 385 (2d Cir.1968) ("It is normally proper for the trial judge to consider the statute of limitations on a motion to amend. To delay until there is a later motion to dismiss because the claim is time-barred would be a wasteful formality.")

Moore filed her original complaint on the last day permitted by Georgia's statute of limitations. Accordingly, the statute of limitations bars the claim asserted in Moore's proposed amended complaint unless the amended complaint relates back to the date of the original complaint. An amendment relates back to the original filing "[w]henever the claim or defense asserted in the amended pleading arose out of the conduct, transaction, or occurrence set forth or attempted to be set forth in the original pleading." Fed.R.Civ.P. 15(c). The critical issue in Rule 15(c) determinations is whether the original complaint gave notice to the defendant of the claim now being asserted. "When new or distinct conduct, transactions, or occurrences are alleged as grounds for recovery, there is no relation back, and recovery under the amended complaint is barred by limitations if it was untimely filed."

Moore relies heavily on Azarbal v. Medical Center of Delaware, Inc., 724 F.Supp. 279 (D.Del.1989), which addressed the doctrine of relation back in the context of a medical malpractice case. In Azarbal, the original complaint alleged negligence in the performance of an amniocentesis on the plaintiff, resulting in injury to the fetus. After the statute of limitations had expired, the plaintiff sought to amend the complaint to add a claim that the doctor failed to obtain her informed consent prior to performing a sterilization procedure on her because the doctor did not tell her that the fetus had probably been injured by the amniocentesis. The district court found that "the original complaint provided adequate notice of any claims Ms. Azarbal would have arising from the amniocentesis, including a claim that Dr. Palacio should have revealed that the procedure had caused fetal injury." Azarbal, supra at 283.

The instant case is clearly distinguishable from Azarbal. Unlike the complaint in Azarbal, the allegations asserted in Moore's original complaint contain nothing to put Dr. Baker on notice that the new claims of negligence might be asserted. Even when given a liberal construction, there is nothing in Moore's original complaint which makes reference to any acts of alleged negligence by Dr. Baker either during or after surgery. ["Moore's original complaint is very specific and focuses solely on Dr. Baker's failure to inform Moore of EDTA therapy as an alternative to surgery. Although the complaint recounts the details of the operation and subsequent recovery, it does not hint that Dr. Baker's actions were negligent. In fact, the only references in the original complaint relating to the surgery or post-operative care suggest that Dr. Baker acted with reasonable care. The complaint states that "the nurses noticed a sudden onset of right sided weakness of which they immediately informed Defendant Baker." "Upon being informed of this Defendant Baker immediately caused Plaintiff to be returned to the operation suite.... Although the clot was promptly removed by Defendant Baker...."] The original complaint focuses on Baker's actions before Moore decided to undergo surgery, but the amended complaint focuses on Baker's actions during and after the surgery. The alleged acts of negligence occurred at different times and involved separate and distinct conduct. In order to recover on the negligence claim contained in her amended complaint, Moore would have to prove completely different facts than would otherwise have been required to recover on the informed consent claim in the original complaint.

We must conclude that Moore's new claim does not arise out of the same conduct, transaction, or occurrence as the claims in the original complaint. Therefore, the amended complaint does not relate back to the original complaint, and the proposed new claims are barred by the applicable statute of limitations. Since the amended complaint could not withstand a motion to dismiss, we hold that the district court did not abuse its discretion in denying Moore's motion to amend her complaint. . . .

Problem Bonerb, a patient at a drug and alcohol rehabilitation facility, slipped and fell while playing basketball on a muddy court at the rehab facility. He sued claiming that the court was negligently maintained. Later, after the statute of limitations had run, he sought to amend his complaint to add a claim for counseling malpractice. May he do so? (See, *Bonerb v. Richard J. Caron Foundation*, 159 F.R.D. 16 (W.D.N.Y. 1994))

Fictitiously Named "Doe" Defendants

Suppose a plaintiff is involved in an automobile accident with another driver. The other driver had a passenger in the back seat. Local laws require drivers in such situations to exchange driver's license information. But there is no requirement that passengers identify themselves to the other driver. If plaintiff sues the other driver and theorizes that the passenger may have contributed to the accident by saying, "all clear" or "hurry up", how can he/she include the "back seat driver" in the complaint without knowing his/her identity?

California allows a plaintiff to name as defendants any number of "John (or Jane) Does" against whom the statute of limitations will then cease to run on any causes of action stated against them. When plaintiff becomes aware that he/she has sued a wrong defendant or has failed to sue a proper defendant, he/she may then merely substitute the name of the new defendants and proceed with the case. (See, Cal.Code.Civ.Proc § 474.)

Streicher v. Tommy's Electric Company
164 Cal.App.3d 876 (1985)

PANELLI, P.J.

Plaintiff appeals from a judgment of dismissal entered after defendants' demurrer to an amended complaint was sustained without leave to amend on the ground the statute of limitations barred the action. We reverse.

Facts

On October 4, 1979, plaintiff Frank Streicher filed a complaint for personal injuries sustained on July 16, 1979, at a construction site when certain radio-controlled overhead garage doors opened causing him to fall from the scaffolding upon which he was working. The complaint named as defendants Shippers Development Company (general contractor), Salinas Steel Builders, Inc. (subcontractor), Jack's Overhead Door Company, Inc. and John Hendrix (independent contractors and installers of the electronic doors), as well as four fictitious business entities (Black, White, Blue, and Grey Companies), three fictitious individuals comprising Grey Company as a partnership (Does One, Two, and Three), and ninety-seven additional fictitious defendants (Does Four through One Hundred).

The first paragraph of the complaint alleged that the true names and capacities of the fictitious defendants were unknown to plaintiff but stated that when these were ascertained plaintiff would move to amend the complaint accordingly. Paragraph six alleged a cause of action for negligence, charging that defendants owned, possessed and controlled the construction site, that they had provided an unsafe workplace through their failure, among other things, to "supervise and control the installation and operation of radio-controlled overhead garage doors" on the worksite, and that such negligence resulted in plaintiff's injuries.

On May 18, 1982, two years and ten months after the accident, and after settlement was obtained with the named defendants, Streicher filed a first amended complaint against respondents Tommy's Electric Company and Shima American Corporation and Does Four through One Hundred. It alleged respondents designed, manufactured, marketed and sold the radio-controlled overhead door openers involved in the accident and that these openers had been defectively designed and would malfunction without human intervention. The amended complaint stated causes of action for negligence, breach of express and implied warranty, and strict products liability.

On June 17, 1982, respondents demurred to the first amended complaint on the ground that the claim was barred by the one-year statute of limitations (Code Civ. Proc., § 340, subd. (3)). Respondents also moved the court to judicially notice, pursuant to

Evidence Code sections 452 and 453, all the pleadings and records in its file on this case including a cross-complaint filed by Jack's Overhead Doors (one of the named defendants) and a complaint in intervention filed by Industrial Indemnity Co. (plaintiff's employer's workers' compensation carrier), both filed in February of 1980, which included respondents among the named defendants and alleged causes of action for indemnity based on a products liability theory.

Respondents argued in their moving papers that since plaintiff's amended complaint did not substitute respondents for any of the fictitiously named defendants in his original complaint, the amended complaint was in fact adding new defendants to the action and that this was not permissible after the running of the one-year statute of limitations. Respondents further argued that even if plaintiff's defective substitution of fictitious defendants was cured, the provisions of Code of Civil Procedure section 474, allowing the amendment to relate back to the filing of the original complaint, did not apply because in February of 1980 plaintiff had notice of respondents' identity through the filing of the cross-complaint and intervention pleadings, yet he had nevertheless failed to exercise due diligence in amending his complaint before the expiration of the statute of limitations in July 1980.

Streicher opposed respondents' demurrer and moved for leave to amend his complaint in order to properly substitute respondents for specifically named fictitious defendants, arguing his failure to do so constituted a procedural error which could be easily cured. Streicher also argued the benefits afforded by section 474 should apply because he was not aware of any facts constituting the basis for a products liability cause of action against respondents until March 30, 1982, when an electronics expert indicated that the electronic door controllers involved in the accident were defective.

The court sustained respondents' demurrer without leave to amend on the ground the statute of limitations barred the action. The court's minute order also noted that plaintiff's early pleadings were consistent with his belief that "before March 30, 1982 ... [he] had no basis for an action against the two defendants." This appeal followed.

Discussion

On appeal, Streicher contends the trial court erroneously sustained the demurrer and abused its discretion in denying him leave to amend the complaint to cure his failure to specifically substitute respondents for fictitious defendants named in the original complaint. We find these contentions meritorious.

Preliminarily we must determine whether Streicher's first amended complaint, absent his defective substitution of respondents for the fictitiously named defendants, relates back to the filing date of the original complaint under section 474, thus defeating the bar of the statute of limitations.

"The purpose of ... section 474 is to enable a plaintiff who is ignorant of the identity of the defendant to file his complaint before his claim is barred by the statute of limitations. There is a strong policy in favor of litigating cases on their merits, and the California courts have been very liberal in permitting the amendment of pleadings to bring in a defendant previously sued by fictitious name." It is also well settled that the amended pleading will relate back to the date of filing of the original complaint provided it seeks recovery on the same general set of facts as alleged in the original complaint. Moreover, it is clear that where the original complaint contains standard Doe allegations alleging negligence theories, it is proper to amend the complaint to bring in other defendants on warranty and products liability; since the amendment involves the same accident and injury, the amendment relates back to satisfy the statute of limitations.

However, in order to claim the benefits of section 474, plaintiff's ignorance of defendant's true name must be genuine and not feigned. We must therefore look to see whether plaintiff knew defendant's true name at the time he filed his original complaint. Plaintiff's requisite ignorance of defendant's name under section 474 has been expansively interpreted by the courts to encompass situations where "'he knew the identity of the person but was ignorant of the facts giving him a cause of action against the person [citations], or knew the name and all the facts but was unaware that the law gave him a cause of action against the fictitiously named defendant and discovered that right by reason of decisions rendered after the commencement of the action. Moreover, section 474's ignorance requirement "is restricted to the knowledge of the plaintiff at the time of filing of the complaint" , "and does not relate to steps that should be taken after the filing of the action."

Guided by the foregoing principles we turn to the case at bar. Streicher's original complaint contained standard "Doe" allegations against fictitious defendants then unknown, as required by section 474. Although the original complaint alleged a cause of action for negligence against all defendants for failing to provide a safe place to work, it was proper to amend the complaint to bring in the defectively substituted defendants on the additional warranty and products liability theories of recovery since the amendment involved the same accident and injury alleged in the original complaint. (See Smeltzley v. Nicholson Mfg. Co., supra, 18 Cal.3d at p. 937.) It is undisputed that at the time Streicher's original complaint was filed he was ignorant of respondents' identity or of their participation in designing, manufacturing or selling the electronic door openers involved in the accident. Likewise Streicher did not know at this time any facts which would indicate the possibility the door openers were defectively designed as such flaw in design was not externally visible.

Respondents contend, nevertheless, that Streicher did not "in good faith" avail himself of the provisions of section 474 because four months after his original complaint was filed he was alerted, through the filing of cross-complaint and intervention pleadings, of respondents' role in manufacturing and distributing the electronic door devices and of the possibility they could be sued under a products liability theory of recovery. As pointed out above, plaintiff's actual knowledge at the time the suit is filed is dispositive in triggering the application of section 474's fictitious defendant provisions Further, it remains undisputed that at the time of the filing of the original complaint Streicher was ignorant of respondents' identity or of their status as manufacturers and distributors of the defective door openers. Moreover, there is no requirement under section 474 that plaintiff exercise reasonable diligence in discovering either the true identity of fictitious defendants or the facts giving him a cause of action against such persons after the filing of a complaint and up to the expiration of the applicable limitation period. As aptly stated by the court in Munoz, supra, "the interjection of a discovery standard into section 474 would lead to the harmful practice in all litigation of requiring that all persons who might conceivably have some connection with the lawsuit be specifically named in order to avoid the sanctions of the failure to comply with the inquiry requirements of section 474."

Respondent also argues that, irrespective of appellant's lack of knowledge of the true identity of the fictitiously named defendants at the time he filed the original complaint, he was nonetheless "dilatory" in filing the amended complaint once he acquired knowledge of the true identity of those defendants fictitiously named. Respondent contends that unreasonable delay in filing the amendment after actual discovery of the true identity of a fictitiously named defendant can bar a plaintiff's resort to the fictitious name procedure. Some authority for this proposition can be found in Barrows v. American Motor Corp., supra, 144 Cal. App.3d at pages 8-9, and in Barnes v. Wilson, supra, 40 Cal. App.3d 199 at page 206. Here, however the trial court was only dealing with a demurrer to the amended complaint. "Defendant's demurrer, however, tests only the sufficiency of the pleadings. Nothing in the pleadings suggests that plaintiff, after learning of his cause of action against defendant, was dilatory in amending his complaint, or that defendant suffered prejudice from such delay. [citation]." (Smeltzley v. Nicholson Mfg. Co., supra, 18 Cal.3d 932, at p. 939, fns. omitted.) Nothing in this record suggests appellant was dilatory in amending his complaint. In fact, the trial court's order states that before March 30, 1982, "[appellant] had no basis for an action against the two defendants." Once he learned the facts giving him a cause of action against respondents on March 30, 1982, his first amended complaint naming respondents as defendants was promptly filed on May 18, 1982, within two months of discovery.

We conclude that, absent Streicher's defective substitution of respondents for the fictitiously named defendants, his first amended complaint relates back to the filing date of the original complaint under section 474, thus defeating the bar of the statute of limitations.

The issue remains whether the court abused its discretion in denying Streicher leave to amend the complaint to cure his failure to properly allege that respondents were being substituted for some of the fictitiously named defendants in the original complaint. Streicher argues this omission constituted a procedural error which was easily curable through amendment. We agree.

"It is axiomatic that if there is a reasonable possibility that a defect in the complaint can be cured by amendment or that the pleading liberally construed can state a cause of action, a demurrer should not be sustained without leave to amend. We are satisfied the amended complaint's allegations sufficiently state a cause of action for products liability against respondents. Moreover, "[a]n amendment substituting the true names of fictitious defendants is not a matter of substance because it does not change the cause of action nor affect the issues raised by the pleadings. Since the defect in the complaint does not affect the substance of its allegations and it is reasonably possible the defect can be cured by amendment, we conclude the trial court abused its discretion in dismissing the action without giving Streicher the opportunity to amend.

The judgment of dismissal is reversed.

CHAPTER 5

JOINDER OF PARTIES AND CLAIMS

Here we explore the exceptions to the rule that "plaintiff is the master of his claim." In other words, it is up to the plaintiff to decide who the parties to the lawsuit will be and which claims will be asserted. In its simplest form, a lawsuit has a single plaintiff asserting a single cause of action against a single defendant. The common law rarely deviated from this form and had strict rules regarding joinder of claims and parties.

Joinder of Claims

FRCP 18 allows a party to join as many claims, counterclaims, cross-claims, and third-party claims as he has against another party. Parties may add as many claims as they wish. The only restriction on joinder of claims in the federal courts is imposed by subject matter jurisdiction limitations. Thus in federal courts, each claim generally must have an independent basis for subject matter jurisdiction. Personal jurisdiction and venue also must be proper as to each claim. (Friedenthal § 6.6) There is no requirement that the claims that are joined be related to each other.

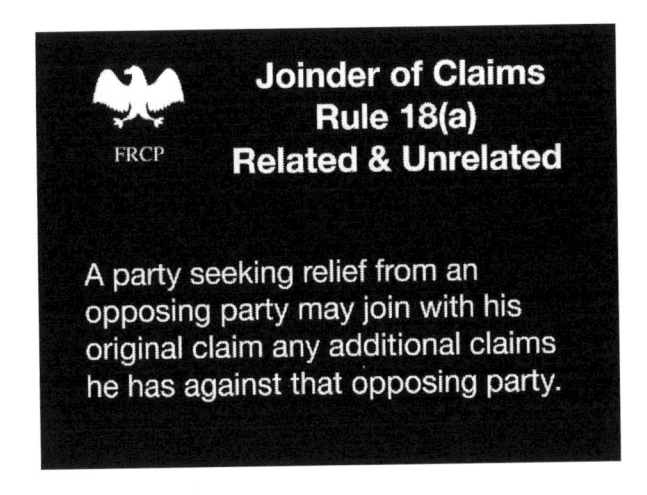

> **Joinder of Claims**
> **Rule 18(a)**
> **Related & Unrelated**
>
> A party seeking relief from an opposing party may join with his original claim any additional claims he has against that opposing party.

Original Claims

Let's take a simple auto collision case. In a hurry to get home after class, you back your car into one of your classmates in the law school parking lot. The other student sues you for the damage to their vehicle. That would be an example of a plaintiff's original claim. Suppose that same plaintiff had sold you some textbooks on credit that you still owed him or her for. Could they include that claim for money owed in the same lawsuit even though it is unrelated to the fender bender? FRCP 18 says yes. Parties may combine or join claims in a single lawsuit regardless of whether they are related or unrelated.

Counterclaims

Suppose further that after being sued you decide it was the plaintiff who was really at fault because they did not turn on the lights to the vehicle. Could you make a claim against them in this lawsuit or would you have to bring a separate lawsuit. The answer is that you have the option to bring it in this lawsuit. Your claim, as a defending party, would be denominated as a "counterclaim." A counterclaim is any affirmative claim for relief asserted by a pleader -- typically the defendant -- in the defensive pleadings against an opposing party -- typically the plaintiff. Counterclaims may be asserted only against opposing parties. Any claim that a defendant has against a plaintiff may be asserted as a counterclaim. (Friedenthal, §§6.7, 6.8)

> **Joinder of Claims**
> **Rule 13**
> **Counterclaims**
>
> FRCP
>
> Authorizes a defending party in a suit to assert claims back against a party who has claimed against him.
>
> Such claims may be either, *compulsory* or *permissive*.

The Federal Rules recognize two different kinds of counterclaims. If defendant's claim arises out of the same transaction or occurrence that gave rise to plaintiff's original claim, it is a "compulsory counterclaim" and it must be asserted as such or be forever barred. Any claim defendant has against plaintiff that does not arise out of the transaction or occurrence that gave rise to plaintiff's original claim is a "permissive counterclaim." Rule 13(b) permits a defendant to assert such a claim as a counterclaim but does not compel him/her to do so. The permissive counterclaim may be asserted in a subsequent lawsuit. (See, Wright, §79)

Plant v. Blazer Financial Services, Inc.
598 F.2d 1357 (1979)

RONEY, Circuit Judge:

In this truth-in-lending case . . .we decide that an action on the underlying debt in default is a compulsory counterclaim that must be asserted in a suit by the debtor on a truth-in-lending cause of action. . . .

On July 17, 1975 plaintiff Theresa Plant executed a note in favor of defendant Blazer Financial Services, Inc. for $2,520.00 to be paid in monthly installments of $105.00. No payments were made on the note. In March 1976 plaintiff commenced a civil action under § 1640 of the Truth-in-Lending Act, 15 U.S.C.A. § 1601 et seq., for failure to make disclosures required by the Act and by Regulation Z, 12 C.F.R. § 226.1 et seq. (1978), promulgated thereunder. Defendant counterclaimed on the note for the unpaid balance. Based on defendant's failure to disclose a limitation on an after-acquired security interest, the trial court held the disclosure inadequate and awarded plaintiff the statutory penalty of $944.76 and $700.00 in attorney's fees. . . .

The trial court, however, offset the plaintiff's award and the attorney's fee award against the judgment for defendant on the counterclaim. From this judgment and setoff, plaintiff appeals on three issues: (1) the jurisdiction of the court to entertain the counterclaim, (2) defenses to the counterclaim under Georgia law, and (3) the offset of attorney's fees.

Plaintiff challenges the trial court's ruling that defendant's counterclaim on the underlying debt was compulsory. The issue is jurisdictional. A permissive counterclaim must have an independent jurisdictional basis, while it is generally accepted that a compulsory counterclaim falls within the ancillary jurisdiction of the federal courts even if it would ordinarily be a matter for state court consideration. In the instant case there is no independent basis since neither federal question nor diversity jurisdiction is available for the counterclaim. Consequently, if the counterclaim were to be treated as permissive, defendant's action on the underlying debt would have to be pursued in the state court.

The issue of whether a state debt counterclaim in a truth-in-lending action is compulsory or permissive is one of first impression in this Circuit, has never, to our knowledge, been decided by a court of appeals, and has received diverse treatment from a great number of district courts. . . .

Rule 13(a), Fed.R.Civ.P., provides that a counterclaim is compulsory if it "arises out of the transaction or occurrence" that is the subject matter of plaintiff's claim. Four tests have been suggested to further define when a claim and counterclaim arise from the same transaction:

1) Are the issues of fact and law raised by the claim and counterclaim largely the same?
2) Would res judicata bar a subsequent suit on defendant's claim absent the compulsory counterclaim rule?
3) Will substantially the same evidence support or refute plaintiff's claim as well as defendant's counterclaim?
4) Is there any logical relation between the claim and the counterclaim?

An affirmative answer to any of the four questions indicates the counterclaim is compulsory.

The test which has commended itself to most courts, including our own, is the logical relation test. The logical relation test is a loose standard which permits "a broad realistic interpretation in the interest of avoiding a multiplicity of suits." 3 Moore's Federal Practice ¶ 13.13 at 300. "The hallmark of this approach is its flexibility." 6 Wright & Miller at 46-47.

In Revere Copper & Brass this Court added a third tier to the counterclaim analysis by further defining "logical relationship" to exist when the counterclaim arises from the same "aggregate of operative facts" in that the same operative facts serves as the basis of both claims or the aggregate core of facts upon which the claim rests activates additional legal rights, otherwise dormant, in the defendant.

Applying the logical relationship test literally to the counterclaim in this case clearly suggests its compulsory character because a single aggregate of operative facts, the loan transaction, gave rise to both plaintiff's and defendant's claim. Because a tallying of the results from the district courts which have decided this question, however, shows that a greater number have found such a counterclaim merely permissive, we subject the relationship between the claims to further analysis.

The split of opinion on the nature of debt counterclaims in truth-in-lending actions appears to be, in large part, the product of competing policy considerations between the objectives of Rule 13(a) and the policies of the Truth-in-Lending Act, and disagreement over the extent to which federal courts should be involved in state causes of action for debt. While Rule 13(a) is intended to avoid multiple litigation by consolidating all controversies between the parties, several courts and commentators have observed that accepting creditors' debt counterclaims may obstruct achievement of the goals of the Truth-in-Lending Act.

> Various arguments are made compositely as follows: The purpose of the Act is to assure a meaningful disclosure of credit terms so that the consumer will be able to compare more readily the various credit terms available to him and avoid the uninformed use of credit.

15 U.S.C.A. § 1601. This purpose is effectuated by debtors' standing in the role of private attorneys general not merely to redress individual injuries but to enforce federal policy. The success of this private enforcement scheme would be undermined if debtors were faced with counterclaims on debts often exceeding the limits of their potential recovery under the Act. The purpose of the Act would suffer further frustration if federal courts were entangled in the myriad factual and legal questions essential to a decision on the debt claims but unrelated to the truth-in-lending violation. In Roberts v.

National School of Radio & Television Broadcasting, 374 F.Supp. 1266 (N.D.Ga.1974), the court also noted the incongruity of enlisting the federal court's resources to assist in debt collection by the very target of the legislation which gives the plaintiff its cause of action.

Several other factors have been cited to offset the attractiveness of treating all related disputes in a single action under Rule 13. For example, courts have predicted a flood of debt counterclaims, greatly increasing the federal court workload. Furthermore, permitting debt counterclaims might destroy truth-in-lending class actions by interjecting vast numbers of individual questions. The judicial economy of consolidated litigation might be countered by the delay of having to provide a jury trial for the debt claim though none is available to the truth-in-lending plaintiff. Other courts have suggested that regarding such debt counterclaims as compulsory would infringe on the power of states to adjudicate disputes grounded in state law.

Courts which have concluded debt counterclaims to be permissive have found the nexus between the truth-in-lending violation and debt obligation too abstract or tenuous to regard the claims as logically related. One claim, they reason, involves the violation of federal law designed to deter lender nondisclosure and facilitate credit shopping and the other concerns merely a default on a private duty.

After careful consideration of the factors relied upon in these cases to find counterclaims permissive, we opt for the analysis applied by district courts in Louisiana, Alabama, Texas and Georgia in determining debt counterclaims to be compulsory...

The results reached in Carter were found "inescapable" in George v. Beneficial Finance Co. of Dallas, 81 F.R.D. 4 (N.D.Tex.1977). Emphasizing the goal of judicial economy furthered by a single presentation of facts, the court observed that "suits on notes will inevitably deal with the circumstance of the execution of the notes and any representation made to `induce' the borrowing."...

We add to these arguments the observation that one of the purposes of the compulsory counterclaim rule is to provide complete relief to the defendant who has been brought involuntarily into the federal court. Absent the opportunity to bring a counterclaim, this party could be forced to satisfy the debtor's truth-in-lending claim without any assurance that his claims against the defaulting debtor arising from the same transaction will be taken into account or even that the funds he has been required to pay will still be available should he obtain a state court judgment in excess of the judgment on the truth-in-lending claim. In addition, a determination that the underlying debt was invalid may have a material effect on the amount of damages a debtor could recover on a truth-in-lending claim.

To permit the debtor to recover from the creditor without taking the original loan into account would be a serious departure from the evenhanded treatment afforded both parties under the Act. Truth-in-lending claims can be brought in either state or federal court. To the extent this dual jurisdiction was intended to permit litigation of truth-in-lending claims in actions on the debt, it reflects a purpose that the debt claim and the truth-in-lending claims be handled together. To the extent it was intended to relieve federal courts of any of this litigation, the purpose would be frustrated by providing a sanctuary from the creditor's claims in one jurisdiction but not in the other. State courts would always have jurisdiction of a creditor's counterclaim. Had Congress intended to insulate recovery in truth-in-lending actions in federal court from the counterclaims of creditors, of which it surely was aware, it could have easily done so.

We conclude that the obvious interrelationship of the claims and rights of the parties, coupled with the common factual basis of the claims, demonstrates a logical relationship between the claim and counterclaim under the test of Revere Copper & Brass. We affirm the trial court's determination that the debt counterclaim is compulsory.

Burlington Northern Railroad Co. v. Strong
907 F.2d 707 (1990)

RIPPLE, Circuit Judge.

John Strong sued his employer, Burlington Northern Railroad Company (Burlington), alleging personal injury tort damages. A jury awarded Mr. Strong $73,000. Thereafter, Burlington moved to set off against the judgment money received by Mr. Strong from a disability insurance program funded by Burlington. The district court denied this motion. Burlington then brought a separate suit to recover the funds. Summary judgment in favor of Burlington for the entire amount of the disability funds was entered on November 30, 1988. Mr. Strong appeals from the district court's judgment in the second suit. For the following reasons, we affirm.

Mr. Strong was a member of the Brotherhood of Maintenance of Way Employees during his employment with Burlington. The union operated under a collective bargaining agreement that applied to all union employees the provisions of the Supplemental Sickness Benefit Agreement of 1973 (1973 Agreement). In turn, the 1973 Agreement provided that the Supplemental Sickness Benefits (SSB) received by employees would not duplicate recovery of lost wages from a disability case.

Mr. Strong was injured in two separate accidents on September 12, 1983 and March 5, 1985 during his employment with Burlington. He brought suit against Burlington to recover for these injuries under the Federal Employers Liability Act (FELA), 45 U.S.C. §§ 51-60. Following a jury trial, Mr. Strong was awarded $73,000 in compensation for the 1983 injury; Burlington was found not liable for the 1985 injury.

After the trial, Burlington moved for a determination that the amount of the judgment ought to be reduced by $11,678.21, the amount paid to Mr. Strong in SSB benefits. The district court held that, "in the absence of a lien or judgment in its favor, [Burlington] is not entitled to withhold the sum of $11,678.21 for any Supplemental Sickness Benefit paid to [Mr. Strong]." However, the district court suggested that Mr. Strong could not succeed in keeping the money if Burlington sued on the contract:

I note that plaintiff's recalcitrance in refusing to remit the $11,678.21 sum allegedly paid out as Supplemental Sickness Benefit payments may well have adverse consequences for plaintiff himself.... [I]t seems clear that defendant can sue on the contract to recover this amount of money from plaintiff, and that if it does so, plaintiff will be subject to additional and probably unnecessary costs for defending a new lawsuit.

Taking its cue from the district court, Burlington sued on the contract to recover the SSB payments. Mr. Strong argued that the railroad's suit was barred by res judicata because such a claim should have been brought as a compulsory counterclaim to the previous FELA suit. However, the court decided that the railroad's claim was a permissive, not compulsory, counterclaim: "Burlington Northern's right to recoup the disability benefits does not arise out of the same occurrence (the accidents) that gave rise to Strong's lawsuit; it derives from the provisions of the Supplemental Sickness Benefit Agreement of May 12, 1973." The court further decided that, even if the claim could be said to be related to the same occurrence, an exception for claims that had not matured at the time of filing the answer would apply. . . .

Mr. Strong argues that Burlington's claim for setoff was a compulsory counterclaim that was waived when Burlington failed to raise it during the first trial (Mr. Strong's FELA trial). See Fed.R.Civ.P. 13(a) Rule 13(a) is "in some ways a harsh rule"[1] if a counterclaim is compulsory and the party does not bring it in the original lawsuit, that claim is thereafter barred. But the rule serves a valuable role in the litigation process, especially in conserving judicial resources. As we have noted, Rule 13(a) "is the result of a balancing between competing interests. The convenience of the party with a compulsory counterclaim is sacrificed in the interest of judicial economy." Martino v. McDonald's Sys., Inc., 598 F.2d 1079, 1082 (7th Cir.), cert. denied, 444 U.S. 966, 100 S.Ct. 455, 62 L.Ed.2d 379 (1979); see also Car Carriers, Inc. v. Ford Motor Co., 789 F.2d 589, 594 n. 7 (7th Cir.1986) (noting that Rule 13(a) "encourages the simultaneous and final resolution of all claims which arise from a common factual background"); Warshawsky & Co. v. Arcata Nat'l Corp., 552 F.2d 1257, 1261 (7th Cir.1977) ("The purpose of the rule is to prevent multiplicity of actions and to achieve resolution in a single lawsuit of all disputes arising out of common matters.") . . .

In order to be a compulsory counterclaim, Rule 13(a) requires that the claim (1) exist at the time of pleading, (2) arise out of the same transaction or occurrence as the opposing party's claim, and (3) not require for adjudication parties over whom the court may not acquire jurisdiction. There is no dispute that the third element — no required third parties — is met in this case. Our disposition therefore must turn on whether the other two requirements are met. We shall discuss them in the same order as the district court: 1) the same transaction and 2) the existence at the time of pleading requirements.

This court has developed a "logical relationship" test to determine whether the "transaction or occurrence" is the same for purposes of Rule 13(a).

> "Courts generally have agreed that the words 'transaction or occurrence' should be interpreted liberally in order to further the general policies of the federal rules and carry out the philosophy of Rule 13(a).... As a word of flexible meaning, 'transaction' may comprehend a series of many occurrences, depending not so much upon the immediateness of their connection as upon their logical relationship. ... [A] counterclaim that has its roots in a separate transaction or occurrence is permissive and is governed by Rule 13(b)."

Gilldorn Sav. Ass'n v. Commerce Sav. Ass'n, 804 F.2d 390, 396 (7th Cir.1986) Despite this liberal construction, we have stressed that our inquiry cannot be a "'wooden application of the common transaction label.'" Rather, we must examine carefully the factual allegations underlying each claim to determine if the logical relationship test is met. . . .

In short, there is no formalistic test to determine whether suits are logically related. A court should consider the totality of the claims, including the nature of the claims, the legal basis for recovery, the law involved, and the respective factual backgrounds. . . .

Even when a counterclaim meets the "same transaction" test, a party need not assert it as a compulsory counterclaim if it has not matured when the party serves his answer. This maturity exception "is derived from the language in the rule limiting its application to claims the pleader has 'at the time of serving the pleading.'" 6 C. Wright, A. Miller & M. Kane, Federal Practice and Procedure § 1411, at 81 (2d ed. 1990). "This exception to the compulsory counterclaim requirement necessarily encompasses a claim that depends upon the outcome of some other lawsuit and thus does not come into existence until the action upon which it is based has terminated."

We believe, in light of the foregoing principles, that the district court correctly concluded that Burlington's claim was not a compulsory counterclaim. We agree with the district court that the claims do not arise out of the same transaction. Burlington's right to recoup does not arise out of the same occurrence that gave rise to Mr. Strong's earlier suit. His suit is grounded in the accidents that resulted in his injury. By contrast, Burlington's suit is grounded in the provisions of the Supplemental Sickness Benefit Agreement of May 12, 1973. The two claims "raise different legal and factual issues governed by different bodies of law." Valencia, 617 F.2d at 1291. "Judicial economy would not be well served in this case as these two actions are based on separate transactions...." Gilldorn Sav. Ass'n, 804 F.2d at 397. They "lack any shared realm of genuine dispute." Valencia, 617 F.2d at 1291

We also agree with the district court that, even if we were to assume, arguendo, that these claims involve the same transaction, Burlington's claim need not have been brought as a counterclaim. It did not exist until the conclusion of the first suit when Mr. Strong obtained his judgment. Thus, the so-called "maturity exception" would permit the maintenance of this second suit. Accordingly, the district court properly determined that the railroad's claim is a permissive counterclaim that was not waived by Burlington's failure to plead it in the FELA case. . . .

For the foregoing reasons, we affirm the judgment of the district court.

Crossclaims

While counterclaims are claims a party may have against an opposing party, FRCP 13 also recognizes that co-parties (e.g. co-defendants or co-plaintiffs) may assert claims against each other. Under FRCP 13(g), a crossclaim against a co-party is allowed only if it is a claim "arising out of the transaction or occurrence that is the subject matter of the original action or of a counterclaim."

Third Party Claims: Impleading "Strangers" Into the Lawsuit

Let's suppose you are the proprietor of a small neighborhood bodega buying your inventory from a big wholesale warehouse. A customer, poisoned by a foreign substance in a can of soup he purchased sues you. Can you pass liability on to the manufacturer of the soup with which you have had no dealings?

This is an example of a situation in which the law permits liability to be passed on to some third party. Impleader is a way of doing that passing on within the scope of the same lawsuit. Of course this could be done in two lawsuits, the first against the primary obligor who would then turn around and sue the secondary obligor in a second suit. FRCP 14 combines these two suits into one. FRCP 14 provides that a defendant can bring in as a third-party defendant one claimed by the defendant to be liable to him for all or part of the plaintiff's claim against the defendant. The rule is not mandatory; defendant may refrain from impleader and assert his claim instead in an independent action if he prefers. (Wright, §76)

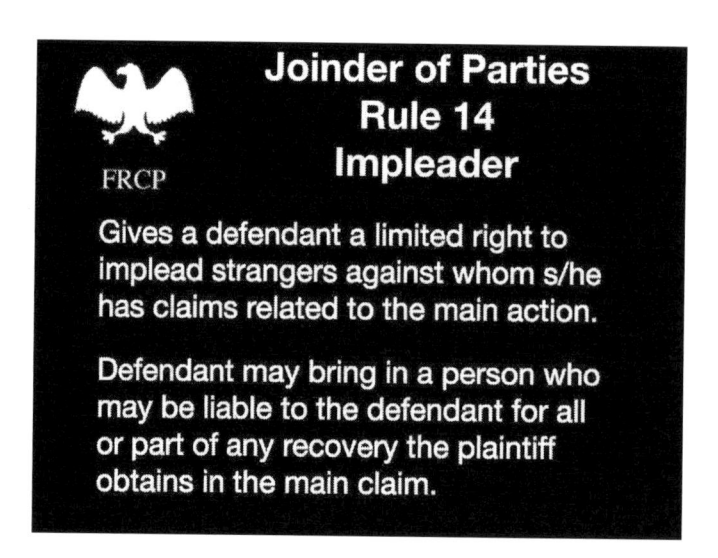

> **Joinder of Parties**
> **Rule 14**
> **Impleader**
>
> FRCP
>
> Gives a defendant a limited right to implead strangers against whom s/he has claims related to the main action.
>
> Defendant may bring in a person who may be liable to the defendant for all or part of any recovery the plaintiff obtains in the main claim.

Impleader seeks to assert a claim against someone who is not already a party to the action. It must involve a transfer of liability based on the plaintiff's original claim. Impleader of a third party because he is directly liable to the plaintiff in the original action is forbidden. (Friedenthal §6.9)

In other words, it is not permissible under FRCP 14 for a defendant to implead a third party that the defendant claims is solely liable to the plaintiff….A proposed third-party plaintiff must allege facts sufficient to establish the derivative or secondary liability of the proposed third-party defendant….Thus, under Rule 14(a), a third-party complaint is appropriate only in cases where the proposed third-party defendant would be secondarily liable to the original defendant in the event the latter is held to be liable to the plaintiff. *(Barab v. Menford,* 98 F.R.D. 455, 456 (E.D. Pa. 1983)

The third-party defendant, who is impleaded under FRCP 14 has the right to assert any defenses which the third-party plaintiff may have to the plaintiff's claim. This protects the impleaded third-party defendant where the third-party plaintiff fails or neglects to assert a proper defense to the plaintiff's action. The third-party defendant also has the right to assert directly against the original plaintiff any claim arising out of the transaction or occurrence that is the subject matter of the plaintiff's claim against the third-party plaintiff. This permits all claims arising out of the same transaction or occurrence to be heard and determined in the same action. (Advisory Committee Notes 1946 Amendment.)

Price v. CTB, Inc.
168 F.Supp.2d 1299 (2001)

DE MENT, District Judge.

Latco, a building contractor, is an original defendant in the underlying action concerning the quality of its workmanship when it constructed chicken houses for various Alabama farmers. The causes of action against Latco include breach of the construction contract, fraudulent misrepresentation of the caliber of materials to be used, and negligence and wantonness in the construction. Latco moved to file a Third-Party Complaint against, inter alios, ITW on February 21, 2001, approximately six months after the case had been removed to the Middle District of Alabama. It failed in its attempt to properly serve ITW until July 19, because it did not name the appropriate agent for service. In the Third-Party Complaint, Latco alleges that ITW, a nail manufacturer, defectively designed the nails used in the construction of the chicken houses. The specific causes of action include breach of warranty, violation of the Alabama Extended Manufacturer's Liability Doctrine, and common law indemnity. ITW argues that it was improperly impleaded under Rule 14 of the Federal Rules of Civil Procedure, . . .

Under Rule 14(a), a defendant may assert a claim against anyone not a party to the original action if that third party's liability is in some way dependent upon the outcome of the original action. There is a limitation on this general statement, however. Even though it may arise out of the same general set of facts as the main claim, a third-party claim will not be permitted when it is based upon a separate and independent claim. Rather, the third-party liability must in some way be derivative of the original claim; a third party may be impleaded only when the original defendant is trying to pass all or part of the liability onto that third party.

Latco argues that ITW is the prototypical third-party defendant under Rule 14. It asserts that ITW can be found liable for the warranty surrounding its products if Latco is first found liable for faulty construction. Furthermore, insists Latco, this derivative liability merely involves a shift in the overall responsibility of the allegedly defective chicken houses. ITW contends, however, that because Rule 14 is merely a procedural rule, the propriety of its application depends upon the existence of a right to indemnity under the substantive law. ITW accurately states the law in this regard, but its conclusion that there is no viable substantive claim under Alabama law is incorrect.

Conceding that Alabama does not recognize a right to contribution among joint tortfeasors, Latco directs the court's attention to the concept of implied contractual indemnity. Under this doctrine, Alabama courts recognize that a manufacturer of a product has impliedly agreed to indemnify the seller when 1) the seller is without fault, 2) the manufacturer is responsible, and 3) the seller has been required to pay a monetary judgment. Under Latco's theory, should it be found liable for its construction of the chicken houses, it can demonstrate that the true fault lies with the nail guns and the nails manufactured by ITW.

Alabama caselaw, not to mention the parties' briefs, is especially sparse with respect to the contours of the doctrine of implied indemnity. However, Illinois courts have applied the doctrine in similar cases, and the court finds no reason to believe that Alabama courts would interpret the common law principles in a different manner.

Indeed, the reasoning of the Supreme Court of Illinois in an almost identical case compels the court to find that impleader is proper here. See Maxfield v. Simmons, 96 Ill.2d 81, 70 Ill.Dec. 236, 449 N.E.2d 110 (1983). In Maxfield, an individual brought suit against a contractor alleging that the latter had constructed the roof of the plaintiff's home in a "poor and shoddy manner." Id. at 110. The contractor, in turn, filed a third-party complaint against the manufacturer and the seller of the roof trusses, alleging that their defective nature entitled the contractor to indemnification....

It must be noted, however, that, under Alabama law, the doctrine permits recovery only when the party to be indemnified is "without fault." Whether, in fact, such a factual scenario will be proven at trial is irrelevant for present purposes. The only issue before the court is whether there exists a legal basis to implead ITW, not whether ITW is, in fact, liable to Latco. Since Rule 14 permits Latco to implead any party who "may be liable," Fed. R.Civ.P. 14(a), it follows that the court must permit development of the factual record so the extent of that liability may be determined....

Furthermore, since Latco has established a basis upon which it may properly implead ITW, the court need not address the applicability of Rule 14 to the other claims in Latco's Third Party Complaint. It is well established that a properly impleaded claim may serve as an anchor for separate and independent claims under Rule 18(a). In short, the court finds that Latco has properly impleaded ITW under Rule 14(a)....

Accordingly, it is CONSIDERED and ORDERED that ITW's Motion To Dismiss be and the same is hereby DENIED.

Note "Rule 14(a) grants federal courts discretion in determining the propriety of a third-party complaint, and in making its determination, a court may consider the burden upon the litigation that might ensue, as well as the merit of the third-party complaint. See generally 6 Charles A. Wright, Arthur R. Miller & Mary Kay Kane, Federal Practice and Procedure § 1443. Rules 21 and 42 further provide original plaintiffs protection against vexatious litigation by permitting the court to drop parties or to sever claims." (*Price v. CTB, Inc.* fn. 3)

Plaintiffs and FRCP 14

Where a third party has been properly brought in, plaintiff may, if he/she chooses, assert directly against the third-party defendant any claim he/she may have against the defendant arising out of the transaction or occurrence that is the subject matter of the plaintiff's claims against the original defendant. (FRCP 14(a).)

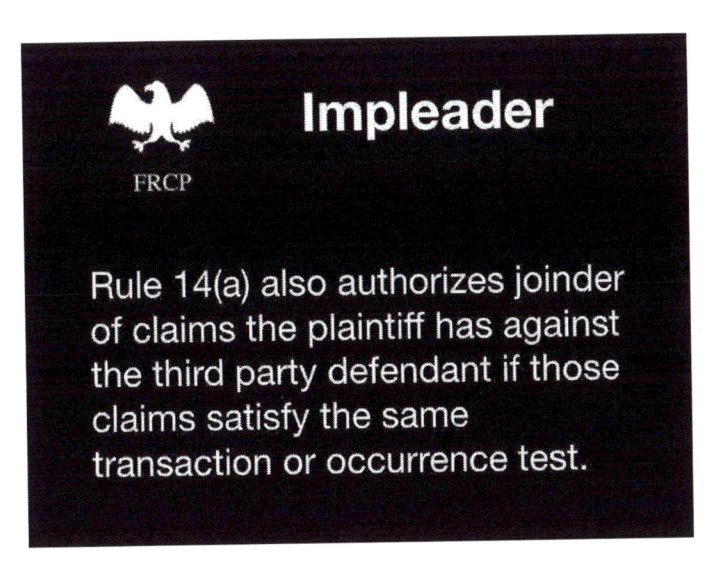

> **Impleader**
> FRCP
>
> Rule 14(a) also authorizes joinder of claims the plaintiff has against the third party defendant if those claims satisfy the same transaction or occurrence test.

    This is a good opportunity to pause and draw the distinction between what is *procedurally* proper and what is *jurisdictionally* proper when it comes to joinder of parties and claims. For example FRCP 13 authorizes the assertion of permissive counterclaims. Thus, permissive counterclaims are procedurally proper. But in a diversity case, a permissive counterclaim for less than $75,000 is not jurisdictionally proper, because it does not satisfy the amount in controversy requirement for diversity cases.

> **More Complex Litigation Rule 14**
> FRCP
>
> Where a third party has been properly brought in, plaintiff may choose to assert directly against the third party defendant any claim s/he may have against him arising out of the transaction or occurrence that is the subject matter of the plaintiff's claims against the original defendant.

    We know that a claim asserted by a plaintiff against a party impleaded under FRCP 14 is procedurally proper. But do federal courts in diversity suits have the jurisdictional power to entertain a claim asserted by a plaintiff against a third-party defendant? Must there be an independent basis for jurisdiction over that claim no matter how entwined it is with the matter already before the court?

Owen Equipment & Erection Co. v. Kroger
437 U.S. 365 (1978)

MR. JUSTICE STEWART delivered the opinion of the Court.

In an action in which federal jurisdiction is based on diversity of citizenship, may the plaintiff assert a claim against a third-party defendant when there is no independent basis for federal jurisdiction over that claim? The Court of Appeals for the Eighth Circuit held in this case that such a claim is within the ancillary jurisdiction of the federal courts. We granted certiorari, 434 U. S. 1008, because this decision conflicts with several recent decisions of other Courts of Appeals.

On January 18, 1972, James Kroger was electrocuted when the boom of a steel crane next to which he was walking came too close to a high-tension electric power line. The respondent (his widow, who is the administratrix of his estate) filed a wrongful-death action in the United States District Court for the District of Nebraska against the Omaha Public Power District (OPPD). Her complaint alleged that OPPD's negligent construction, maintenance, and operation of the power line had caused Kroger's death. Federal jurisdiction was based on diversity of citizenship, since the respondent was a citizen of Iowa and OPPD was a Nebraska corporation.

OPPD then filed a third-party complaint pursuant to Fed. Rule Civ. Proc. 14 (a) against the petitioner, Owen Equipment and Erection Co. (Owen), alleging that the crane was owned and operated by Owen, and that Owen's negligence had been the proximate cause of Kroger's death. OPPD later moved for summary judgment on the respondent's complaint against it. While this motion was pending, the respondent was granted leave to file an amended complaint naming Owen as an additional defendant. Thereafter, the District Court granted OPPD's motion for summary judgment in an unreported opinion. The case thus went to trial between the respondent and the petitioner alone.

The respondent's amended complaint alleged that Owen was "a Nebraska corporation with its principal place of business in Nebraska." Owen's answer admitted that it was "a corporation organized and existing under the laws of the State of Nebraska," and denied every other allegation of the complaint. On the third day of trial, however, it was disclosed that the petitioner's principal place of business was in Iowa, not Nebraska, and that the petitioner and the respondent were thus both citizens of Iowa. The petitioner then moved to dismiss the complaint for lack of jurisdiction. The District Court reserved decision on the motion, and the jury thereafter returned a verdict in favor of the respondent. In an unreported opinion issued after the trial, the District Court denied the petitioner's motion to dismiss the complaint.

The judgment was affirmed on appeal. The Court of Appeals held that under this Court's decision in Mine Workers v. Gibbs, 383 U. S. 715, the District Court had jurisdictional power, in its discretion, to adjudicate the respondent's claim against the petitioner because that claim arose from the "core of 'operative facts' giving rise to both [respondent's] claim against OPPD and OPPD's claim against Owen." It further held that the District Court had properly exercised its discretion in proceeding to decide the case even after summary judgment had been granted to OPPD, because the petitioner had concealed its Iowa citizenship from the respondent. Rehearing en banc was denied by an equally divided court.

It is undisputed that there was no independent basis of federal jurisdiction over the respondent's state-law tort action against the petitioner, since both are citizens of Iowa. And although Fed. Rule Civ. Proc. 14 (a) permits a plaintiff to assert a claim against a third-party defendant, see n. 2, supra, it does not purport to say whether or not such a claim requires an independent basis of federal jurisdiction. Indeed, it could not determine that question, since it is axiomatic that the Federal Rules of Civil Procedure do not create or withdraw federal jurisdiction. . . .

The relevant statute in this case, 28 U. S. C. § 1332 (a) (1), confers upon federal courts jurisdiction over "civil actions where the matter in controversy exceeds the sum or value of $10,000 . . . and is between . . . citizens of different States." This statute and its predecessors have consistently been held to require complete diversity of citizenship. That is, diversity jurisdiction does not exist unless each defendant is a citizen of a different State from each plaintiff. Over the years Congress has repeatedly re-enacted or amended the statute conferring diversity jurisdiction, leaving intact this rule of complete diversity. Whatever may have been the original purposes of diversity-of-citizenship jurisdiction, this subsequent history clearly demonstrates a congressional mandate that diversity jurisdiction is not to be available when any plaintiff is a citizen of the same State as any defendant. Thus it is clear that the respondent could not originally have brought suit in federal court naming Owen and OPPD as codefendants, since citizens of Iowa would have been on both sides of the litigation. Yet the identical lawsuit resulted when she amended her complaint. Complete diversity was destroyed just as surely as if she had sued Owen initially. In either situation, in the plain language of the statute, the "matter in controversy" could not be "between . . . citizens of different States."

It is a fundamental precept that federal courts are courts of limited jurisdiction. The limits upon federal jurisdiction, whether imposed by the Constitution or by Congress, must be neither disregarded nor evaded. Yet under the reasoning of the Court of Appeals in this case, a plaintiff could defeat the statutory requirement of complete diversity by the simple expedient of suing only those defendants who were of diverse citizenship and waiting for them to implead nondiverse defendants. If, as the Court of Appeals thought, a "common nucleus of operative fact" were the only requirement for ancillary jurisdiction in a diversity case, there would be no principled reason why the respondent in this case could not have joined her cause of action against Owen in her original complaint as ancillary to her claim against OPPD. Congress' requirement of complete diversity would thus have been evaded completely.

It is true, as the Court of Appeals noted, that the exercise of ancillary jurisdiction over nonfederal claims has often been upheld in situations involving impleader, cross-claims or counterclaims.[1] But in determining whether jurisdiction over a nonfederal claim exists, the context in which the nonfederal claim is asserted is crucial. And the claim here arises in a setting quite different from the kinds of nonfederal claims that have been viewed in other cases as falling within the ancillary jurisdiction of the federal courts.

First, the nonfederal claim in this case was simply not ancillary to the federal one in the same sense that, for example, the impleader by a defendant of a third-party defendant always is. A third-party complaint depends at least in part upon the resolution of the primary lawsuit. See n. 3, supra. Its relation to the original complaint is thus not mere factual similarity but logical dependence. The respondent's claim against the petitioner, however, was entirely separate from her original claim against OPPD, since the petitioner's liability to her depended not at all upon whether or not OPPD was also liable. Far from being an ancillary and dependent claim, it was a new and independent one.

Second, the nonfederal claim here was asserted by the plaintiff, who voluntarily chose to bring suit upon a state-law claim in a federal court. By contrast, ancillary jurisdiction typically involves claims by a defending party hauled into court against his will, or by another person whose rights might be irretrievably lost unless he could assert them in an ongoing action in a federal court. A plaintiff cannot complain if ancillary jurisdiction does not encompass all of his possible claims in a case such as this one, since it is he who has chosen the federal rather than the state forum and must thus accept its limitations. "[T]he efficiency plaintiff seeks so avidly is available without question in the state courts."

It is not unreasonable to assume that, in generally requiring complete diversity, Congress did not intend to confine the jurisdiction of federal courts so inflexibly that they are unable to protect legal rights or effectively to resolve an entire, logically entwined lawsuit. Those practical needs are the basis of the doctrine of ancillary jurisdiction. But neither the convenience of litigants nor considerations of judicial economy can suffice to justify extension of the doctrine of ancillary jurisdiction to a plaintiff's cause of action against a citizen of the same State in a diversity case. Congress has established the basic rule that diversity jurisdiction exists under 28 U. S. C. § 1332 only when there is complete diversity of citizenship. "The policy of the statute calls for its strict construction." To allow the requirement of complete diversity to be circumvented as it was in this case would simply flout the congressional command

Accordingly, the judgment of the Court of Appeals is reversed.

It is so ordered.

Problem In 1990 Congress amended the supplemental jurisdiction statute. Carefully read 28 U.S.C. § 1367. What would be the outcome if Mrs. Kroger tried to implead Owen Equipment in her diversity case? Is the rule different in federal question cases?

Joinder of Parties
Permissive Joinder of Parties

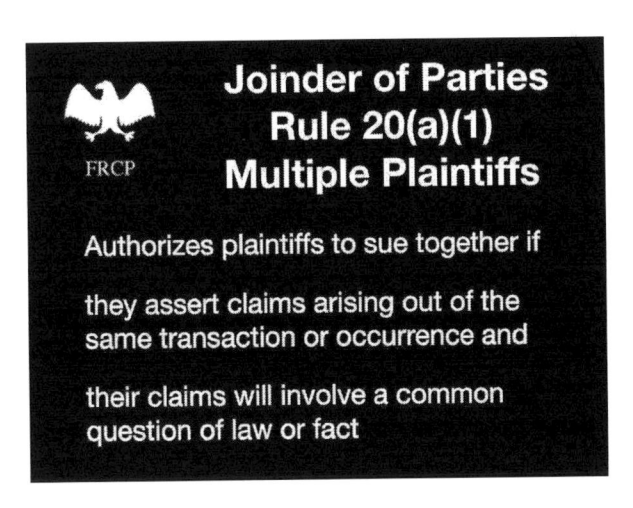

> **Joinder of Parties**
> **Rule 20(a)(1)**
> **Multiple Plaintiffs**
>
> Authorizes plaintiffs to sue together if
>
> they assert claims arising out of the same transaction or occurrence and
>
> their claims will involve a common question of law or fact

FRCP 20 deals with permissive joinder of parties. The plaintiff has the option whether to join a party if the tests of Rule 20 are met. Rule 20(a) applies to joinder of both plaintiffs and defendants. It creates two tests for joinder. 1) There must be some question of law or fact common to all parties which will arise in the action. 2) There must be some right to relief asserted on behalf of each of the plaintiffs and against each of the defendants, relating to or arising out of a single transaction or occurrence or series of transactions or occurrences. These tests are cumulative and both of them must be satisfied to permit joinder. (Wright, §71) The purpose of Rule 20 is to promote trial convenience and expedite the final determination of disputes, thereby preventing multiple lawsuits.

Mosley v. General Motors Corp.
497 F.2d 1330 (1974)

ROSS, Circuit Judge.

Nathaniel Mosley and nine other persons joined in bringing this action individually and as class representatives alleging that their rights guaranteed under 42 U.S.C. § 2000e et seq. and 42 U.S.C. § 1981 were denied by General Motors and Local 25, United Automobile, Aerospace and Agriculture Implement Workers of America [Union] by reason of their color and race. Each of the ten named plaintiffs had, prior to the filing of the complaint, filed a charge with the Equal Employment Opportunity Commission [EEOC] asserting the facts underlying these claims. Pursuant thereto, the EEOC made a reasonable cause finding that General Motors, Fisher Body Division and Chevrolet Division, and the Union had engaged in unlawful employment practices in violation of Title VII of the Civil Rights Act of 1964. Accordingly, the charging parties were notified by EEOC of their right to institute a civil action in the appropriate federal district court. . . .

Pursuant thereto, the EEOC made a reasonable cause finding that General Motors, Fisher Body Division and Chevrolet Division, and the Union had engaged in unlawful employment practices in violation of Title VII of the Civil Rights Act of 1964. Accordingly, the charging parties were notified by EEOC of their right to institute a civil action in the appropriate federal district court . . .

In each of the first eight counts of the twelve-count complaint, eight of the ten plaintiffs alleged that General Motors, Chevrolet Division, had engaged in unlawful employment practices by: "discriminating against Negroes as regards promotions, terms and conditions of employment"; "retaliating against Negro employees who protested actions made unlawful by Title VII of the Act and by discharging some because they protested said unlawful acts"; "failing to hire Negro employees as a class on the basis of race"; "failing to hire females as a class on the basis of sex"; "discharging Negro employees on the basis of race"; and "discriminating against Negroes and females in the granting of relief time." Each additionally charged that the defendant Union had engaged in unlawful employment practices "with respect to the granting of relief time to Negro and female employees" and "by failing to pursue 6a grievances." The remaining two plaintiffs made similar allegations against General Motors, Fisher Body Division. All of the individual plaintiffs requested injunctive relief, back pay, attorneys fees and costs. Counts XI and XII of the complaint were class action counts against the two individual divisions of General Motors. They also sought declaratory and injunctive relief, back pay, attorneys fees and costs. . . .

The district court ordered that "insofar as the first ten counts are concerned, those ten counts shall be severed into ten separate causes of action," and each plaintiff was directed to bring a separate action based upon his complaint, duly and separately filed. The court also ordered that the class action would not be dismissed, but rather would be left open "to each of the plaintiffs herein, individually or collectively . . . to allege a separate cause of action on behalf of any class of persons which such plaintiff or plaintiffs may separately or individually represent."

In reaching this conclusion on joinder, the district court followed the reasoning of Smith v. North American Rockwell Corp., 50 F.R.D. 515 (N.D.Okla.1970), which, in a somewhat analogous situation, found there was no right to relief arising out of the same transaction, occurrence or series of transactions or occurrences, and that there was no question of law or fact common to all plaintiffs sufficient to sustain joinder under Federal Rule of Civil Procedure 20(a). Similarly, the district court here felt that the plaintiffs' joint actions against General Motors and the Union presented a variety of issues having little relationship to one another; that they had only one common problem, i. e. the defendant; and that as pleaded the joint actions were completely unmanageable.

Upon entering the order, and upon application of the plaintiffs, the district court found that its decision involved a controlling question of law as to which there is a substantial ground for difference of opinion and that any of the parties might make application for appeal under 28 U.S.C. § 1292(b). We granted the application to permit this interlocutory appeal and for the following reasons we affirm in part and reverse in part.

Rule 20(a) of the Federal Rules of Civil Procedure provides:

All persons may join in one action as plaintiffs if they assert any right to relief jointly, severally, or in the alternative in respect of or arising out of the same transaction, occurrence, or series of transactions or occurrences and if any question of law or fact common to all these persons will arise in the action. . . .

Additionally, Rule 20(b) and Rule 42(b) vest in the district court the discretion to order separate trials or make such other orders as will prevent delay or prejudice. In this manner, the scope of the civil action is made a matter for the discretion of the district court, and a determination on the question of joinder of parties will be reversed on appeal only upon a showing of abuse of that discretion. To determine whether the district court's order was proper herein, we must look to the policy and law that have developed around the operation of Rule 20.

The purpose of the rule is to promote trial convenience and expedite the final determination of disputes, thereby preventing multiple lawsuits. 7 C. Wright, Federal Practice and Procedure § 1652 at 265 (1972). Single trials generally tend to lessen the delay, expense and inconvenience to all concerned. Reflecting this policy, the Supreme Court has said:

> Under the Rules, the impulse is toward entertaining the broadest possible scope of action consistent with fairness to the parties; joinder of claims, parties and remedies is strongly encouraged. United Mine Workers of America v. Gibbs, 383 U.S. 715, 724, 86 S.Ct. 1130, 1138, 16 L.Ed.2d 218 (1966).

Permissive joinder is not, however, applicable in all cases. The rule imposes two specific requisites to the joinder of parties: (1) a right to relief must be asserted by, or against, each plaintiff or defendant relating to or arising out of the same transaction or occurrence, or series of transactions or occurrences; and (2) some question of law or fact common to all the parties must arise in the action.

In ascertaining whether a particular factual situation constitutes a single transaction or occurrence for purposes of Rule 20, a case by case approach is generally pursued. 7 C. Wright, Federal Practice and Procedure § 1653 at 270 (1972). No hard and fast rules have been established under the rule. However, construction of the terms "transaction or occurrence" as used in the context of Rule 13(a) counterclaims offers some guide to the application of this test. For the purposes of the latter rule, "Transaction" is a word of flexible meaning. It may comprehend a series of many occurrences, depending not so much upon the immediateness of their connection as upon their logical relationship. Moore v. New York Cotton Exchange, 270 U.S. 593, 610, 46 S.Ct. 367, 371, 70 L.Ed. 750 (1926). Accordingly, all "logically related" events entitling a person to institute a legal action against another generally are regarded as comprising a transaction or occurrence. 7 C. Wright, Federal Practice and Procedure § 1653 at 270 (1972). The analogous interpretation of the terms as used in Rule 20 would permit all reasonably related claims for relief by or against different parties to be tried in a single proceeding. Absolute identity of all events is unnecessary.

This construction accords with the result reached in United States v. Mississippi, 380 U.S. 128, 85 S.Ct. 808, 13 L. Ed.2d 717 (1965), a suit brought by the United States against the State of Mississippi, the election commissioners, and six voting registrars of the State, charging them with engaging in acts and practices hampering and destroying the right of black citizens of Mississippi to vote. The district court concluded that the complaint improperly attempted to hold the six county registrars jointly liable for what amounted to nothing more than individual torts committed by them separately against separate applicants. In reversing, the Supreme Court said:

> But the complaint charged that the registrars had acted and were continuing to act as part of a state-wide system designed to enforce the registration laws in a way that would inevitably deprive colored people of the right to vote solely because of their color. On such an allegation the joinder of all the registrars as defendants in a single suit is authorized by Rule 20(a) of the Federal Rules of Civil Procedure . . . . These registrars were alleged to be carrying on activities which part of a series of transactions or occurrences were the validity of which depended to a large extent upon "question[s] of law or fact common to all of them."

Here too, then, the plaintiffs have asserted a right to relief arising out of the same transactions or occurrences. Each of the ten plaintiffs alleged that he had been injured by the same general policy of discrimination on the part of General Motors and the Union. Since a "state-wide system designed to enforce the registration laws in a way that would inevitably deprive colored people of the right to vote" was determined to arise out of the same series of transactions or occurrences, we conclude that a company-wide policy purportedly designed to discriminate against blacks in employment similarly arises out of the same series of transactions or occurrences. Thus the plaintiffs meet the first requisite for joinder under Rule 20(a).

The second requisite necessary to sustain a permissive joinder under the rule is that a question of law or fact common to all the parties will arise in the action. The rule does not require that all questions of law and fact raised by the dispute be common. Yet, neither does it establish any qualitative or quantitative test of commonality. For this reason, cases construing the parallel requirement under Federal Rule of Civil Procedure 23(a) provide a helpful framework for construction of the commonality required by Rule 20. In general, those cases that have focused on Rule 23(a)(2) have given it a permissive application so that common questions have been found to exist in a wide range of context. 7 C. Wright, Federal Practice and Procedure § 1763 at 604 (1972). Specifically, with respect to employment discrimination cases under Title VII, courts have found that the discriminatory character of a defendant's conduct is basic to the class, and the fact that the individual class members may have suffered different effects from the alleged discrimination is immaterial for the purposes of the prerequisite. Hicks v. Crown Zellerbach Corp., 49 F.R.D. 184, 187-188 (E.D.La.1968). In this vein, one court has said:

[A]lthough the actual effects of a discriminatory policy may thus vary throughout the class; the existence of the discriminatory policy threatens the entire class. And whether the Damoclean threat of a racially discriminatory policy hangs over the racial class is a question of fact common to all the members of the class.

The right to relief here depends on the ability to demonstrate that each of the plaintiffs was wronged by racially discriminatory policies on the part of the defendants General Motors and the Union. The discriminatory character of the defendants' conduct is thus basic to each plaintiff's recovery. The fact that each plaintiff may have suffered different effects from the alleged discrimination is immaterial for the purposes of determining the common question of law or fact. Thus, we conclude that the second requisite for joinder under Rule 20(a) is also met by the complaint.

For the reasons set forth above, we conclude that the district court abused its discretion in severing the joined actions. The difficulties in ultimately adjudicating damages to the various plaintiffs are not so overwhelming as to require such severance. If appropriate, separate trials may be granted as to any particular issue after the determination of common questions.

The judgment of the district court disallowing joinder of the plaintiffs' individual actions is reversed and remanded with directions to permit the plaintiffs to proceed jointly. . . .

Baughman v. Lee County, Mississippi
554 F.Supp.2d 652 (2008)

MICHAEL P. MILLS, Chief Judge.

This cause comes before the court on the motion of defendant Lee County, Mississippi to sever, pursuant to Fed.R.Civ.P. 21. Plaintiffs Melanie Baughman et al have responded in opposition to the motion, and the court, having considered the memoranda and submissions of the parties, concludes that the motion is well taken and should be granted.

This is, inter alia, a 42 U.S.C. § 1983 action involving twenty-seven plaintiffs, each of whom alleges that he or she was unnecessarily strip-searched at the Lee County Jail, in violation of his or her Constitutional rights. A party seeking joinder of claimants under Rule 20 must establish (1) a right to relief arising out of the same transaction or occurrence, or series of transactions or occurrences, and (2) some question of law or fact common to all persons seeking to be joined. See Fed. R.Civ.P. 20(a). In deciding whether claims should be severed pursuant to Rule 21, this court determines (1) whether the claims arise out of the same transaction or occurrence; (2) whether the claims present some common questions of law or fact; (3) whether settlement of the claims or judicial economy would be facilitated; (4) whether prejudice would be avoided if severance were granted; and (5) whether different witnesses and documentary proof are required for separate claims.

In analyzing the joinder issues in this case, the court finds persuasive the reasoning of Magistrate Judge Robert H. Walker in McFarland, a Hurricane Katrina case in which hundreds of plaintiffs sought to join together to assert insurance fraud and other claims against State Farm. This case, like McFarland, involves plaintiffs who assert what are superficially similar claims but which will require different fact witnesses and individualized proof regarding damages. This lawsuit does not arise from a single incident in which large numbers of inmates were strip-searched at the same time. To the contrary, the complaint alleges a series of allegedly unlawful strip searches which took place between 2005 and 2007, and each incident will require individualized proof regarding the circumstances and nature of the strip search in question. Moreover, each plaintiff alleges that he or she suffered emotional distress damages as a result of being strip searched, and federal law requires that, to recover emotional distress damages, a § 1983 plaintiff must demonstrate a "specific discernable injury to [his] emotional state" resulting from a constitutional violation, proven with evidence regarding the "nature and extent" of the harm. Patterson v. P.H.P. Healthcare Corp., 90 F.3d 927, 938-40 (5th Cir.1996).

The foregoing considerations make it clear that, as in McFarland, the similarity between the claims of the various plaintiffs in this case is more illusory than real. As noted by Judge Walker in McFarland:

> The Court concludes that the Plaintiffs should be required to file separate complaints. Although there may be some common issues of law and fact, the Court finds that the Plaintiffs have not met the same transaction or occurrence prong of Rule 20(a). In a superficial sense, the hurricane was a common occurrence; however, the storm was vastly different in its effect depending on the specific geographic location of each particular home. Although Plaintiffs each held basically the same standard homeowner's policy, each insurance contract is a separate transaction.... Likewise, any alleged negligent or fraudulent misrepresentations by insurance agents constitute separate transactions or occurrences.

In the court's view, Judge Walker's observations apply equally to the claims of the plaintiffs in this case.

In opposing severance, plaintiffs' primary argument is that it would be costly in time and money to try these lawsuits individually. However, it is not a goal of the federal judiciary to implement justice on the cheap by compromising the basic integrity of the judicial process. The court has little doubt that a jury would find it impossible to give plaintiffs' claims the individual attention and scrutiny which they deserve if they were joined together in the manner sought. Differing facts among the claimants would likely far exceed common facts. Mississippi state courts have, in recent years, moved away from the "herd justice" approach once prevailing in those courts. There is little doubt that plaintiffs would be unable to maintain these mass-joined claims in Mississippi state court. No valid reason dictates that Mississippi federal courts should be any less attentive to ensuring that juries are not overwhelmed by mass-joined actions such as the present one. Defendant's motion to sever should be granted.

Having granted defendant's motion to sever, this court will follow Judge Walker's approach in McFarland to implement this severance. It is therefore ordered that:

(1) All plaintiffs' claims in Civil Action No. 1:07cv239 shall be severed into individual actions, one for each plaintiff, and the Clerk shall assign a new civil action number for each severed claim.

(2) The Clerk shall copy the pleadings and exhibits from Civil Action No. 1:07cv239, which shall then be included as part of the record for each severed action. Each of the previous filings will be deemed filed in the new cases as of the dates shown on the docket sheet for Civil Action No. 1:07cv239.

(3) The current case, No. 1:07cv239, shall be closed upon the individual cases being severed and replaced by the new filings.

(4) Within (30) days of this Order, Plaintiffs shall file an amended complaint and filing fee in each new civil action.

(5) All pre-discovery disclosure of case information or other cooperative discovery devices provided for by the Uniform Local Rules of the United States District Courts of Mississippi 26.1(A) and Federal Rules of Civil Procedure 26(a)(1) which have not been previously furnished by the parties shall be disclosed pursuant to said rules. Should the court find that common questions of law or fact exist in separate cases, the court may then order those cases consolidated as provided in Fed.R.Civ.P. 42(a).

(6) All severed cases shall remain assigned to United States District Judge Michael P. Mills and United States Magistrate Judge S. Allan Alexander.

Compulsory Joinder of Parties

Under FRCP 19, there are some instances where parties must be joined. This compulsory joinder of parties is an exception to the usual practice that leaves a plaintiff free to decide who shall be the parties to his lawsuit. Whether a party must be joined is determined by whether the party is classified as merely *necessary* or, on the other hand, *indispensable*.

Necessary parties are those parties who must be joined if feasible but whose nonjoinder will not result in dismissal. Indispensable parties are those parties whose joinder will be compelled even at the cost of dismissing the action. I.e., parties in whose absence the court cannot proceed. The label "indispensable" is used if the action should be dismissed unless the party is joined. The label "necessary" is used if the party is one who ought to be joined if this is possible. (Wright, § 70) If it is not possible the action may nevertheless proceed.

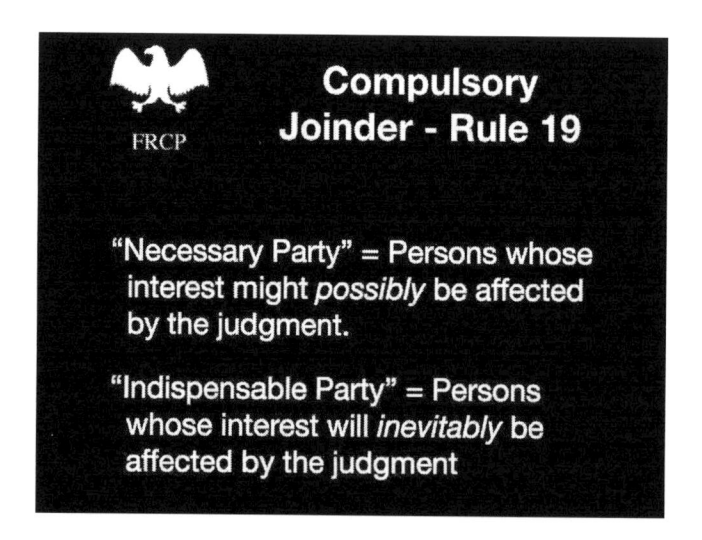

> **Compulsory Joinder - Rule 19**
> FRCP
>
> "Necessary Party" = Persons whose interest might *possibly* be affected by the judgment.
>
> "Indispensable Party" = Persons whose interest will *inevitably* be affected by the judgment

Whenever feasible, the persons materially interested in the subject of an action should be joined as parties so that they may be heard and a complete disposition made. When this comprehensive joinder cannot be accomplished—a situation which may be encountered in Federal courts because of limitations on service of process, subject matter jurisdiction, and venue—the case should be examined pragmatically and a choice made between the alternatives of proceeding with the action in the absence of particular interested persons, and dismissing the action. (Advisory Committee Notes, 1966 Amendment.)

FRCP 19 stresses the desirability of joining those persons in whose absence the court would be obliged to grant partial or "hollow" rather than complete relief to the parties before the court. The interests that are being furthered here are not only those of the parties, but also that of the public in avoiding repeated lawsuits on the same essential subject matter.

If a person as described in FRCP subdivision (a)(1)(2) is amenable to service of process and his joinder would not deprive the court of jurisdiction the court should order him to be brought into the action. When a person as described in subdivision (a)(1)–(2) cannot be made a party, the court is to determine whether in equity and good conscience the action should proceed among the parties already before it, or should be dismissed. If the court determines that the action should be dismissed, then the absentee party is said to be "indispensable." (See, Advisory Committee Notes, 1966 Amendment)

Temple v. Synthes Corp., Ltd.
498 U.S. 5 (1990)

PER CURIAM.

Petitioner Temple, a Mississippi resident, underwent surgery in October 1986 in which a "plate and screw device" was implanted in his lower spine. The device was manufactured by respondent Synthes Corp., Ltd. (U. S. A.) (Synthes), a Pennsylvania corporation. Dr. S. Henry LaRocca performed the surgery at St. Charles General Hospital in New Orleans, Louisiana. Following surgery, the device's screws broke off inside Temple's back.

Temple filed suit against Synthes in the United States District Court for the Eastern District of Louisiana. The suit, which rested on diversity jurisdiction, alleged defective design and manufacture of the device. At the same time, Temple filed a state administrative proceeding against Dr. LaRocca and the hospital for malpractice and negligence. At the conclusion of the administrative proceeding, Temple filed suit against the doctor and the hospital in Louisiana state court.

Synthes did not attempt to bring the doctor and the hospital into the federal action by means of a third-party complaint, as provided in Federal Rule of Civil Procedure 14(a). Instead, Synthes filed a motion to dismiss Temple's federal suit for failure to join necessary parties pursuant to Federal Rule of Civil Procedure 19. Following a hearing, the District Court ordered Temple to join the doctor and the hospital as defendants within 20 days or risk dismissal of the lawsuit. According to the court, the most significant reason for requiring joinder was the interest of judicial economy. App. to Pet. for Cert. A-12. The court relied on this Court's decision in Provident Tradesmens Bank & Trust Co. v. Patterson, 390 U. S. 102 (1968), wherein we recognized that one focus of Rule 19 is "the interest of the courts and the public in complete, consistent, and efficient settlement of controversies." When Temple failed to join the doctor and the hospital, the court dismissed the suit with prejudice.

Temple appealed, and the United States Court of Appeals for the Fifth Circuit affirmed. The court deemed it "obviously prejudicial to the defendants to have the separate litigations being carried on," because Synthes' defense might be that the plate was not defective but that the doctor and the hospital were negligent, while the doctor and the hospital, on the other hand, might claim that they were not negligent but that the plate was defective. The Court of Appeals found that the claims overlapped and that the District Court therefore had not abused its discretion in ordering joinder under Rule 19. A petition for rehearing was denied.

In his petition for certiorari to this Court, Temple contends that it was error to label joint tortfeasors as indispensable parties under Rule 19(b) and to dismiss the lawsuit with prejudice for failure to join those parties. We agree. Synthes does not deny that it, the doctor, and the hospital are potential joint tortfeasors. It has long been the rule that it is not necessary for all joint tortfeasors to be named as defendants in a single lawsuit. Nothing in the 1966 revision of Rule 19 changed that principle. The Advisory Committee Notes to Rule 19(a) explicitly state that "a tortfeasor with the usual `joint-and-several' liability is merely a permissive party to an action against another with like liability." 28 U. S. C. App., p. 595. There is nothing in Louisiana tort law to the contrary.

The opinion in Provident Bank, supra, does speak of the public interest in limiting multiple litigation, but that case is not controlling here. There, the estate of a tort victim brought a declaratory judgment action against an insurance company. We assumed that the policyholder was a person "who, under § (a), should be `joined if feasible.'" and went on to discuss the appropriate analysis under Rule 19(b), because the policyholder could not be joined without destroying diversity. After examining the factors set forth in Rule 19(b), we determined that the action could proceed without the policyholder; he therefore was not an indispensable party whose absence required dismissal of the suit.

Here, no inquiry under Rule 19(b) is necessary, because the threshold requirements of Rule 19(a) have not been satisfied. As potential joint tortfeasors with Synthes, Dr. LaRocca and the hospital were merely permissive parties. The Court of Appeals erred by failing to hold that the District Court abused its discretion in ordering them joined as defendants and in dismissing the action when Temple failed to comply with the court's order. For these reasons, we grant the petition for certiorari, reverse the judgment of the Court of Appeals for the Fifth Circuit, and remand for further proceedings consistent with this opinion.

It is so ordered.

Helzberg's Diamond Shops, Inc. v. Valley West Des Moines Shopping Center, Inc.
564 F.2d 816 (1977)

ALSOP, District Judge.

On February 3, 1975, Helzberg's Diamond Shops, Inc. (Helzberg), a Missouri corporation, and Valley West Des Moines Shopping Center, Inc. (Valley West), an

Iowa corporation, executed a written Lease Agreement. The Lease Agreement granted Helzberg the right to operate a full line jewelry store at space 254 in the Valley West Mall in West Des Moines, Iowa. Section 6 of Article V of the Lease Agreement provides:

> [Valley West] agrees it will not lease premises in the shopping center for use as a catalog jewelry store nor lease premises for more than two full line jewelry stores in the shopping center in addition to the leased premises. This clause shall not prohibit other stores such as department stores from selling jewelry from catalogs or in any way restrict the shopping center department stores.

Subsequently, Helzberg commenced operation of a full line jewelry store in the Valley West Mall.

Between February 3, 1975 and November 2, 1976 Valley West and two other corporations entered into leases for spaces in the Valley West Mall for use as full line jewelry stores. Pursuant to those leases the two corporations also initiated actual operation of full line jewelry stores.

On November 2, 1976, Valley West and Kirk's Incorporated, Jewelers, an Iowa corporation, doing business as Lord's Jewelers (Lord's), entered into a written Lease Agreement. The Lease Agreement granted Lord's the right to occupy space 261 in the Valley West Mall. Section 1 of Article V of the Lease Agreement provides that Lord's will use space 261

> . . . only as a retail specialty jewelry store (and not as a catalogue or full line jewelry store) featuring watches, jewelry (and the repair of same) and incidental better gift items.

However, Lord's intended to open and operate what constituted a full line jewelry store at space 261.

In an attempt to avoid the opening of a fourth full line jewelry store in the Valley West Mall and the resulting breach of the Helzberg-Valley West Lease Agreement, Helzberg instituted suit seeking preliminary and permanent injunctive relief restraining Valley West's breach of the Lease Agreement. The suit was filed in the United States District Court for the Western District of Missouri. Subject matter jurisdiction was invoked pursuant to 28 U.S.C. § 1332 based upon diversity of citizenship between the parties and an amount in controversy which exceeded $10,000. Personal jurisdiction was established by service of process on Valley West pursuant to the Missouri "long arm" statute, Rev.Stat.Mo. § 506.500 et seq. (1977). Rule 4(e), Fed.R.Civ.P.

Valley West moved to dismiss pursuant to Rule 19 because Helzberg had failed to join Lord's as a party defendant. [Lord's was not subject to the personal jurisdiction of the District Court.] That motion was denied. The District Court went on to order that

> pending the determination of [the] action on the merits, that [Valley West] be, and it is hereby, enjoined and restrained from allowing, and shall take all necessary steps to prevent, any other tenant in its Valley West Mall (including but not limited to Kirk's Incorporated, Jewelers, d/b/a Lord's Jewelers) to open and operate on March 30, 1977, or at any other time, or to be operated during the term of [Helzberg's] present leasehold, a fourth full line jewelry store meaning a jewelry store offering for sale at retail a broad range of jewelry items at various prices such as diamonds and diamond jewelry, precious and semi-precious stones, watches, rings, gold jewelry, costume jewelry, gold chains, pendants, bracelets, belt buckles, tie tacs, tie slides and earrings, provided, however, nothing contained herein shall be construed to enjoin [Valley West] from allowing the opening in said Valley West Mall of a small store, known by [Valley West] as a boutique, which sells limited items such as only Indian jewelry, only watches, only earrings, or only pearls.

From this order Valley West appeals.

It is clear that Valley West is entitled to appeal from the order granting preliminary injunctive relief. 28 U.S.C. § 1292(a)(1). However, Valley West does not attack the propriety of the issuance of a preliminary injunction directly; instead, it challenges the District Court's denial of its motion to dismiss for failure to join an indispensable party and argues that the District Court's order fails for lack of specificity in describing the acts of Valley West to be restrained.

Ordinarily, the denial of a motion to dismiss is not reviewable. However, because the denial of Valley West's motion to dismiss enters into and becomes a part of the District Court's order granting preliminary injunctive relief and because the granting of preliminary injunctive relief is itself appealable, we can and will review the order denying Valley West's motion to dismiss. Rule 19, Fed.R.Civ.P., provides in pertinent part:

> (a) A person who is subject to service of process and whose joinder will not deprive the court of jurisdiction over the subject matter of the action shall be joined as a party in the action if (1) in his absence complete relief cannot be accorded among those already parties, or (2) he claims an interest relating to the subject of the action and is so situated that the disposition of the action in his absence may (i) as a practical matter impair or impede his ability to protect that interest or (ii) leave any of the persons already parties subject to a substantial risk of incurring double, multiple, or otherwise inconsistent obligations by reason of his claimed interest. . . .
>
> (b) If a person as described in subdivision (a)(1)-(2) hereof cannot be made a party, the court shall determine whether in equity and good conscience the action should proceed among the parties before it, or should be dismissed, the absent person being

thus regarded as indispensable. The factors to be considered by the court include: first, to what extent a judgment rendered in the person's absence might be prejudicial to him or those already parties; second, the extent to which, by protective provisions in the judgment, by the shaping of relief, or other measures, the prejudice can be lessened or avoided; third, whether a judgment rendered in the person's absence will be adequate; fourth, whether the plaintiff will have an adequate remedy if the action is dismissed for nonjoinder.

Because Helzberg was seeking and the District Court ordered injunctive relief which may prevent Lord's from operating its jewelry store in the Valley West Mall in the manner in which Lord's originally intended, the District Court correctly concluded that Lord's was a party to be joined if feasible. See Rule 19(a)(2)(i), Fed.R.Civ.P. Therefore, because Lord's was not and is not subject to personal jurisdiction in the Western District of Missouri, the District Court was required to determine whether or not Lord's should be regarded as indispensable. After considering the factors which Rule 19(b) mandates be considered, the District Court concluded that Lord's was not to be regarded as indispensable. We agree.

The determination of whether or not a person is an indispensable party is one which must be made on a case-by-case basis and is dependent upon the facts and circumstances of each case. An analysis of the facts and circumstances of the case before us lead us to conclude that Lord's was not an indispensable party and that, therefore, the District Court did not err in denying Valley West's motion to dismiss.

Rule 19(b) requires the court to look first to the extent to which a judgment rendered in Lord's absence might be prejudicial to Lord's or to Valley West. Valley West argues that the District Court's order granting preliminary injunctive relief does prejudice Lord's and may prejudice Valley West. We do not agree.

It seems axiomatic that none of Lord's rights or obligations will be ultimately determined in a suit to which it is not a party. Even if, as a result of the District Court's granting of the preliminary injunction, Valley West should attempt to terminate Lord's leasehold interest in space 261 in the Valley West Mall, Lord's will retain all of its rights under its Lease Agreement with Valley West. None of its rights or obligations will have been adjudicated as a result of the present proceedings, proceedings to which it is not a party. Therefore, we conclude that Lord's will not be prejudiced in a way contemplated by Rule 19(b) as a result of this action.

Likewise, we think that Lord's absence will not prejudice Valley West in a way contemplated by Rule 19(b). Valley West contends that it may be subjected to inconsistent obligations as a result of a determination in this action and a determination in another forum that Valley West should proceed in a fashion contrary to what has been ordered in these proceedings.

It is true that the obligations of Valley West to Helzberg, as determined in these proceedings, may be inconsistent with Valley West's obligations to Lord's. However, we are of the opinion that any inconsistency in those obligations will result from Valley West's voluntary execution of two Lease Agreements which impose inconsistent obligations rather than from Lord's absence from the present proceedings.

Helzberg seeks only to restrain Valley West's breach of the Lease Agreement to which Helzberg and Valley West were the sole parties. Certainly, all of the rights and obligations arising under a lease can be adjudicated where all of the parties to the lease are before the court. Thus, in the context of these proceedings the District Court can determine all of the rights and obligations of both Helzberg and Valley West based upon the Lease Agreement between them, even though Lord's is not a party to the proceedings.

Valley West's contention that it may be subjected to inconsistent judgments if Lord's should choose to file suit elsewhere and be awarded judgment is speculative at best. In the first place, Lord's has not filed such a suit. Secondly, there is no showing that another court is likely to interpret the language of the two Lease Agreements differently from the way in which the District Court would. Therefore, we also conclude that Valley West will suffer no prejudice as a result of the District Court's proceeding in Lord's absence. Any prejudice which Valley West may suffer by way of inconsistent judgments would be the result of Valley West's execution of Lease Agreements which impose inconsistent obligations and not the result of the proceedings in the District Court.

Rule 19(b) also requires the court to consider ways in which prejudice to the absent party can be lessened or avoided. The District Court afforded Lord's an opportunity to intervene in order to protect any interest it might have in the outcome of this litigation. Lord's chose not to do so. In light of Lord's decision not to intervene we conclude that the District Court acted in such a way as to sufficiently protect Lord's interests.

Similarly, we also conclude that the District Court's determinations that a judgment rendered in Lord's absence would be adequate and that there is no controlling significance to the fact that Helzberg would have an adequate remedy in the Iowa courts were not erroneous. It follows that the District Court's conclusion that in equity and good conscience the action should be allowed to proceed was a correct one.

In sum, it is generally recognized that a person does not become indispensable to an action to determine rights under a contract simply because that person's rights or obligations under an entirely separate contract will be affected by the result of the action. This principle applies to an action against a lessor who has entered into other leases which also may be affected by the result in the action in which the other lessees are argued to be indispensable parties. We conclude that the District Court properly denied the motion to dismiss for failure to join an indispensable party.

Valley West also argues that the District Court's order does not comply with the specificity provisions of Rule 65(d), Fed. R.Civ.P. Valley West contends that the terms of the order fail to apprise it of the behavior which the order requires it to perform. Valley West claims that Rule 65(d) mandates that the District Court spell out the "necessary steps" which it is to take to prevent the opening of a fourth full line jewelry store and define the term "full line jewelry store."

Rule 65(d) provides in pertinent part:
Every order granting an injunction . . . shall be specific in terms; shall describe in reasonable detail . . . the act or acts sought to be restrained . . ..

These provisions require specificity and are designed to prevent uncertainty and confusion on the part of those to whom the injunction is directed and to avoid the possible founding of a contempt citation on a decree too vague to be understood. They require that those enjoined receive explicit notice of precisely what conduct is outlawed.

We think that the District Court's order measures up to the statutory standard. Although the order does not spell out the steps which Valley West is to take, it does provide Valley West with explicit notice that it is not to allow the opening or operation of a fourth full line jewelry store in the Valley West Mall. In addition, Valley West's protestations notwithstanding, it is difficult to imagine how the District Court might have more adequately defined the term "full line jewelry store."

In view of the foregoing, it follows that the judgment of the District Court is affirmed.

Affirmed.

Intervention

"Ordinarily, a nonparty has no legal interest in a judgment in an action between others. Such a judgment does not determine the nonparty's rights and obligations under the rules of *res judicata* and he may so assert if the judgment is relied upon against him. But in some situations, one's interests, particularly in one's own personal legal status or claims to property, may be placed in practical jeopardy by a judgment between others." (James & Hazard § 12.15, p. 681)

Intervention is the procedure that permits someone who is not a party to an action to enter the lawsuit in order to protect his/her interests.

The general purpose of FRCP 24(a)(2) is to entitle an absentee, purportedly represented by a party, to intervene in the action if he could establish with fair probability that the representation was inadequate. Thus, where an action is being prosecuted or defended by a trustee, a beneficiary of the trust should have a right to intervene if he can show that the trustee's representation of his interest probably is inadequate; similarly a member of a class should have the right to intervene in a class action if he can show the inadequacy of the representation of his interest by the representative parties before the court. The representation whose adequacy comes into question under the rule is not confined to formal representation like that provided by a trustee for his beneficiary or a representative party in a class action for a member of the class. A party to an action may provide practical representation to the absentee seeking intervention although no such formal relationship exists between them, and the adequacy of this practical representation will then have to be weighed. (Advisory Committee Notes, 1966 Amendment)

FRCP 24 distinguishes between two types of intervention: intervention as a matter of right and permissive intervention.

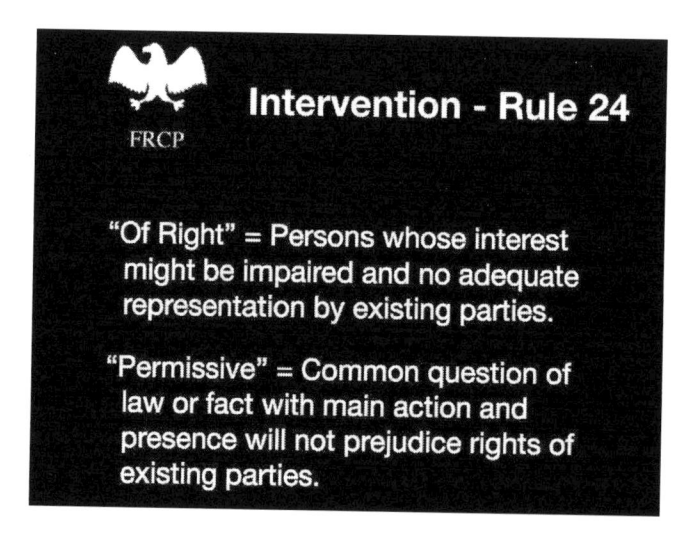

> **Intervention - Rule 24**
> FRCP
>
> "Of Right" = Persons whose interest might be impaired and no adequate representation by existing parties.
>
> "Permissive" = Common question of law or fact with main action and presence will not prejudice rights of existing parties.

When intervention is of right, the nonparty's right to participate should predominate. Note that 24(a)(1) recognizes that a statute may grant the right to intervene. E.g., 28 U.S.C. 2403 gives the U.S. the right to intervene when the constitutionality of a statute is challenged.

When intervention is determined to be permissive only, the court first must ascertain whether the interests of the original parties will be prejudiced by allowing the outsider access to the litigation. (See FRCP 24(b); Friedenthal §6.10))

As you read the next case, ask yourself what are the three requirements of FRCP 24(a)(2) that must be satisfied in order to entitle a party to intervene?

Natural Resources Defense Council, Inc. v. United States Nuclear Regulatory Commission
578 F.2d 1341 (1978)

WILLIAM E. DOYLE, Circuit Judge.

The American Mining Congress and Kerr-McGee Nuclear Corporation seek review of the order of the United States District Court for the District of New Mexico denying their motions to intervene was a matter of right or on a permissive basis, pursuant to Rule 24(a)(2) and (b), Fed.R.Civil Proc.

The underlying action in which the movants requested intervention was instituted by the Natural Resources Defense Council, Inc., and others. In the action, declaratory and injunctive relief is directed to the United States Nuclear Regulatory Commission (NRC) and the New Mexico Environmental Improvement Agency (NMEIA), prohibiting those agencies from issuing licenses for the operation of uranium mills in New Mexico without first preparing environmental impact statements. Kerr-McGee and United Nuclear are potential recipients of the licenses.

Congress, in the Atomic Energy Act of 1954, 42 U.S.C. §§ 2011-2296, has authorized the NRC to issue such licenses. NMEIA is involved because under § 274(b) of the Act, 42 U.S.C. § 2021(b) (1970), the NRC is authorized to enter into agreements with the states allowing the states to issue licenses. Such agreements have been made with about 25 states including New Mexico. Thus, the action below in effect seeks to prevent the use of § 274(b) of the Act so as to avoid the requirement of an impact statement for which provision is made in the National Environmental Policy Act. . . .

The relief sought by the plaintiffs' complaint is, first, that NRC's involvement in the licensing procedure in New Mexico is, notwithstanding the delegation to the state, sufficient to constitute major federal action, whereby the impact statement requirement is not eliminated. Second, that if an impact statement is not required in connection with the granting of licenses, the New Mexico program is in conflict with § 274(d)(2) of the Atomic Energy Act of 1954, 42 U.S.C. § 2021(d)(2) (1970).

The motion of United Nuclear Corporation to intervene is not opposed by the parties and was granted. On May 3, 1977, the date that the complaint herein was filed, NMEIA granted a license to United Nuclear to operate a uranium mill at Church Rock, New Mexico. The complaint seeks to enjoin the issuance of the license thus granted.

It was after that that Kerr-McGee Nuclear Corporation, Anaconda Company, Gulf Oil Corporation, Phillips Petroleum Company, and the American Mining Congress filed motions to intervene. These motions, insofar as they sought intervention as of right, were denied on the ground that the interests of the parties or movants would be adequately represented by United Nuclear. Permissive intervention was also denied. Kerr-McGee and the American Mining Congress both appeal denial of both intervention as of right and permissive intervention.

Our issue is a limited one. We merely construe and weigh Rule 24(a) of the Fed.R.Civ.P. (intervention as of right) and decide in light of the facts and considerations presented whether the denial of intervention was correct. The Rule provides as follows:

Upon timely application anyone shall be permitted to intervene in an action: (1) when a statute of the United States confers an unconditional right to intervene; or (2) when the applicant claims an interest relating to the property or transaction which is the subject of the action and he is so situated that the disposition of the action may as a practical matter impair or impede his ability to protect that interest, unless the applicant's interest is adequately represented by existing parties.

We do not have a subsection (1) situation involving a statutory conferring of right to intervene. Accordingly, we must consider the standards set forth in subsection (2), which are:

1. Whether the applicant claims an interest relating to the property or transaction which is the subject of the action.

2. Whether the claimants are so situated that the disposition of the action may as a practical matter impair or impede their ability to protect that interest.

3. Whether their interest is not adequately represented by existing parties.

The district court's order denying intervention by the several corporations focused on whether the interest of the party seeking to intervene was adequately represented by a fellow member of the industry. Our relatively recent decision in National Farm Lines v. ICC, 564 F.2d 381 (10th Cir. 1977), was held not determinative because the movants for intervention would be represented by a fellow member of the industry rather than by the United States Government, whose interests were different in National Farm Lines. The court decided that the interests of the movants were adequately protected by United Nuclear, which possessed the necessary experience and knowledge in a complex area of business, whereby the representative's capability was competent to meet the demands. The court thought that to allow the intervention would engender delay and produce unwieldy procedure; and that the movants' requirements were met by allowing the filing of amicus curiae briefs.

Our conclusion is that the interests of movants in the subject matter is sufficient to satisfy the requirements of Rule 24 and that the threat of loss of their interest and inability to participate is of such magnitude as to impair their ability to advance their interest.

. . . Strictly to require that the movant in intervention have a direct interest in the outcome of the lawsuit strikes us as being too narrow a construction of Rule 24(a)(2). . . .

In our case the matter of immediate interest is, of course, the issuance and delivery of the license sought by United Nuclear. However, the consequence of the litigation could well be the imposition of the requirement that an environmental impact statement be prepared before granting any uranium mill license in New Mexico, or, secondly, it could result in an injunction terminating or suspending the agreement between NRC and NMEIA. Either consequence would be felt by United Nuclear and to some degree, of course, by Kerr-McGee, which is said to be one of the largest holders of uranium properties in New Mexico. It operates a uranium mill in Grants, New Mexico, pursuant to an NMEIA license, which application for renewal is pending. A decision in favor of the plaintiffs, which is not unlikely, could have a profound effect upon Kerr-McGee. Hence, it does have an interest within the meaning of Rule 24(a)(2). This interest of Kerr-McGee is in sharp contrast to the minimal interest which was present in Allard, wherein it was an interest of environmental groups in the protection of living birds. This was considered insufficient to justify intervention in a case involving feathers which are part of Indian artifacts. Their interest was said to be limited to a general interest in the public. Id. at 1334. The interest asserted on behalf of Kerr-McGee and the American Mining Congress is one which is a genuine threat to Kerr-McGee and the members of the American Mining Congress to a substantial degree.

We do not suggest that Kerr-McGee could expect better treatment from state authorities than federal. We do recognize that a change in procedure would produce impairing complications.

The next question is whether, assuming the existence of an interest, the chance of impairment is sufficient to fulfill the requirement of Rule 24(a)(2).

. . .If the relief sought by the plaintiffs is granted, there can be little question but that the interests of the American Mining Congress and of Kerr-McGee would be affected. Plaintiffs contend, however, that appellants would not be bound by such a result if they are not participants. Kerr-McGee points out that even though it may not be res judicata, still it would have a stare decisis effect. Moreover, with NRC and NMEIA as parties, the result might be more profound than stare decisis.

It should be pointed out that the Rule refers to impairment "as a practical matter." Thus, the court is not limited to consequences of a strictly legal nature. The court may consider any significant legal effect in the applicant's interest and it is not restricted to a rigid res judicata test. Hence, the stare decisis effect might be sufficient to satisfy the requirement. It is said that where, as here, the case is of first impression, the stare decisis effect would be important.

Finally, the considerations for requiring an environmental impact statement will be relatively the same in respect to the issuance of a uranium mining license in every instance. Hence, to say that it can be repeatedly litigated is not an answer, for the chance of getting a contrary result in a case which is substantially similar on its facts to one previously adjudicated seems remote.

We are of the opinion, therefore, that appellants have satisfied the impairment criterion.

The final question is whether the trial court was correct in its conclusion that United Nuclear would adequately represent Kerr-McGee and the American Mining Congress.

The finding and conclusion was that the representation would be adequate because United Nuclear, a fellow member of the industry, has interests which were the same as those of the appellants and possessed the same level of knowledge and experience with the ability and willingness to pursue the matter and could adequately represent Kerr-McGee and the members of the American Mining Congress. . . .

United Nuclear is situated somewhat differently in this case than are the other members of the industry since it has been granted its license. From this it is urged by Kerr-McGee that United Nuclear may be ready to compromise the case by obtaining a mere declaration that while environmental impact statements should be issued, this requirement need be prospective only, whereby it would not affect them. While we see this as a remote possibility, we gravely doubt that United Nuclear would opt for such a result. It is true, however, that United Nuclear has a defense of laches that is not available to Kerr-McGee or the others.

7A C. Wright & A. Miller, Federal Practice & Procedure, § 1909, at 524 (1972), says:

> [I]f [an applicant's] interest is similar to, but not identical with, that of one of the parties, a discriminating judgment is required on the circumstances of the particular case, but he ordinarily should be allowed to intervene unless it is clear that the party will provide adequate representation for the absentee.

While the interest of the two applicants may appear similar, there is no way to say that there is no possibility that they will not be different and the possibility of divergence of interest need not be great in order to satisfy the burden of the applicants under National Farm Lines, supra.

There are other reasons for allowing intervention. There is some value in having the parties before the court so that they will be bound by the result. American Mining Congress represents a number of companies having a wide variety of interests. This can, therefore, provide a useful supplement to the defense of the case. The same can be said of Kerr-McGee.

The trial court was concerned that the addition of these movants would make the litigation unwieldy. If the intervenors are limited to this group, unwieldiness does not become a problem which the trial court cannot control. It does not appear that there would be a need for additional parties in view of the presence of the American Mining Congress. While we do not express an opinion on the possibilities of further additions, we wish to make clear that the present holdings that the two applicants should be allowed to intervene does not say that others should be added. . . .

The order of the district court is reversed and the cause is remanded with instructions to the trial court to grant the appellants, Kerr-McGee's and American Mining Congress', motions to intervene

Introduction to *Martin v. Wilks* May a litigant be bound by a previous decision because, although technically a nonparty, he/she purposely bypassed an adequate opportunity to intervene?

Martin v. Wilks
490 U.S. 755 (1989)

CHIEF JUSTICE REHNQUIST delivered the opinion of the Court.

A group of white firefighters sued the city of Birmingham, Alabama (City), and the Jefferson County Personnel Board (Board) alleging that they were being denied promotions in favor of less qualified black firefighters. They claimed that the City and the Board were making promotion decisions on the basis of race in reliance on certain consent decrees, and that these decisions constituted impermissible racial discrimination in violation of the Constitution and federal statutes. The District Court held that the white firefighters were precluded from challenging employment decisions taken pursuant to the decrees, even though these firefighters had not been parties to the proceedings in which the decrees were entered. We think this holding contravenes the general rule that a person cannot be deprived of his legal rights in a proceeding to which he is not a party.

The litigation in which the consent decrees were entered began in 1974, when the Ensley Branch of the National Association for the Advancement of Colored People and seven black individuals filed separate class-action complaints against the City and the Board. They alleged that both had engaged in racially discriminatory hiring and promotion practices in various public service jobs in violation of Title VII of the Civil Rights Act of 1964, 42 U. S. C. § 2000e et seq., and other federal law. After a bench trial on some issues, but before judgment, the parties entered into two consent decrees, one between the black individuals and the City and the other between them and the Board. These proposed decrees set forth an extensive remedial scheme, including long-term and interim annual goals for the hiring of blacks as firefighters. The decrees also provided for goals for promotion of blacks within the fire department.

The District Court entered an order provisionally approving the decrees and directing publication of notice of the upcoming fairness hearings. App. 694-696. Notice of the hearings, with a reference to the general nature of the decrees, was published in two local newspapers. At that hearing, the Birmingham Firefighters Association (BFA) appeared and filed objections as amicus curiae. After the hearing, but before final approval of the decrees, the BFA and two of its members also moved to intervene on the ground that the decrees would adversely affect their rights. The District Court denied the motions as untimely and approved the decrees. United States v. Jefferson County, 28 FEP Cases 1834 (ND Ala. 1981). Seven white firefighters, all members of the BFA, then filed a complaint against the City and the Board seeking injunctive relief against enforcement of the decrees. The seven argued that the decrees would operate to illegally discriminate against them; the District Court denied relief.

Both the denial of intervention and the denial of injunctive relief were affirmed on appeal. The District Court had not abused its discretion in refusing to let the BFA intervene, thought the Eleventh Circuit, in part because the firefighters could "institut[e] an independent Title VII suit, asserting specific violations of their rights." And, for the same reason, petitioners had not adequately shown the potential for irreparable harm from the operation of the decrees necessary to obtain injunctive relief.

A new group of white firefighters, the Wilks respondents, then brought suit against the City and the Board in District Court. They too alleged that, because of their race, they were being denied promotions in favor of less qualified blacks in violation of federal law. The Board and the City admitted to making race-conscious employment decisions but argued that the decisions were unassailable because they were made pursuant to the consent decrees. A group of black individuals, the Martin petitioners, were allowed to intervene in their individual capacities to defend the decrees.

The defendants moved to dismiss the reverse discrimination cases as impermissible collateral attacks on the consent decrees. The District Court denied the motions, ruling that the decrees would provide a defense to claims of discrimination for employment decisions "mandated" by the decrees, leaving the principal issue for trial whether the challenged promotions were indeed required by the decrees. App. 237-239, 250. After trial the District Court granted the motion to dismiss. App. to Pet. for Cert. 67a. The court concluded that "if in fact the City was required to [make promotions of blacks] by the consent decree, then they would not be guilty of [illegal] racial discrimination" and that the defendants had "establish[ed] that the promotions of the black individuals. . . were in fact required by the terms of the consent decree."

On appeal, the Eleventh Circuit reversed. It held that, "[b]ecause . . . [the Wilks respondents] were neither parties nor privies to the consent decrees, . . . their independent claims of unlawful discrimination are not precluded." In re Birmingham Reverse Discrimination Employment Litigation, 833 F. 2d 1492, 1498 (1987). The court explicitly rejected the doctrine of "impermissible collateral attack" espoused by other Courts of Appeals to immunize parties to a consent decree from charges of discrimination by nonparties for actions taken pursuant to the decree. Ibid. Although it recognized a "strong public policy in favor of voluntary affirmative action plans," the panel acknowledged that this interest "must yield to the policy against requiring third parties to submit to bargains in which their interest were either ignored or sacrificed." Ibid. The court remanded the case for trial of the discrimination claims, suggesting that the operative law for judging the consent decrees was that governing voluntary affirmative-action plans. Id., at 1497.

We granted certiorari, 487 U. S. 1204 (1988), and now affirm the Eleventh Circuit's judgment. All agree that "[i]t is a principle of general application in Anglo-American jurisprudence that one is not bound by a judgment in personam in a litigation in which he is not designated as a party or to which he has not been made a party by service of process." Hansberry v. Lee, 311 U. S. 32, 40 (1940). This rule is part of our "deep-rooted historic tradition that everyone should have his own day in court." 18 C. Wright, A. Miller, & E. Cooper, Federal Practice and Procedure § 4449, p. 417 (1981) (hereafter 18 Wright). A judgment or decree among parties to a lawsuit resolves issues as among them, but it does not conclude the rights of strangers to those proceedings.

Petitioners argue that, because respondents failed to timely intervene in the initial proceedings, their current challenge to actions taken under the consent decree constitutes an impermissible "collateral attack." They argue that respondents were aware that the underlying suit might affect them, and if they chose to pass up an opportunity to intervene, they should not be permitted to later litigate the issues in a new action. The position has sufficient appeal to have commanded the approval of the great majority of the Federal Courts of Appeals,[3] but we agree with the contrary view expressed by the Court of Appeals for the Eleventh Circuit in these cases.

We begin with the words of Justice Brandeis in Chase National Bank v. Norwalk, 291 U. S. 431 (1934):

"The law does not impose upon any person absolutely entitled to a hearing the burden of voluntary intervention in a suit to which he is a stranger. . . . Unless duly summoned to appear in a legal proceeding, a person not a privy may rest assured that a judgment recovered therein will not affect his legal rights." Id. at 441.

While these words were written before the adoption of the Federal Rules of Civil Procedure, we think the Rules incorporate the same principle; a party seeking a judgment binding on another cannot obligate that person to intervene; he must be joined. Against the background of permissive intervention set forth in Chase National Bank, the drafters cast Rule 24, governing intervention, in permissive terms. See Fed. Rule Civ. Proc. 24(a) (intervention as of right) ("Upon timely application anyone shall be permitted to intervene"); Fed. Rule Civ. Proc. 24(b) (permissive intervention) ("Upon timely application anyone may be permitted to intervene"). They determined that the concern for finality and completeness of judgments would be "better [served] by mandatory joinder procedures." 18 Wright § 4452, p. 453. Accordingly, Rule 19(a) provides for mandatory joinder in circumstances where a judgment rendered in the absence of a person may "leave. . . persons already parties subject to a substantial risk of incurring . . . inconsistent obligations. . . ." Rule 19(b) sets forth the factors to be considered by a court in deciding whether to allow an action to proceed in the absence of an interested party.

Joinder as a party, rather than knowledge of a lawsuit and an opportunity to intervene, is the method by which potential parties are subjected to the jurisdiction of the court and bound by a judgment or decree. The parties to a lawsuit presumably know better than anyone else the nature and scope of relief sought in the action, and at whose expense such relief might be granted. It makes sense, therefore, to place on them a burden of bringing in additional parties where such a step is indicated, rather than placing on potential additional parties a duty to intervene when they acquire knowledge of the lawsuit. The linchpin of the "impermissible collateral attack" doctrine — the attribution of preclusive effect to a failure to intervene — is therefore quite inconsistent with Rule 19 and Rule 24.

* * *

Petitioners contend that a different result should be reached because the need to join affected parties will be burdensome and ultimately discouraging to civil rights litigation. Potential adverse claimants may be numerous and difficult to identify; if they are not joined, the possibility for inconsistent judgments exists. Judicial resources will be needlessly consumed in relitigation of the same question.

Even if we were wholly persuaded by these arguments as a matter of policy, acceptance of them would require a rewriting rather than an interpretation of the relevant Rules. But we are not persuaded that their acceptance would lead to a more satisfactory method of handling cases like these. It must be remembered that the alternatives are a duty to intervene based on knowledge, on the one hand, and some form of joinder, as the Rules presently provide, on the other. No one can seriously contend that an employer might successfully defend against a Title VII claim by one group of employees on the ground that its actions were required by an earlier decree entered in a suit brought against it by another, if the later group did not have adequate notice or knowledge of the earlier suit.

* * *

Nor do we think that the system of joinder called for by the Rules is likely to produce more relitigation of issues than the converse rule. The breadth of a lawsuit and concomitant relief may be at least partially shaped in advance through Rule 19 to avoid needless clashes with future litigation. And even under a regime of mandatory intervention, parties who did not have adequate knowledge of the suit would relitigate issues. Additional questions about the adequacy and timeliness of knowledge would inevitably crop up. We think that the system of joinder presently contemplated by the Rules best serves the many interests involved in the run of litigated cases, including cases like the present ones.

Petitioners also urge that the congressional policy favoring voluntary settlement of employment discrimination claims, . . . also supports the "impermissible collateral attack" doctrine. But once again it is essential to note just what is meant by "voluntary settlement." A voluntary settlement in the form of a consent decree between one group of employees and their employer cannot possibly "settle," voluntarily or otherwise, the conflicting claims of another group of employees who do not join in the agreement. This is true even if the second group of employees is a party to the litigation:

"[P]arties who choose to resolve litigation through settlement may not dispose of the claims of a third party... without that party's agreement. A court's approval of a consent decree between some of the parties therefore cannot dispose of the valid claims of nonconsenting intervenors." Firefighters v. Cleveland, 478 U. S. 501, 529 (1986).

Insofar as the argument is bottomed on the idea that it may be easier to settle claims among a disparate group of affected persons if they are all before the court, joinder bids fair to accomplish that result as well as a regime of mandatory intervention.

For the foregoing reasons we affirm the decision of the Court of Appeals for the Eleventh Circuit. That court remanded the case for trial of the reverse discrimination claims. Petitioners point to language in the District Court's findings of fact and conclusions of law which suggests that respondents will not prevail on the merits. We agree with the view of the Court of Appeals, however, that the proceedings in the District Court may have been affected by the mistaken view that respondents' claims on the merits were barred to the extent they were inconsistent with the consent decree.

Affirmed.

Notes and Questions

A person is entitled to intervene when his position is comparable to that of a "necessary" party as defined by Rule 19(a). If the stranger would be substantially affected in a practical sense by the determination made in an action, he should, as a general rule, be entitled to intervene. (Advisory Committee Note to Rule 24.)

After *Martin v. Wilks*, a party seeking a judgment binding on another cannot obligate that person to intervene under FRCP 24, rather he/she must be joined pursuant to FRCP 19).

In light of this, if the plaintiffs in the original suit had wanted to make any judgment binding up on the absent fire-fighters what should plaintiffs have done?

Procedure for Intervention The party desiring to intervene must serve a motion for leave to intervene upon all parties, stating the ground for intervention and accompanied by a pleading setting forth the claim or defense for which intervention is sought. (FRCP 24(c); Wright, §75)

Interpleader

Let's suppose that after the conclusion of class your Civil Procedure instructor (who is always last to leave the classroom) discovers a $100 bill on the floor. At the next class meeting he announces that he found it and asks who it belongs to. Several students claim to be the owner. What is the instructor to do? Rather than risk giving the money to the wrong claimant the instructor could follow the procedure provided for in FRCP 22 (assuming the requirements of diversity jurisdiction were otherwise satisfied) and deposit the money with the court and let the claimants fight it out over ownership.

A common scenario for interpleader are competing claimants for the proceeds of an insurance policy. An insurer faced with conflicting but mutually exclusive claims to a policy could deposit the proceeds with the court and let the claimants litigate rightful entitlement to the proceeds. The case that follows is a variation on that: an insurer confronted with the problem of allocating a fund among various claimants whose independent claims may exceed the amount of the fund.

State Farm Fire & Casualty Co. v. Tashire
386 U.S. 523 (1967)

MR. JUSTICE FORTAS delivered the opinion of the Court.

Early one September morning in 1964, a Greyhound bus proceeding northward through Shasta County, California, collided with a southbound pickup truck. Two of the passengers aboard the bus were killed. Thirty-three others were injured, as were the bus driver, the driver of the truck and its lone passenger. One of the dead and 10 of the injured passengers were Canadians; the rest of the individuals involved were citizens of five American States. The ensuing litigation led to the present case, which raises important questions concerning administration of the interpleader remedy in the federal courts.

The litigation began when four of the injured passengers filed suit in California state courts, seeking damages in excess of $1,000,000. Named as defendants were Greyhound Lines, Inc., a California corporation; Theron Nauta, the bus driver; Ellis Clark, who drove the truck; and Kenneth Glasgow, the passenger in the truck who was apparently its owner as well. Each of the individual defendants was a citizen and resident of Oregon. Before these cases could come to trial and before other suits were filed in California or elsewhere, petitioner State Farm Fire & Casualty Company, an Illinois corporation, brought this action in the nature of interpleader in the United States District Court for the District of Oregon.

In its complaint State Farm asserted that at the time of the Shasta County collision it had in force an insurance policy with respect to Ellis Clark, driver of the truck, providing for bodily injury liability up to $10,000 per person and $20,000 per occurrence and for legal representation of Clark in actions covered by the policy. It asserted that actions already filed in California and others which it anticipated would be filed far exceeded in aggregate damages sought the amount of its maximum liability under the policy. Accordingly, it paid into court the sum of $20,000 and asked the court (1) to require all claimants to establish their claims against Clark and his insurer in this single proceeding and in no other, and (2) to discharge State Farm from all further obligations under its policy—including its duty to defend Clark in lawsuits arising from the accident. Alternatively, State Farm expressed its conviction that the policy issued to Clark excluded from coverage accidents resulting from his operation of a truck which belonged to another and was being used in the business of another. The complaint, therefore, requested that the court decree that the insurer owed no duty to Clark and was not liable on the policy, and it asked the court to refund the $20,000 deposit.

Joined as defendants were Clark, Glasgow, Nauta, Greyhound Lines, and each of the prospective claimants. Jurisdiction was predicated upon 28 U. S. C. § 1335, the federal interpleader statute, and upon general diversity of citizenship, there being diversity between two or more of the claimants to the fund and between State Farm and all of the named defendants.

An order issued, requiring the defendants to show cause why they should not be restrained from filing or prosecuting "any proceeding in any state or United States Court affecting the property or obligation involved in this interpleader action, and specifically against the plaintiff and the defendant Ellis D. Clark." Personal service was effected on each of the American defendants, and registered mail was employed to reach the 11 Canadian claimants. Defendants Nauta, Greyhound, and several of the injured passengers responded, contending that the policy did cover this accident and advancing various arguments for the position that interpleader was either impermissible or inappropriate in the present circumstances. Greyhound, however, soon switched sides and moved that the court broaden any injunction to include Nauta and Greyhound among those who could not be sued except within the confines of the interpleader proceeding.

When a temporary injunction along the lines sought by State Farm was issued by the United States District Court for the District of Oregon, the present respondents moved to dismiss the action and, in the alternative, for a change of venue—to the Northern District of California, in which district the collision had occurred. After a hearing, the court declined to dissolve the temporary injunction, but continued the motion for a change of venue. The injunction was later broadened to include the protection sought by Greyhound but modified to permit the filing—although not the prosecution—of suits. The injunction, therefore, provided that all suits against Clark, State Farm, Greyhound, and Nauta be prosecuted in the interpleader proceeding.

On interlocutory appeal, the Court of Appeals for the Ninth Circuit reversed. 363 F. 2d 7. The court found it unnecessary to reach respondents' contentions relating to service of process and the scope of the injunction, for it concluded that interpleader was not available in the circumstances of this case. It held that in States like Oregon which do not permit "direct action" suits against insurance companies until judgments are obtained against the insured, the insurance companies may not invoke federal interpleader until the claims against the insured, the alleged tortfeasor, have been reduced to judgment. Until that is done, said the court, claimants with unliquidated tort claims are not "claimants" within the meaning of § 1335, nor are they "persons having claims against the plaintiff" within the meaning of Rule 22 of the Federal Rules of Civil Procedure. Id., at 10. In accord with that view, it directed dissolution of the temporary injunction and dismissal of the action. Because the Court of Appeals' decision on this point conflicts with those of other federal courts and concerns a matter of significance to the administration of federal interpleader, we granted certiorari. 385 U. S. 811 (1966). Although we reverse the decision of the Court of Appeals upon the jurisdictional question, we direct a substantial modification of the District Court's injunction for reasons which will appear.

Before considering the issues presented by the petition for certiorari, we find it necessary to dispose of a question neither raised by the parties nor passed upon by the courts below. Since the matter concerns our jurisdiction, we raise it on our own motion. The interpleader statute, 28 U. S. C. § 1335, applies where there are "Two or more adverse claimants, of diverse citizenship . . . ." This provision has been uniformly construed to require only "minimal diversity," that is, diversity of citizenship between two or more claimants, without regard to the circumstance that other rival claimants may be co-citizens. The language of the statute, the legislative purpose broadly to remedy the problems posed by multiple claimants to a single fund, and the consistent judicial interpretation tacitly accepted by Congress, persuade us that the statute requires no more. There remains, however, the question whether such a statutory construction is consistent with Article III of our Constitution, which extends the federal judicial power to "Controversies. . . between Citizens of different States . . . and between a State, or the Citizens thereof, and foreign States, Citizens or Subjects." In Strawbridge v. Curtiss, 3 Cranch 267 (1806), this Court held that the diversity of citizenship statute required "complete diversity": where co-citizens appeared on both sides of a dispute, jurisdiction was lost. But Chief Justice Marshall there purported to construe only "The words of the act of congress," not the Constitution itself. And in a variety of contexts this Court and the lower courts have concluded that Article III poses no obstacle to the legislative extension of federal jurisdiction, founded on diversity, so long as any two adverse parties are not co-citizens. Accordingly, we conclude that the present case is properly in the federal courts.

We do not agree with the Court of Appeals that, in the absence of a state law or contractual provision for "direct action" suits against the insurance company, the company must wait until persons asserting claims against its insured have reduced those claims to judgment before seeking to invoke the benefits of federal interpleader....

Considerations of judicial administration demonstrate the soundness of this view which, in any event, seems compelled by the language of the present statute, which is remedial and to be liberally construed. Were an insurance company required to await reduction of claims to judgment, the first claimant to obtain such a judgment or to negotiate a settlement might appropriate all or a disproportionate slice of the fund before his fellow claimants were able to establish their claims. The difficulties such a race to judgment pose for the insurer, and the unfairness which may result to some claimants, were among the principal evils the interpleader device was intended to remedy.

The fact that State Farm had properly invoked the interpleader jurisdiction under § 1335 did not, however, entitle it to an order both enjoining prosecution of suits against it outside the confines of the interpleader proceeding and also extending such protection to its insured, the alleged tortfeasor. Still less was Greyhound Lines entitled to have that order expanded so as to protect itself and its driver, also alleged to be tortfeasors, from suits brought by its passengers in various state or federal courts. Here, the scope of the litigation, in terms of parties and claims, was vastly more extensive than the confines of the "fund," the deposited proceeds of the insurance policy. In these circumstances, the mere existence of such a fund cannot, by use of interpleader, be employed to accomplish purposes that exceed the needs of orderly contest with respect to the fund.

There are situations, of a type not present here, where the effect of interpleader is to confine the total litigation to a single forum and proceeding. One such case is where a stakeholder, faced with rival claims to the fund itself, acknowledges—or denies—his liability to one or the other of the claimants. In this situation, the fund itself is the target of the claimants. It marks the outer limits of the controversy. It is, therefore, reasonable and sensible that interpleader, in discharge of its office to protect the fund, should also protect the stakeholder from vexatious and multiple litigation. In this context, the suits sought to be enjoined are squarely within the language of 28 U. S. C. § 2361, which provides in part:

> "In any civil action of interpleader or in the nature of interpleader under section 1335 of this title, a district court may issue its process for all claimants and enter its order restraining them from instituting or prosecuting any proceeding in any State or United States court affecting the property, instrument or obligation involved in the interpleader action...."

But the present case is another matter. Here, an accident has happened. Thirty-five passengers or their representatives have claims which they wish to press against a variety of defendants: the bus company, its driver, the owner of the truck, and the truck driver. The circumstance that one of the prospective defendants happens to have an insurance policy is a fortuitous event which should not of itself shape the nature of the ensuing litigation. For example, a resident of California, injured in California aboard a bus owned by a California corporation should not be forced to sue that corporation anywhere but in California simply because another prospective defendant carried an insurance policy. And an insurance company whose maximum interest in the case cannot exceed $20,000 and who in fact asserts that it has no interest at all, should not be allowed to determine that dozens of tort plaintiffs must be compelled to press their claims—even those claims which are not against the insured and which in no event could be satisfied out of the meager insurance fund—in a single forum of the insurance company's choosing. There is nothing in the statutory scheme, and very little in the judicial and academic commentary upon that scheme, which requires that the tail be allowed to wag the dog in this fashion.

State Farm's interest in this case, which is the fulcrum of the interpleader procedure, is confined to its $20,000 fund. That interest receives full vindication when the court restrains claimants from seeking to enforce against the insurance company any judgment obtained against its insured, except in the interpleader proceeding itself. To the extent that the District Court sought to control claimants' lawsuits against the insured and other alleged tortfeasors, it exceeded the powers granted to it by the statutory scheme.

We recognize, of course, that our view of interpleader means that it cannot be used to solve all the vexing problems of multiparty litigation arising out of a mass tort. But interpleader was never intended to perform such a function, to be an all-purpose "bill of peace." Had it been so intended, careful provision would necessarily have been made to insure that a party with little or no interest in the outcome of a complex controversy should not strip truly interested parties of substantial rights— such as the right to choose the forum in which to establish their claims, subject to generally applicable rules of jurisdiction, venue, service of process, removal, and change of venue. None of the legislative and academic sponsors of a modern federal interpleader device viewed their accomplishment as a "bill of peace," capable of sweeping dozens of lawsuits out of the various state and federal courts in which they were brought and into a single interpleader proceeding. . . .

In light of the evidence that federal interpleader was not intended to serve the function of a "bill of peace" in the context of multiparty litigation arising out of a mass tort, of the anomalous power which such a construction of the statute would give the stakeholder, and of the thrust of the statute and the purpose it was intended to serve, we hold that the interpleader statute did not authorize the injunction entered in the present case. Upon remand, the injunction is to be modified consistently with this opinion.

The judgment of the Court of Appeals is reversed, and the case is remanded to the United States District Court for proceedings consistent with this opinion.

It is so ordered.

Statutory or Rule Interpleader?

As you have seen in the previous case interpleader comes in two "flavors." Statutory and rule interpleader. Rule 22 interpleaders are subject to the normal rules for subject matter jurisdiction (diversity between all plaintiffs and all defendants); personal jurisdiction (jurisdiction within the state); and venue (residency of all defendants, or where the claim arises). Statutory Interpleader broadens the circumstances in which interpleader is available, requiring only "minimal" diversity among adverse claimants and reducing the amount in controversy requirement to a mere $500. The chart below notes the distinctions.

DISTINCTIONS BETWEEN RULE AND STATUTORY INTERPLEADER

	Rule Interpleader	**Statutory Interpleader**
Diversity Requirement	Complete diversity between stakeholder and claimants	Minimal diversity among adverse claimants
Amount-in-Controversy Requirement	Greater than $75,000	At least $500
Personal Jurisdiction	Governed by FRCP 4(k) [typically tied to the reach of the forum state]	Nationwide
Venue	Limited according to 28 USC § 1391	Anywhere any claimant resides
Enjoining Claimants	Governed by the Anti-Injunction Act and Rule 65	Authorized under 28 USC § 2361

Problem Robyn Davis was the named beneficiary of a $95,000 life insurance policy on her late husband. However, Ms. Davis has been arrested and charged with killing him. Pursuant to Louisiana law, a beneficiary of the life insurance policy cannot recover the proceeds if he or she is deemed to have been criminally responsible for the death of the insured. With Ms. Davis' entitlement to the proceeds in question, Farm Bureau

Insurance, who issued the policy, would like to deposit the proceeds in court and let Ms. Davis and the decedent's other heirs litigate entitlement to the proceeds. Does federal subject matter exist under either rule or statutory interpleader? What additional facts would you need to know? (See, *Southern Farm Bureau Life Ins. Co. v. Davis,* 2010 WL 1245024 (W.D. La. 2010)

CHAPTER 6

CLASS ACTIONS

In the last chapter, we studied joinder of parties and claims. In this chapter, we circle back to joinder of parties to examine what has become a specialized form of civil litigation, the class action.

The class action is a device by which a group of persons (usually plaintiffs) who are similarly situated may band together for purposes of litigation. They may have suffered similar common injuries which would be economically unfeasible to pursue individually, or a common issue of law or fact may determine the validity of their claims. The class action provides a method whereby a group of people may redress their individual injuries (provided they have something in common) which would otherwise be too small to warrant separate lawsuits. In other words, class actions permit the plaintiffs to pool claims which would be uneconomical to litigate individually. (*Phillips Petroleum v. Shutts*, 472 U.S. 797 (1985).)

This next case explores the due process concerns that are raised by class actions. As we learned when we studied personal jurisdiction, in order to subject an individual to a binding judgment the court must give them notice, and an opportunity to be heard. In other words, one is not bound by a judgment in a litigation in which he/she is not designated as a party, or to which he/she has not been made a party by service of process. (*Pennoyer v. Neff*) However, classes of persons can be so numerous that individual members of the class may not learn of the pendency of the class action yet they may find themselves bound by a judgment or settlement. How does that square with due process?

Hansberry v. Lee
311 U.S. 32 (1940)

MR. JUSTICE STONE delivered the opinion of the Court.

The question is whether the Supreme Court of Illinois, by its adjudication that petitioners in this case are bound by a judgment rendered in an earlier litigation to which they were not parties, has deprived them of the due process of law guaranteed by the Fourteenth Amendment.

Respondents brought this suit in the Circuit Court of Cook County, Illinois, to enjoin the breach by petitioners of an agreement restricting the use of land within a described area of the City of Chicago, which was alleged to have been entered into by some five hundred of the landowners. The agreement stipulated that for a specified period no part of the land should be "sold, leased to or permitted to be occupied by any person of the colored race," and provided that it should not be effective unless signed by the "owners of 95 per centum of the frontage" within the described area. The bill of complaint set up that the owners of 95 per cent of the frontage had signed; that respondents are owners of land within the restricted area who have either signed the agreement or acquired their land from others who did sign; and that petitioners Hansberry, who are Negroes, have, with the alleged aid of the other petitioners and with knowledge of the agreement, acquired and are occupying land in the restricted area formerly belonging to an owner who had signed the agreement.

To the defense that the agreement had never become effective because owners of 95 per cent of the frontage had not signed it, respondents pleaded that that issue was res judicata by the decree in an earlier suit. To this, petitioners pleaded, by way of rejoinder, that they were not parties to that suit or bound by its decree, and that denial of their right to litigate, in the present suit, the issue of performance of the condition precedent to the validity of the agreement would be a denial of due process of law guaranteed by the Fourteenth Amendment. It does not appear, nor is it contended that any of petitioners is the successor in interest to or in privity with any of the parties in the earlier suit.

The circuit court, after a trial on the merits, found that owners of only about 54 per cent of the frontage had signed the agreement, and that the only support of the judgment in the Burke case was a false and fraudulent stipulation of the parties that owners of 95 per cent had signed. But it ruled that the issue of performance of the condition precedent to the validity of the agreement was res judicata as alleged and entered a decree for respondents. The Supreme Court of Illinois affirmed. 372 Ill. 369; 24 N.E.2d 37. We granted certiorari to resolve the constitutional question. . . .

From this the Supreme Court of Illinois concluded in the present case that Burke v. Kleiman was a "class" or "representative" suit, and that in such a suit, "where the remedy is pursued by a plaintiff who has the right to represent the class to which he belongs, other members of the class are bound by the result in the case unless it is reversed or set aside on direct proceedings"; that petitioners in the present suit were members of the class represented by the plaintiffs in the earlier suit and consequently were bound by its decree . . .

State courts are free to attach such descriptive labels to litigations before them as they may choose and to attribute to them such consequences as they think appropriate under state constitutions and laws, subject only to the requirements of the Constitution of the United States. But when the judgment of a state court, ascribing to the judgment of another court the binding force and effect of res judicata is challenged for want of due process it becomes the duty of this Court to examine the course of procedure in both litigations to ascertain whether the litigant whose rights have thus been adjudicated has been afforded such notice and opportunity to be heard as are requisite to the due process which the Constitution prescribes.

It is a principle of general application in Anglo-American jurisprudence that one is not bound by a judgment in personam in a litigation in which he is not designated as a party or to which he has not been made a party by service of process. Pennoyer v. Neff, 95 U.S. 714. A judgment rendered in such circumstances is not entitled to the full faith and credit which the Constitution and statute of the United States, R.S. § 905, 28 U.S.C. § 687, prescribe, and judicial action enforcing it against the person or property of the absent party is not that due process which the Fifth and Fourteenth Amendments require.

To these general rules there is a recognized exception that, to an extent not precisely defined by judicial opinion, the judgment in a "class" or "representative" suit, to which some members of the class are parties, may bind members of the class or those represented who were not made parties to it.

The class suit was an invention of equity to enable it to proceed to a decree in suits where the number of those interested in the subject of the litigation is so great that their joinder as parties in conformity to the usual rules of procedure is impracticable. Courts are not infrequently called upon to proceed with causes in which the number of those interested in the litigation is so great as to make difficult or impossible the joinder of all because some are not within the jurisdiction or because their whereabouts is unknown or where if all were made parties to the suit its continued abatement by the death of some would prevent or unduly delay a decree. In such cases where the interests of those not joined are of the same class as the interests of those who are, and where it is considered that the latter fairly represent the former in the prosecution of the litigation of the issues in which all have a common interest, the court will proceed to a decree. . . .

[T]here is scope within the framework of the Constitution for holding in appropriate cases that a judgment rendered in a class suit is res judicata as to members of the class who are not formal parties to the suit. Here, as elsewhere, the Fourteenth Amendment does not compel state courts or legislatures to adopt any particular rule for establishing the conclusiveness of judgments in class suits; nor does it compel the adoption of the particular rules thought by this Court to be appropriate for the federal courts. With a proper regard for divergent local institutions and interests, this Court is justified in saying that there has been a failure of due process only in those cases where it cannot be said that the procedure adopted, fairly insures the protection of the interests of absent parties who are to be bound by it.

It is familiar doctrine of the federal courts that members of a class not present as parties to the litigation may be bound by the judgment where they are in fact adequately represented by parties who are present, or where they actually participate in the conduct of the litigation in which members of the class are present as parties, or where the interest of the members of the class, some of whom are present as parties, is joint, or where for any other reason the relationship between the parties present and those who are absent is such as legally to entitle the former to stand in judgment for the latter.

In all such cases, so far as it can be said that the members of the class who are present are, by generally recognized rules of law, entitled to stand in judgment for those who are not, we may assume for present purposes that such procedure affords a protection to the parties who are represented, though absent, which would satisfy the requirements of due process and full faith and credit Nor do we find it necessary for the decision of this case to say that, when the only circumstance defining the class is that the determination of the rights of its members turns upon a single issue of fact or law, a state could not constitutionally adopt a procedure whereby some of the members of the class could stand in judgment for all, provided that the procedure were so devised and applied as to insure that those present are of the same class as those absent and that the litigation is so conducted as to insure the full and fair consideration of the common issue. We decide only that the procedure and the course of litigation sustained here by the plea of res judicata do not satisfy these requirements.

The restrictive agreement did not purport to create a joint obligation or liability. If valid and effective its promises were the several obligations of the signers and those claiming under them. The promises ran severally to every other signer. It is plain that in such circumstances all those alleged to be bound by the agreement would not constitute a single class in any litigation brought to enforce it. Those who sought to secure its benefits by enforcing it could not be said to be in the same class with or represent those whose interest was in resisting performance, for the agreement by its terms imposes obligations and confers rights on the owner of each plot of land who signs it. If those who thus seek to secure the benefits of the agreement were rightly regarded by the state Supreme Court as constituting a class, it is evident that those signers or their successors who are interested in challenging the validity of the agreement and resisting its performance are not of the same class in the sense that their interests are identical so that any group who had elected to enforce rights conferred by the agreement could be said to be acting in the interest of any others who were free to deny its obligation.

Because of the dual and potentially conflicting interests of those who are putative parties to the agreement in compelling or resisting its performance, it is impossible to say, solely because they are parties to it, that any two of them are of the same class. Nor without more, and with the due regard for the protection of the rights of absent parties which due process exacts, can some be permitted to stand in judgment for all.

It is one thing to say that some members of a class may represent other members in a litigation where the sole and common interest of the class in the litigation, is either to assert a common right or to challenge an asserted obligation. It is quite another to hold that all those who are free alternatively either to assert rights or to challenge them are of a single class, so that any group, merely because it is of the class so constituted, may be deemed adequately to represent any others of the class in litigating their interests in either alternative. Such a selection of representatives for purposes of litigation, whose substantial interests are not necessarily or even probably the same as those whom they are deemed to represent, does not afford that protection to absent parties which due process requires. The doctrine of representation of absent parties in a class suit has not hitherto been thought to go so far. Apart from the opportunities it would afford for the fraudulent and collusive sacrifice of the rights of absent parties, we think that the representation in this case no more satisfies the requirements of due process than a trial by a judicial officer who is in such situation that he may have an interest in the outcome of the litigation in conflict with that of the litigants.

The plaintiffs in the Burke case sought to compel performance of the agreement in behalf of themselves and all others similarly situated. They did not designate the defendants in the suit as a class or seek any injunction or other relief against others than the named defendants, and the decree which was entered did not purport to bind others. In seeking to enforce the agreement the plaintiffs in that suit were not representing the petitioners here whose substantial interest is in resisting performance. The defendants in the first suit were not treated by the pleadings or decree as representing others or as foreclosing by their defense the rights of others; and, even though nominal defendants, it does not appear that their interest in defeating the contract outweighed their interest in establishing its validity. For a court in this situation to ascribe to either the plaintiffs or defendants the performance of such functions on behalf of petitioners here, is to attribute to them a power that it cannot be said that they had assumed to exercise, and a responsibility which, in view of their dual interests it does not appear that they could rightly discharge.

Reversed.

The Problem of Personal Jurisdiction in the Class Action

Phillips Petroleum Co. v. Shutts
472 U.S. 797 (1985)

JUSTICE REHNQUIST delivered the opinion of the Court.

Petitioner is a Delaware corporation which has its principal place of business in Oklahoma. During the 1970's it produced or purchased natural gas from leased land located in 11 different States and sold most of the gas in interstate commerce. Respondents are some 28,000 of the royalty owners possessing rights to the leases from which petitioner produced the gas; they reside in all 50 States, the District of Columbia, and several foreign countries. Respondents brought a class action against petitioner in the Kansas state court, seeking to recover interest on royalty payments which had been delayed by petitioner. They recovered judgment in the trial court, and the Supreme Court of Kansas affirmed the judgment over petitioner's contentions that the Due Process Clause of the Fourteenth Amendment prevented Kansas from adjudicating the claims of all the respondents, and that the Due Process Clause and the Full Faith and Credit Clause of Article IV of the Constitution prohibited the application of Kansas law to all of the transactions between petitioner and respondents. We granted certiorari to consider these claims. . . .

After the class was certified respondents provided each class member with notice through first-class mail. The notice described the action and informed each class member that he could appear in person or by counsel; otherwise each member would be represented by Shutts and the Andersons, the named plaintiffs. The notices also stated that class members would be included in the class and bound by the judgment unless they "opted out" of the lawsuit by executing and returning a "request for exclusion" that was included with the notice. The final class as certified contained 28,100 members; 3,400 had "opted out" of the class by returning the request for exclusion, and notice could not be delivered to another 1,500 members, who were also excluded. Less than 1,000 of the class members resided in Kansas. Only a minuscule amount, approximately one quarter of one percent, of the gas leases involved in the lawsuit were on Kansas land. . . .

After petitioner's mandamus petition to decertify the class was denied, the case was tried to the court. The court found petitioner liable under Kansas law for interest on the suspended royalties to all class members. . . .

Petitioner raised two principal claims in its appeal to the Supreme Court of Kansas. It first asserted that the Kansas trial court did not possess personal jurisdiction over absent plaintiff class members as required by International Shoe Co. v. Washington and similar cases. Related to this first claim was petitioner's contention that the "opt-out" notice to absent class members, which forced them to return the request for exclusion in order to avoid the suit, was insufficient to bind class members who were not residents of Kansas or who did not possess "minimum contacts" with Kansas. Second, petitioner claimed that Kansas courts could not apply Kansas law to every claim in the dispute. The trial court should have looked to the laws of each State where the leases were located to determine, on the basis of conflict of laws principles, whether interest on the suspended royalties was recoverable, and at what rate. . . .

Reduced to its essentials, petitioner's argument is that unless out-of-state plaintiffs affirmatively consent, the Kansas courts may not exert jurisdiction over their claims. Petitioner claims that failure to execute and return the "request for exclusion" provided with the class notice cannot constitute consent of the out-of-state plaintiffs; thus Kansas courts may exercise jurisdiction over these plaintiffs only if the plaintiffs possess the sufficient "minimum contacts" with Kansas as that term is used in cases involving personal jurisdiction over out-of-state defendants. E. g., International Shoe Co. v. Washington, 326 U. S. 310 (1945); Shaffer v. Heitner, 433 U. S. 186 (1977); World-Wide Volkswagen Corp. v. Woodson, 444 U. S. 286 (1980). Since Kansas had no prelitigation contact with many of the plaintiffs and leases involved, petitioner claims that Kansas has exceeded its jurisdictional reach and thereby violated the due process rights of the absent plaintiffs. . . .

Although the cases like Shaffer and Woodson which petitioner relies on for a minimum contacts requirement all dealt with out-of-state defendants or parties in the procedural posture of a defendant, petitioner claims that the same analysis must apply to absent class-action plaintiffs. In this regard petitioner correctly points out that a chose in action is a constitutionally recognized property interest possessed by each of the plaintiffs. An adverse judgment by Kansas courts in this case may extinguish the chose in action forever through res judicata. Such an adverse judgment, petitioner claims, would be every bit as onerous to an absent plaintiff as an adverse judgment on the merits would be to a defendant. Thus, the same due process protections should apply to absent plaintiffs: Kansas should not be able to exert jurisdiction over the plaintiffs' claims unless the plaintiffs have sufficient minimum contacts with Kansas.

We think petitioner's premise is in error. The burdens placed by a State upon an absent class-action plaintiff are not of the same order or magnitude as those it places upon an absent defendant. An out-of-state defendant summoned by a plaintiff is faced with the full powers of the forum State to render judgment against it. The defendant must generally hire counsel and travel to the forum to defend itself from the plaintiff's claim or suffer a default judgment. The defendant may be forced to participate in extended and often costly discovery and will be forced to respond in damages or to comply with some other form of remedy imposed by the court should it lose the suit. The defendant may also face liability for court costs and attorney's fees.

A class-action plaintiff, however, is in quite a different posture. . . .

In sharp contrast to the predicament of a defendant haled into an out-of-state forum, the plaintiffs in this suit were not haled anywhere to defend themselves upon pain of a default judgment. As commentators have noted, from the plaintiffs' point of view a class action resembles a "quasi-administrative proceeding, conducted by the judge."

A plaintiff class in Kansas and numerous other jurisdictions cannot first be certified unless the judge, with the aid of the named plaintiffs and defendant, conducts an inquiry into the common nature of the named plaintiffs' and the absent plaintiffs' claims, the adequacy of representation, the jurisdiction possessed over the class, and any other matters that will bear upon proper representation of the absent plaintiffs' interest. See, e. g., Kan. Stat. Ann. § 60-223 (1983); Fed. Rule Civ. Proc. 23. Unlike a defendant in a civil suit, a class-action plaintiff is not required to fend for himself. See Kan. Stat. Ann.

§ 60-223(d) (1983). The court and named plaintiffs protect his interests. Indeed, the class-action defendant itself has a great interest in ensuring that the absent plaintiffs' claims are properly before the forum. . . .

The concern of the typical class-action rules for the absent plaintiffs is manifested in other ways. Most jurisdictions, including Kansas, require that a class action, once certified, may not be dismissed or compromised without the approval of the court. In many jurisdictions such as Kansas the court may amend the pleadings to ensure that all sections of the class are represented adequately. Kan. Stat. Ann. § 60-223(d) (1983); see also, e. g., Fed. Rule Civ. Proc. 23(d).

Besides this continuing solicitude for their rights, absent plaintiff class members are not subject to other burdens imposed upon defendants. They need not hire counsel or appear. They are almost never subject to counter-claims or cross-claims, or liability for fees or costs. Absent plaintiff class members are not subject to coercive or punitive remedies. Nor will an adverse judgment typically bind an absent plaintiff for any damages, although a valid adverse judgment may extinguish any of the plaintiff's claims which were litigated. . . .

In most class actions an absent plaintiff is provided at least with an opportunity to "opt out" of the class, and if he takes advantage of that opportunity he is removed from the litigation entirely. This was true of the Kansas proceedings in this case. . . .

Because States place fewer burdens upon absent class plaintiffs than they do upon absent defendants in non-class suits, the Due Process Clause need not and does not afford the former as much protection from state-court jurisdiction as it does the latter. The Fourteenth Amendment does protect "persons," not "defendants," however, so absent plaintiffs as well as absent defendants are entitled to some protection from the jurisdiction of a forum State which seeks to adjudicate their claims. In this case we hold that a forum State may exercise jurisdiction over the claim of an absent class-action plaintiff, even though that plaintiff may not possess the minimum contacts with the forum which would support personal jurisdiction over a defendant. If the forum State wishes to bind an absent plaintiff concerning a claim for money damages or similar relief at law, it must provide minimal procedural due process protection. The plaintiff must receive notice plus an opportunity to be heard and participate in the litigation, whether in person or through counsel. The notice must be the best practicable, "reasonably calculated, under all the circumstances, to apprise interested parties of the pendency of the action and afford them an opportunity to present their objections." Mullane, 339 U. S., at 314-315; cf. Eisen v.Carlisle & Jacquelin, 417 U. S. 156, 174-175 (1974). The notice should describe the action and the plaintiffs' rights in it. Additionally, we hold that due process requires at a minimum that an absent plaintiff be provided with an opportunity to remove himself from the class by executing and returning an "opt out" or "request for exclusion" form to the court. Finally, the Due

Process Clause of course requires that the named plaintiff at all times adequately represent the interests of the absent class members.

We think that the procedure followed by Kansas, where a fully descriptive notice is sent first-class mail to each class member, with an explanation of the right to "opt out," satisfies due process. . . .

The Kansas courts applied Kansas contract and Kansas equity law to every claim in this case, notwithstanding that over 99% of the gas leases and some 97% of the plaintiffs in the case had no apparent connection to the State of Kansas except for this lawsuit. Petitioner protested that the Kansas courts should apply the laws of the States where the leases were located, or at least apply Texas and Oklahoma law because so many of the leases came from those States. The Kansas courts disregarded this contention and found petitioner liable for interest on the suspended royalties as a matter of Kansas law, and set the interest rates under Kansas equity principles. . . .

We make no effort to determine for ourselves which law must apply to the various transactions involved in this lawsuit, and we reaffirm our observation in Allstate that in many situations a state court may be free to apply one of several choices of law. But the constitutional limitations laid down in cases such as Allstate and Home Ins. Co. v. Dick, supra, must be respected even in a nationwide class action.

We therefore affirm the judgment of the Supreme Court of Kansas insofar as it upheld the jurisdiction of the Kansas courts over the plaintiff class members in this case and reverse its judgment insofar as it held that Kansas law was applicable to all of the transactions which it sought to adjudicate. We remand the case to that court for further proceedings not inconsistent with this opinion.

It is so ordered.

Jurisdiction Over Class Actions in Federal Courts

How do the diversity jurisdiction requirements apply to class actions? Only the *citizenship* of the named representatives is to be considered, it is no objection to jurisdiction that other members of the class, not named as parties, are of such citizenship that would defeat diversity. Similarly, for purposes of *venue*, only the residence of the named parties is considered.

Amount in controversy. Federal courts have original jurisdiction in class actions in which "any member of a class of plaintiffs is a citizen of a State different from any defendant," and the aggregated claims of the plaintiffs exceeds the sum or value of $5,000,000, exclusive of interest and costs. (28 U.S.C. §1332(d))

> **CLASS ACTIONS AND DIVERSITY**
>
> "Bare" diversity
>
> Amount in controversy exceeds $5,000,000

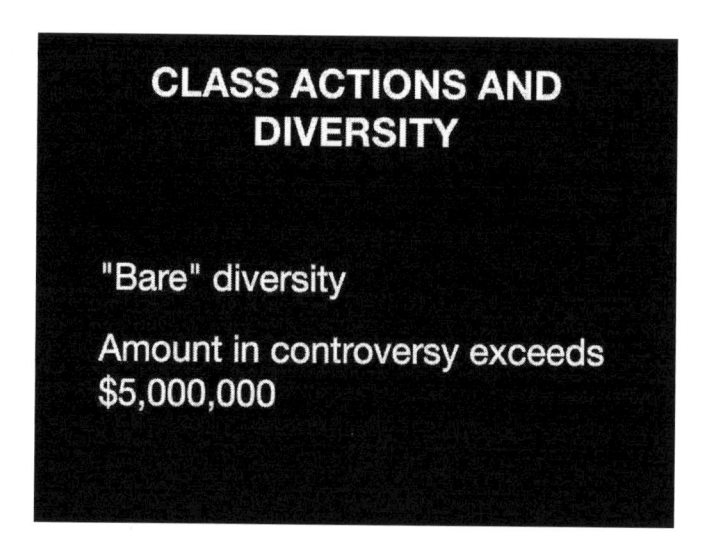

Standard Fire Insurance Co v. Knowles
568 US 588 (2012)

Justice BREYER delivered the opinion of the Court.

The Class Action Fairness Act of 2005 (CAFA) provides that the federal "district courts shall have original jurisdiction" over a civil "class action" if, among other things, the "matter in controversy exceeds the sum or value of $5,000,000." 28 U.S.C. § 1332(d)(2), (d)(5). The statute adds that "to determine whether the matter in controversy exceeds the sum or value of $5,000,000," the "claims of the individual class members shall be aggregated." § 1332(d)(6).

The question presented concerns a class-action plaintiff who stipulates, prior to certification of the class, that he, and the class he seeks to represent, will not seek damages that exceed $5 million in total. Does that stipulation remove the case from CAFA's scope? In our view, it does not.

In April 2011 respondent, Greg Knowles, filed this proposed class action in an Arkansas state court against petitioner, the Standard Fire Insurance Company. Knowles claimed that, when the company had made certain homeowner's insurance loss payments, it had unlawfully failed to include a general contractor fee. And Knowles sought to certify a class of "hundreds, and possibly thousands" of similarly harmed Arkansas policyholders. App. to Pet. for Cert. 66. In describing the relief sought, the complaint says that the "Plaintiff and Class stipulate they will seek to recover total aggregate damages of less than five million dollars." An attached affidavit stipulates that Knowles "will not at any time during this case ... seek damages for the class ... in excess of $5,000,000 in the aggregate."

On May 18, 2011, the company, pointing to CAFA's jurisdictional provision, removed the case to Federal District Court. See 28 U.S.C. § 1332(d); § 1453. . . .

The company appealed from the remand order, but the Eighth Circuit declined to hear the appeal. See 28 U.S.C. § 1453(c)(1) (2006 ed., Supp. V) (providing discretion to hear an appeal from a remand order). The company petitioned for a writ of certiorari. And, in light of divergent views in the lower courts, we granted the writ.

CAFA provides the federal district courts with "original jurisdiction" to hear a "class action" if the class has more than 100 members, the parties are minimally diverse, and the "matter in controversy exceeds the sum or value of $5,000,000." 28 U.S.C. § 1332(d)(2), (d)(5)(B). To "determine whether the matter in controversy" exceeds that sum, "the claims of the individual class members shall be aggregated." § 1332(d)(6). And those "class members" include "persons (named or unnamed) who fall within the definition of the proposed or certified class." § 1332(d)(1)(D) (emphasis added).

The District Court in this case found that resulting sum would have exceeded $5 million but for the stipulation. And we must decide whether the stipulation makes a critical difference.

In our view, it does not. Our reason is a simple one: Stipulations must be binding. The stipulation Knowles proffered to the District Court, however, does not speak for those he purports to represent.

That is because a plaintiff who files a proposed class action cannot legally bind members of the proposed class before the class is certified.

Because his precertification stipulation does not bind anyone but himself, Knowles has not reduced the value of the putative class members' claims. For jurisdictional purposes, our inquiry is limited to examining the case "as of the time it was filed in state court," At that point, Knowles lacked the authority to concede the amount-in-controversy issue for the absent class members. The Federal District Court, therefore, wrongly concluded that Knowles' precertification stipulation could overcome its finding that the CAFA jurisdictional threshold had been met.

Knowles concedes that "[f]ederal jurisdiction cannot be based on contingent future events." Brief for Respondent 20. Yet the two legal principles to which we have just referred — that stipulations must be binding and that a named plaintiff cannot bind precertification class members — mean that the amount to which Knowles has stipulated is in effect contingent.

If, for example, as Knowles' complaint asserts, "hundreds, and possibly thousands" of persons in Arkansas have similar claims, App. to Pet. for Cert. 66, and if each of those claims places a significant sum in controversy, the state court might certify the class and permit the case to proceed, but only on the condition that the stipulation be excised. Or a court might find that Knowles is an inadequate representative due to the artificial cap he purports to impose on the class' recovery. Similarly, another class member could intervene with an amended complaint (without a stipulation), and the District Court might permit the action to proceed with a new representative. See 5 A. Conte & H. Newberg, Class Actions § 16:7, p. 154 (4th ed. 2002) ("[M]embers of a class have a right to intervene if their interests are not adequately represented by existing parties"). Even were these possibilities remote in Knowles' own case, there is no reason to think them farfetched in other cases where similar stipulations could have more dramatic amount-lowering effects.

The strongest counterargument, we believe, takes a syllogistic form: First, this complaint contains a presently nonbinding stipulation that the class will seek damages that amount to less than $5 million. Second, if the state court eventually certifies that class, the stipulation will bind those who choose to remain as class members. Third, if the state court eventually insists upon modification of the stipulation (thereby permitting class members to obtain more than $5 million), it will have in effect created a new, different case. Fourth, CAFA, however, permits the federal court to consider only the complaint that the plaintiff has filed, i.e., this complaint, not a new, modified (or amended) complaint that might eventually emerge.

Our problem with this argument lies in its conclusion. We do not agree that CAFA forbids the federal court to consider, for purposes of determining the amount in controversy, the very real possibility that a nonbinding, amount-limiting, stipulation may not survive the class certification process. This potential outcome does not result in the creation of a new case not now before the federal court. To hold otherwise would, for CAFA jurisdictional purposes, treat a nonbinding stipulation as if it were binding, exalt form over substance, and run directly counter to CAFA's primary objective: ensuring "Federal court consideration of interstate cases of national importance." § 2(b)(2), 119 Stat. 5. It would also have the effect of allowing the subdivision of a $100 million action into 21 just-below-$5-million state-court actions simply by including nonbinding stipulations; such an outcome would squarely conflict with the statute's objective. . . .

Knowles also points out that federal courts permit individual plaintiffs, who are the masters of their complaints, to avoid removal to federal court, and to obtain a remand to state court, by stipulating to amounts at issue that fall below the federal jurisdictional requirement. That is so.("If [a plaintiff] does not desire to try his case in the federal court he may resort to the expedient of suing for less than the jurisdictional amount, and though he would be justly entitled to more, the defendant cannot remove"). But the key characteristic about those stipulations is that they are legally binding on all plaintiffs. See 14AA C. Wright, A. Miller, & E. Cooper, Federal Practice and Procedure § 3702.1, p. 335 (4th ed.2011) (federal court, as condition for remand, can insist on a "binding affidavit or stipulation that the plaintiff will continue to claim less than the jurisdictional amount" (emphasis added)). That essential feature is missing here, as Knowles cannot yet bind the absent class. . . .

In sum, the stipulation at issue here can tie Knowles' hands, but it does not resolve the amount-in-controversy question in light of his inability to bind the rest of the class. For this reason, we believe the District Court, when following the statute to aggregate the proposed class members' claims, should have ignored that stipulation. Because it did not, we vacate the judgment below and remand the case for further proceedings consistent with this opinion.

It is so ordered.

Rule 23

FRCP 23(a) states the prerequisites for maintaining any class action in terms of the numerousness of the class making joinder of the members impracticable, the existence of questions common to the class, and the desired qualifications of the representative parties. (Notes of Advisory Committee on Rules—1966 Amendment)

Determining whether a lawsuit should be treated as a class action is a two-stage process.

1. Are the prerequisites of FRCP 23(a) met? 2. Does the lawsuit fall within the definition of one of the permissible types of class actions listed in FRCP 23(b)? (Friedenthal, § 16.2)

Subdivision (a) of FRCP 23

Subdivision (a) states the prerequisites for maintaining any class action in terms of the numerousness of the class making joinder of the members impracticable, the existence of questions common to the class, and the desired qualifications of the representative parties.

Class Actions Rule 23 Prerequisites (FRCP)

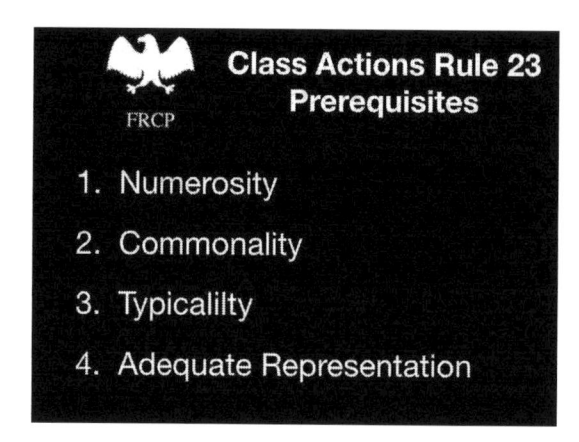

1. Numerosity
2. Commonality
3. Typicalilty
4. Adequate Representation

The adequacy-of-representation requirement "tend[s] to merge" with the commonality and typicality criteria of Rule 23(a), which "serve as guideposts for determining whether . . . maintenance of a class action is economical and whether the named plaintiff's claim and the class claims are so interrelated that the interests of the class members will be fairly and adequately protected in their absence." (*General Telephone Co. of Southwest v. Falcon*, 457 U. S. 147, 157, n. 13 (1982). The adequacy heading also factors in competency and conflicts of class counsel.

Subdivision (b) of FRCP 23

In addition to satisfying the requirements of FRCP 23(a), the party seeking class certification still has to show that the litigation fits within one of the three categories of FRCP 23(b).

Subdivision (b)(1) addresses the difficulties which would be likely to arise if resort were had to separate actions by or against the individual members of the class. These difficulties furnish the reasons for, and the principal key to, the propriety and value of utilizing the class-action device. The considerations stated under clauses (A) and (B) are comparable to certain of the elements which define the persons whose joinder in an action is desirable as stated in Rule 19(a). (Advisory Committee Notes, 1966 Amendment)

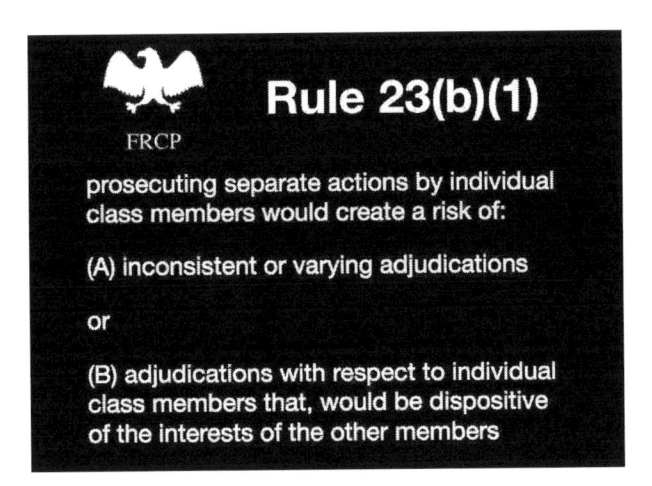

> **Rule 23(b)(1)**
> FRCP
>
> prosecuting separate actions by individual class members would create a risk of:
>
> (A) inconsistent or varying adjudications
>
> or
>
> (B) adjudications with respect to individual class members that, would be dispositive of the interests of the other members

With regard to subdivision (A), one person may have rights against, or be under duties toward, numerous persons constituting a class, and be so positioned that conflicting or varying adjudications in lawsuits with individual members of the class might establish incompatible standards to govern his conduct. The class action device can be used effectively to obviate the actual or virtual dilemma which would thus confront the party opposing the class. (Advisory Committee Notes, 1966 Amendment)

Subdivision (B) takes in situations where the judgment in a nonclass action by or against an individual member of the class, while not technically concluding the other members, might do so as a practical matter. The vice of an individual actions would lie in the fact that the other members of the class, thus practically concluded, would have had no representation in the lawsuit. (Advisory Committee Notes, 1966 Amendment)

> **Rule 23(b)(2)(3)**
> FRCP
>
> (2) final injunctive relief is appropriate respecting the class as a whole; or
>
> (3) the court finds that the questions of law or fact common to class members predominate over any questions affecting only individual members, and that a class action is superior to other available methods

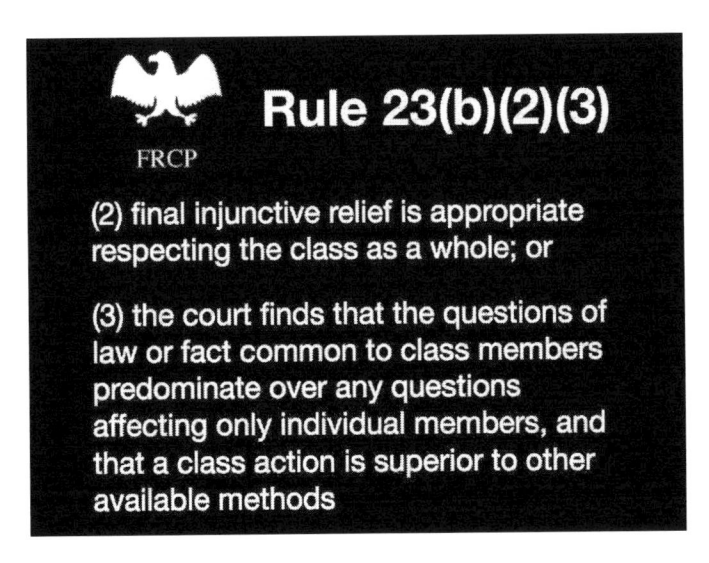

Subdivision (b)(2) is intended to reach situations where a party has taken action or refused to take action with respect to a class, and final relief of an injunctive nature or of a corresponding declaratory nature, settling the legality of the behavior with respect to the class as a whole, is appropriate. Illustrative are various actions in the civil-rights field where a party is charged with discriminating unlawfully against a class, usually one whose members are incapable of specific enumeration. Subdivision (b)(2) is not limited to civil-rights cases. Thus an action looking to specific or declaratory relief could be brought by a numerous class of purchasers, say retailers of a given description, against a seller alleged to have undertaken to sell to that class at prices higher than those set for other purchasers, say retailers of another description, when the applicable law forbids such a pricing differential. (Advisory Committee Notes, 1966 Amendment)

Subdivision (b)(3) encompasses those cases in which a class action would achieve economies of time, effort, and expense, and promote, uniformity of decision as to persons similarly situated, without sacrificing procedural fairness or bringing about other undesirable results. (Claims for money damages.) (Advisory Committee Notes, 1966 Amendment)

The predominance requirement of subdivision (b)(3) is similar to the requirement of Rule 23(a)(3) that "claims or defenses" of the named representatives must be "typical of the claims or defenses of the class." The words "claims or defenses" in this context—just as in the context of Rule 24(b)(2) governing permissive intervention—"manifestly refer to the kinds of claims or defenses that can be raised in courts of law as part of an actual or impending law suit." (*Diamond v. Charles*, 476 U. S. 54, 76-77 (1986) (O'Connor, J., concurring in part and concurring in judgment).

The criteria set out in subdivision (b) are alternative rather than cumulative; once the four requirements of subdivision (a) are met, only one of the three subsections of subdivision (b) need be satisfied for the class action to proceed.

Chandler v. Southwest Jeep-Eagle, Inc.
162 F.R.D. 302 (N.D. Ill. 1995)

RUBEN CASTILLO, District Judge

Plaintiff Raymond Chandler ("Chandler") sues defendants Southwest Jeep-Eagle, Inc. ("Southwest") and Calumet National Bank ("Calumet") seeking redress for alleged misrepresentations and unfair and deceptive practices in connection with Southwest's standard retail installment contract. Counts I and II of the complaint, the class claims, are alleged only against Southwest. Count I alleges that Southwest made certain misrepresentations in its retail installment contracts in violation of the Truth in Lending Act, ("TILA"). Count II alleges that the misrepresentations amounted to deceptive practices under the Illinois Consumer Fraud and Deceptive Business Practices Act, 815 ILCS 505/1 et seq. ("Consumer Fraud Act"). . . .

Pursuant to Federal Rule of Civil Procedure 23, Chandler moves for class certification with respect to counts I and II. . . .

With respect to count I, the TILA claim, the proposed class includes anyone whose retail installment contract is dated on or after October 12, 1993, one year prior to the date Chandler filed his original complaint. With respect to count II, the Consumer Fraud Act claim, the proposed class includes anyone whose retail installment contract was outstanding on or after October 12, 1991, three years prior to the date Chandler filed his original complaint. The different temporal parameters of the two classes is a product of the different statutes of limitation for TILA and the Consumer Fraud Act. . . .

Background

Southwest operates an automobile dealership. Calumet is a nationally chartered bank. On May 23, 1994, Chandler purchased from Southwest a used Chrysler automobile to be used for personal, family and household purposes. At the time he purchased the car, Chandler signed Southwest's standard motor vehicle retail installment sales contract, which was subsequently assigned to Calumet. Chandler also informed Southwest that he wished to purchase a full warranty from Chrysler that would be transferable to another authorized Chrysler dealership for the purpose of repairs. Southwest informed Chandler that the price for a full warranty was $1,780.40 and provided Chandler with its standard service contract, on which the fee amount was listed under the subheading "Amounts Paid to Others for You," along with taxes, insurance premiums, and license, title, registration and filing fees, none of which were negotiable. Chandler signed the contract and paid the $1,780.40 fee to Southwest.

Chandler alleges, however, that Southwest only transferred a small portion of the $1,780.40 to Chrysler, retaining the balance, and that the fee amount was actually unilaterally determined by Southwest and therefore negotiable. Chandler charges that the method by which the cost was listed on the contract is misleading, unfair and deceptive. He alleges that Southwest intended him and other purchasers to rely on the misleading, unfair and deceptive representation and thus not attempt to negotiate the price of the service contract, allowing Southwest routinely to overcharge customers. He further alleges that had he known that the cost of the service contract was negotiable, neither he nor the average consumer would have paid as much. . . .

Analysis
Class Certification for Counts I and II

The party seeking class certification bears the burden of establishing that certification is proper.

Rule 23 requires a two-step analysis to determine whether class certification is appropriate. First, the action must satisfy all four requirements of Rule 23(a). That is, "the plaintiff must meet the prerequisites of numerosity, commonality, typicality, and adequacy of representation." "All of these elements are prerequisites to certification; failure to meet any one of these precludes certification as a class." second, the action must satisfy one of the conditions of Rule 23(b). Chandler seeks certification under Rule 23(b)(3), which requires that questions of law or fact common to class members predominate over questions affecting only individual members, and that a class action be superior to other available methods for the fair and efficient adjudication of the controversy.

Chandler maintains that all of the requirements of Rule 23(a) and (b)(3) are met. Southwest contends that Chandler fails to meet any of Rule 23's requirements. Accordingly, we address each of the requirements for Rule 23(b)(3) certification in turn below.

A. Numerosity

Rule 23's first express requirement is that the class be "so numerous that joinder of all members is impracticable." FED. R.CIV.P. 23(a)(1). The issue of whether the numerosity requirement is satisfied is extremely fact-specific. Courts have granted class certification to groups smaller than 30, As a general proposition, although the numerosity analysis does not rest on any magic number, permissive joinder is usually deemed impracticable where the class members number 40 or more. That standard is met in this case.

Southwest concedes that the proposed class would consist of approximately 50 members for purposes of the TILA claim [count I] and approximately 150 members for purposes of the Consumer Fraud Act claim [count II] but argues that these classes are insufficiently numerous to warrant certification. Southwest cites Marcial, In re Cardinal Indus., and Liberty Lincoln-Mercury as support for its argument. However, in each of these cases, class certification was denied for reasons unrelated to numerosity. Moreover, the facts of this case are significantly different than those presented in the cases cited by Southwest. In the instant case, the dispute concerns a standard form document signed by all proposed class members, who are otherwise unrelated and would unlikely be motivated to bring individual actions given the relatively small size of the claim. These factors militate in favor of class certification even where the number of class members is relatively small. In the instant case, the Court finds that the proposed classes are sufficiently numerous to make joinder impracticable. Accordingly, we find the numerosity requirement to be satisfied.

B. Commonality

Rule 23(a)(2) requires the presence of questions of law or fact common to the class. A "common nucleus of operative fact" is generally enough to satisfy the commonality requirement. A common nucleus of operative fact is typically found where, as in the instant case, the defendants have engaged in standardized conduct toward members of the proposed class.

In the instant case, all proposed class members purchased a standard service contract from Southwest. Thus, their claims all involve the common question of whether the disclosure provisions of Southwest's standard retail installment contract violated TILA and/or the Consumer Fraud Act. Southwest contends that the commonality requirement is not met because each class member must prove reliance and actual damages. It is well-established, however, that the presence of some individualized issues does not overshadow the common nucleus of operative fact presented when the defendant has engaged in standardized conduct toward the class. Accordingly, we find that the commonality requirement is satisfied.

C. Typicality

Rule 23(a)(3) requires that the representative plaintiff's claims be typical of those of the class. This requirement focuses on whether the named representative's claim has the same essential characteristics of the claims of the class at large. A plaintiff's claim is typical "if it arises from the same event or practice or course of conduct that gives rise to the claims of other class members and his or her claims are based on the same legal theory. "In this case, the legal theory underlying Chandler's class claims is that the standard retail installment contract provided to him and all other proposed class members violated TILA and/or the Consumer Fraud Act. Plainly, Chandler's TILA and Consumer Fraud Act claims arise out of the same course of conduct giving rise to the claims of the other class members. Southwest maintains, however, that Chandler is an atypical class representative because his own deposition testimony suggests that he did not rely on (or was not misled by) any alleged misrepresentation

It is clear that Chandler has fairly alleged that he relied upon and was deceived by Southwest's misrepresentation. Furthermore, Southwest reads Chandler's testimony selectively. In his deposition, Chandler clearly states that he believed that the amount charged would be transferred to the service contract provider. Although Southwest may ultimately prove that Chandler did not rely on the alleged misrepresentation, the determination of whether Chandler is a typical class member for purposes of class certification does not depend on the resolution of the merits of the case. The typicality requirement is satisfied.

D. Adequacy of Representation

Rule 23(a)(4)'s adequacy requirement has three elements: (1) the chosen class representative cannot have antagonistic or conflicting claims with other members of the class, (2) the named representative must have a "sufficient interest in the outcome to ensure vigorous advocacy," Riordan, 113 F.R.D. 60, 64 (N.D.Ill. 1986); and, (3) counsel for the named plaintiff must be competent, experienced, qualified, and generally able to conduct the proposed litigation vigorously. Southwest challenges Chandler's ability to satisfy the last of these three requirements. Southwest notes that at least one judge has expressed doubt regarding Chandler's counsel's ability to represent a class. Notwithstanding the foregoing, this Court is satisfied that Chandler's attorneys have demonstrated that they possess the necessary qualifications to represent adequately a class of consumers under TILA and the Consumer Fraud Act. Chandler's attorneys have successfully prosecuted numerous consumer class actions — including actions before this Court. Accordingly, we find that Chandler has met his burden of satisfying Rule 23(a)(4)'s adequacy of representation requirement.

E. Predominance of Common Questions of Law or Fact

Class certification pursuant to Rule 23(b)(3) requires a determination that "questions of law or fact common to the members of the class predominate over any questions affecting only individual members, and that a class action is superior to other methods for the fair and efficient adjudication of the controversy." FED.R.CIV.P. 23(b)(3).

1. Common Questions of Law and Fact Predominate

Considerable overlap exists between Rule 23(a)(2)'s commonality prerequisite and 23(b)(3). Rule 23(a)(2) requires that common questions exist; Rule 23(b)(3) requires that they predominate. Many of the issues raised by Southwest relating to the relative importance of common issues have been addressed and disposed of above in the Court's discussion of Rule (a)(2)'s commonality requirement.

In considering whether common questions of law or fact predominate, the common issues need not be dispositive of the entire litigation. Riordan, 113 F.R.D. 60, 65 (N.D.Ill. 1986). "Instead, resolution of the predominance question tends to focus on the form trial in the issues would take, with consideration of whether the action would be manageable.'

The predominance requirement is generally satisfied where a "common nucleus of operative fact" exists among all class members for which the law provides a remedy. Both TILA and the Consumer Fraud Act claims lend themselves readily to the finding that a common issue predominates over individual issues, as the principal question presented is whether the disclosure provisions of Southwest's standard retail installment contract provided to Chandler and all the proposed class members violated TILA and/or the Consumer Fraud Act.

Southwest suggests that the damages claimed by each class member can only be calculated by determining the extent of each individual's actual reliance on the alleged misrepresentation, and thus that common questions do not predominate. The Illinois Supreme Court has held, however, that reliance is not an element of a Consumer Fraud Act claim. The question of reliance and individualized damages therefore does not arise at all in relation to the Consumer Fraud Act claim. With respect to the TILA claim, we note that predominance is not precluded even if individualized proof of damages is required. As long as the allocation of individualized damages does not create problems of unmanageability, which it does not in this case, a court may grant class certification. For the foregoing reasons, this Court finds the predominance requirement to be satisfied.

2. Class Action is Superior to Other Methods of Litigating This Matter

Rule 23(b)(3) provides a non-exhaustive list of factors for courts to consider in determining the superiority of class actions to individual litigation. These factors include the interest of individual members in individually controlling the litigation, the desirability of concentrating the litigation in the particular forum, and the manageability of the class action. FED.R.CIV.P. 23(b)(3).

The Court finds that a class action is superior to other methods of litigating this matter for several reasons. First, as should be clear from the foregoing discussion, this case poses no unusual manageability concerns arising from either the size of the class or the adjudication of damages. Second, most of the proposed class members are individual consumers who are probably unaware of their rights under TILA and the Consumer Fraud Act. A class action would help to ensure that their rights are protected. Third, the size of each individual claim is relatively small. Class members, even if aware of their rights, likely would lack the initiative to bring suit individually. Fourth, efficiency and consistency concerns favor trying the legality of a document challenged by all class members in one litigation, rather than forcing each proposed class member to litigate his or her claim individually. In view of these considerations, the Court finds Rule 23(b)(3)'s superiority element to be satisfied.

Having determined that all of the prerequisites of Rule 23(a) are satisfied and that the action also meets the conditions of Rule 23(b)(3), the Court grants plaintiffs motion for class certification for counts I and II. This action may be maintained as a class action with the class defined, as in plaintiff's motion and memorandum in support of class certification, as follows:

(1) Count I: All individuals who purchased a service contract from the defendant by means of a standard retail installment contract, dated on or after October 12, 1993, in which the TILA disclosures represented that the defendant paid an amount to a third party in exchange for a service contract that was different from the amount actually paid.

(2) Count II: All individuals who purchased a service contract from the defendant by means of a standard retail installment contract, outstanding on or after October 12, 1991, in which the TILA disclosures represented that the defendant paid an amount to a third party in exchange for a service contract that was different from the amount actually paid. . . .

CONCLUSION

Chandler's motion for class certification is granted.

Wal-Mart Stores, Inc. v. Dukes
564 US 338 (2011)

Justice SCALIA delivered the opinion of the Court.

We are presented with one of the most expansive class actions ever. The District Court and the Court of Appeals approved the certification of a class comprising about one and a half million plaintiffs, current and former female employees of petitioner Wal-Mart who allege that the discretion exercised by their local supervisors over pay and promotion matters violates Title VII by discriminating against women. In addition to injunctive and declaratory relief, the plaintiffs seek an award of backpay. We consider whether the certification of the plaintiff class was consistent with Federal Rules of Civil Procedure 23(a) and (b)(2).

I
A

Petitioner Wal-Mart is the Nation's largest private employer. It operates four types of retail stores throughout the country: Discount Stores, Supercenters, Neighborhood Markets, and Sam's Clubs. Those stores are divided into seven nationwide divisions, which in turn comprise 41 regions of 80 to 85 stores apiece. Each store has between 40 and 53 separate departments and 80 to 500 staff positions. In all, Wal-Mart operates approximately 3,400 stores and employs more than one million people.

Pay and promotion decisions at Wal-Mart are generally committed to local managers' broad discretion, which is exercised "in a largely subjective manner." Local store managers may increase the wages of hourly employees (within limits) with only limited corporate oversight. As for salaried employees, such as store managers and their deputies, higher corporate authorities have discretion to set their pay within preestablished ranges.

Promotions work in a similar fashion. Wal-Mart permits store managers to apply their own subjective criteria when selecting candidates as "support managers," which is the first step on the path to management. Admission to Wal-Mart's management training program, however, does require that a candidate meet certain objective criteria, including an above-average performance rating, at least one year's tenure in the applicant's current position, and a willingness to relocate. But except for those requirements, regional and district managers have discretion to use their own judgment when selecting candidates for management training. Promotion to higher office—e.g., assistant manager, co-manager, or store manager—is similarly at the discretion of the employee's superiors after prescribed objective factors are satisfied.

B

The named plaintiffs in this lawsuit, representing the 1.5 million members of the certified class, are three current or former Wal-Mart employees who allege that the company discriminated against them on the basis of their sex by denying them equal pay or promotions, in violation of Title VII of the Civil Rights Act of 1964 . . .

Betty Dukes began working at a Pittsburg, California, Wal-Mart in 1994. She started as a cashier, but later sought and received a promotion to customer service manager. After a series of disciplinary violations, however, Dukes was demoted back to cashier and then to greeter. Dukes concedes she violated company policy but contends that the disciplinary actions were in fact retaliation for invoking internal complaint procedures and that male employees have not been disciplined for similar infractions. Dukes also claims two male greeters in the Pittsburgh store are paid more than she is.

Christine Kwapnoski has worked at Sam's Club stores in Missouri and California for most of her adult life. She has held a number of positions, including a supervisory position. She claims that a male manager yelled at her frequently and screamed at female employees, but not at men. The manager in question "told her to `doll up,' to wear some makeup, and to dress a little better."

The final named plaintiff, Edith Arana, worked at a Wal-Mart store in Duarte, California, from 1995 to 2001. In 2000, she approached the store manager on more than one occasion about management training but was brushed off. Arana concluded she was being denied opportunity for advancement because of her sex. She initiated internal complaint procedures, whereupon she was told to apply directly to the district manager if she thought her store manager was being unfair. Arana, however, decided against that and never applied for management training again. In 2001, she was fired for failure to comply with Wal-Mart's timekeeping policy.

These plaintiffs, respondents here, do not allege that Wal-Mart has any express corporate policy against the advancement of women. Rather, they claim that their local managers' discretion over pay and promotions is exercised disproportionately in favor of men, leading to an unlawful disparate impact on female employees, And, respondents say, because Wal-Mart is aware of this effect, its refusal to cabin its managers' authority amounts to disparate treatment. Their complaint seeks injunctive and declaratory relief, punitive damages, and backpay. It does not ask for compensatory damages.

Importantly for our purposes, respondents claim that the discrimination to which they have been subjected is common to all Wal-Mart's female employees. The basic theory of their case is that a strong and uniform "corporate culture" permits bias against women to infect, perhaps subconsciously, the discretionary decision making of each one of Wal-Mart's thousands of managers—thereby making every woman at the company the victim of one common discriminatory practice. Respondents therefore wish to litigate the Title VII claims of all female employees at Wal-Mart's stores in a nationwide class action.

C

Class certification is governed by Federal Rule of Civil Procedure 23. Under Rule 23(a), the party seeking certification must demonstrate, first, that:

"(1) the class is so numerous that joinder of all members is impracticable,

"(2) there are questions of law or fact common to the class,

"(3) the claims or defenses of the representative parties are typical of the claims or defenses of the class, and

"(4) the representative parties will fairly and adequately protect the interests of the class".

Second, the proposed class must satisfy at least one of the three requirements listed in Rule 23(b). Respondents rely on Rule 23(b)(2), which applies when "the party opposing the class has acted or refused to act on grounds that apply generally to the class, so that final injunctive relief or corresponding declaratory relief is appropriate respecting the class as a whole."

Invoking these provisions, respondents moved the District Court to certify a plaintiff class consisting of "`[a]ll women employed at any Wal-Mart domestic retail store at any time since December 26, 1998, who have been or may be subjected to Wal-Mart's challenged pay and management track promotions policies and practices.'" As evidence that there were indeed "questions of law or fact common to" all the women of Wal-Mart, as Rule 23(a)(2) requires, respondents relied chiefly on three forms of proof: statistical evidence about pay and promotion disparities between men and women at the company, anecdotal reports of discrimination from about 120 of Wal-Mart's female employees, and the testimony of a sociologist, Dr. William Bielby, who conducted a "social framework analysis" of Wal-Mart's "culture" and personnel practices, and concluded that the company was "vulnerable" to gender discrimination.

Wal-Mart unsuccessfully moved to strike much of this evidence. It also offered its own countervailing statistical and other proof in an effort to defeat Rule 23(a)'s requirements of commonality, typicality, and adequate representation. Wal-Mart further contended that respondents' monetary claims for backpay could not be certified under Rule 23(b)(2), first because that Rule refers only to injunctive and declaratory relief, and second because the backpay claims could not be manageably tried as a class without depriving Wal-Mart of its right to present certain statutory defenses. With one limitation not relevant here, the District Court granted respondents' motion and certified their proposed class.

D

A divided *en banc* Court of Appeals substantially affirmed the District Court's certification order. . . .

. . . [T]he Court of Appeals determined that the action could be manageably tried as a class action because the District Court could adopt the approach the Ninth Circuit approved in Hilao v. Estate of Marcos, 103 F.3d 767, 782-787 (1996). There compensatory damages for some 9,541 class members were calculated by selecting 137 claims at random, referring those claims to a special master for valuation, and then extrapolating the validity and value of the untested claims from the sample set. . . .

I

The class action is "an exception to the usual rule that litigation is conducted by and on behalf of the individual named parties only." In order to justify a departure from that rule, "a class representative must be part of the class and `possess the same interest and suffer the same injury' as the class members." Rule 23(a) ensures that the named plaintiffs are appropriate representatives of the class whose claims they wish to litigate. The Rule's four requirements—numerosity, commonality, typicality, and adequate representation—"effectively `limit the class claims to those fairly encompassed by the named plaintiff's claims.'"

A

The crux of this case is commonality—the rule requiring a plaintiff to show that "there are questions of law or fact common to the class." Rule 23(a)(2) That language is easy to misread, since "[a]ny competently crafted class complaint literally raises common `questions.'" Nagareda, Class Certification in the Age of Aggregate Proof, 84 N.Y.U.L.Rev. 97, 131-132 (2009). For example: Do all of us plaintiffs indeed work for Wal-Mart? Do our managers have discretion over pay? Is that an unlawful employment practice? What remedies should we get? Reciting these questions is not sufficient to obtain class certification. Commonality requires the plaintiff to demonstrate that the class members "have suffered the same injury," This does not mean merely that they have all suffered a violation of the same provision of law. Title VII, for example, can be violated in many ways—by intentional discrimination, or by hiring and promotion criteria that result in disparate impact, and by the use of these practices on the part of many different superiors in a single company. Quite obviously, the mere claim by employees of the same company that they have suffered a Title VII injury, or even a disparate-impact Title VII injury, gives no cause to believe that all their claims can productively be litigated at once. Their claims must depend upon a common contention—for example, the assertion of discriminatory bias on the part of the same supervisor. That common contention, moreover, must be of such a nature that it is capable of class wide resolution—which means that determination of its truth or falsity will resolve an issue that is central to the validity of each one of the claims in one stroke.

> What matters to class certification ... is not the raising of common `questions'—even in droves—but, rather the capacity of a class wide proceeding to generate common answers apt to drive the resolution of the litigation. Dissimilarities within the proposed class are what have the potential to impede the generation of common answers.

Rule 23 does not set forth a mere pleading standard. A party seeking class certification must affirmatively demonstrate his compliance with the Rule—that is, he must be prepared to prove that there are in fact sufficiently numerous parties, common questions of law or fact, etc. We recognized in Falcon that "sometimes it may be necessary for the court to probe behind the pleadings before coming to rest on the certification question," and that certification is proper only if "the trial court is satisfied, after a rigorous analysis, that the prerequisites of Rule 23(a) have been satisfied," ("[A]ctual, not presumed, conformance with Rule 23(a) remains ... indispensable"). Frequently that "rigorous analysis" will entail some overlap with the merits of the plaintiff's underlying claim. That cannot be helped. "`[T]he class determination generally involves considerations that are enmeshed in the factual and legal issues comprising the plaintiff's cause of action.'" Nor is there anything unusual about that consequence: The necessity of touching aspects of the merits in order to resolve preliminary matters, e.g. Jurisdiction and venue, is a familiar feature of litigation.

In this case, proof of commonality necessarily overlaps with respondents' merits contention that Wal-Mart engages in a pattern or practice of discrimination. That is so because, in resolving an individual's Title VII claim, the crux of the inquiry is "the reason for a particular employment decision," Here respondents wish to sue about literally millions of employment decisions at once. Without some glue holding the alleged reasons for all those decisions together, it will be impossible to say that examination of all the class members' claims for relief will produce a common answer to the crucial question why was I disfavored.

B

This Court's opinion in Falcon describes how the commonality issue must be approached. There an employee who claimed that he was deliberately denied a promotion on account of race obtained certification of a class comprising all employees wrongfully denied promotions and all applicants wrongfully denied jobs. We rejected that composite class for lack of commonality and typicality, explaining:

"Conceptually, there is a wide gap between (a) an individual's claim that he has been denied a promotion [or higher pay] on discriminatory grounds, and his otherwise unsupported allegation that the company has a policy of discrimination, and (b) the existence of a class of persons who have suffered the same injury as that individual, such that the individual's claim and the class claim will share common questions of law or fact and that the individual's claim will be typical of the class claims."

Falcon suggested two ways in which that conceptual gap might be bridged. First, if the employer "used a biased testing procedure to evaluate both applicants for employment and incumbent employees, a class action on behalf of every applicant or employee who might have been prejudiced by the test clearly would satisfy the commonality and typicality requirements of Rule 23(a)." Second, "[s]ignificant proof that an employer operated under a general policy of discrimination conceivably could justify a class of both applicants and employees if the discrimination manifested itself in hiring and promotion practices in the same general fashion, such as through entirely subjective decision-making processes." We think that statement precisely describes respondents' burden in this case. The first manner of bridging the gap obviously has no application here; Wal-Mart has no testing procedure or other companywide evaluation method that can be charged with bias. The whole point of permitting discretionary decision-making is to avoid evaluating employees under a common standard.

The second manner of bridging the gap requires "significant proof" that Wal-Mart "operated under a general policy of discrimination." That is entirely absent here. Wal-Mart's announced policy forbids sex discrimination, see App. 1567a-1596a, and as the District Court recognized the company imposes penalties for denials of equal employment opportunity, 222 F.R.D., at 154. The only evidence of a "general policy of discrimination" respondents produced was the testimony of Dr. William Bielby, their sociological expert. Relying on "social framework" analysis, Bielby testified that Wal-Mart has a "strong corporate culture," that makes it "'vulnerable'" to "gender bias." He could not, however, "determine with any specificity how regularly stereotypes play a meaningful role in employment decisions at Wal-Mart. At his deposition... Dr. Bielby conceded that he could not calculate whether 0.5 percent or 95 percent of the employment decisions at Wal-Mart might be determined by stereotyped thinking." 222 F.R.D. 189, 192 (N.D.Cal.2004). The parties dispute whether Bielby's testimony even met the standards for the admission of expert testimony under Federal Rule of Civil Procedure 702 and our Daubert case, see Daubert v. Merrell Dow Pharmaceuticals, Inc., 509 U.S. 579, 113 S.Ct. 2786, 125 L.Ed.2d 469 (1993). The District Court concluded that Daubert did not apply to expert testimony at the certification stage of class-action proceedings. 222 F.R.D., at 191. We doubt that is so, but even if properly considered, Bielby's testimony does nothing to advance respondents' case. "[W]hether 0.5 percent or 95 percent of the employment decisions at Wal-Mart might be determined by stereotyped thinking" is the essential question on which respondents' theory of commonality depends. If Bielby admittedly has no answer to that question, we can safely disregard what he has to say. It is worlds away from "significant proof" that Wal-Mart "operated under a general policy of discrimination."

C

The only corporate policy that the plaintiffs' evidence convincingly establishes is Wal-Mart's "policy" of allowing discretion by local supervisors over employment matters. On its face, of course, that is just the opposite of a uniform employment practice that would provide the commonality needed for a class action; it is a policy against having uniform employment practices. It is also a very common and presumptively reasonable way of doing business—one that we have said "should itself raise no inference of discriminatory conduct,"

To be sure, we have recognized that, "in appropriate cases," giving discretion to lower-level supervisors can be the basis of Title VII liability under a disparate-impact theory—since "an employer's undisciplined system of subjective decision making [can have] precisely the same effects as a system pervaded by impermissible intentional discrimination." But the recognition that this type of Title VII claim "can" exist does not lead to the conclusion that every employee in a company using a system of discretion has such a claim in common. . . .

Respondents have not identified a common mode of exercising discretion that pervades the entire company—aside from their reliance on Dr. Bielby's social frameworks analysis that we have rejected. In a company of Wal-Mart's size and geographical scope, it is quite unbelievable that all managers would exercise their discretion in a common way without some common direction. Respondents attempt to make that showing by means of statistical and anecdotal evidence, but their evidence falls well short.

The statistical evidence consists primarily of regression analyses performed by Dr. Richard Drogin, a statistician, and Dr. Marc Bendick, a labor economist. Drogin conducted his analysis region-by-region, comparing the number of women promoted into management positions with the percentage of women in the available pool of hourly workers. After considering regional and national data, Drogin concluded that "there are statistically significant disparities between men and women at Wal-Mart... [and] these disparities ... can be explained only by gender discrimination." 603 F.3d, at 604 (internal quotation marks omitted). Bendick compared work-force data from Wal-Mart and competitive retailers and concluded that Wal-Mart "promotes a lower percentage of women than its competitors."

Even if they are taken at face value, these studies are insufficient to establish that respondents' theory can be proved on a class wide basis. In Falcon, we held that one named plaintiff's experience of discrimination was insufficient to infer that "discriminatory treatment is typical of [the employer's employment] practices." A similar failure of inference arises here. As Judge Ikuta observed in her dissent, "[i]nformation about disparities at the regional and national level does not establish the existence of disparities at individual stores, let alone raise the inference that a companywide policy of discrimination is implemented by discretionary decisions at the store and district level." A regional pay disparity, for example, may be attributable to only a small set of Wal-Mart stores, and cannot by itself establish the uniform, store-by-store disparity upon which the plaintiffs' theory of commonality depends. . . .

"[T]he plaintiff must begin by identifying the specific employment practice that is challenged." (approving that statement), superseded by statute on other grounds, 42 U.S.C. § 2000e-2(k). That is all the more necessary when a class of plaintiffs is sought to be certified. Other than the bare existence of delegated discretion, respondents have identified no "specific employment practice"—much less one that ties all their 1.5 million claims together. Merely showing that Wal-Mart's policy of discretion has produced an overall sex-based disparity does not suffice. . . .

Respondents' anecdotal evidence suffers from the same defects, and in addition is too weak to raise any inference that all the individual, discretionary personnel decisions are discriminatory. . . . Here . . . respondents filed some 120 affidavits reporting experiences of discrimination—about 1 for every 12,500 class members—relating to only some 235 out of Wal-Mart's 3,400 stores. More than half of these reports are concentrated in only six States (Alabama, California, Florida, Missouri, Texas, and Wisconsin); half of all States have only one or two anecdotes; and 14 States have no anecdotes about Wal-Mart's operations at all. Even if every single one of these accounts is true, that would not demonstrate that the entire company "operate[s] under a general policy of discrimination," ...

In sum, we agree with Chief Judge Kozinski that the members of the class:

> held a multitude of different jobs, at different levels of Wal-Mart's hierarchy, for variable lengths of time, in 3,400 stores, sprinkled across 50 states, with a kaleidoscope of supervisors (male and female), subject to a variety of regional policies that all differed .... Some thrived while others did poorly. They have little in common but their sex and this lawsuit.

III

We also conclude that respondents' claims for backpay were improperly certified under Federal Rule of Civil Procedure 23(b)(2). Our opinion in Ticor Title Ins. Co. v. Brown, 511 U.S. 117, 121, 114 S.Ct. 1359, 128 L.Ed.2d 33 (1994) (per curiam)expressed serious doubt about whether claims for monetary relief may be certified under that provision. We now hold that they may not, at least where (as here) the monetary relief is not incidental to the injunctive or declaratory relief.

A

Rule 23(b)(2) allows class treatment when "the party opposing the class has acted or refused to act on grounds that apply generally to the class, so that final injunctive relief or corresponding declaratory relief is appropriate respecting the class as a whole." One possible reading of this provision is that it applies only to requests for such injunctive or declaratory relief and does not authorize the class certification of monetary claims at all. We need not reach that broader question in this case, because we think that, at a minimum, claims for individualized relief (like the backpay at issue here) do not satisfy the Rule. The key to the (b)(2) class is "the indivisible nature of the injunctive or declaratory remedy warranted—the notion that the conduct is such that it can be enjoined or declared unlawful only as to all of the class members or as to none of them." Nagareda, 84 N.Y.U.L.Rev., at 132. In other words, Rule 23(b)(2) applies only when a single injunction or declaratory judgment would provide relief to each member of the class. It does not authorize class certification when each individual class member would be entitled to a different injunction or declaratory judgment against the defendant. Similarly, it does not authorize class certification when each class member would be entitled to an individualized award of monetary damages.

That interpretation accords with the history of the Rule. Because Rule 23 "stems from equity practice" that predated its codification, Amchem Products, Inc. v. Windsor, 521 U.S. 591, 613, 117 S.Ct. 2231, 138 L.Ed.2d 689 (1997), in determining its meaning we have previously looked to the historical models on which the Rule was based. As we observed in Amchem, "[c]ivil rights cases against parties charged with unlawful, class-based discrimination are prime examples" of what (b)(2) is meant to capture. In particular, the Rule reflects a series of decisions involving challenges to racial segregation—conduct that was remedied by a single class wide order. In none of the cases cited by the Advisory Committee as examples of (b)(2)'s antecedents did the plaintiffs combine any claim for individualized relief with their class wide injunction.

Permitting the combination of individualized and class wide relief in a (b)(2) class is also inconsistent with the structure of Rule 23(b). Classes certified under (b)(1) and (b)(2) share the most traditional justifications for class treatment—that individual adjudications would be impossible or unworkable, as in a(b)(1) class, or that the relief sought must perforce affect the entire class at once, as in a (b)(2) class. For that reason these are also mandatory classes: The Rule provides no opportunity for (b)(1) or (b)(2) class members to opt out and does not even oblige the District Court to afford them notice of the action. Rule 23(b)(3), by contrast, is an "adventuresome innovation" of the 1966 amendments, , framed for situations "in which `class-action treatment is not as clearly called for'," It allows class certification in a much wider set of circumstances but with greater procedural protections. Its only prerequisites are that "the questions of law or fact common to class members predominate over any questions affecting only individual members, and that a class action is superior to other available methods for fairly and efficiently adjudicating the controversy." Rule 23(b)(3). And unlike (b)(1) and (b)(2) classes, the (b)(3) class is not mandatory; class members are entitled to receive "the best notice that is practicable under the circumstances" and to withdraw from the class at their option. See Rule 23(c)(2)(B).

Given that structure, we think it clear that individualized monetary claims belong in Rule 23(b)(3). The procedural protections attending the (b)(3) class—predominance, superiority, mandatory notice, and the right to opt out—are missing from (b)(2) not because the Rule considers them unnecessary, but because it considers them unnecessary to a (b)(2) class. When a class seeks an indivisible injunction benefitting all its members at once, there is no reason to undertake a case-specific inquiry into whether class issues predominate or whether class action is a superior method of adjudicating the dispute. Predominance and superiority are self-evident. But with respect to each class member's individualized claim for money, that is not so—which is precisely why (b)(3) requires the judge to make findings about predominance and superiority before allowing the class. Similarly, (b)(2) does not require that class members be given notice and opt-out rights, presumably because it is thought (rightly or wrongly) that notice has no purpose when the class is mandatory, and that depriving people of their right to sue in this manner complies with the Due Process Clause. In the context of a class action predominantly for money damages we have held that absence of notice and opt-out violates due process. While we have never held that to be so where the monetary claims do not predominate, the serious possibility that it may be so provides an additional reason not to read Rule 23(b)(2) to include the monetary claims here. . . .

B

Against that conclusion, respondents argue that their claims for backpay were appropriately certified as part of a class under Rule 23(b)(2) because those claims do not "predominate" over their requests for injunctive and declaratory relief. They rely upon the Advisory Committee's statement that Rule 23(b)(2) "does not extend to cases in which the appropriate final relief relates exclusively or predominantly to money damages." . . .

Respondents' predominance test, moreover, creates perverse incentives for class representatives to place at risk potentially valid claims for monetary relief. In this case, for example, the named plaintiffs declined to include employees' claims for compensatory damages in their complaint. That strategy of including only backpay claims made it more likely that monetary relief would not "predominate." But it also created the possibility (if the predominance test were correct) that individual class members' compensatory-damages claims would be precluded by litigation they had no power to hold themselves apart from. If it were determined, for example, that a particular class member is not entitled to backpay because her denial of increased pay or a promotion was not the product of discrimination, that employee might be collaterally estopped from independently seeking compensatory damages based on that same denial. That possibility underscores the need for plaintiffs with individual monetary claims to decide for themselves whether to tie their fates to the class representatives' or go it alone—a choice Rule 23(b)(2) does not ensure that they have. . . .

C

The Court of Appeals believed that it was possible to replace such proceedings with Trial by Formula. A sample set of the class members would be selected, as to whom liability for sex discrimination and the backpay owing as a result would be determined in depositions supervised by a master. The percentage of claims determined to be valid would then be applied to the entire remaining class, and the number of (presumptively) valid claims thus derived would be multiplied by the average backpay award in the sample set to arrive at the entire class recovery— without further individualized proceedings. 603 F.3d, at 625-627. We disapprove that novel project. Because the Rules Enabling Act forbids interpreting Rule 23 to "abridge, enlarge or modify any substantive right," 28 U.S.C. § 2072(b); a class cannot be certified on the premise that Wal-Mart will not be entitled to litigate its statutory defenses to individual claims. And because the necessity of that litigation will prevent backpay from being "incidental" to the class wide injunction, respondents' class could not be certified even assuming, arguendo, that "incidental" monetary relief can be awarded to a 23(b)(2) class.

* * *

The judgment of the Court of Appeals is

Reversed.

The Requirement of Notice in Class Actions

Depending upon the type of class action, notice to members of the class may or may not be required. The present rule expressly requires notice only in actions certified under Rule 23(b)(3). (Claims for monetary damages.) For class actions certified under Rules 23(b)(1) or (b)(2) (common fund or regulatory actions affecting members of the class) subdivision (d)(2) does not require notice at any stage, but rather calls attention to its availability and invokes the court's discretion as to whether to require it. To the degree that there is cohesiveness or unity in the class and the representation is effective, the need for notice to the class will tend toward a minimum.

Under Rule 23(c)(2), notice must be ordered, and is not merely discretionary, to give the members in a subdivision (b)(3) class action an opportunity to secure exclusion from the class. This mandatory notice pursuant to subdivision (c)(2), together with any discretionary notice which the court may find it advisable to give under subdivision (d)(2), is designed to fulfill requirements of due process to which the class action procedure is of course subject. If a Rule 23(b)(3) class is certified in conjunction with a (b)(2) class, the (c)(2)(B) notice requirements must be satisfied as to the (b)(3) class.

For class actions maintained under Rule 23 (b)(3) the notice setting forth the alternatives open to the members of the class, is to be the best practicable under the circumstances, and shall include individual notice to the members who can be identified through reasonable effort. The court is required to direct notice to the members of the class of the right of each member to be excluded from the class upon his request. Notice to members of the class need not comply with the formalities for service of process.

Reasonable settlement notice may require individual notice in the manner required by Rule 23(c)(2)(B) for certification notice to a Rule 23(b)(3) class. Individual notice is appropriate, for example, if class members are required to take action—such as filing claims—to participate in the judgment, or if the court orders a settlement opt-out opportunity under Rule 23(e)(3). (See, Notes of Advisory Committee on Rules to Rule 23)

Rule 23(c)(2)(B) was amended in 2018 to take account of changes in technology. The rule continues to call for giving class members "the best notice that is practicable." It does not specify any particular means as preferred. Although it may sometimes be true that electronic methods of notice, for example email, are the most promising, it is important to keep in mind that a significant portion of class members in certain cases may have limited or no access to email or the Internet.

Instead of preferring any one means of notice, therefore, the amended rule relies on courts and counsel to focus on the means or combination of means most likely to be effective in the case before the court. Courts should exercise discretion to select appropriate means of giving notice. In providing the court with sufficient information to enable it to decide whether to give notice to the class of a proposed class-action settlement under Rule 23(e)(1), it would ordinarily be important to include details about the proposed method of giving notice and to provide the court with a copy of each notice the parties propose to use.

In determining whether the proposed means of giving notice is appropriate, the court should also give careful attention to the content and format of the notice and, if notice is given under both Rule 23(e)(1) and Rule 23(c)(2)(B), any claim form class members must submit to obtain relief.

Counsel should consider which method or methods of giving notice will be most effective; simply assuming that the "traditional" methods are best may disregard contemporary communication realities. The ultimate goal of giving notice is to enable class members to make informed decisions about whether to opt out or, in instances where a proposed settlement is involved, to object or to make claims. Rule 23(c)(2)(B) directs that the notice be "in plain, easily understood language." Means, format, and content that would be appropriate for class members likely to be sophisticated, for example in a securities fraud class action, might not be appropriate for a class having many members likely to be less sophisticated. (Advisory Committee Notes, 2018 Amendments)

Settlement of the Class Action

A class action may not be dismissed or compromised without the approval of the court and notice of the proposed dismissal or compromise must be given to all members of the class. [Rule 23(e).] (Wright §72) This is contrary to the usual rule in civil litigation that the parties are free to dismiss or settle a lawsuit as they see fit, and approval of the judge is not required. The rule for class actions requiring the judge's blessing is designed to prevent an unjust settlement resulting from the class representatives becoming faint hearted or having been bought off by their opponents. In scrutinizing the settlement, the judge acts as a guardian for the interests of the absent class members. (Friendenthal §16.7.)

The central concern in reviewing a proposed class-action settlement is that it be fair, reasonable, and adequate. The court must make findings that support the conclusion that the settlement is fair, reasonable, and adequate. The findings must be set out in sufficient detail to explain to class members and the appellate court the factors that bear on applying the standard.

Rule 23(e)(4) confirms the right of class members to object to a proposed settlement, voluntary dismissal, or compromise. Objections may be withdrawn, but court approval is sometimes necessary in order to withdraw. An objector should be free to withdraw on concluding that an objection is not justified. But Rule 23(e)(5)(B)(i) requires court approval of any payment or other consideration in connection with withdrawing the objection. (See, Advisory Committee Notes, 2018 Amendment.)

Amchem Products, Inc. v. Windsor
521 U.S. 591 (1997)

Justice Ginsburg, delivered the opinion of the Court.

This case concerns the legitimacy under Rule 23 of the Federal Rules of Civil Procedure of a class-action certification sought to achieve global settlement of current and future asbestos-related claims. The class proposed for certification potentially encompasses hundreds of thousands, perhaps millions, of individuals tied together by this commonality: Each was, or someday may be, adversely affected by past exposure to asbestos products manufactured by one or more of 20 companies. Those companies, defendants in the lower courts, are petitioners here. . . .

I
A

The settlement-class certification we confront evolved in response to an asbestos-litigation crisis. A United States Judicial Conference Ad Hoc Committee on Asbestos Litigation, appointed by The Chief Justice in September 1990, described facets of the problem in a 1991 report:

"[This] is a tale of danger known in the 1930s, exposure inflicted upon millions of Americans in the 1940s and 1950s, injuries that began to take their toll in the 1960s, and a flood of lawsuits beginning in the 1970s. On the basis of past and current filing data, and because of a latency period that may last as long as 40 years for some asbestos related diseases, a continuing stream of claims can be expected. The final toll of asbestos related injuries is unknown. Predictions have been made of 200,000 asbestos disease deaths before the year 2000 and as many as 265,000 by the year 2015.

"The most objectionable aspects of asbestos litigation can be briefly summarized: dockets in both federal and state courts continue to grow; long delays are routine; trials are too long; the same issues are litigated over and over; transaction costs exceed the victims' recovery by nearly two to one; exhaustion of assets threatens and distorts the process; and future claimants may lose altogether." Report of The Judicial Conference Ad Hoc Committee on Asbestos Litigation 2-3 (Mar. 1991).

Real reform, the report concluded, required federal legislation creating a national asbestos dispute-resolution scheme. . . . to this date, no congressional response has emerged.

In the face of legislative inaction, the federal courts—lacking authority to replace state tort systems with a national toxic tort compensation regime—endeavored to work with the procedural tools available to improve management of federal asbestos litigation. Eight federal judges, experienced in the superintendence of asbestos cases, urged the Judicial Panel on Multidistrict Litigation (MDL Panel), to consolidate in a single district all asbestos complaints then pending in federal courts. Accepting the recommendation, the MDL Panel transferred all asbestos cases then filed, but not yet on trial in federal courts to a single district, the United States District Court for the Eastern District of Pennsylvania; pursuant to the transfer order, the collected cases were consolidated for pretrial proceedings before Judge Weiner. The order aggregated pending cases only; no authority resides in the MDL Panel to license for consolidated proceedings claims not yet filed.

B

After the consolidation, attorneys for plaintiffs and defendants formed separate steering committees and began settlement negotiations. . . . Settlement talks thus concentrated on devising an administrative scheme for disposition of asbestos claims not yet in litigation. In these negotiations, counsel for masses of inventory plaintiffs endeavored to represent the interests of the anticipated future claimants, although those lawyers then had no attorney-client relationship with such claimants.

Once negotiations seemed likely to produce an agreement purporting to bind potential plaintiffs, CCR agreed to settle, through separate agreements, the claims of plaintiffs who had already filed asbestos-related lawsuits. In one such agreement, CCR defendants promised to pay more than $200 million to gain release of the claims of numerous inventory plaintiffs. After settling the inventory claims, CCR, together with the plaintiffs' lawyers CCR had approached, launched this case, exclusively involving persons outside the MDL Panel's province—plaintiffs without already pending lawsuits.

C

The class action thus instituted was not intended to be litigated. Rather, within the space of a single day, January 15, 1993, the settling parties—CCR defendants and the representatives of the plaintiff class described below—presented to the District Court a complaint, an answer, a proposed settlement agreement, and a joint motion for conditional class certification.

The complaint identified nine lead plaintiffs, designating them and members of their families as representatives of a class comprising all persons who had not filed an asbestos related lawsuit against a CCR defendant as of the date the class action commenced, but who (1) had been exposed— occupationally or through the occupational exposure of a spouse or household member—to asbestos or products containing asbestos attributable to a CCR defendant, or (2) whose spouse or family member had been so exposed. Untold numbers of individuals may fall within this description. All named plaintiffs alleged that they or a member of their family had been exposed to asbestos-containing products of CCR defendants. More than half of the named plaintiffs alleged that they or their family members had already suffered various physical injuries as a result of the exposure. The others alleged that they had not yet manifested any asbestos-related condition. The complaint delineated no subclasses; all named plaintiffs were designated as representatives of the class as a whole.

The complaint invoked the District Court's diversity jurisdiction. . . .

A stipulation of settlement accompanied the pleadings; it proposed to settle, and to preclude nearly all class members from litigating against CCR companies, all claims not filed before January 15, 1993, involving compensation for present and future asbestos-related personal injury or death. An exhaustive document exceeding 100 pages, the stipulation presents in detail an administrative mechanism and a schedule of payments to compensate class members who meet defined asbestos-exposure and medical requirements. The stipulation describes four categories of compensable disease: mesothelioma; lung cancer; certain "other cancers" (colon rectal, laryngeal, esophageal, and stomach cancer); and "non-malignant conditions" (asbestosis and bilateral pleural thickening). Persons with "exceptional" medical claims— claims that do not fall within the four described diagnostic categories—may in some instances qualify for compensation, but the settlement caps the number of "exceptional" claims CCR must cover.

For each qualifying disease category, the stipulation specifies the range of damages CCR will pay to qualifying claimants. Payments under the settlement are not adjustable for inflation. Mesothelioma claimants—the most highly compensated category—are scheduled to receive between $20,000 and $200,000. The stipulation provides that CCR is to propose the level of compensation within the prescribed ranges; it also establishes procedures to resolve disputes over medical diagnoses and levels of compensation. . . .

Class members are to receive no compensation for certain kinds of claims, even if otherwise applicable state law recognizes such claims. Claims that garner no compensation under the settlement include claims by family members of asbestos-exposed individuals for loss of consortium and claims by so-called "exposure-only" plaintiffs for increased risk of cancer, fear of future asbestos-related injury, and medical monitoring. "Pleural" claims, which might be asserted by persons with asbestos-related plaques on their lungs but no accompanying physical impairment, are also excluded. Although not entitled to present compensation, exposure-only claimants and pleural claimants may qualify for benefits when and if they develop a compensable disease and meet the relevant exposure and medical criteria. Defendants forgo defenses to liability, including statute of limitations pleas.

Class members, in the main, are bound by the settlement in perpetuity, while CCR defendants may choose to withdraw from the settlement after ten years.

A small number of class members—only a few per year—may reject the settlement and pursue their claims in court. Those permitted to exercise this option, however, may not assert any punitive damages claim or any claim for increased risk of cancer. Aspects of the administration of the settlement are to be monitored by the AFL—CIO and class counsel. Class counsel are to receive attorneys' fees in an amount to be approved by the District Court.

D

On January 29, 1993, as requested by the settling parties, the District Court conditionally certified, under Federal Rule of Civil Procedure 23(b)(3), an encompassing opt-out class. . . .Judge Weiner assigned to Judge Reed, also of the Eastern District of Pennsylvania, "the task of conducting fairness proceedings and of determining whether the proposed settlement is fair to the class." . . .

Reasoning that the representative plaintiffs "have a strong interest that recovery for all of the medical categories be maximized because they may have claims in any, or several categories," the District Court found "no antagonism of interest between class members with various medical conditions, or between persons with and without currently manifest asbestos impairment." Declaring class certification appropriate and the settlement fair, the District Court preliminarily enjoined all class members from commencing any asbestos-related suit against the CCR defendants in any state or federal court.

The objectors appealed. The United States Court of Appeals for the Third Circuit vacated the certification, holding that the requirements of Rule 23 had not been satisfied.

The Court of Appeals . . . found that "serious intra-class conflicts preclude[d] th[e] class from meeting the adequacy of representation requirement" of Rule 23(a)(4).

III

To place this controversy in context, we briefly describe the characteristics of class actions for which the Federal Rules provide. Rule 23, governing federal-court class actions, stems from equity practice and gained its current shape in an innovative 1966 revision. . . .

In the decades since the 1966 revision of Rule 23, class action practice has become ever more "adventuresome" as a means of coping with claims too numerous to secure their "just, speedy, and inexpensive determination" one by one. See Fed. Rule Civ. Proc. 1. The development reflects concerns about the efficient use of court resources and the conservation of funds to compensate claimants who do not line up early in a litigation queue. . . .

Among current applications of Rule 23(b)(3), the "settlement only" class has become a stock device. Although all Federal Circuits recognize the utility of Rule 23(b)(3) settlement classes, courts have divided on the extent to which a proffered settlement affects court surveillance under Rule 23's certification criteria. . . .

IV

We granted review to decide the role settlement may play, under existing Rule 23, in determining the propriety of class certification. . . .

Confronted with a request for settlement-only class certification, a district court need not inquire whether the case, if tried, would present intractable management problems, see Fed. Rule Civ. Proc. 23(b)(3)(D), for the proposal is that there be no trial. But other specifications of the Rule— those designed to protect absentees by blocking unwarranted or overbroad class definitions—demand undiluted, even heightened, attention in the settlement context. Such attention is of vital importance, for a court asked to certify a settlement class will lack the opportunity, present when a case is litigated, to adjust the class, informed by the proceedings as they unfold. See Rule 23(c), (d).

And, of overriding importance, courts must be mindful that the Rule as now composed sets the requirements they are bound to enforce. Federal Rules take effect after an extensive deliberative process involving many reviewers: a Rules Advisory Committee, public commenters, the Judicial Conference, this Court, the Congress. See 28 U. S. C. §§ 2073, 2074. The text of a rule thus proposed and reviewed limits judicial inventiveness. Courts are not free to amend a rule outside the process Congress ordered, a process properly tuned to the instruction that rules of procedure "shall not abridge . . . any substantive right." § 2072(b).

Rule 23(e), [at the time of decision] on settlement of class actions, read[ ] in its entirety: "A class action shall not be dismissed or compromised without the approval of the court, and notice of the proposed dismissal or compromise shall be given to all members of the class in such manner as the court directs." This prescription was designed to function as an additional requirement, not a superseding direction, for the "class action" to which Rule 23(e) refers is one qualified for certification under Rule 23(a) and (b). Cf. Eisen, 417 U. S., at 176-177 (adequate representation does not eliminate additional requirement to provide notice). Subdivisions (a) and (b) focus court attention on whether a proposed class has sufficient unity so that absent members can fairly be bound by decisions of class representatives. That dominant concern persists when settlement, rather than trial, is proposed.

The safeguards provided by the Rule 23(a) and (b) class qualifying criteria, we emphasize, are not impractical impediments—checks shorn of utility—in the settlement-class context. . . .

Federal courts, in any case, lack authority to substitute for Rule 23's certification criteria a standard never adopted— that if a settlement is "fair," then certification is proper. Applying to this case criteria the rule makers set, we conclude that the Third Circuit's appraisal is essentially correct. Although that court should have acknowledged that settlement is a factor in the calculus, a remand is not warranted on that account. The Court of Appeals' opinion amply demonstrates why—with or without a settlement on the table— the sprawling class the District Court certified does not satisfy Rule 23's requirements.

A

We address first the requirement of Rule 23(b)(3) that "[common] questions of law or fact . . . predominate over any questions affecting only individual members." The District Court concluded that predominance was satisfied based on two factors: class members' shared experience of asbestos exposure and their common "interest in receiving prompt and fair compensation for their claims, while minimizing the risks and transaction costs inherent in the asbestos litigation process as it occurs presently in the tort system." The settling parties also contend that the settlement's fairness is a common question, predominating over disparate legal issues that might be pivotal in litigation but become irrelevant under the settlement.

The predominance requirement stated in Rule 23(b)(3), we hold, is not met by the factors on which the District Court relied. The benefits asbestos-exposed persons might gain from the establishment of a grand-scale compensation scheme is a matter fit for legislative consideration, see supra, at 598, but it is not pertinent to the predominance inquiry. That inquiry trains on the legal or factual questions that qualify each class member's case as a genuine controversy, questions that preexist any settlement. . . .

B

Nor can the class approved by the District Court satisfy Rule 23(a)(4)'s requirement that the named parties "will fairly and adequately protect the interests of the class." The adequacy inquiry under Rule 23(a)(4) serves to uncover conflicts of interest between named parties and the class they seek to represent. . . .

As the Third Circuit pointed out, named parties with diverse medical conditions sought to act on behalf of a single giant class rather than on behalf of discrete subclasses. In significant respects, the interests of those within the single class are not aligned. Most saliently, for the currently injured, the critical goal is generous immediate payments. That goal tugs against the interest of exposure-only plaintiffs in ensuring an ample, inflation-protected fund for the future. . . .

The settling parties, in sum, achieved a global compromise with no structural assurance of fair and adequate representation for the diverse groups and individuals affected. Although the named parties alleged a range of complaints, each served generally as representative for the whole, not for a separate constituency. . . .

The Third Circuit found no assurance here—either in the terms of the settlement or in the structure of the negotiations—that the named plaintiffs operated under a proper understanding of their representational responsibilities. That assessment, we conclude, is on the mark.

C

Because we have concluded that the class in this case cannot satisfy the requirements of common issue predominance and adequacy of representation, we need not rule, definitively, on the notice given here. In accord with the Third Circuit, however, see we recognize the gravity of the question whether class action notice sufficient under the Constitution and Rule 23 could ever be given to legions so unselfconscious and amorphous.

V

The argument is sensibly made that a nationwide administrative claims processing regime would provide the most secure, fair, and efficient means of compensating victims of asbestos exposure. Congress, however, has not adopted such a solution. And Rule 23, which must be interpreted with fidelity to the Rules Enabling Act and applied with the interests of absent class members in close view, cannot carry the large load

CCR, class counsel, and the District Court heaped upon it. As this case exemplifies, the rule makers' prescriptions for class actions may be endangered by "those who embrace [Rule 23] too enthusiastically just as [they are by] those who approach [the Rule] with distaste." C. Wright, Law of Federal Courts 508 (5th ed. 1994)....

In re: Prudential Ins. Co. America Sales Practice Litigation Agent Action
148 F.3d 283 (1998)

SCIRICA, Circuit Judge

This is an appeal from the approval of the settlement of a nationwide class action lawsuit against Prudential Life Insurance Company alleging deceptive sales practices affecting over 8 million claimants throughout the fifty states and the District of Columbia.

The class is comprised of Prudential policyholders who allegedly were the victims of fraudulent and misleading sales practices employed by Prudential's sales force. The challenged sales practices consisted primarily of churning, vanishing premiums and fraudulent investment plans, and each cause of action is based on fraud or deceptive conduct. There are no allegations of personal injury; there are no futures classes. The settlement creates an alternative dispute resolution mechanism and establishes protocols to determine the kind and amount of relief to be granted. The relief awarded includes full compensatory damages consisting of what plaintiffs thought they were purchasing from the insurance agent. There is no cap on the amount of compensatory damages for those who qualify, and although punitive damages are not included in the settlement, Prudential has agreed to pay a remediation amount in addition to the payments made through dispute resolution process...

Appellants, members of the certified class who object to the settlement, challenge [among other things] ... the fairness of the settlement itself....

V. THE FAIRNESS OF THE PROPOSED SETTLEMENT

Even if it has satisfied the requirements for certification under Rule 23, a class action cannot be settled without the approval of the court and a determination that the proposed settlement is "fair, reasonable and adequate. "Rule 23(e) imposes on the trial judge the duty of protecting absentees, which is executed by the court's assuring the settlement represents adequate compensation for the release of the class claims."

In deciding the fairness of a proposed settlement, we have said that "[t]he evaluating court must, of course, guard against demanding too large a settlement based on its view of the merits of the litigation; after all, settlement is a compromise, a yielding of the highest hopes in exchange for certainty and resolution." At the same time, we have noted that cases such as this, where the parties simultaneously seek certification and settlement approval, require "courts to be even more scrupulous than usual" when they examine the fairness of the proposed settlement. This heightened standard is designed to ensure that class counsel has demonstrated "sustained advocacy" throughout the course of the proceedings and has protected the interests of all class members.

"The decision of whether to approve a proposed settlement of a class action is left to the sound discretion of the district court." Because of the district court's proximity to the parties and to the nuances of the litigation, we accord great weight to the court's factual findings.

As the district court recognized, our decision in Girsh sets out appropriate factors to be considered when determining the fairness of a proposed settlement. Those factors are:

(1) the complexity, expense and likely duration of the litigation ...; (2) the reaction of the class to the settlement ...; (3) the stage of the proceedings and the amount of discovery completed ...; (4) the risks of establishing liability ...; (5) the risks of establishing damages ...; (6) the risks of maintaining the class action through trial ...; (7) the ability of the defendants to withstand a greater judgment; (8) the range of reasonableness of the settlement fund in light of the best possible recovery ...; (9) the range of reasonableness of the settlement fund to a possible recovery in light of all the attendant risks of litigation....

Girsh, 521 F.2d at 157 (quoting City of Detroit v. Grinnell Corp., 495 F.2d 448, 463 (2d Cir.1974)) (the "Girsh factors"). The court examined each of these factors and found "the Proposed Settlement is indeed fair, reasonable, and adequate and should be approved."

In addition to the Girsh analysis, the district court offered other reasons for its conclusion that the settlement was fair and reasonable. Describing the proposed settlement as "exceptional," the court noted the settlement's structure was based on the class action settlements approved in Willson v. New York Life Ins. Co., No. 94-127804, 1995 N.Y. Misc. LEXIS 652 (N.Y.Sup.Ct. Feb. 1, 1996), aff'd, 228 A.D.2d 368, 644 N.Y.S.2d 617 (1st Dept.), and Michaels v. Pheonix Home Life Ins. Co., No. 95-5318, 1997 N.Y. Misc. LEXIS 171 (N.Y.Sup.Ct. Jan. 3, 1997), both of which received the praise of "[c]ourts, academic and industry experts, and various independent organizations." The court also relied on the expertise of the insurance regulators from the fifty states and the District of Columbia, all of whom endorsed the settlement.

The court found the terms of the settlement "benefit the class enormously," emphasizing the uncapped nature of the relief, the fairness of the ADR process, and the availability of Basic Claim Relief to those class members who either elect not to participate in the ADR process or who cannot demonstrate they have a compensable claim. The court found this relief was enhanced by the inclusion of "Additional Remediation Amounts," which it described as the "punitive damage counterpart to the Proposed Settlement," and by Prudential's agreement to pay all attorneys' fees and costs associated with the settlement. Finally, the court emphasized the settlement provided class members the opportunity to file claims immediately after court approval of the settlement, rather than waiting through what no doubt would be protracted litigation.

Krell raises several challenges to the district court's fairness determination First, Krell claims the district court applied several of the Girsh factors improperly, and in some cases not at all, and that it erred by not creating a separate subclass to address replacement claims. Krell Brief at 43-50. Second, he contends the district court's fairness determination violated the McCarran-Ferguson Act and the Rules Enabling Act by altering the substantive contractual and statutory insurance rights of the class. Finally, Krell alleges the certification and fairness proceedings lacked due process.

A. The Girsh Factors

Although Krell has not directly challenged the court's analysis with respect to each of the nine Girsh factors, we will examine each of them in turn.

1. The complexity and duration of the litigation

Citing the myriad complex legal and factual issues which would arise at trial, the district court found the "anticipated complexity, costs, and time necessary to try this case greatly substantiate the fairness of the settlement." The court found that litigation would require expensive and time-consuming discovery, would necessitate the use of several expert witnesses, and would not be completed for years. Consequently, the court concluded this factor weighed in favor of settlement.

We agree. Examining the sheer magnitude of the proposed settlement class as well as the complexity of the issues raised, we conclude the trial of this class action would be a long, arduous process requiring great expenditures of time and money on behalf of both the parties and the court. The prospect of such a massive undertaking clearly counsels in favor of settlement.

2. The reaction of the class to the settlement

This factor attempts to gauge whether members of the class support the settlement. Although the response rate in a 23(b)(3) class action is relevant to the fairness determination, "a combination of observations about the practical realities of class actions has led a number of courts to be considerably more cautious about inferring support from a small number of objectors to a sophisticated settlement."

The district court found that, of the 8 million policyholders to whom Prudential sent the class notice, approximately 19,000 policyholders or 0.2 per cent of the class opted out. The court also noted that approximately 300 policyholders filed objections to the settlement. The court found the small percentage of opt outs and objectors was "truly insignificant," and noted that the "most vociferous objectors to the Proposed Settlement are a handful of litigants represented by counsel in cases that compete with or overlap the claims asserted in the Second Amended Complaint." Consequently, the court concluded the limited number of objections filed also weighed in favor of approving the settlement.

We see no abuse of discretion. While we do not read too much into the low rate of response, we believe the district court properly analyzed this factor.

3. The stage of the proceedings and amount of discovery completed

The parties must have an "adequate appreciation of the merits of the case before negotiating." To ensure that a proposed settlement is the product of informed negotiations, there should be an inquiry into the type and amount of discovery the parties have undertaken. Krell contends that class counsel's discovery was insufficient to support the proposed settlement, claiming that Lead Counsel's pre-settlement discovery consisted only of 70 boxes of documents received in August 1996 pursuant to informal letter requests, and a number of meetings with Prudential's chairman, Arthur Ryan. Krell questions how Lead Counsel could have been in "second stage settlement negotiations" before receiving Prudential's production of over 1 million documents, videotapes, audio tapes and computer tapes in mid-August. Finally, Krell contends there was no vigorous, adversarial discovery because "virtually all of Prudential's discovery obligations" were stayed between October 1995 and September 10, 1996, and the parties didn't agree on a free exchange of information until August 20, 1996, only a few weeks before the proposed settlement was announced.

The district court found that "counsel for plaintiffs and Prudential did not commence serious settlement discussions until 18 months of vigorous litigation had transpired," noting the parties had filed and argued a multitude of motions, including consolidation motions, jurisdictional motions, motions to stay competing class actions, case management motions, and Prudential's motion to dismiss under F.R.C.P. 12(b)(6). In addition to its in-court efforts, the district court concluded that class counsel's pursuit of discovery also supported the settlement. The court found class counsel reviewed a multitude of documents provided by Prudential, conducted its own interviews with hundreds of current and former Prudential employees, took twenty depositions, and had access to all of the materials collected by the Task Force. The district court also found class counsel took sufficient time to review the discovery materials it collected, noting that class counsel refused to discuss settlement on two separate occasions because it believed it needed further discovery. Finally, the court found class counsels' "use of informal discovery was especially appropriate in this case because the Court stayed plaintiffs' right to formal discovery for many months, and because informal discovery could provide the information that plaintiffs needed." Based on the foregoing, the district court concluded "the volume and substance of Class Counsel's knowledge of this case are unquestionably adequate to support this settlement." We see no error here.

4. The risks of establishing liability and damages

The fourth and fifth Girsh factors survey the possible risks of litigation in order to balance the likelihood of success and the potential damage award if the case were taken to trial against the benefits of an immediate settlement. Examining plaintiffs' ability to establish liability and damages at trial, the court concluded "the risks of establishing liability weigh in favor of approving the settlement."

We believe the district court properly examined the risks faced by the putative class. The court found plaintiffs would face a difficult burden at trial demonstrating, inter alia,(1) class members were deceived by Prudential's written disclosures and illustrations; (2) their contract claims were not barred by the parol evidence rule because they conflict with the unambiguous language in the insurance contracts; (3) the necessary reliance to support their federal securities claims; and (4) their federal securities claims were not barred by the one year statute of limitations and the three year statute of repose. As further evidence of the barriers facing plaintiffs, the district court took notice of a similar life insurance sales practice case in Alabama state court in which the judge overturned a substantial jury verdict against Prudential. We believe the district court offered substantial reasons for its findings.

a. Replacement Claims

Krell argues the district court failed to consider separately the likelihood of success at trial for those class members who alleged "replacement claims," contending those claims require a lesser degree of proof and may be established by an objective review of the documents in Prudential's files. Both Prudential and Lead Counsel contend that "replacement policyholders faced similar burdens to those of other Class Members in establishing liability and damages against Prudential."

The district court did not believe that "replacement claims" are easier to prove and therefore required separate consideration. We agree. Krell offers no authority or analysis to support this blanket assertion. In addition, the findings of the Multi-State Task Force undermine Krell's argument.

The primary focus of the Multi-State Task Force was the practice known as "churning" or "twisting," which it defined as "the sale of any policy based upon incomplete or misleading comparisons." Task Force Report at 35. According to the Multi-State Task Force Report, the transactions most frequently the subject of churning or twisting complaints were financed sales and abbreviated payment plans. Replacement transactions are a subcategory of financed sales in which at least 25% of an existing policy's value is used to fund the purchase of a new policy.

The Task Force Report makes clear that "none of these types of sales, financed, replacement or abbreviated pay, is in violation of the replacement regulation if properly done." It also notes that, during the late 1970s and early 1980's, the previous industry-wide disinclination for replacement sales began to give way. In 1978, for example, the National Association of Insurance Commissioners modified its model replacement regulations to reflect the growing acceptance of replacement sales, provided those sales were accompanied by necessary information and disclosure to allow consumers to "make an informed choice."

Turning to its examination of Prudential, the Task Force acknowledged its goal was "to determine whether during the sale of new policies, those involving financing or replacement, consumers were adequately advised of the potential failings of the new policies or the funding basis on which they were sold." The Report notes that although all of the required disclosure forms may have been completed and filed by Prudential, "[o]ne must look beyond the required forms to determine whether or not presentations were accurate and not misleading." In its discussion of the remediation protocol, the Task Force explained "the documentation received from Prudential did not always support the consumer's assertion," and consequently "[w]hat was or was not agreed upon at the time of sale became a question of fact." (noting that while "some replacements may have been appropriate ... misrepresentation is never appropriate," and thus "the challenge is to distinguish appropriate replacement activity.")

Consequently, it appears that misrepresentation, rather than compliance with bookkeeping requirements, was the primary concern of the Task Force examination of Prudential's replacement sales. As the Task Force Report states, it is incorrect "to assume that in any and every case where a replacement was not identified or the regulatory requirements were not met, the policyholder did not understand the transaction or that it was not properly explained." We also find it significant that the state insurance regulators who crafted the initial Task Force Report did not incorporate a lesser burden of proof or otherwise distinguish "replacement claims" from other types of claims. Consequently, we believe the district court properly considered the role of replacement claims when analyzing the fourth and fifth Girsh factors.

5. The risks of maintaining the class action through trial

Under Rule 23, a district court may decertify or modify a class at any time during the litigation if it proves to be unmanageable. In this instance, the district court concluded that although "this case is manageable as a class action and the class action device is the most appropriate means to adjudicate this controversy, as the case evolves, maintaining the class action may become unworkable" and require decertification. The court also noted Prudential had sought to preserve its objections to class certification and would likely contest certification if the case proceeded to trial. Consequently, the court concluded that there was a risk the case might eventually be decertified, all of which weighed in favor of settlement.

Although we agree with the district court's analysis and find there was some risk of decertification which supports settlement, we pause to comment on the application of this factor in "settlement-only" class actions following the Supreme Court's decision in Amchem. Because the district court always possesses the authority to decertify or modify a class that proves unmanageable, examination of this factor in the standard class action would appear to be perfunctory. There will always be a "risk" or possibility of decertification, and consequently the court can always claim this factor weighs in favor of settlement. The test becomes even more "toothless" after Amchem. The Supreme Court in Amchem held a district court could take settlement into consideration when deciding whether to certify a class, and that, "[c]onfronted with a request for settlement-only class certification, a district court need not inquire whether the case, if tried, would present intractable management problems ... for the proposal is that there be no trial." It would seem, therefore, that after Amchem the manageability inquiry in settlement-only class actions may not be significant.

6. The ability of the defendants to withstand a greater judgment

The district court found "Prudential's ability to withstand a greater judgment is a matter of concern." Noting that the settlement was valued between $1 billion and $2 billion, the court found a larger judgment could negatively impact Prudential's declining credit rating. The court also expressed concern that, because Prudential is a mutual insurer, non-class member policyholders could conceivably be adversely affected by an excessive settlement in the form of lower dividends.

Krell claims the district court erred by finding that Prudential could not withstand a greater judgment because "neither Lead Counsel nor Prudential submitted any reliable evidence of the true value of the ADR relief." Krell Brief at 50. Krell speculates that even the $410 million minimum is inaccurate because it does not account for "profits, if any" generated by Basic Claim Relief.

We see no error here. As the district court noted, the value of the proposed settlement is difficult to determine because both the compensatory relief available under the ADR and the additional relief available through Basic Claim Relief are uncapped. The parties' experts offered valuations between $1 and $2 billion, with an absolute minimum of

$410 million. While these numbers are imprecise, they are a sufficient basis for the district court to decide whether Prudential could withstand a greater judgment. In addition, Prudential's credit rating during the course of the litigation may be an appropriate indicator, among others, for the court's consideration, and its decline would support the court's analysis.

7. *The range of reasonableness of the settlement fund in light of the best possible recovery and all the attendant risks of litigation*

The last two Girsh factors ask whether the settlement is reasonable in light of the best possible recovery and the risks the parties would face if the case went to trial. In order to assess the reasonableness of a proposed settlement seeking monetary relief, "the present value of the damages plaintiffs would likely recover if successful, appropriately discounted for the risk of not prevailing, should be compared with the amount of the proposed settlement." On appeal, Krell argues the district court declined to address this issue, instead finding the analysis unnecessary because all injured policyholders would receive full compensatory relief.

Krell has mischaracterized the district court's opinion. The district court applied the final two Girsh factors, although it did not attempt to reduce its analysis to a concrete formula. The district court found that calculating the best possible recovery for the class in the aggregate would be "exceedingly speculative," and in this instance such a calculation was unnecessary because the reasonableness of the settlement could be fairly judged. The court instead examined the nature of the settlement and the range of possible outcomes for those participating in either the ADR process or Basic Claim Relief and concluded that "an individual's recovery exceeds the value of the best possible recovery discounted by the risks of litigation."

For example, the court found class members who have clear claims against Prudential will receive scores of "3" and will "receive a choice between full rescissionary or compensatory relief plus interest." Thus they will receive full compensation without paying attorneys fees and without undue delay. The court concluded this relief "is not only fair, it is exceptional." Those class members who received a score of "2" — where the evidence on balance supports the claim — would receive 50% of their damages without having to pay litigation costs or fees, an award the court concluded was equivalent to what the claimant would have received at trial. ("The 50% award plus 100% interest is equivalent to a full award minus litigation costs, attorneys' fees, and the price of delay."). The court also found the settlement was fair for those receiving a score of "1" in the ADR process and for those electing Basic Claim Relief — those who would not have had a claim or not elected to bring one — because the Basic Claim Relief recovery is greater than what they would have gotten at trial.

We believe the district court adequately addressed these factors and agree its examination "accounts appropriately for the nuances of this Proposed Settlement." As the court noted, both the structure of the settlement and the uncapped nature of the relief provided make it difficult to determine accurately the actual value of the settlement. Consequently, the traditional calculus suggested by the Manual for Complex Litigation 2d and adopted by this Court in G.M. Trucks cannot be applied to this case. But we cannot find the district court abused its discretion when it found that the remedies available under the proposed settlement provided extraordinary relief. When balanced against the best possible recovery and the risks of taking this case to trial, these remedies weighed in favor of the proposed settlement.

It is worth noting that since Girsh was decided in 1975, there has been a sea-change in the nature of class actions, especially with respect to mass torts. In this regard, it may be useful to expand the traditional Girsh factors to include, when appropriate, these factors among others: the maturity of the underlying substantive issues, as measured by experience in adjudicating individual actions, the development of scientific knowledge, the extent of discovery on the merits, and other factors that bear on the ability to assess the probable outcome of a trial on the merits of liability and individual damages; the existence and probable outcome of claims by other classes and subclasses; the comparison between the results achieved by the settlement for individual class or subclass members and the results achieved — or likely to be achieved — for other claimants; whether class or subclass members are accorded the right to opt out of the settlement; whether any provisions for attorneys' fees are reasonable; and whether the procedure for processing individual claims under the settlement is fair and reasonable. Of these factors, the only one relevant here is the fairness and reasonableness of the ADR procedure. See also discussion supra § V.D.

Surrendering the Right to Bring a Class Action

American Express Co. v. Italian Colors Restaurant
570 US 228 (2013)

Justice SCALIA delivered the opinion of the Court.

We consider whether a contractual waiver of class arbitration is enforceable under the Federal Arbitration Act when the plaintiff's cost of individually arbitrating a federal statutory claim exceeds the potential recovery.

I

Respondents are merchants who accept American Express cards. Their agreement with petitioners — American Express and a wholly owned subsidiary — contains a clause that requires all disputes between the parties to be resolved by arbitration. The agreement also provides that "[t]here shall be no right or authority for any Claims to be arbitrated on a class action basis."

Respondents brought a class action against petitioners for violations of the federal antitrust laws. According to respondents, American Express used its monopoly power in the market for charge cards to force merchants to accept credit cards at rates approximately 30% higher than the fees for competing credit cards. This tying arrangement, respondents said, violated § 1 of the Sherman Act. They sought treble damages for the class under § 4 of the Clayton Act.

Petitioners moved to compel individual arbitration under the Federal Arbitration Act (FAA), 9 U.S.C. § 1 et seq. In resisting the motion, respondents submitted a declaration from an economist who estimated that the cost of an expert analysis necessary to prove the antitrust claims would be "at least several hundred thousand dollars, and might exceed $1 million," while the maximum recovery for an individual plaintiff would be $12,850, or $38,549 when trebled. The District Court granted the motion and dismissed the lawsuits. The Court of Appeals reversed and remanded for further proceedings. It held that because respondents had established that "they would incur prohibitive costs if compelled to arbitrate under the class action waiver," the waiver was unenforceable and the arbitration could not proceed.

We granted certiorari, vacated the judgment, and remanded for further consideration in light of Stolt-Nielsen S.A. v. AnimalFeeds Int'l Corp., 559 U.S. 662, 130 S.Ct. 1758, 176 L.Ed.2d 605 (2010), which held that a party may not be compelled to submit to class arbitration absent an agreement to do so. The Court of Appeals stood by its reversal, stating that its earlier ruling did not compel class arbitration. It then sua sponte reconsidered its ruling in light of AT&T Mobility LLC v. Concepcion, 563 U.S. ___, 131 S.Ct. 1740, 179 L.Ed.2d 742 (2011), which held that the FAA pre-empted a state law barring enforcement of a class-arbitration waiver. Finding AT&T Mobility inapplicable because it addressed pre-emption, the Court of Appeals reversed for the third time. It then denied rehearing en banc with five judges dissenting. We granted certiorari to consider the question "[w]hether the Federal Arbitration Act permits courts ... to invalidate arbitration agreements on the ground that they do not permit class arbitration of a federal-law claim,"

II

Congress enacted the FAA in response to widespread judicial hostility to arbitration. See AT&T Mobility, supra, As relevant here, the Act provides:

"A written provision in any maritime transaction or contract evidencing a transaction involving commerce to settle by arbitration a controversy thereafter arising out of such contract or transaction... shall be valid, irrevocable, and enforceable, save upon such grounds as exist at law or in equity for the revocation of any contract." 9 U.S.C. § 2.

This text reflects the overarching principle that arbitration is a matter of contract. And consistent with that text, courts must "rigorously enforce" arbitration agreements according to their terms, Dean Witter Reynolds Inc. v. Byrd, 470 U.S. 213, 221, 105 S.Ct. 1238, 84 L.Ed.2d 158 (1985), including terms that "specify with whom [the parties] choose to arbitrate their disputes," Stolt-Nielsen, supra, at 683, and "the rules under which that arbitration will be conducted," Volt Information Sciences, Inc. v. Board of Trustees of Leland Stanford Junior Univ., 489 U.S. 468, 479, 109 S.Ct. 1248, 103 L.Ed.2d 488 (1989). That holds true for claims that allege a violation of a federal statute, unless the FAA's mandate has been "'overridden by a contrary congressional command.'"

III

No contrary congressional command requires us to reject the waiver of class arbitration here. Respondents argue that requiring them to litigate their claims individually — as they contracted to do — would contravene the policies of the antitrust laws. But the antitrust laws do not guarantee an affordable procedural path to the vindication of every claim. Congress has taken some measures to facilitate the litigation of antitrust claims — for example, it enacted a multiplied-damages remedy. See 15 U.S.C. § 15 (treble damages). In enacting such measures, Congress has told us that it is willing to go, in certain respects, beyond the normal limits of law in advancing its goals of deterring and remedying unlawful trade practice. But to say that Congress must have intended whatever departures from those normal limits advance antitrust goals is simply irrational. "[N]o legislation pursues its purposes at all costs." Rodriguez v. United States, 480 U.S. 522, 525-526, 107 S.Ct. 1391, 94 L.Ed.2d 533 (1987) (per curiam).

The antitrust laws do not "evinc[e] an intention to preclude a waiver" of class-action procedure. Mitsubishi Motors Corp. v. Soler Chrysler-Plymouth, Inc., 473 U.S. 614, 628, 105 S.Ct. 3346, 87 L.Ed.2d 444 (1985). The Sherman and Clayton Acts make no mention of class actions. In fact, they were enacted decades before the advent of Federal Rule of Civil Procedure 23, which was "designed to allow an exception to the usual rule that litigation is conducted by and on behalf of the individual named parties only." Califano v. Yamasaki, 442 U.S. 682, 700-701, 99 S.Ct. 2545, 61 L.Ed.2d 176 (1979). The parties here agreed to arbitrate pursuant to that "usual rule," and it would be remarkable for a court to erase that expectation.

Nor does congressional approval of Rule 23 establish an entitlement to class proceedings for the vindication of statutory rights. To begin with, it is likely that such an entitlement, invalidating private arbitration agreements denying class adjudication, would be an "abridg[ment]" or "modif[ication]" of a "substantive right" forbidden to the Rules, see 28 U.S.C. § 2072(b). But there is no evidence of such an entitlement in any event. The Rule imposes stringent requirements for certification that in practice exclude most claims. And we have specifically rejected the assertion that one of those requirements (the class-notice requirement) must be dispensed with because the "prohibitively high cost" of compliance would "frustrate [plaintiff's] attempt to vindicate the policies underlying the antitrust" laws. Eisen v. Carlisle & Jacquelin, 417 U.S. 156, 166-168, 175-176, 94 S.Ct. 2140, 40 L.Ed.2d 732 (1974). One might respond, perhaps, that federal law secures a nonwaivable opportunity to vindicate federal policies by satisfying the procedural strictures of Rule 23 or invoking some other informal class mechanism in arbitration. But we have already rejected that proposition in AT&T Mobility, 563 U.S., at ___, 131 S.Ct., at 1748.

IV

Our finding of no "contrary congressional command" does not end the case. Respondents invoke a judge-made exception to the FAA which, they say, serves to harmonize competing federal policies by allowing courts to invalidate agreements that prevent the "effective vindication" of a federal statutory right. Enforcing the waiver of class arbitration bars effective vindication, respondents contend, because they have no economic incentive to pursue their antitrust claims individually in arbitration.

The "effective vindication" exception to which respondents allude originated as dictum in Mitsubishi Motors, where we expressed a willingness to invalidate, on "public policy" grounds, arbitration agreements that "operat[e] ... as a prospective waiver of a party's right to pursue statutory remedies." Dismissing concerns that the arbitral forum was inadequate, we said that "so long as the prospective litigant effectively may vindicate its statutory cause of action in the arbitral forum, the statute will continue to serve both its remedial and deterrent function." Subsequent cases have similarly asserted the existence of an "effective vindication" exception, see, e.g., 14 Penn Plaza LLC v. Pyett, 556 U.S. 247, 273-274, 129 S.Ct. 1456, 173 L.Ed.2d 398 (2009); Gilmer v. Interstate/Johnson Lane Corp., 500 U.S. 20, 28, 111 S.Ct. 1647, 114 L.Ed.2d 26 (1991), but have similarly declined to apply it to invalidate the arbitration agreement at issue.

And we do so again here. As we have described, the exception finds its origin in the desire to prevent "prospective waiver of a party's right to pursue statutory remedies," Mitsubishi Motors, supra, That would certainly cover a provision in an arbitration agreement forbidding the assertion of certain statutory rights. And it would perhaps cover filing and administrative fees attached to arbitration that are so high as to make access to the forum impracticable. See Green Tree Financial Corp.-Ala. v. Randolph, 531 U.S. 79, 90, 121 S.Ct. 513, 148 L.Ed.2d 373 (2000) ("It may well be that the existence of large arbitration costs could preclude a litigant ... from effectively vindicating her federal statutory rights"). But the fact that it is not worth the expense involved in proving a statutory remedy does not constitute the elimination of the right to pursue that remedy. The class-action waiver merely limits arbitration to the two contracting parties. It no more eliminates those parties' right to pursue their statutory remedy than did federal law before its adoption of the class action for legal relief in 1938, see Fed. Rule Civ. Proc. 23, 28 U.S.C., p. 864 (1938 ed., Supp V); 7A C. Wright, A. Miller, & M. Kane, Federal Practice and Procedure § 1752, p. 18 (3d ed. 2005). Or, to put it differently, the individual suit that was considered adequate to assure "effective vindication" of a federal right before adoption of class-action procedures did not suddenly become "ineffective vindication" upon their adoption. . . .

Truth to tell, our decision in AT&T Mobility all but resolves this case. There we invalidated a law conditioning enforcement of arbitration on the availability of class procedure because that law "interfere[d] with fundamental attributes of arbitration." "[T]he switch from bilateral to class arbitration," we said, "sacrifices the principal advantage of arbitration — its informality — and makes the process slower, more costly, and more likely to generate procedural morass than final judgment." We specifically rejected the argument that class arbitration was necessary to prosecute claims "that might otherwise slip through the legal system."

* * *

The regime established by the Court of Appeals' decision would require — before a plaintiff can be held to contractually agreed bilateral arbitration — that a federal court determine (and the parties litigate) the legal requirements for success on the merits claim-by-claim and theory-by-theory, the evidence necessary to meet those requirements, the cost of developing that evidence, and the damages that would be recovered in the event of success. Such a preliminary litigating hurdle would undoubtedly destroy the prospect of speedy resolution that arbitration in general and bilateral arbitration in particular was meant to secure. The FAA does not sanction such a judicially created superstructure.

The judgment of the Court of Appeals is reversed.

It is so ordered.

CHAPTER 7

PROVISIONAL REMEDIES

The filing of a lawsuit seldom results in instant gratification. Lawsuits take a while to wind through the courts. It can typically take a year or longer for a lawsuit to go all the way to trial, verdict, and judgment. In the meantime, there is the risk that any assets which the defendant possesses (especially when it is claimed that the defendant is holding property that belongs to the plaintiff) will be dissipated. To guard against the possibility of dissipation the plaintiff may, in limited circumstances, resort to what are referred to as temporary or provisional remedies.

However, plaintiff's resort to provisional remedies may collide with a defendant's Fifth and Fourteenth amendment right not to be deprived of property without due process of law. Provisional remedies often raise the question of whether there has been a taking of property without the procedural due process that is required by the Constitution.

This next case involves a procedure known as "garnishment," which is an order issued to a third party (typically the defendant's employer) not to pay the defendant money due to him or her, because the plaintiff has a claim on it.

ATTACHMENT AND GARNISHMENT

Sniadach v. Family Finance Corp.
395 U.S. 337 (1969)

MR. JUSTICE DOUGLAS delivered the opinion of the Court.

Respondents instituted a garnishment action against petitioner as defendant and Miller Harris Instrument Co., her employer, as garnishee. The complaint alleged a claim of $420 on a promissory note. The garnishee filed its answer stating it had wages of $63.18 under its control earned by petitioner and unpaid, and that it would pay one-half to petitioner as a subsistence allowance and hold the other half subject to the order of the court.

Petitioner moved that the garnishment proceedings be dismissed for failure to satisfy the due process requirements of the Fourteenth Amendment. The Wisconsin Supreme Court sustained the lower state court in approving the procedure. The case is here on a petition for a writ of certiorari.

The Wisconsin statute gives a plaintiff 10 days in which to serve the summons and complaint on the defendant after service on the garnishee. In this case petitioner was served the same day as the garnishee. She nonetheless claims that the Wisconsin garnishment procedure violates that due process required by the Fourteenth Amendment, in that notice and an opportunity to be heard are not given before the in rem seizure of the wages. What happens in Wisconsin is that the clerk of the court issues the summons at the request of the creditor's lawyer; and it is the latter who by serving the garnishee sets in motion the machinery whereby the wages are frozen. They may, it is true, be unfrozen if the trial of the main suit is ever had and the wage earner wins on the merits. But in the interim the wage earner is deprived of his enjoyment of earned wages without any opportunity to be heard and to tender any defense he may have, whether it be fraud or otherwise.

Such summary procedure may well meet the requirements of due process in extraordinary situations. But in the present case no situation requiring special protection to a state or creditor interest is presented by the facts; nor is the Wisconsin statute narrowly drawn to meet any such unusual condition. Petitioner was a resident of this Wisconsin community and in personam jurisdiction was readily obtainable.

The question is not whether the Wisconsin law is a wise law or unwise law. Our concern is not what philosophy Wisconsin should or should not embrace. We do not sit as a super-legislative body. In this case the sole question is whether there has been a taking of property without that procedural due process that is required by the Fourteenth Amendment. We have dealt over and over again with the question of what constitutes "the right to be heard" within the meaning of procedural due process. See Mullane v. Central Hanover Trust Co., 339 U. S. 306, 314. In the latter case we said that the right to be heard "has little reality or worth unless one is informed that the matter is pending and can choose for himself whether to appear or default, acquiesce or contest." In the context of this case the question is whether the interim freezing of the wages without a chance to be heard violates procedural due process.

A procedural rule that may satisfy due process for attachments in general, does not necessarily satisfy procedural due process in every case. The fact that a procedure would pass muster under a feudal regime does not mean it gives necessary protection to all property in its modern forms. We deal here with wages—a specialized type of property presenting distinct problems in our economic system. We turn then to the nature of that property and problems of procedural due process.

A prejudgment garnishment of the Wisconsin type is a taking which may impose tremendous hardship on wage earners with families to support. Until a recent Act of Congress,[of which forbids discharge of employees on the ground that their wages have been garnished, garnishment often meant the loss of a job. Over and beyond that was the great drain on family income. As stated by Congressman Reuss:

"The idea of wage garnishment in advance of judgment, of trustee process, of wage attachment, or whatever it is called is a most inhuman doctrine. It compels the wage earner, trying to keep his family together, to be driven below the poverty level."

Recent investigations of the problem have disclosed the grave injustices made possible by prejudgment garnishment whereby the sole opportunity to be heard comes after the taking. Congressman Sullivan, Chairman of the House Subcommittee on Consumer Affairs who held extensive hearings on this and related problems stated:

"What we know from our study of this problem is that in a vast number of cases the debt is a fraudulent one, saddled on a poor ignorant person who is trapped in an easy credit nightmare, in which he is charged double for something he could not pay for even if the proper price was called for, and then hounded into giving up his pound of flesh, and being fired besides." 114 Cong. Rec. 1832.

The leverage of the creditor on the wage earner is enormous. The creditor tenders not only the original debt but the "collection fees" incurred by his attorneys in the garnishment proceedings:

"The debtor whose wages are tied up by a writ of garnishment, and who is usually in need of money, is in no position to resist demands for collection fees. If the debt is small, the debtor will be under considerable pressure to pay the debt and collection charges in order to get his wages back. If the debt is large, he will often sign a new contract of 'payment schedule' which incorporates these additional charges." Apart from those collateral consequences, it appears that in Wisconsin the statutory exemption granted the wage earner is "generally insufficient to support the debtor for any one week."

The result is that a prejudgment garnishment of the Wisconsin type may as a practical matter drive a wage-earning family to the wall. Where the taking of one's property is so obvious, it needs no extended argument to conclude that absent notice and a prior hearing this prejudgment garnishment procedure violates the fundamental principles of due process.

Reversed.

Fuentes v. Shevin
407 U.S. 67 (1972)

MR. JUSTICE STEWART delivered the opinion of the Court.

We here review the decisions of two three-judge federal District Courts that upheld the constitutionality of Florida and Pennsylvania laws authorizing the summary seizure of goods or chattels in a person's possession under a writ of replevin. Both statutes provide for the issuance of writs ordering state agents to seize a person's possessions, simply upon the ex parte application of any other person who claims a right to them and posts a security bond. Neither statute provides for notice to be given to the possessor of the property, and neither statute gives the possessor an opportunity to challenge the seizure at any kind of prior hearing. The question is whether these statutory procedures violate the Fourteenth Amendment's guarantee that no State shall deprive any person of property without due process of law.

The appellant . . . Margarita Fuentes, is a resident of Florida. She purchased a gas stove and service policy from the Firestone Tire and Rubber Co. (Firestone) under a conditional sales contract calling for monthly payments over a period of time. A few months later, she purchased a stereophonic phonograph from the same company under the same sort of contract. The total cost of the stove and stereo was about $500, plus an additional financing charge of over $100. Under the contracts, Firestone retained title to the merchandise, but Mrs. Fuentes was entitled to possession unless and until she should default on her installment payments.

For more than a year, Mrs. Fuentes made her installment payments. But then, with only about $200 remaining to be paid, a dispute developed between her and Firestone over the servicing of the stove. Firestone instituted an action in a small-claims court for repossession of both the stove and the stereo, claiming that Mrs. Fuentes had refused to make her remaining payments. Simultaneously with the filing of that action and before Mrs. Fuentes had even received a summons to answer its complaint, Firestone obtained a writ of replevin ordering a sheriff to seize the disputed goods at once.

In conformance with Florida procedure, Firestone had only to fill in the blanks on the appropriate form documents and submit them to the clerk of the small-claims court. The clerk signed and stamped the documents and issued a writ of replevin. Later the same day, a local deputy sheriff and an agent of Firestone went to Mrs. Fuentes' home and seized the stove and stereo.

Shortly thereafter, Mrs. Fuentes instituted the present action in a federal district court, challenging the constitutionality of the Florida prejudgment replevin procedures under the Due Process Clause of the Fourteenth Amendment. She sought declaratory and injunctive relief against continued enforcement of the procedural provisions of the state statutes that authorize prejudgment replevin.

* * *

Under the Florida statute challenged here, "[a]ny person whose goods or chattels are wrongfully detained by any other person . . . may have a writ of replevin to recover them . . . ." There is no requirement that the applicant make a convincing showing before the seizure that the goods are, in fact, "wrongfully detained." Rather, Florida law automatically relies on the bare assertion of the party seeking the writ that he is entitled to one and allows a court clerk to issue the writ summarily. It requires only that the applicant file a complaint, initiating a court action for repossession and reciting in conclusory fashion that he is "lawfully entitled to the possession" of the property, and that he file a security bond "in at least double the value of the property to be replevied conditioned that plaintiff will prosecute his action to effect and without delay and that if defendant recovers judgment against him in the action, he will return the property, if return thereof is adjudged, and will pay defendant all sums of money recovered against plaintiff by defendant in the action." Fla. Stat. Ann. § 78.07 (Supp. 1972-1973).

On the sole basis of the complaint and bond, a writ is issued "command[ing] the officer to whom it may be directed to replevy the goods and chattels in possession of defendant . . . and to summon the defendant to answer the complaint." Fla. Stat. Ann. § 78.08 (Supp. 1972-1973). If the goods are "in any dwelling house or other building or enclosure," the officer is required to demand their delivery; but, if they are not delivered, "he shall cause such house, building or enclosure to be broken open and shall make replevin according to the writ . . . ."

Thus, at the same moment that the defendant receives the complaint seeking repossession of property through court action, the property is seized from him. He is provided no prior notice and allowed no opportunity whatever to challenge the issuance of the writ. After the property has been seized, he will eventually have an opportunity for a hearing, as the defendant in the trial of the court action for repossession, which the plaintiff is required to pursue. And he is also not wholly without recourse in the meantime. For under the Florida statute, the officer who seizes the property must keep it for three days, and during that period the defendant may reclaim possession of the property by posting his own security bond in double its value. But if he does not post such a bond, the property is transferred to the party who sought the writ, pending a final judgment in the underlying action for repossession.

* * *

Although these prejudgment replevin statutes are descended from the common-law replevin action of six centuries ago, they bear very little resemblance to it. Replevin at common law was an action for the return of specific goods wrongfully taken or "distrained." Typically, it was used after a landlord (the "distrainor") had seized possessions from a tenant (the "distrainee") to satisfy a debt allegedly owed. If the tenant then instituted a replevin action and posted security, the landlord could be ordered to return the property at once, pending a final judgment in the underlying action. However, this prejudgment replevin of goods at common law did not follow from an entirely ex parte process of pleading by the distrainee. For "[t]he distrainor could always stop the action of replevin by claiming to be the owner of the goods; and as this claim was often made merely to delay the proceedings, the writ de proprietate probanda was devised early in the fourteenth century, which enabled the sheriff to determine summarily the question of ownership. If the question of ownership was determined against the distrainor the goods were delivered back to the distrainee [pending final judgment]." 3 W. Holdsworth, History of English Law 284 (1927).

Prejudgment replevin statutes like those of Florida and Pennsylvania are derived from this ancient possessory action in that they authorize the seizure of property before a final judgment. But the similarity ends there. As in the present cases, such statutes are most commonly used by creditors to seize goods allegedly wrongfully detained—not wrongfully taken—by debtors. At common law, if a creditor wished to invoke state power to recover goods wrongfully detained, he had to proceed through the action of debt or detinue. These actions, however, did not provide for a return of property before final judgment. And, more importantly, on the occasions when the common law did allow prejudgment seizure by state power, it provided some kind of notice and opportunity to be heard to the party then in possession of the property, and a state official made at least a summary determination of the relative rights of the disputing parties before stepping into the dispute and taking goods from one of them.

For more than a century the central meaning of procedural due process has been clear: "Parties whose rights are to be affected are entitled to be heard; and in order that they may enjoy that right they must first be notified." It is equally fundamental that the right to notice and an opportunity to be heard "must be granted at a meaningful time and in a meaningful manner."

The primary question in the present cases is whether these state statutes are constitutionally defective in failing to provide for hearings "at a meaningful time." The Florida replevin process guarantees an opportunity for a hearing after the seizure of goods, and the Pennsylvania process allows a post-seizure hearing if the aggrieved party shoulders the burden of initiating one. But neither the Florida nor the Pennsylvania statute provides for notice or an opportunity to be heard before the seizure. The issue is whether procedural due process in the context of these cases requires an opportunity for a hearing before the State authorizes its agents to seize property in the possession of a person upon the application of another.

The constitutional right to be heard is a basic aspect of the duty of government to follow a fair process of decision-making when it acts to deprive a person of his possessions. The purpose of this requirement is not only to ensure abstract fair play to the individual. Its purpose, more particularly, is to protect his use and possession of property from arbitrary encroachment— to minimize substantively unfair or mistaken deprivations of property, a danger that is especially great when the State seizes goods simply upon the application of and for the benefit of a private party. So viewed, the prohibition against the deprivation of property without due process of law reflects the high value, embedded in our constitutional and political history, that we place on a person's right to enjoy what is his, free of governmental interference.

The requirement of notice and an opportunity to be heard raises no impenetrable barrier to the taking of a person's possessions. But the fair process of decision-making that it guarantees works, by itself, to protect against arbitrary deprivation of property. For when a person has an opportunity to speak up in his own defense, and when the State must listen to what he has to say, substantively unfair and simply mistaken deprivations of property interests can be prevented. It has long been recognized that "fairness can rarely be obtained by secret, one-sided determination of facts decisive of rights. . . . [And n]o better instrument has been devised for arriving at truth than to give a person in jeopardy of serious loss notice of the case against him and opportunity to meet it."

If the right to notice and a hearing is to serve its full purpose, then, it is clear that it must be granted at a time when the deprivation can still be prevented. At a later hearing, an individual's possessions can be returned to him if they were unfairly or mistakenly taken in the first place. Damages may even be awarded to him for the wrongful deprivation. But no later hearing and no damage award can undo the fact that the arbitrary taking that was subject to the right of procedural due process has already occurred. "This Court has not . . . embraced the general proposition that a wrong may be done if it can be undone."

This is no new principle of constitutional law. The right to a prior hearing has long been recognized by this Court under the Fourteenth and Fifth Amendments. Although the Court has held that due process tolerates variances in the form of a hearing "appropriate to the nature of the case," Mullane v. Central Hanover Tr. Co., 339 U. S. 306, 313, and "depending upon the importance of the interests involved and the nature of the subsequent proceedings [if any]," Boddie v. Connecticut, 401 U. S. 371, 378, the Court has traditionally insisted that, whatever its form, opportunity for that hearing must be provided before the deprivation at issue takes effect.

* * *

The Florida and Pennsylvania prejudgment replevin statutes fly in the face of this principle. To be sure, the requirements that a party seeking a writ must first post a bond, allege conclusorily that he is entitled to specific goods, and open himself to possible liability in damages if he is wrong, serve to deter wholly unfounded applications for a writ. But those requirements are hardly a substitute for a prior hearing, for they test no more than the strength of the applicant's own belief in his rights. Since his private gain is at stake, the danger is all too great that his confidence in his cause will be misplaced. Lawyers and judges are familiar with the phenomenon of a party mistakenly but firmly convinced that his view of the facts and law will prevail, and therefore quite willing to risk the costs of litigation. Because of the understandable, self-interested fallibility of litigants, a court does not decide a dispute until it has had an opportunity to hear both sides—and does not generally take even tentative action until it has itself examined the support for the plaintiff's position. The Florida and Pennsylvania statutes do not even require the official issuing a writ of replevin to do that much.

The minimal deterrent effect of a bond requirement is, in a practical sense, no substitute for an informed evaluation by a neutral official. More specifically, as a matter of constitutional principle, it is no replacement for the right to a prior hearing that is the only truly effective safeguard against arbitrary deprivation of property. While the existence of these other, less effective, safeguards may be among the considerations that affect the form of hearing demanded by due process, they are far from enough by themselves to obviate the right to a prior hearing of some kind.

* * *

A deprivation of a person's possessions under a prejudgment writ of replevin, at least in theory, may be only temporary. The Florida and Pennsylvania statutes do not require a person to wait until a post-seizure hearing and final judgment to recover what has been replevied. Within three days after the seizure, the statutes allow him to recover the goods if he, in return, surrenders other property—a payment necessary to secure a bond in double the value of the goods seized from him. But it is now well settled that a temporary, nonfinal deprivation of property is nonetheless a "deprivation" in the terms of the Fourteenth Amendment. Sniadach v. Family Finance Corp., 395 U. S. 337; Bell v. Burson, 402 U. S. 535. Both Sniadach and Bell involved takings of property pending a final judgment in an underlying dispute. In both cases, the challenged statutes included recovery provisions, allowing the defendants to post security to quickly regain the property taken from them. Yet the Court firmly held that these were deprivations of property that had to be preceded by a fair hearing.

The present cases are no different. When officials of Florida or Pennsylvania seize one piece of property from a person's possession and then agree to return it if he surrenders another, they deprive him of property whether or not he has the funds, the knowledge, and the time needed to take advantage of the recovery provision. The Fourteenth Amendment draws no bright lines around three-day, 10-day or 50-day deprivations of property. Any significant taking of property by the State is within the purview of the Due Process Clause. While the length and consequent severity of a deprivation may be another factor to weigh in determining the appropriate form of hearing, it is not decisive of the basic right to a prior hearing of some kind.

* * *

There are "extraordinary situations" that justify postponing notice and opportunity for a hearing. Boddie v. Connecticut, 401 U. S., at 379. These situations, however, must be truly unusual. Only in a few limited situations has this Court allowed outright seizure without opportunity for a prior hearing. First, in each case, the seizure has been directly necessary to secure an important governmental or general public interest. Second, there has been a special need for very prompt action. Third, the State has kept strict control over its monopoly of legitimate force: the person initiating the seizure has been a government official responsible for determining, under the standards of a narrowly drawn statute, that it was necessary and justified in the particular instance. Thus, the Court has allowed summary seizure of property to collect the internal revenue of the United States, to meet the needs of a national war effort, to protect against the economic disaster of a bank failure, and to protect the public from misbranded drugs and contaminated food.

The Florida and Pennsylvania prejudgment replevin statutes serve no such important governmental or general public interest. They allow summary seizure of a person's possessions when no more than private gain is directly at stake. The replevin of chattels, as in the present cases, may satisfy a debt or settle a score. But state intervention in a private dispute hardly compares to state action furthering a war effort or protecting the public health.

Nor do the broadly drawn Florida and Pennsylvania statutes limit the summary seizure of goods to special situations demanding prompt action. There may be cases in which a creditor could make a showing of immediate danger that a debtor will destroy or conceal disputed goods. But the statutes before us are not "narrowly drawn to meet any such unusual condition." Sniadach v. Family Finance Corp., supra, at 339. And no such unusual situation is presented by the facts of these cases.

The statutes, moreover, abdicate effective state control over state power. Private parties, serving their own private advantage, may unilaterally invoke state power to replevy goods from another. No state official participates in the decision to seek a writ; no state official reviews the basis for the claim to repossession; and no state official evaluates the need for immediate seizure. There is not even a requirement that the plaintiff provide any information to the court on these matters. The State acts largely in the dark.

* * *

We hold that the Florida and Pennsylvania prejudgment replevin provisions work a deprivation of property without due process of law insofar as they deny the right to a prior opportunity to be heard before chattels are taken from their possessor. Our holding, however, is a narrow one. We do not question the power of a State to seize goods before a final judgment in order to protect the security interests of creditors so long as those creditors have tested their claim to the goods through the process of a fair prior hearing. The nature and form of such prior hearings, moreover, are legitimately open to many potential variations and are a subject, at this point, for legislation—not adjudication. Since the essential reason for the requirement of a prior hearing is to prevent unfair and mistaken deprivations of property, however, it is axiomatic that the hearing must provide a real test. "[D]ue process is afforded only by the kinds of `notice' and `hearing' that are aimed at establishing the validity, or at least the probable validity, of the underlying claim against the alleged debtor before he can be deprived of his property . . . ." Sniadach v. Family Finance Corp., supra, at 343 (Harlan, J., concurring).

For the foregoing reasons, the judgments of the District Courts are vacated and these cases are remanded for further proceedings consistent with this opinion.

It is so ordered.

Mitchell v. W.T. Grant Co.
416 U.S. 600 (1974)

MR. JUSTICE WHITE delivered the opinion of the Court.

In this case, a state trial judge in Louisiana ordered the sequestration of personal property on the application of a creditor who had made an installment sale of the goods to petitioner and whose affidavit asserted delinquency and prayed for sequestration to enforce a vendor's lien under state law. The issue is whether the sequestration violated the Due Process Clause of the Fourteenth Amendment because it was ordered ex parte, without prior notice or opportunity for a hearing.

On February 2, 1972, respondent W. T. Grant Co. filed suit in the First City Court of the City of New Orleans, Louisiana, against petitioner, Lawrence Mitchell. The petition alleged the sale by Grant to Mitchell of a refrigerator, range, stereo, and washing machine, and an overdue and unpaid balance of the purchase price for said items in the amount of $574.17. Judgment for that sum was demanded. It was further alleged that Grant had a vendor's lien on the goods and that a writ of sequestration should issue to sequester the merchandise pending the outcome of the suit. The accompanying affidavit of Grant's credit manager swore to the truth of the facts alleged in the complaint. It also asserted that Grant had reason to believe petitioner would "encumber, alienate or otherwise dispose of the merchandise described in the foregoing petition during the pendency of these proceedings, and that a writ of sequestration is necessary in the premises." Based on the foregoing petition and affidavit, and without prior notice to Mitchell or affording him opportunity for hearing, the judge of the First City Court, Arthur J. O'Keefe, then signed an order that "a writ of sequestration issue herein" and that "the Constable of this court sequester and take into his possession the articles of merchandise described in the foregoing petition, upon plaintiff furnishing bond in the amount of $1,125." Bond in that amount having been filed by the respondent, the writ of sequestration issued, along with citation to petitioner Mitchell, citing him to file a pleading or make appearance in the First City Court of the city of New Orleans within five days. The citation recited the filing of the writ of sequestration and the accompanying affidavit, order, and bond. On March 3 Mitchell filed a motion to dissolve the writ of sequestration issued on February 2. The motion asserted that the personal property at issue had been seized under the writ on February 7, 1972, and claimed, first, that the goods were exempt from seizure under state law and, second, that the seizure violated the Due Process Clauses of the State and Federal Constitutions in that it had occurred without prior notice and opportunity to defend petitioner's right to possession of the property.

The motion came on for hearing on March 14. It was then stipulated that a vendor's lien existed on the items, arguments of counsel were heard, and on March 16 the motion to dissolve was denied. The goods were held not exempt from seizure under state law. The trial court also ruled that "the provisional seizure enforced through sequestration" was not a denial of due process of law. "To the contrary," the trial judge said, "plaintiff insured defendant's right to due process by proceeding in accordance with Louisiana Law as opposed to any type of self-help seizure which would have denied defendant possession of his property without due process." The appellate courts of Louisiana refused to disturb the rulings of the trial court, the Supreme Court of Louisiana expressly rejecting petitioner's due process claims pressed under the Federal Constitution. We granted certiorari and now affirm the judgment of the Louisiana Supreme Court.

Petitioner's basic proposition is that because he had possession of and a substantial interest in the sequestered property, the Due Process Clause of the Fourteenth Amendment necessarily forbade the seizure without prior notice and opportunity for a hearing. In the circumstances presented here, we cannot agree.

Petitioner no doubt "owned" the goods he had purchased under an installment sales contract, but his title was heavily encumbered. The seller, W. T. Grant Co., also had an interest in the property, for state law provided it with a vendor's lien to secure the unpaid balance of the purchase price. Because of the lien, Mitchell's right to possession and his title were subject to defeasance in the event of default in paying the installments due from him. His interest in the property, until the purchase price was paid in full, was no greater than the surplus remaining, if any, after foreclosure and sale of the property in the event of his default and satisfaction of outstanding claims. The interest of Grant, as seller of the property and holder of a vendor's lien, was measured by the unpaid balance of the purchase price. The monetary value of that interest in the property diminished as payments were made, but the value of the property as security also steadily diminished over time as it was put to its intended use by the purchaser.

Plainly enough, this is not a case where the property sequestered by the court is exclusively the property of the defendant debtor. The question is not whether a debtor's property may be seized by his creditors, pendente lite, where they hold no present interest in the property sought to be seized. The reality is that both seller and buyer had current, real interests in the property, and the definition of property rights is a matter of state law. Resolution of the due process question must take account not only of the interests of the buyer of the property but those of the seller as well.

With this duality in mind, we are convinced that the Louisiana sequestration procedure is not invalid, either on its face or as applied. Sequestration under the

Louisiana statutes is the modern counterpart of an ancient civil law device to resolve conflicting claims to property. Historically, the two principal concerns have been that, pending resolution of the dispute, the property would deteriorate or be wasted in the hands of the possessor and that the latter might sell or otherwise dispose of the goods. A minor theme was that official intervention would forestall violent self-help and retaliation.

Louisiana statutes provide for sequestration where "one claims the ownership or right to possession of property, or a mortgage, lien, or privilege thereon . . . if it is within the power of the defendant to conceal, dispose of, or waste the property or the revenues therefrom, or remove the property from the parish, during the pendency of the action." The writ, however, will not issue on the conclusory allegation of ownership or possessory rights. Article 3501[4] provides that the writ of sequestration shall issue "only when the nature of the claim and the amount thereof, if any, and the grounds relied upon for the issuance of the writ clearly appear from specific facts" shown by a verified petition or affidavit. In the parish where this case arose, the clear showing required must be made to a judge, and the writ will issue only upon his authorization and only after the creditor seeking the writ has filed a sufficient bond to protect the vendee against all damages in the event the sequestration is shown to have been improvident.

The writ is obtainable on the creditor's ex parte application, without notice to the debtor or opportunity for a hearing, but the statute entitles the debtor immediately to seek dissolution of the writ, which must be ordered unless the creditor "proves the grounds upon which the writ was issued," the existence of the debt, lien, and delinquency, failing which the court may order return of the property and assess damages in favor of the debtor, including attorney's fees.

The debtor, with or without moving to dissolve the sequestration, may also regain possession by filing his own bond to protect the creditor against interim damage to him should he ultimately win his case and have judgment against the debtor for the unpaid balance of the purchase price which was the object of the suit and of the sequestration.

In our view, this statutory procedure effects a constitutional accommodation of the conflicting interests of the parties. We cannot accept petitioner's broad assertion that the Due Process Clause of the Fourteenth Amendment guaranteed to him the use and possession of the goods until all issues in the case were judicially resolved after full adversary proceedings had been completed. It is certainly clear under this Court's precedents that issues can be limited in actions for possession. Indeed, in Grant Timber & Mfg. Co. v. Gray, 236 U. S. 133 (1915) (Holmes, J.), the Court upheld such limitations in possessory actions for real property in Louisiana. Petitioner's claim must accordingly be narrowed to one for a hearing on the issues in the possessory action—default, the existence of a lien, and possession of the debtor—before property is taken.

* * *

Petitioner asserts that his right to a hearing before his possession is in any way disturbed is nonetheless mandated by a long line of cases in this Court, culminating in Sniadach v. Family Finance Corp., 395 U. S. 337 (1969), and Fuentes v. Shevin, 407 U. S. 67 (1972). The pre-Sniadach cases are said by petitioner to hold that "the opportunity to be heard must precede any actual deprivation of private property." Their import, however, is not so clear as petitioner would have it: they merely stand for the proposition that a hearing must be had before one is finally deprived of his property and do not deal at all with the need for a pretermination hearing where a full and immediate post-termination hearing is provided. The usual rule has been "[w]here only property rights are involved, mere postponement of the judicial enquiry is not a denial of due process, if the opportunity given for ultimate judicial determination of liability is adequate." . . ."We have repeatedly held that no hearing at the preliminary stage is required by due process so long as the requisite hearing is held before the final administrative order becomes effective." "It is sufficient, where only property rights are concerned, that there is at some stage an opportunity for a hearing and a judicial determination."

* * *

In Sniadach v. Family Finance Corp., supra, it was said that McKay and like cases dealt with "[a] procedural rule that may satisfy due process for attachments in general" but one that would not "necessarily satisfy procedural due process in every case," nor one that "gives necessary protection to all property in its modern forms." 395 U. S., at 340. Sniadach involved the prejudgment garnishment of wages—"a specialized type of property presenting distinct problems in our economic system." Ibid. Because "[t]he leverage of the creditor on the wage earner is enormous" and because "prejudgment garnishment of the Wisconsin type may as a practical matter drive a wage-earning family to the wall," it was held that the Due Process Clause forbade such garnishment absent notice and prior hearing. Id., at 341-342. In Sniadach, the Court also observed that garnishment was subject to abuse by creditors without valid claims, a risk minimized by the nature of the security interest here at stake and the protections to the debtor offered by Louisiana procedure. Nor was it apparent in Sniadach with what speed the debtor could challenge the validity of the garnishment, and obviously the creditor's claim could not rest on the danger of destruction of wages, the property seized, since their availability to satisfy the debt remained within the power of the debtor who could simply leave his job. The suing creditor in Sniadach had no prior interest in the property attached, and the opinion did not purport to govern the typical case of the installment seller who brings a suit to collect an unpaid balance and who does not seek to attach wages pending the outcome of the suit but to repossess the sold property on which he had retained a lien to secure the purchase price. This very case soon came before the Court in Fuentes v. Shevin, where the constitutionality of the Florida and Pennsylvania replevin statutes was at issue. Those statutes permitted the secured installment seller to repossess the goods sold, without notice or hearing and without judicial order or supervision, but with the help of the sheriff operating under a writ issued by the court clerk at the behest of the seller. Because carried out without notice or opportunity for hearing and without judicial participation, this kind of seizure was held violative of the Due Process Clause. This holding is the mainstay of petitioner's submission here. But we are convinced that Fuentes was decided against a factual and legal background sufficiently different from that now before us and that it does not require the invalidation of the Louisiana sequestration statute, either on its face or as applied in this case.

The Florida law under examination in Fuentes authorized repossession of the sold goods without judicial order, approval, or participation. A writ of replevin was employed, but it was issued by the court clerk. As the Florida law was perceived by this Court, "[t]here is no requirement that the applicant make a convincing showing before the seizure," the law required only "the bare assertion of the party seeking the writ that he is entitled to one" as a condition to the clerk's issuance of the writ. Id., at 74. The Court also said that under the statute the defendant-buyer would "eventually" have an opportunity for a hearing, "as the defendant in the trial of the court action for repossession . . . ." The Pennsylvania law was considered to be essentially the same as that of Florida except that it did "not require that there ever be opportunity for a hearing on the merits of the conflicting claims to possession of the replevied property." The party seeking the writ was not obliged to initiate a court action for repossession, was not required formally to allege that he was entitled to the property and had only to file an affidavit of the value of the property sought to be replevied. The Court distinguished the Pennsylvania and Florida procedures from that of the common law where, the Court said, "a state official made at least a summary determination of the relative rights of the disputing parties before stepping into the dispute and taking goods from one of them."

The Louisiana sequestration statute followed in this case mandates a considerably different procedure. A writ of sequestration is available to a mortgage or lien holder to forestall waste or alienation of the property, but, different from the Florida and Pennsylvania systems, bare, conclusory claims of ownership or lien will not suffice under the Louisiana statute. Article 3501 authorizes the writ "only when the nature of the claim and the amount thereof, if any, and the grounds relied upon for the issuance of the writ clearly appear from specific facts" shown by verified petition or affidavit. Moreover, in the parish where this case arose, the requisite showing must be made to a judge, and judicial authorization obtained. Mitchell was not at the unsupervised mercy of the creditor and court functionaries. The Louisiana law provides for judicial control of the process from beginning to end.[12] This control is one of the measures adopted by the State to minimize the risk that the ex parte procedure will lead to a wrongful taking. It is buttressed by the provision that should the writ be dissolved there are "damages for the wrongful issuance of a writ" and for attorney's fees "whether the writ is dissolved on motion or after trial on the merits."

The risk of wrongful use of the procedure must also be judged in the context of the issues which are to be determined at that proceeding. In Florida and Pennsylvania property was only to be replevied in accord with state policy if it had been "wrongfully detained." This broad "fault" standard is inherently subject to factual determination and adversarial input. . . . In Fuentes this fault standard for replevin was thought ill-suited for preliminary ex parte determination. In Louisiana, on the other hand, the facts relevant to obtaining a writ of sequestration are narrowly confined. As we have indicated, documentary proof is particularly suited for questions of the existence of a vendor's lien and the issue of default. There is thus far less danger here that the seizure will be mistaken and a corresponding decrease in the utility of an adversary hearing which will be immediately available in any event.

Of course, as in Fuentes, consideration of the impact on the debtor remains. Under Louisiana procedure, however, the debtor, Mitchell, was not left in limbo to await a hearing that might or might not "eventually" occur, as the debtors were under the statutory schemes before the Court in Fuentes. Louisiana law expressly provides for an immediate hearing and dissolution of the writ "unless the plaintiff proves the grounds upon which the writ was issued."

To summarize, the Louisiana system seeks to minimize the risk of error of a wrongful interim possession by the creditor. The system protects the debtor's interest in every conceivable way, except allowing him to have the property to start with, and this is done in pursuit of what we deem an acceptable arrangement pendente lite to put the property in the possession of the party who furnishes protection against loss or damage to the other pending trial on the merits.

The Court must be sensitive to the possible consequences, already foreseen in antiquity, of invalidating this state statute. Doing so might not increase private violence, but self-help repossession could easily lessen protections for the debtor. Here, the initial hardship to the debtor is limited, the seller has a strong interest, the process proceeds under judicial supervision and management, and the prevailing party is protected against all loss. Our conclusion is that the Louisiana standards regulating the use of the writ of sequestration are constitutional. Mitchell was not deprived of procedural due process in this case. The judgment of the Supreme Court of Louisiana is affirmed.

So ordered.

NOTES What factors led the court in *Mitchell* to conclude the Louisiana procedure for pre-judgment seizure was constitutional while the procedures in *Sniadach* and *Fuentes* were held to be unconstitutional?

In *Mathews v. Eldridge*, 424 U. S. 319, 335 (1976), the Court set forth three factors that normally determine whether an individual has received the "process" that the Constitution finds "due":

"First, the private interest that will be affected by the official action; second, the risk of an erroneous deprivation of such interest through the procedures used, and the probable value, if any, of additional or substitute procedural safeguards; and finally, the Government's interest, including the function involved and the fiscal and administrative burdens that the additional or substitute procedural requirement would entail."

By weighing these concerns, courts can determine whether a State has met the "fundamental requirement of due process" — "the opportunity to be heard `at a meaningful time and in a meaningful manner.'" *Id.*, at 333.

PROBLEM On August 13, 1998, a Los Angeles police officer ordered Edwin David's automobile towed from a spot where parking was forbidden. After paying $134.50, David recovered his car. David, believing that the trees obstructed his view of the "no parking" sign, requested a hearing to recover the money. On September 9, 1998 — 27 days after the vehicle was towed — the city held the hearing and denied David's claim. David then brought a lawsuit in Federal District Court under 42 U. S. C. § 1983, arguing that the city, in failing to provide a sufficiently prompt hearing, had violated his federal right to "due process of law." How should the court rule? (See, *City of Los Angeles v. David* 538 U.S. 715 (2003)

PRELIMINARY INJUNCTIONS AND TEMPORARY RESTRAINING ORDERS

INTRODUCTION

The purpose of the preliminary injunction is to maintain the status quo between the litigants pending final determination of the case. *United Mine Workers* (1947) 330 U.S. 258 affirmed the power of a court of equity to issue an order to preserve the status quo in order to protect its ability to render judgment in a case over which it might have jurisdiction. The authority of a court to issue a preliminary injunction is governed by FRCP 65(a).

Winter v. Natural Resources Defense Council, Inc.,
555 U.S. 7, 129 S.Ct. 365 (2008)

"To be prepared for war is one of the most effectual means of preserving peace." 1 Messages and Papers of the Presidents 57 (J. Richardson comp. 1897). So said George Washington in his first Annual Address to Congress, 218 years ago. One of the most important ways the Navy prepares for war is through integrated training exercises at sea. These exercises include training in the use of modern sonar to detect and track enemy submarines, something the Navy has done for the past 40 years. The plaintiffs, respondents here, complained that the Navy's sonar-training program harmed marine mammals, and that the Navy should have prepared an environmental impact statement before commencing its latest round of training exercises. The Court of Appeals upheld a preliminary injunction imposing restrictions on the Navy's sonar training, even though that court acknowledged that "the record contains no evidence that marine mammals have been harmed" by the Navy's exercises.

The Court of Appeals was wrong, and its decision is reversed.

The Navy deploys its forces in "strike groups," which are groups of surface ships, submarines, and aircraft centered around either an aircraft carrier or an amphibious assault ship. Seamless coordination among strike-group assets is critical. Before deploying a strike group, the Navy requires extensive integrated training in analysis and prioritization of threats, execution of military missions, and maintenance of force protection.

Antisubmarine warfare is currently the Pacific Fleet's top war-fighting priority. Modern diesel-electric submarines pose a significant threat to Navy vessels because they can operate almost silently, making them extremely difficult to detect and track. Potential adversaries of the United States possess at least 300 of these submarines.

The most effective technology for identifying submerged diesel-electric submarines within their torpedo range is active sonar, which involves emitting pulses of sound underwater and then receiving the acoustic waves that echo off the target. Active sonar is a particularly useful tool because it provides both the bearing and the distance of target submarines; it is also sensitive enough to allow the Navy to track enemy submarines that are quieter than the surrounding marine environment. This case concerns the Navy's use of "mid-frequency active" (MFA) sonar, which transmits sound waves at frequencies between 1 kHz and 10 kHz.

Not surprisingly, MFA sonar is a complex technology, and sonar operators must undergo extensive training to become proficient in its use. Sonar reception can be affected by countless different factors, including the time of day, water density, salinity, currents, weather conditions, and the contours of the sea floor. Id., at 278a-279a. When working as part of a strike group, sonar operators must be able to coordinate with other Navy ships and planes while avoiding interference. The Navy conducts regular training exercises You under realistic conditions to ensure that sonar operators are thoroughly skilled in its use in a variety of situations.

The waters off the coast of southern California (SOCAL) are an ideal location for conducting integrated training exercises, as this is the only area on the west coast that is relatively close to land, air, and sea bases, as well as amphibious landing areas. At issue in this case are the Composite Training Unit Exercises and the Joint Tactical Force Exercises, in which individual naval units (ships, submarines, and aircraft) train together as members of a strike group. A strike group cannot be certified for deployment until it has successfully completed the integrated training exercises, including a demonstration of its ability to operate under simulated hostile conditions. In light of the threat posed by enemy submarines, all strike groups must demonstrate proficiency in antisubmarine warfare. Accordingly, the SOCAL exercises include extensive training in detecting, tracking, and neutralizing enemy submarines. The use of MFA sonar during these exercises is "mission-critical," given that MFA sonar is the only proven method of identifying submerged diesel-electric submarines operating on battery power.

Sharing the waters in the SOCAL operating area are at least 37 species of marine mammals, including dolphins, whales, and sea lions. The parties strongly dispute the extent to which the Navy's training activities will harm those animals or disrupt their behavioral patterns. The Navy emphasizes that it has used MFA sonar during training exercises in SOCAL for 40 years, without a single documented sonar-related injury to any marine mammal. The Navy asserts that, at most, MFA sonar may cause temporary hearing loss or brief disruptions of marine mammals' behavioral patterns.

The plaintiffs are the Natural Resources Defense Council, Inc., Jean-Michael Cousteau (an environmental enthusiast and filmmaker), and several other groups devoted to the protection of marine mammals and ocean habitats. They contend that MFA sonar can cause much more serious injuries to marine mammals than the Navy acknowledges, including permanent hearing loss, decompression sickness, and major behavioral disruptions. According to the plaintiffs, several mass strandings of marine mammals (outside of SOCAL) have been "associated" with the use of active sonar. They argue that certain species of marine mammals — such as beaked whales — are uniquely susceptible to injury from active sonar; these injuries would not necessarily be detected by the Navy, given that beaked whales are "very deep divers" that spend little time at the surface.

The procedural history of this case is rather complicated. The Marine Mammal Protection Act of 1972 (MMPA), 86 Stat. 1027, generally prohibits any individual from "taking" a marine mammal, defined as harassing, hunting, capturing, or killing it. 16 U.S.C. §§ 1362(13), 1372(a). The Secretary of Defense may "exempt any action or category of actions" from the MMPA if such actions are "necessary for national defense." § 1371(f)(1). In January 2007, the Deputy Secretary of Defense — acting for the Secretary — granted the Navy a 2-year exemption from the MMPA for the training exercises at issue in this case. Pet.App. 219a-220a. The exemption was conditioned on the Navy adopting several mitigation procedures, . . .

The National Environmental Policy Act of 1969 (NEPA), requires federal agencies "to the fullest extent possible" to prepare an environmental impact statement (EIS) for "every ... major Federal actio[n] significantly affecting the quality of the human environment." 42 U.S.C. § 4332(2)(C) (2000 ed.). An agency is not required to prepare a full EIS if it determines — based on a shorter environmental assessment (EA) — that the proposed action will not have a significant impact on the environment. 40 CFR §§ 1508.9(a), 1508.13 (2007).

In February 2007, the Navy issued an EA concluding that the 14 SOCAL training exercises scheduled through January 2009 would not have a significant impact on the environment. . .

Shortly after the Navy released its EA, the plaintiffs sued the Navy, seeking declaratory and injunctive relief on the grounds that the Navy's SOCAL training exercises violated NEPA, the Endangered Species Act of 1973(ESA), and the Coastal Zone Management Act of 1972 (CZMA). The District Court granted plaintiffs' motion for a preliminary injunction and prohibited the Navy from using MFA sonar during its remaining training exercises. The court held that plaintiffs had "demonstrated a probability of success" on their claims under NEPA and the CZMA. The court also determined that equitable relief was appropriate because, under Ninth Circuit precedent, plaintiffs had established at least a "'possibility'" of irreparable harm to the environment. Based on scientific studies, declarations from experts, and other evidence in the record, the District Court concluded that there was in fact a "near certainty" of irreparable injury to the environment, and that this injury outweighed any possible harm to the Navy.

The Navy filed an emergency appeal, and the Ninth Circuit stayed the injunction pending appeal. After hearing oral argument, the Court of Appeals agreed with the District Court that preliminary injunctive relief was appropriate. The appellate court concluded, however, that a blanket injunction prohibiting the Navy from using MFA sonar in SOCAL was overbroad, and remanded the case to the District Court "to narrow its injunction so as to provide mitigation conditions under which the Navy may conduct its training exercises."

On remand, the District Court entered a new preliminary injunction allowing the Navy to use MFA sonar only as long as it implemented . . . mitigation measures.

The Court of Appeals further determined that plaintiffs had carried their burden of establishing a "possibility" of irreparable injury. Even under the Navy's own figures, the court concluded, the training exercises would cause 564 physical injuries to marine mammals, as well as 170,000 disturbances of marine mammals' behavior. Lastly, the Court of Appeals held that the balance of hardships and consideration of the public interest weighed in favor of the plaintiffs. The court emphasized that the negative impact on the Navy's training exercises was "speculative," since the Navy has never before operated under the procedures required by the District Court. In particular, the court determined that: (1) The 2,200-yard shutdown zone imposed by the District Court was unlikely to affect the Navy's operations, because the Navy often shuts down its MFA sonar systems during the course of training exercises; and (2) the power-down requirement during significant surface ducting conditions was not unreasonable because such conditions are rare, and the Navy has previously certified strike groups that had not trained under such conditions. The Ninth Circuit concluded that the District Court's preliminary injunction struck a proper balance between the competing interests at stake.

We granted certiorari and now reverse and vacate the injunction.

A plaintiff seeking a preliminary injunction must establish that he is likely to succeed on the merits, that he is likely to suffer irreparable harm in the absence of preliminary relief, that the balance of equities tips in his favor, and that an injunction is in the public interest.

The District Court and the Ninth Circuit concluded that plaintiffs have shown a likelihood of success on the merits of their NEPA claim. The Navy strongly disputes this determination, arguing that plaintiffs' likelihood of success is low because the CEQ reasonably concluded that "emergency circumstances" justified alternative arrangements to NEPA compliance. Plaintiffs' briefs before this Court barely discuss the ground relied upon by the lower courts — that the plain meaning of "emergency circumstances" does not encompass a court order that was "entirely predictable" in light of the parties' litigation history. Instead, plaintiffs contend that the CEQ's actions violated the separation of powers by readjudicating a factual issue already decided by an Article III court. Moreover, they assert that the CEQ's interpretations of NEPA are not entitled to deference because the CEQ has not been given statutory authority to conduct adjudications.

The District Court and the Ninth Circuit also held that when a plaintiff demonstrates a strong likelihood of prevailing on the merits, a preliminary injunction may be entered based only on a "possibility" of irreparable harm. The lower courts held that plaintiffs had met this standard because the scientific studies, declarations, and other evidence in the record established to "a near certainty" that the Navy's training exercises would cause irreparable harm to the environment.

The Navy challenges these holdings, arguing that plaintiffs must demonstrate a likelihood of irreparable injury — not just a possibility — in order to obtain preliminary relief. On the facts of this case, the Navy contends that plaintiffs' alleged injuries are too speculative to give rise to irreparable injury, given that ever since the Navy's training program began 40 years ago, there has been no documented case of sonar-related injury to marine mammals in SOCAL. And even if MFA sonar does cause a limited number of injuries to individual marine mammals, the Navy asserts that plaintiffs have failed to offer evidence of species-level harm that would adversely affect their scientific, recreational, and ecological interests. For their part, plaintiffs assert that they would prevail under any formulation of the irreparable injury standard, because the District Court found that they had established a "near certainty" of irreparable harm.

We agree with the Navy that the Ninth Circuit's "possibility" standard is too lenient. Our frequently reiterated standard requires plaintiffs seeking preliminary relief to demonstrate that irreparable injury is likely in the absence of an injunction. Issuing a preliminary injunction based only on a possibility of irreparable harm is inconsistent with our characterization of injunctive relief as an extraordinary remedy that may only be awarded upon a clear showing that the plaintiff is entitled to such relief.

It is not clear that articulating the incorrect standard affected the Ninth Circuit's analysis of irreparable harm. Although the court referred to the "possibility" standard, and cited Circuit precedent along the same lines, it affirmed the District Court's conclusion that plaintiffs had established a "'near certainty'" of irreparable harm...

As explained in the next section, even if plaintiffs have shown irreparable injury from the Navy's training exercises, any such injury is outweighed by the public interest and the Navy's interest in effective, realistic training of its sailors. A proper consideration of these factors alone requires denial of the requested injunctive relief. For the same reason, we do not address the lower courts' holding that plaintiffs have also established a likelihood of success on the merits.

A preliminary injunction is an extraordinary remedy never awarded as of right. In each case, courts "must balance the competing claims of injury and must consider the effect on each party of the granting or withholding of the requested relief." "In exercising their sound discretion, courts of equity should pay particular regard for the public consequences in employing the extraordinary remedy of injunction." In this case, the District Court and the Ninth Circuit significantly understated the burden the preliminary injunction would impose on the Navy's ability to conduct realistic training exercises, and the injunction's consequent adverse impact on the public interest in national defense...

This case involves "complex, subtle, and professional decisions as to the composition, training, equipping, and control of a military force," which are "essentially professional military judgments." We "give great deference to the professional judgment of military authorities concerning the relative importance of a particular military interest." As the Court emphasized just last Term, "neither the Members of this Court nor most federal judges begin the day with briefings that may describe new and serious threats to our Nation and its people."

Here, the record contains declarations from some of the Navy's most senior officers, all of whom underscored the threat posed by enemy submarines and the need for extensive sonar training to counter this threat...

These interests must be weighed against the possible harm to the ecological, scientific, and recreational interests that are legitimately before this Court...

While we do not question the seriousness of these interests, we conclude that the balance of equities and consideration of the overall public interest in this case tip strongly in favor of the Navy. For the plaintiffs, the most serious possible injury would be harm to an unknown number of the marine mammals that they study and observe. In contrast, forcing the Navy to deploy an inadequately trained antisubmarine force jeopardizes the safety of the fleet. Active sonar is the only reliable technology for detecting and tracking enemy diesel-electric submarines, and the President — the Commander in Chief — has determined that training with active sonar is "essential to national security."

The public interest in conducting training exercises with active sonar under realistic conditions plainly outweighs the interests advanced by the plaintiffs. Of course, military interests do not always trump other considerations, and we have not held that they do. In this case, however, the proper determination of where the public interest lies does not strike us as a close question. . . .

As noted above, we do not address the underlying merits of plaintiffs' claims. While we have authority to proceed to such a decision at this point, doing so is not necessary here. In addition, reaching the merits is complicated by the fact that the lower courts addressed only one of several issues raised, and plaintiffs have largely chosen not to defend the decision below on that ground.[5]

At the same time, what we have said makes clear that it would be an abuse of discretion to enter a permanent injunction, after final decision on the merits, along the same lines as the preliminary injunction. An injunction is a matter of equitable discretion; it does not follow from success on the merits as a matter of course. ("[A] federal judge sitting as chancellor is not mechanically obligated to grant an injunction for every violation of law"). . .

The judgment of the Court of Appeals is reversed, and the preliminary injunction is vacated to the extent it has been challenged by the Navy.

It is so ordered.

TEMPORARY RESTRAINING ORDERS

FRCP 65(b) authorizes a court to issue a temporary restraining order. Temporary restraining orders (TROs) are granted after a brief hearing where evidence may be presented by affidavit. TROs may be granted without a hearing or notice provided there is some exigent circumstance or necessity. TRO's can last no longer than 14 days, and may be renewed once, for an additional 14 days. A party that needs the benefits of a TRO for longer than the aggregate 28 days must seek a preliminary injunction under FRCP 65(a).)

A temporary restraining order may be issued without any notice when the circumstances warrant. In view of the possibly drastic consequence of a temporary restraining order, the opposition should be heard, if feasible, before the order is granted. Many judges have properly insisted that, when time does not permit of formal notice of the application to the adverse party, some expedient, such as telephonic notice to the attorney for the adverse party, be resorted to if this can reasonably be done. On occasion, however, temporary restraining orders have been issued without any notice when it was feasible for some fair, although informal, notice to be given. Before notice can be dispensed with, the applicant's counsel must give his certificate as to any efforts made to give notice and the reasons why notice should not be required. This certificate is in addition to the requirement of an affidavit or verified complaint setting forth the facts as to the irreparable injury which would result before the opposition could be heard. (Notes of Advisory Committee on Rules—1966 Amendment)

Since both a preliminary injunction or a TRO can be granted before a full hearing on the merits, F.R.C.P. 65(c) requires a bond in order to ensure that the plaintiff will be able to pay all or at least some of the damages that the defendant incurs from the preliminary injunction if it turns out to have been wrongfully issued. The U.S. Supreme Court has held that a party injured by the issuance of an injunction later determined to be erroneous has no action for damages in the absence of a bond. *W.R. Grace & Co. v. Local Union 759, United Rubber Workers,* 461 U.S. 757 (1983). State statutes may create express exceptions to the requirement that a bond be posted. See, e.g., Cal.Code.Civ.Proc. § 529(b).

F.R.C.P 65 (d) provides that injunctions and restraining orders shall be "binding only upon the parties to the action, their officers, agents, servants, employees, and attorneys, and upon those persons in active concert or participation with them who receive actual notice of the order by personal service or otherwise." A TRO or preliminary injunction is binding only on those "who receive actual notice of the order by personal service or otherwise."

This page left intentionally blank.

CHAPTER 8

DISCOVERY

Discovery is the process by which the parties may learn what evidence their opponents and other parties to the lawsuit may possess or know of which will support their claims, contentions and defenses. In modern civil litigation, the discovery process is probably the most time-consuming (and oftentimes most costly) phase of litigation. Under FRCP 26, a party is entitled to discover not only material which is relevant and admissible at trial, but also to discover information which "appears reasonably calculated to lead to the discovery of admissible evidence."

DISCOVERY PROCEDURES AND METHODS

Discovery is a self-executing process, meaning the parties initiate and control discovery and only ask the intervention of the court in the event of a dispute. FRCP 26(a)(1) requires that a party must, "without awaiting a discovery request" reveal to the other party certain basic information supporting that party's claims or defenses. Such information typically includes, but is not limited to, names of witnesses, the existence of documents and bases for damage calculations. For example, a plaintiff must disclose information that he or she "may use to support" his or her claims. That will include the identity and contact information for the witnesses one might use, a description and the location of his or her medical and wage records, and a calculation of his or her damage claims.

Additionally, the following discovery methods are recognized by rule:

DEPOSITIONS BY ORAL EXAMINATION

A party may, by oral questions, depose (take the sworn testimony) of any person, including a party. (FRCP 30; Cal.Code.Civ.Proc. § 2025.010)

INTERROGATORIES

A self-executing procedure for submission of written questions to a party to be answered under oath. (FRCP 33; Cal.Code.Civ.Proc. § 2030)

Demands to Inspect or Produce Documents

A party may make inspection demands on "any other party to the action" to produce and permit the party making the request to inspect and copy, any designated documents. (FRCP 34; Cal.Code.Civ.Proc. § 2031.010)

Requests for Admission

A written request that a party admit genuineness of relevant documents or truth of relevant matters. FRCP 36(a) provides that one party may serve upon any other party a written request to admit the truth of certain matters of fact that are in dispute or to admit the genuineness of any relevant document. The party who receives the request to admit must respond under oath and in timely fashion, admitting or denying each matter for which an admission is requested. The responding party may also object to a request because improperly phrased (as "vague," "ambiguous", etc.) or because it seeks privileged or protected information. (FRCP 36; Cal.Code.Civ.Proc. § 2033.010)

Physical and Mental Examinations

Procedure by motion for court order, on showing of good cause, to obtain a mental or physical examination of a party or controlled person whose condition is in controversy in the pending action. (FRCP 35; Cal.Code.Civ.Proc. § 2032.010)

The Scope of Discovery

Discovery may cover not only evidence for use at the trial but also inquiry into matters in themselves inadmissible as evidence but that will lead to the discovery of such evidence. The purpose of discovery is to allow a broad search for facts, the names of witnesses, or any other matters which may aid a party in the preparation or presentation of his case. (Engl v. Aetna Life Ins. Co. (C.C.A.2d, 1943) 139 F.(2d) 469)

Scope of Discovery

Parties may obtain discovery regarding any nonprivileged matter that is relevant to any party's claim or defense.

Evidence need not be admissible at trial in order to be discoverable.

Privileged information may not be discovered.

Butler v. Rigsby
1998 U.S. Dist. LEXIS 4618 (E.D. La. 1998)

VANCE, J.

American Medical Group ("AMG") and Midtown Health Care ("MHC") object to Magistrate Judge Chasez's ruling of February 20, 1998. For the reasons that follow, Magistrate Judge Chasez's order is affirmed in part, and reversed in part.

I. Background

This lawsuit arises out of an automobile accident. [Butler and others, alleging injuries from a collision involving a gravel truck, sued Rigsby, the truck driver, and his employer.] AMG and MHC are not parties to this lawsuit, but doctors from both groups provided medical treatment to all of the plaintiffs. Defendants filed identical notices of depositions on AMG and MHC, in which defendants requested certain documents and information....

AMG and MHC moved the Court for a protective order prohibiting defendants from discovering the information requested....Magistrate Judge Chasez concluded that most of the information was discoverable. Specifically, she ordered the following:

AMG and MHC are to provide defendants with a computer printout listing their current patients....In addition, AMG and MHC are to provide defendants with a listing of the total number of patients referred to them by Jose Castro, Evan Tolchinsky, and/or the Personal Injury Law Center ("PILC") between July 1, 1995 and June 30, 1996. At the deposition of AMG and MHC...defendants may inquire as to the net income of those two entities and what percentage of the net income is litigation-related....

Order, Feb. 18, 1998 (Rec. Doc. No. 139).

AMG and MHC object to the Magistrate Judge's ruling. They insist that the information is not relevant to the lawsuit, it is unduly burdensome to non-parties, and some of the information is privileged....

II. Discussion

B. Scope of Discovery in General

The Federal Rules contemplate liberal discovery and provide for a flexible treatment of relevance. Under Rule 26(b)(1) of the Federal Rules of Civil Procedure, the scope of discovery includes any matter, not privileged, that is relevant to ["any party's claim or defense—including the existence, description, nature, custody, condition, and location of any books, documents, or other tangible things and the identity and location of persons who know of any discoverable matter"]. Fed. R. Civ. P. 26(b)(1). The rules make clear that the discovery need not be admissible at trial "[if the discovery] appears reasonably calculated to lead to the discovery of admissible evidence."

Discovery may be limited by the court if it determines that "the discovery sought is unreasonably cumulative or duplicative." Fed. R. Civ. P. 26(b)[(2)(C)(i)]. The court may also restrict discovery if it concludes that "the burden or expense of the proposed discovery outweighs its likely benefit, taking into account the needs of the case, the amount in controversy, the parties['] resources, the importance of the issues at stake in the litigation, and the importance of the proposed discovery in resolving the issues." [Rule 26(b)(2)(C)(iii).] Further, the federal rules provide that the court "may make any order which justice requires to protect a party or person from annoyance, embarrassment, oppression, or undue burden or expense." Fed. R. Civ. P. 26(c)[(1)].

C. The Discovery in Dispute

1. A Listing of the Total Number of Patients Referred to AMG and/or MHC by Castro, Tolchinsky, and/or the PILC

AMG and MHC argue that this information has no relevance to plaintiffs' lawsuit, and the request is unduly burdensome. Defendants contend that they seek this information in order to show that the medical groups receive substantial income from the attorneys who initially represented the plaintiffs in this matter, and they argue that such evidence is relevant to show potential bias.

Magistrate Judge Chasez's conclusion that the sought-after information was discoverable was not contrary to law. Evidence of a special relationship between an expert witness and legal counsel is relevant to demonstrate the possible bias of the expert witness, and discovery that is reasonably calculated to lead to such evidence should be permitted....

Further, it was not clearly erroneous for Magistrate Judge Chasez to conclude that the expense or burden of producing this information did not outweigh its likely benefits....However, in light of the medical groups' concerns of time and expense and the sworn affidavit that states that compiling the requested information would require that each individual chart be manually pulled and reviewed, the Court orders that defendants shall pay one-half the costs associated with composing the list of the total number of patients....

2. The Net Income of the Entities and the Percentage of Net Income That [Is] Litigation Related

Allowing the discovery of this information was neither contrary to law nor clearly erroneous. The courts have held that the amount of income derived from services related to testifying as an expert witness is relevant to show bias or financial interest....

3. A Computer Printout of AMG's and MHC's Current Patients

Magistrate Judge Chasez ordered that the medical groups are to provide defendants with a computer printout listing their current patients as well as any patient lists that were previously generated. AMG and MHC insist that lists of their current or past patients are privileged from discovery pursuant to La. R.S. 13:3734. The Court agrees and concludes that the magistrate judge's ruling was contrary to law. Rule 501 of the Federal Rules of Evidence provides that [the state law of privilege—here, that of Louisiana—shall govern in diversity cases]....

...Louisiana courts have broadly interpreted the scope of the health care provider-patient privilege. [Louisiana's] First Circuit Court of Appeal has concluded that "when an individual walks into a doctor's office and opens his mouth, that everything spilling out of it, whether it be his identity or his false teeth..., is presumptively privileged and beyond the reach of discovery." Sarphie v. Rowe, 618 So. 2d 905, 908 (La. App. 1st Cir.), writ denied, 620 So. 2d 1324 (La. 1993)....

In light of this precedent, the Court concludes that the AMG/MHC lists of current and/or past patients is privileged, and the information is therefore not discoverable. Moreover, this Court does not see how the identity of these patients could be relevant to this litigation in any event. Magistrate Judge Chasez's order compelling AMG and MHC to disclose their patient lists was contrary to law, and it is reversed.

For all of the foregoing reasons,

IT IS ORDERED that Magistrate Judge Chasez's ruling of February 20, 1998 is affirmed in part, and reversed in part, in accordance with the Court's conclusions as set forth above.

Favale v. Roman Catholic Diocese of Bridgeport
233 F.R.D. 243 (D. Conn. 2005)

SQUATRITO, J.

Now pending in the above-captioned matter is plaintiffs' motion to compel and defendant's motion for a protective order.... For the reasons that follow, plaintiffs' motion to compel is DENIED and defendant's motion for a protective order is GRANTED.

Background

Plaintiff Maryann Favale worked as an administrative assistant at Saint Joseph's

School in Brookfield, Connecticut, for approximately twenty-one years. During this time period, in November of 2002, Sister Bernice Stobierski became the new interim principal. Then, in May 2003, Sister Stobierski assumed the position of full-time principal. Maryann Favale alleges that Sister Stobierski subjected her to "severe and repeated sexual harassment" in the workplace from December 2002 to June 2003. Specifically, plaintiff alleges that Sister Stobierski touched her inappropriately, made sexually suggestive comments, exhibited lewd behavior, and requested physical affection. Plaintiff first informed her employer, the Roman Catholic Diocese of Bridgeport, ("the Diocese") of the alleged sexual harassment on June 11, 2003. Maryann Favale, who no longer works at Saint Joseph's School, seeks damages against the Diocese for sexual harassment, retaliation, defamation, intentional and negligent infliction of emotional distress, negligent hiring, negligent supervision, and other causes of action. In addition, co-plaintiff Mark Favale asserts a claim for loss of consortium against the defendant. Sister Stobierski is not a party to this case.

Plaintiffs now seek to compel Sister Stobierski to testify to any prior treatment she may have received for her alleged anger management history and psychological or psychiatric conditions. Plaintiffs also move to compel the Diocese to produce any records it has of any such treatment. [The Diocese objects to both motions to compel on relevance grounds, among others.]...

Sister Stobierski's Testimony

Plaintiffs assert that Sister Stobierski's testimony regarding the treatment she received for her alleged anger management, psychological, and psychiatric conditions is relevant to their claims of negligent hiring and negligent supervision. To assert a negligent hiring claim under Connecticut law, a plaintiff must "[p]lead and prove that she was injured by the defendant's own negligence in failing to select as its employee a person who was fit and competent to perform the job in question and that her injuries resulted from the employee's unfit or incompetent performance of his work." Similarly, Connecticut law requires that a plaintiff bringing a negligent supervision claim plead and prove that he suffered an injury due to the defendant's failure to supervise an employee whom the defendant had a duty to supervise. A defendant does not owe a duty of care to protect a plaintiff from another employee's tortious acts unless the defendant knew or reasonably should have known of the employee's propensity to engage in that type of tortious conduct.

Both negligent hiring and negligent supervision claims turn upon the type of wrongful conduct that actually precipitated the harm suffered by plaintiff. "It is well settled that defendants cannot be held liable for their alleged negligent hiring, training, supervision or retention of an employee accused of wrongful conduct unless they had notice of said employee's propensity for the type of behavior causing the plaintiff's harm."

Plaintiffs allege that the defendant negligently hired and supervised an individual who was not fit to be the principal of an elementary school. They contend that the "defendant knew or reasonably should have known that Sister Stobierski was unfit to be the principal of St. Joseph's School as a result of her prior emotional and anger management issues, and limited school administration experience."...Yet, plaintiffs do not allege that Sister Stobierski's prior emotional and anger management issues harmed plaintiff.

Rather, the only type of harm alleged to have been suffered by Maryann Favale was harm resulting from repeated acts of sexual harassment, and plaintiffs do not maintain that Sister Stobierski's alleged anger management and psychological or psychiatric conditions contributed to the sexual harassment. Accordingly, Sister Stobierski's testimony pertaining to the treatment she allegedly received for her anger management, psychological, or psychiatric conditions is not relevant because it does not pertain to the defense or claim of any party.

Indeed, even if the Diocese was aware of Sister Stobierski's alleged anger management history or psychological or psychiatric conditions, this knowledge would have no bearing on plaintiffs' claims for negligent supervision and negligent hiring because the wrongful conduct of which the Diocese would have had notice was not the same type of wrongful conduct that caused Maryann Favale harm. Notice of Sister Stobierski's alleged anger management history or psychological or psychiatric conditions does not equate to notice of Sister Stobierski's propensity to commit acts of sexual harassment. The Diocese's objection to plaintiffs' motion to compel the testimony of Sister Stobierski is sustained, and plaintiffs' motion is denied.

The Production of Defendant's Records Relating to Sister Stobierski

Plaintiffs assert that any documentation that the Roman Catholic Diocese of Bridgeport may have regarding Sister Stobierski's treatment for anger management or psychological and psychiatric conditions is relevant to their claims of negligent hiring and negligent supervision. The elements of these claims are discussed above.... [E]ven if the defendant possessed documents relating to treatment Sister Stobierski received for her alleged anger management or psychological and psychiatric conditions, these records would not establish Sister Stobierski's propensity for the type of behavior that caused Maryann Favale harm because they would not demonstrate a propensity for sexual harassment. Again, it is significant that plaintiffs do not allege that Maryann Favale was harmed by Sister Stobierski's alleged inability to control her anger or her alleged psychological or psychiatric conditions. Sexual harassment is the only type of harm alleged by plaintiffs....

Defendant's motion for a protective order is granted. A protective order shall enter barring future discovery into Sister Stobierski's anger management or psychological and psychiatric treatment as the court finds that this information is profoundly personal and, as stated herein, not relevant to the claims in this case.

LIMITATIONS ON DISCOVERY

All provisions as to scope of discovery are subject to the initial qualification that the court may limit discovery in accordance with the Federal Rules. FRCP 26(c) confers broad powers on the courts to regulate or prevent discovery even though the materials sought are within the scope of 26(b), and these powers have always been freely exercised. For example, a party's income tax return is generally held not privileged, 2A Barron & Holtzoff, Federal Practice and Procedure, §65.2 (Wright ed. 1961), and yet courts have recognized that interests in privacy may call for a measure of extra protection. E.g., Wiesenberger v. W. E. Hutton & Co., 35 F.R.D. 556 (S.D.N.Y. 1964). Similarly, the courts have, in appropriate circumstances, protected materials that are primarily of an impeaching character. These two types of materials merely illustrate the many situations, not capable of governance by precise rule, in which courts must exercise judgment. (Notes of Advisory Committee on Rules—1970 Amendment)

Discovery and Privacy

FRCP 26(c) permits a party to seek a protective order (an order that certain matters not be inquired into) and gives the judge broad power to prevent abusive discovery. Rule 35 places limits on the use of discovery to compel physical or mental examinations. A protective order may be sought by any person against whom discovery is sought, party or nonparty. The burden is on the person seeking the protective order to show that it is necessary "to protect a party or person from annoyance, embarrassment, oppression or undue burden or expense." The types of protective orders available include but are not limited to orders that: "That discovery not be had."; "That the discovery may be had only on specified terms and conditions, including a designation of the time or place."; "That certain matters not be inquired into, or that the scope of the discovery be limited to certain matters."

Morales v. Superior Court
99 Cal.App.3d 283 (1979)

Petitioner James Morales seeks a writ of mandate commanding respondent court to vacate its order compelling him to answer interrogatories. The interrogatories were propounded by real party Teresi Trucking, Inc., one of several defendants in a wrongful death action brought by petitioner and his three minor children to recover damages resulting from the death of Phyllis Morales, petitioner's late wife. For the reasons to be explained, we have concluded that the interrogatories must be further limited, but that as so limited, they must be answered by petitioner.

Interrogatory No. 2 demands that the petitioner state the name, current address and telephone number of each woman he dated during his marriage to Phyllis Morales and the calendar dates upon which he saw these women socially. Interrogatory No. 3 asks whether during the period of his marriage to Phyllis Morales the petitioner had sexual relations with women other than Phyllis Morales and if so demands that he state the names, current addresses and telephone numbers of each woman with whom he had sexual relations during that time and the date or dates of the sexual relations with each woman so identified.

The petitioner objected to each of these interrogatories "on the grounds that it cannot possibly lead to any relevant discoverable evidence and it may violate the rights of privacy of certain individuals."

In the trial court the real party in interest filed a motion for an order compelling answers to the interrogatories. The motion was granted with the following limitation: "... Answers limited to contacts with other women within two years before decedent's death."

The question before us is whether a plaintiff in a wrongful death action may be compelled to disclose information regarding his extramarital sexual activities during the period of his marriage to decedent. This question has not previously been answered in California.

The petitioner bases his request upon a right to privacy in sexual relations and the right to associational privacy. In our examination of this question we follow the reasoning and apply the tests of Britt v. Superior Court (1978) 20 Cal.3d 844 [143 Cal. Rptr. 695, 574 P.2d 766]. In that case, the Supreme Court reversed the order of the superior court compelling plaintiffs to disclose names and identities of associations and persons with whom the plaintiffs had affiliated. The case involved a group of homeowners who sued the San Diego Unified Port District, which controlled the San Diego airport, for diminution of property values, personal injuries and emotional disturbance allegedly caused by the operation of the airport. The court found that the right of associational privacy is not absolute but that the government bears a heavy burden in demonstrating the justification for compelling disclosure. The court went on to find that to justify impairment of the right of privacy, there must be a present compelling state interest.

The Supreme Court held that when a litigant invokes judicial assistance to discover, in the context of civil litigation, matters which are within a constitutionally protected zone of privacy, such discovery "must be justified by a compelling state interest and must be precisely tailored to avoid undue infringement of constitutional rights." (Id., at pp. 864-865.)

We direct our attention first to relevancy.

1. (1) THE INQUIRY IS RELEVANT TO THE ISSUE BEFORE THE TRIAL COURT.

In Benwell v. Dean (1967) 249 Cal. App.2d 345 at page 349[57 Cal. Rptr. 394], the court stated: "... the statutory and exclusive measure of damages in actions for wrongful death is that embodied in Code of Civil Procedure section 377, which is 'such damages ... as under all the circumstances ... may be just.' Damages under the provisions of this section 'are measured by the financial benefits the heirs were receiving at the time of death, those reasonably to be expected in the future, and the monetary equivalent of loss of comfort, society and protection' (Stathos v. Lemich, 213 Cal. App.2d 52, 56 ...); as, stated in Cervantes v. Maco Gas Co., 177 Cal. App.2d 246 ..., such damages are 'what the heirs received at the time of the death of the decedent and what the heirs would have received had the decedent lived.' With respect to the loss of comfort, society and protection, this element of pecuniary loss recoverable under section 377 has an actual value which cannot be compensated for by merely nominal damages.

The question of whether extramarital sexual conduct affected the relationship is one of fact to be decided by the trier of fact. Evidence of such conduct is relevant to the nature of the personal relationship and thus as to whether there was any loss of love, companionship, comfort, affection, society, solace, moral support or enjoyment of sexual relations.

There is evidence that this is not simply a "fishing expedition." In the deposition of Cynthia Morales, who married petitioner after decedent's death but who is now divorced from him, there is an indication that during his marriage to decedent petitioner dated and "possibly had frequent sexual relations" with other women.

However, not all such evidence is necessarily relevant. Some limitation of the time to be covered by the discovery may properly be required. What happened 10 years before the decedent's death may or may not have relevance. This is so because the appropriate inquiry in the wrongful death case is the nature of the relationship at date of death. We do not attempt to say what period is proper. What is proper in a given case depends upon the facts of the case. The two-year limitation imposed by the trial court in this case does not appear to us to be unreasonable or improper. Of course, we are discussing this matter for purposes of discovery only. (2) As observed in Fults v. Superior Court (1979) 88 Cal. App.3d 899 at page 902 [152 Cal. Rptr. 210]: "... relevancy at trial and relevancy for purposes of discovery are two different things. 'An appellate court cannot reverse a trial court's grant of discovery under a "relevancy" attack unless it concludes that the answers sought by a given line of questioning cannot as a reasonable possibility lead to the discovery of admissible evidence or be helpful in preparation for trial.'

3) This does not end our inquiry. "When compelled disclosure intrudes on constitutionally protected areas, it cannot be justified solely on the ground that it may lead to relevant information."

Our second inquiry then is whether one or more constitutionally protected zones of privacy are involved.

2. THERE IS A PROTECTED RIGHT OF PRIVACY UNDER THE FACTS OF THIS CASE.

The right of privacy is secured by article I, section 1, of the California Constitution. This was added to the California Constitution in 1974. However, privacy was identified as a right protected by the federal Constitution in Griswold v. Connecticut (1965) 381 U.S. 479 [14 L.Ed.2d 510, 85 S.Ct. 1678], and its application to sexual matters has been steadily expanded The right of privacy in sexual matters is not limited to the marital relationship As was said in Fults v. Superior Court, supra, 88 Cal. App.3d 899 at page 904: "... [T]hese interrogatories deal with a well established `zone of privacy,' one's sexual relations."

The right to associational privacy was recognized in Britt. "As both the United States Supreme Court and this court have observed time and again, however, First Amendment freedoms, such as the right of association, `are protected not only against heavy-handed frontal attack, but also from being stifled by more subtle governmental interference.' Indeed, numerous cases establish that compelled disclosure of an individual's private associational affiliations and activities, ... frequently poses one of the most serious threats to the free exercise of this constitutionally endowed right." Since the associational privacy for which protection is requested in this case is concerned with association for extramarital activities, we treat the rights as merging for purposes of our consideration. (4) We follow the holdings that there is a right to privacy in sexual matters and that it is not limited to the marital relationship. However, we believe that the right is not absolute. As the Britt decision said: "Of course, as with all other First Amendment rights, the right of associational privacy is not absolute, and past cases recognize that under some circumstances disclosure may permissibly be compelled. Because of the constitutional interests at stake, however, the authorities establish that private association affiliations and activities ... `are presumptively immune from inquisition....' and thus the government bears the burden of demonstrating the justification for compelling disclosure. Moreover, the cases also make clear that in this context the government's burden is a particularly heavy one: `[T]o justify any impairment there must be present [a] "compelling state interest ... [which] justifies the substantial infringement of ... First Amendment rights. It is basic that no showing merely of a rational relationship to some colorable state interest would suffice; in this highly sensitive constitutional area `[o]nly the gravest abuses, endangering paramount interests, give occasion for permissible limitation,' [citation].'" We believe the same principle and the same tests apply to privacy in sexual matters.

We turn then to the question of the state interest in invasion of the right in the present case.

3. (5) THERE IS A COMPELLING STATE INTEREST SUPPORTING INTRUSION INTO THE PETITIONER'S CONSTITUTIONALLY PROTECTED RIGHT OF PRIVACY.

The state is said to have a compelling interest in "facilitating the ascertainment of truth in connection with legal proceedings." In the Britt case it was stated that a trial court could properly compel disclosure of protected associational activities when they were directly relevant and disclosure of the plaintiff's affiliation is essential to the fair resolution of the lawsuit. The petitioner here contends that unfairness would result rather than fairness because there would be prejudice from the disclosure to the jury or trial court of any extramarital activity. On the other hand, the real party in interest argues that unfairness would result if petitioner is allowed to paint an unrealistic picture of his relationship with his deceased wife.

(6) We are mindful that some detriment to petitioner's interest, and possibly to that of his children, may result. If answers are required for preparation of a fair trial and detriment results from such answers in order to obtain that preparation, the detriment will have to be suffered.

We find that the inquiries here could, as a reasonable possibility, lead to the discovery of potentially admissible evidence or be helpful in preparation for trial.

We then come to the fourth question and decide:

4. (7) THE ORDER BELOW WAS NOT DRAWN WITH THE REQUIRED NARROW SPECIFICITY.

"'Precision of [compelled disclosure] is required so that the exercise of our precious freedoms will not be unduly curtailed except to the extent necessitated by the legitimate governmental objective.'"

The privacy proposed to be invaded in this case is not that of the petitioner alone. If petitioner is required to answer the interrogatories as they are presently framed, he might have to divulge the names, addresses and phone numbers of other people. Their rights also deserve protection. As to them, there is no argument that the right to privacy has been forfeited by filing a lawsuit.

Further, the governmental objective of a fair trial in this case will be served if the petitioner is required to state whether, during some relevant period he dated other women, and, if so, when; and if during such relevant period he had extramarital contacts and, if so, when; without giving the names, addresses, or phone numbers of such people, if they exist. This information will permit defendants to explore the impairment of the relationship between petitioner and his deceased spouse by means consistent with the right of privacy of others. We are aware that requiring these limited answers will, to an extent, expose whatever there may be of a portion of petitioner's life which he may have regarded as protected. We believe the place at which we have drawn the line meets the needs of a fair trial while protecting petitioner's right of privacy to some extent and wholly protecting the rights of others.

For now we rule only that a fair resolution of the lawsuit requires exploration of the nature of the relationship between the deceased wife and her plaintiff husband by some exploration of possible outside sexual activity...

Let a writ issue directing the Superior Court of Kern County to modify its order so that plaintiff will not be required to give the names, addresses, or telephone numbers of anyone in response to interrogatories 2 or 3. The writ is otherwise denied.

Renfifo v. Erevos Enterprises, Inc.
2007 WL 894376 (S.D.N.Y. Mar. 20, 2007)

ELLIS, M.J.

Plaintiff, Willy Rengifo ("Rengifo") [who brings this action against his former employers to recover unpaid overtime wages under the federal Fair Labor Standards Act (FLSA) and New York Labor Law, among other claims] requests this Court to issue a protective order pursuant to Federal Rule of Civil Procedure 26(c) barring discovery related to his immigration status, social security number, and authorization to work in the United States....

Rule 26(c) authorizes courts, for good cause, to "make any order which justice requires to protect a party or person from annoyance, embarrassment, oppression, or undue burden or expense, including...that certain matters not be inquired into, or that the scope of the disclosure or discovery be limited to certain matters...." Fed. R. Civ. P. 26(c). "[T]he burden is upon the party seeking non-disclosure or a protective order to show good cause." Dove v. Atlantic Capital Corp., 963 F.2d 15, 19 (2d Cir. 1992) (citations omitted).

Rengifo argues that discovery related to his immigration status, authorization to work in this country, and social security number are not relevant to his right to recover unpaid wages. Further, Rengifo argues that the intimidating effect of requiring disclosure of immigration status is sufficient to establish "good cause" when the question of immigration status only goes to a collateral issue. Defendants argue that documents containing Rengifo's social security number or tax identification number, such as tax returns, are relevant to the issue of whether he is entitled to overtime wages, which is a central issue in this case. Additionally, defendants argue that the validity of Rengifo's social security number, his immigration status and authorization to work in this country are relevant to his credibility....

Courts have recognized the in terrorem effect of inquiring into a party's immigration status and authorization to work in this country when irrelevant to any material claim because it presents a "danger of intimidation [that] would inhibit plaintiffs in pursuing their rights." Liu v. Donna Karan International, Inc., 207 F. Supp. 2d 191, 193 (S.D.N.Y. 2002) (citations omitted). Here, Rengifo's immigration status and authority to work is a collateral issue. The protective order becomes necessary as "[i]t is entirely likely that any undocumented [litigant] forced to produce documents related to his or her immigration status will withdraw from the suit rather than produce such documents and face...potential deportation." Topo v. Dhir, 210 F.R.D. 76, 78 (S.D.N.Y. 2002)....

Rengifo also seeks to prevent disclosure of his social security number or tax identification number. Defendants note that, in support of his claim for unpaid overtime wages, Rengifo has produced an incomplete set of pay stubs that do not reflect all of the compensation he has received from corporate defendants, and that he has not produced any records regarding the number of hours he has worked on a weekly basis. Defendants contend, therefore, that discovery of documents containing his tax identification number or social security number, such as tax returns, is necessary and relevant to obtain this information. [The court rejects defendants' argument, reasoning that t]he information sought is not relevant to the claims in this case. Even if it were, however, the corporate defendants possess relevant data on hours and compensation, and there is no reason to assume that defendants' records are less reliable than any records maintained by Rengifo....

Defendants also assert that the documents requested would allow them to test the truthfulness of Rengifo's representations to his employer. They argue that by applying for a job and providing his social security number, Rengifo represented to defendants that he was a legal resident and they are entitled to test the truthfulness of that information. Defendants further argue that if Rengifo filed tax returns, this information would be relevant to his overtime claim, but if he failed to file tax returns, this fact would affect the veracity of statements he would potentially make at trial.

While it is true that credibility is always at issue, that "does not by itself warrant unlimited inquiry into the subject of immigration status when such examination would impose an undue burden on private enforcement of employment discrimination laws." Avila-Blum v. Casa de Cambio Delgado, Inc., 236 F.R.D. 190, 192 (S.D.N.Y. 2006). A party's attempt to discover tax identification numbers on the basis of testing credibility appears to be a back door attempt to learn of immigration status. Further, the opportunity to test the credibility of a party based on representations made when seeking employment does not outweigh the chilling effect that disclosure of immigration status has on employees seeking to enforce their rights. "While documented workers face the possibility of retaliatory discharge for an assertion of their labor and civil rights, undocumented workers confront the harsher reality that, in addition to possible discharge, their employer will likely report them to the INS and they will be subjected to deportation proceedings or criminal prosecution." Rivera v. NIBCO, Inc., 364 F.3d 1057, 1064 (9th Cir. 2004). Granting employers the right to inquire into immigration status in employment cases would allow them to implicitly raise threats of such negative consequences when a worker reports illegal practices. Id. at 1065.

While defendants suggest a compromise whereby discovery would be limited to the present litigation and not disclosed to any third party for any purpose beyond this litigation, the limitation does not abate the chilling effect of such disclosure. "Even if the parties were to enter into a confidentiality agreement restricting the disclosure of such discovery…, there would still remain 'the danger of intimidation, the danger of destroying the cause of action' and would inhibit plaintiffs in pursuing their rights." Liu, 207 F. Supp. 2d at 193 (quoting Ansoumana v. Gristede's Operating Corp., 201 F.R.D. 81 (S.D.N.Y. 2001)). This Court finds that defendants' opportunity to test the credibility of Rengifo does not outweigh the public interest in allowing employees to enforce their rights.

For the foregoing reasons, Rengifo's application for a protective order barring defendants from inquiring into his immigration status, social security number or tax identification number, and authorization to work in the United States is GRANTED.

TRIAL PREPARATION MATERIAL

Some of the most controversial and vexing problems to emerge from the discovery rules have arisen out of requests for the production of documents or things prepared in anticipation of litigation or for trial. Two verbally distinct doctrines have developed, each conferring a qualified immunity on these materials—the "good cause" requirement in Rule 34 (now generally held applicable to discovery of documents via deposition under Rule 45 and interrogatories under Rule 33) and the work-product doctrine of *Hickman v. Taylor, supra*. Both demand a showing of justification before production can be had, the one of "good cause" and the other variously described in the *Hickman* case: "necessity or justification," "denial * * * would unduly prejudice the preparation of petitioner's case," or "cause hardship or injustice." (Notes of Advisory Committee on Rules—1970 Amendment)

> **Work Product**
>
> Ordinarily, a party may not discover documents and tangible things that are prepared in anticipation of litigation or for trial by or for another party or its representative.

Hickman v. Taylor
329 U.S. 495 (1947)

Mr. Justice MURPHY delivered the opinion of the Court.

This case presents an important problem under the Federal Rules of Civil Procedure, as to the extent to which a party may inquire into oral and written statements of witnesses, or other information, secured by an adverse party's counsel in the course of preparation for possible litigation after a claim has arisen....

On February 7, 1943, the tug "J.M. Taylor" sank while engaged in helping to tow a car float of the Baltimore & Ohio Railroad across the Delaware River at Philadelphia. The accident was apparently unusual in nature, the cause of it still being unknown. Five of the nine crew members were drowned. Three days later the tug owners and the underwriters employed a law firm, of which respondent Fortenbaugh is a member, to defend them against potential suits by representatives of the deceased crew members and to sue the railroad for damages to the tug.

A public hearing was held on March 4, 1943, before the United States Steamboat Inspectors, at which the four survivors were examined. This testimony was recorded and made available to all interested parties. Shortly thereafter, Fortenbaugh privately interviewed the survivors and took statements from them with an eye toward the anticipated litigation; the survivors signed these statements on March 29. Fortenbaugh also interviewed other persons believed to have some information relating to the accident and in some cases he made memoranda of what they told him. At the time when Fortenbaugh secured the statements of the survivors, representatives of two of the deceased crew members had been in communication with him. Ultimately claims were presented by representatives of all five of the deceased; four of the claims, however, were settled without litigation. The fifth claimant, petitioner herein, brought suit in a federal court under the Jones Act on November 26, 1943, naming as defendants the two tug owners, individually and as partners, and the railroad.

One year later, petitioner filed 39 interrogatories directed to the tug owners. The 38th interrogatory read: "State whether any statements of the members of the crews of the Tugs 'J.M. Taylor' and 'Philadelphia' or of any other vessel were taken in connection with the towing of the car float and the sinking of the Tug 'John M. Taylor.' [Plaintiff also asked for] exact copies of all such statements if in writing, and if oral, set forth in detail the exact provisions of any such oral statements or reports."...

The tug owners, through Fortenbaugh,...while admitting that statements of the survivors had been taken,...declined to summarize or set forth the contents. They did so on the ground that such requests called "for privileged matter obtained in preparation for litigation" and constituted "an attempt to obtain indirectly counsel's private files." It was claimed that answering these requests "would involve practically turning over not only the complete files, but also the telephone records and, almost, the thoughts of counsel."...[When the district court ordered Fortenbaugh to produce the requested statements, he refused, and the court ordered him imprisoned until he complied (but stayed the order pending an appeal).]

The pre-trial deposition-discovery mechanism established by Rules 26 to 37 is one of the most significant innovations of the Federal Rules of Civil Procedure. Under the prior federal practice, the pre-trial functions of notice-giving issue-formulation and fact-revelation were performed primarily and inadequately by the pleadings. Inquiry into the issues and the facts before trial was narrowly confined and was often cumbersome in method. The new rules, however, restrict the pleadings to the task of general notice-giving and invest the deposition-discovery process with a vital role in the preparation for trial. The various instruments of discovery now serve (1) as a device, along with the pre-trial hearing under Rule 16, to narrow and clarify the basic issues between the parties, and (2) as a device for ascertaining the facts, or information as to the existence or whereabouts of facts, relative to those issues. Thus civil trials in the federal courts no longer need be carried on in the dark. The way is now clear, consistent with recognized privileges, for the parties to obtain the fullest possible knowledge of the issues and facts before trial....

We agree, of course, that the deposition-discovery rules are to be accorded a broad and liberal treatment. No longer can the time-honored cry of "fishing expedition" serve to preclude a party from inquiring into the facts underlying his opponent's case. Mutual knowledge of all the relevant facts gathered by both parties is essential to proper litigation. To that end, either party may compel the other to disgorge whatever facts he has in his possession. The deposition-discovery procedure simply advances the stage at which the disclosure can be compelled from the time of trial to the period preceding it, thus reducing the possibility of surprise. But discovery, like all matters of procedure, has ultimate and necessary boundaries. As indicated by Rules [26(c) and 30(d)], limitations inevitably arise when it can be shown that the examination is being conducted in bad faith or in such a manner as to annoy, embarrass or oppress the person subject to the inquiry. And as Rule 26(b) provides, further limitations come into existence when the inquiry touches upon the irrelevant or encroaches upon the recognized domains of privilege.

We also agree that the memoranda, statements and mental impressions in issue in this case fall outside the scope of the attorney-client privilege and hence are not protected from discovery on that basis. It is unnecessary here to delineate the content and scope of that privilege as recognized in the federal courts. For present purposes, it suffices to note that the protective cloak of this privilege does not extend to information which an attorney secures from a witness while acting for his client in anticipation of litigation. Nor does this privilege concern the memoranda, briefs, communications and other writings prepared by counsel for his own use in prosecuting his client's case; and it is equally unrelated to writings which reflect an attorney's mental impressions, conclusions, opinions or legal theories.

But the impropriety of invoking that privilege does not provide an answer to the problem before us. Petitioner has made more than an ordinary request for relevant, non-privileged facts in the possession of his adversaries or their counsel. He has sought discovery as of right of oral and written statements of witnesses whose identity is well known and whose availability to petitioner appears unimpaired. He has sought production of these matters after making the most searching inquiries of his opponents as to the circumstances surrounding the fatal accident, which inquiries were sworn to have been answered to the best of their information and belief. Interrogatories were directed toward all the events prior to, during and subsequent to the sinking of the tug. Full and honest answers to such broad inquiries would necessarily have included all pertinent information gleaned by Fortenbaugh through his interviews with the witnesses. Petitioner makes no suggestion, and we cannot assume, that the tug owners or Fortenbaugh were incomplete or dishonest in the framing of their answers. In addition, petitioner was free to examine the public testimony of the witnesses taken before the United States Steamboat Inspectors. We are thus dealing with an attempt to secure the production of written statements and mental impressions contained in the files and the mind of the attorney Fortenbaugh without any showing of necessity or any indication or claim that denial of such production would unduly prejudice the preparation of petitioner's case or cause him any hardship or injustice. For aught that appears, the essence of what petitioner seeks either has been revealed to him already through the interrogatories or is readily available to him direct from the witnesses for the asking....

In our opinion, neither Rule 26 nor any other rule dealing with discovery contemplates production under such circumstances. That is not because the subject matter is privileged or irrelevant, as those concepts are used in these rules. Here is simply an attempt, without purported necessity or justification, to secure written statements, private memoranda and personal recollections prepared or formed by an adverse party's counsel in the course of his legal duties. As such, it falls outside the arena of discovery and contravenes the public policy underlying the orderly prosecution and defense of legal claims. Not even the most liberal of discovery theories can justify unwarranted inquiries into the files and the mental impressions of an attorney.

Historically, a lawyer is an officer of the court and is bound to work for the advancement of justice while faithfully protecting the rightful interests of his clients. In performing his various duties, however, it is essential that a lawyer work with a certain degree of privacy, free from unnecessary intrusion by opposing parties and their counsel. Proper preparation of a client's case demands that he assemble information, sift what he considers to be the relevant from the irrelevant facts, prepare his legal theories and plan his strategy without undue and needless interference. That is the historical and the necessary way in which lawyers act within the framework of our system of jurisprudence to promote justice and to protect their clients' interests. This work is reflected, of course, in interviews, statements, memoranda, correspondence, briefs, mental impressions, personal beliefs, and countless other tangible and intangible ways—aptly though roughly termed by the Circuit Court of Appeals in this case as the "work product of the lawyer." Were such materials open to opposing counsel on mere demand, much of what is now put down in writing would remain unwritten. An attorney's thoughts, heretofore inviolate, would not be his own. Inefficiency, unfairness and sharp practices would inevitably develop in the giving of legal advice and in the preparation of cases for trial. The effect on the legal profession would be demoralizing. And the interests of the clients and the cause of justice would be poorly served.

We do not mean to say that all written materials obtained or prepared by an adversary's counsel with an eye toward litigation are necessarily free from discovery in all cases. Where relevant and non-privileged facts remain hidden in an attorney's file and where production of those facts is essential to the preparation of one's case, discovery may properly be had. Such written statements and documents might, under certain circumstances, be admissible in evidence or give clues as to the existence or location of relevant facts. Or they might be useful for purposes of impeachment or corroboration. And production might be justified where the witnesses are no longer available or can be reached only with difficulty. Were production of written statements and documents to be precluded under such circumstances, the liberal ideals of the deposition-discovery portions of the Federal Rules of Civil Procedure would be stripped of much of their meaning. But the general policy against invading the privacy of an attorney's course of preparation is so well recognized and so essential to an orderly working of our system of legal procedure that a burden rests on the one who would invade that privacy to establish adequate reasons to justify production through a subpoena or court order....

But as to oral statements made by witnesses to Fortenbaugh, whether presently in the form of his mental impressions or memoranda, we do not believe that any showing of necessity can be made under the circumstances of this case so as to justify production....

Denial of production of this nature does not mean that any material, non-privileged facts can be hidden from the petitioner in this case. He need not be unduly hindered in the preparation of his case, in the discovery of facts or in his anticipation of his opponents' position. Searching interrogatories directed to Fortenbaugh and the tug owners, production of written documents and statements upon a proper showing and direct interviews with the witnesses themselves all serve to reveal the facts in Fortenbaugh's possession to the fullest possible extent consistent with public policy. Petitioner's counsel frankly admits that he wants the oral statements only to help prepare himself to examine witnesses and to make sure that he has overlooked nothing. That is insufficient under the circumstances to permit him an exception to the policy underlying the privacy of Fortenbaugh's professional activities. If there should be a rare situation justifying production of these matters, petitioner's case is not of that type....

NOTES Protected against disclosure from discovery are the mental impressions, conclusions, opinions, or legal theories concerning the litigation of an attorney or other representative of a party. The *Hickman* opinion drew special attention to the need for protecting an attorney against discovery of memoranda prepared from recollection of oral interviews. The courts have steadfastly safeguarded against disclosure of lawyers' mental impressions and legal theories, as well as mental impressions and subjective evaluations of investigators and claim-agents. (See, Notes of Advisory Committee on Rules—1970 Amendment.)

> **Work Product**
>
> There is an absolute privilege for writings that reflect the attorney's impressions, conclusions, opinions, legal research, or theories. Such information is not discoverable under any circumstances.

Nacht & Lewis Architects, Inc., v. Superior Court
47 Cal.App.4th 214 (1996)

PUGLIA, P.J.

Real party in interest (plaintiff) filed a civil complaint against petitioners (defendants) regarding her former employment with defendant Nacht & Lewis Architects, Inc. In response to Judicial Council approved form interrogatory No. 12.1, defendants provided the names of seven persons who witnessed, or who defendants claimed had knowledge of, the "incident," defined as "the circumstances and events surrounding the alleged accident, injury, or other occurrence or breach of contract giving rise to this action or proceeding." However, defendants objected to and refused to answer interrogatories requesting the identity of and information regarding individuals interviewed concerning the incident (form interrogatory No. 12.2) and individuals from whom written or recorded statements were obtained concerning the incident (form interrogatory No. 12.3). Defendants' responses to interrogatories Nos. 12.2 and 12.3 were identical: "Counsel for the Defendants has conducted interviews of employees of Nacht & Lewis Architects. The information collected from the interviews is protected by the attorney-client privilege and work product doctrine."

By order dated March 7, 1996, the respondent court granted plaintiff's motion to compel further responses to interrogatories Nos. 12.2 and 12.3. (1) Defendants contend the court's order violates the qualified work product privilege. We agree the respondent court erred in compelling further response to interrogatory No. 12.2. Compelled production of a list of potential witnesses interviewed by opposing counsel would necessarily reflect counsel's evaluation of the case by revealing which witnesses or persons who claimed knowledge of the incident (already identified by defendants' response to interrogatory No. 12.1) counsel deemed important enough to interview. (Cf. City of Long Beach v. Superior Court (1976) 64 Cal. App.3d 65, 73 [134 Cal. Rptr. 468] [compelled production of list of witnesses to be called at trial impermissibly reveals counsel's evaluation of the strengths and weaknesses of his case].)

(2) The issue is more subtle as to interrogatory No. 12.3. In their response to that interrogatory defendants did not state that their attorney took notes or otherwise recorded his interviews with employees of Nacht & Lewis, but that their attorney collected information from the interviews. Though imprecise, the language is susceptible to the interpretation that defendants' counsel collected from the employees statements the employees had previously written or recorded themselves.

The distinction is significant. A list of the potential witnesses interviewed by defendants' counsel which interviews counsel recorded in notes or otherwise would constitute qualified work product because it would tend to reveal counsel's evaluation of the case by identifying the persons who claimed knowledge of the incident from whom counsel deemed it important to obtain statements. Moreover, any such notes or recorded statements taken by defendants' counsel would be protected by the absolute work product privilege because they would reveal counsel's "impressions, conclusions, opinions, or legal research or theories" within the meaning of Code of Civil Procedure section 2018, subdivision (c).

On the other hand, a list of potential witnesses who turned over to counsel their independently prepared statements would have no tendency to reveal counsel's evaluation of the case. Such a list would therefore not constitute qualified work product. Moreover, unlike interview notes prepared by counsel, statements written or recorded independently by witnesses neither reflect an attorney's evaluation of the case nor constitute derivative material, and therefore are neither absolute nor qualified work product. The respondent court should compel further response to interrogatory No. 12.3 only to the extent the court determines defendants' counsel obtained an independently written or recorded statement from one or more of the employees interviewed by counsel.

Finally, we decline to consider whether the respondent court erred in denying defendants' motion to compel further responses to interrogatories. Defendants fail to demonstrate harm sufficient to warrant pretrial review, i.e., no privilege has been threatened, and defendants have not been denied discovery in that they may serve plaintiff with special interrogatories to obtain the information they seek.

We have previously notified the parties we were considering issuing a peremptory writ of mandate in the first instance, stayed the order compelling defendants' further responses to interrogatories Nos. 12.2 and 12.3, and provided plaintiff with the opportunity to file opposition to the petition. Having complied with the procedural requirements delineated in Palma v. U.S. Industrial Fasteners, Inc. (1984) 36 Cal.3d 171 [203 Cal. Rptr. 626, 681 P.2d 893], we are authorized to issue a peremptory writ of mandate in the first instance.

Let a peremptory writ of mandate issue directing the respondent superior court to vacate that portion of its order filed March 7, 1996, granting plaintiff's motion to compel further responses to interrogatories Nos. 12.2 and 12.3, to enter a new order denying plaintiff's motion to compel further response to interrogatory No. 12.2, and to take further action consistent with this opinion regarding interrogatory No. 12.3. Upon this decision becoming final, the stay previously issued is vacated.

NOTES An exception to the work product privilege enables a party or a nonparty witness to secure production of his or her own statement without any special showing of hardship or good cause. (See, Notes of Advisory Committee on Rules—1970 Amendment.)

Dowden v. Superior Court
73 Cal.App.4th 126 (1999)

RYLAARSDAM, J.

Petitioner filed a petition for writ of mandate seeking relief from an order granting a motion to compel production of a diary. Petitioner, who is an in propria persona litigant, claims a work product privilege under Code of Civil Procedure section 2018. (All further statutory references are to the Code of Civil Procedure.) Without determining whether his diary is in fact work product, we conclude that litigants appearing in propria persona may assert section 2018's work product privilege. We grant the petition and remand the matter to the trial court to conduct an in camera review of the diary to determine whether it contains matter which is privileged under section 2018.

FACTS

Real party in interest Daniel Dowden, plaintiff in the underlying action, and petitioner Douglas Dowden, defendant, are brothers. Following their mother's death they allegedly agreed to divide certain property held in joint tenancy. Real party in interest claimed petitioner breached the agreement and sued him for property damage and breach of contract. Petitioner cross-complained for conversion and breach of contract. Petitioner is represented by attorneys in his capacity as a defendant but appears in propria persona as a cross-complainant. Petitioner's attorney allegedly advised him to keep a diary in anticipation of litigating his claims against real party in interest.

Real party in interest filed a motion to compel production of the diary. Petitioner opposed the motion, arguing the diary was entitled to a work product privilege under section 2018. The dispute was submitted to a referee. The referee recommended compelling production of the diary because he interpreted section 2018's privilege to be available only to attorneys. The trial court adopted the referee's recommendation and granted real party in interest's motion.

DISCUSSION

The Use of the Word "Attorney" in Section 2018 is Ambiguous
The construction and interpretation of a statute is a question of law, which the Court of Appeal considers de novo.

Section 2018 provides a privilege for matter prepared in anticipation of litigation. (See Fellows v. Superior Court (1980) 108 Cal.App.3d 55, 62, 166 Cal.Rptr. 274.) It reads, in part, "[i]t is the policy of this state to (1) preserve the rights of attorneys to prepare cases for trial with that degree of privacy necessary to encourage them to prepare their cases thoroughly and to investigate not only the favorable but the unfavorable aspects of those cases; and (2) to prevent attorneys from taking undue advantage of their adversary's industry and efforts." (§ 2018, subd. (a).) Therefore, "[a]ny writing that reflects an attorney's impressions, conclusions, opinions, or legal research or theories shall not be discoverable under any circumstances." (§ 2018, subd. (c).) Other types of work product are not discoverable unless "denial of discovery will unfairly prejudice the party seeking discovery...." (§ 2018, subd. (b).)

When interpreting a statute, "we turn first to the statutory language, since the words the Legislature chose are the best indicators of its intent." "When statutory language is clear and unambiguous, there is no need for construction...." However, if the language is ambiguous, we "may resort to extrinsic sources, including the ostensible objects to be achieved and the legislative history."

Real party interest contends the plain language of section 2018 establishes that the privilege applies only to licensed attorneys, and therefore, petitioner is not entitled to the work product privilege. However, section 2018 does not define the term attorney. In ordinary parlance, the term "attorney" means "attorney at law," or "lawyer." (Black's Law Dict. (5th ed.1979) pp. 117-118.) At least one other jurisdiction includes in the definition of "attorney" any "party prosecuting or defending an action in person." (See, e.g. N.Y. CPLR § 105.)

On its face the statute may not seem ambiguous, but an ambiguity arises because other provisions of the Code of Civil Procedure and California Rules of Court which require that "attorneys" follow certain procedures, apply to litigants appearing in propria persona as well. (See, e.g. § 1952.2; Cal. Rules of Court, rules 15(b), 217 & 219; Cal. Standards Jud. Admin, § 9.) Moreover, "[a] lay person,... who exercises the privilege of trying his own case must expect and receive the same treatment as if represented by an attorney—no different, no better, no worse." Because the term "attorney" has been applied to other statutes without distinguishing between attorneys and litigants appearing in propria persona, the term is ambiguous, and it is necessary to look at section 2018's legislative history to determine whether the Legislature intended to limit the work product privilege to attorneys.

Section 2018's Legislative History Supports Applying the Privilege to Unrepresented Litigants

The United States Supreme Court first recognized a privilege for work product in Hickman v. Taylor (1947) 329 U.S. 495, 67 S.Ct. 385, 91 L.Ed. 451. After Hickman, and prior to the adoption of section 2016, 2018's predecessor, California courts struggled to develop a work product doctrine. In Holm v. Superior Court (1954) 42 Cal.2d 500, 267 P.2d 1025, California's Supreme Court created a privilege similar to the federal work product privilege but based on the attorney-client privilege.

In Holm, the court held photographs and an accident report prepared for counsel's assistance in defending an action were within the attorney-client privilege. (Holm v. Superior Court, supra, 42 Cal.2d at p. 510, 267 P.2d 1025.) The practical effect of Holm was to protect certain material now considered work product as if it were an attorney-client communication. For example, in Heffron v. Los Angeles Transit Lines (1959) 170 Cal.App.2d 709, 339 P.2d 567, a statement by defendant's employee concerning an accident was held to be privileged because it had been prepared as part of a procedure followed in anticipation of litigation. The court, in deciding the statement was privileged, noted the "[defendant's] dominant purpose in obtaining and preserving the driver's statement was that it might be transmitted as a communication to the attorneys designated by its insurance carrier for use in the performance of professional responsibilities in defending [defendant] against a potential claim. [Citations.] The driver's statement evidently set forth ` ... his version of the accident and thus clearly is at the very heart of the attorney client privilege.' " (Id. at pp. 717-718, 339 P.2d 567.)

At about the same time, the concept of a separate privilege for work product was also beginning to take form in California's courts. In Trade Center Properties, Inc. v. Superior Court (1960) 185 Cal.App.2d 409, 8 Cal.Rptr. 345, the court recognized that policy considerations separate from those of the attorney-client privilege existed for protecting work product. In that case, the plaintiff sought to depose defendant's attorney and sought production of files the attorney had compiled in preparation for litigation. The court held the attorney could not be deposed and the files were not discoverable. In reaching its decision, the court rejected defendant's argument that the files fell within the attorney-client privilege. The court stated, "[n]o conceivable extension of the broadest view of the language of prediscovery cases relied upon by real parties in interest [citation] can extend the attorney-client privilege to the communications of the independent nonparty witness here involved. [¶] However, sound reasons of policy support the trial court's determination.... [¶] What petitioner here seeks is the right to take the deposition of his adversary's attorney upon matters pertaining to the latter's preparation for trial. Whether to protect the work product of that attorney or to restrict the picking of his brains, the court clearly should bar such a proceeding except upon a showing of extremely good cause." (Id. at p. 411, 8 Cal.Rptr. 345.) Despite its decision, the court noted that it was not adopting the entirety of the Hickman rule. (Ibid.)

While the concept of work product was being developed by the courts, California's Legislature was also preparing to enact the Discovery Act. Under that proposed legislation, certain work product would be absolutely protected based on the attorney-client privilege. (Stats.1957, ch. 1904, § 3, pp. 3322-3323; see Holm v. Superior Court, supra, 42 Cal.2d at pp. 509-510, 267 P.2d 1025; see also Pruitt, Lawyers' Work Product (1962) 37 State Bar J. 228, 235-236.) This initial concept differed from the federal rules which granted only a qualified protection founded on Hickman's work product doctrine. (Hickman v. Taylor, supra, 329 U.S. 495, 67 S.Ct. 385, 91 L.Ed. 451.) Concerned that Hickman 's lower level of protection for work product would influence California law, the California State Bar proposed and the Legislature adopted an amendment to the Discovery Act. This amendment, although arguably intended to protect work product as attorney-client privileged communications pursuant to the ruling in Holm, did not expressly do so; nor did the new statute use the term "work product." (Stats. 1957, ch. 1904, § 3, pp. 3322-3323; see also Pruitt, Lawyers' Work Product, supra, 37 State Bar J. at p. 235.)

Subsequent to the enactment of the Discovery Act of 1957, in Greyhound Corp. v. Superior Court (1961) 56 Cal.2d 355, 15 Cal.Rptr. 90, 364 P.2d 266 and Suezaki v. Superior Court (1962) 58 Cal.2d 166, 23 Cal.Rptr. 368, 373 P.2d 432, the California Supreme Court redefined its ruling in Holm. The language of Holm suggested that pictures and other objects were incorporated into "communications" and therefore privileged. (Holm v. Superior Court, supra, 42 Cal.2d at pp. 508-509, 267 P.2d 1025.) In Greyhound, the Supreme Court reached a contrary conclusion in holding that statements of witnesses taken by defense investigators were not within the attorney-client privilege. It also questioned the validity of the Holm holding, that photographs transmitted to counsel to assist him in defending an action were within the attorney-client privilege, and determined that the work product privilege was not the law of California. In Suezaki the Supreme Court took another step to reduce the protection for work product. It stated that "simply because the subject matter sought to be discovered is the "work product' of the attorney it is not privileged."

Whereas after Holm certain work product had been absolutely privileged, after Greyhound and Suezaki work product was only one factor to be used by the trial court in the exercise of its discretion in determining whether or not discovery should be granted. The development of the work product doctrine in California prevented incorporating federal decisions. (See Pruitt, Lawyers' Work Product, supra, 37 State Bar J. at pp. 233-236.) Therefore, work product was not protected under Hickman, and its protection was only available where the material sought to be produced fit under the attorney-client privilege umbrella.

==In response to these decisions, the California State Bar sponsored an amendment to the Discovery Act to create a separate privilege for materials prepared in anticipation of litigation.== The proposed amendment provided: "[I]t is the policy of this state (i) to preserve the rights of parties and their attorneys to prepare cases for trial with that degree of privacy necessary to encourage them to prepare their cases thoroughly and to investigate not only the favorable but the unfavorable aspects of such cases and (ii) to so limit discovery that one party or his attorney may not take undue advantage of this [sic] adversary's industry or efforts. Accordingly, the following shall not be discoverable unless the court determines that denial of discovery will unfairly prejudice the party seeking discovery in preparing his claim or defense or will result in an injustice: [¶] (1) The work product of an attorney...." (Committee Report-Administration of Justice (1962) 37 State Bar J. 585, 586-587, italics added.)

The State Bar proposed the amendment to "... protect the lawyer's normal work processes ... [and] to establish a more desirable balance between `discovery' and the right of litigants and prospective litigants to obtain advice of experts, make investigations and do other acts, without fear of unlimited or indiscriminate disclosures to, and use by adversaries." (Committee Report-Administration of Justice, supra, 37 State Bar J. at p. 586, italics added.) Moreover, "... discovery may be limited or denied when the facts indicate that `one litigant is attempting to take advantage of the other' or that there is `an abusive attempt to "ride free" on the opponent's industry.' [Citation.]" (Id. at p. 588, italics added.)

In 1963, the Legislature adopted the State Bar's amendment almost verbatim. The amendment reiterated the need to protect the privacy and work efforts of attorneys. (Former Code Civ. Proc, § 2016, subds. (b) & (g), amended by Stats.1990, ch. 207, § 1, pp. 1364-1395.) Since 1963, excluding some cosmetic changes, what is now section

2018 has not changed. "In the absence of any indication of legislative intent ... [the] court should consider the general purpose of the statute, as well as the consequences of alternative constructions, as guides to interpretation." (In re Marriage of Harris (1977) 74 Cal.App.3d 98, 101-102, 141 Cal. Rptr. 333.) Since the Legislature enacted the State Bar's proposal almost verbatim, the State Bar's report may be used as an interpretive aid. The report expresses concern over litigants, as well as of attorneys, having unrestrained access by their opponents to materials prepared in anticipation of litigation.

Section 2018's stated purpose and the underlying reasons for its creation emphasize the need to "limit[ ] discovery so that 'the stupid or lazy practitioner may not take undue advantage of his adversary's efforts....'" (Pruitt, Lawyers' Work Product, supra, 37 State Bar J. at pp. 240-241.) Such a policy is important not only for attorneys, but also for litigants acting in propria persona. A litigant needs the same opportunity to research relevant law and to prepare his or her case without then having to give that research to an adversary making a discovery request.

Case Law Supports Applying the Privilege to Unrepresented Litigants

* * *

In Mack v. Superior Court (1968) 259 Cal.App.2d 7, 66 Cal.Rptr. 280, which was decided after the 1963 amendment created an explicit work product privilege, the court stated, "[t]he work product privilege was created for the protection of the client as well as the attorney...." (Id at p. 10, 66 Cal.Rptr. 280.) Lohman v. Superior Court, supra, 81 Cal.App.3d 90, 146 Cal. Rptr. 171, disagreed with this statement, but Fellows v. Superior Court, supra, 108 Cal.App.3d 55, 166 Cal.Rptr. 274, criticized Lohman for misreading Mack. Fellows notes, "[t]he language of Mack to the effect that the privilege was created in the interest of protecting the client as well as the attorney provides a basis for a judicial interpretation of ... section [2018] to permit a client to claim the attorney's work product privilege whenever the attorney is not present to claim it himself." (Fellows v. Superior Court supra, 108 Cal.App.3d at p. 64, 166 Cal.Rptr. 274.) The reasoning in Fellows reinforces the rationale that the work product privilege is intended for the protection of litigants, not just attorneys.

In interpreting section 2018, California courts have looked to its intended purpose when determining who may assert a work product privilege. For example, several cases have held that a party who was previously represented by an attorney has standing to assert a privilege as to the attorney's work product as a means of furthering the statute's intended purpose. "[T]he work product privilege... exist[s] ... to promote the adversary system." Allowing litigants appearing in propria persona to assert the privilege furthers that purpose.

Other Considerations Do Not Militate Against Applying the Privilege to Unrepresented Litigants

Real party argues a litigant appearing in propria persona should not be entitled to a work product privilege because, unlike a licensed attorney, such a litigant is not an officer of the court and is not subject to discipline for violating discovery orders. Although a litigant appearing in propria persona is not subject to discipline by the State Bar, the trial court may grant sanctions for failure to obey a discovery order. (See § 2017.)

Real party next contends that granting a work product privilege to litigants appearing in propria persona would curtail discovery. He argues that, because parties in a suit generally have the most information, allowing a litigant to assert a work product privilege would unfairly limit the discovery efforts of the opposing party acting with an attorney. In making this argument, real party assumes that a litigant appearing in propria persona would be given carte blanche to limit discoverable material. Not so. Since "work product" is not defined, whether specific material is work product must be resolved on a case-by-case basis. If the material sought would be subject to discovery from a represented party, it will be discoverable from a litigant appearing in propria persona.

In determining whether particular matter is privileged as work product, the reviewing court should be guided by the underlying policies of section 2018. Specifically, the policy of promoting diligence in preparing one's own case, rather than depending on an adversary's efforts. A practical guide for ascertaining its scope is found in Mack v. Superior Court, supra, 259 Cal.App.2d at pp. 10-11, 66 Cal.Rptr. 280 and Fellows v. Superior Court, supra, 108 Cal.App.3d at pp. 69-70, 166 Cal.Rptr. 274. In Mack, the court indicated that material of a derivative character, such as diagrams prepared for trial, audit reports, appraisals, and other expert opinions, developed on the initiative of counsel in preparing for trial, are protected as work product. (Mack v. Superior Court, supra, 259 Cal.App.2d at pp. 10-11, 66 Cal.Rptr. 280; see also Fellows v. Superior Court, supra, 108 Cal.App.3d at pp. 69-70, 166 Cal.Rptr. 274.)

An in camera review is the proper method for determining whether specific items are subject to a work product privilege. If the material is not absolutely privileged under section 2018, subdivision (c), the party seeking discovery may obtain discovery by showing that denial of such discovery would "unfairly prejudice the party ...." (§ 2018, subd. (b).)

Despite real party in interest's contentions, the policy rationale for section 2018 supports interpreting the statute as protecting the work product of an unrepresented litigant.

DISPOSITION

Without determining whether the diary is in fact work product, we hold that in propria persona litigants may assert section 2018's work product privilege. Since the

[handwritten: what is an in camera review?]

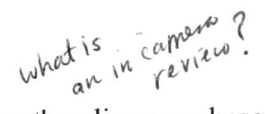

trial court's ruling was based on the conclusion that petitioner was not entitled to assert the work product privilege, we remand the matter to that court to conduct an in camera review of the diary to determine whether it contains matter which is privileged under section 2018. Our stay order is vacated and, the alternative writ is discharged.

EXPERT WITNESSES

FRCP 26(a)(2)(b)(4) requires experts witnesses who are expected to testify at trial, to produce some form of initial written report describing their conclusions about the case and requiring that, after such report is available, the experts submit to a deposition. Ninety days before trial a party must supply the name and resume of any expert witnesses they expect to call at trial supplying all the information required in Rule 26(a)(2)(B), which includes a written report explaining the nature and basis for the expert's testimony. The party must thereafter make the expert available for deposition by the other parties. (FRCP 26(a)(2)(C).)

On the other hand, a non-testifying expert is generally immune from discovery. Facts or opinions may be obtained from an expert who has been retained in anticipation of litigation but who is not expected to testify only "upon a showing of exceptional circumstances under which it is impracticable for the party seeking discovery to obtain facts or opinions on the same subject by other means." (Friedenthal §7.6,; Wright §81)

> **Expert Witnesses**
>
> A party must disclose to the other parties the identity of any witness it may use at trial to present evidence as an expert witness.

> **Expert Witnesses**
>
> Facts or opinions may be obtained from an expert who has been retained in anticipation of litigation but who is not expected to testify only "upon a showing of exceptional circumstances under which it is impracticable for the party seeking discovery to obtain facts or opinions on the same subject by other means."

Thompson v. The Haskell Co.
65 Fair Empl. Prac. Cas. (BNA) 1088 (M.D. Fla. 1994)

SNYDER, M.J.

This cause is before the Court on Plaintiff's Motion for Protective Order filed on May 13, 1994 (hereinafter Motion). Plaintiff seeks to shield from discovery documents related to her in the possession of Lauren Lucas, Ph.D., a psychologist. She contends that Rule 26(b)(4) of the Federal Rules of Civil Procedure (FRCP) protects the psychological records in Dr. Lucas' possession. In particular, Plaintiff represents Dr. Lucas was retained by her prior counsel to perform a diagnostic review and personality profile, and that, after seeing Plaintiff on one occasion on June 15, 1992, Dr. Lucas prepared a report for her prior counsel.

Rule 26(b)(4)[(D)] of the FRCP provides:

[Expert Employed Only for Trial Preparation. Ordinarily, a party may not, by interrogatories or deposition, discover facts known or opinions held by an expert who has been retained or specially employed by another party in anticipation of litigation or to prepare for trial and who is not expected to be called as a witness at trial. But a party may do so only:

(i) as provided in Rule 35(b); or

(ii) on showing exceptional circumstances under which it is impracticable for the party to obtain facts or opinions on the same subject by other means.]

Assuming arguendo that Dr. Lucas' report is covered by Rule 26(b)(4), it would nevertheless be discoverable under the circumstances presented in this case. In the instant lawsuit, Plaintiff alleges that, as a result of sexual harassment by co-defendant Zona, a supervisor in the employ of the Defendant, she was "reduced to a severely depressed emotional state and her employment was terminated when she did not acquiesce to the advances of [Zona]." Complaint, filed on September 23, 1993, at 6. According to a complaint filed with the Jacksonville Equal Opportunity Commission, Plaintiff apparently was terminated from her position with Defendant Haskell Company on June 5, 1992. Thus, her mental and emotional state ten days later on June 15, 1992, the date on which she was examined by Dr. Lucas, is highly probative with regard to the above-quoted allegation, which is essential to her case.

This highly probative information is discoverable notwithstanding Rule 26(b)(4), moreover, given the nature of the report at issue. Apparently, no other comparable report was prepared during the weeks immediately following Plaintiff's discharge. Thus, the Defendant could not obtain the information contained in Dr. Lucas' report by other means. In a case almost on all fours with the instant one, the Court recognized that even "independent examinations...pursuant to Rule 35 would not contain equivalent information." Dixon v. Cappellini, 88 F.R.D. 1, 3 (M.D. Pa. 1980). Under these facts, it appears there are exceptional circumstances favoring disclosure of Dr. Lucas' report, and that the Defendant could not obtain comparable information by other means. Accordingly, the Motion is DENIED....

NOTES Rule 26(b)(4)(B) provides work-product protection for drafts of expert reports or disclosures. This protection applies to all witnesses identified under Rule 26(a)(2)(A), whether they are required to provide reports under Rule 26(a)(2)(B) or are the subject of disclosure under Rule 26(a)(2)(C). It applies regardless of the form in which the draft is recorded, whether written, electronic, or otherwise. It also applies to drafts of any supplementation under Rule 26(e). (See, Advisory Committee Notes on Rules—2010 Amendment)

Chiquita International Ltd. v. M/V Bolero Reefer
1994 U.S. Dist. LEXIS 5820 (S.D.N.Y. 1994)

FRANCIS, M.J.

This is a maritime action in which the shipper, Chiquita International Ltd. ("Chiquita"), sues the carrier, International Reefer Services, S.A. ("International Reefer"), for cargo loss and damage. Chiquita alleges that International Reefer was engaged to transport 154,660 boxes of bananas from Puerto Bolivar, Ecuador to Bremerhaven, Germany aboard the M/V Bolero Reefer. However, because of alleged malfunctions of the vessel's loading cranes and side-ports, only 111,660 boxes were loaded. Thus, 43,000 boxes of bananas were left on the wharf and were later disposed of. The cargo that did arrive in Germany was allegedly in poor condition.

International Reefer has submitted a letter in support of an application to compel discovery of Joseph Winer. Mr. Winer is a marine surveyor who examined the vessel and loading gear at Chiquita's request shortly after the vessel arrived in Bremerhaven. International Reefer seeks Mr. Winer's deposition and production of the file he assembled in connection with his inspection. Chiquita has objected to these demands on the ground that Mr. Winer is a non-testifying expert as to whom discovery is closely circumscribed by Rule 26(b)(4)([D]) of the Federal Rules of Civil Procedure. International Reefer replies that Mr. Winer is a fact witness rather than an expert. Moreover, even if he is an expert, International Reefer argues that the fact that he is the only surveyor who observed the vessel shortly after it docked is an exceptional circumstance warranting discovery....

[The opinion quotes Rule 26(b)(4)(D).]

[A] non-testifying expert is generally immune from discovery.
Mr. Winer qualifies as such an expert. He is a marine engineer who was specifically engaged by Chiquita to examine the vessel in connection with the cargo loss claim. He

is clearly an "expert" in that he brought his technical background to bear in observing the condition of the gear and offering his opinion to Chiquita. He does not forfeit this status merely because he made a personal examination of the vessel and therefore learned "facts," rather than simply offering an opinion based on the observations of others. Rule 26(b)(4)[(D)] generally precludes discovery of "facts known or opinions" held by a non-testifying expert, and so it anticipates that such an expert may make his or her own investigation. Thus, the relevant distinction is not between fact and opinion testimony but between those witnesses whose information was obtained in the normal course of business and those who were hired to make an evaluation in connection with expected litigation. See Harasimowicz v. McAllister, 78 F.R.D. 319, 320 (E.D. Pa. 1978) (medical examiner subject to ordinary discovery on routine autopsy); Congrove v. St. Louis-San Francisco Railway, 77 F.R.D. 503, 504-05 (W.D. Mo. 1978) (treating physician subject to ordinary discovery). Here, Mr. Winer falls into the latter category and Rule 26(b)(4)[(D)] therefore applies.

International Reefer nevertheless contends that discovery should be permitted under the "exceptional circumstances" clause of the rule, since no other marine surveyor viewed the vessel shortly after docking. This argument would have merit if International Reefer had been precluded from sending its own expert to the scene by forces beyond its control. Thus, for example, in Sanford Construction Co. v. Kaiser Aluminum & Chemical Sales, Inc., 45 F.R.D. 465, 466 (E.D. Ky. 1968), the court found there to be exceptional circumstances where the plaintiff allowed its own expert to examine the item at issue while barring the defendant's experts until the item was no longer accessible.

However, that is not the case here. The vessel and equipment were at least as available to International Reefer as to Chiquita from the time of loading. Indeed, during the three-week voyage to Bremerhaven, International Reefer's employees had the exclusive opportunity to examine the loading cranes. Under these circumstances, the failure of International Reefer to engage its own marine surveyor in a timely manner should not be rewarded by permitting discovery of Chiquita's expert. To do so would permit the exceptional circumstances exception to swallow Rule 26(b)(4)[(D)].

Finally, International Reefer maintains that even if it is foreclosed from deposing Mr. Winer, it should be given access to his file. However, Rule 26(b)(4)[(D)] applies to document discovery as well as to depositions. Nevertheless, International Reefer is correct that information does not become exempt from discovery merely because it is conveyed to a non-testifying expert. Thus, while the file may contain Mr. Winer's recorded observations and opinions which need not be disclosed, it may also include discoverable information provided to Mr. Winer by others. Such documents shall be produced.

Conclusion

For the reasons set forth above, International Reefer's application to take the deposition of Joseph Winer is denied. By May 13, 1994, Chiquita shall produce from Mr. Winer's file those documents that do not reflect his observations and opinions or are otherwise privileged. Chiquita shall prepare a log of any documents withheld, identifying them with the specificity required by Local Rule 46(e).

SO ORDERED.

Ensuring Compliance and Controlling Discovery Abuses

Sanctions for Discovery Violations

Rosales v. Thermex-Thermatron
67 Cal.App.4th 187 (1998)

GILBERT, Associate Justice.

In this product liability case, judgment was awarded to plaintiff for injuries she suffered from a product manufactured by defendant's corporate predecessor 24 years earlier. Defendant had continued to distribute the same products of the corporation it had acquired. Its acquisition of the predecessor corporation had destroyed plaintiffs remedy against that corporation. . .

[During discovery plaintiff propounded to defendant 136 requests for admissions that directly related to the issue of successor liability. Rather than admit, the defendant denied the requests forcing the plaintiff to introduce evidence at trial to establish the necessary facts to support liability.] At the conclusion of the trial, the court awarded plaintiff her additional costs that she incurred in having to produce evidence at trial with regard to the issue of successor liability.]

On appeal the defendant . . .contends the trial court abused its discretion in awarding sanctions for refusal to admit to successor liability.

Code of Civil Procedure section 2033, subdivision (o) allows the trial court to grant sanctions against a party who fails to admit pursuant to a request for admissions to the truth of any matter where the matter is proven to be true. The subdivision requires sanctions unless, among other exceptions, the admission sought was of no substantial importance or the party failing to make the admission had reasonable grounds to believe it would prevail on the matter.

If a party who denies a request for admission lacks personal knowledge but had available sources of information and failed to make a reasonable investigation, the failure will justify an award of sanctions. In order to be of substantial importance, a request for admission should have some direct relationship to an issue which, if not proven, would have altered the results of the case. There is no requirement, however, that the fact in question is one that would have altered the determination of the ultimate issue.

Here Rosales made 136 requests for admissions that directly related to the issue of successor liability. It is not necessary to review each request and response. The following examples will suffice:

Nineteen times Thermex-Thermatron responded that it was not Thermatron. But Thermex-Thermatron's attorney stated in his summation to the jury, "They are Thermatron. [¶] They testified they're Thermatron." Thermex-Thermatron even denied that it was listed in specified telephone directories under "Thermatron Division of Solidyne, Inc." The denial was quite obviously false.

In general, Thermex-Thermatron denied in its responses to the requests for admissions any knowledge of any of the operations of Sealomatic or any of the Solidyne divisions. This was even though Jack Palmer, the officer and part owner who answered the requests, began working for Sealomatic in 1960 and worked for Solidyne and its subsidiary. It was obvious at trial that Palmer had a great deal more information than his responses to the requests for admissions indicated. He tried to explain the discrepancy. He said that at trial he was answering from his personal knowledge, but in answering the requests for admissions he was acting as an officer of Thermex-Thermatron. He said he answered the requests for admissions honestly as far as all the owners of Thermex-Thermatron were concerned, but that if some of the owners did not know the answer, he did not admit to the request. He said he did not remember whether he undertook any investigation.

Palmer's testimony is tantamount to a confession that his responses to the requests for admissions were deceptive.

Thermex-Thermatron's claim that its liability under Ray was at least arguable misses the point. That the ultimate issue may be arguable does not justify deceptive responses to particular requests for admissions.

Thermex-Thermatron places much emphasis on the trial court's statement that "the defense admitted it was a successor in interest to the above entities in its opening statement." Thermex-Thermatron complains that its attorney made no such admission in the opening statement. But Palmer's testimony shows that his answers were deceptive. It is hard to think of a more compelling case for sanctions.

Litigation is supposed to be a search for truth. Here the defense abandoned its part of the search in favor of tactics that made plaintiffs pretrial discovery more burdensome. It is appropriate that the defense now pay for that burden.

The judgment is affirmed. Costs on appeal are awarded to respondent.

SANCTIONS FOR FAILING TO PRESERVE EVIDENCE

Zubulake v. UBS Warburg LLP
229 F.R.D. 422 (S.D.N.Y. 2003)

SCHEINDLIN, J.

...What is true in love is equally true at law: Lawyers and their clients need to communicate clearly and effectively with one another to ensure that litigation proceeds efficiently. When communication between counsel and client breaks down, conversation becomes "just crossfire," and there are usually casualties.

I. Introduction

This is the fifth written opinion in this case, a relatively routine employment discrimination dispute in which discovery has now lasted over two years. Laura Zubulake is once again moving to sanction UBS for its failure to produce relevant information and for its tardy production of such material....

II. Facts

...Zubulake is an equities trader specializing in Asian securities who is suing her former employer for gender discrimination, failure to promote, and retaliation under federal, state, and city law.

A. Background

Zubulake filed an initial charge of gender discrimination with the EEOC on August 16, 2001. Well before that, however—as early as April 2001—UBS employees were on notice of Zubulake's impending court action. After she received a right-to-sue letter from the EEOC, Zubulake filed this lawsuit on February 15, 2002.

Fully aware of their common law duty to preserve relevant evidence, UBS's in-house attorneys gave oral instructions in August 2001—immediately after Zubulake filed her EEOC charge—instructing employees not to destroy or delete material potentially relevant to Zubulake's claims, and in fact to segregate such material into separate files for the lawyers' eventual review.... [These same instructions were reiterated in August

2001, and again in February, August, and September of 2002.]

B. Procedural History

In Zubulake I, I addressed Zubulake's claim that relevant e-mails had been deleted from UBS's active servers and existed only on "inaccessible" archival media (i.e., backup tapes). Arguing that e-mail correspondence that she needed to prove her case existed only on those backup tapes, Zubulake called for their production. UBS moved for a protective order shielding it from discovery altogether or, in the alternative, shifting the cost of backup tape restoration onto Zubulake. Because the evidentiary record was sparse, I ordered UBS to bear the costs of restoring a sample of the backup tapes.

After the sample tapes were restored, UBS continued to press for cost shifting with respect to any further restoration of backup tapes. In Zubulake III, I ordered UBS to bear the lion's share of restoring certain backup tapes because Zubulake was able to demonstrate that those tapes were likely to contain relevant information.... In the restoration effort, the parties discovered that certain backup tapes [were] missing. They also discovered a number of e-mails on the backup tapes that were missing from UBS's active files, confirming Zubulake's suspicion that relevant e-mails were being deleted or otherwise lost.

Zubulake III begat Zubulake IV, where Zubulake moved for sanctions as a result of UBS's failure to preserve all relevant backup tapes, and UBS's deletion of relevant e-mails. Finding fault in UBS's document preservation strategy but lacking evidence that the lost tapes and deleted e-mails were particularly favorable to Zubulake, I ordered UBS to pay for the re-deposition of several key UBS employees—Varsano, Chapin, Hardisty, Kim, and Tong—so that Zubulake could inquire about the newly-restored e-mails.

C. The Instant Dispute

The essence of the current dispute is that during the re-depositions required by Zubulake IV, Zubulake learned about more deleted e-mails and about the existence of e-mails preserved on UBS's active servers that were, to that point, never produced. In sum, Zubulake has now presented evidence that UBS personnel deleted relevant e-mails, some of which were subsequently recovered from backup tapes (or elsewhere) and thus produced to Zubulake long after her initial document requests, and some of which were lost altogether. Zubulake has also presented evidence that some UBS personnel did not produce responsive documents to counsel until recently, depriving Zubulake of the documents for almost two years.... Zubulake now moves for sanctions as a result of UBS's purported discovery failings. In particular, she asks—as she did in Zubulake IV—that an adverse inference instruction be given to the jury that eventually hears this case.

III. Legal Standard

Spoliation is the destruction or significant alteration of evidence, or the failure to preserve property for another's use as evidence in pending or reasonably foreseeable litigation. The determination of an appropriate sanction for spoliation, if any, is confined to the sound discretion of the trial judge, and is assessed on a case-by-case basis. The authority to sanction litigants for spoliation arises jointly under the Federal Rules of Civil Procedure and the court's inherent powers.

The spoliation of evidence germane to proof of an issue at trial can support an inference that the evidence would have been unfavorable to the party responsible for its destruction. A party seeking an adverse inference instruction (or other sanctions) based on the spoliation of evidence must establish the following three elements: (1) that the party having control over the evidence had an obligation to preserve it at the time it was destroyed; (2) that the records were destroyed with a "culpable state of mind" and (3) that the destroyed evidence was "relevant" to the party's claim or defense such that a reasonable trier of fact could find that it would support that claim or defense.

In this circuit, a "culpable state of mind" for purposes of a spoliation inference includes ordinary negligence. When evidence is destroyed in bad faith (i.e., intentionally or willfully), that fact alone is sufficient to demonstrate relevance. By contrast, when the destruction is negligent, relevance must be proven by the party seeking the sanctions....

IV. Discussion

...In Zubulake IV, I summarized a litigant's preservation obligations:

Once a party reasonably anticipates litigation, it must suspend its routine document retention/destruction policy and put in place a "litigation hold" to ensure the preservation of relevant documents. As a general rule, that litigation hold does not apply to inaccessible backup tapes (e.g., those typically maintained solely for the purpose of disaster recovery), which may continue to be recycled on the schedule set forth in the company's policy. On the other hand, if backup tapes are accessible (i.e., actively used for information retrieval), then such tapes would likely be subject to the litigation hold.

A party's discovery obligations do not end with the implementation of a "litigation hold"—to the contrary, that's only the beginning....

Once a "litigation hold" is in place, a party and her counsel must make certain that all sources of potentially relevant information are identified and placed "on hold," to the extent required in Zubulake IV. To do this, counsel must become fully familiar with her client's document retention policies, as well as the client's data retention architecture. This will invariably involve speaking with information technology personnel, who can explain system-wide backup procedures and the actual (as opposed to theoretical) implementation of the firm's recycling policy. It will also involve communicating with the "key players" in the litigation, in order to understand how they stored information. In this case, for example, some UBS employees created separate computer files pertaining to Zubulake, while others printed out relevant e-mails and retained them in hard copy only. Unless counsel interviews each employee, it is impossible to determine whether all potential sources of information have been inspected....

To the extent that it may not be feasible for counsel to speak with every key player, given the size of a company or the scope of the lawsuit, counsel must be more creative.... [I]t is not sufficient to notify all employees of a litigation hold and expect that the party will then retain and produce all relevant information. Counsel must take affirmative steps to monitor compliance so that all sources of discoverable information are identified and searched. This is not to say that counsel will necessarily succeed in locating all such sources, or that the later discovery of new sources is evidence of a lack of effort. But counsel and client must take some reasonable steps to see that sources of relevant information are located.

...The continuing duty to supplement disclosures strongly suggests that parties also have a duty to make sure that discoverable information is not lost. Indeed, the notion of a "duty to preserve" connotes an ongoing obligation. Obviously, if information is lost or destroyed, it has not been preserved....

There are thus a number of steps that counsel should take to ensure compliance with the preservation obligation. While these precautions may not be enough (or may be too much) in some cases, they are designed to promote the continued preservation of potentially relevant information in the typical case.

First, counsel must issue a "litigation hold" at the outset of litigation or whenever litigation is reasonably anticipated. The litigation hold should be periodically re-issued so that new employees are aware of it, and so that it is fresh in the minds of all employees.

Second, counsel should communicate directly with the "key players" in the litigation, i.e., the people identified in a party's initial disclosure and any subsequent supplementation thereto. Because these "key players" are the "employees likely to have relevant information," it is particularly important that the preservation duty be communicated clearly to them. As with the litigation hold, the key players should be periodically reminded that the preservation duty is still in place.

Finally, counsel should instruct all employees to produce electronic copies of their relevant active files. Counsel must also make sure that all backup media which the party is required to retain is identified and stored in a safe place....

As more fully described above, UBS's in-house counsel issued a litigation hold in August 2001 and repeated that instruction several times from September 2001 through September 2002. Outside counsel also spoke with some (but not all) of the key players in August 2001. Nonetheless, certain employees unquestionably deleted e-mails. Although many of the deleted e-mails were recovered from backup tapes, a number of backup tapes—and the e-mails on them—are lost forever. Other employees, notwithstanding counsel's request that they produce their files on Zubulake, did not do so....

Counsel failed to communicate the litigation hold order to all key players. They also failed to ascertain each of the key players' document management habits. By the same token, UBS employees—for unknown reasons—ignored many of the instructions that counsel gave. This case represents a failure of communication, and that failure falls on counsel and client alike.

At the end of the day, however, the duty to preserve and produce documents rests on the party. Once that duty is made clear to a party, either by court order or by instructions from counsel, that party is on notice of its obligations and acts at its own peril. Though more diligent action on the part of counsel would have mitigated some of the damage caused by UBS's deletion of e-mails, UBS deleted the e-mails in defiance of explicit instructions not to.

Because UBS personnel continued to delete relevant e-mails, Zubulake was denied access to e-mails to which she was entitled. Even those e-mails that were deleted but ultimately salvaged from other sources...were produced 22 months after they were initially requested. The effect of losing potentially relevant e-mails is obvious, but the effect of late production cannot be underestimated either.... I therefore conclude that UBS acted willfully in destroying potentially relevant information, which resulted either in the absence of such information or its tardy production.... Because UBS's spoliation was willful, the lost information is presumed to be relevant....

Having concluded that UBS was under a duty to preserve the e-mails and that it deleted presumably relevant e-mails willfully, I now consider the full panoply of available sanctions. In doing so, I recognize that a major consideration in choosing an appropriate sanction—along with punishing UBS and deterring future misconduct—is to restore Zubulake to the position that she would have been in had UBS faithfully discharged its discovery obligations. That being so, I find that the following sanctions are warranted.

First, the jury empanelled to hear this case will be given an adverse inference instruction with respect to e-mails deleted after August 2001, and in particular, with respect to e-mails that were irretrievably lost when UBS's backup tapes were recycled. [An adverse inference instruction would tell the jury to infer that these lost and destroyed e-mails would have been favorable to the plaintiff.] No one can ever know precisely what was on those tapes, but the content of e-mails recovered from other sources—along with the fact that UBS employees willfully deleted e-mails—is sufficiently favorable to Zubulake that I am convinced that the contents of the lost tapes would have been similarly, if not more, favorable.

Second, Zubulake argues that the e-mails that were produced, albeit late, "are brand new and very significant to Ms. Zubulake's retaliation claim and would have affected [her] examination of every witness...in this case."...These arguments stand unrebutted and are therefore adopted in full by the Court. Accordingly, UBS is ordered to pay the costs of any depositions or re-depositions required by the late production.

Third, UBS is ordered to pay the costs of this motion.

Finally, I note that UBS's belated production has resulted in a self-executing sanction. Not only was Zubulake unable to question UBS's witnesses using the newly produced e-mails, but UBS was unable to prepare those witnesses with the aid of those e-mails. Some of UBS's witnesses, not having seen these e-mails, have already given deposition testimony that seems to contradict the newly discovered evidence....

NOTES ON DISCOVERY SANCTIONS

FRCP 37 provides generally for sanctions against parties or persons unjustifiably resisting discovery.

Sanctions imposed for discovery violations typically include:

(1) directing that facts be taken as established for purposes of the action;
(2) prohibiting the disobedient party from supporting or opposing designated claims or defenses, or from introducing designated matters in evidence;
(3) striking pleadings in whole or in part;
(4) staying further proceedings until the order is obeyed;
(5) dismissing the action or proceeding in whole or in part;
(6) rendering a default judgment against the disobedient party; or
(7) treating as contempt of court the failure to obey any order

On many occasions, to be sure, the dispute over discovery between the parties is genuine, though ultimately resolved one way or the other by the court. In such cases, the losing party is substantially justified in carrying the matter to court. But the rules should deter the abuse implicit in carrying or forcing a discovery dispute to court when no genuine dispute exists. And the potential or actual imposition of expenses is virtually the sole formal sanction in the rules to deter a party from pressing to a court hearing frivolous requests for or objections to discovery. Expenses should ordinarily be awarded unless a court finds that the losing party acted justifiably in carrying his point to court.

At the same time, a necessary flexibility is maintained, since the court retains the power to find that other circumstances make an award of expenses unjust—as where the prevailing party also acted unjustifiably. (Advisory Committee Notes, 1970 Amendment)

This Page Left Intentionally Blank

CHAPTER 9

RESOLUTION WITHOUT TRIAL

DEFAULT AND DEFAULT JUDGMENTS

Many defendants will timely respond to the plaintiff's complaint thus setting in motion the processes and procedures you have studied up to this point. However, a surprising number of defendants will do nothing in response to the complaint thus exposing them to having their default entered and ultimately a default judgment.

Defaults are governed by FRCP 55. It applies to any party against whom a judgment for affirmative relief is requested. When a party against whom a judgment for affirmative relief is sought has failed to plead or otherwise defend, the clerk must enter the party's default upon a proper application by the plaintiff.

Note that the clerk's entry of default only cuts off the defendant's right to file an answer or another responsive pleading. Obtaining an actual default judgment based upon the defendant's failure to timely respond requires an additional step. And defaults can be set aside upon a showing of good cause. (See, FRCP 55(c); 60(b); Cal.Code.Civ.Proc. sec. 473.)

Beeman v. Burling
216 Cal.App.3d 1586 (1990)

KLINE, P.J.

Appellant Spencer M. Burling appeals a default judgment rendered against him in the amount of $197,044.01. He asserts (1) the default judgment must be vacated because he was not personally served with the statement of damages and because respondent's proof at the default hearing amounted to a de facto amendment of the complaint, which should have revived appellant's ability to respond; (2) the judgment relies upon two sections of the San Francisco Rent Ordinance that are unconstitutional; (3) the judgment exceeds the relief demanded and thus must be reduced; and (4) the court abused its discretion in denying relief from default under Code of Civil Procedure section 473. We affirm.

BACKGROUND

Appellant purchased an apartment building at 76 Deming Street in March 1986. On approximately March 24 he served an eviction notice upon respondent John Beeman, indicating he wished to occupy respondent's unit himself.[1] Respondent moved out of the apartment on April 1. Respondent testified that although appellant did move into the vacated apartment, he lived there for less than three months. The San Francisco Rent Ordinance (Rent Ordinance) requires an owner to reside for 12 months in an apartment that has been vacated pursuant to an "owner move-in" eviction notice.

On May 20, 1986 appellant served an eviction notice upon another tenant, Richard Kronstedt. Mr. Kronstedt testified that the notice indicated appellant's business partner was intending to occupy that unit. He vacated the apartment on approximately June 12, 1986. Similarly, in June 1986 another tenant, Steve Munnell, received an "owner move-in" eviction notice from appellant's business partners, Emmett Hayes and Robert Hill.

In August 1986 respondent sued appellant for wrongful eviction. Following appellant's motion to strike respondent filed a first amended complaint. The amended complaint alleged that appellant had wrongfully evicted respondent with the intention of renting the vacated unit at a higher rental and thus increasing the building's overall value. The complaint set forth 14 causes of action, including actions for negligence, constructive eviction, fraud and violation of the Rent Ordinance. Respondent sought special and general damages according to proof, punitive damages and treble statutory damages under the Rent Ordinance.

Appellant demurred and moved to strike portions of the amended complaint. Following a hearing on January 20, 1987 the court overruled the demurrer, granted the motion to strike in part and ordered appellant to respond to the complaint within 30 days.

Four other tenants of 76 Deming Street also filed suit against appellant alleging similar causes of action. All were represented by the attorney representing respondent. Counsel eventually agreed that appellant would respond to all of the complaints on or before May 16, 1987. Timely answers were filed in three of the pending cases. On May 22 respondent's counsel served appellant's counsel, Mr. Zimmerman, with statements of damages in the instant case and in the case filed by another tenant, Richard Kronstedt. Respondent also offered, pursuant to Code of Civil Procedure section 998, to settle the matter for $30,000. On June 19, respondent's counsel wrote to Zimmerman, warning that he would take appellant's default in the Kronstedt and Beeman cases if no response was filed by June 17. No answers were filed.

Appellant's counsel did not respond to the default warning because he was distracted by the hospitalization of his girlfriend on June 20. During the hospitalization his girlfriend's young daughter was left in the care of her grandfather, who is mentally impaired, and counsel was required to assume significant responsibility for the care of the child.

According to Zimmerman's declaration, during this time he believed an answer had been properly filed in this matter. He did not notice any letters threatening a default until he received a request to enter default on July 1, 1987. Respondent's counsel refused to have the default set aside, stating his client would not permit him to do so; however, counsel did grant appellant's attorney an extension to respond in the Kronstedt matter. By his own admission, Zimmerman "simply blocked the case out of [his] mind" and did not file a motion to have the default set aside.

A hearing on the default judgment was held on October 21, 1987. Respondent and three other tenants testified regarding the eviction notices they received when they lived at 76 Deming Street. Stephen Munnell asserted that appellant was "unpleasant" and "threatening" and "did everything to make [the tenants] feel completely uneasy." Richard Kronstedt described appellant's "intimidating manner" and stated he was "very rude [and] very abrupt." Maurice Jarrett also complained that he felt threatened by appellant and was intimidated by appellant yelling at the tenants that they were to "'get out or else.'" The witnesses also testified that following respondent's eviction appellant did not occupy respondent's apartment for a continuous 12-month period, a fact which under the Rent Ordinance raises a presumption that the eviction was not a valid "owner-occupy" eviction. Based on this evidence the court awarded respondent $197,044.01 in damages, costs and disbursements.

Appellant was unaware of these proceedings and did not learn of the judgment until he retained new counsel on November 2, 1987. His new counsel moved for relief from default on the grounds that (1) the default was taken in violation of Code of Civil Procedure section 425.11, which, he alleges, has been construed to require personal service of a statement of damages; and (2) an answer was not filed due to his former counsel's excusable mistake and neglect, which warrants the granting of relief from default under Code of Civil Procedure section 473. The court denied the motion on the ground that appellant had not demonstrated the default resulted from counsel's excusable neglect.

* * *

This timely appeal followed.

DISCUSSION

A. Procedural Irregularities

1. Service pursuant to Code of Civil Procedure section 425.11.

Code of Civil Procedure section 425.11 provides, in pertinent part, that "the plaintiff shall give notice to the defendant of the amount of special and general damages sought to be recovered (1) before a default may be taken...."[2] Appellant argues, . . .that respondent's service of the statement of damages was insufficient since it was mailed to appellant's counsel, rather than personally served upon appellant.

In Engebretson, the court determined that where a defendant has failed to appear, personal service of an amended complaint is a prerequisite to a valid default judgment. (The court reasoned that nonappearing and defaulting defendants, who already have decided to permit a default judgment for the amount originally sought, might not pay adequate attention to an amendment served by mail, since they may mistakenly view it as merely a procedural step to obtaining the default judgment. In Plotitsa, the court used the same reasoning in holding that the defendants, who had not made an appearance in the action, were entitled to personal service of the statement of damages required prior to entry of a default judgment.

Despite the fact that Engebretson and Plotitsa both involved nonappearing defendants, appellant urges us to extend this rule to defendants who have appeared in the action. He argues the purpose of Code of Civil Procedure section 425.11 — to give the defendant one "last clear chance" to respond to the allegations — applies with even greater force to a litigant who has appeared and thus expressed his desire to present a defense.

We disagree with appellant's argument. Appellant does not deny that he made an appearance in this action when he filed a demurrer and motion to strike. (Code Civ. Proc., § 1014 ["A defendant appears in an action when he ... demurs [or] files a notice of motion to strike ..."].) He also does not dispute the fact that he was represented by counsel. He is therefore unlike the defendants in Plotitsa, who made no appearance and were unrepresented by counsel. Moreover, in Plotitsa there was a question as to whether service upon the defendants was effective; in the instant case the statutory notice admittedly was received, but went unheeded. On the facts presented we see no reason to extend Plotitsa to require personal service upon a defendant who, by filing a demurrer and a motion to strike, has made an appearance in the action.

Appellant admits his attorney was properly served with — and actually received — a statement of damages prior to the default. Thus, appellant's problem arises not from the mode of service, but from appellant's attorney's failure to respond to the threatened default. We therefore reject appellant's contention and conclude the statement of damages was properly served by mail upon appellant's counsel.

2. Variances between allegations and proof.

Appellant maintains that because the evidence presented at the default hearing went beyond the scope of the complaint it was tantamount to an amendment, which should revive his right to answer. In particular, appellant complains that (1) testimony concerning the conduct of his business partners was introduced, although the complaint was not amended to name those individuals; and (2) tenants other than respondent testified regarding their dealings with appellant and his partners despite the fact that such testimony did not relate to the allegedly wrongful evictions and could not properly be used to support an award of punitive damages to respondent.

A substantive amendment to a complaint supersedes the original complaint, and effectively "opens the default," which permits the defaulting defendant to answer. The purpose of this rule is to insure the defendant has an opportunity to reassess the action in light of the changes made in the complaint.

The rule has no application in this case because the "amendments" appellant focuses on did not result in any substantive changes and did not expose appellant to any greater or different liability than was presented by the complaint on file. Accordingly, there was no need to open the default to allow a reassessment of the action. While certain of the witnesses testified regarding the conduct of Emmett Hayes and Robert Hill, appellant's purported business associates, such references did not affect appellant's exposure and did not amount to a de facto amendment which added these men as defendants. Moreover, appellant was on notice that his agents and employees would be implicated since the complaint alleged that appellant and his agents together had engaged in unlawful business practices which resulted in respondent's losses. As such, the use of their actual names did not change the substance of the complaint or in any way surprise or disadvantage appellant.

Appellant also objects to testimony by tenants other than respondent concerning threatening or intimidating encounters with appellant and his partners. He argues only testimony directly relating to the assertedly wrongful evictions ought to have been used, and objects to the evidence concerning incidents involving tenants other than respondent. We find this argument unpersuasive.

First, appellant admits that evidence concerning his efforts to wrongfully evict other tenants from their apartments is relevant to respondent's claim that appellant engaged in an unlawful course of conduct under Business and Professions Code section 17200. Thus, the court did not err in permitting such testimony at the hearing. Moreover, after reviewing the record and the trial court's conclusions it is apparent the error, if any, in admitting this testimony was harmless. The evidence was presented to support respondent's claim that appellant's actions were willful and malicious, which would justify an award of punitive damages. However, the court specifically indicated that it was not awarding punitive damages because it considered the treble damages under the Rent Ordinance sufficient. Thus, the damage award was unaffected by the evidence of intimidation offered by the other tenants: under the Rent Ordinance respondent would have been entitled to the identical award based solely on the fact that he was wrongfully evicted based on the false assertion that respondent's unit was to be owner-occupied.

* * *

1. Award of excessive special damages.

Appellant next asserts the court erred in awarding $42,948 in special damages when respondent only sought $25,000. He points out that where the award resulting from a default judgment exceeds the relief sought the award must be amended to conform to the requirements of Code of Civil Procedure section 580.[8] (Furthermore, in Plotitsa v. Superior Court, supra, 140 Cal. App.3d 755, 761-762 the court held that a statement of damages which did not include a breakdown between general and special damages as provided in Code of Civil Procedure section 425.11 was insufficient. The court stated, "[a]lthough sections 425.10 and 425.11 are silent as to the purpose of requiring a statement of both special and general damages sought, it certainly appears that such information aids a defendant in evaluating the validity of plaintiff's damage claims with regard to their provability."

Respondent's complaint sought "actual and special damages, including, but not limited to, moving expenses, increased housing costs for an inferior residence, expenses for installing telephone and utilities, loss of earnings, loss of business goodwill and identity, business expenses arising out of relocation, and higher utility costs." (6a) "General damages are 'those which necessarily result from the act complained of,' and are implied by law to have thereby accrued to plaintiff. (7) Special damages, on the other hand, are defined as damages which do not arise from the wrongful act itself, but depend on the circumstances peculiar to the infliction of each respective injury." "'Special damages' refers to out-of pocket losses that can be documented by bills, receipts, cancelled checks, and business and wage records. Special damages generally include medical and related expense, loss of income, and the loss or cost of services. (6b) [¶] 'General damages' refers to damages for harm or loss such as pain, suffering, emotional distress, and other forms of detriment that are sometimes characterized as 'subjective' or not directly quantifiable."

Appellant argues the sum of the damages awarded for increased housing costs, moving expenses, loss of earnings and mental anguish, all assertedly special damages, exceeds the $25,000 sought in the statement of damages. In response, respondent maintains that only the damages awarded for mental anguish are properly characterized as special damages, and asserts the other items all are general damages well within the $400,000 sought in the statement of damages.

First, both parties are mistaken in characterizing the award of damages for mental anguish as special, rather than general, damages. As earlier noted, general damages are those losses which naturally flow from the injury and which are not quantifiable by reference to bills or receipts. Thus, damages for pain, suffering and emotional distress are paradigmatic examples of general damages.

Two of the remaining items comprising the damage award, moving expenses and actual loss of earnings prior to the default hearing, are clearly special damages, as they are based on actual out-of-pocket losses proved by reference to receipts and business records. For similar reasons, the other two types of damages awarded, for the present cash value of future lost earnings and the present cash value of the lost future possessory interest in the rent controlled apartment, are general damages. Unlike the moving expenses and lost earnings, which compensate for actual monetary losses already incurred, these damages compensate for future losses that can be estimated but not fixed. Because these losses have not yet been incurred they cannot be proved by receipts, bills or other financial records, but are nonetheless awarded because they are considered a natural and proximate result of the eviction. As such, they are general damages.

In sum, the only special damages awarded were for moving expenses ($800) and for actual lost earnings prior to the October 1987 hearing ($2,000), a total of $2,800, well within the $25,000 of special damages sought in the statement of damages.

* * *

D. Denial of Motion for Relief from Default

On January 13, 1988 a hearing was held on appellant's motion for relief from default under Code of Civil Procedure section 473. At that time the court heard arguments from counsel and denied the motion, concluding appellant had not made the requisite showing of excusable neglect. Appellant now asserts this was error.

"It is axiomatic that a motion for relief from default under section 473 is addressed to the sound discretion of the trial court. The exercise of that discretion will not be disturbed on appeal absent a clear showing of abuse." "[A] party who seeks relief under section 473 on the basis of mistake or inadvertence of counsel must demonstrate that such mistake, inadvertence, or general neglect was excusable `because the negligence of the attorney ... is imputed to his client and may not be offered by the latter as a basis for relief.' The client's redress for inexcusable neglect by counsel is, of course, an action for malpractice."

In the instant case appellant's counsel was warned on June 19, 1987 that a default would be taken on June 27. The default was in fact entered on July 1. Although appellant's counsel was informed that a prove-up hearing would be scheduled for October and was called by opposing counsel in September to ascertain whether he would be bringing a Code of Civil Procedure section 473 motion prior to the hearing, appellant's counsel did not take any steps to have the default set aside.

While appellant contends that his counsel's girlfriend's hospitalization led to the default, that does not explain why counsel failed to respond to the first amended complaint from February through June. Moreover, since counsel's friend was only hospitalized from June 20 to June 24, and was then released without restriction, it is not apparent why counsel was unable to respond between June 24 and July 1, when the default was entered. Finally, there is no reason offered for counsel's failure to promptly seek relief from the default once he returned to his business and realized his error.[11] Excusable neglect is an "act or omission which might have been committed by a reasonably prudent person under the same circumstances." In the absence of any reasonable explanation for the attorney's errors the court was entirely justified in finding the neglect inexcusable and denying appellant's request to be relieved of the default.

Finally, appellant argues he was abandoned by his attorney and should therefore not be charged with or penalized for counsel's errors. In support of this claim he cites Daley v. County of Butte (1964) 227 Cal. App.2d 380 [38 Cal. Rptr. 693], where the court found the plaintiff's attorneys guilty of gross misconduct which resulted in dismissal of the action due to a lack of prosecution. Plaintiff moved for relief from default, which was denied. On appeal the court observed that the attorneys had never personally appeared on any motion or in any pretrial conference and had never communicated with the court concerning any of the calendar hearings or pretrial conferences pertaining to the case. The attorneys also held plaintiff's requested substitution of attorneys for over five months without acting on it until defendant moved for dismissal. Under these circumstances the court held the plaintiff had been deprived of effective representation and would not be charged with the misconduct of her "nominal counsel of record." Accordingly, the court reversed the trial court's denial of plaintiff's motion under Code of Civil Procedure section 473.

Daley is inapposite. Here, unlike counsel in Daley, Attorney Zimmerman continued to act, albeit ineffectively, as appellant's representative. For example, when Zimmerman finally realized on June 27 that a default was imminent, he phoned respondent's attorney and asked to have appellant relieved of the default. Soon thereafter respondent's attorney spoke with Zimmerman concerning settlement of the case. When respondent's counsel met Zimmerman in late August or September of 1987 he said he intended to bring a motion for relief under Code of Civil Procedure section 473. On September 24 Zimmerman repeated this intention to respondent's attorney during a telephone conversation. At the section 473 hearing appellant's new counsel explicitly admitted there were "ongoing settlement negotiations" between Zimmerman and respondent's counsel after the July 1 default.

In Carroll v. Abbott Laboratories, our Supreme Court reviewed Daley and concluded that "the Daley exception should be narrowly applied, lest negligent attorneys find that the simplest way to gain the twin goals of rescuing clients from defaults and themselves from malpractice liability, is to rise to ever greater heights of incompetence and professional irresponsibility...." With this guideline in mind we cannot say the court erred in concluding appellant had not been abandoned within the meaning of Daley v. County of Butte, supra.

At oral argument appellant's counsel informed the court and opposing counsel that an amendment to Code of Civil Procedure section 473 that became effective after the completion of briefing in this case made relief from default mandatory whenever the attorney attests that his mistake, inadvertence, surprise or neglect resulted in the default at issue. She argued that because appellant's trial counsel had sworn that the default resulted from his neglect appellant was entitled to the benefit of the amendment.

In 1988, Code of Civil Procedure section 473 was amended to provide that: "Notwithstanding any other requirements of this section, the court shall, whenever an application for relief is timely, in proper form, and accompanied by an attorney's sworn affidavit attesting to his or her mistake, inadvertence, surprise or neglect, vacate any resulting default judgment entered against his or her client unless the court finds that the default was not in fact caused by the attorney's mistake, inadvertence, surprise or neglect. The court shall, whenever relief is granted based on an attorney's affidavit of fault, direct the attorney to pay reasonable compensatory legal fees and costs to opposing counsel or parties." This amendment became effective January 1, 1989.

The amendment changes the prior statute in two significant ways. While the preamendment statute provided that a court "may" relieve a party or his legal representative from a judgment taken through "mistake, inadvertence, surprise or excusable neglect," the amendment states that the court "shall" vacate any judgment resulting from an attorney's "mistake, inadvertence, surprise or neglect." Thus, while the prior law was discretionary, the amendment is couched in mandatory terms. Whereas the prior statute only recognized excusable neglect, the amendment provides relief for defaults founded on an attorney's neglect, regardless whether it may be characterized as excusable.

Appellant asserts that, pursuant to this amendment, relief from default must be granted unless the court finds the default did not in fact result from the attorney's mistake, inadvertence, surprise or neglect. The legislative history of the amendment supports that position; respondent does not offer a contrary interpretation, but only argues the amendment ought not be applied retroactively to relieve appellant's default.

* * *

[T]he amended version of Code of Civil Procedure section 473 cannot be applied retroactively to provide appellant relief from default.

* * *

The judgment is affirmed.

Peralta v. Heights Medical Center
485 U.S. 80 (1988)

Justice WHITE delivered the opinion of the Court.

Heights Medical Center, Inc. (hereafter appellee) sued appellant Peralta in February 1982, to recover some $5600 allegedly due under appellant's guarantee of a hospital debt incurred by one of his employees. Citation issued, the return showing personal, but untimely, service. Appellant did not appear or answer, and on July 20, 1982, default judgment was entered for the amount claimed, plus attorney's fees and costs.

In June 1984, appellant began a bill of review proceeding in the Texas courts to set aside the default judgment and obtain the relief. In the second amended petition, it was alleged that the return of service itself showed a defective service and that appellant in fact had not been personally served at all. The judgment was therefore void under Texas law. It was also alleged that the judgment was abstracted and recorded in the county real property records, thereby creating a cloud on appellant's title, that a writ of attachment was issued, and that, unbeknownst to him, his real property was sold to satisfy the judgment and for much less than its true value. Appellant prayed that the default judgment be vacated, the abstract of judgment be expunged from the county real property records, the constable's sale be voided, and that judgment for damages be entered against the Medical Center and Mr. and Mrs. Paul Seng-Ngan Chen, the purchasers at the constable's sale and appellees here.

Appellee filed a motion for summary judgment asserting that in a bill of review proceeding such as appellant filed, it must be shown that the petitioner had a meritorious defense to the action in which judgment had been entered, that petitioner was prevented from proving his defense by the fraud, accident, or wrongful act of the opposing party, and that there had been no fault or negligence on petitioner's part. Although it was assumed for the purposes of summary judgment that there had been defective service and that this lapse excused proof of the second and third requirement for obtaining a bill of review, it was assertedly necessary, nevertheless, to show a meritorious defense, which appellant had conceded he did not have.

..."An elementary and fundamental requirement of due process in any proceeding which is to be accorded finality is notice reasonably calculated, under the circumstances, to apprise interested parties of the pendency of the action and afford them the opportunity to present their objections." Mullane v. Central Hanover Bank & Trust Co. [supra page 161]. Failure to give notice violates "the most rudimentary demands of due process of law." Armstrong v. Manzo, 380 U.S. 545, 550 (1965). See also...Pennoyer v. Neff.

The Texas courts nevertheless held, as appellee urged them to do, that to have the judgment set aside, appellant was required to show that he had a meritorious defense, apparently on the ground that without a defense, the same judgment would again be entered on retrial and hence appellant had suffered no harm from the judgment entered without notice. But this reasoning is untenable. As appellant asserts, had he had notice of the suit, he might have impleaded the employee whose debt had been guaranteed, worked out a settlement, or paid the debt. He would also have preferred to sell his property himself in order to raise funds rather than to suffer it sold at a constable's auction.

Nor is there any doubt that the entry of the judgment itself had serious consequences. It is not denied that the judgment was entered on the county records, became a lien on appellant's property, and was the basis for issuance of a writ of execution under which appellant's property was promptly sold, without notice. Even if no execution sale had yet occurred, the lien encumbered the property and impaired appellant's ability to mortgage or alienate it; and state procedures for creating and enforcing such liens are subject to the strictures of due process. Here, we assume that the judgment against him and the ensuing consequences occurred without notice to appellant, notice at a meaningful time and in a meaningful manner that would have given him an opportunity to be heard....

...The Texas court held that the default judgment must stand absent a showing of a meritorious defense to the action in which judgment was entered without proper notice to appellant, a judgment that had substantial adverse consequences to appellant. By reason of the Due Process Clause of the Fourteenth Amendment, that holding is plainly infirm. Where a person has been deprived of property in a manner contrary to the most basic tenets of due process, "it is no answer to say that in his particular case due process of law would have led to the same result because he had no adequate defense upon the merits." Coe v. Armour Fertilizer Works, 237 U.S. 413, 424 (1915). As we observed in Armstrong v. Manzo, only "wip[ing] the slate clean...would have restored the petitioner to the position he would have occupied had due process of law been accorded to him in the first place." The Due Process Clause demands no less in this case.

The judgment below is reversed.

ARBITRATION

Alternative Dispute Resolution (ADR) has gained popularity as a way to avoid the vicissitudes of civil litigation. By pursuing ADR parties can often resolve their cases more quickly and with less expense than full-on civil litigation. One method of ADR is arbitration where the parties agree to have their case decided by a neutral (oftentimes a retired judge or a legally trained arbitrator). However, in return for what is arguably a speedier and more efficient system of justice, the parties who submit to arbitration often give up rights they could have exercised had they proceeded in the civil court system. Parties can agree in advance of any dispute breaking out to participate in arbitration.

Sometimes this agreement to arbitrate is done knowingly but in many cases it is done unwittingly.

Ferguson v. Countrywide Credit Industries, Inc.
298 F.3d 778 (9th Cir. 2002)

PREGERSON, J.

Misty Ferguson filed a complaint against Countrywide Credit Industries, Inc. and her supervisor, Leo DeLeon, alleging causes of action under federal and state law for sexual harassment, retaliation, and hostile work environment. Countrywide filed a petition for an order compelling arbitration of Ferguson's claims. The district court denied Countrywide's petition on the grounds that Countrywide's arbitration agreement is unenforceable based on the doctrine of unconscionability.

I. Factual and Procedural History

When Ferguson was hired she was required to sign Countrywide's Conditions of Employment, which states in relevant part: "I understand that in order to work at Countrywide I must execute an arbitration agreement."

The district court denied Countrywide's petition to compel arbitration. It ruled that the arbitration agreement is unenforceable because it is unconscionable under Armendariz v. Foundation Health Psychcare Services, Inc., 24 Cal. 4th 83 (2000).

II. Unconscionability

The FAA compels judicial enforcement of a wide range of written arbitration agreements. Section 2 of the FAA provides, in relevant part, that arbitration agreements "shall be valid, irrevocable, and enforceable, save upon such grounds that exist at law or in equity for the revocation of any contract." 9 U.S.C. §2. In determining the validity of an agreement to arbitrate, federal courts "should apply ordinary state-law principles that govern the formation of contracts." First Options of Chicago, Inc. v. Kaplan, 514 U.S. 938, 944 (1995). "Thus, generally applicable defenses, such as unconscionability, may be applied to invalidate arbitration agreements without contravening the FAA." Doctor's Assocs., Inc. v. Casarotto, 517 U.S. 681, 687 (1996). California courts may invalidate an arbitration clause under the doctrine of unconscionability. This doctrine, codified by the California Legislature in California Civil Code 1670.5(a), provides:

if the court as a matter of law finds the contract or any clause of the contract to have been unconscionable at the time it was made, the court may refuse to enforce the contract, or may enforce the remainder of the contract without the unconscionable clause, or it may so limit the application of any unconscionable clause as to avoid any unconscionable result.

This statute, however, does not define unconscionability. Instead, we look to the California Supreme Court's decision in Armendariz, which provides the definitive pronouncement of California law on unconscionability to be applied to mandatory arbitration agreements, such as the one at issue in this case. In order to render a contract unenforceable under the doctrine of unconscionability, there must be both a procedural and substantive element of unconscionability. These two elements, however, need not both be present in the same degree. Thus, for example, the more substantively oppressive the contract term, the less evidence of procedural unconscionability is required to come to the conclusion that the term is unenforceable.

1. Procedural Unconscionability

Procedural unconscionability concerns the manner in which the contract was negotiated and the circumstances of the parties at that time. A determination of whether a contract is procedurally unconscionable focuses on two factors: oppression and surprise. Oppression arises from an inequality of bargaining power which results in no real negotiation and an absence of meaningful choice. Surprise involves the extent to which the supposedly agreed-upon terms of the bargain are hidden in the prolix printed form drafted by the party seeking to enforce the disputed terms.

In Circuit City Stores, Inc. v. Adams, 279 F.3d 889, 892 (9th Cir.), cert. denied, 535 U.S. 1112 (2002), we held that the arbitration agreement at issue satisfied the elements of procedural unconscionability under California law. We found the agreement to be procedurally unconscionable because Circuit City, which possesses considerably more bargaining power than nearly all of its employees or applicants, drafted the contract and uses it as its standard arbitration agreement for all of its new employees. The agreement is a prerequisite to employment, and job applicants are not permitted to modify the agreement's terms—they must take the contract or leave it.

2. Substantive Unconscionability

Substantive unconscionability focuses on the terms of the agreement and whether those terms are so one-sided as to shock the conscience. Just before oral argument was heard in this case, the California Court of Appeal held in another case that Countrywide's arbitration agreement was unconscionable. See Mercuro v. Superior Court, 96 Cal. App. 4th 167 (2002).

a. One-Sided Coverage of Arbitration Agreement

Countrywide's arbitration agreement specifically covers claims for breach of express or implied contracts or covenants, tort claims, claims of discrimination or harassment based on race, sex, age, or disability, and claims for violation of any federal, state, or other governmental constitution, statute, ordinance, regulation, or public policy. On the other hand, the arbitration agreement specifically excludes claims for workers' compensation or unemployment compensation benefits,6 injunctive and/or other equitable relief for intellectual property violations, unfair competition and/or the use and/or unauthorized disclosure of trade secrets or confidential information. We adopt the California appellate court's holding in Mercuro, that Countrywide's arbitration agreement was unfairly one-sided and, therefore, substantively unconscionable because the agreement "compels arbitration of the claims employees are most likely to bring against Countrywide...[but] exempts from arbitration the claims Countrywide is most likely to bring against its employees."

b. Arbitration Fees

In Armendariz, the California Supreme Court held that:

when an employer imposes mandatory arbitration as a condition of employment, the arbitration agreement or arbitration process cannot generally require the employee to bear any type of expense that the employee would not be required to bear if he or she were free to bring the action in court. This rule will ensure that employees bringing [discrimination] claims will not be deterred by costs greater than the usual costs incurred during litigation, costs that are essentially imposed on an employee by the employer.

Countrywide's arbitration agreement has a provision that requires the employee to "pay to NAF [National Arbitration Forum] its filing fee up to a maximum of $125.00 when the Claim is filed. The Company shall pay for the first hearing day. All other arbitration costs shall be shared equally by the Company and the Employee." Countrywide argues that this provision is not so one-sided as to "shock the conscience" and, therefore, is enforceable.

However, Armendariz holds that a fee provision is unenforceable when the employee bears any expense beyond the usual costs associated with bringing an action in court. NAF imposes multiple fees which would bring the cost of arbitration for Ferguson into the thousands of dollars.7...

Because the only valid fee provision is one in which an employee is not required to bear any expense beyond what would be required to bring the action in court, we affirm the district court's conclusion that "the original fee provision...appears clearly to violate the Armendariz standard."

c. One-Sided Discovery Provision

Ferguson also argues that the discovery provision in the arbitration agreement is one-sided and, therefore, unconscionable. The discovery provision states that "a deposition of a corporate representative shall be limited to no more than four designated subjects," but does not impose a similar limitation on depositions of employees. Ferguson also notes that the arbitration agreement sets mutual limitations (e.g., no more than three depositions) and mutual advantages (e.g., unlimited expert witnesses) which favor Countrywide because it is in a superior position to gather information regarding its business practices and employees' conduct, and has greater access to funds to pay for expensive expert witnesses.

Ferguson urges this court to affirm the district court's ruling that the discovery provision is unconscionable on the ground that the limitations and mutual advantages on discovery are unfairly one-sided and have no commercial justification other than "maximizing employer advantage," which is an improper basis for such differences under Armendariz. Countrywide argues to the contrary that the arbitration agreement provides for ample discovery by employees.

In Armendariz, the California Supreme Court held that employees are "at least entitled to discovery sufficient to adequately arbitrate their statutory claims, including access to essential documents and witnesses." Adequate discovery, however, does not mean unfettered discovery. As Armendariz recognized, an arbitration agreement might specify "something less than the full panoply of discovery provided in the California Code of Civil Procedure."

In Mercuro, the California Court of Appeals applied the parameters set forth in Armendariz to Countrywide's discovery provisions. It concluded that "without evidence showing how these discovery provisions are applied in practice, we are not prepared to say they would not necessarily prevent Mercuro from vindicating his statutory rights." Mercuro relied heavily on the ability of the arbitrator to extend the discovery limits for "good cause." In fact, Mercuro ultimately left it up to the arbitrator to balance the need for simplicity in arbitration with the discovery necessary for a party to vindicate her claims. Following the Court in Mercuro, we too find that Countrywide's discovery provisions may afford Ferguson adequate discovery to vindicate her claims.

Nevertheless, we recognize an insidious pattern in Countrywide's arbitration agreement. Not only do these discovery provisions appear to favor Countrywide at the expense of its employees, but the entire agreement seems drawn to provide Countrywide with undue advantages should an employment-related dispute arise. Aside from merely availing itself of the cost-saving benefits of arbitration, Countrywide has sought to advantage itself substantively by tilting the playing field.

While many of its arbitration provisions appear equally applicable to both parties, these provisions may work to curtail the employee's ability to substantiate any claim against the employer. We follow Mercuro in holding that the discovery provisions alone are not unconscionable, but in the context of an arbitration agreement which unduly favors Countrywide at every turn, we find that their inclusion reaffirms our belief that the arbitration agreement as a whole is substantively unconscionable.

Conclusion

The district court's denial of Countrywide's petition to compel arbitration on the ground that Countrywide's arbitration agreement is unenforceable under the doctrine of unconscionability is AFFIRMED.

AT&T Mobility LLC v. Concepcion
131 S. Ct. 1740 (2011)

Justice SCALIA delivered the opinion of the Court.

Section 2 of the Federal Arbitration Act (FAA) makes agreements to arbitrate "valid, irrevocable, and enforceable, save upon such grounds as exist at law or in equity for the revocation of any contract." 9 U.S.C. §2. We consider whether the FAA prohibits States from conditioning the enforceability of certain arbitration agreements on the availability of classwide arbitration procedures.

I

In February 2002, Vincent and Liza Concepcion entered into an agreement for the sale and servicing of cellular telephones with AT&T Mobility LCC (AT&T). The contract provided for arbitration of all disputes between the parties, but required that claims be brought in the parties' "individual capacity, and not as a plaintiff or class member in any purported class or representative proceeding."2 The agreement authorized AT&T to make unilateral amendments, which it did to the arbitration provision on several occasions. The version at issue in this case reflects revisions made in December 2006, which the parties agree are controlling.

The revised agreement provides that customers may initiate dispute proceedings by completing a one-page Notice of Dispute form available on AT&T's Web site. AT&T may then offer to settle the claim; if it does not, or if the dispute is not resolved within 30 days, the customer may invoke arbitration by filing a separate Demand for Arbitration, also available on AT&T's Web site. In the event the parties proceed to arbitration, the agreement specifies that AT&T must pay all costs for nonfrivolous claims; that arbitration must take place in the county in which the customer is billed; that, for claims of $10,000 or less, the customer may choose whether the arbitration proceeds in person, by telephone, or based only on submissions; that either party may bring a claim in small claims court in lieu of arbitration; and that the arbitrator may award any form of individual relief, including injunctions and presumably punitive damages. The agreement, moreover, denies AT&T any ability to seek reimbursement of its attorney's fees, and, in the event that a customer receives an arbitration award greater than AT&T's last written settlement offer, requires AT&T to pay a $7,500 minimum recovery and twice the amount of the claimant's attorney's fees.3

The Concepcions purchased AT&T service, which was advertised as including the provision of free phones; they were not charged for the phones, but they were charged $30.22 in sales tax based on the phones' retail value. In March 2006, the Concepcions filed a complaint against AT&T in the United States District Court for the Southern District of California. The complaint was later consolidated with a putative class action alleging, among other things, that AT&T had engaged in false advertising and fraud by charging sales tax on phones it advertised as free.

In March 2008, AT&T moved to compel arbitration under the terms of its contract with the Concepcions. The Concepcions opposed the motion, contending that the arbitration agreement was unconscionable and unlawfully exculpatory under California law because it disallowed classwide procedures. The District Court denied AT&T's motion. It described AT&T's arbitration agreement favorably, noting, for example, that the informal dispute-resolution process was "quick, easy to use" and likely to "promp[t] full or…even excess payment to the customer without the need to arbitrate or litigate"; that the $7,500 premium functioned as "a substantial inducement for the consumer to pursue the claim in arbitration" if a dispute was not resolved informally; and that consumers who were members of a class would likely be worse off. Nevertheless, relying on the California Supreme Court's decision in Discover Bank v. Superior Court, 36 Cal. 4th 148 (2005), the court found that the arbitration provision was unconscionable because AT&T had not shown that bilateral arbitration adequately substituted for the deterrent effects of class actions.

The Ninth Circuit affirmed, also finding the provision unconscionable under California law as announced in Discover Bank [and holding] that the Discover Bank rule was not preempted by the FAA because that rule was simply "a refinement of the unconscionability analysis applicable to contracts generally in California."… We granted certiorari.

II

The FAA was enacted in 1925 in response to widespread judicial hostility to arbitration agreements. Section 2, the "primary substantive provision of the Act," provides, in relevant part, as follows:

"A written provision in any maritime transaction or a contract evidencing a transaction involving commerce to settle by arbitration a controversy thereafter arising out of such contract or transaction…shall be valid, irrevocable, and enforceable, save upon such grounds as exist at law or in equity for the revocation of any contract."

We have described this provision as reflecting both a "liberal federal policy favoring arbitration," and the "fundamental principle that arbitration is a matter of contract." In line with these principles, courts must place arbitration agreements on an equal footing with other contracts, and enforce them according to their terms.

The final phrase of §2, however, permits arbitration agreements to be declared unenforceable "upon such grounds as exist at law or in equity for the revocation of any contract." This saving clause permits agreements to arbitrate to be invalidated by "generally applicable contract defenses, such as fraud, duress, or unconscionability," but not by defenses that apply only to arbitration or that derive their meaning from the fact that an agreement to arbitrate is at issue. The question in this case is whether §2 preempts California's rule classifying most collective-arbitration waivers in consumer contracts as unconscionable. We refer to this rule as the Discover Bank rule.

In Discover Bank, the California Supreme Court applied [its] framework to class-action waivers in arbitration agreements and held as follows:

[W]hen the waiver is found in a consumer contract of adhesion in a setting in which disputes between the contracting parties predictably involve small amounts of damages, and when it is alleged that the party with the superior bargaining power has carried out a scheme to deliberately cheat large numbers of consumers out of individually small sums of money, then…the waiver becomes in practice the exemption of the party "from responsibility for [its] own fraud, or willful injury to the person or property of another." Under these circumstances, such waivers are unconscionable under California law and should not be enforced (quoting Cal. Civ. Code Ann. §1668)….

III

A

The Concepcions argue that the Discover Bank rule, given its origins in California's unconscionability doctrine and California's policy against exculpation, is a ground that "exist[s] at law or in equity for the revocation of any contract" under FAA §2. Moreover, they argue that even if we construe the Discover Bank rule as a prohibition on collective-action waivers rather than simply an application of unconscionability, the rule would still be applicable to all dispute-resolution contracts, since California prohibits waivers of class litigation as well.

When state law prohibits outright the arbitration of a particular type of claim, the analysis is straightforward: The conflicting rule is displaced by the FAA. But the inquiry becomes more complex when a doctrine normally thought to be generally applicable, such as duress or, as relevant here, unconscionability, is alleged to have been applied in a fashion that disfavors arbitration. In Perry v. Thomas, 482 U.S. 483 (1987), for example, we noted that the FAA's preemptive effect might extend even to grounds traditionally thought to exist "'at law or in equity for the revocation of any contract.'" We said that a court may not "rely on the uniqueness of an agreement to arbitrate as a basis for a state-law holding that enforcement would be unconscionable, for this would enable the court to effect what...the state legislature cannot."

An obvious illustration of this point would be a case finding unconscionable or unenforceable as against public policy consumer arbitration agreements that fail to provide for judicially monitored discovery. The rationalizations for such a holding are neither difficult to imagine nor different in kind from those articulated in Discover Bank. A court might reason that no consumer would knowingly waive his right to full discovery, as this would enable companies to hide their wrongdoing. Or the court might simply say that such agreements are exculpatory—restricting discovery would be of greater benefit to the company than the consumer, since the former is more likely to be sued than to sue. And, the reasoning would continue, because such a rule applies the general principle of unconscionability or public-policy disapproval of exculpatory agreements, it is applicable to "any" contract and thus preserved by §2 of the FAA. In practice, of course, the rule would have a disproportionate impact on arbitration agreements; but it would presumably apply to contracts purporting to restrict discovery in litigation as well.

Other examples are easy to imagine. The same argument might apply to a rule classifying as unconscionable arbitration agreements that fail to abide by the Federal Rules of Evidence, or that disallow an ultimate disposition by a jury (perhaps termed "a panel of twelve lay arbitrators" to help avoid preemption). Such examples are not fanciful, since the judicial hostility towards arbitration that prompted the FAA had manifested itself in "a great variety" of "devices and formulas" declaring arbitration against public policy. And although these statistics are not definitive, it is worth noting that California's courts have been more likely to hold contracts to arbitrate unconscionable than other contracts.

The Concepcions suggest that all this is just a parade of horribles, and no genuine worry. "Rules aimed at destroying arbitration" or "demanding procedures incompatible with arbitration," they concede, "would be preempted by the FAA because they cannot sensibly be reconciled with Section 2." The "grounds" available under §2's saving clause, they admit, "should not be construed to include a State's mere preference for procedures that are incompatible with arbitration and 'would wholly eviscerate arbitration agreements.'"

We largely agree. Although §2's saving clause preserves generally applicable contract defenses, nothing in it suggests an intent to preserve state-law rules that stand as an obstacle to the accomplishment of the FAA's objectives. As we have said, a federal statute's saving clause "'cannot in reason be construed as [allowing] a common law right, the continued existence of which would be absolutely inconsistent with the provisions of the act. In other words, the act cannot be held to destroy itself.'"

We differ with the Concepcions only in the application of this analysis to the matter before us. We do not agree that rules requiring judicially monitored discovery or adherence to the Federal Rules of Evidence are "a far cry from this case." The overarching purpose of the FAA, evident in the text of §§2, 3, and 4, is to ensure the enforcement of arbitration agreements according to their terms so as to facilitate streamlined proceedings. Requiring the availability of classwide arbitration interferes with fundamental attributes of arbitration and thus creates a scheme inconsistent with the FAA.

B

The "principal purpose" of the FAA is to "ensur[e] that private arbitration agreements are enforced according to their terms." This purpose is readily apparent from the FAA's text. Section 2 makes arbitration agreements "valid, irrevocable, and enforceable" as written (subject, of course, to the saving clause); §3 requires courts to stay litigation of arbitral claims pending arbitration of those claims "in accordance with the terms of the agreement"; and §4 requires courts to compel arbitration "in accordance with the terms of the agreement" upon the motion of either party to the agreement (assuming that the "making of the arbitration agreement or the failure…to perform the same" is not at issue). In light of these provisions, we have held that parties may agree to limit the issues subject to arbitration, to arbitrate according to specific rule, and to limit with whom a party will arbitrate its disputes.

The point of affording parties discretion in designing arbitration processes is to allow for efficient, streamlined procedures tailored to the type of dispute. It can be specified, for example, that the decisionmaker be a specialist in the relevant field, or that proceedings be kept confidential to protect trade secrets. And the informality of arbitral proceedings is itself desirable, reducing the cost and increasing the speed of dispute resolution.

The dissent quotes Dean Witter Reynolds Inc. v. Byrd, 470 U.S. 213, 219 (1985), as "'reject[ing] the suggestion that the overriding goal of the Arbitration Act was to promote the expeditious resolution of claims.'" That is greatly misleading. After saying (accurately enough) that "the overriding goal of the Arbitration Act was [not] to promote the expeditious resolution of claims," but to "ensure judicial enforcement of privately made agreements to arbitrate," Dean Witter went on to explain: "This is not to say that Congress was blind to the potential benefit of the legislation for expedited resolution of disputes. Far from it…." The concluding paragraph of this part of its discussion begins as follows:

We therefore are not persuaded by the argument that the conflict between two goals of the Arbitration Act—enforcement of private agreements and encouragement of efficient and speedy dispute resolution—must be resolved in favor of the latter in order to realize the intent of the drafters.

In the present case, of course, those "two goals" do not conflict—and it is the dissent's view that would frustrate both of them.

Contrary to the dissent's view, our cases place it beyond dispute that the FAA was designed to promote arbitration. They have repeatedly described the Act as "embod[ying] [a] national policy favoring arbitration," and "a liberal federal policy favoring arbitration agreements, notwithstanding any state substantive or procedural policies to the contrary."...Thus, in Preston v. Ferrer, holding preempted a state-law rule requiring exhaustion of administrative remedies before arbitration, we said: "A prime objective of an agreement to arbitrate is to achieve 'streamlined proceedings and expeditious results,'" which objective would be "frustrated" by requiring a dispute to be heard by an agency first. That rule, we said, would "at the least, hinder speedy resolution of the controversy."5

California's Discover Bank rule similarly interferes with arbitration. Although the rule does not require classwide arbitration, it allows any party to a consumer contract to demand it ex post. The rule is limited to adhesion contracts, Discover Bank, 36 Cal. 4th, at 162-163, but the times in which consumer contracts were anything other than adhesive are long past. The rule also requires that damages be predictably small, and that the consumer allege a scheme to cheat consumers. Discover Bank, supra, at 162-163. The former requirement, however, is toothless and malleable (the Ninth Circuit has held that damages of $4000 are sufficiently small, see Oestreicher v. Alienware Corp.), and the latter has no limiting effect, as all that is required is an allegation. Consumers remain free to bring and resolve their disputes on a bilateral basis under Discover Bank, and some may well do so; but there is little incentive for lawyers to arbitrate on behalf of individuals when they may do so for a class and reap far higher fees in the process. And faced with inevitable class arbitration, companies would have less incentive to continue resolving potentially duplicative claims on an individual basis.

Although we have had little occasion to examine classwide arbitration, our decision in Stolt-Nielsen is instructive...[where we] held that the agreement at issue, which was silent on the question of class procedures, could not be interpreted to allow them because the "changes brought about by the shift from bilateral arbitration to class-action arbitration" are "fundamental." This is obvious as a structural matter: Classwide arbitration includes absent parties, necessitating additional and different procedures and involving higher stakes. Confidentiality becomes more difficult. And while it is theoretically possible to select an arbitrator with some expertise relevant to the class-certification question, arbitrators are not generally knowledgeable in the often-dominant procedural aspects of certification, such as the protection of absent parties. The conclusion follows that class arbitration, to the extent it is manufactured by Discover Bank rather than consensual, is inconsistent with the FAA....

First, the switch from bilateral to class arbitration sacrifices the principal advantage of arbitration—its informality—and makes the process slower, more costly, and more likely to generate procedural morass than final judgment....A cursory comparison of bilateral and class arbitration illustrates the difference. According to the American Arbitration Association (AAA), the average consumer arbitration between January and August 2007 resulted in a disposition on the merits in six months, four months if the arbitration was conducted by documents only. AAA, Analysis of the AAA's Consumer Arbitration Caseload, online at http://www.adr.org/si.asp?id=5027 (all Internet materials as visited Apr. 25, 2011, and available in Clerk of Court's case file). As of September 2009, the AAA had opened 283 class arbitrations. Of those, 121 remained active, and 162 had been settled, withdrawn, or dismissed. Not a single one, however, had resulted in a final award on the merits....

Second, class arbitration requires procedural formality. The AAA's rules governing class arbitrations mimic the Federal Rules of Civil Procedure for class litigation....

Third, class arbitration greatly increases risks to defendants. Informal procedures do of course have a cost: The absence of multilayered review makes it more likely that errors will go uncorrected. Defendants are willing to accept the costs of these errors in arbitration, since their impact is limited to the size of individual disputes, and presumably outweighed by savings from avoiding the courts. But when damages allegedly owed to tens of thousands of potential claimants are aggregated and decided at once, the risk of an error will often become unacceptable. Faced with even a small chance of a devastating loss, defendants will be pressured into settling questionable claims....

The dissent claims that class proceedings are necessary to prosecute small-dollar claims that might otherwise slip through the legal system....But States cannot require a procedure that is inconsistent with the FAA, even if it is desirable for unrelated reasons....

Because it "stands as an obstacle to the accomplishment and execution of the full purposes and objectives of Congress," California's Discover Bank rule is preempted by the FAA. The judgment of the Ninth Circuit is reversed, and the case is remanded for further proceedings consistent with this opinion.

It is so ordered.

SCOPE OF REVIEW OF THE ARBITRATOR'S DECISION

Ferguson v. Writers Guild of America, West
226 Cal. App. 3d 1382, 277 Cal. Rptr. 450 (1991)

KLEIN (B.), J.A.

I

Larry Ferguson appeals from a judgment of the superior court denying his petition for a writ of mandate directed to respondent Writers Guild of America, West, Inc.

Ferguson, a screenwriter, was engaged by Paramount Pictures Corporation to write a screenplay for a feature-length theatrical motion picture entitled "Beverly Hills Cop II." When the picture was completed, the Writers Guild, on April 27, 1987, determined the writing credits for the picture as follows: Screenplay by Larry Ferguson and Warren Skaaren; Story by Eddie Murphy & Robert D. Wachs.

Ferguson then commenced this proceeding by filing a petition for writ of mandate in the superior court on May 15, 1987. In his petition he asked the court to issue a peremptory writ of mandate requiring the Writers Guild to set aside its credit determination and make a new determination giving Ferguson sole screenplay credit and sole story credit....

II

The process for determining writing credits for theatrical motion picture scripts is governed in this case by two documents. The first is the 369-page theatrical and television basic agreement, reached in 1985 by 241 producing companies, represented by the Alliance of Motion Picture and Television Producers, Inc.; 3 television networks; Writers Guild of America, West, Inc.; and Writers Guild of America, East, Inc. The second document is the Writers Guild West's 11-page credits manual, dated December 31, 1980.

The basic agreement contains, in a section entitled theatrical schedule A, detailed provisions concerning writing credits for feature-length theatrical photo-plays. Under schedule A, the production company must notify all participating writers of its tentative credits determination. Any of the writers may then file with the production company and the Writers Guild a written request for arbitration of credits....

The credits manual, discussed below, sets forth the procedures the Writers Guild has adopted....The credit arbitration is administered by the Writers Guild's credit arbitration secretary. When a credit arbitration is requested, this officer sends the parties to the arbitration a screen arbiter's list, containing the names of all potential arbitrators. These are Writers Guild members with credit arbitration experience or with at least three screenplay credits of their own. This list comprised at least 400 names in 1987. Each party can peremptorily disqualify a reasonable number of persons from the list. From the remaining potential arbitrators, the secretary selects three, endeavoring to select individuals experienced in the type of writing involved in the particular case.

The secretary delivers to the three arbitrators all script, outline, and story material prepared or used in the creation of the screenplay, together with source material (writings upon which the screenplay or story is based). These documents are supplied to the Writers Guild by the production company, and each participant in the credit arbitration may examine them to assure the inclusion of everything he or she has written. Any dispute over the "authenticity, identification, sequence, authorship or completeness" of literary material to be included is resolved by a special three-member committee, which conducts for that purpose a prearbitration hearing, at which all affected writers may present testimony and other evidence.

The arbitrators also receive the production company's statement of tentative credits; a copy of the credits manual; and the statements of the parties, which are confidential. The secretary designates a member of the Writers Guild's Screen Writers' credits committee to act as consultant to the arbitrators on procedure, precedent, policies, and rules, and to aid the arbitrators toward a majority decision.

The three arbitrators hold no hearing, and they deliberate independently of each other. Indeed, each remains unaware of the identity of the other two (unless, after they reach their decisions, the consultant convenes a meeting with the three). Each arbitrator notifies the secretary of his or her determination. The secretary then informs the parties of the decision of the majority of the arbitrators.

Within 24 hours thereafter, any party may request the convening of a policy review board, consisting of three members of the Writers Guild's credits committee including that committee's chairman or vice-chairman. The policy review board does not examine the script, story, or source material; indeed, its members are forbidden to read these. Its function is solely to detect any substantial deviation from the policy of the Writers Guild or from the procedure set forth in the credits manual. The policy review board has authority to direct the arbitration committee to reconsider the case or to order a fresh arbitration by a new triumvirate. The policy review board is not empowered to reverse the decision of an arbitration committee in matters of judgment. A decision of the policy review board approving a credit determination is final.

III

With his petition, Ferguson furnished the superior court with all screenplay and story materials, so the court could make the proper credit decisions under Writers Guild standards. Thus, to determine the correct story credit, the court was invited to ascertain which writings represented "a contribution distinct from screenplay and consisting of basic narrative, idea, theme or outline indicating character development and action."...

Ferguson contends, in the alternative, that the Writers Guild's credit determination process was infected by procedural improprieties and irregularities, and asks us to order the Writers Guild to conduct the credit arbitration anew. The asserted procedural defects are these: (1) the credit arbitration secretary improperly cast herself in the role of consultant to the arbitration committee and had improper substantive communications with the three arbitrators; (2) Ferguson was unfairly denied a postponement of the arbitration to assemble additional story materials and prepare his confidential statement for the arbitrators; (3) the arbitrators were given insufficient time to review the materials Ferguson submitted; (4) the Writers Guild took no steps to ensure the three arbitrators were disinterested and unbiased; (5) the arbitrators were not provided with copies of schedule A or the credits Manual; (6) the Writers Guild incorrectly treated as story material a memorandum in which Paramount executive David Kirkpatrick recounted a story idea told him orally by Murphy and Wachs; and (7) the Writers Guild improperly denied Ferguson's request that the arbitrators be given a second memorandum in which Paramount executive Michael Roberts remarked that Paramount "threw out" the screenplay drafted by the writers it had previously engaged and hired Ferguson "to write an entirely new draft." Ferguson presents a final contention, challenging as error the rulings of the superior court denying his requests (a) to take the deposition of Warren Skaaren, the writer awarded shared screenplay credit, and (b) to compel the Writers Guild to reveal the identity of the three arbitrators, presumably so Ferguson could take their depositions.

IV

Before ruling on these contentions, we must consider the proper scope of judicial review of the Writers Guild's credit determination in this case. We agree with the Writers Guild's position that under schedule A and the credits manual, disputes over writing credits for feature-length photoplays are nonjusticiable. As judges we are no doubt as capable as any lay person of studying screenplays, outlines, and other literary material to assess the relative contributions of the participating writers. The membership of the Writers Guild, however, have agreed among themselves (by approving the credits manual) and with the producers' association (by entering into schedule A of the basic agreement) that this delicate task is to be performed by arbitration committees composed of experienced Writers Guild members. The professional writers who constitute the Writers Guild have thus decided[,] quite appropriately we think[,] that the credit-determination process can be handled both more skillfully, more expeditiously, and more economically by Writers Guild arbitration committees than by courts. The finality provisions of schedule A and the credits manual, quoted earlier, demonstrate the Writers Guild membership's intention that credit disputes be resolved without resort to ruinously expensive litigation. The scope of judicial review in a particular case, then, is limited to a determination whether there has been a material breach of the terms of the credits manual, which binds the Writers Guild as well as its members. This limited scope of review is similar to that employed in judicial review of more traditional arbitrations. There the court does not review the merits of the arbitrators' award; it examines only whether the parties in fact agreed to submit their controversy to arbitration, whether the procedures employed deprived the objecting party of a fair opportunity to be heard, and whether the arbitrators exceeded their powers. (See Code Civ. Proc., §§1286-1286.8; Morris v. Zuckerman, 69 Cal. 2d 686, 691 (1968).)

V

In examining Ferguson's claims of procedural irregularities, we bear in mind that the procedures employed in the present arbitration have already been reviewed for correctness by the Writers Guild's own policy review board. The court accords considerable deference to the decision of the policy review board, because of its members' expertise in the interpretation and application of schedule A and the credits manual....

Even were we to reach the merits of Ferguson's seven claims, we would find them devoid of merit. Judicial review of the Writers Guild's credits determination is restricted to considering whether the party challenging the determination has demonstrated a material and prejudicial departure from the procedures specified in the credits manual. Applying this standard, we have determined that the record sustains none of Ferguson's seven procedural contentions.

Ferguson's remaining grievance is that he should have been told the names of the arbitrators.... We reject this position....

With respect to the identity of the arbitrators, the credits manual unequivocally specifies that the three arbitrators are not to be informed of each other's identities, and the Writers Guild has sufficiently established that, though not also stated in the credits manual, its unvarying and well-known rule has long been that the identities of the arbitrators are also not disclosed to the parties to the arbitration nor to anyone else inside or outside the Writers Guild. The Writers Guild's insistence on this practice is supported by important and legitimate considerations, including the necessity that arbitrators be entirely freed from both real and perceived dangers of pressure, retaliation, and litigation. While it is unusual to have an arbitration procedure in which the parties cannot appear in person before the arbitrators and cannot learn the arbitrators' identities, discovery of the names of the arbitrators in a Writers Guild credit arbitration could serve no legitimate function. Ferguson apparently wishes to ask the arbitrators, inter alia, to explain and justify their conclusions regarding the various writers' contributions to the final screenplay. Even when an arbitration is conducted under more familiar rules, though, such as the commercial arbitration rules of the American Arbitration Association, the losing party is not permitted to conduct an inquisition into the

CHAPTER 9 RESOLUTION WITHOUT TRIAL   413

arbitrators' thought processes in reaching their award.

Appellant's request to dismiss the appeal is denied, and the judgment is affirmed....

SUMMARY JUDGMENT

Under summary judgment, any party to an action, whether plaintiff or defendant, may move the court for summary judgment in his or her favor on a cause of action (i.e., claim) or defense. The court must grant the motion if all the papers submitted show that there is no triable issue as to any material fact and that the moving party is entitled to a judgment as a matter of law. The moving party must support the motion with evidence including affidavits, declarations, admissions, answers to interrogatories, depositions, and matters of which judicial notice must or may be taken. In sum, summary judgment is appropriate in any case where the material facts are undisputed and the only issues in the case are issues of law. (See FRCP 56; Cal.Code.Civ.Proc. sec 437c) FRCP 56 provides that summary judgment shall be granted if the pleadings, depositions, answers to interrogatories, and admissions together with affidavits show that there is no genuine issue as to any material fact.

Summary judgment may be requested not only as to an entire case but also as to a claim, defense, or part of a claim or defense.

Celotex Corp. v. Catrett
477 U.S. 317 (1986)

REHNQUIST, J.

...Respondent commenced this lawsuit in September 1980, alleging that the death...of her husband...resulted from his exposure to products containing asbestos manufactured or distributed by 15 named corporations....Petitioner's motion [for summary judgment]...argued that summary judgment was proper because respondent had "failed to produce evidence that any [Celotex] product... was the proximate cause of the injuries alleged...." In particular, petitioner noted that respondent had failed to identify, in answering interrogatories specifically requesting such information, any witnesses who could testify about the decedent's exposure to petitioner's asbestos products. In response to petitioner's summary judgment motion, respondent then produced three documents which she claimed "demonstrate that there is a genuine material factual dispute" as to whether the decedent had ever been exposed to petitioner's asbestos products. The three documents included a transcript of a deposition of the decedent, a letter from an official of one of the decedent's former employers whom petitioner planned to call as a trial witness, and a letter from an insurance company to respondent's attorney, all tending to establish that the decedent had been exposed to petitioner's asbestos products in Chicago. Petitioner, in turn, argued that the three documents were inadmissible hearsay and thus could not be considered in opposition to the summary judgment motion.

...The District Court granted...the motion...because "there [was] no showing that the plaintiff was exposed to the defendant Celotex's product in the District of Columbia or elsewhere within the statutory period." [The court of appeals reversed.] According to the majority, Rule 56(e) of the Federal Rules of Civil Procedure, and this Court's decision in Adickes v. S.H. Kress & Co., 398 U.S. 144, 159 (1970), establish that "the party opposing the motion for summary judgment bears the burden of responding only after the moving party has met its burden of coming forward with proof of the absence of any genuine issues of material fact." 244 U.S. App. D.C., at 163, 756 F.2d, at 184 (emphasis in original; footnote omitted). The majority therefore declined to consider petitioner's argument that none of the evidence produced by respondent in opposition to the motion for summary judgment would have been admissible at trial.

...We think that the position taken by the majority of the Court of Appeals is inconsistent with the standard for summary judgment set forth in Rule 56[(a)] of the Federal Rules of Civil Procedure....In our view, the plain language of Rule 56[(a)] mandates the entry of summary judgment, after adequate time for discovery...against a party who fails to make a showing sufficient to establish the existence of an element essential to that party's case, and on which that party will bear the burden of proof at trial. In such a situation, there can be "no genuine [dispute] as to any material fact," since a complete failure of proof concerning an essential element of the nonmoving party's case necessarily renders all other facts immaterial. The moving party is "entitled to judgment as a matter of law" because the nonmoving party has failed to make a sufficient showing on an essential element of her case with respect to which she has the burden of proof. "[The] standard [for granting summary judgment] mirrors the standard for a directed verdict under Federal Rule of Civil Procedure 50(a)...." Anderson v. Liberty Lobby, 477 U.S. 242, 250 (1986).

Of course, a party seeking summary judgment always bears the initial responsibility of informing the district court of the basis for its motion, and identifying those portions of ["particular parts of materials in the record, including depositions, documents, electronically stored information, affidavits or declarations, stipulations... admissions, interrogatory answers [quoting Rule 56(c)(1)]"] which it believes demonstrate the absence of a genuine [dispute]. But unlike the Court of Appeals, we find no express or implied requirement in Rule 56 that the moving party support its motions with affidavits or other similar materials negating the opponent's claim. On the contrary, Rule 56(c), which refers to "pleadings, depositions, answers to interrogatories and admission on file, together with the affidavits if any", suggests the absence of such a requirement....One of the principal purposes of the summary judgment rule is to isolate and dispose of factually unsupported claims or defenses, and we think it should be interpreted in a way that enables it to accomplish this purpose....

We do not mean that the nonmoving party must produce evidence in a form that would be admissible at trial in order to avoid summary judgment. Obviously, Rule 56 does not require the nonmoving party to depose her own witness. Rule 56[(a)] permits a proper summary judgment motion to be opposed by any of the kinds of evidentiary materials listed in Rule 56(c), except the mere pleadings themselves....

The Court of Appeals in this case felt itself constrained, however, by language in Adickes v. S. H. Kress & Co., 398 U.S. 144 (1970). There we held that summary judgment had been improperly entered in favor of the defendant....Adickes... said..."both the commentary on and the background of the 1963 Amendment conclusively show that it was not intended to modify the burden of the moving party...to show initially the absence of a genuine issue concerning any material fact." We think that this statement is accurate in a literal sense....But we do not think the Adickes language quoted above should be construed to mean that the burden is on the party moving for summary judgment to produce evidence showing the absence of a genuine issue of material fact, even with respect to an issue on which the nonmoving party bears the burden of proof. Instead, as we have explained, the burden on the moving party may be discharged by "showing"—that is, pointing out to the District Court—that there is an absence of evidence to support the nonmoving party's case....

Our conclusion is bolstered by the fact that district courts are widely acknowledged to possess the power to enter summary judgments sua sponte, so long as the losing party was on notice that she had to come forward with all of her evidence. It would surely defy common sense to hold that the District Court could have entered summary judgment sua sponte in favor of petitioner in the instant case, but that petitioner's filing of a motion requesting such a disposition precluded the District Court from ordering it.

Respondent commenced this action in September 1980, and petitioner's motion was filed in September 1981. The parties had conducted discovery, and no serious claim can be made that the respondent was in any sense "railroaded" by a premature motion for summary judgment. Any potential problem with such premature motions can be adequately dealt with under Rule 56[(d)], which allows a summary judgment motion to be denied, or the hearing on the motion to be continued, if the nonmoving party has not had an opportunity to make full discovery.

In this Court, respondent's brief and oral argument have been devoted as much to the proposition that an adequate showing of exposure to petitioner's asbestos products was made as to the proposition that no such showing should have been required. But the Court of Appeals declined to address either....We think the Court of Appeals...is better suited than we are to make these determinations in the first instance....Summary judgment procedure is properly regarded not as a disfavored procedural shortcut, but rather as an integral part of the Federal Rules as a whole, which are designed "to secure the just, speedy and inexpensive determination of every action." Fed. Rule Civ. Proc. 1. Before the shift to "notice pleading" accomplished by the Federal Rules, motions to dismiss a complaint or to strike a defense were the principal tools by which factually insufficient claims or defenses could be isolated and prevented from going to trial....But with the advent of "notice pleading," the motion to dismiss seldom fulfills this function any more, and its place has been taken by the motion for summary judgment....

The judgment of the Court of Appeals is accordingly reversed, and the case is remanded for further proceedings consistent with this opinion.

Aguilar v. Atlantic Richfield Co.
25 Cal.4th 826 (2001)

MOSK, J.

* * *

This is an antitrust action arising from a complaint filed by Theresa Aguilar on behalf of herself and all of the other, by her estimate, 24 million retail consumers of California Air Resources Board, or CARB, gasoline—collectively, Aguilar—against Atlantic Richfield Company, Chevron Corporation, Exxon Corporation, Mobil Oil Corporation, Union Oil Company of California (later succeeded by 76 Products Company), Shell Oil Company, Texaco Refining and Marketing, Inc., Tosco Corporation, and Ultramar Inc.—collectively, the petroleum companies...

[B]ecause our review focuses on the law that courts must apply in ruling on motions for summary judgment in all actions including the present, and not on the application of such law in this particular one, we need not state the facts in detail and at length....

On June 7, 1996, on behalf of herself and all other retail consumers of CARB gasoline, Aguilar filed an unverified complaint, with a demand for trial by jury, against the petroleum companies in the Superior Court of San Diego County. In the complaint, as subsequently amended into its operative form, she alleged facts for a primary cause of action for violation of section 1 of the Cartwright Act asserting in substance that the petroleum companies had entered into an unlawful conspiracy to restrict the output of CARB gasoline and to raise its price— specifically, a conspiracy among competitors that is unlawful per se without regard to any of its effects. She also alleged facts for a derivative cause of action for violation of the unfair competition law asserting in substance that the conspiracy in question, even if not unlawful under the Cartwright Act, was unlawful at least under the unfair competition law itself.

The petroleum companies each answered, denying all of the allegations referred to above.

Later, the petroleum companies each moved the superior court for summary judgment. In support, they each presented evidence including declarations by officers or managers or similar employees with responsibility in the premises, generally stating on personal knowledge how the company made its capacity, production, and pricing decisions about CARB gasoline, asserting that it did so independently, and denying that it did so collusively with any of the others. Aguilar opposed the motions. In support, she presented evidence including the companies' gathering and dissemination of capacity, production, and pricing information, through the independently owned and operated Oil Price Information Service, or OPIS, and otherwise; their use of common consultants; and, perhaps most prominently, their execution of exchange agreements—under which, for example, two companies may trade, with or without a price differential, products of the same type in different geographical areas and/or at different times or products of different types in the same geographical area and/or at the same time—including any consequent activity, or lack of activity, in the spot market, where individual wholesale bulk sales and purchases are transacted. She also presented related evidence in the form of opinion by experts.

After a hearing, the superior court issued an order granting the petroleum companies summary judgment...

III

Our task in this cause is to clarify the law that courts must apply in ruling on motions for summary judgment, both in actions generally and specifically in antitrust actions for unlawful conspiracy.

The purpose of the law of summary judgment is to provide courts with a mechanism to cut through the parties' pleadings in order to determine whether, despite their allegations, trial is in fact necessary to resolve their dispute.

* * *

In 1986, the United States Supreme Court handed down a trio of decisions dealing with the law of summary judgment in the federal courts: Matsushita Elec. Industrial Co. v. Zenith Radio (1986) 475 U.S. 574, 106 S.Ct. 1348, 89 L.Ed.2d 538 (hereafter sometimes Matsushita); Anderson v. Liberty Lobby, Inc. (1986) 477 U.S. 242, 106 S.Ct. 2505, 91 L.Ed.2d 202 (hereafter sometimes Anderson); and Celotex Corp. v. Catrett (1986) 477 U.S. 317, 106 S.Ct. 2548, 91 L.Ed.2d 265 (hereafter sometimes Celotex).

The purpose of federal summary judgment law, which is identical to the purpose of ours, is to provide courts with a mechanism to cut through the parties' pleadings in order to determine whether, despite their allegations, trial is in fact necessary to resolve their dispute. (Fed. Rules Civ.Proc., rule 56, 28 U.S.C.; Advisory Com. Notes, 1963 amend, to rule 56(e))

Under federal summary judgment law, which is similar to ours, any party to an action, whether plaintiff or defendant, "may., move" the court "for a summary judgment in [his] favor" on a claim (i.e., cause of action) or defense. The court must "render[ ]" the "judgment sought" "forthwith" . . . "if the pleadings, depositions, answers to interrogatories, and admissions on file, together with the affidavits, if any, show" that "there is no genuine issue as to any material fact" —that is, there is no issue requiring a trial as to any fact that is necessary under the pleadings and, ultimately, the law and that the "moving party is entitled to a judgment as a matter of law". The moving party may "support" the motion with evidence in the form of "affidavits" and also with the "pleadings, depositions, answers to interrogatories, and admissions on file" Likewise, any "adverse party" may "oppos[e]" the motion with "affidavits" and also with the "pleadings, depositions, answers to interrogatories, and admissions on file." An adverse party who chooses to oppose the motion must be allowed a reasonable opportunity to do so. When the moving party so makes and supports the motion, the opposing party "may not rest upon the mere allegations or denials of his "pleading," but his "response" by "affidavits" or by "depositions, answers to interrogatories, [or] admissions on file" "must set forth specific facts showing that there is a genuine issue for trial". In ruling on the motion, the court must consider all of the evidence and all of the inferences reasonably drawn therefrom and must view such evidence in the light most favorable to the opposing party.

In Celotex, Anderson, and Matsushita, the Supreme Court clarified federal summary judgment law, and liberalized the granting of such motions.

Together, Celotex, Anderson, and Matsushita operate generally, to the following effect: From commencement to conclusion, the moving party bears the burden of persuasion that there is no genuine issue of material fact and that he is entitled to judgment as a matter of law. There is a genuine issue of material fact if, and only if, the evidence would allow a reasonable trier of fact to find the underlying fact in favor of the party opposing the motion in accordance with the applicable standard of proof. Initially, the moving party bears a burden of production to make a prima facie showing of the nonexistence of any genuine issue of material fact. If he carries his burden of production, he causes a shift: the opposing party is then subjected to a burden of production of his own to make a prima facie showing of the existence of a genuine issue of material fact. How each party may carry his burden of persuasion and/or production depends on which would bear what burden of proof at trial. Thus, if a plaintiff who would bear the burden of proof by a preponderance of evidence at trial moves for summary judgment, he must present evidence that would require a reasonable trier of fact to find any underlying material fact more likely than not. By contrast, if a defendant moves for summary judgment against such a plaintiff, he may present evidence that would require such a trier of fact not to find any underlying material fact more likely than not. In the alternative, he may simply point out—he is not required to present evidence — that the plaintiff does not possess, and cannot reasonably obtain, evidence that would allow such a trier of fact to find any underlying material fact more likely than not.

* * *

At the time of Celotex, Anderson, and Matsushita, summary judgment law in this state differed from its federal counterpart in various particulars, and was more restrictive of the granting of such motions as a result. For example, a plaintiff moving for summary judgment had to disprove any defense asserted by the defendant as well as prove each element of his own cause of action. For his part, a defendant moving for summary judgment had to "conclusively negate"—to quote the potentially misleading phrase— an element of the plaintiffs cause of action. To do so, the defendant had to present evidence, and not simply point out that the plaintiff did not possess, and could not reasonably obtain, needed evidence. (See Code Civ. Proc., § 437c, subd. (b))

In the wake of Celotex, Anderson, and Matsushita, as we recently noted in Guz v. Bechtel National, Inc. (2000) 24 Cal.4th 317, 335, footnote 7, 100 Cal.Rptr.2d 352, 8 P.3d 1089 (hereafter sometimes Guz), summary judgment law has been amended, most significantly in 1992 and 1993, . . .

The purpose of the 1992 amendment was "to move summary judgment law" in this state "closer" to its "federal" counterpart as clarified in Celotex, Anderson, and Matsushita, in order to liberalize the granting of such motions. The purpose of the 1993 amendment was to move it even closer. Behind each of these amendments, Celotex figured prominently. Albeit less prominently, Anderson and Matsushita figured as well.

* * *

In moving for summary judgment, a "plaintiff ... has met" his "burden of showing that there is no defense to a cause of action if he "has proved each element of the cause of action entitling" him "to judgment on that cause of action. Once the plaintiff ... has met that burden, the burden shifts to the defendant ... to show that a triable issue of one or more material facts exists as to that cause of action or a defense thereto. The defendant ... may not rely upon the mere allegations or denials" of his "pleadings to show that a triable issue of material fact exists but, instead," must "set forth the specific facts showing that a triable issue of material fact exists as to that cause of action or a defense thereto." (Code Civ. Proc., § 437c, subd. (o)(D.)

Similarly, in moving for summary judgment, a "defendant ... has met" his "burden of showing that a cause of action has no merit if he "has shown that one or more elements of the cause of action ... cannot be established, or that there is a complete defense to that cause of action. Once the defendant ... has met that burden, the burden shifts to the plaintiff ... to show that a triable issue of one or more material facts exists as to that cause of action or a defense thereto. The plaintiff ... may not rely upon the mere allegations or denials" of his "pleadings to show that a triable issue of material fact exists but, instead," must "set forth the specific facts showing that a triable issue of material fact exists as to that cause of action or a defense thereto." (Code Civ. Proc., § 437c, subd. (o)(2).)

In light of the foregoing, we believe that summary judgment law in this state now conforms, largely but not completely, to its federal counterpart as clarified and liberalized in Celotex, Anderson, and Matsushita. The language added by the 1992 and 1993 amendments, which follows the substance of those decisions, supports our view. The legislative history of the bills that would result in those amendments provides confirmation, making plain that they "follow" their "example." (Sen. Com. on Judiciary, Analysis of Assem. Bill No. 2616 (1991-1992 Reg. Sess.) as amended Aug. 12, 1992, p. 9.)[10]

First, and generally, from commencement to conclusion, the party moving for summary judgment bears the burden of persuasion that there is no triable issue of material fact and that he is entitled to judgment as a matter of law.. . . A defendant bears the burden of persuasion that "one or more elements of the "cause of action" in question "cannot be established," or that "there is a complete defense" thereto. (Id., § 437c, subd. (o)(2).)

Second, and generally, the party moving for summary judgment bears an initial burden of production to make a prima facie showing of the nonexistence of any triable issue of material fact; if he carries his burden of production, he causes a shift, and the opposing party is then subjected to a burden of production of his own to make a prima facie showing of the existence of a triable issue of material fact. . . . A prima facie showing is one that is sufficient to support the position of the party in question. . . . No more is called for.

Third, and generally, how the parties moving for, and opposing, summary judgment may each carry their burden of persuasion and/or production depends on which would bear what burden of proof at trial. . . . Thus, if a plaintiff who would bear the burden of proof by a preponderance of evidence at trial moves for summary judgment, he must present evidence that would require a reasonable trier of fact to find any underlying material fact more likely than not—otherwise, he would not be entitled to judgment as a matter of law, but would have to present his evidence to a trier of fact. By contrast, if a defendant moves for summary judgment against such a plaintiff, he must present evidence that would require a reasonable trier of fact not to find any underlying material fact more likely than not—otherwise, he would not be entitled to judgment as a matter of law, but would have to present his evidence to a trier of fact.

* * *

It follows that summary judgment law in this state now conforms, largely but not completely, to its federal counterpart as clarified and liberalized in Celotex, Anderson, and Matsushita.

For example, summary judgment law in this state no longer requires a plaintiff moving for summary judgment to disprove any defense asserted by the defendant as well as prove each element of his own cause of action. In this particular, it now accords with federal law. All that the plaintiff need do is to "prove[ ] each element of the cause of action." (Code Civ. Proc., § 437c, subd. (o)(1).)[18]

Neither does summary judgment law in this state any longer require a defendant moving for summary judgment to conclusively negate an element of the plaintiffs cause of action. In this particular too, it now accords with federal law. All that the defendant need do is to "show[ ] that one or more elements of the cause of action ... cannot be established" by the plaintiff. (Code Civ. Proc., § 437c, subd. (o)(2).) In other words, all that the defendant need do is to show that the plaintiff cannot establish at least one element of the cause of action—for example, that the plaintiff cannot prove element X. . . .

Summary judgment law in this state, however, continues to require a defendant moving for summary judgment to present evidence, and not simply point out that the plaintiff does not possess, and cannot reasonably obtain, needed evidence. In this particular at least, it still diverges from federal law. For the defendant must "support[ ]" the "motion" with evidence including "affidavits, declarations, admissions, answers to interrogatories, depositions, and matters of which judicial notice" must or may "be taken." (Code Civ. Proc., § 437c, subd. (b).) The defendant may, but need not, present evidence that conclusively negates an element of the plaintiffs cause of action. The defendant may also present evidence that the plaintiff does not possess, and cannot reasonably obtain, needed evidence—as through admissions by the plaintiff following extensive discovery to the effect that he has discovered nothing.[24] But, as Fairbank v. Wunderman Cato Johnson (9th Cir.2000) 212 F.3d 528 concludes, the defendant must indeed present "evidence": Whereas, under federal law, `pointing out through argument' may be sufficient under state law, it is not.

To speak broadly, all of the foregoing discussion of summary judgment law in this state, like that of its federal counterpart, may be reduced to, and justified by, a single proposition: If a party moving for summary judgment in any action, including an antitrust action for unlawful conspiracy, would prevail at trial without submission of any issue of material fact to a trier of fact for determination, then he should prevail on summary judgment. In such a Justice Chin stated in his concurring opinion in Guz, the "court should grant" the motion "and avoid a ... trial" rendered "useless" by nonsuit or directed verdict or similar device.

* * *

The petroleum companies carried their burden of persuasion to show that there was no triable issue of material fact and that they were entitled to judgment as a matter of law as to Aguilar's unfair competition law cause of action. They did so by doing so as to her Cartwright Act cause of action. Again, they carried their burden of production to make a prima facie showing of the absence of any conspiracy, but she did not carry her shifted burden of production to make a prima facie showing of the presence of an unlawful one.

* * *

V

For the reasons stated above, we conclude that we must affirm the judgment of the Court of Appeal...

Houchens v. American Home Assurance Co.
927 F.2d 163 (4th Cir. 1991)

ERVIN, J.

Alice Houchens brought suit against American Home Assurance Company ("American") for breach of contract involving two insurance policies in the United States District Court for the Eastern District of Virginia. American made a motion for summary judgment, and a hearing was held on the motion. The district court granted American's motion for summary judgment, and Houchens appealed. Finding no error in the granting of summary judgment in favor of American, we affirm.

I

Coulter Houchens disappeared in August 1980 and has not been heard from since. His wife, Alice Houchens, is trying to collect upon either of two life insurance policies issued by American, which covered Mr. Houchens. One policy was an occupational accidental injury and death insurance policy. The other policy was a non-occupational accident insurance policy....Both policies required that the insured's death be caused by accident in order to be covered.

Evidence shows that Mr. Houchens was...[employed by the] International Civil Aviation Organization in Montreal, Canada (ICAO)...[and] stationed in Dharan, Saudi Arabia.

Sometime around August 14, 1980, Mr. Houchens received a week of vacation leave. He traveled to Bangkok, Thailand on or before August 14 via Thai Airlines.

Immigration records show that he arrived in Bangkok on August 15, 1980. His entry permit was valid through August 29, 1980.

No one has heard from Mr. Houchens since that time. The State Department, the FBI, ICAO, Mrs. Houchens, and the Red Cross have searched for him to no avail. In 1988, Mrs. Houchens brought an action to declare Mr. Houchens legally dead under Virginia law. On April 29, 1988, an order was issued by the Circuit Court of Loudoun County, Virginia, declaring that Mr. Houchens is presumed to have died between August 15 and August 29, 1980.

Houchens sued American for breach of contract because American refused to pay under either of two accidental death policies covering Mr. Houchens, which were issued by American. Both policies provided coverage in the event of death by accident. American maintained that there was no evidence of Mr. Houchens' death, nor was there evidence of accidental death. American moved for summary judgment, and the district court granted the motion. This appeal followed....

II

Section 64.1-105 of the Virginia Code provides that a person who has been missing for 7 years is presumed to be dead. Va. Code Ann. §64.1-105 (1987). Therefore, Mr. Houchens is presumed to be dead, and Mrs. Houchens is entitled to that presumption. However, in order for Mrs. Houchens to recover under the American policies, she must prove that Mr. Houchens died as a result of an accident. The term "accident" is not defined in the policies. In such cases, the courts of Virginia have said that an accident is an "event that takes place without one's foresight or expectation; an undesigned, sudden, and unexpected event." Harris v. Bankers Life & Cas. Co., 222 Va. 45, 46 (1981) (quoting Ocean Accident & Guaranty Corp. v. Glover, 165 Va. 283, 285 (1935)).

"Under the general rule...a beneficiary who makes a death claim under an accident policy or the double indemnity clause of a life policy, has the burden of proving that the insured's death was caused by violent, external and accidental means within the terms of the policy." Life & Cas. Ins. Co. of Tennessee v. Daniel, 209 Va. 332, 335 (1968). Therefore, the burden is on Mrs. Houchens to prove that her husband died by accidental means.

The district court granted summary judgment to American in this case under the rationale of Celotex Corp. v. Catrett, 477 U.S. 317 (1986). The Supreme Court set out the standard for granting summary judgment as follows:

In our view, the plain language of Rule 56[(a)] mandates the entry of summary judgment, after adequate time for discovery and upon motion, against a party who fails to make a showing sufficient to establish the existence of an element essential to that party's case, and on which that party will bear the burden of proof at trial.

We elaborated on that standard in Helm v. Western Maryland Ry. Co.:

> The appellate court, therefore, must reverse the grant of summary judgment if it appears from the record that there is an unresolved issue of material fact; the inferences to be drawn from the underlying facts contained in the materials before the trial court must be viewed in the light most favorable to the party opposing the motion.

On this appeal, then, we must view the evidence in the light most favorable to Houchens to ascertain whether she made a sufficient showing that Mr. Houchens died accidentally.

Mrs. Houchens asserts that the presumption that Mr. Houchens is dead somehow translates into the presumption that he died accidentally; therefore, she made a sufficient showing. She relies upon three cases from the western part of the country as support for the fact that she met her burden. [The court described these cases—Martin, Englehart, and Valley National.]

These three cases are readily distinguishable from the case at bar. Here, there is only evidence of a disappearance. Mr. Houchens went to Bangkok and was never heard from again. There are no bizarre circumstances surrounding his disappearance. He was not last seen in a position of peril as in Martin. He simply vanished. The circumstances surrounding his disappearance do not give us a clue that he actually died, as did the circumstances in Martin, Englehart, and Valley National. Viewed in the light most favorable to Mrs. Houchens, we can only conclude that Mr. Houchens disappeared, and then presume that he died under Virginia law. We cannot conclude that he died accidentally....

This is a case where the inferences show equal support for opposing conclusions. Mr. Houchens might have died accidentally. However, it is equally likely that he was murdered, that he died of natural causes, that he took his own life, or that he just went away somewhere and lives yet. "It is our function...to ascertain whether the evidence, considered in the light most favorable toward plaintiff affords room for men of reasonable minds to conclude that there is a greater probability that the ultimate fact did happen than that it did not happen." [quoting one of the distinguishable cases]. The ultimate fact at issue here is whether the death occurred by accident. We cannot conclude that there is a greater probability that the death was caused by accident than by other means.

The Virginia Supreme Court gave guidance in this area in General Accident & Casualty Corp. v. Murray, 120 Va. 115, [126] (1916). There the court wrote:

> The right to recover upon the policy sued on must be established by a preponderance of the evidence deduced in the case, and not be based merely upon conjecture, guess or random judgment, that is, upon mere supposition without a single known fact.

The [burden is upon plaintiff] to bring herself within the provisions of the contract of insurance by proving an accidental injury to the assured, and there is no presumption to aid her in this proof, since the well-established rule of law, according to all the authorities, is, that when death occurs it is presumed to be the result of natural dissolution rather than of accidental injury....

III

To summarize, Houchens relies on the presumption given her by §64-1.105 of the Virginia Code to establish that Mr. Houchens is dead. She then relies upon the facts surrounding his disappearance as a basis for a jury finding that his death was accidental. However, the meager circumstances would not allow a jury to reasonably conclude that it is more likely that Mr. Houchens died from an accident than in some other manner. Because of the sparse evidence concerning his disappearance, we cannot say that the district court erred in granting summary judgment in favor of American under the Celotex standard. Therefore, the order of the district court is affirmed....

Tolan v. Cotton
134 S. Ct. 1861 (2014)

PER CURIAM.

During the early morning hours of New Year's Eve, 2008, police sergeant Jeffrey Cotton fired three bullets at Robert Tolan; one of those bullets hit its target and punctured Tolan's right lung. At the time of the shooting, Tolan was unarmed on his parents' front porch about 15 to 20 feet away from Cotton. Tolan sued, alleging that Cotton had exercised excessive force in violation of the Fourth Amendment. The District Court granted summary judgment to Cotton. In articulating the factual context of the case, the Fifth Circuit failed to adhere to the axiom that in ruling on a motion for summary judgment, "[t]he evidence of the nonmovant is to be believed, and all justifiable inferences are to be drawn in his favor." Anderson v. Liberty Lobby, Inc., 477 U.S. 242, 255 (1986). For that reason, we vacate its decision and remand the case for further proceedings consistent with this opinion.

I
A

The following facts, which we view in the light most favorable to Tolan, are taken from the record evidence and the opinions below. At around 2:00 on the morning of December 31, 2008, John Edwards, a police officer, was on patrol in Bellaire, Texas, when he noticed a black Nissan sport utility vehicle turning quickly onto a residential street. The officer watched the vehicle park on the side of the street in front of a house. Two men exited: Tolan and his cousin, Anthony Cooper.

Edwards attempted to enter the license plate number of the vehicle into a computer in his squad car. But he keyed an incorrect character; instead of entering plate number 696BGK, he entered 695BGK. That incorrect number matched a stolen vehicle of the same color and make. This match caused the squad car's computer to send an automatic message to other police units, informing them that Edwards had found a stolen vehicle.

Edwards exited his cruiser, drew his service pistol and ordered Tolan and Cooper to the ground. He accused Tolan and Cooper of having stolen the car. Cooper responded, "That's not true." And Tolan explained, "That's my car." Tolan then complied with the officer's demand to lie face-down on the home's front porch.

As it turned out, Tolan and Cooper were at the home where Tolan lived with his parents. Hearing the commotion, Tolan's parents exited the front door in their pajamas. In an attempt to keep the misunderstanding from escalating into something more, Tolan's father instructed Cooper to lie down, and instructed Tolan and Cooper to say nothing. Tolan and Cooper then remained face-down.

Edwards told Tolan's parents that he believed Tolan and Cooper had stolen the vehicle. In response, Tolan's father identified Tolan as his son, and Tolan's mother explained that the vehicle belonged to the family and that no crime had been committed. Tolan's father explained, with his hands in the air, "[T]his is my nephew. This is my son. We live here. This is my house." Tolan's mother similarly offered, "[S]ir this is a big mistake. This car is not stolen.... That's our car."

While Tolan and Cooper continued to lie on the ground in silence, Edwards radioed for assistance. Shortly thereafter, Sergeant Jeffrey Cotton arrived on the scene and drew his pistol. Edwards told Cotton that Cooper and Tolan had exited a stolen vehicle. Tolan's mother reiterated that she and her husband owned both the car Tolan had been driving and the home where these events were unfolding. Cotton then ordered her to stand against the family's garage door. In response to Cotton's order, Tolan's mother asked, "[A]re you kidding me? We've lived her[e] 15 years. We've never had anything like this happen before."

The parties disagree as to what happened next. Tolan's mother and Cooper testified during Cotton's criminal trial that Cotton grabbed her arm and slammed her against the garage door with such force that she fell to the ground. Tolan similarly testified that Cotton pushed his mother against the garage door. In addition, Tolan offered testimony from his mother and photographic evidence to demonstrate that Cotton used enough force to leave bruises on her arms and back that lasted for days. By contrast, Cotton testified in his deposition that when he was escorting the mother to the garage, she flipped her arm up and told him to get his hands off her. He also testified that he did not know whether he left bruises but believed that he had not.

The parties also dispute the manner in which Tolan responded. Tolan testified in his deposition and during the criminal trial that upon seeing his mother being pushed, he rose to his knees. Edwards and Cotton testified that Tolan rose to his feet.

Both parties agree that Tolan then exclaimed, from roughly 15 to 20 feet away, "[G]et your fucking hands off my mom." The parties also agree that Cotton then drew his pistol and fired three shots at Tolan. Tolan and his mother testified that these shots came with no verbal warning. One of the bullets entered Tolan's chest, collapsing his right lung and piercing his liver. While Tolan survived, he suffered a life-altering injury that disrupted his budding professional baseball career and causes him to experience pain on a daily basis.

B

In May 2009, Cooper, Tolan, and Tolan's parents filed this suit in the Southern District of Texas, alleging claims under Rev. Stat. §1979, 42 U.S.C. §1983. Tolan claimed, among other things, that Cotton had used excessive force against him in violation of the Fourth Amendment. After discovery, Cotton moved for summary judgment.

The District Court granted summary judgment to Cotton. It reasoned that Cotton's use of force was not unreasonable and therefore did not violate the Fourth Amendment. The Fifth Circuit affirmed.

In reaching this conclusion, the Fifth Circuit began by noting that at the time Cotton shot Tolan, "it was...clearly established that an officer had the right to use deadly force if that officer harbored an objective and reasonable belief that a suspect presented an 'immediate threat to [his] safety.'" The Court of Appeals reasoned that Tolan failed to overcome th[at] bar because "an objectively-reasonable officer in Sergeant Cotton's position could have...believed" that Tolan "presented an 'immediate threat to the safety of the officers.'" In support of this conclusion, the court relied on the following facts: the front porch had been "dimly-lit"; Tolan's mother had "refus[ed] orders to remain quiet and calm"; and Tolan's words had amounted to a "verba[l] threa[t]." Most critically, the court also relied on the purported fact that Tolan was "moving to intervene in" Cotton's handling of his mother, and that Cotton therefore could reasonably have feared for his life. Accordingly, the court held, Cotton did not violate clearly established law in shooting Tolan....

II
B

In holding that Cotton's actions did not violate clearly established law, the Fifth Circuit failed to view the evidence at summary judgment in the light most favorable to Tolan with respect to the central facts of this case. By failing to credit evidence that contradicted some of its key factual conclusions, the court improperly "weigh[ed] the evidence" and resolved disputed issues in favor of the moving party, Anderson, 477 U.S., at 249.

First, the court relied on its view that at the time of the shooting, the Tolans' front porch was "dimly-lit." The court appears to have drawn this assessment from Cotton's statements in a deposition that when he fired at Tolan, the porch was "'fairly dark,'" and lit by a gas lamp that was "'decorative.'" In his own deposition, however, Tolan's father was asked whether the gas lamp was in fact "more decorative than illuminating." He said that it was not. Moreover, Tolan stated in his deposition that two floodlights shone on the driveway during the incident, and Cotton acknowledged that there were two motion-activated lights in front of the house. And Tolan confirmed that at the time of the shooting, he was "not in darkness."

Second, the Fifth Circuit stated that Tolan's mother "refus[ed] orders to remain quiet and calm," thereby "compound[ing]" Cotton's belief that Tolan "presented an immediate threat to the safety of the officers." But here, too, the court did not credit directly contradictory evidence. Although the parties agree that Tolan's mother repeatedly informed officers that Tolan was her son, that she lived in the home in front of which he had parked, and that the vehicle he had been driving belonged to her and her husband, there is a dispute as to how calmly she provided this information. Cotton stated during his deposition that Tolan's mother was "very agitated" when she spoke to the officers. By contrast, Tolan's mother testified at Cotton's criminal trial that she was neither "aggravated" nor "agitated."

Third, the Court concluded that Tolan was "shouting," and "verbally threatening" the officer, in the moments before the shooting. The court noted, and the parties agree, that while Cotton was grabbing the arm of his mother, Tolan told Cotton, "[G]et your fucking hands off my mom." But Tolan testified that he "was not screaming." And a jury could reasonably infer that his words, in context, did not amount to a statement of intent to inflict harm. Tolan's mother testified in Cotton's criminal trial that he slammed her against a garage door with enough force to cause bruising that lasted for days. A jury could well have concluded that a reasonable officer would have heard Tolan's words not as a threat, but as a son's plea not to continue any assault of his mother.

Fourth, the Fifth Circuit inferred that at the time of the shooting, Tolan was "moving to intervene in Sergeant Cotton's" interaction with his mother. The court appears to have credited Edwards' account that at the time of the shooting, Tolan was on both feet "[i]n a crouch" or a "charging position" looking as if he was going to move forward. Tolan testified at trial, however, that he was on his knees when Cotton shot him, a fact corroborated by his mother. Tolan also testified in his deposition that he "wasn't going anywhere," and emphasized that he did not "jump up."

Considered together, these facts lead to the inescapable conclusion that the court below credited the evidence of the party seeking summary judgment and failed properly to acknowledge key evidence offered by the party opposing that motion. And while "this Court is not equipped to correct every perceived error coming from the lower federal courts," Boag v. MacDougall, 454 U.S. 364, 366 (1982) (O'Connor, J., concurring), we intervene here because the opinion below reflects a clear misapprehension of summary judgment standards in light of our precedents.

The witnesses on both sides come to this case with their own perceptions, recollections, and even potential biases. It is in part for that reason that genuine disputes are generally resolved by juries in our adversarial system. By weighing the evidence and reaching factual inferences contrary to Tolan's competent evidence, the court below neglected to adhere to the fundamental principle that at the summary judgment stage, reasonable inferences should be drawn in favor of the nonmoving party.

Applying that principle here, the court should have acknowledged and credited Tolan's evidence with regard to the lighting, his mother's demeanor, whether he shouted words that were an overt threat, and his positioning during the shooting....The judgment of the United States Court of Appeals for the Fifth Circuit is vacated, and the case is remanded for further proceedings consistent with this opinion.

Bias v. Advantage International, Inc.
905 F.2d 1558 (D.C. Cir. 1990)

SENTELLE, J.

This case arises out of the tragic death from cocaine intoxication of University of Maryland basketball star Leonard K. Bias ("Bias"). James Bias, as Personal Representative of the Estate of Leonard K. Bias, deceased ("the Estate"), appeals an order of the District Court for the District of Columbia which granted summary judgment to defendants Advantage International, Inc. ("Advantage") and A. Lee Fentress....For the reasons which follow, we affirm....

I. Background

On April 7, 1986, after the close of his college basketball career, Bias entered into a representation agreement with Advantage whereby Advantage agreed to advise and represent Bias in his affairs. Fentress was the particular Advantage representative servicing the Bias account. On June 17 of that year Bias was picked by the Boston Celtics in the first round of the National Basketball Association draft. On the morning of June 19, 1986, Bias died of cocaine intoxication. The Estate sued Advantage and Fentress for...injuries allegedly arising out of the representation arrangement between Bias and the defendants.

[T]he Estate alleges that, prior to Bias's death, Bias and his parents directed Fentress to obtain a one-million dollar life insurance policy on Bias's life, that Fentress represented to Bias and Bias's parents that he had secured such a policy, and that in reliance on Fentress's assurances, Bias's parents did not independently seek to buy an insurance policy on Bias's life....[D]efendants...did not secure any life insurance coverage for Bias prior to his death....

The District Court awarded the defendants summary judgment....With respect to the [life insurance] claim, the District Court held, in effect, that the Estate did not suffer any damage from the defendants' alleged failure to obtain life insurance for Bias because, even if the defendants had tried to obtain a one-million dollar policy on Bias's life, they would not have been able to do so. The District Court based this conclusion on the facts, about which it found no genuine issue, that Bias was a cocaine user and that no insurer in 1986 would have issued a one-million dollar life insurance policy, or "jumbo" policy, to a cocaine user unless the applicant made a misrepresentation regarding the applicant's use of drugs, thereby rendering the insurance policy void....

The Estate appeals...the District Court's conclusions, arguing that there is a genuine issue as to Bias's insurability....

II. Summary Judgment Standard

The Supreme Court has stated that the moving party always bears the initial responsibility of informing the district court of the basis for its motion and identifying those portions of the record which it believes demonstrate the absence of a genuine issue of material fact. Celotex Corp. v. Catrett. The Supreme Court also explained that summary judgment is appropriate, no matter which party is the moving party, where a party fails to make a showing sufficient to establish the existence of an element essential to that party's case, and on which that party will bear the burden of proof at trial. Thus, the moving party must explain its reasons for concluding that the record does not reveal any genuine issues of material fact, and must make a showing supporting its claims insofar as those claims involve issues on which it will bear the burden at trial.

Once the moving party has carried its burden, the responsibility then shifts to the nonmoving party to show that there is, in fact, a genuine issue of material fact. The Supreme Court has directed that the nonmoving party "must do more than simply show that there is some metaphysical doubt as to the material facts." Matsushita Elec. Industrial Co. v. Zenith Radio, 475 U.S. 574, 586 (1986). The nonmoving party "must come forward with 'specific facts showing that there is a genuine issue for trial.'" (emphasis in original). In evaluating the nonmovant's proffer, a court must of course draw from the evidence all justifiable inferences in favor of the nonmovant. Anderson v. Liberty Lobby, Inc., 477 U.S. 242, 255 (1986).

III. The Insurance Issue

The District Court's determination that there was no genuine issue involving Bias's insurability rests on two subsidiary conclusions: First, the District Court concluded that there was no genuine issue as to the fact that Bias was a drug user. Second, the District Court held that there was no dispute about the fact that as a drug user, Bias could not have obtained a jumbo life insurance policy. We can only affirm the District Court's award of summary judgment to the defendants on the insurance issue if both of these conclusions were correct.

A. Bias's Prior Drug Use

The defendants in this case offered the eyewitness testimony of two former teammates of Bias, Terry Long and David Gregg, in order to show that Bias was a cocaine user during the period prior to his death. Long and Gregg both described numerous occasions when they saw Bias ingest cocaine, and Long testified that he was introduced to cocaine by Bias and that Bias sometimes supplied others with cocaine.

Although on appeal the Estate attempts to discredit the testimony of Long and Gregg, the Estate did not seek to impeach the testimony of these witnesses before the District Court, and the Estate made no effort to depose these witnesses. Instead, the Estate offered affidavits from each of Bias's parents stating that Bias was not a drug user; the deposition testimony of Bias's basketball coach, Charles "Lefty" Driesell, who testified that he knew Bias well for four years and never knew Bias to be a user of drugs at any time prior to his death; and the results of several drug tests administered to Bias during the four years prior to his death which may have shown that, on the occasions when the tests were administered, there were no traces in Bias's system of the drugs for which he was tested.

Because the Estate's generalized evidence that Bias was not a drug user did not contradict the more specific testimony of teammates who knew Bias well and had seen him use cocaine on particular occasions, the District Court determined that there was no genuine issue as to the fact that Bias was a drug user. We agree.

There is no question that the defendants satisfied their initial burden on the issue of Bias's drug use. The testimony of Long and Gregg clearly tends to show that Bias was a cocaine user. We also agree with the District Court that the Estate did not rebut the defendants' showing. The testimony of Bias's parents to the effect that they knew Bias well and did not know him to be a drug user does not rebut the Long and Gregg testimony about Bias's drug use on particular occasions. The District Court properly held that rebuttal testimony either must come from persons familiar with the particular events to which the defendants' witnesses testified or must otherwise cast more than metaphysical doubt on the credibility of that testimony. Bias's parents and coach did not have personal knowledge of Bias's activities at the sorts of parties and gatherings about which Long and Gregg testified. The drug test results offered by the Estate may show that Bias had no cocaine in his system on the dates when the tests were administered, but, as the District Court correctly noted, these tests speak only to Bias's abstention during the periods preceding the tests. The tests do not rebut the Long and Gregg testimony that on a number of occasions Bias ingested cocaine in their presence.

The Estate could have deposed Long and Gregg, or otherwise attempted to impeach their testimony. The Estate also could have offered the testimony of other friends or teammates of Bias who were present at some of the gatherings described by Long and Gregg, who went out with Bias frequently, or who were otherwise familiar with his social habits. The Estate did none of these things. The Estate is not entitled to reach the jury merely on the supposition that the jury might not believe the defendants' witnesses. We thus agree with the District Court that there was no genuine issue of fact concerning Bias's status as a cocaine user.

B. The Availability of a Jumbo Policy in Light of Bias's Prior Drug Use...

The defendants offered evidence that every insurance company inquires about the prior drug use of an applicant for a jumbo policy at some point in the application process.... The Estate's evidence that some insurance companies existed in 1986 which did not inquire about prior drug use at certain particular stages in the application process does not undermine the defendant's claim that at some point in the process every insurance company did inquire about drug use, particularly where a jumbo policy was involved. The Estate failed to name a single particular company or provide other evidence that a single company existed which would have issued a jumbo policy in 1986 without inquiring about the applicant's drug use. Because the Estate has failed to do more than show that there is "some metaphysical doubt as to the material facts," Matsushita Elec., the District Court properly concluded that there was no genuine issue of material fact as to the insurability of a drug user....

In order to withstand a summary judgment motion once the moving party has made a prima facie showing to support its claims, the nonmoving party must come forward with specific facts showing that there is a genuine issue for trial. Fed. R. Civ. P. 56(e). The Estate has failed to come forward with such facts in this case, relying instead on bare arguments and allegations or on evidence which does not actually create a genuine issue for trial. For this reason, we affirm the District Court's award of summary judgment to the defendants in this case.

TIMING OF THE MOTION FOR SUMMARY JUDGMENT

FEDERAL COURT

FRCP 56 allows a party to move for summary judgment at any time, even as early as the commencement of the action. If the motion seems premature both subdivision (c)(1) and FRCP 6(b) allow the court to extend the time to respond. The rule does set a presumptive deadline at 30 days after the close of all discovery. (Committee Notes on Rules—2009 Amendment) The presumptive timing rules are default provisions that may be altered by an order in the case or by local rule.

CALIFORNIA STATE COURT

The motion for summary judgment may be made at any time after 60 days have elapsed since the general appearance in the action or proceeding of each party against whom the motion is directed. The motion shall be heard no later than 30 days before the date of trial. Notice of the motion and supporting papers shall be served on all other parties to the action at least 75 days before the time appointed for hearing. (CCP §437c(a))

This page left intentionally blank.

CHAPTER 10

THE TRIAL

PRETRIAL CONFERENCES AND ORDERS

FRCP 16 makes scheduling and case management an express goal of pretrial procedure. This is done by shifting the emphasis away from a conference focused solely on the trial and toward a process of judicial management that embraces the entire pretrial phase, especially motions and discovery. Note the mandatory scheduling order described in FRCP 16(b). A scheduling conference may be requested either by the judge or a party within 90 days after the summons and complaint are filed, or 60 days after any defendant has appeared. If a scheduling conference is not arranged within that time and the case is not exempted by local rule, a scheduling order must be issued under FRCP 16(b), after some communication with the parties, which may be by may be held in person, by telephone, or by more sophisticated electronic means, rather than in person. The judge and attorneys are required to develop a timetable for the matters listed in FRCP 16(b)(1)–(3). As indicated in FRCP 16(b)(4)–(5), the order may also deal with a wide range of other matters. The court must issue a written scheduling order even if no scheduling conference is called. The order normally will "control the subsequent course of the action." Once formulated, pretrial orders should not be changed lightly. (Notes of Advisory Committee on Rules)

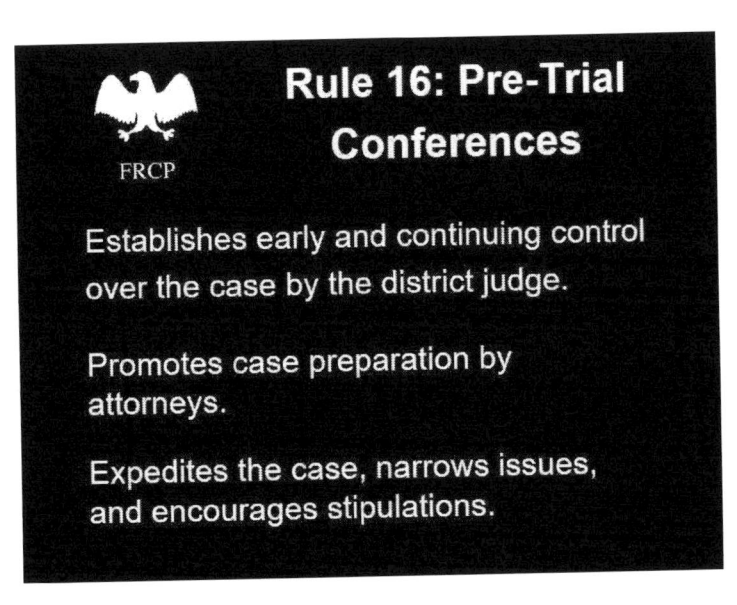

> **Rule 16: Pre-Trial Conferences**
>
> Establishes early and continuing control over the case by the district judge.
>
> Promotes case preparation by attorneys.
>
> Expedites the case, narrows issues, and encourages stipulations.

Monfore v. Phillips
778 F.3d 849 (10th Cir. 2015)

GORSUCH, J.

Sherman Shatwell went to the hospital complaining of neck pain. Tests showed he probably had throat cancer. It was treatable but required immediate attention. Thanks to a variety of bureaucratic blunders the news never made it to him. Instead, Mr. Shatwell was sent home with a prescription for antibiotics. By the time he learned the truth a year later, it was too late.

Eventually, his widowed wife pursued negligence claims against the doctors and hospital. Through twenty months of motions practice and discovery and all the way through their submissions for the final pretrial order the defendants maintained a unified front, denying any negligence by anyone. Then, two weeks before trial, some of the defendants settled. Dr. Kenneth Phillips wasn't one of those. Left to stand trial and with just days before jury selection, he sought permission to amend the pretrial order so he could revamp his trial strategy. Now he wanted to pursue a defense pinning the blame on the absent settling defendants, arguing that they were indeed negligent and that they—not he—should be held responsible for any damages. Dr. Phillips's motion to amend the final pretrial order sought permission to introduce new jury instructions, exhibits, and witnesses aimed at advancing this new defense. But the district court denied the motion and at the trial's end the jury found him liable for damages of a little over $1 million. Dr. Phillips now asks us to overturn the judgment, contending that the district court's refusal to amend the final pretrial order and allow his new defense amounts to reversible error.

Final pretrial orders seek to "formulate a trial plan." Fed. R. Civ. P. 16(e). In their complaints and answers lawyers and parties today often list every alternative and contradictory claim or defense known to the law; during discovery they sometimes depose every potential witness still breathing and collect every bit and byte of evidence technology, time, and money will allow. Final pretrial orders seek to tame such exuberant modern pretrial practices and focus the mind on the impending reality of trial. "The casual pleading [and discovery] indulged by the courts under the Federal Rules...has quite naturally led to"—some might say required—"more and more emphasis on pre-trial hearings and statements to define the issues" for trial. Meadow Gold Prods. Co. v. Wright, 278 F.2d 867, 868-69 (D.C. Cir. 1960). Leaving the reins so loose at the front end of the case requires some method of gathering them up as the end approaches. At trial you just can't argue every contradictory and mutually exclusive claim or defense you were able to conjure in your pleadings: juries would lose faith in your credibility. Neither can you present the millions of documents and the scores of witnesses you were able to dig up in discovery: no sensible judge would tolerate it. Final pretrial orders encourage both sides to edit their scripts, peel away any pleading and discovery bluster, and disclose something approximating their real trial intentions to opposing counsel and the court. Toward those ends, the parties are often asked—as they were in this case—to specify the witnesses and exhibits, supply the proposed jury instructions, and identify the claims and defenses they actually intend to introduce at trial.

While pretrial orders entered earlier in the life of a case often deal with interstitial questions like discovery staging and motions practice and are relatively easy to amend as a result, a final pretrial order focused on formulating a plan for an impending trial may be amended "only to prevent manifest injustice." Fed. R. Civ. P. 16(e). Even that standard isn't meant to preclude any flexibility—trials are high human dramas; surprises always emerge; and no judge worth his salt can forget or fail to sympathize with the challenges the trial lawyer confronts. For all our extensive pretrial procedures, even the most meticulous trial plan today probably remains no more reliable a guide than the script in a high school play—provisional at best and with surprising deviations guaranteed. At the same time, the standard for modifying a final pretrial order is as high as it is to ensure everyone involved has sufficient incentive to fulfill the order's dual purposes of encouraging self-editing and providing reasonably fair disclosure to the court and opposing parties alike of their real trial intentions. This court will review a district court's decision to amend or not to amend a pretrial order only for abuse of discretion.

We see nothing like that here. Dr. Phillips says that he was surprised when his co-defendants left him to stand trial and that the court was insufficiently sympathetic to his desire to revamp his trial strategy in light of the last-minute settlement. But can a partial settlement really come as a surprise in an age when virtually all cases settle in part or in whole, many on the eve of trial? Especially in multiparty litigation, where an incentive exists to break ranks, settle relatively cheaply, and leave others on the hook before the jury? The truth is, what happened in this case was hardly unforeseeable. Like many before him in multi-defendant cases, Dr. Phillips initially saw profit in presenting a united front with his co-defendants only to regret the decision later. United front defenses often present a tempting choice at the outset of multiparty cases and through discovery. Parties can pool their resources and efforts in joint defense arrangements. Besides, no one likes to throw overboard someone else in the same boat. But the complications associated with this strategic choice often come home to roost as trial nears. An attractive partial settlement may be dangled before one defendant and not others. The settling defendant may get a good deal, replenish an opponent's litigation coffers depleted through exhausting pretrial litigation, and leave others exposed at trial for the bulk of the plaintiff's damages. Remaining defendants can be left wishing for a defense or evidence or witnesses forgone. If a remaining defendant's attorney counted on a colleague working for a settling party to do the heavy lifting at trial he may feel flat-footed when it comes to examining witnesses and arguing motions. Even if all the defendants do go to trial, failing to obtain experts and gather evidence to show contributory negligence by co-defendants can exact its toll and lead to regret. Multiparty litigation presents a variety of collective action problems and other strategic pitfalls and those Dr. Phillips encountered here are well known, not the stuff of surprise.

It's hard, as well, to ignore the prejudice the other side can experience in these circumstances. Dr. Phillips effectively sought to force the plaintiff to prepare for an entirely different trial on a few days' notice. For the better part of two years the defendants presented a united front. Even in their final pretrial order submissions they didn't designate experts to suggest one or another of the codefendants acted unprofessionally. They didn't submit documents to prove such a claim. They didn't propose jury instructions asking that someone else be held accountable. The closest they came to suggesting contributory negligence was to prepare boilerplate blaming unspecified others for Mr. Shatwell's injuries. Beyond that, through the long months of discovery and into their final Rule 16(e) submissions, nothing. In these circumstances, the plaintiff and her lawyers had some reasonable expectations about what trial would look like and the sort of evidence they would—and would not—need. They knew they'd need to prove negligence by the defendants who chose to go to trial but they wouldn't have to worry about finger pointing between defendants; trial would present one set of challenges but not another.

It may be that the district court could have allowed Dr. Phillips to rejigger his defense at the last minute and afforded the plaintiff more time to prepare for it. But we do not see why that outcome was mandatory. A district court does not abuse its discretion in holding a party to a long-scheduled trial and to the strategy he articulated though pleading and discovery and in the face of such obvious risks, especially when indulging an eleventh-hour strategic shift would mean either imposing prejudice on the other side or inviting more delay. So beware: when a fellow litigant settles on the eve of trial you can't bank on the right to claim surprise and rewrite your case from top to bottom.

Many of Dr. Phillips's remaining arguments echo his Rule 16 complaint and fail with it....

Problem Levi McKey rented a dwelling house from Kenneth Fairbairn. Agnes Littlejohn, McKey's mother-in-law, occupied a bedroom and other space on the second floor. On February 20, 1958, apparently as a result of a snow storm, moisture on an area "about twice the size of a pie" was noticed on a wall of Mrs. Littlejohn's bedroom. There was no moisture on the floor. This condition was reported to Fairbarin and within a week his representative inspected the premises, discovered the dampness on the wall of Mrs. Littlejohn's room, but found no leak in the roof. He agreed to eliminate the cause of the dampness. On the night of February 26, 1958, an all-night rain fell, as a result of which the roof developed a leak and the floor of Mrs. Littlejohn's bedroom became wet. Upon arising the next morning and discovering the floor's condition, Mrs. Littlejohn went over it twice with a mop. Having left the room for a short time, she returned to awaken her grandson, who was sleeping there, and to get her coat. She slipped on the wet floor and fell, sustaining certain injuries.

Littlejohn brought suit to recover damages from the owner of the house and her agent. In her complaint, she alleged that the floor on which she slipped and fell:

". . . was wet and dangerous due to a leaking roof which the defendants, or either them, knew or should have known in time to have repaired said damage."

At the pre-trial conference plaintiff's attorney indicated he would be relying on a negligence theory in order to establish defendant's liability. Later in the trial, plaintiff's attorney moved to amend the pre-trial order to permit him to introduce certain sections of the District of Columbia Housing Regulations which requires that roofs shall be leakproof, and that rain water shall be drained so as not to cause wet walls or ceilings. The trial judge denied the motion on the grounds that this was a change in the theory of liability, and directed a verdict for the defendant. Assuming this was a change of theory, was the trial judge correct in refusing allow that evidence to be introduced? (See, *McKey v. Fairbairn,* 345 F.2d 739 (1965)

THE JUDGE

In both the federal and state court systems a judge is assigned to handle a case from start to finish. The selection of the judge is typically random and is made at or soon after the time of filing of the complaint. What if a party is unhappy with the judge who has been assigned to hear the case? Is there anything they can do about it? The answer is almost always, "not much."

28 U.S. Code § 455 (a) provides that, "Any justice, judge, or magistrate judge of the United States shall disqualify himself in any proceeding in which his impartiality might reasonably be questioned." 28 U.S. Code § 455 (b) also lists five specific circumstances where a judge is required to recuse him or herself from hearing a matter. In other words, in federal court, judges can only be disqualified or recused for cause. If a judge refuses to voluntarily recuse him or herself any party may challenge the judge. But in the federal courts, the hearing on whether a judge should be required to recuse is heard by the judge assigned to the case who is being challenged. Good luck with that!

In California state court, trial judges can be peremptorily challenged (that is, without a showing of any actual bias or cause) in addition to being subject to recusal because of actual bias or cause. (See, Cal.Code.Civ.Proc. §§170.5 and 170.6.) Peremptory challenges must be made within a very short time of assignment of a judge to a case. Hence, the parties do not have an opportunity to sample the judge's early rulings in the case to see which way the wind is blowing, before deciding whether or not to exercise their one peremptory challenge. Challenges of actual bias or cause can be made at any time and are unlimited. And unlike federal court, a challenge for cause in state court (in the event the judge refuses to recuse him or herself) is heard and ruled upon by another judge.

THE RIGHT TO A TRIAL BY JURY

The right to a jury trial is founded in the Seventh Amendment. That amendment does not "create" the right to a trial by jury. Rather it "preserves" the right as it existed at common law in 1791 the date of the Seventh Amendment's ratification. By "common law" the framers of the Constitution meant, suits in which legal rights were to be ascertained and determined in contrast to those where equitable rights alone were recognized and equitable remedies were administered. (*Parsons v. Bedford* 7 L.3d. 732, 737 (1830).) Hence, under the old system of separate courts for law and equity, the right to a jury trial only existed for actions at law. There was no right to a jury trial for actions brought in equity.

Although the Federal Rules abolish the procedural distinctions between law and equity and substitute a single form of action, they do not abrogate the differences between the substantive and remedial rules of the two systems. Since a party may now enter a single court with both legal and equitable claims the question recurs as to when there is a right to a jury trial.

The same court may try both legal and equitable causes in the same action. When one or more issues common to both legal and equitable claims exist, the legal claim should be tried first, in order to avoid depriving the party of a determination by a jury on the common issue. I.e., it is the issue to be adjudicated, not the underlying nature of the case, that is determinative of the right to jury trial. (*Beacon Theatres, Inc. v. Westover,* 359 U.S. 500 (1959)

To determine whether a statutory action is more similar to cases that were tried in courts of law than to suits tried in courts of equity, the Court must examine both the nature of the action and of the remedy sought. (*Tull v. United States,* 481 U.S. 412 (1987)

Dairy Queen, Inc. v. Wood, 369 U.S. 469 (1962) shortly followed *Beacon*. It involved a licensing agreement for the trademark "Dairy Queen." Plaintiff sued for a breach of contract seeking injunctions restraining defendant from further use of the name and an accounting to determine the exact sum owed the plaintiff. The trial court struck the defendant's demand for a jury trial. The Supreme Court reversed, it reasoned that the accounting claim was merely a disguise for a damage claim.

Ross v. Bernhard, 396 U.S. 531 (1970) extended the *Beacon-Dairy Queen* doctrine to stockholder derivative suits, which traditionally had been the exclusive province of equity. The Court ruled "the right of jury trial attaches to those issues in derivative actions as to which the corporation if it had been suing in its own right, would have been entitled to a jury."

Although the thrust of the 7th Amendment was to preserve the right to jury trial as it existed in 1791, it has long been settled that the right extends beyond the common-law forms of action recognized at that time. By common law the Framers meant not merely suits, which the common law recognized among its old and settled proceedings, but suits in which legal rights were to be ascertained and determined. The 7th Amendment does apply to actions enforcing statutory rights, and requires a jury trial upon demand, if the statute creates legal rights and remedies, enforceable in an action for damages in the ordinary courts of law. When Congress provides for enforcement of statutory rights in an ordinary civil action there is no functional justification for denying the jury trial right, a jury trial must be available if the action involves rights and remedies of the sort typically enforced in an action at law. Hence, a right to a jury trial is not restricted to those common law actions that actually existed in 1791. (*Curtis v. Loether,* 415 U.S. 189 (1974)

In California the right to a trial by jury is declared by Section 16 of Article I of the California Constitution. (See, Cal.Code.Civ.Proc. § 631)

C & K Engineering Contractors v. Amber Steel Company, Inc.
23 Cal.3d 1 (1978)

RICHARDSON, J.

The issue posed by this case is whether or not defendant was improperly denied its constitutional right to a jury trial. (Cal. Const., art. I, § 16.) We will conclude that because plaintiff's suit for damages for breach of contract was based entirely upon the equitable doctrine of promissory estoppel (see Drennan v. Star Paving Co. (1958) 51 Cal.2d 409 [333 P.2d 757]), the gist of the action must be deemed equitable in nature and, under well established principles, neither party was entitled to a jury trial as a matter of right.

Plaintiff, a general contractor, solicited bids from defendant and other subcontractors for the installation of reinforcing steel in the construction of a waste water treatment plant in Fresno County. Plaintiff included defendant's bid in its master bid, which was ultimately accepted by the public sanitation district, the proposed owner of the plant. After defendant refused to perform in accordance with its bid on the subcontract, plaintiff brought the present action to recover $102,660 in damages for defendant's alleged breach of contract. (A second cause of action, claiming defendant's negligence in preparing its bid, was dismissed during trial and is not presently at issue.)

The allegations of plaintiff's first cause of action may be summarized: defendant submitted a written bid of $139,511 for the work; defendant gave a subsequent "verbal promise" that the work would be performed for the bid price; plaintiff "reasonably relied" on defendant's bid and promise in submitting its master bid; defendant knew or should have known that plaintiff would submit a master bid based upon defendant's bid;

defendant refused to perform in accordance with its bid; plaintiff was required to expend $242,171 to perform the reinforcing steel work; as a result plaintiff was damaged in the amount of $102,660; and "Injustice can be avoided only by enforcement of defendant's promise to perform...."

Defendant's answer to the complaint alleged its bid was the result of an "honest mistake" in calculation; plaintiff knew of the mistake but failed to notify defendant or permit it to revise its bid as is customary in the industry; and plaintiff's conduct in this regard should bar it from recovering damages.

Defendant demanded a jury trial. The trial court, deeming the case to be essentially in equity, denied the request but empaneled an advisory jury to consider the sole issue of plaintiff's reasonable reliance on defendant's promise. The jury found that plaintiff reasonably relied to its detriment on defendant's bid. The trial court adopted this finding and entered judgment in plaintiff's favor for $102,620, the approximate amount of its prayer, together with interest and costs. Defendant appeals.

Defendant's primary contention is that it was improperly denied a jury trial of plaintiff's action for damages. In resolving this contention we first review the nature and derivation of the doctrine of promissory estoppel. Thereafter, we discuss certain authorities governing the right to jury trial in this state. As will appear, we have concluded that by reason of the essentially equitable nature of the doctrine and plaintiff's exclusive reliance upon it in the present action, the case was properly triable by the court with an advisory jury.

* * *

We conclude, . . . that the doctrine of promissory estoppel is essentially equitable in nature, developed to provide a remedy (namely, enforcement of a gratuitous promise) which was not generally available in courts of law prior to 1850. We now move to an examination of the authorities on the subject of the right to a jury trial, to determine whether the equitable nature of plaintiff's action precluded a jury trial as a matter of right.

2. Right to Jury Trial

The right to a jury trial is guaranteed by our Constitution. (Cal. Const., art. 1, § 16.) We have long acknowledged that the right so guaranteed, however, is the right as it existed at common law in 1850, when the Constitution was first adopted, "and what that right is, is a purely historical question, a fact which is to be ascertained like any other social, political or legal fact."

As we stated in People v. One 1941 Chevrolet Coupe, supra, 37 Cal.2d 283, "'If the action has to deal with ordinary common-law rights cognizable in courts of law, it is to that extent an action at law. In determining whether the action was one triable by a jury at common law, the court is not bound by the form of the action but rather by the nature of the rights involved and the facts of the particular case — the gist of the action. A jury trial must be granted where the gist of the action is legal, where the action is in reality cognizable at law.'" (P. 299, fn. omitted, italics added.) On the other hand, if the action is essentially one in equity and the relief sought "depends upon the application of equitable doctrines," the parties are not entitled to a jury trial. Although we have said that "the legal or equitable nature of a cause of action ordinarily is determined by the mode of relief to be afforded" the prayer for relief in a particular case is not conclusive Thus, "The fact that damages is one of a full range of possible remedies does not guarantee ... the right to a jury...."

In the present case, the complaint purports to seek recovery of damages for breach of contract, in form an action at law in which a right to jury trial ordinarily would exist. As we have seen, however, the complaint seeks relief which was available only in equity, namely, the enforcement of defendant's gratuitous promise to perform its bid through application of the equitable doctrine of promissory estoppel. Although there is no direct authority on point, several cases have held that actions based upon the analogous principle of equitable estoppel may be tried by the court without a jury.

Defendant responds by relying primarily upon certain dictum in Raedeke, supra, which also concerned an action based on promissory estoppel. The Raedeke complaint alleged dual theories of traditional breach of contract and promissory estoppel. We stressed that the "resolution of the instant case did not depend entirely upon the application of equitable principles; the doctrine of promissory estoppel was only one of two alternative theories of recovery." Accordingly, we held in Raedeke that plaintiffs were entitled to a jury trial, and that the trial court erred in treating the jury's findings and verdict as advisory only. In a footnote, however, we added the following dictum: "Moreover, even as to plaintiffs' reliance upon promissory estoppel, there is some basis for holding that the action remained one at law. 'The fact that equitable principles are applied in the action does not necessarily identify the resultant relief as equitable. [Citations.] Equitable principles are a guide to courts of law as well as of equity. [Furthermore, the incidental adoption of equitable sounding measures to effect the application of equitable principles in an action at law, such as for damages, does not change the character of that action.

The foregoing general principles do not alter our conclusion that the present action is, essentially, one recognized only in courts of equity and, despite plaintiff's request for damages, is not an "action at law" involving, to use the Raedeke language, the "incidental adoption of equitable sounding measures." Defendant before us has argued that because plaintiff sought to recover damages rather than to compel defendant to perform its bid, plaintiff requested relief which is available at common law. Yet, as we have seen, damages at law were unavailable in actions for breach of a gratuitous promise. The only manner in which damages have been recognized in such cases of gratuitous promises is by application of the equitable doctrine of promissory estoppel which renders such promises legally binding. Without the employment of this doctrine, essentially equitable, there was no remedy at all. As illustrated by the express language of section 90 of the Restatement of Contracts, promissory estoppel is used to avoid injustice "by enforcement of the promise."

Furthermore, the addition, in such cases, of a prayer for damages does not convert what is essentially an equitable action into a legal one for which a jury trial would be available. This was demonstrated in a recent case, Southern Pac. Transportation Co. v. Superior Court, supra, 58 Cal. App.3d 433, wherein plaintiff sought damages as a good faith improver of land owned by another person. (See Code Civ. Proc., § 871.1 et seq.) The appellate court rejected the contention that plaintiff's request for damages necessarily identified the action as one at law. The court first noted that since the good faith improver statute had no counterpart in English common law, "classification of the action as either legal or equitable depends upon characterization of the nature of the relief sought." (P. 437.)

The Southern Pac. Transportation court properly observed that under the statute, the trial court must "effect such an adjustment of the rights, equities, and interests" of the parties as was consistent with substantial justice. (Code Civ. Proc., § 871.5.) Thus, the action was essentially one calling for the exercise of equitable principles. The court added, "The fact that damages is one of a full range of possible remedies does not guarantee real parties the right to a jury," since "there is no possibility of severing the legal from the equitable. The trier of fact must determine whether to quiet title in the improver on the condition he pay to the landowner the value of the unimproved land, or whether and in what amount, to award damages to the improver, or whether to require a completely different form of relief.... Such a determination is not susceptible of division into one component to be resolved by the court and another component to be determined by a jury. Only one decision can be made, and it must make a proper adjustment of the 'rights, equities, and interests' of all the parties involved." (Pp. 437-438.) The court concluded that in view of the various equitable considerations involved, it would be "an impossible task" for a jury to resolve the dispute. (P. 438.)

Similarly, in the present case, the trier of fact is called upon to determine whether "injustice can be avoided only by enforcement of [defendant's] promise." (Rest., Contracts, § 90.) The "gist" of such an action is equitable. Both historically and functionally, the task of weighing such equitable considerations is to be performed by the trial court, not the jury. We conclude that the trial court properly treated the action as equitable in nature, to be tried by the court with or without an advisory jury as the court elected.

MAKING THE DEMAND FOR A JURY TRIAL

One who is entitled to a trial by jury must assert their right to it by a demand in writing not later than 14 days after the service of the last pleading" or he will be deemed to have waived the right. (FRCP 38(b).) In California, the procedure for demanding a right to jury trial is set forth in the Code of Civil Procedure. (Cal.Code.Civ.Proc. § 631)

CHALLENGING THE JURY'S VERDICT IN THE TRIAL COURT - JUDICIAL CONTROL OF JURY ACTION

MOTIONS FOR JUDGMENT AS A MATTER OF LAW

FRCP 50 provides that a party may move for judgment as a matter of law. (A Rule 50 motion was formerly known by the terms directed verdict and judgment notwithstanding the verdict [JNOV].) Motion for judgment as a matter of law is a mechanism by which the judge controls the jury. This motion may be made by either party at the close of their opponent's evidence. For the motion to be granted the court must find that there is insufficient evidence to go to the jury or that the evidence is so compelling that only one result could follow. Rule 50 specifies that judgment as a matter of law may be entered when "there is no legally sufficient evidentiary basis for a reasonable jury to find for" the nonmoving party. In other words, the motion will be granted if the opponent's evidence is so weak that no reasonable jury could have reached a verdict for him.

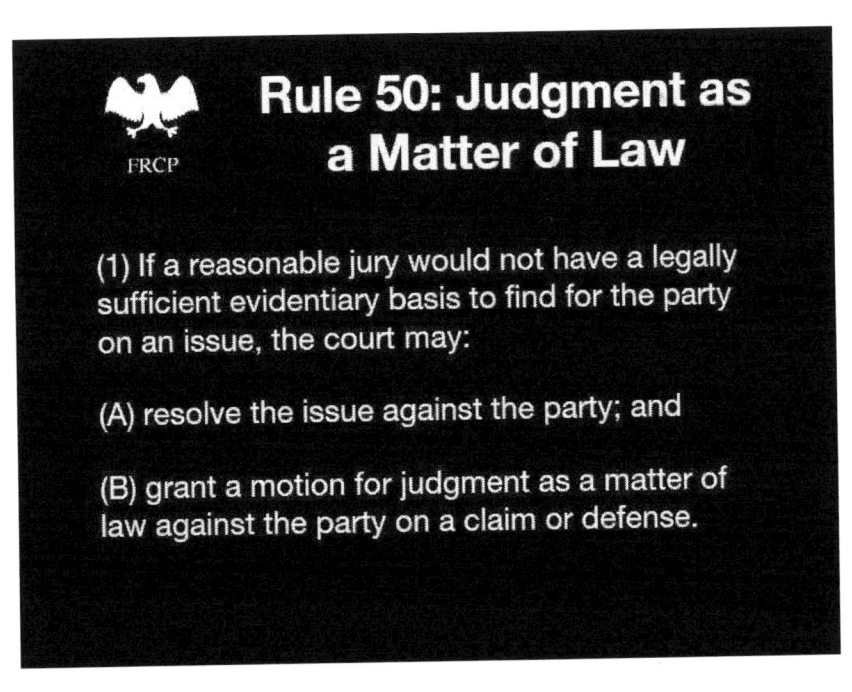

> **Rule 50: Judgment as a Matter of Law** (FRCP)
>
> (1) If a reasonable jury would not have a legally sufficient evidentiary basis to find for the party on an issue, the court may:
>
> (A) resolve the issue against the party; and
>
> (B) grant a motion for judgment as a matter of law against the party on a claim or defense.

FRCP 50(a)(1) authorizes the court to consider a motion for judgment as a matter of law as soon as a party has completed a presentation on a fact essential to that party's case. FRCP 50(a)(2) requires that motion for judgment as a matter of law must be made prior to the close of the trial, subject to renewal after a jury verdict has been rendered. The purpose of this requirement is to assure the responding party an opportunity to cure any deficiency in that party's proof that may have been overlooked until called to the party's attention by a late motion for judgment.

When the motion is made after the verdict is rendered it seeks a judgment contrary to the verdict on the ground that there was insufficient evidence for the jury to find as it did. (See, Friedenthal § 12.3) The post-verdict motion is a renewal of an earlier motion made at the close of the evidence.

Reid v. San Pedro, Los Angeles & Salt Lake Railroad
39 Utah 617, 118 P. 1009 (1911)

This action was brought by respondent to recover damages for the killing of certain cattle by the trains of appellant....

It is alleged in the first cause of action that appellant's railroad passes through certain lands in Salt Lake County, Utah, owned and improved by private owners; that appellant carelessly and negligently permitted the fence along its line of railroad where the same passes through the lands mentioned to be broken and in poor repair and become down so that cattle had an easy passage through the same; that appellant "carelessly and negligently left and permitted to remain open a gate along the line of said railway at said point and plaintiff (respondent) does not know, and therefore is unable to state, whether the fence was down or the gate left open, and because thereof a three year old heifer of the plaintiff strayed on the right of way of said defendant company, and defendant so carelessly and negligently operated its train that it ran on and over said heifer"....

[There was a verdict for plaintiff, and defendant appealed from the judgment entered on the verdict.]

MCCARTY, J.

It is contended on behalf of appellant that the evidence is insufficient to support the verdict because it fails to show where and under what circumstances the cattle sued for got upon the right of way.

The evidence shows that the cow mentioned in the first cause of action was being pastured on land that was fenced, improved, and owned by a private party, and through which appellant's railroad was constructed and maintained; that respondent did not own the land, but was pasturing her stock thereon by permission of the owner at the time the cow was killed; that the fence inclosing appellant's right of way was down and out of repair about one mile west of the point where the cow was killed; that two gates opening into the right of way in the immediate vicinity of the place where the accident occurred, which were installed and maintained by appellant for the benefit and convenience of the owner of the land through which the railroad passes and upon which the cow was being pastured, had been left open almost continuously prior to the accident.

It is not contended, nor even suggested, that these gates, which were in good condition, were used or left open by appellant. In fact, the evidence, what there is on this point, tends to show that the appellant was in no wise responsible for the gates being left open. Respondent contends that the judgment, in so far as it is based on the first cause of action, should be affirmed regardless of whether the cow got on the right of way through the broken fence or the open gate. In his brief counsel for respondent says: "In the first cause of action the evidence showed the fence down and gate open....It is immaterial whether the heifer strayed on through an inviting open gate or an enticing open fence;...either gives the verdict to the plaintiff." Comp. Laws 1907, §456xl, provides:

Whenever such railroad company shall provide gates for private crossings for the convenience of the owner of the lands through which such railroad passes, such owner shall keep such gates closed at all times when not in actual use, and if such owner fail to keep such gates closed, and in consequence thereof his animal strays upon such railroad, and is killed or injured, such owner shall not be entitled to recover damages therefor.

Under this statute, if the cow entered upon the right of way through the open gate, appellant cannot be held liable for her loss; there being no evidence of negligence on the part of trainmen at the time she was killed.

There is no direct evidence as to where the cow got on to the right of way. It is conceded, however, that she was killed in the immediate vicinity of the gate mentioned, and, as shown by the evidence, about one mile from the point where the fence inclosing the right of way was down and out of repair. The inference, therefore, is just as strong, if not stronger, that she entered upon the right of way through the open gate as it is that she entered through the fence at the point where it was out of repair. The plaintiff held the affirmative and the burden was on her to establish the liability of the defendant by a preponderance of the evidence. It is a familiar rule that where the undisputed evidence of the plaintiff, from which the existence of an essential fact is sought to be inferred, points with equal force to two things, one of which renders the defendant liable and the other not, the plaintiff must fail. So in this case, in order to entitle respondent to recover, it was essential for her to show by a preponderance of the evidence that the cow entered upon the right of way through the broken down fence. This the respondent failed to do.

We are of the opinion that the verdict rendered on the first cause of action is not supported by the evidence, and that the trial court should have directed a verdict for appellant on that cause of action in accordance with appellant's request....

Pennsylvania Railroad v. Chamberlain
288 U.S. 333 (1933)

Mr. Justice SUTHERLAND delivered the opinion of the Court.

This is an action brought by respondent against petitioner to recover for the death of a brakeman, alleged to have been caused by petitioner's negligence. The complaint alleges that the deceased, at the time of the accident resulting in his death, was assisting in the yard work of breaking up and making up trains and in the classifying and assorting of cars operating in interstate commerce; that in pursuance of such work, while riding a cut of cars, other cars ridden by fellow employees were negligently caused to be brought into violent contact with those upon which deceased was riding, with the result that he was thrown therefrom to the railroad track and run over by a car or cars, inflicting injuries from which he died.

At the conclusion of the evidence, the trial court directed the jury to find a verdict in favor of petitioner. Judgment upon a verdict so found was reversed by the court of appeals, Judge Swan dissenting.

That part of the yard in which the accident occurred contained a lead track and a large number of switching tracks branching therefrom. The lead track crossed a "hump," and the work of car distribution consisted of pushing a train of cars by means of a locomotive to the top of the "hump," and then allowing the cars, in separate strings, to descend by gravity, under the control of hand brakes, to their respective destinations in the various branch tracks. Deceased had charge of a string of two gondola cars, which he was piloting to track 14. Immediately ahead of him was a string of seven cars, and behind him a string of nine cars, both also destined for track 14. Soon after the cars ridden by deceased had passed to track 14, his body was found on that track some distance beyond the switch. He had evidently fallen onto the track and been run over by a car or cars.

The case for respondent rests wholly upon the claim that the fall of deceased was caused by a violent collision of the string of nine cars with the string ridden by deceased. Three employees, riding the nine-car string, testified positively that no such collision occurred. They were corroborated by every other employee in a position to see, all testifying that there was no contact between the nine-car string and that of the deceased. The testimony of these witnesses, if believed, establishes beyond doubt that there was no collision between these two strings of cars, and that the nine-car string contributed in no way to the accident. The only witness who testified for the respondent was one Bainbridge; and it is upon his testimony alone that respondent's right to recover is sought to be upheld. His testimony is concisely stated, in its most favorable light for respondent, in the prevailing opinion below by Judge Learned Hand, as follows:

The plaintiff's only witness to the event, one Bainbridge, then employed by the road, stood close to the yardmaster's office, near the "hump." He professed to have paid little attention to what went on, but he did see the deceased riding at the rear of his cars, whose speed when they passed him he took to be about eight or ten miles. Shortly thereafter a second string passed which was shunted into another track and this was followed by the nine, which, according to the plaintiff's theory, collided with the deceased's. After the nine cars had passed at a somewhat greater speed than the deceased's, Bainbridge paid no more attention to either string for a while, but looked again when the deceased, who was still standing in his place, had passed the switch and onto the assorting track where he was bound. At that time his speed had been checked to about three miles, but the speed of the following nine cars had increased. They were just passing the switch, about four or five cars behind the deceased. Bainbridge looked away again and soon heard what he described as a "loud crash," not however an unusual event in a switching yard. Apparently this did not cause him at once to turn, but he did so shortly thereafter, and saw the two strings together still moving, and the deceased no longer in sight. Later still his attention was attracted by shouts and he went to the spot and saw the deceased between the rails. Until he left to go to the accident, he had stood fifty feet to the north of the track where the accident happened, and about nine hundred feet from where the body was found.

The court, although regarding Bainbridge's testimony as not only "somewhat suspicious in itself, but its contradiction...so manifold as to leave little doubt," held, nevertheless, that the question was one of fact depending upon the credibility of the witnesses, and that it was for the jury to determine, as between the one witness and the many, where the truth lay. The dissenting opinion of Judge Swan proceeds upon the theory that Bainbridge did not testify that in fact a collision had taken place, but inferred it because he heard a crash, and because thereafter the two strings of cars appeared to him to be moving together. It is correctly pointed out in that opinion, however, that the crash might have come from elsewhere in the busy yard and that Bainbridge was in no position to see whether the two strings of cars were actually together; that Bainbridge repeatedly said he was paying no particular attention; and that his position was such, being 900 feet from the place where the body was found and less than 50 feet from the side of the track in question, that he necessarily saw the strings of cars at such an acute angle that it would be physically impossible even for an attentive observer to tell whether the forward end of the nine-car cut was actually in contact with the rear end of the two-car cut. The dissenting opinion further points out that all the witnesses who were in a position to see testified that there was no collision; that respondent's evidence was wholly circumstantial, and the inferences which might otherwise be drawn from it were shown to be utterly erroneous unless all of petitioner's witnesses were willful perjurers. "This is not a case," the opinion proceeds, "where direct testimony to an essential fact is contradicted by direct testimony of other witnesses, though even there it is conceded a directed verdict might be proper in some circumstances. Here, when all the testimony was in, the circumstantial evidence in support of negligence was thought by the trial judge to be so insubstantial and insufficient that it did not justify submission to the jury." We thus summarize and quote from the prevailing and dissenting opinions, because they present the divergent views to be considered in reaching a correct determination of the question involved. It, of course, is true, generally, that where there is a direct conflict of testimony upon a matter of fact, the question must be left to the jury to determine, without regard to the number of witnesses upon either side. But here there really is no conflict in the testimony as to the facts. The witnesses for petitioner flatly testified that there was no collision between the nine-car and the two-car strings. Bainbridge did not say there was such a collision. What he said was that he heard a "loud crash," which did not cause him at once to turn, but that shortly thereafter he did turn and saw the two strings of cars moving together with the deceased no longer in sight; that there was nothing unusual about the crash of cars—it happened every day; that there was nothing about this crash to attract his attention except that it was extra loud; that he paid no attention to it; that it was not sufficient to attract his attention. The record shows that there was a continuous movement of cars over and down the "hump," which were distributed among a large number of branch tracks within the yard, and that any two strings of these cars moving upon the same track might have come together and caused the crash which Bainbridge heard. There is no direct evidence that in fact the crash was occasioned by a collision of the two strings in question; and it is perfectly clear that no such fact was brought to Bainbridge's attention as a perception of the physical sense of sight or of hearing. At most there was an inference to that effect drawn from observed facts which gave equal support to the opposite inference that the crash was occasioned by the coming together of other strings of cars entirely away from the scene of the accident, or of the two-car string ridden by deceased and the seven-car string immediately ahead of it.

We, therefore, have a case belonging to that class of cases where proven facts give equal support to each of two inconsistent inferences; in which event, neither of them being established, judgment, as a matter of law, must go against the party upon whom rests the necessity of sustaining one of these inferences as against the other, before he is entitled to recover.

The rule is succinctly stated in Smith v. First National Bank in Westfield, 99 Mass. 605, 611-612, quoted in the Des Moines National Bank case [United States F. & G. Co. v. Des Moines National Bank, 145 F. 273, 280 (8th Cir. 1906)]:

There being several inferences deducible from the facts which appear, and equally consistent with all those facts, the plaintiff has not maintained the proposition upon which alone he would be entitled to recover. There is strictly no evidence to warrant a jury in finding that the loss was occasioned by negligence and not by theft. When the evidence tends equally to sustain either of two inconsistent propositions, neither of them can be said to have been established by legitimate proof. A verdict in favor of the party bound to maintain one of those propositions against the other is necessarily wrong.

That Bainbridge concluded from what he himself observed that the crash was due to a collision between the two strings of cars in question is sufficiently indicated by his statements. But this, of course, proves nothing, since it is not allowable for a witness to resolve the doubt as to which of two equally justifiable inferences shall be adopted by drawing a conclusion, which, if accepted, will result in a purely gratuitous award in favor of the party who has failed to sustain the burden of proof cast upon him by the law.

And the desired inference is precluded for the further reason that respondent's right of recovery depends upon the existence of a particular fact which must be inferred from proven facts, and this is not permissible in the face of the positive and otherwise uncontradicted testimony of unimpeached witnesses consistent with the facts actually proved, from which testimony it affirmatively appears that the fact sought to be inferred did not exist....

Not only is Bainbridge's testimony considered as a whole suspicious, insubstantial and insufficient, but his statement that when he turned shortly after hearing the crash the two strings were moving together is simply incredible, if he meant thereby to be understood as saying that he saw the two in contact; and if he meant by the words "moving together" simply that they were moving at the same time in the same direction but not in contact, the statement becomes immaterial. As we have already seen he was paying slight and only occasional attention to what was going on. The cars were 800 or 900 feet from where he stood and moving almost directly away from him, his angle of vision being only 3°03 from a straight line. At that sharp angle and from that distance, near dusk of a misty evening (as the proof shows), the practical impossibility of the witness being able to see whether the front of the nine-car string was in contact with the back of the two-car string is apparent. And, certainly, in the light of these conditions, no verdict based upon a statement so unbelievable reasonably could be sustained as against the positive testimony to the contrary of unimpeached witnesses, all in a position to see, as this witness was not, the precise relation of the cars to one another. The fact that these witnesses were employees of the petitioner, under the circumstances here disclosed, does not impair this conclusion. Chesapeake & Ohio Ry. v. Martin, 283 U.S. 209, 216-220....

Leaving out of consideration, then, the inference relied upon, the case for respondent is left without any substantial support in the evidence, and a verdict in her favor would have rested upon mere speculation and conjecture. This, of course, is inadmissible.

The judgment of the Circuit Court of Appeals is reversed and that of the District Court is affirmed.

POST VERDICT MOTIONS FOR JUDGMENT AS A MATTER OF LAW

Often it appears to the court or to the moving party that a motion for judgment as a matter of law made at the close of the evidence should be reserved for a post-verdict decision. This is so because a jury verdict for the moving party moots the issue and because a pre-verdict ruling gambles that a reversal may result in a new trial that might have been avoided. For these reasons, the court may often wisely decline to rule on a motion for judgment as a matter of law made at the close of the evidence, and it is not inappropriate for the moving party to suggest such a postponement of the ruling until after the verdict has been rendered. (Notes of Advisory Committee on Rules—1991 Amendment)

Norton v. Snapper Power Equipment
806 F.2d 1545 (11th Cir. 1987)

CLARK, J.

Plaintiff James L. Norton was injured while using a riding lawn mower manufactured by defendant Snapper Power Equipment. The issue on appeal is whether the district court erred in granting a judgment notwithstanding the verdict to Snapper on Norton's strict liability claim. We reverse.

I. Facts

Norton was, and still is, in the commercial lawn mowing business. He bought a Snapper riding mower in July 1981. On January 24, 1983, Norton was using this mower to clear leaves from a yard...adjacent to a creek. At the end of his third circular route through the yard, he drove up an incline, traveling in the direction away from the creek. Norton testified that as he reached the top of the incline, approximately six feet from the creek, the mower began to slide backwards toward the creek. Norton says he applied the brakes, but he continued to slide backwards. The lawn mower, with Norton still aboard, crashed into the creek. Norton testified that he kept both hands on the handle bars until the impact of the mower hitting the water knocked him off the seat....[A]t some point during this crash, Norton's hand was caught in the lawn mower's blades, thereby amputating four of his fingers. It is not known...precisely how the injury occurred....

At the close of the plaintiff's case, and again at the close of all evidence, Snapper moved for a directed verdict. The court dismissed Norton's negligence and warranty claims, but left the strict liability "defect" claim for the jury. The jury returned a verdict for Norton, holding Snapper liable for 80% of the injuries.

Immediately after dismissing the jury, the district court indicated it would enter a judgment notwithstanding the verdict.

[Plaintiff appealed from this ruling.]

II. Substantive Objections to Judgment Notwithstanding the Verdict

The test for granting a judgment notwithstanding the verdict is the same as the test for granting a directed verdict. The court considers the evidence in the light most favorable to the non-moving party and should grant the judgment notwithstanding the verdict only where the evidence so strongly and so favorably points in the favor of the moving party that reasonable people could not arrive at a contrary verdict....

The issues in this case were: (1) whether the failure to install "dead man" devices rendered the 1981 Snapper mower defective; and (2) if the lawn mower was defective, whether the lack of a "dead man" control caused Norton's injury....

Norton claims the Snapper mower was unreasonably dangerous because it did not have a "dead man" device. Although there are several types of such devices, the basic principle is the same in each type. In order to keep the lawn mower blades spinning, the operator has to remain in a certain position or has to continuously apply pressure to a pedal or handle. When the operator disengages the blades, they are quickly brought to a stop. The 1981 Snapper mowers were designed so that the blades would spin for three to five seconds after the power was turned off. Norton offered evidence that more sophisticated "dead man" devices are able to stop the blades in less than one second after the operator applies the brakes or releases the handle.

[After reviewing the law on product defects, the appellate court concluded that the jury could reasonably have found the mower defective. The court then considers whether a jury could reasonably have found that the defect caused Norton's injury.]

...Since Norton did not know exactly when or how his hand got caught in the blades, and since a reconstruction of the accident was impossible, Snapper contends that the jury could not determine whether a blade stopping device would have eliminated or lessened Norton's injury.

Snapper correctly points out that "plaintiffs are not entitled to a verdict based on speculation and conjecture." Fenner v. General Motors Corp., 657 F.2d 647, 651 (5th Cir. 1981), cert. denied, 455 U.S. 942 (1982)....The jury is, however, permitted to "reconstruct the series of events by drawing an inference upon an inference." Id. at 650.

In Fenner, plaintiff contended his automobile veered off the highway because of a defective steering mechanism. The steering problem would only manifest itself if a stone got caught in the steering mechanism. Because plaintiff's vehicle was not examined by any experts and since plaintiff's experts were only able to say that theoretically the accident could have been caused by a stone in the steering mechanism, the district court entered a judgment notwithstanding the verdict for defendant....

The causation evidence in this case, although circumstantial, was far more impressive than the evidence presented in Fenner. Norton testified that the lawn mower slid six feet from the top of the hill into the creek....Expert testimony revealed that when Norton applied the brakes, an effective dead man device could have stopped the blades in as little as .7 seconds. The blades on the 1981 Snapper would continue to spin for three to five seconds....Each of Snapper's experts testified that, given the amount of time the mower would have taken to slide six feet and given Norton's testimony that both of his hands were on the handle bars until the mower hit the creek, a two or three second difference in blade stopping time would have avoided the injury....Snapper was given every opportunity to point out the weaknesses in Norton's proof, but apparently was unpersuasive....

Reversed and Remanded.

Lind v. Schenley Industries
278 F.2d 79 (3d Cir. 1960)

[Lind, a sales manager for the defendant liquor company, alleged that it had promised him an increase in pay and a share of commissions but had then breached that promise. The alleged promises were oral. Lind and his then-secretary, Mrs. Kennan, testified to such promises. Schenley's agents denied making them. The jury found a contract; a damage award followed. Schenley moved both for judgment notwithstanding the verdict and, alternatively, for a new trial. The trial judge granted the j.n.o.v., and, in the alternative, a new trial (see Rule 50(c), which authorizes such dual contingent rulings). The plaintiff appealed.]

BIGGS, J....

The district court granted the alternative motion for a new trial because it found the jury's verdict (1) contrary to the weight of the evidence, (2) contrary to law and (3) a result of error in the admission of evidence....

[The court first ruled on points (2) and (3) above, holding that it had been error to grant the j.n.o.v. for Schenley and a new trial on these grounds.]

The remaining basis for ordering a new trial is that the verdict was against the weight of the evidence. It is frequently stated that a motion for a new trial on this ground ordinarily is nonreviewable because within the discretion of the trial court. But this discretion must still be exercised in accordance with ascertainable legal standards and if an appellate court is shown special or unusual circumstances which clearly indicate an abuse of discretion in that the trial court failed to apply correctly the proper standards, reversal is possible. Concededly appellate courts rarely find that the trial court abused its discretion.

In Commercial Credit Corp. v. Pepper, Judge Borah stated:

It is a principle well recognized in the federal courts that the granting or refusing of a new trial is a matter resting within the discretion of the trial court. The term "discretion," however, when invoked as a guide to judicial action, means a sound discretion, exercised with regard to what is right and in the interests of justice. And an appellate court is not bound to stay its hand and place its stamp of approval on a case when it feels that injustice may result. Quite to the contrary, it is definitely recognized in numerous decisions that an abuse of discretion is an exception to the rule that the granting or refusing of a new trial is not assignable as error.

Thus an appellate court must still rule upon the propriety of an order for a new trial, even though the grounds for reversal are exceedingly narrow. But before any rational decision can be made, the reviewing court must know what standards the trial judge is bound to apply when ruling upon a motion for a new trial. These standards necessarily vary according to the grounds urged in support of the new trial. There is, however, little authority on what standards are to be applied in ruling on a motion for new trial on the grounds that the verdict is against the weight of the evidence beyond the simple maxim that the trial judge has wide discretion. The few available authorities are conflicting. Professor Moore concludes that while the trial judge has a responsibility for the result at least equal to that of the jury he should not set the verdict aside as contrary to the weight of the evidence and order a new trial simply because he would have come to a different conclusion if he were the trier of the facts. Professor Moore states in this connection:

[S]ince the credibility of witnesses is peculiarly for the jury it is an invasion of the jury's province to grant a new trial merely because the evidence was sharply in conflict. The trial judge, exercising a mature judicial discretion, should view the verdict in the overall setting of the trial; consider the character of the evidence and the complexity or simplicity of the legal principles which the jury was bound to apply to the facts; and abstain from interfering with the verdict unless it is quite clear that the jury has reached a seriously erroneous result. The judge's duty is essentially to see that there is no miscarriage of justice. If convinced that there has been then it is his duty to set the verdict aside; otherwise not.

Professor Moore's views are logical and persuasive and buttressed by some decisional authority....

What we have stated demonstrates that there is no consensus of opinion as to the exact standards to be used by a trial court in granting a new trial and that the criteria to be employed by an appellate tribunal charged with reviewing the trial judge's decision in this respect are equally indefinite. New trials granted because (1) a jury verdict is against the weight of the evidence may be sharply distinguished from (2) new trials ordered for other reasons: for example, evidence improperly admitted, prejudicial statements by counsel, an improper charge to the jury or newly discovered evidence. In the first instance given it is the jury itself which fails properly to perform the functions confided to it by law. In the latter instances something occurred in the course of the trial which resulted or which may have resulted in the jury receiving a distorted, incorrect, or an incomplete view of the operative facts, or some undesirable element obtruded itself into the proceedings creating a condition whereby the giving of a just verdict was rendered difficult or impossible. In the latter instances, (2), supra, the trial court delivered the jury from a possibly erroneous verdict arising from circumstances over which the jury had no control. Under these conditions there is no usurpation by the court of the prime function of the jury as the trier of the facts and the trial judge necessarily must be allowed wide discretion in granting or refusing a new trial.

But where no undesirable or pernicious element has occurred or been introduced into the trial and the trial judge nonetheless grants a new trial on the ground that the verdict was against the weight of the evidence, the trial judge in negating the jury's verdict has, to some extent at least, substituted his judgment of the facts and the credibility of the witnesses for that of the jury. Such an action effects a denigration of the jury system and to the extent that new trials are granted the judge takes over, if he does not usurp, the prime function of the jury as the trier of the facts. It then becomes the duty of the appellate tribunal to exercise a closer degree of scrutiny and supervision than is the case where a new trial is granted because of some undesirable or pernicious influence obtruding into the trial. Such a close scrutiny is required in order to protect the litigants' right to jury trial.

Where a trial is long and complicated and deals with a subject matter not lying within the ordinary knowledge of jurors a verdict should be scrutinized more closely by the trial judge than is necessary where the litigation deals with material which is familiar and simple, the evidence relating to ordinary commercial practices. An example of subject matter unfamiliar to a layman would be a case requiring a jury to pass upon the nature of an alleged newly discovered organic compound in an infringement action. A prime example of subject matter lying well within the comprehension of jurors is presented by the circumstances at bar.

The subject matter of the litigation before us is simple and easily comprehended by any intelligent layman. The jury's main function was to determine the veracity of the witnesses: i.e., what testimony should be believed. If Lind's testimony and that of Mrs. Kennan, Kaufman's secretary, was deemed credible, Lind presented a convincing, indeed an overwhelming case. We must conclude that the jury did believe this testimony and that the court below substituted its judgment for that of the jury on this issue and thereby abused its legal discretion.

The judgment of the court below will be reversed and the case will be remanded with the direction to the court below to reinstate the verdict and judgment in favor of Lind.

MOTION FOR A NEW TRIAL

The trial judge has the power to grant a motion for a new trial when errors or irregularities have occurred during the proceedings. Under the federal rules a motion for new trial must be served within 28 days from the entry of judgment (FRCP 59(b).) The most frequent ground for granting of a new trial is that the verdict is against the weight of the evidence. Also, any prejudicial error of law which would be ground for a reversal on appeal will also be a ground for a new trial.

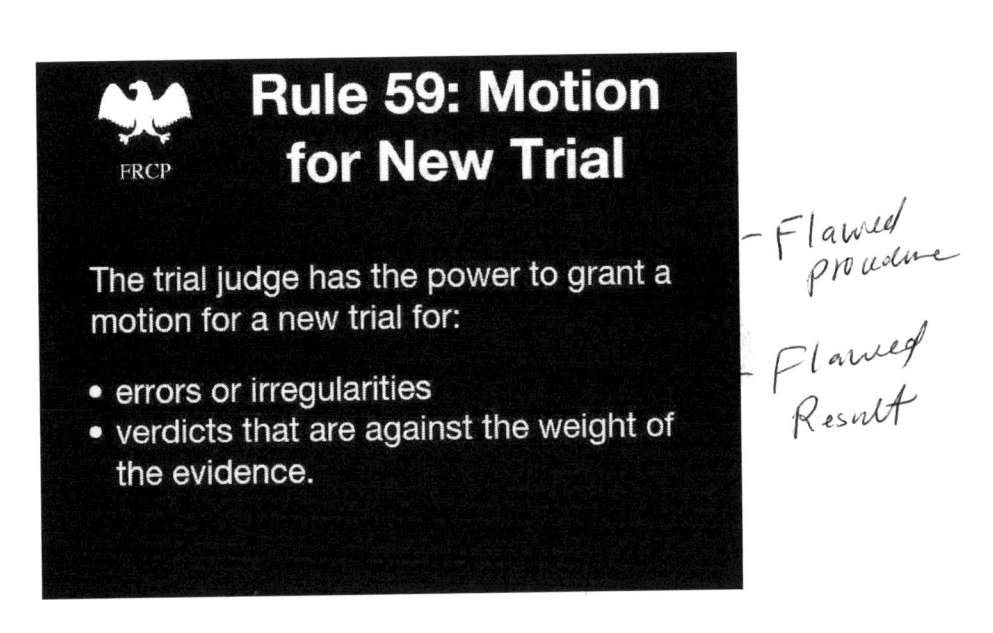

> **Rule 59: Motion for New Trial** (FRCP)
>
> The trial judge has the power to grant a motion for a new trial for:
> - errors or irregularities
> - verdicts that are against the weight of the evidence.

[Handwritten margin notes: "Flawed procedure" / "Flawed Result"]

Peterson v. Wilson
141 F.3d 573 (5th Cir. 1998)

WIENER, J....

I. Facts and Proceedings

Peterson filed this suit in district court under 42 U.S.C. §§1983 and 1988, as well as the First, Fifth, and Fourteenth Amendments of the United States Constitution after he was fired as grant director at Texas Southern University (TSU). He claims that his property interest in his employment at TSU was damaged or destroyed when it was arbitrarily and capriciously terminated....After five days of trial, conducted by the magistrate judge with the consent of the parties, the jury found for Peterson and awarded him $152,235 for lost pay and benefits and $35,000 for past and future mental anguish. Following the verdict, Wilson renewed his motion for j.m.l. and supplemented it with his bare-bones alternative motion for a new trial.

Some four months later, in January 1996, the district court granted the new trial, ostensibly in response to Wilson's motion, but in actuality on its own motion: The substantive language of the district court's order granting a new trial eschews any conclusion other than that the ruling was granted sua sponte, and that it was not granted for insufficiency of the evidence or because the jury verdict was against the great weight of the evidence, but rather for the following reason:

The court concludes, based on the jury's verdict and comments the jurors made to the court after returning the verdict [and outside the presence of the parties and their respective counsel], that the jury completely disregarded the Court's instructions. Instead, it appears that the jury considered improper factors in reaching its verdict. Accordingly, the Court deems it in the interest of justice to grant a new trial (emphasis added).

…The inference is inescapable that, to impeach the jury's verdict, the district court relied on information gleaned from the jurors themselves during the court's post-verdict, ex parte meeting with the jury. The court voided the verdict because, in the court's own words, the jury "completely disregarded the Court's instructions." Peterson timely filed a motion for reconsideration, which the district court did not grant. The case was retried in June 1996, and ended in a jury verdict in favor of Wilson, rejecting Peterson's claims.…

The jury, as the finder of facts and the maker of all credibility calls, reached its verdict in the first trial on the basis of the following record facts and inferences.

Peterson is well educated, well trained, and widely experienced in his field of concentration, which is grant administration for institutions of higher education. When Peterson joined TSU in 1983 he assumed responsibility for administering grants, principally Title III grants. In addition, he was in charge of student affairs and was responsible for determining the residency status of foreign students. Peterson also supervised finances of the university and was in charge of Institutional Research. As Title III Director, Peterson generally reported directly to the Vice President for Academic Affairs: first Clarkson, then Moore, and eventually, Wilson. The programs supported by Title III grants included faculty development, equipment purchases, and institutional research, providing millions of dollars annually for expenditures at TSU.…

Without reiterating every detail of the relevant testimony and documents, it suffices that the evidence heard and obviously credited by the jury painted a picture of Peterson as a highly principled, apolitical, objective grant administrator who repeatedly refused to "play ball" with high ranking TSU administrators when they attempted to obtain expensive equipment for unauthorized personal use or sought to have unauthorized job positions created and funded with grant money for their special "friends." The jury also heard and obviously credited testimony of both direct and implied threats by Wilson of adverse job actions, including firing, that Peterson was in jeopardy of incurring if, on reflection, he should fail or refuse to accede to requests that would require the unauthorized expenditure of grant funds.

The termination letter of January 3, 1991, from Wilson to Peterson purported to outline nine items constituting "cause" for the firing, each of which was set forth in a report prepared and submitted on request by one Joyce Deyon with whom, it turned out, Wilson never conferred after receiving the report. Wilson testified that he accepted the report and made his judgment based on it.

The jury heard testimony and saw documents which, if believed—as the jury apparently did—methodically refuted or explained away each of the nine purported causes for termination and revealed that Wilson did not even understand some of the items. The jury also heard evidence which, if credited, was sufficient to support a conclusion that the termination and its purported causes were pretext intended to cover Wilson's retaliation and desire to accomplish his actual or implied threats of getting rid of Peterson and replacing him with a grant director who would be more of a team player, i.e., would be more amenable to funding equipment purchases and job creations for "friends" of the higher-ups in the TSU administration with grant money.

That the jury unquestionably credited the testimony and documentation supporting Peterson's version of the facts and rejected Wilson's is confirmed by the "Yes" answer to Interrogatory No. I-A, "Do you find from a preponderance of the evidence that Dr. Bobby Wilson acted arbitrarily and capriciously in terminating Dr. Peterson?" In the interrogatory that followed, the jury awarded Peterson $152,235 in lost pay and benefits, and $35,000 for past and future mental anguish.

II. Analysis

...We review the district court's grant of a new trial for abuse of discretion. "It is a well-settled rule in this circuit that 'a verdict can be against the "great weight of the evidence," and thus justify a new trial, even if there is substantial evidence to support it.'" What courts cannot do—and what the district court here never purported to do—is to grant a new trial "simply because [the court] would have come to a different conclusion than the jury did."...

The district court's succinct but cryptic, three-sentence explanation for granting a new trial demonstrates beyond question that, following the verdict, the court impermissibly met with and interrogated the jurors outside the presence of the parties and their respective counsel, and then proceeded to act in direct reliance on the jurors' comments as though they constituted newly discovered evidence of a kind that the court could properly consider. It was not. The conclusion is inescapable that, in impeaching the jury's verdict in this case, the district court relied on information obtained from the jurors in the court's post-verdict, ex parte meeting with them and that, by definition, any information thus obtained had to come directly from their internal deliberations qua jurors.

1. Jury Impeachment

Rule 606(b) of the Federal Rules of Evidence (F.R.E.) tightly controls impeachment of jury verdicts. This rule states, in pertinent part:

Upon an inquiry into the validity of a verdict..., a juror may not testify as to any matter or statement occurring during the course of the jury's deliberations or to the effect of anything upon that or any other juror's mind or emotions as influencing the juror to assent to or dissent from the verdict...or concerning the juror's mental processes in connection therewith, except that a juror may testify on the question whether extraneous prejudicial information was improperly brought to the jury's attention or whether any outside influence was improperly brought to the jury's attention or whether any outside influence was improperly brought to bear upon any juror. Nor may a juror's affidavit or evidence of any statement by the juror concerning a matter about which the juror would be precluded from testifying be received for these purposes....

The landmark Supreme Court case on this issue is Tanner v. United States. After acknowledging that "[b]y the beginning of this century, if not earlier, the near-universal and firmly established common-law rule in the United States flatly prohibited the admission of juror testimony to impeach a jury verdict," the Court observed that "Federal Rule of Evidence 606(b) is grounded in the common-law rule against admission of jury testimony to impeach a verdict and the exception for juror testimony relating to extraneous influences." Following Tanner, and more closely on point, we held in Robles v. Exxon Corp. that receiving testimony from the jurors after they have returned their verdict, for the purpose of ascertaining that the jury misunderstood its instructions, is absolutely prohibited by F.R.E. 606(b). We underscored that holding by noting that "the legislative history of the rule unmistakably points to the conclusion that Congress made a conscious decision to disallow juror testimony as to the jurors' mental processes or fidelity to the court's instructions." What is pellucid here, from the court's own unequivocal and unambiguous words, is that the jurors' statements to the court related directly to matters that transpired in the jury room, that these matters comprehended the mental processes of the jurors in their deliberations on the case, and that the jurors' statements formed the foundation of the court's impeachment of the verdict grounded in the jury's lack of "fidelity to the court's instructions." We cannot conceive of an example more explicitly violative of Robles....

[The Court of Appeals concluded that the district court did not find that the verdict was against the great weight of the evidence and that, even if it had, such a decision was contrary to the record.] We are thus left with no choice but to reverse the district court's grant of a new trial, vacate the court's judgment rendered on the basis of the jury verdict in the second trial, and reinstate the results of the first trial. We therefore remand this case to the district court for entry of judgment in favor of Peterson and against Wilson in the principal sum of $187,235 ($152,235 for lost pay and benefits and $35,000 for past and future mental anguish), and for the assessment of appropriate interest and costs, including reasonable attorneys' fees incurred by Peterson in both trials and on appeal.

Grounds for a New Trial (As listed in (Cal.Code.Civ.Proc. § 657.)

(1) Irregularity of the proceedings;

(2) Misconduct of jury;

(3) Accident or surprise;

(4) Newly discovered evidence;

(5) Insufficient evidence;

(6) Verdict against law;

(7) Error in law;

(8) Excessive or inadequate damages.

FRCP 59 does not list the grounds for which a new trial may be granted. (Wright § 95) In federal courts common law must be looked to in determining the available grounds.

Tribble v. Bruin
279 F.2d 424 (1960)

SOBELOFF, Chief Judge.

This appeal raises a procedural problem relating to the power of the District Court to act upon a motion for a new trial after this court issued its mandate in an earlier appeal.

The background of this protracted litigation may be briefly summarized. On the night of July 1, 1954, plaintiff, Nancy Bruin, was injured by a tractor-trailer while crossing a street intersection in Bluffton, South Carolina. She subsequently sued the owner of the trailer, G. P. Tribble, and its operator, Allen Harper, to recover actual and punitive damages. The case was tried in the District Court on January 30 and 31, 1956, and at the close of the testimony, the defendants moved for a directed verdict. Denying the motion, the District Judge submitted the case to the jury, which returned a verdict for the plaintiff in the amount of $1,380.85 actual damages and $1,000 punitive damages. Thereafter, defendants moved under Rule 50(b) for a judgment n. o. v. and, in the alternative, for a new trial. The plaintiff also moved for a new trial, on the ground that the verdict was inadequate.

The District Judge, thinking the plaintiff guilty of gross contributory negligence as a matter of law, granted defendants' motion for judgment n. o. v. He found it unnecessary to pass on defendants' alternative motion for a new trial. As to the plaintiff's motion for a new trial, the Judge later explained:

"* * * I did not rule upon plaintiff's motion for a new trial since I decided that the defendants were entitled to a judgment notwithstanding the verdict. I did feel and announce that if the plaintiff was entitled to a verdict, the verdict of the jury was inadequate in view of the serious injuries she received."

From the entry of the judgment against her, plaintiff appealed, assigning error to the District Court in holding her guilty of gross contributory negligence as a matter of law. On the appeal, this court held, in an opinion filed on November 7, 1956, that the questions of contributory negligence and last clear chance were sufficiently in doubt to require their submission to the jury. The opinion concluded as follows:

"The judgment of the District Court will be reversed and the case will be remanded with directions to reinstate the verdict of the jury and enter judgment thereon.
"Reversed and Remanded."

The mandate of the court, issued on December 10, 1956, declared:

"* * * It is now here ordered and adjudged by this Court that the judgment of the said District Court appealed from, in this cause, be, and the same is hereby, reversed with costs; and that this cause be, and the same is hereby, remanded to the United States District Court for the Eastern District of South Carolina, at Charleston, with directions to reinstate the verdict of the jury and enter judgment thereon in accordance with the opinion of the Court filed herein."

Upon the filing of the mandate, plaintiff requested the District Court to rule on her motion for a new trial based on the ground of the inadequacy of the verdIct. Several hearings took place before the District Judge, who held the matter under advisement. For reasons which are unexplained, the District Judge did not enter judgment in accordance with the mandate until August 1, 1959; he still had not passed on the question of a new trial. Subsequently, plaintiff renewed her motion for a new trial, and on November 30, 1959, the District Judge signed an order setting aside the judgment and granting plaintiff a new trial.

The defendant brings this appeal, contending that the District Judge lacked the power to grant a new trial, after our mandate, rightly or wrongly, instructed him to reinstate the jury verdict and enter judgment thereon.

Initially, it should be observed that the District Judge ought to have ruled on the new trial motions when he granted the defendants' motion for judgment n. o. v. In the leading case of Montgomery Ward & Co. v. Duncan, 1940, 311 U.S. 243, 61 S.Ct. 189, 85 L.Ed. 147, the Supreme Court held that if alternative motions are presented under Rule 50(b) for judgment n. o. v. and for a new trial, the District Judge should rule on the motion for judgment, and "[w]hatever his ruling thereon he should also rule on the motion for a new trial, indicating the grounds of his decision." Where, as here, in addition to alternative motions by the losing party there is also a motion for new trial by his adversary, the District Judge should pass on all the motions, stating the grounds for each decision. Such a practice not only conforms to the requirements laid down in Montgomery Ward & Co. v. Duncan, but is conducive to "the just, speedy, and inexpensive determination of every action." F.R.Civ.P., Rule 1.

We note further that when our opinion was filed, with its direction to reinstate the jury verdict, plaintiff's proper course was to petition this court for a rehearing or modification of the mandate on the ground that the new trial motion, based on insufficiency of damages, had not been acted upon below or considered by us, and should not be precluded. Strictly speaking, plaintiff's motion for a new trial was not timely when renewed in the District Court after judgment was entered. F.R. Civ.P., Rule 59(b). Nevertheless, in the interests of justice, we will consider the renewed motion as one seeking relief under Rule 60.

* * *

Turning, therefore, to the merits of the question, the District Judge, as already mentioned, should have ruled on plaintiff's new trial motion when he granted defendants' motion for judgment n. o. v. On the first appeal, only one question was argued before us, stated in plaintiff's brief as follows:

"Did the trial judge err in holding and ruling that the plaintiff was guilty of contributory willfulness as a matter of law and granting defendants' motion for judgment notwithstanding the verdict?"

Though the plaintiff's motion for a new trial was mentioned incidentally in the statement of the case and in the conclusion of the plaintiff's brief, no point or controversy was presented in respect to this. It cannot be seriously questioned that our court did not advert to the motion or intend to pass on its merits. If it had been drawn to our notice, we would certainly have remanded the case to the District Judge so that he might rule upon the motion. Furthermore, if the plaintiff had filed a timely petition for a rehearing or modification of the mandate, as above suggested, we would no doubt have decided that action by the District Court upon her motion, which was not passed upon below or considered by us, should not be foreclosed. However, the failure of the mandate to reserve the motion was not called to our attention until now. Instead, the plaintiff renewed her motion in the District Court, where a ruling was delayed, for one reason or another, for almost three years. In these circumstances, we hold that plaintiff's motion is entitled to consideration by the District Court under Rule 60(b) (6). The rule, as we have seen, is broad enough to allow a judgment to be vacated "to accomplish justice."

In summary, while the District Court was powerless to pass on plaintiff's motion without leave from this court, we now decide that the motion warranted the District Court's consideration, and a grant of leave by us is appropriate.

We might therefore remand the case to the District Judge so that he could rule on the motion, yet we hesitate unnecessarily to prolong this already extended litigation. On two occasions, once informally after the trial and again in the order appealed from, the District Court has determined that the plaintiff is entitled to a new trial because the jury verdict was inadequate to compensate her for the serious injuries sustained. The District Court has doubtless weighed all the relevant considerations before entering its order of November 30, 1959. In the circumstances, instead of remanding with leave to take the action already deliberately taken, we affirm that order.

Order vacating judgment and granting new trial affirmed and case remanded for further proceedings.

COMBINING THE MOTIONS FOR JUDGMENT AS A MATTER OF LAW AND MOTION FOR A NEW TRIAL

FRCP 50(e) provides: If the court denies the motion for judgment as a matter of law, the prevailing party may, as appellee, assert grounds entitling it to a new trial should the appellate court conclude that the trial court erred in denying the motion. If the appellate court reverses the judgment, it may order a new trial, direct the trial court to determine whether a new trial should be granted, or direct the entry of judgment.

Subdivision (e) deals with the situation where judgment has been entered on the jury verdict, the motion for judgment as a matter of law and any motion for a new trial having been denied by the trial court. The verdict-winner, as appellee (the non-appealing party) besides seeking to uphold the judgment, may urge upon the appellate court that in case the trial court is found to have erred in entering judgment on the verdict, there are grounds for granting him a new trial instead of directing the entry of judgment for his opponent. In appropriate cases, the appellate court is not precluded from itself directing that a new trial be had. Nor is it precluded in proper cases from remanding the case for a determination by the trial court as to whether a new trial should be granted. The latter course is advisable where the grounds urged are suitable for the exercise of trial court discretion. (Notes of Advisory Committee on Rules—1963 Amendment)

CHAPTER 11

APPEAL

Appeal is the process by which a litigant who is unhappy with the decision of the trial court and feels it is erroneous, may have that decision reviewed by a higher court.

WHO CAN APPEAL?

Only parties aggrieved or harmed by the judgment can appeal from it. Winning parties may not obtain review of findings deemed erroneous if those findings are not necessary to the decree. (Friedenthal, §13.4)

According to Cal.Code.Civ.Proc § 902 "any party aggrieved" may appeal. A party is not aggrieved by a judgment granting it all relief sought, and cannot therefore appeal from it. Likewise, a party is not aggrieved by a judgment or order to which the party has consented or stipulated. Nor can a party appeal from a judgment which does not adversely affect him.

> **Appeals**
> **The Requirement of an Adverse Decision**
>
> Only parties aggrieved or harmed by the judgment can appeal from it.
>
> Winning parties may not obtain review of findings deemed erroneous.

Aetna Casualty & Surety Co. v. Cunningham
224 F.2d 478 (5th Cir. 1955)

[In large building projects, the owner or developer frequently requires that its main contractor take out an insurance policy to cover the possibility that the contractor will be unable to complete the project. If this happens, the policy provides funds so others can complete the project. In Cunningham the contractor failed to complete the project, and Aetna, the insurer, stepped in. After the dust settled (so to speak) and the project was completed with Aetna's money, Aetna tried to recover $32,000—the amount of its loss—from the contractor. At trial Aetna presented two theories for recovery: that the terms of the insurance contract permitted such recovery; and that, without regard to the policy terms, the contractor/insured had committed fraud in applying for the policy and that Aetna's loss was traceable to that fraud. (Aetna did not seek punitive damages on the fraud claim.) The district court found for Aetna on the contract claim but ruled that the contractor had not committed fraud. Both Aetna and the contractor appealed; an issue on appeal was which party could raise which contentions of error on appeal. Note that (1) failed construction contractors often file for bankruptcy protection from their creditors and (2) under some conditions liabilities incurred as a result of fraud are not discharged in bankruptcy.]

At the outset there is some doubt as to whether Aetna can appeal from the judgment which was in its favor in the amount prayed. If the relief granted was all to which Aetna was entitled, the mere fact that it was granted on one ground rather than on another would not make Aetna an aggrieved party on appeal. But amount is not the sole measure of the relief to which a party may be entitled. The judgment may have different qualities and legal consequences dependent on the claim on which it is based. At the beginning of the trial, Aetna's counsel, in response to an inquiry from the court, frankly stated his reason for insisting on the tort claim for fraud and deceit, "Because if we get a straight contract judgment it would be dischargeable in bankruptcy."...

It would be premature for us to pass upon the effect of bankruptcy on a judgment on either claim, or upon whether the finding that Cunningham's representations were not fraudulent would be res judicata as to the operation of a discharge in bankruptcy. It is enough at this time for us to hold that, if Aetna was denied judgment of the quality to which it laid claim [i.e., the fraud claim], it is a party aggrieved on appeal....

The law is fashioned to work substantial justice in real transactions. We hold, therefore, that when, as a practical matter, the denial of any one claim results in the plaintiff not getting the relief to which it claims to be entitled, whether in the amount or in the quality of the judgment, it has a right to be heard on appeal....

THE FINAL ORDER RULE

Title 28 U.S.C. §1291 provides for appeal to the courts of appeals only from "final decisions of the district courts of the United States." For purposes of §1291, a final judgment is generally regarded as "a decision by the District Court that 'ends the litigation on the merits and leaves nothing for the court to do but execute the judgment.'" (Catlin v. United States, 324 U.S. 229, 233 (1945).)

Appeals

The Requirement of Finality

Appeals lie only from "final decisions."

"One which ends the litigation on the merits and leaves nothing for the court to do but execute the judgment."

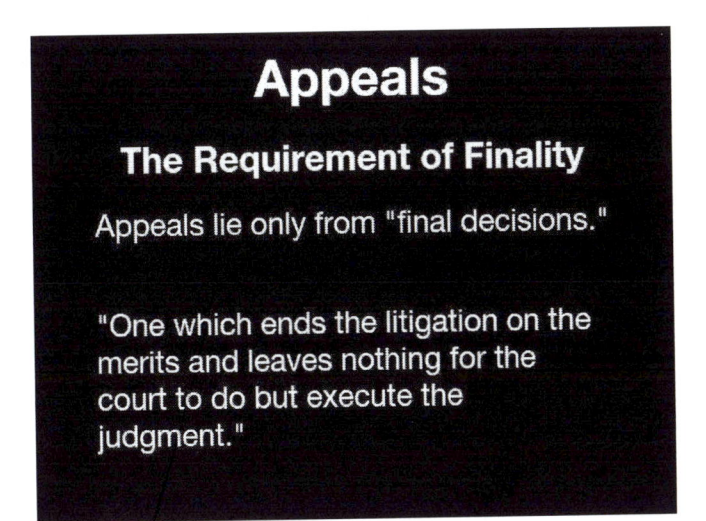

Reise v. Board of Regents of The University of Wisconsin
957 F.2d 293 (7th Cir. 1992)

EASTERBROOK, J.

E.H. Reise, who was graduated in the top 5% of his class from the Law School of the University of Wisconsin at Madison, applied for a position on its faculty. The Law School did not hire him. He believes that his race and sex account for the decision, that in recent years the Law School has been unwilling to consider anyone, no matter how skilled, who is not black, female, or otherwise eligible for preferential treatment. According to Reise, only one of the last thirteen appointments to the faculty has been a white male, and that appointment was made in 1985. The Law School says that the persons it hired are better lawyers and scholars than Reise. The district court has set a trial for this coming April to get at the truth.

[Reise has filed an appeal]...asking us to reverse the judge's order that he submit to a mental examination under Fed. R. Civ. P. 35. Reise demands $4 million in compensatory damages on account of the mental anguish, emotional distress, and illness that he says he has endured as a result of the Law School's decision not to hire him. Not surprisingly, the Law School wants to obtain a medical opinion on Reise's mental state, so that it may present evidence on that subject at trial. Reise insists that because he is over his distress and is not seeking damages on account of his current mental condition, an examination would reveal nothing of value. Again not surprisingly, the Law School is not content with Reise's say-so and wants to check. The district judge, siding with the Law School, ordered Reise to undergo an examination.

Although Reise contends that the examination is unnecessary and that the judge should at all events have ensured that the physician would be independent of the University, we shall have nothing to say about [those contentions]. Details of discovery are a long way from final decision [and the discovery order is therefore "interlocutory" and the Court of Appeal thus lacks jurisdiction to consider Reise's argument, 28 U.S.C. §1291]....

It is too late in the day to waste words explaining why interlocutory orders, and discovery orders in particular, are not appealable despite their irreversible costs. Because almost all interlocutory appeals from discovery orders would end in affirmance (the district court possesses discretion, and review is deferential), the costs of delay via appeal, and the costs to the judicial system of entertaining these appeals, exceed in the aggregate the costs of the few erroneous discovery orders that might be corrected were appeals available....

Discovery orders, including orders to submit to an examination, are readily reviewable after final decision. A party aggrieved by the order assures eventual review by refusing to comply. The district judge then imposes sanctions under Fed. R. Civ. P. 37(b)(2). The probable sanction in a case such as this is an order striking Reise's claim for damages on account of mental and physical distress. If Reise should prevail on the merits but not obtain damages because of the order striking his claim, he may obtain full review on appeal: if the district judge abused his discretion in requiring Reise to submit to an examination, we will remand for further proceedings. True, this procedure creates a potential for two trials, but then so does any other discovery order, or an order disqualifying or failing to disqualify counsel, or any order granting or denying partial summary judgment.... And requiring the complaining party to take some risk—to back up his belief with action—winnows weak claims. Only persons who have substantial objections to the examination and believe their legal positions strong will follow a path that could end in defeat. Among those who take the risk by balking at the order, some will lose on the merits, and their discovery disputes will become moot. Most of the remaining cases will end in affirmance, given deferential review. The number of retrials entailed by the procedure is small, the number of appeals avoided large.

As an order to submit to a physical or mental examination is not appealable.... Appeal No. 91-3844 is dismissed for want of jurisdiction.

EXCEPTIONS TO THE FINAL JUDGMENT RULE

FRCP 54(b) provides that a trial court in an action with multiple claims or parties may identify as appealable a particular order issued with respect to a claim or party by making an express direction for the entry of a judgment as to that claim or party involved and by certifying that there is no just reason to delay an appeal. In the absence of this trial court certification no appeal will lie. (Friedenthal § 13.1) Rule 54(b) allows appeal from a portion of a case that could have been brought as a separate action. It simply removes the penalty that liberal joinder would inflict if it prevented separate appeals in portions of a case that could have been separate cases.

Liberty Mutual Insurance Co. v. Wetzel
424 U.S. 737 (1976)

Mr. Justice REHNQUIST delivered the opinion of the Court.

Respondents filed a complaint in the United States District Court for the Western District of Pennsylvania in which they asserted that petitioner's employee insurance benefits and maternity leave regulations discriminated against women in violation of Title VII of the Civil Rights Act of 1964, as amended by the Equal Employment Opportunity Act of 1972. The District Court ruled in favor of respondents on the issue of petitioner's liability under that Act, and petitioner appealed to the Court of Appeals for the Third Circuit. That court held that it had jurisdiction of petitioner's appeal under 28 U.S.C. §1291, and proceeded to affirm on the merits the judgment of the District Court. We granted certiorari and heard argument on the merits. Though neither party has questioned the jurisdiction of the Court of Appeals to entertain the appeal, we are obligated to do so on our own motion if a question thereto exists. Because we conclude that the District Court's order was not appealable to the Court of Appeals, we vacate the judgment of the Court of Appeals with instructions to dismiss petitioner's appeal from the order of the District Court.

Respondents' complaint, after alleging jurisdiction and facts deemed pertinent to their claim, prayed for a judgment against petitioner embodying the following relief:

(a) requiring that defendant establish non-discriminatory hiring, payment, opportunity, and promotional plans and programs;

(b) enjoining the continuance by defendant of the illegal acts and practices alleged herein;

(c) requiring that defendant pay over to plaintiffs and to the members of the class the damages sustained by plaintiffs and the members of the class by reason of defendant's illegal acts and practices, including adjusted back pay, with interest, and an additional equal amount as liquidated damages, and exemplary damages;

(d) requiring that defendant pay to plaintiffs and to the members of the class the costs of this suit and a reasonable attorney's fee, with interest; and

(e) such other and further relief as the Court deems appropriate.

After extensive discovery, respondents moved for partial summary judgment only as to the issue of liability. Fed. Rule Civ. Proc. 56[(a)]. The District Court on January 9, 1974, finding no issues of material fact in dispute, entered an order to the effect that petitioner's pregnancy-related policies violated Title VII of the Civil Rights Act of 1964. It also ruled that Liberty Mutual's hiring and promotion policies violated Title

VII. Petitioner thereafter filed a motion for reconsideration which was denied by the District Court. Its order of February 20, 1974, denying the motion for reconsideration, contains the following concluding language:

In its Order the court stated it would enjoin the continuance of practices which the court found to be in violation of Title VII. The Plaintiffs were invited to submit the form of the injunction order and the Defendant has filed Notice of Appeal and asked for stay of any injunctive order. Under these circumstances the court will withhold the issuance of the injunctive order and amend the Order previously issued under the provisions of Fed. R. Civ. P. 54(b), as follows:

And now this 20th day of February, 1974, it is directed that final judgment be entered in favor of Plaintiffs that Defendant's policy of requiring female employees to return to work within three months of delivery of a child or be terminated is in violation of the provisions of Title VII of the Civil Rights Act of 1964; that Defendant's policy of denying disability income protection plan benefits to female employees for disabilities related to pregnancies or childbirth is in violation of Title VII of the Civil Rights Act of 1964 and that it is expressly directed that Judgment be entered for the Plaintiffs upon these claims of Plaintiffs' Complaint; there being no just reason for delay.

It is obvious from the District Court's order that respondents, although having received a favorable ruling on the issue of petitioner's liability to them, received none of the relief which they expressly prayed for in the portion of their complaint set forth above. They requested an injunction, but did not get one; they requested damages, but were not awarded any; they requested attorneys' fees, but received none.

Counsel for respondents when questioned during oral argument in this Court suggested that at least the District Court's order of February 20 amounted to a declaratory judgment on the issue of liability pursuant to the provisions of 28 U.S.C. §2201. Had respondents sought only a declaratory judgment, and no other form of relief, we would of course have a different case. But even if we accept respondents' contention that the District Court's order was a declaratory judgment on the issue of liability, it nonetheless left unresolved respondents' requests for an injunction, for compensatory and exemplary damages, and for attorneys' fees. It finally disposed of none of respondents' prayers for relief.

The District Court and the Court of Appeals apparently took the view that because the District Court made the recital required by Fed. Rule Civ. Proc. 54(b) that final judgment be entered on the issue of liability, and that there was no just reason for delay, the orders thereby became appealable as a final decision pursuant to 28 U.S.C. §1291. We cannot agree with this application of the Rule and statute in question.

Rule 54(b)2 "does not apply to a single claim action....It is limited expressly to multiple claims actions in which 'one or more but less than all' of the multiple claims have been finally decided and are found otherwise to be ready for appeal." Here, however, respondents set forth but a single claim: that petitioner's employee insurance benefits and maternity leave regulations discriminated against its women employees in violation of Title VII of the Civil Rights Act of 1964. They prayed for several different types of relief in the event that they sustained the allegations of their complaint, see Fed. Rule Civ. Proc. 8(a)(3), but their complaint advanced a single legal theory which was applied to only one set of facts.4 Thus, despite the fact that the District Court undoubtedly made the findings required under the Rule had it been applicable, those findings do not in a case such as this make the order appealable pursuant to 28 U.S.C. §1291.

We turn to consider whether the District Court's order might have been appealed by petitioner to the Court of Appeals under any other theory. The order, viewed apart from its discussion of Rule 54(b), constitutes a grant of partial summary judgment limited to the issue of petitioner's liability. Such judgments are by their term interlocutory, and where assessment of damages or awarding of other relief remains to be resolved have never been considered to be "final" within the meaning of 28 U.S.C. §1292. Thus the only possible authorization for an appeal from the District Court's order would be pursuant to the provisions of 28 U.S.C. §1292.

If the District Court had granted injunctive relief but had not ruled on respondents' other requests for relief, this interlocutory order would have been appealable under §1292(a)(1).5 As noted above, the court did not issue an injunction. It might be argued that the order of the District Court, insofar as it failed to include the injunctive relief requested by respondents, is an interlocutory order refusing an injunction within the meaning of §1292(a)(1). But even if this would have allowed respondents to then obtain review in the Court of Appeals, there was no denial of any injunction sought by Petitioner and it could not avail itself of that grant of jurisdiction.

Nor was this order appealable pursuant to 28 U.S.C. §1292(b).6 Although the District Court's findings made with a view to satisfying Rule 54(b) might be viewed as substantial compliance with the certification requirement of that section, there is no showing in this record that petitioner made application to the Court of Appeals within the 10 days therein specified. And that court's holding that its jurisdiction was pursuant to §1291 makes it clear that it thought itself obliged to consider on the merits petitioner's appeal. There can be no assurance that had the other requirements of §1292(b) been complied with, the Court of Appeals would have exercised its discretion to entertain the interlocutory appeal.

Were we to sustain the procedure followed here, we would condone a practice whereby a district court in virtually any case before it might render an interlocutory decision on the question of liability of the defendant, and the defendant would thereupon be permitted to appeal to the court of appeals without satisfying any of the requirements that Congress carefully set forth. We believe that Congress, in enacting present §§1291 and 1292 of Title 28, has been well aware of the dangers of an overly rigid insistence upon a "final decision" for appeal in every case, and has in those sections made ample provision for appeal of orders which are not "final" so as to alleviate any possible hardship. We would twist the fabric of the statute more than it will bear if we were to agree that the District Court's order of February 20, 1974, was appealable to the Court of Appeals.

The judgment of the Court of Appeals is therefore vacated, and the case is remanded with instructions to dismiss the petitioner's appeal. It is so ordered.

PRACTICAL FINALITY

Lauro Lines S.R.L. v. Chasser
490 U.S. 495 (1989)

Justice BRENNAN delivered the opinion of the Court.

We granted certiorari to consider whether an interlocutory order of a United States District Court denying a defendant's motion to dismiss a damages action on the basis of a contractual forum-selection clause is immediately appealable under 28 U.S.C. §1291 as a collateral final order. We hold that it is not.

I

The individual respondents were, or represent the estates of persons who were, passengers aboard the cruise ship Achille Lauro when it was hijacked by terrorists in the Mediterranean in October 1985. Petitioner Lauro Lines s.r.l., an Italian company, owns the Achille Lauro. Respondents filed suits against Lauro Lines in the District Court for the Southern District of New York to recover damages for injuries sustained as a result of the hijacking, and for the wrongful death of passenger Leon Klinghoffer. Lauro Lines moved before trial to dismiss the actions, citing the forum-selection clause printed on each passenger ticket. This clause purported to obligate the passenger to institute any suit arising in connection with the contract in Naples, Italy, and to renounce the right to sue elsewhere.

The District Court denied petitioner's motions to dismiss, holding that the ticket as a whole did not give reasonable notice to passengers that they were waiving the opportunity to sue in a domestic forum. Without moving for certification for immediate appeal pursuant to 28 U.S.C. §1292(b), Lauro Lines sought to appeal the District Court's orders. The Court of Appeals for the Second Circuit dismissed petitioner's appeal on the ground that the District Court's orders denying petitioner's motions to dismiss were interlocutory and not appealable under §1291. The court held that the orders did not fall within the exception to the rule of nonappealability carved out for collateral final orders in Cohen v. Beneficial Industrial Loan Corp., 337 U.S. 541 (1949). We granted certiorari to resolve a disagreement among the Courts of Appeals. We now affirm.

II

Title 28 U.S.C. §1291 provides for appeal to the courts of appeals only from "final decisions of the district courts of the United States." For purposes of §1291, a final judgment is generally regarded as "a decision by the District Court that 'ends the litigation on the merits and leaves nothing for the court to do but execute the judgment.'" Van Cauwenberghe v. Biard, 486 U.S. 517, 521 (1988), quoting Catlin v. United States, 324 U.S. 229, 233 (1945). An order denying a motion to dismiss a civil action on the ground that a contractual forum-selection clause requires that such suit be brought in another jurisdiction is not a decision on the merits that ends the litigation. On the contrary, such an order "ensures that litigation will continue in the District Court." Gulfstream Aerospace Corp. v. Mayacamas Corp., 485 U.S. 271, 275 (1988). Section 1291 thus permits an appeal only if an order denying a motion to dismiss based upon a forum-selection clause falls within the "narrow exception to the normal application of the final judgment rule [that] has come to be known as the collateral order doctrine." Midland Asphalt Corp. v. United States, 489 U.S. 794, 798 (1989). That exception is for a "small class" of prejudgment orders that "finally determine claims of right separable from, and collateral to, rights asserted in the action, [and that are] too important to be denied review and too independent of the cause itself to require that appellate consideration be deferred until the whole case is adjudicated." Cohen, supra, at 546. We have held that to fall within the Cohen exception, an order must satisfy at least three conditions: "It must 'conclusively determine the disputed question,' 'resolve an important issue completely separate from the merits of the action,' and 'be effectively unreviewable on appeal from a final judgment.'" Richardson-Merrell Inc. v. Koller, 472 U.S. 424, 431 (1985), quoting Coopers & Lybrand v. Livesay, 437 U.S. 463, 468 (1978). For present purposes, we need not decide whether an order denying a dismissal motion based upon a contractual forum-selection clause conclusively determines a disputed issue, or whether it resolves an important issue that is independent of the merits of the action, for the District Court's orders fail to satisfy the third requirement of the collateral order test.

We recently reiterated the "general rule" that an order is "effectively unreviewable" only "where the order at issue involves 'an asserted right the legal and practical value of which would be destroyed if it were not vindicated before trial.'" Midland Asphalt Corp., quoting United States v. MacDonald, 435 U.S. 850, 860 (1978). If it is eventually decided that the District Court erred in allowing trial in this case to take place in New York, petitioner will have been put to unnecessary trouble and expense, and the value of its contractual right to an Italian forum will have been diminished. It is always true, however, that "there is value…in triumphing before trial, rather than after it," MacDonald, supra, at 860, n.7, and this Court has declined to find the costs associated with unnecessary litigation to be enough to warrant allowing the immediate appeal of a pretrial order. See Richardson-Merrell Inc., supra, at 436 ("the possibility that a ruling may be erroneous and may impose additional litigation expense is not sufficient to set aside the finality requirement imposed by Congress" in §1291). Instead, we have insisted that the right asserted be one that is essentially destroyed if its vindication must be postponed until trial is completed.

We have thus held in cases involving criminal prosecutions that the deprivation of a right not to be tried is effectively unreviewable after final judgment and is immediately appealable. Similarly, in civil cases, we have held that the denial of a motion to dismiss based upon a claim of absolute immunity from suit is immediately appealable prior to final judgment, "for the essence of absolute immunity is its possessor's entitlement not to have to answer for his conduct in a civil damages action." Mitchell v. Forsyth, 472 U.S. 511, 525 (1985). And claims of qualified immunity may be pursued by immediate appeal, because qualified immunity too "is an immunity from suit." On the other hand, we have declined to hold the collateral order doctrine applicable where a district court has denied a claim, not that the defendant has a right not to be sued at all, but that the suit against the defendant is not properly before the particular court because it lacks jurisdiction. In Van Cauwenberghe v. Biard, 486 U.S. 517 (1988), a civil defendant moved for dismissal on the ground that he had been immune from service of process because his presence in the United States had been compelled by extradition to face criminal charges. We noted that, after Mitchell, "[t]he critical question...is whether 'the essence' of the claimed right is a right not to stand trial," 486 U.S., at 524, and held that the immunity from service of process defendant asserted did not amount to an immunity from suit—even though service was essential to the trial court's jurisdiction over the defendant.

Lauro Lines argues here that its contractual forum-selection clause provided it with a right to trial before a tribunal in Italy, and with a concomitant right not to be sued anywhere else. This "right not to be haled for trial before tribunals outside the agreed forum," petitioner claims, cannot effectively be vindicated by appeal after trial in an improper forum. There is no obviously correct way to characterize the right embodied in petitioner's forum-selection provision: "all litigants who have a meritorious pretrial claim for dismissal can reasonably claim a right not to stand trial." Van Cauwenberghe. The right appears most like that to be free from trial if it is characterized—as by petitioner—as a right not to be sued at all except in a Neapolitan forum. It appears less like a right not to be subjected to suit if characterized—as by the Court of Appeals—as "a right to have the binding adjudication of claims occur in a certain forum." Even assuming that the former characterization is proper, however, petitioner is obviously not entitled under the forum-selection clause of its contract to avoid suit altogether, and an entitlement to avoid suit is different in kind from an entitlement to be sued only in a particular forum. Petitioner's claim that it may be sued only in Naples, while not perfectly secured by appeal after final judgment, is adequately vindicable at that stage—surely as effectively vindicable as a claim that the trial court lacked personal jurisdiction over the defendant—and hence does not fall within the third prong of the collateral order doctrine.

Petitioner argues that there is a strong federal policy favoring the enforcement of foreign forum-selection clauses, citing The Bremen v. Zapata Off-Shore Co., 407 U.S. 1 (1972), and that "the essential concomitant of this strong federal policy…is the right of immediate appellate review of district court orders denying their enforcement." A policy favoring enforcement of forum-selection clauses, however, would go to the merits of petitioner's claim that its ticket-agreement requires that any suit be filed in Italy and that the agreement should be enforced by the federal courts. Immediate appealability of a prejudgment order denying enforcement, insofar as it depends upon satisfaction of the third prong of the collateral order test, turns on the precise contours of the right asserted, and not upon the likelihood of eventual success on the merits. The Court of Appeals properly dismissed petitioner's appeal, and its judgment is affirmed.

OTHER EXCEPTIONS TO THE FINAL JUDGMENT RULE

INJUNCTIONS 28 U.S.C. 1292(A)

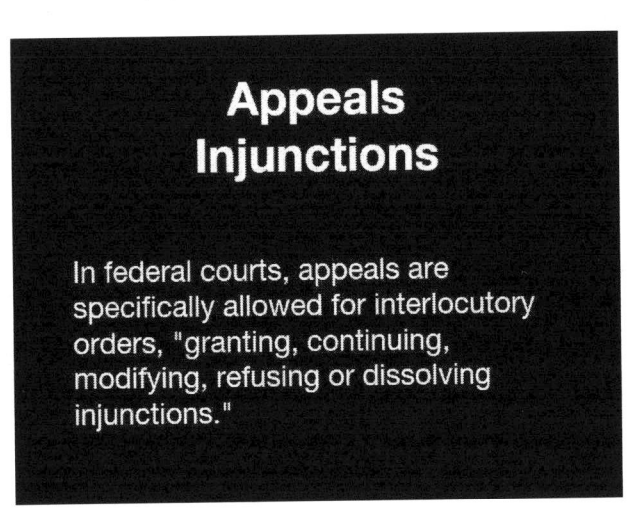

> **Appeals Injunctions**
>
> In federal courts, appeals are specifically allowed for interlocutory orders, "granting, continuing, modifying, refusing or dissolving injunctions."

INTERLOCUTORY APPEALS UNDER 28 U.S.C. 1292(B)

28 U.S.C. 1292(b) grants discretion to the courts of appeals to review any interlocutory order in a civil case if the trial judge, in making the order, has stated in writing that the order involves a controlling question of law as to which there is substantial ground for difference of opinion and that an immediate appeal from the order may materially advance the ultimate termination of the litigation. 1292(b) allows discretionary appeals from interlocutory orders when both the trial and appellate courts agree that an appeal is appropriate.

For section 1292(b) to apply there must be (1) a "controlling question of law." Many cases have held a 1292(b) appeal not proper on matters that lie within the discretion of the district court. (2) There must be a "difference of opinion" about the controlling question of law. i.e., it must not be a question which is controlled by clear precedent. (3) It must be thought that immediate appeal "may materially advance the ultimate termination of the litigation." Hence, the appeal must carry the potential of avoiding litigation altogether. (Wright § 102)

SHORT CIRCUITING THE APPEALS PROCESS THROUGH WRITS

The last category of exceptions to the final judgment rule involves applications to the appellate courts for writs of mandamus or prohibition to reverse some intermediate court ruling. Technically this is not an appeal but an original proceeding in the appellate court seeking an order directing the judge to enter or vacate a particular order. (Friedenthal § 13.3)

The remedy of mandamus is a drastic one, to be invoked only in extraordinary situations. The writ has traditionally been used in the federal courts only to confine an inferior court to a lawful exercise of its proscribed jurisdiction or to compel it to exercise its authority when it is its duty to do so. Only exceptional circumstances amounting to a judicial usurpation of power will justify the invocation of mandamus. Issuance of the writ is in a large part a matter of discretion with the court to which the petition is addressed. (*Kerr. v. U.S. District Court,* 426 U.S. 394 (1976). The party seeking issuance of the writ must have no other adequate means to attain the relief he desires. He must satisfy the burden of showing that his right to issuance of the writ is clear and indisputable.

Omaha Indemnity Company v. Superior Court
209 Cal.App.3d 1266 (1989)

GILBERT, J.

An attorney files a writ petition with the Court of Appeal pointing out an apparent error of the trial court. The Court of Appeal summarily denies the petition. The bewildered attorney asks, "Why?"

If this case does not answer the question, we hope the following rule will at least assuage counsel's frustration: (1) Error by the trial judge does not of itself ensure that a writ petition will be granted. A remedy will not be deemed inadequate merely because additional time and effort would be consumed by its being pursued through the ordinary course of the law. (Rescue Army v. Municipal Court (1946) 28 Cal.2d 460 [171 P.2d 8].)

In this action, plaintiffs are suing defendants for negligence. They are also suing defendants' insurance company in a cause of action for declaratory relief. Plaintiffs claim that they are third party beneficiaries of this insurance contract. The trial court has denied the motion of the insurance company to sever the declaratory relief cause of action, and the insurance company therefore seeks relief by way of extraordinary writ. We initially denied the writ, but after our Supreme Court directed us to issue an alternative writ, we shall now grant a writ of mandate.

BACKGROUND

Real parties Frank and Margaret Greinke owned rental property in the City of Santa Maria. In July of 1980, the Greinkes leased the premises to K.R. Trefts and Patricia M. Trefts. The lease agreement required the Trefts to purchase a general liability insurance policy for the mutual benefit of landlord and tenant. In July of 1982, Omaha Indemnity Company, an insurance company, issued a general liability policy to the Trefts.

The Greinkes claim that, on or about July 17, 1986, they became aware of damage to their property caused by an oil spill. They contend that the oil spill occurred during the Trefts' occupation of the property. The Greinkes demanded that Omaha compensate them, under the terms of the insurance policy, for the damage to the property. Omaha has purportedly denied coverage under the policy.

On March 14, 1988, the Greinkes sued the Trefts for damage resulting from the oil spill. They also sued Omaha for declaratory relief of their rights under the terms of the insurance contract.

Omaha demurred to the declaratory relief cause of action. In its demurrer it asserted that the Greinkes were not parties to the contract of insurance and, therefore, had no standing to pursue a claim for declaratory relief. It contended that the Greinkes had alleged neither interest in the insurance policy nor a denial of coverage. Thus, Omaha reasoned that there is no case or controversy pending against it.

The trial court was correct in overruling the demurrer. The Greinkes allege that they are the intended beneficiaries of the insurance policy and that Omaha had denied them coverage. In such instances, an action for declaratory relief is appropriate.

In the alternative, Omaha moved to sever the declaratory relief action from the tort lawsuit. Omaha claimed that it would suffer prejudice should the lawsuit against both itself and the Trefts go forward. Further, it pointed out that severance would promote judicial economy in that there would be no need to try the declaratory relief action should the tenants be found not liable.

Although Omaha has requested our review of this ruling, it has neglected to supply us with a copy of the reporter's transcript. This did not simplify our task of review. (See

Sherwood v. Superior Court (1979) 24 Cal.3d 183, 186-187 [154 Cal. Rptr. 917, 593 P.2d 862].)

On August 2, 1988, we denied a petition for writ of mandate. On September 29, 1988, the Supreme Court granted a petition for review. It then ordered the case retransferred to us with the direction to issue an alternative writ in light of Evidence Code section 1155 and Moradi-Shalal v. Fireman's Fund Ins. Companies (1988) 46 Cal.3d 287, 306 [250 Cal. Rptr. 116, 758 P.2d 58].

DISCUSSION

A. Motion to Sever

Code of Civil Procedure section 1048, subdivision (b) states, in pertinent part: "The court, in furtherance of convenience or to avoid prejudice, or when separate trials will be conducive to expedition and economy, may order a separate trial of any cause of action...."

In a negligence action, Evidence Code section 1155 precludes the use of evidence that a tortfeasor has insurance for the injury that he has allegedly caused. "The evidence [of a party being insured] is regarded as both irrelevant and prejudicial to the defendant." (1 Witkin, Cal. Evidence (3d ed. 1986) § 417, p. 391.)

Our Supreme Court has stated that the suing of an insured for negligence and the insurer for bad faith in the same lawsuit "'... obviously violate[s] both the letter and spirit of [Evid. Code, § 1155].' [Royal Globe Ins. Co. v. Superior Court (1979) 23 Cal.3d 880, 891 (153 Cal. Rptr. 842, 592 P.2d 329).] ... `... [U]ntil the liability of the insured is first determined, the defense of the insured may be seriously hampered by discovery initiated by the injured claimant against the insurer.' [Citation.]" (Moradi-Shalal v. Fireman's Fund Ins. Companies, supra, 46 Cal.3d at p. 306, italics in original.)

"It is within the discretion of the court to order a severance and separate trials of such actions [citations], and the exercise of such discretion will not be interfered with on appeal except when there has been a manifest abuse thereof. [Citation.]" (McLellan v. McLellan (1972) 23 Cal. App.3d 343, 353 [100 Cal. Rptr. 258].) (4a) Although we find that the trial court abused its discretion when it denied Omaha's motion to sever, relief by way of extraordinary writ should not be considered a foregone conclusion.

B. Relief by Way of Extraordinary Writ - Why It Is Hard to Get, and Why We Initially Denied the Petition

Approximately 90 percent of petitions seeking extraordinary relief are denied. (See Cal. Civil Writ Practice (Cont.Ed.Bar 1987) § 2.2, p. 50.) Only rarely does the court give detailed reasons for its rejection of a petition. Instead, counsel is usually notified in a terse minute order or postcard that the petition is denied.

Although, as a rule, the court states no reason for its denial of a petition, it will on occasion refer to an authority in support of its order of denial. This oblique message, ostensibly designed to enlighten, often has the opposite effect and promotes anxiety among those attorneys unable to tolerate either uncertainty or ambiguity.

Case law has done little to explain why appellate courts deny writ petitions. The subject is most commonly broached in those cases in which relief has been granted. The appellate court in dicta will briefly explain why extraordinary relief is typically not available. The discussion primarily centers on the unique circumstances of the case at hand that were found to warrant extraordinary relief.

Just as case law has been disappointing as a source of information concerning the mysteries of the writ, so have attempts to impart information by hierophants of appellate practice. Those who have tried to extract a coherent set of rules from cases and treatises on writs have found it easier to comprehend a "washing bill in Babylonic cuneiform." (Gilbert & Sullivan, Pirates of Penzance (1879).)

The large number of rejections of writ petitions demonstrates that courts will not use their scarce resources to second-guess every ruling and order of the trial court, particularly when to do so would save neither time nor aid in the resolution of a lawsuit. (E.g., see Dondi Properties Corp. v. Commerce Sav. and Loan Ass'n (N.D.Tex. 1988) 121 F.R.D. 284, 286.)

Writ relief, if it were granted at the drop of a hat, would interfere with an orderly administration of justice at the trial and appellate levels. Reviewing courts have been cautioned to guard against the tendency to take "'... too lax a view of the "extraordinary" nature of prerogative writs ...'" lest they run the risk of fostering the delay of trials, vexing litigants and trial courts with multiple proceedings, and adding to the delay of judgment appeals pending in the appellate court.

"If the rule were otherwise, in every ordinary action a defendant whenever he chose could halt the proceeding in the trial court by applying for a writ of prohibition to stop the ordinary progress of the action toward a judgment until a reviewing tribunal passed upon an intermediate question that had arisen. If such were the rule, reviewing courts would in innumerable cases be converted from appellate courts to nisi prius tribunals."

Particularly today, "in an era of excessively crowded lower court dockets, it is in the interest of the fair and prompt administration of justice to discourage piecemeal litigation." (Kerr v. United States District Court (1976) 426 U.S. 394, 403 [48 L.Ed.2d 725, 732, 96 S.Ct. 2119].)

Were reviewing courts to treat writs in the same manner as they do appeals, these courts would be trapped in an appellate gridlock. This in turn would cause ordinary appeals, waiting for review, to be shunted to the sidelines. One writer sees a writ petition as being a device used to "cut into line" ahead of those litigants awaiting determination of postjudgment appeals.

The Court of Appeal is generally in a far better position to review a question when called upon to do so in an appeal instead of by way of a writ petition. When review takes place by way of appeal, the court has a more complete record, more time for deliberation and, therefore, more insight into the significance of the issues. "Unlike the ordinary appeal which moves in an orderly, predictable pattern onto and off the appellate court's calendar, writ proceedings follow no set procedural course." (

Further, some issues may diminish in importance as a case proceeds towards trial. Petitioners seeking extraordinary writs do not always consider that a purported error of a trial judge may (1) be cured prior to trial, (2) have little or no effect upon the outcome of trial, or (3) be properly considered on appeal.

An unrestrained exercise of the power to grant extraordinary writs carries the potential to undermine the relationship between trial and appellate courts. Writ petitions "'have the unfortunate consequence of making the judge a litigant, obliged to obtain personal counsel or to leave his defense to one of the litigants [appearing] before him' in the underlying case. [Citations.]" Judges should be umpires rather than players.

In order to confine the use of mandamus to its proper office, the Supreme Court, in various cases, has stated general criteria for determining the propriety of an extraordinary writ: (1) the issue tendered in the writ petition is of widespread interest or presents a significant and novel constitutional issue 2) the trial court's order deprived petitioner of an opportunity to present a substantial portion of his cause of action; (3) conflicting trial court interpretations of the law require a resolution of the conflict; (4) the trial court's order is both clearly erroneous as a matter of law and substantially prejudices petitioner's case; (5) the party seeking the writ lacks an adequate means, such as a direct appeal, by which to attain relief; and (6) the petitioner will suffer harm or prejudice in a manner that cannot be corrected on appeal. The extent to which these criteria apply depends on the facts and circumstances of the case.

To adequately and intelligently decide the issues in this case or any other case, the court must have a complete record. Here, we did not have a copy of the reporter's transcript, and consequently did not know whether the court had even denied the motion to sever. The minute order states only that the court did not grant the demurrer.

After the Supreme Court remanded the matter to this court, at oral argument the parties stipulated that respondent court had denied the motion to sever. This was helpful, but we still do not know upon what grounds the trial judge made his decision.

It is true that mandate, in certain instances, provides a more effective remedy than does appeal for the purpose of reviewing an order denying severance. If, however, the trial court here denied the motion for severance without prejudice to bring the motion at a later time, writ relief would be inappropriate.

Under such circumstances, the failure to order severance would not meet the definition of an "irreparable injury." It would constitute, at best, an "irreparable inconvenience." Upon proper application at a later time, Omaha may have succeeded in obtaining an order for severance. A trial court is entitled to change its mind before judgment (and may vacate a prior order for consolidation and order severance.

Here, however, there is no indication that the motion was denied without prejudice.

The Supreme Court's order directing that an alternative writ be issued constitutes a determination that, in the ordinary course of the law, the petitioner is without an adequate remedy.

Let a writ of mandate issue ordering respondent superior court to grant the motion to sever. The stay of proceedings is dissolved.

SCOPE OF REVIEW
LAW AND FACT

FRCP 52(a)(6) provides that: findings of fact must not be set aside unless clearly erroneous, and the reviewing court must give due regard to the trial court's opportunity to judge the witnesses' credibility. The "clearly erroneous" rule applies in all nonjury cases even when findings are based solely on documentary evidence or on inferences from undisputed facts. See, e.g., *Maxwell v. Sumner*, 673 F.2d 1031, 1036 (9th Cir.), cert. denied, 459 U.S. 976 (1982)

Anderson v. Bessemer City
470 U.S. 564 (1985)

Justice WHITE delivered the opinion of the Court.

[A] District Court's finding of discriminatory intent in an action brought under Title VII of the Civil Rights Act of 1964…is a factual finding that may be overturned on appeal only if it is clearly erroneous. In this case, the Court of Appeals for the Fourth Circuit concluded that there was clear error in a District Court's finding of discrimination and reversed. Because our reading of the record convinces us that the Court of Appeals misapprehended and misapplied the clearly-erroneous standard, we reverse.

I

[Bessemer City sought a new Recreation Director. Ms. Anderson was the only woman to apply for the job. A five-member committee interviewed the eight applicants and chose a male, and Ms. Anderson sued, alleging discrimination.]

...After a 2-day trial, during which the court heard testimony from petitioner, Mr. Kincaid [the successful applicant], and the five members of the selection committee, the court issued a brief memorandum of decision setting forth its finding that petitioner...had been denied the position...on account of her sex....[The judge also requested] that petitioner's counsel submit proposed findings of fact and conclusions of law expanding upon those set forth in the memorandum....[This procedure led to several rounds of proposed findings by plaintiff and objections by defendant. Finally,] the court issued its own findings of fact and conclusions of law.

...[T]he court's finding that petitioner had been denied employment...because of her sex rested on a number of subsidiary findings[: (1) that Ms. Anderson "had been better qualified than Mr. Kincaid" (the court detailed the careers of each); (2) that "male committee members had in fact been biased against" Ms. Anderson because she was a woman, a finding based "in part on the testimony of one of the committee members that he believed it would have been 'real hard' for a woman to handle the job and that he would not want his wife to have to perform" its duties; (3) that Ms. Anderson "alone among the applicants...had been asked whether she realized the job would involve night work and travel and whether her husband approved of her applying for the job" (there was some dispute about whether Mr. Kincaid was asked an analogous question but the trial court concluded that it was "not a serious inquiry"); and (4)] that the reasons offered by the male committee members for their choice of Mr. Kincaid were pretextual. The court rejected the proposition that Mr. Kincaid's degree in physical education justified his choice, as the evidence suggested that where male candidates were concerned, the committee valued experience more highly than formal education....

The Fourth Circuit reversed...[holding that three of] the District Court's crucial findings were clearly erroneous: the finding that petitioner was the most qualified candidate, the finding that petitioner had been asked questions that other applicants were spared, and the finding that the male committee members were biased against hiring a woman....

II

We must deal at the outset with the Fourth Circuit's suggestion that "close scrutiny of the record in this case [was] justified by the manner in which the opinion was prepared"—that is, by the District Court's adoption of petitioner's proposed findings of fact and conclusions of law.

We too, have criticized courts for their verbatim adoption of findings of fact prepared by prevailing parties....Nonetheless, our previous discussions of the subject suggest that even when the trial judge adopts the proposed findings verbatim, the findings are those of the court and may be reversed only if clearly erroneous....

In any event, the District Court in this case does not appear to have uncritically accepted findings prepared without judicial guidance....

III

Because a finding of intentional discrimination is a finding of fact, the standard governing appellate review...is that set forth in Federal Rule of Civil Procedure 52(a): "Findings of fact shall not be set aside unless clearly erroneous, and due regard shall be given to the opportunity of the trial court to judge the credibility of the witnesses."...

Although the meaning of the phrase "clearly erroneous" is not immediately apparent, certain general principles...may be derived from our cases. The foremost of these principles, as the Fourth Circuit itself recognized, is that a "finding is 'clearly erroneous' when although there is evidence to support it, the reviewing court on the entire evidence is left with the definite and firm conviction that a mistake has been committed." United States v. United States Gypsum Co., 333 U.S. 364, 395 (1948)....Where there are two permissible views of the evidence, the factfinder's choice between them cannot be clearly erroneous.

This is so even when the district court's findings do not rest on credibility determinations, but are based instead on physical or documentary evidence or inferences from other facts. To be sure, various Courts of Appeals have on occasion asserted the theory that an appellate court may exercise de novo review over findings not based on credibility determinations....

The rationale for deference to the original finder of fact is not limited to the superiority of the trial judge's position to make determinations of credibility. The trial judge's major role is the determination of fact, and with experience in fulfilling that role comes expertise. Duplication of the trial judge's efforts in the court of appeals would very likely contribute only negligibly to the accuracy of fact determination at a huge cost in diversion of judicial resources....As the Court has stated in a different context, the trial on the merits should be "the 'main event'...rather than a 'tryout on the road.'" Wainwright v. Sykes, 433 U.S. 72, 90 (1977)....

IV

Application of the foregoing principles to the facts of the case lays bare the errors committed....[T]he Fourth Circuit improperly conducted what amounted to a de novo weighing of the evidence in the record. The District Court's finding was based on essentially undisputed evidence regarding the respective backgrounds of petitioner and Mr. Kincaid and the duties...of Recreation Director. The District Court, after considering the evidence, concluded that the position...carried with it broad responsibilities for creating and managing a recreation program involving not only athletics, but also other activities for citizens of all ages and interests. The court determined that petitioner's more varied educational and employment background and her extensive involvement in a variety of civic activities left her better qualified to implement such a rounded program....

The Fourth Circuit, reading the same record, concluded that the basic duty of Recreation Director was to implement an athletic program....Accordingly, it seemed evident to the Court of Appeals that Mr. Kincaid was in fact better qualified than [Ms. Anderson].

Based on our reading of the record, we cannot say that either interpretation of the facts is illogical or implausible. Each has support in inferences that may be drawn from the facts in the record....The question we must answer, however, is not whether the Fourth Circuit's interpretation of the facts was clearly erroneous, but whether the District Court's finding was clearly erroneous....

Somewhat different concerns are raised by the Fourth Circuit's treatment of the District Court's finding that petitioner, alone among the applicants..., was asked questions regarding her spouse's feelings....Here the error of the Court of Appeals was its failure to give due regard to the ability of the District Court to interpret and discern the credibility of oral testimony....The Court of Appeals rested its rejection of the District Court's finding...on its own interpretation of testimony by Mrs. Boone....

Mrs. Boone's testimony on this point, which is set forth in the margin,3 is certainly not free from ambiguity. But Mrs. Boone several times stated that other candidates had not been questioned about the reaction of their wives—at least "not in the same context."...Whether the judge's interpretation is actually correct is impossible to tell from the paper record, but it is easy to imagine that the tone of voice in which the witness related her comment, coupled with her immediate denial that she had questioned Mr. Kincaid on the subject, might have conclusively established that the remark was a facetious one. We therefore cannot agree that the judge's conclusion that the remark was facetious was clearly erroneous....

The Fourth Circuit's refusal to accept the District Court's finding that the committee members were biased against hiring a woman was based to a large extent on its rejection of the finding that petitioner had been subjected to questioning that the other applicants were spared. Given that that finding was not clearly erroneous, the finding of bias cannot be termed erroneous....

Our determination that the findings of the District Court regarding petitioner's qualifications, the conduct of her interview, and the bias of the male committee members were not clearly erroneous leads us to conclude that the court's finding that petitioner was discriminated against on account of her sex was also not clearly erroneous....

In so holding, we do not assert that our knowledge of what happened 10 years ago in Bessemer City is superior to that of the Court of Appeals; nor do we claim to have greater insight than the Court of Appeals into the state of mind of the men on the selection committee....Even the trial judge, who has heard the witnesses directly...cannot always be confident that he "knows" what happened. Often, he can only determine whether the plaintiff has succeeded in presenting an account of the facts that is more likely to be true than not. Our task—and the task of appellate tribunals generally—is more limited still: we must determine whether the trial judge's conclusions are clearly erroneous. On the record before us, we cannot say that they are. Accordingly, the judgment of the Court of Appeals is reversed.

THE HARMLESS ERROR DOCTRINE

Not all errors committed at trial constitute grounds for reversal. Only those errors which are prejudicial to the rights of the complaining party are reversible. (28 U.S. Code § 2111; FRCP 61)

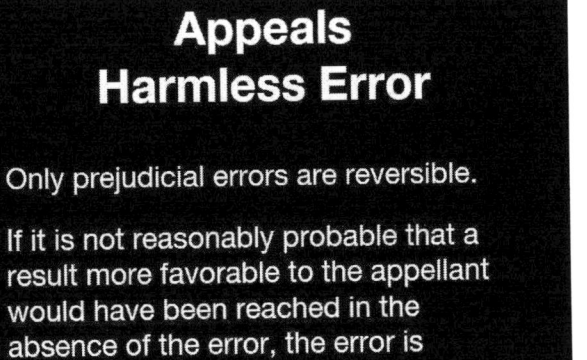

> **Appeals**
> **Harmless Error**
>
> Only prejudicial errors are reversible.
>
> If it is not reasonably probable that a result more favorable to the appellant would have been reached in the absence of the error, the error is harmless.

The "harmless error" rule provides that based on an examination of the entire record, if it is not reasonably probable that a result more favorable to the appellant would have been reached in the absence of the error, the error is harmless and the decision of the lower court will be upheld. I.e., error in the lower court does not call for reversal unless it is prejudicial. Reversible error is a relative concept and whether a slight or gross error is ground for reversal depends upon the circumstances of each case. Even substantial error which would be prejudicial is not grounds for reversal where the error was invited, waived or cured.

Harnden v. Jayco, Inc.
496 F.3d 579 (6th Cir. 2007)

MARTIN, JR., J.

Plaintiff Glenn Harnden appeals the district court's order granting summary judgment to defendant Jayco as to Harnden's claims based on alleged defects in a Jayco-manufactured Recreational Vehicle. For the reasons below, we Affirm the judgment of the district court.

Factual and Procedural Background

Harnden purchased a new 2001 Jayco Eagle Recreational Vehicle. Harnden returned it several times for repair of various defects. [When these repairs allegedly failed to fix the vehicle, Harden sued Ford, which made the chassis and motor, Jayco, which made the body, and Bridges, the dealer who sold the vehicle to Harnden.]

Harnden filed a complaint in Michigan state court alleging (1) breach of contract; (2) violation of the Michigan Consumer Protection Act; (3) breach of written warranty under the Magnuson-Moss Warranty Act, 15 U.S.C. §2301 et seq.; (4) revocation of acceptance; (5) breach of implied warranty; (6) breach of express warranty; (7) breach of implied warranty of merchantability; and (8) violation of the [Michigan] Motor Vehicle Service and Repair Act 2004. The [case was removed] to federal court based on Harnden's federal claim [with supplemental jurisdiction attaching to the related state-law claims].

[All claims against Ford and Bridges were either dropped by the plaintiff or dismissed by the court.] Jayco moved for summary judgment on all claims against it, relying in part on an expert report prepared by Randy Zonker, a Jayco employee. Harnden now appeals the district court's order granting Jayco summary judgment.

Admissibility of Randy Zonker's Report

A report detailing a series of tests performed by Jayco employee Randy Zonker was submitted along with Jayco's Motion for Summary Judgment. Based on these tests, Zonker ultimately concluded that in his expert opinion the RV was in good condition. He noted just two minor leaks, neither of which was a substantial defect. Zonker reported that neither defect substantially impaired the value of the RV and that both were common in the RV industry. Further, one leak did not affect a Jayco-manufactured part and thus was not covered by the warranty. Zonker concluded that repairing a leaky compartment manufactured by Jayco would be easy, in that "[m]ost likely, the compartment just needs some more sealant at the lip, where the door closes." Zonker recommended that in order to be sure the problem was fixed, he would remove some of the molding in the exterior of the compartment and then clean and seal the entire compartment. He claimed that this repair, plus re-testing, would cost no more than $250. Harnden has offered no evidence rebutting Zonker's conclusions that these were the only defects, that these defects were insubstantial, and that these defects were easily repairable for little cost.

Jayco and Harnden dispute the admissibility of this report. At the summary judgment hearing, Harnden's attorney objected to the admission of the expert report because it was not in the form of an affidavit or sworn statement, as required under Fed. R. Civ. P. 56(c). Thus, according to Harnden, Zonker's report was inadmissible hearsay. Jayco's attorney responded that he was willing to submit the report in an admissible form, but the district court did not take him up on his offer. The district court considered Zonker's report in conducting its analysis.

Even if Zonker's unsworn testimony was in the form of inadmissible evidence for purposes of Rule 56, thus rendering its consideration to be in error, such error may be considered harmless if it "[do[es] not affect any party's substantial rights]." See Fed. R. Civ. P. 61; United States v. Markwood, 48 F.3d 969, 981 (6th Cir. 1995) (holding that reversal is required only where the district court's error affected a party's substantial rights and the party was prejudiced by the district court's error).

We hold that admission of this report was harmless error. Notably, sending this case back to the district court will simply result in the affidavit being re-submitted in admissible form, and the district court granting summary judgment again. We reject Harnden's contention that if Jayco were given the opportunity to re-file its motion with the report in admissible form, Harnden would have the opportunity to "present additional evidence showing that summary judgment is improper that is not currently part of the record." Appellant's Reply Br. at 11. First, this argument implies that Zonker's report was a surprise for which Harnden did not have adequate time to prepare; but, in fact, Jayco submitted this report along with its motion for summary judgment. Harnden knew of the content of Zonker's report well in advance, and had ample time to procure his own expert report and/or evidence.2 Thus, Harnden appears to be arguing that had Jayco submitted this same report at the same time, but in admissible form, Harnden would have obtained an expert of his own. Given that Harnden had advance warning of Zonker's testimony, we cannot find that the district court's error affected Harnden's substantial rights, and most certainly, Harnden was not prejudiced by this error.

Conclusion

For the foregoing reasons, we affirm the judgment of the district court.

This page left intentionally blank.

CHAPTER 12

FORMER ADJUDICATION
(THE BINDING EFFECT OF JUDGMENTS)

The doctrine of res judicata prevents a litigant from getting yet another day in court after the first lawsuit is concluded by giving a different reason than he or she gave in the first for recovery of damages for the same invasion of his right. The rule provides that when a court of competent jurisdiction has entered a final judgment on the merits of a cause of action, the parties to the suit and their privies are bound "not only as to every matter which was offered and received to sustain or defeat the claim or demand, but as to any other admissible matter which might have been offered for that purpose." A final judgment on the merits bars further claims by the same parties based on the same cause of action.

Res judicata prevents a plaintiff from suing on a claim that already has been decided and also prevents a defendant from raising any new defense to defeat the enforcement of an earlier judgment. It also precludes relitigation of any issue, regardless of whether the second action is on the same claim as the first one, if that particular issue actually was contested and decided in the first action. (Friedenthal § 14.1) Former adjudication is an analogue of the criminal law concept of double jeopardy.

A judgment in a prior suit between the same parties is final not only as to all matters that were in fact offered and received to sustain or defeat the claim but also as to all matters that might have been offered for that purpose. A party may not litigate a claim and then, upon an unsuccessful disposition, revive the same cause of action with a new theory.

TERMINOLOGY

Res judicata A general term referring to all of the ways in which one judgment will have a binding effect on another.

Claim preclusion (true res judicata) A valid and final judgment on a claim precludes a second action on that claim or any part of it. Claim preclusion is divided into two areas, bar and merger.

Merger When a plaintiff prevails on a claim the claim is "merged" into the judgment in his favor. The claim is extinguished and replaced by the judgment.

Bar If a plaintiff loses his claim is said to be "barred" by the adverse judgment so that no further suit can be brought on the claim.

Issue preclusion (Collateral estoppel) Preclusion of matters that have once been decided.

Four Factors Are Considered in Determining the Validity of a Plea of Claim Preclusion:

1) Was the claim decided in the prior suit the same claim being presented in the action in question?

2) Was there a final judgment on the merits?

3) Was the party against whom the plea was asserted a party or in privity with a party to the prior suit?

4) Was the party against whom the plea was asserted given a fair opportunity to be heard on the issue?

Four Prerequisites of Claim Preclusion:

1) There must be a final judgment;

2) on the merits;

3) the claims must be the same in the first and second suits;

4) the parties in the second action must be the same as (or in privity with) those in the prior action.

IDENTITY OF CLAIMS

Ison v. Thomas
2007 WL 1194374 (Ky. App. 2007)

ABRAMSON, J.

George Ison appeals from a January 30, 2006 summary judgment of the Pendleton Circuit Court dismissing his claim against Anthony Thomas for personal injury damages. Ison contends that the trial court misapplied the rule against splitting one's cause of action, an aspect of the doctrine of res judicata. We disagree and so affirm.

Ison alleges that in July 2003 Thomas injured him in an automobile accident on Kentucky Highway 9 near Foster in Pendleton County. Soon after the accident, in August 2003, Ison sued Thomas and Thomas's insurer for losses arising from the damage to Ison's vehicle….A jury awarded him about $5,000.00 for his property losses….Ison brought the present personal injury action against Thomas in April 2005. The trial court, noting the long standing rule in Kentucky that "one may not split up his cause of action and have it tried piecemeal," Hays v. Sturgill, 302 Ky. 31, 34 (1946), ruled that Ison's personal injury claim was part of the same cause of action as his property damage claim and so had merged with the prior judgment. We agree.

As the Kentucky Court of Appeals, then the state's highest Court, stated in Hays: when a matter is in litigation, parties are required to bring forward their whole case; and the plea of res judicata applies not only to the points upon which the court was required by the parties to form an opinion and pronounce judgment, but to every point which properly belonged to the subject of litigation, and which the parties, exercising reasonable diligence, might have brought forward at the time.

Applying this rule in Kirchner v. Riherd, 702 S.W.2d 33 (Ky. 1985), a case, like this one, involving an automobile accident and successive suits for property and personal injury damages, our Supreme Court ruled that "the law will not permit a party who has sued for a part of an entire demand to sue for the residue in another action." In [that case] the Court reaffirmed its adoption of Restatement (Second), Judgments, §24 (1982), which provides in part that:

[w]hen a valid and final judgment rendered in an action extinguishes the plaintiff's claim…the claim extinguished includes all rights of the plaintiff to remedies against the defendant with respect to all or any part of the transaction, or series of connected transactions, out of which the action arose.

Our Supreme Court so held in Kirchner, and the trial court did not err by so holding here.

Ison's contention that the rule against splitting one's cause of action does not apply if the plaintiff prevails in the prior action is without merit….If the plaintiff prevails on his initial claim, other claims arising from the same transaction are said to merge with his judgment, and if the plaintiff loses initially, that judgment is said to bar any such subsequent claim. Restatement (Second), Judgments, §§18, 19 (1982). In either case, the subsequent action is precluded.

Finally, Ison contends that Thomas waived the affirmative res judicata defense by failing to plead it in his answer to Ison's complaint. He notes, correctly, that CR 8.03

[analogous to Federal Rule 8(c)(1)] requires affirmative defenses such as res judicata to be "set forth affirmatively" in the answer, that is, that the pleading should give fair notice of the particular defense and a short statement of its grounds....We agree with Ison that Thomas's Answer...did not satisfy a notice standard for any particular affirmative defense. Nevertheless, CR 8.03 is not to be applied mechanically, and waiver need not be found where the affirmative defense is raised by timely motion that does not prejudice the plaintiff.

In this case, Thomas raised the res judicata defense in a motion for summary judgment in September 2005, only about five months into the case and before either party had expended much on discovery....

In sum, our law requires that all claims against a single defendant arising from a single negligent incident be brought in a single action. Ison improperly split his claim for property damages from his claim for personal injury damages, where both claims arose against a single defendant as a result of a single automobile accident. The damages claims should have been brought together, and because they were not, the trial court correctly ruled that the subsequent action is barred. Accordingly, we affirm the January 30, 2006 order of the Pendleton Circuit Court.

ALL CONCUR.

NOTES Under the Restatement, all claims arising from a single "transaction"—broadly defined to include matters related in time, space, origin, and motivation—must be litigated in a single, initial lawsuit, or be barred from being raised in subsequent litigation. Restatement (Second) of Judgments §§24, 25 (1982)

As we have seen, under the Restatement approach, which has been adopted in a majority of jurisdictions, a claim or cause of action is coterminous with the transaction or occurrence that caused the plaintiff's damage. By contrast, California courts analyze a cause of action for purposes of res judicata according to "primary rights." In California and other primary rights jurisdictions, certain rights are accorded "primary" status; these rights include the right to be free from injury to person and the right to be free from injury to property. The number of primary rights violated is significant because it determines the number of causes of action a plaintiff has in California. The victim's primary rights to be free from personal injury and free from injury to property were violated in the above-described accident, and the victim therefore has two causes of action.

Sawyer v. First City Financial Corporation, LTD
124 Cal.App.3d 390 (1981)

FROELICH, J

Plaintiffs appeal from adverse summary judgment rulings in favor of all defendants. An understanding of the litigation requires an analysis of two separate cases involving essentially the same parties, of which the present appeal relates specifically to the second. For reference purposes these two cases will be called Sawyer I and Sawyer II. Each case arises from the same general factual background.

* * *

Sawyer I

Sawyer I was commenced in July of 1975. The defendants were F.C. Financial Associates, its parent First City, and, later, another subsidiary of First City (all sometimes called herein Financial); and Toronto Dominion Bank of California (Bank). The several causes of action all were based upon contractual theories.

* * *

The case was tried in February of 1978. By stipulation the issues were severed for trial and dispositive issues were presented to a judge, sitting without jury. The judgment rendered in March of 1978, focused upon the issue of the validity of the waiver by Sawyers of their right to a deficiency judgment. This waiver was found to be effective and judgment was rendered in favor of all defendants on all causes of action. Following affirmance on appeal, the judgment became final in December of 1979.

Sawyer II

Sawyer II was filed in January of 1978. Entitled "Complaint for Damages Based Upon Conspiracy and Fraud," it joined as defendants all of the parties named in Sawyer I and in addition the ultimate purchaser Ehrlich and his corporation, Lexington Properties; the new financier of the development, Lomitas Properties; and a number of officers and directors of the Financial companies and the Bank. Three of the causes of action of this new lawsuit are based upon an alleged conspiracy among the defendants to cause a default in the Bank's note and trust deed, hold a sham sale, and take other action for the purpose of eliminating the obligation to the Sawyers. The only essential difference in the three causes of action is the date of commencement of the alleged conspiracy — one alleging the evil motives from the very start of the land acquisition transaction, a second alleging commencement of the conspiracy when Financial defaulted on its note payments, and a third alleging commencement of the conspiracy at the time of the foreclosure sale. The fourth cause of action uses the same factual allegations as the basis for a claim of intentional interference with contractual relation (Financial's note obligation to the Sawyers). Damages alleged are the same as in Sawyer I except that additional punitive damages are sought.

The procedural history of Sawyer II is detailed as follows:

1. Promptly upon filing Sawyer II, counsel sought to consolidate with Sawyer I, and moved for a continuance of the trial of Sawyer I. This motion was opposed by the defendants, who objected because the issues and causes of action of Sawyer II were different from those of Sawyer I, and also because the case, then pending for two and one-half years, was scheduled for trial nine days later. The court denied a motion to continue the trial of Sawyer I, and it was tried without consolidation with Sawyer II.

2. In January of 1980, the Bank and its officers moved for summary judgment in Sawyer II upon the ground of the res judicata effect of Sawyer I. . .

* * *

2. In January of 1980, the Bank and its officers moved for summary judgment in Sawyer II upon the ground of the res judicata effect of Sawyer I, . . . The Honorable Douglas Woodworth denied the motion based upon res judicata

3. In May of 1980, a separate motion for summary judgment was filed by the Financial corporations on the ground that Sawyer I was res judicata to the issues of Sawyer II — that the plaintiffs had split their cause of action by attempting to relitigate the same issues in a second lawsuit. The bank officers (whose motion for reconsideration was then pending before Judge Woodworth) joined in this motion, and it was set for hearing before the Honorable Franklin B. Orfield. On July 25, 1980, Judge Orfield ruled in favor of all defendants on the ground of res judicata . . .

Appellants appeal from the summary judgments of both Judge Woodworth (dismissing the Bank) and Judge Orfield (dismissing all parties), and also from a discovery ruling (described infra). Many bases of appeal are urged: The central and most important issue, however, is the question of res judicata. As reviewed in 3 Witkin, California Procedure (2d ed. 1971) Pleading, section 32 et seq., page 1715, a single cause of action cannot be split and made the subject of several suits. If a primary right is so split, determination of the issues in the first suit will be res judicata to the attempt to relitigate them in the second suit. Where the plaintiff has several causes of action, however, even though they may arise from the same factual setting, and even though they might have been joined in one suit under permissive joinder provisions, the plaintiff is privileged to bring separate actions based upon each separate cause.

A valid final judgment on the merits in favor of a defendant serves as a complete bar to further litigation on the same cause of action. (Slater v. Blackwood (1975) 15 Cal.3d

791, 795 [126 Cal. Rptr. 225, 543 P.2d 593].) The question in this and similar cases, of course, is whether the attempted second litigation involves the "same cause of action." A "cause of action" is conceived as the remedial right in favor of a plaintiff for the violation of one "primary right." That several remedies may be available for violation of one "primary right" does not create additional "causes of action." However, it is also true that a given set of facts may give rise to the violation of more than one "primary right," thus giving a plaintiff the potential of two separate lawsuits against a single defendant. (See 3 Witkin, supra, p. 1707 et seq.)

The theoretical discussion of what constitutes a "primary right" is complicated by historical precedent in several well-litigated areas establishing the question of "primary rights" in a manner perhaps contrary to the result that might be reached by a purely logical approach. For instance, the primary right to be free from personal injury has been construed as to embrace all theories of tort which might have given rise to the injury. In Panos v. Great Western Packing Co. (1943) 21 Cal.2d 636 [134 P.2d 242], the plaintiff was injured in a meat packing house. His first cause of action was based upon alleged negligence of the packing house in permitting third parties to come upon the premises and operate equipment. A defense judgment was then held to bar a second suit based upon an entirely different factual theory of negligence — that the defendant itself had negligently operated the equipment. In Slater v. Blackwood, supra, 15 Cal.3d 791, a defense judgment in a suit based upon violation of the guest statute (intoxication or willful misconduct) was held to bar a second suit (after the guest statute was held unconstitutional) based upon allegations of ordinary negligence.

Other examples of torts resulting in easily conceptualized types of damages have been settled, one way or the other, by precedent. While one act of tortious conduct might well be deemed to violate only one "primary right" — the right to be free from the particular unlawful conduct — the resultant (1) injury to person and (2) damage to property have been deemed creative of separate causes of action. On the other hand, one course of wrongful conduct which damages several pieces of property traditionally gives rise to only one cause of action. (See 3 Witkin, supra, at pp. 1720-1721, and cases cited therein.)

Other classes of litigation, however, with perhaps less historical or precedential background, are not so well defined in terms of deciding how many "primary rights" derive from a single factual transaction. The tort in Agarwal v. Johnson (1979) 25 Cal.3d 932 [160 Cal. Rptr. 141, 603 P.2d 58], was unfair treatment of a minority race employee by an employer. Plaintiff's first action was in federal court for back wages under the authority of the federal Civil Rights Act. The state Supreme Court determined this was no bar to a second suit in superior court for general and punitive damages for defamation and intentional infliction of emotional distress. Although the same set of facts is presented in each claim, one primary right is created by the federal statute prohibiting discriminatory employment practices; and the second primary right is grounded in state common law. Also, the "harm suffered" was deemed separable —

damages for lost wages in the federal action, and damages for injury to reputation and peace of mind in the state case. Compare Mattson v. City of Costa Mesa (1980) 106 Cal. App.3d 441 [164 Cal. Rptr. 913], where the actionable facts consisted of an unlawful arrest of the plaintiff and his abuse in confinement. His first action in federal court under the authority of the Civil Rights Act was held to be a bar to a subsequent suit in state court for negligence, assault and battery. The court found that the "primary rights" giving rise to the state common law tort action were the same as those reflected in the Civil Rights Act, and that the civil rights action was "simply a different way of expressing an invasion of the same primary rights or the assertion of a different legal theory for recovery." (Id., at pp. 447-448.) In City of Los Angeles v. Superior Court (1978) 85 Cal. App.3d 143, 153 [149 Cal. Rptr. 320], a federal civil rights action followed by a superior court common law tort action, both involving wrongful seizure of personal property, the appellate court reached the same conclusion and applied the bar of res judicata on the ground that "the civil rights action was designed to vindicate precisely the same interests in ... personal property that (the plaintiff) seeks to vindicate in the matter before us."

One would assume that the question of litigation of claims arising from one transaction first on the basis of contract, and then on alleged tort theories, would have received substantial appellate attention. authorities, however, are surprisingly sparse. The Restatement of the Law, Judgments (1942) chapter 3, section 63, provides several illustrations involving actions to cancel a deed. A failure to sustain the first action on contractual grounds (i.e., failure of execution or delivery of the deed) is held to bar a subsequent action based upon fraudulent procurement — thus suggesting that the "primary right" is the right to cancel the deed (as applied to our case, to validate the note) and that this gives rise to only one cause of action, whether it be framed in contract or tort.

* * *

The case before us is not one in which the same factual structure is characterized in one complaint as a breach of contract and in another as a tort. The first action is solely on contract and is based upon the note, deed of trust, and loan and development agreement. At the time of trial the principal issue litigated was the effectiveness of the waiver of deficiency judgment, and this issue was presented in the context of contractual theories. There was no contention and no evidence was presented relating to a possible invalidation of the waiver on grounds of fraud, misrepresentation or any other tort.

Sawyer II, of course, had as its object collection of the same promissory note which was the subject matter of Sawyer I; but the basis of the claim is completely different, and rests upon a completely separate set of facts. The complaint assumes and admits that the forms of the waiver of deficiency and the subordination are technically appropriate and enforceable. The pleading reaches beyond these documents, however, to highlight other conduct of the parties alleged to be tortious. The core of the alleged wrongful conduct is an agreement among the parties to conduct what is characterized as a sham foreclosure sale, the only substantive effect of which would be secretly to discharge the obligation to Sawyer, leaving all other parties in essentially the same position as prior to the sale. Surely one's breach of contract by failing to pay a note violates a "primary right" which is separate from the "primary right" not to have the note stolen. That the two causes of action might have been joined in one lawsuit under our permissive joinder provisions (see 3 Witkin, supra, at p. 1915) does not prevent the plaintiff from bringing them in separate suits if he elects to do so. While the monetary loss may be measurable by the same promissory note amount, and hence in a general sense the same "harm" has been done in both cases, theoretically the plaintiffs have been "harmed" differently by tortious conduct destroying the value of the note, than by the contractual breach of simply failing to pay it. We conclude, therefore, that Sawyer II is based upon a separate and severable cause of action from that litigated in Sawyer I, and that it was error to grant summary judgment on the ground of res judicata.

NOTES Perhaps the most frequently encountered application of the primary rights approach involves a tort victim who simultaneously suffers both personal injury and property damage caused by the defendant's single act. A typical example is negligence litigation arising out of the crash of two cars, where one driver sues the other. The resulting personal injury to the plaintiff driver is a separate primary right from the property damage to the plaintiff's car, and may be pursued in two separate lawsuits. See *Holmes v. David H. Bricker Inc.*, 70 Cal. 2d 786, 76 Cal. Rptr. 431, 452 P.2d 647 (1969). However, a breach of contract that results in injury to person and property violates only one primary right, and therefore gives rise to only one cause of action. Id.

Frier v. City of Vandalia
770 F.2d 699 (7th Cir. 1985)

EASTERBROOK, J.

The City of Vandalia is fairly small (the population is less than 2,500), and apparently its police have maintained informal ways. When Charles Frier parked one of his cars in a narrow street, which forced others to drive on someone else's lawn to get around Frier's car, the police left two notes at Frier's house asking him to move the car. That did not work, so an officer called a local garage, which towed the car back to the garage. The officer left a note, addressed to "Charlie," telling him where he could find the car. The officer did not issue a citation for illegal parking, however; he later testified that he wanted to make it easier for Frier to retrieve the car.

Frier balked at paying the $10 fee the garage wanted. He also balked at keeping his cars out of the street. The police had garages tow four of them in 1983—a 1963 Ford Falcon, a 1970 Plymouth Duster, a 1971 Opal GT, and a 1971 Dodge van. Instead of paying the garages, Frier filed suits in the courts of Illinois seeking replevin. Each suit named as defendants the City of Vandalia and the garage that had towed the car.

One of the suits (which sought to replevy two cars) was dismissed voluntarily when Frier got his cars back. We do not know whether he paid for the tows and the subsequent daily storage fees or whether the garage thought it cheaper to surrender the cars than to defend the suit. The other two cases were consolidated and litigated. The police testified to the circumstances under which they had called for the tows. The court concluded that the police properly took the cars into the City's possession to remove obstructions to the alley, and it declined to issue the writ of replevin because the City had the right to remove the cars from the street. Frier then retrieved another car;1 so far as we can tell, a garage still has the 1970 Plymouth Duster.

After losing in state court, Frier turned to federal court. His [federal] complaint maintained that the City had not offered him a hearing either before or after it took the cars and that it is the "official policy" of the City not to do so. The complaint invoked the Due Process Clause of the Fourteenth Amendment and 42 U.S.C. §1983, and it sought equitable relief in addition to $100,000 in compensatory and $100,000 in punitive damages. The district court, after reviewing the transcript of the replevin action, dismissed the complaint for failure to state a claim on which relief may be granted. (Because the judge considered the transcript he should have treated the motion to dismiss as one for summary judgment. We analyze the decision as if he had done so.) The court found that Frier had notice of each tow and knew how to get his cars back. Frier also had a full hearing in the replevin action on the propriety of the tows. Although the judicial hearing came approximately one month after the tows, the court thought the delay permissible.

A month is a long wait for a hearing when the subject is an automobile. The automobile is "property" within the meaning of the Due Process Clause, and the City therefore must furnish appropriate process. Sutton v. City of Milwaukee, 672 F.2d 644 (7th Cir. 1982), holds that a hearing is not necessary before the police tow a car but suggests that one must be furnished promptly after the tow. Sutton also suggests, in line with many other cases, that the City must establish the process and tender an opportunity for a hearing; it may not sit back and wait for the aggrieved person to file a suit.

The City, for its part, maintains that a few isolated tows without hearings are not the "policy" of the City and may not be imputed to it, and that anyway a month's delay in holding a hearing about seized property is permissible....

A court ought not resolve a constitution[al] dispute unless that is absolutely necessary. Here it is not. Frier had his day in court in the replevin action. The City has argued that this precludes further suits. (The City raised this argument in the motion to dismiss, which is irregular but not fatally so. See Fed. R. Civ. P. 8(c).) The district court bypassed this argument because, it believed, Frier could not have asserted his constitutional arguments in a replevin action. This is only partially correct.

Frier could not have obtained punitive damages or declaratory relief in a suit limited to replevin. But he was free to join one count seeking such relief with another seeking replevin. See Welch v. Brunswick Corp., 10 Ill. App. 3d 693 (1st Dist. 1973), revd. in part on other grounds, 57 Ill. 2d 461 (1974); Hanaman v. Davis, 20 Ill. App. 2d 111 (2d Dist. 1959), both of which allow one count seeking replevin to be joined with another count seeking different relief. As we show below, the law of Illinois, which under 28 U.S.C. §1738 governs the preclusive effect to be given to the judgment in the replevin actions, see Marrese v. American Academy of Orthopaedic Surgeons, 470 U.S. 373 (1985), would bar this suit. The City therefore is entitled to prevail on the ground of claim preclusion, although the district court did not decide the case on that ground. See Massachusetts Mutual Life Insurance Co. v. Ludwig, 426 U.S. 479 (1976).

Illinois recognizes the principles of claim preclusion (also called res judicata or estoppel by judgment). Jones v. City of Alton, 757 F.2d 878, 884-85 (7th Cir. 1985) (summarizing the law of preclusion in Illinois). One suit precludes a second "where the parties and the cause of action are identical." "Causes of action are identical where the evidence necessary to sustain a second verdict would sustain the first, i.e., where the causes of action are based upon a common core of operative facts." Two suits may entail the same "cause of action" even though they present different legal theories, and the first suit "operates as an absolute bar to a subsequent action...

'not only as to every matter which was offered and received to sustain or defeat the claim or demand, but as to any other admissible matter which might have been offered for that purpose.'"...

The City was a defendant in each replevin action. Frier could have urged constitutional grounds as reasons for replevin.[2] He also could have joined a constitutional claim seeking punitive damages and declaratory relief to his demand for replevin, and therefore he had a full and fair opportunity to litigate (unlike Jones v. City of Alton, where procedural obstacles impeded litigation of the federal claim). The actions also involve both the same "common core of operative facts" and the same transactions. Frier argues that the City towed his cars wrongfully. Each complaint seeking replevin asserted [that] Frier owned each car and that it had not been "seized under lawful process"—in other words, that there had been no citation and no hearing at which anyone had found that the cars were illegally parked. The replevin statute requires a plaintiff to show that the property was taken without "lawful process." Ill. Rev. Stat., ch. 110, §19-104. "Process," even in its technical sense, initiates or follows a hearing. Had there been process and a hearing at which a magistrate found the cars to have been illegally parked, Frier would have had no claim for replevin no matter how strongly he contested the substantive issue. The "operative facts" in the replevin and §1983 actions therefore are the same. Frier urges that he owned the car (the property interest) and that the City did not offer him a hearing to adjudicate the legality of his parking (the absence of due process).

The replevin actions diverged from the path of this §1983 suit only because the state judge adjudicated on the merits the propriety of the seizures. Having found the seizures proper, the judge had no occasion to determine whether the City should have offered Frier an earlier hearing. But this divergence does not mean that the two legal theories require a different "core of operative facts."...

To the extent there is any doubt about this, we look...to the purpose of doctrines of preclusion. Claim preclusion is designed to impel "parties to consolidate all closely related matters into one suit." This prevents the oppression of defendants by multiple cases, which may be easy to file and costly to defend. There is no assurance that a second or third case will be decided more accurately than the first and so there is no good reason to incur the costs of litigation more than once. When the facts and issues of all theories of liability are closely related, one case is enough. Here the replevin theory contained the elements that make up a due process theory, and we are therefore confident that the courts of Illinois would treat both theories as one "cause of action." The final question is whether it makes a difference that only two of the replevin actions went to judgment, while here Frier challenges the towing of four cars. Under Illinois law the answer is no. The defendant may invoke claim preclusion when the plaintiff litigated in the first suit a subset of all available disputes between the parties. See Baird & Warner, Inc. v. Addison Industrial Park, Inc., 70 Ill. App. 3d 59 (1st Dist. 1979), which holds that a suit on three of six disputed parcels of land precludes a subsequent suit on all six. We doubt that Illinois would see difference between three lots out of six and two cars out of four.

If Frier had filed the current suit in state court, he would have lost under the doctrine of claim preclusion. Under 28 U.S.C. §1738 he therefore loses in federal court as well.

AFFIRMED.

IDENTITY OF PARTIES

The general rule is that a judgment has no binding effect upon anyone who was not a party to the action. A stranger cannot take advantage of a judgment, nor can it be enforced against him. Consequently, the principle of claim preclusion does not apply unless the parties in the subsequent suit are identical with the parties in the first suit. If the subsequent suit involves different parties, those parties cannot be bound by the prior judgment.

> **Claim Preclusion**
> **Identity of Parties**
>
> The general rule is that a judgment has no binding effect upon anyone who was not a party to the action.
>
> The rules of claim preclusion do not apply unless the parties in the subsequent suit are identical with the parties in the first suit.

Taylor v. Sturgell
553 U.S. 880 (2008)

Justice GINSBURG delivered the opinion of the Court.

"It is a principle of general application in Anglo-American jurisprudence that one is not bound by a judgment in personam in a litigation in which he is not designated as a party or to which he has not been made a party by service of process." Hansberry v. Lee, 311 U.S. 32, 40 (1940). Several exceptions, recognized in this Court's decisions, temper this basic rule. In a class action, for example, a person not named as a party may be bound by a judgment on the merits of the action, if she was adequately represented by a party who actively participated in the litigation. In this case, we consider for the first time whether there is a "virtual representation" exception to the general rule against precluding nonparties. Adopted by a number of courts, including the courts below in the case now before us, the exception so styled is broader than any we have so far approved....

We disapprove the doctrine of preclusion by "virtual representation," and hold, based on the record as it now stands, that the judgment against Herrick does not bar Taylor from maintaining this suit.

I

The Freedom of Information Act (FOIA) accords "any person" a right to request any records held by a federal agency. 5 U.S.C. §552(a)(3)(A) (2006 ed.). No reason need be given for a FOIA request, and unless the requested materials fall within one of the Act's enumerated exemptions, see §552(a)(3)(E), (b), the agency must "make the records promptly available" to the requester, §552(a)(3)(A). If an agency refuses to furnish the requested records, the requester may file suit in federal court and obtain an injunction "order[ing] the production of any agency records improperly withheld." §552(a)(4)(B).

The courts below held the instant FOIA suit barred by the judgment in earlier litigation seeking the same records. Because the lower courts' decisions turned on the connection between the two lawsuits, we begin with a full account of each action.

A

The first suit was filed by Greg Herrick, an antique aircraft enthusiast and the owner of an F-45 airplane, a vintage model manufactured by the Fairchild Engine and Airplane Corporation (FEAC) in the 1930's. In 1997, seeking information that would help him restore his plane to its original condition, Herrick filed a FOIA request asking the Federal Aviation Administration (FAA) for copies of any technical documents about the F-45 contained in the agency's records.

To gain a certificate authorizing the manufacture and sale of the F-45, FEAC had submitted to the FAA's predecessor, the Civil Aeronautics Authority, detailed specifications and other technical data about the plane. Hundreds of pages of documents produced by FEAC in the certification process remain in the FAA's records. The FAA denied Herrick's request, however, upon finding that the documents he sought are subject to FOIA's exemption for "trade secrets and commercial or financial information obtained from a person and privileged or confidential," 5 U.S.C. §552(b)(4) (2006 ed.)....

[When Herrick filed suit,] the District Court granted summary judgment to the FAA [rejecting Herrick's argument that a 1955 letter from Fairchild to a government agency had waived any protection.] [T]he Tenth Circuit...affirmed....

B

Less than a month later, on August 22, petitioner Brent Taylor—a friend of Herrick's and an antique aircraft enthusiast in his own right—submitted a FOIA request seeking the same documents Herrick had unsuccessfully sued to obtain. When the FAA failed to respond, Taylor filed a complaint in the U.S. District Court for the District of Columbia. Like Herrick, Taylor argued that FEAC's 1955 letter had stripped the records of their trade-secret status. But Taylor also sought to litigate...two issues concerning recapture of protected status that Herrick had failed to raise in his appeal to the Tenth Circuit.

After Fairchild intervened as a defendant, the District Court in D.C. concluded that Taylor's suit was barred by claim preclusion; accordingly, it granted summary judgment to Fairchild and the FAA....

The record before the District Court in Taylor's suit revealed the following facts about the relationship between Taylor and Herrick: Taylor is the president of the Antique Aircraft Association, an organization to which Herrick belongs; the two men are "close associate[s]"; Herrick asked Taylor to help restore Herrick's F-45, though they had no contract or agreement for Taylor's participation in the restoration; Taylor was represented by the lawyer who represented Herrick in the earlier litigation; and Herrick apparently gave Taylor documents that Herrick had obtained from the FAA during discovery in his suit....

Applying this test to the record in Taylor's case, the D.C. Circuit found both of the necessary conditions for virtual representation well met....

II

The preclusive effect of a federal-court judgment is determined by federal common law. See Semtek Int'l Inc. v. Lockheed Martin Corp., 531 U.S. 497, 507-508 (2001). For judgments in federal-question cases—for example, Herrick's FOIA suit—federal courts participate in developing "uniform federal rule[s]" of res judicata, which this Court has ultimate authority to determine and declare. Id. at 508.3 The federal common law of preclusion is, of course, subject to due process limitations. See Richards v. Jefferson County, 517 U.S. 793, 797 (1996).

Taylor's case presents an issue of first impression in this sense: Until now, we have never addressed the doctrine of "virtual representation" adopted (in varying forms) by several Circuits and relied upon by the courts below. Our inquiry, however, is guided by well-established precedent regarding the propriety of nonparty preclusion. We review that precedent before taking up directly the issue of virtual representation.

A

The preclusive effect of a judgment is defined by claim preclusion and issue preclusion, which are collectively referred to as "res judicata."4...By "preclud[ing] parties from contesting matters that they have had a full and fair opportunity to litigate," these two doctrines protect against "the expense and vexation attending multiple lawsuits, conserv[e] judicial resources, and foste[r] reliance on judicial action by minimizing the possibility of inconsistent decisions."

A person who was not a party to a suit generally has not had a "full and fair opportunity to litigate" the claims and issues settled in that suit. The application of claim and issue preclusion to nonparties thus runs up against the "deep-rooted historic tradition that everyone should have his own day in court." Richards. Indicating the strength of that tradition, we have often repeated the general rule that "one is not bound by a judgment in personam in a litigation in which he is not designated as a party or to which he has not been made a party by service of process." Hansberry; Martin v. Wilks, 490 U.S. 755, 761 (1989).

B

Though hardly in doubt, the rule against nonparty preclusion is subject to exceptions. For present purposes, the recognized exceptions can be grouped into six categories.5 [The Court listed (1) agreement by the parties to be bound by a prior action; (2) preexisting "substantive legal relationships" (such as preceding and succeeding owners of property); (3) adequate representation by someone with the same interests who was a party (such as trustees, guardians, and other fiduciaries); (4) a party "assuming control" over prior litigation; (5) a party who loses an individual suit then sues again, this time as the representative of a class; and (6) special statutory schemes such as bankruptcy and probate proceedings, provided those proceedings comport with due process.]

III

Reaching beyond these six established categories, some lower courts have recognized a "virtual representation" exception to the rule against nonparty preclusion. Decisions of these courts, however, have been far from consistent....

The D.C. Circuit, the FAA, and Fairchild have presented three arguments in support of an expansive doctrine of virtual representation. We find none of them persuasive.

A

The D.C. Circuit purported to ground its virtual representation doctrine in this Court's decisions stating that, in some circumstances, a person may be bound by a judgment if she was adequately represented by a party to the proceeding yielding that judgment. But the D.C. Circuit's definition of "adequate representation" strayed from the meaning our decisions have attributed to that term....

The D.C. Circuit misapprehended Richards....[O]ur holding that the Alabama Supreme Court's application of res judicata to nonparties violated due process turned on the lack of either special procedures to protect the nonparties' interests or an understanding by the concerned parties that the first suit was brought in a representative capacity....

B

Fairchild and the FAA do not argue that the D.C. Circuit's virtual representation doctrine fits within any of the recognized grounds for nonparty preclusion. Rather, they ask us to abandon the attempt to delineate discrete grounds and clear rules altogether. Preclusion is in order, they contend, whenever "the relationship between a party and a non-party is 'close enough' to bring the second litigant within the judgment." Courts should make the "close enough" determination, they urge, through a "heavily fact-driven" and "equitable" inquiry....

We reject this argument for three reasons. First, our decisions emphasize the fundamental nature of the general rule that a litigant is not bound by a judgment to which she was not a party....

Our second reason for rejecting a broad doctrine of virtual representation rests on the limitations attending nonparty preclusion based on adequate representation. A party's representation of a nonparty is "adequate" for preclusion purposes only if, at a minimum: (1) the interests of the nonparty and her representative are aligned, see Hansberry; and (2) either the party understood herself to be acting in a representative capacity or the original court took care to protect the interests of the nonparty, see Richards. In addition, adequate representation sometimes requires (3) notice of the original suit to the persons alleged to have been represented.6 In the class-action context, these limitations are implemented by the procedural safeguards contained in Federal Rule of Civil Procedure 23.

An expansive doctrine of virtual representation, however, would "recogniz[e], in effect, a common-law kind of class action." That is, virtual representation would authorize preclusion based on identity of interests and some kind of relationship between parties and nonparties, shorn of the procedural protections prescribed in Hansberry, Richards, and Rule 23. These protections, grounded in due process, could be circumvented were we to approve a virtual representation doctrine that allowed courts to "create de facto class actions at will."

Third, a diffuse balancing approach to nonparty preclusion would likely create more headaches than it relieves. Most obviously, it could significantly complicate the task of district courts faced in the first instance with preclusion questions. An all-things-considered balancing approach might spark wide-ranging, time-consuming, and expensive discovery tracking factors potentially relevant under seven- or five-prong tests....

C

Finally...the FAA maintains that nonparty preclusion should apply more broadly in "public-law" litigation than in "private-law" controversies. To support this position, the FAA offers two arguments. First, the FAA urges, our decision in Richards acknowledges that, in certain cases, the plaintiff has a reduced interest in controlling the litigation "because of the public nature of the right at issue."...

[W]e said in Richards only that, for the type of public-law claims there envisioned, [state and federal legislatures] are free to adopt procedures limiting repetitive litigation [involving public rights]....It hardly follows, however, that this Court should proscribe or confine successive FOIA suits by different requesters. Indeed, Congress' provision for FOIA suits with no statutory constraint on successive actions counsels against judicial imposition of constraints through extraordinary application of the common law of preclusion.

The FAA next argues that "the threat of vexatious litigation is heightened" in public-law cases because "the number of plaintiffs with standing is potentially limitless."...

But we are not convinced that this risk justifies departure from the usual rules governing nonparty preclusion. First, stare decisis will allow courts swiftly to dispose of repetitive suits brought in the same circuit. Second, even when stare decisis is not dispositive, "the human tendency not to waste money will deter the bringing of suits based on claims or issues that have already been adversely determined against others." This intuition seems to be borne out by experience: The FAA has not called our attention to any instances of abusive FOIA suits in the Circuits that reject the virtual-representation theory respondents advocate here.

IV

For the foregoing reasons, we disapprove the theory of virtual representation on which the decision below rested. The preclusive effects of a judgment in a federal-question case decided by a federal court should instead be determined according to the established grounds for nonparty preclusion described in this opinion....

We now turn back to Taylor's action to determine whether his suit is such a case, or whether the result reached by the courts below can be justified on one of the recognized grounds for nonparty preclusion.

A

It is uncontested that four of the six grounds for nonparty preclusion have no application here....

That leaves only the fifth category: preclusion because a nonparty to an earlier litigation has brought suit as a representative or agent of a party who is bound by the prior adjudication. Taylor is not Herrick's legal representative and he has not purported to sue in a representative capacity. He concedes, however, that preclusion would be appropriate if respondents could demonstrate that he is acting as Herrick's "undisclosed agen[t]."...

We therefore remand to give the courts below an opportunity to determine whether Taylor, in pursuing the instant FOIA suit, is acting as Herrick's agent. Taylor concedes that such a remand is appropriate....

* * *

For the reasons stated, the judgment of the United States Court of Appeals for the District of Columbia Circuit is vacated, and the case is remanded for further proceedings consistent with this opinion.

It is so ordered.

Searle Brothers v. Searle
588 P.2d 689 (1978)

ELLETT, Chief Justice:

This case is before this Court on appeal from a final order of the trial court which dismissed the plaintiff's amended complaint with prejudice and held that a prior judgment of the same court rendered in a divorce case wherein the defendants in this case were the parties there, was res judicata as to the appellants here.

In the prior case of Searle v. Searle (a divorce action), the court determined that a particular piece of property commonly known as the "Slaugh House" and recorded in the name of the defendant, Woodey B. Searle (who is the father of the appellants in the instant matter) was part of the marital property, and awarded the same to Edlean Searle (who is the mother of the appellants and also the respondent in the instant matter). The divorce was appealed to this Court and was affirmed in all respects.

Appellants instituted this suit claiming that an undivided one-half interest in the "Slaugh House" was a partnership asset of Diamond Hills Motel (owned by the Searle Brothers partnership) and had been paid for with partnership funds. The trial court held that res judicata applied and that appellants were collaterally estopped from bringing this suit.

Appellants have appealed this judgment, claiming that the trial court erred in that the appellants were not parties to the divorce action and could not be bound by the decree entered therein.

In general, a divorce decree, like other final judgments, is conclusive as to parties and their privies and operates as a bar to any subsequent action. In order for res judicata to apply, both suits must involve the same parties or their privies and also the same cause of action; and this precludes the relitigation of all issues that could have been litigated as well as those that were, in fact, litigated in the prior action. If the subsequent suit involves different parties, those parties cannot be bound by the prior judgment.

Collateral estoppel, on the other hand, arises from a different cause of action and prevents parties or their privies from relitigating facts and issues in the second suit that were fully litigated in the first suit. This means that the plea of collateral estoppel can be asserted only against a party in the subsequent suit who was also a party or in privity with a party in the prior suit.

In Bernhard v. Bank of America Nat'l Trust & Savings Association the California Supreme Court considered the question of the applicability of res judicata as a basis for applying the collateral estoppel doctrine and identified the following three tests as being determinative:

1. Was the issue decided in the prior adjudication identical with the one presented in the action in question?
2. Was there a final judgment on the merits?
3. Was the party against whom the plea is asserted a party or in privity with a party to the prior adjudication?

In a subsequent opinion, the California Supreme Court recognized the necessity for a fourth test: "Was the issue in the first case competently, fully, and fairly litigated?" These four tests have been adopted by the majority of jurisdictions as the correct standard to apply. As to the second test above, there is no dispute that the divorce decree rendered in the former suit was a final judgment on the merits. Points One and Four will be discussed infra. Under the third test, it is clear that the appellants in this action were not parties to the first action; hence, the only way they can be barred or estopped from pursuing the second suit is if they were "in privity" with the parties to the divorce action.

The legal definition of a person in privity with another, is a person so identified in interest with another that he represents the same legal right. This includes a mutual or successive relationship to rights in property. Our Court has said that as applied to judgments or decrees of court, privity means "one whose interest has been legally represented at the time."

In the case before us, appellants' interest was neither mutual nor successive. They claim no part of the interest owned by Woodey B. Searle, but assert their own, independent and separate partnership interest in 50 percent of the property involved. The rights are similar but not identical. The property interest arose before the commencement of the first action, not subsequent thereto, so that appellants cannot be regarded as in privity and subject to the judgment rendered therein. Furthermore, under [Utah law] partners are co-owners of specific partnership property which is directly opposite to successive interests.

The first and fourth tests previously outlined also do not permit the application of collateral estoppel in this case. The partnership interest was not legally represented in the prior divorce suit. Woodey B. Searle, the defendant in the prior action, was acting in his individual capacity as the husband of the plaintiff and was not acting in a representative capacity for the partnership. Respondent urges that Woodey B. Searle was acting as agent for the partnership; hence, the partnership is bound by his action or inaction in the prior litigation. However, the general rule is that agents and principals do not have any mutual or successive relationship to rights of property and are not, as a consequence thereof, in privity with each other. Therefore, the principal is not bound by any judgment obtained against an agent, unless the principal became a party or privy thereto by actually and openly defending the action.

The right to intervene as a party in the prior suit does not bind the party in the subsequent suit where he failed to so intervene. 46 Am.Jur.2d, Judgments, Sec. 530 discusses this point as follows:

A party to the principal case is regarded as a stranger to the judgment rendered in the previous action where he was not directly interested in the subject matter thereof, and had no right to make defense, adduce testimony, cross-examine witnesses, control the proceedings or appeal from the judgment, even though he could have made himself a party to the previous action. The right to intervene in an action does not, in the absence of its exercise, subject one possessing it to the risk of being bound by the result of the litigation, under the doctrine of res judicata... .

The foregoing rule has been adopted by this Court.

Collateral estoppel is not available to defeat appellants' claim since the partners were not made parties to the first suit and there is not sufficient evidence in the record to show that the interest of the partnership in the "Slaugh House" was ever litigated. The standard rule was reiterated by this Court earlier this year in Ruffinengo v. Miller when we said:

Collateral estoppel is not a defense against a litigant who was not a party to the action and judgment claimed to have created an estoppel.

In the matter now before us, no trial was held. On the date set for trial, the court instructed the counsel for both parties to attempt to settle the case and that if they failed to reach an agreement, to submit memoranda to the court addressed solely to the issue of the res judicata effect of the divorce action. The parties were not afforded an opportunity to present testimony or to make a proffer on proof. In its Amended Order, the court stated:

... Memoranda was submitted by counsel for both the plaintiff and the defendant. The transcript of testimony of the previous divorce action between the plaintiff's parents was referred to.

... From the undisputed facts presented in counsel's memoranda, the court further finds that the doctrine of collateral estoppel appears in the instant case and is a bar to the plaintiff's claim.

It also appears from this Order that the court relied entirely on counsels' memoranda, which memoranda contained references to the previous litigation but which were not necessarily examined independently by the trial court. We dealt with a similar problem in Parrish v. Layton City Corp. wherein we stated:

> ... The mere fact that there was a record of another action on file in the clerk's office did not place these records in evidence.... Since the record of the prior action was not before the trial court, there is no basis to sustain the determination that plaintiff's claim was barred by the doctrine of res judicata.

Appellants cannot be bound by the decree entered in the previous suit nor are they estopped from litigating their own claim against the property in a subsequent suit since they were not parties or privies in the first action, and the issue raised in the second action was never litigated in the prior proceeding. The trial court erred in holding that the doctrines of res judicata and collateral estoppel barred the appellants from pursuing their suit. In making this ruling, we do not express an opinion as to whether or not the property in question was an asset of the partnership.

The judgment is reversed and remanded for trial. Costs are awarded to appellants.

THE REQUIREMENT THAT THE JUDGMENT BE "ON THE MERITS"

The requirement that a judgment, to be res judicata, must be rendered "on the merits" guarantees to every plaintiff the right once to be heard on the substance of his claim. Generally speaking, this means that a case must be decided on its substantive merits. Cases which are decided on grounds of practice, procedure, jurisdiction or form are not accorded res judicata effect.

Gargallo v. Merrill Lynch, Pierce, Fenner & Smith
918 F.2d 658 (6th Cir. 1990)

RYAN, J.

This case presents the interesting dual questions 1) whether a federal court must apply federal or state claim preclusion law in deciding 2) whether a prior state court judgment upon subject matter over which only a federal court has jurisdiction is a bar to a subsequent federal court claim upon the identical cause of action.... The district court dismissed the suit below on grounds of res judicata as to Merrill Lynch....

I

Miguel Gargallo opened a "margin brokerage account" with Merrill Lynch in 1976. He maintained the account until 1980, when his investments apparently went awry and losses occurred, resulting in a debt of some $17,000 owed to Merrill Lynch....When the obligation was not paid, the brokerage firm filed suit for collection in the Court of Common Pleas, Franklin County, Ohio. In response, Mr. Gargallo filed an answer and counterclaim against Merrill Lynch, alleging that Merrill Lynch caused his losses through "negligence, misrepresentations, and churning," and that the firm had violated...federal securities laws. After a considerable history of discovery difficulties, the state court dismissed Mr. Gargallo's counterclaim "with prejudice," citing Ohio Civil Rule 37 [substantially identical to Federal Rule 37], for refusal to comply with Merrill Lynch's discovery requests and the court's discovery orders....

Mr. Gargallo...then filed a complaint in the United States District Court, Southern District of Ohio, charging Merrill Lynch and its account executive, Larry Tyree, with violating [federal securities laws]...based on the same transactions at issue in the state litigation. After preparing a thoughtful written opinion, the district court dismissed the suit against Merrill Lynch on res judicata grounds, finding that the "issues, facts and evidence to sustain this action are identical to the claims asserted [against the brokerage firm] in [Mr. Gargallo's] counterclaim that was dismissed with prejudice by the state court." This appeal followed.

II

There is no dispute in this case about the essential facts relating to the summary judgment, and the ultimate issue is: whether the district court correctly dismissed the plaintiff's claims on res judicata...grounds....

A. Claim Preclusion

The federal securities law violations asserted against Merrill Lynch...in this litigation are the same, for all practical purposes, as those Mr. Gargallo previously asserted in the counterclaim he filed in the Franklin County court. For reasons we shall discuss shortly, Ohio claim preclusion law ultimately determines the outcome of this case. Consequently, we must decide whether the Franklin County court judgment dismissing Mr. Gargallo's first lawsuit would operate as a bar, under Ohio claim preclusion rules, to the action brought in the district court, now under review, had it been brought in an Ohio court....

In Ohio, the requirements for application of the doctrine of claim preclusion, or res judicata as the earlier Ohio court termed it, are the same as those applicable in a federal court:

The doctrine of res judicata is that an existing final judgment rendered upon the merits, without fraud or collusion, by a court of competent jurisdiction, is conclusive of rights, questions and facts in issue, as to the parties and their privies, in all other actions in the same or any other judicial tribunal of concurrent jurisdiction. Under Ohio law, the dismissal with prejudice of Mr. Gargallo's Common Pleas Court counterclaim for noncompliance with Ohio's Civil Rule 37 was a "final judgment rendered upon the merits."

...We agree with the district court that the "issues, facts, and evidence to sustain this action are identical to the claims asserted...in [plaintiff's state] counterclaim," and we are satisfied that the federal claim or cause of action giving rise to this appeal is the same claim or cause of action that was asserted in the counterclaim dismissed in the state court litigation.

Thus, we have no question that, absent any regard for subject matter jurisdiction, Ohio claim preclusion law would bar the claim asserted in Mr. Gargallo's district court complaint had it been filed in an Ohio court.

B. Federal Exclusivity

However, the district court in which plaintiff brought his claim is not an Ohio court but a federal tribunal. Consequently, we are faced with the more difficult issue of whether a federal district court may give claim preclusive effect to an Ohio judgment regarding federal securities laws that are within the exclusive jurisdiction of the federal courts. The first rule in determining whether a prior state court judgment has preclusive effect in a federal court is that the full faith and credit statute, 28 U.S.C. §1738,3 requires a federal court to give a state court judgment the same preclusive effect such judgment would have in a state court....And the rule is no less applicable in a case in which the state court was without jurisdiction to entertain the exclusively federal claim it adjudicated....

Marrese v. [American] Academy of Orthopaedic Surgeons, 470 U.S. 373 (1985)...requires...that a federal court must determine whether to give claim preclusive effect to a state court judgment upon a cause of action over which the state court had no subject matter jurisdiction by determining whether the state court would give preclusive effect to such a judgment....

Ohio appears to subscribe to the Restatement (Second) of Judgments position that a judgment rendered by a court lacking subject matter jurisdiction ought not be given preclusive effect. Addressing whether an Ohio judgment in an action commenced after expiration of the applicable limitations period was entitled to claim preclusive effect, the Ohio Supreme Court stated:

It is not contended that the judgment in the prior action [in this case] was void because of some defect relating to the jurisdiction of either court therein, in which case the judgment could not operate as an estoppel as to a particular fact or issue; nor could it operate as res judicata as to a cause of action.

It seems clear, therefore, that in Ohio a final judgment by a court of that state, upon a cause of action over which the adjudicating court had no subject matter jurisdiction, does not have claim preclusive effect in any subsequent proceedings....

In summary, we hold that the Ohio court judgment, dismissing, with prejudice, Mr. Gargallo's federal securities law claims against Merrill Lynch...may not be given claim preclusive effect in a subsequent federal court action asserting those same claims because Ohio courts would not give claim preclusive effect to a prior final judgment upon a cause of action over which the Ohio court had no subject matter jurisdiction....

[Reversed and remanded.]

ISSUE PRECLUSION - COLLATERAL ESTOPPEL

The doctrine of issue preclusion (also called collateral estoppel) allows the judgment in a prior action to operate as an estoppel as to those facts or questions actually litigated and determined in the prior action. In other words, under certain conditions, issues determined in lawsuits cannot be relitigated in subsequent lawsuits.

Prerequisites for Issue Preclusion

(1) The issue in the second case must be the same as the issue in the first.

(2) The issue must have been actually litigated.

(3) The issue must have been actually decided.

(4) The issue must have been necessary to the court's judgment.

The purpose of the doctrine of issue preclusion is to protect a party from being subjected to harassment by being compelled to litigate the same controversy more than once. (*Belliston v. Texaco, Inc.*, Utah, 521 P.2d 379 (1974))

Does Issue Preclusion Apply?

(1) Was the issue decided in the prior adjudication identical with the one presented in the action in question?

(2) Was there a final judgment on the merits?

(3) Was the party against whom the plea is asserted a party or in privity with a party to the prior adjudication?

(4) Was the issue in the first case competently, fully and fairly litigated?

IDENTITY OF PARTIES AND MUTUALITY OF PRECLUSION

Under traditional issue preclusion principles, a party may be estopped from relitigating an issue that he had litigated in a prior suit and lost. The general rule was that estoppel must be mutual, i.e., the only parties who could invoke collateral estoppel were those who were involved in the suit in which the issue was initially decided. I.e., parties are bound, nonparties are not. (Wright, § 100A). However, many jurisdictions have abandoned the mutuality requirement.

Briefit

Bernhard v. Bank of America
19 Cal.2d 807 (1942)

TRAYNOR, J.

In June, 1933, Mrs. Clara Sather, an elderly woman, made her home with Mr. and Mrs. Charles O. Cook in San Dimas, California. Because of her failing health, she authorized Mr. Cook and Dr. Joseph Zeiler to make drafts jointly against her commercial account in the Security First National Bank of Los Angeles. On August 24, 1933, Mr. Cook opened a commercial account at the First National Bank of San Dimas in the name of "Clara Sather by Charles O. Cook." No authorization for this account was ever given to the bank by Mrs. Sather. Thereafter, a number of checks drawn by Cook and Zeiler on Mrs. Sather's commercial account in Los Angeles were deposited in the San Dimas account and checks were drawn upon that account signed "Clara Sather by Charles O. Cook" to meet various expenses of Mrs. Sather.

On October 26, 1933, a teller from the Los Angeles Bank called on Mrs. Sather at her request to assist in transferring her money from the Los Angeles Bank to the San Dimas Bank. In the presence of this teller, the cashier of the San Dimas Bank, Mr. Cook, and her physician, Mrs. Sather signed by mark an authorization directing the Security First National Bank of Los Angeles to transfer the balance of her savings account in the amount of $4,155.68 to the First National Bank of San Dimas. She also signed an order for this amount on the Security First National Bank of San Dimas "for credit to the account of Mrs. Clara Sather." The order was credited by the San Dimas Bank to the account of "Clara Sather by Charles O. Cook." Cook withdrew the entire balance from that account and opened a new account in the same bank in the name of himself and his wife. He subsequently withdrew the funds from this last mentioned account and deposited them in a Los Angeles Bank in the names of himself and his wife.

Mrs. Sather died in November, 1933. Cook qualified as executor of the estate and proceeded with its administration. After a lapse of several years he filed an account at the instance of the probate court accompanied by his resignation. The account made no mention of the money transferred by Mrs. Sather to the San Dimas Bank; and Helen Bernhard, Beaulah Bernhard, Hester Burton, and Iva LeDoux, beneficiaries under Mrs. Sather's will, filed objections to the account for this reason. After a hearing on the objections the court settled the account, and as part of its order declared that the decedent during her lifetime had made a gift to Charles O. Cook of the amount of the deposit in question.

After Cook's discharge, Helen Bernhard was appointed administratrix with the will annexed. She instituted this action against defendant, the Bank of America, successor to the San Dimas Bank, seeking to recover the deposit on the ground that the bank was indebted to the estate for this amount because Mrs. Sather never authorized its withdrawal. In addition to a general denial, defendant pleaded two affirmative defenses: (1) that the money on deposit was paid out to Charles O. Cook with the consent of Mrs. Sather and (2) that this fact is res judicata by virtue of the finding of the probate court in the proceeding to settle Cook's account that Mrs. Sather made a gift of the money in question to Charles O. Cook and "owned no sums of money whatsoever" at the time of her death. . . . The trial court overruled the demurrers and objection to the evidence, and gave judgment for defendant on the ground that Cook's ownership of the money was conclusively established by the finding of the probate court. Plaintiff has appealed, denying that the doctrine of res judicata is applicable to the instant case or that there was a valid gift of the money to Cook by Mrs. Sather.

Plaintiff contends that the doctrine of res judicata does not apply because the defendant who is asserting the plea was not a party to the previous action nor in privity with a party to that action and because there is no mutuality of estoppel.

The doctrine of res judicata precludes parties or their privies from relitigating a cause of action that has been finally determined by a court of competent jurisdiction. Any issue necessarily decided in such litigation is conclusively determined as to the parties or their privies if it is involved in a subsequent lawsuit on a different cause of action. The rule is based upon the sound public policy of limiting litigation by preventing a party who has had one fair trial on an issue from again drawing it into controversy. The doctrine also serves to protect persons from being twice vexed for the same cause. It must, however, conform to the mandate of due process of law that no person be deprived of personal or property rights by a judgment without notice and an opportunity to be heard.

Many courts have stated the facile formula that the plea of res judicata is available only when there is privity and mutuality of estoppel. Under the requirement of privity, only parties to the former judgment or their privies may take advantage of or be bound by it. A party in this connection is one who is "directly interested in the subject matter, and had a right to make defense, or to control the proceeding, and to appeal from the judgment." A privy is one who, after rendition of the judgment, has acquired an interest in the subject matter affected by the judgment through or under one of the parties, as by inheritance, succession, or purchase. The estoppel is mutual if the one taking advantage of the earlier adjudication would have been bound by it, had it gone against him.

The criteria for determining who may assert a plea of res judicata differ fundamentally from the criteria for determining against whom a plea of res judicata may be asserted. The requirements of due process of law forbid the assertion of a plea of res judicata against a party unless he was bound by the earlier litigation in which the matter was decided. He is bound by that litigation only if he has been a party thereto or in privity with a party thereto. There is no compelling reason, however, for requiring that the party asserting the plea of res judicata must have been a party, or in privity with a party, to the earlier litigation.

No satisfactory rationalization has been advanced for the requirement of mutuality. Just why a party who was not bound by a previous action should be precluded from asserting it as res judicata against a party who was bound by it is difficult to comprehend. Many courts have abandoned the requirement of mutuality and confined the requirement of privity to the party against whom the plea of res judicata is asserted. . . . The courts of most jurisdictions have in effect accomplished the same result by recognizing a broad exception to the requirements of mutuality and privity, namely, that they are not necessary where the liability of the defendant asserting the plea of res judicata is dependent upon or derived from the liability of one who was exonerated in an earlier suit brought by the same plaintiff upon the same facts. Typical examples of such derivative liability are master and servant, principal and agent, and indemnitor and indemnitee. Thus, if a plaintiff sues a servant for injuries caused by the servant's alleged negligence within the scope of his employment, a judgment against the plaintiff on the grounds that the servant was not negligent can be pleaded by the master as res judicata if he is subsequently sued by the same plaintiff for the same injuries. Conversely, if the plaintiff first sues the master, a judgment against the plaintiff on the grounds that the servant was not negligent can be pleaded by the servant as res judicata if he is subsequently sued by the plaintiff. In each of these situations the party asserting the plea of res judicata was not a party to the previous action nor in privity with such a party under the accepted definition of a privy set forth above. Likewise, the estoppel is not mutual since the party asserting the plea, not having been a party or in privity with a party to the former action, would not have been bound by it had it been decided the other way. The cases justify this exception on the ground that it would be unjust to permit one who has had his day in court to reopen identical issues by merely switching adversaries.

In determining the validity of a plea of res judicata three questions are pertinent: Was the issue decided in the prior adjudication identical with the one presented in the action in question? Was there a final judgment on the merits? Was the party against whom the plea is asserted a party or in privity with a party to the prior adjudication? . . .

In the present case, therefore, the defendant is not precluded by lack of privity or of mutuality of estoppel from asserting the plea of res judicata against the plaintiff. Since the issue as to the ownership of the money is identical with the issue raised in the probate proceeding, and since the order of the probate court settling the executor's account was a final adjudication of this issue on the merits, it remains only to determine whether the plaintiff in the present action was a party or in privity with a party to the earlier proceeding. The plaintiff has brought the present action in the capacity of administratrix of the estate. In this capacity she represents the very same persons and interests that were represented in the earlier hearing on the executor's account. In that proceeding plaintiff and the other legatees who objected to the executor's account represented the estate of the decedent. They were seeking not a personal recovery but, like the plaintiff in the present action, as administratrix, a recovery for the benefit of the legatees and creditors of the estate, all of whom were bound by the order settling the account. The plea of res judicata is therefore available against plaintiff as a party to the former proceeding, despite her formal change of capacity. "Where a party though appearing in two suits in different capacities is in fact litigating the same right, the judgment in one estops him in the other."

The judgment is affirmed.

> **Issue Preclusion**
> **Nonmutuality**
>
> Collateral estoppel runs against anyone who has fully and fairly litigated an issue in an earlier action.

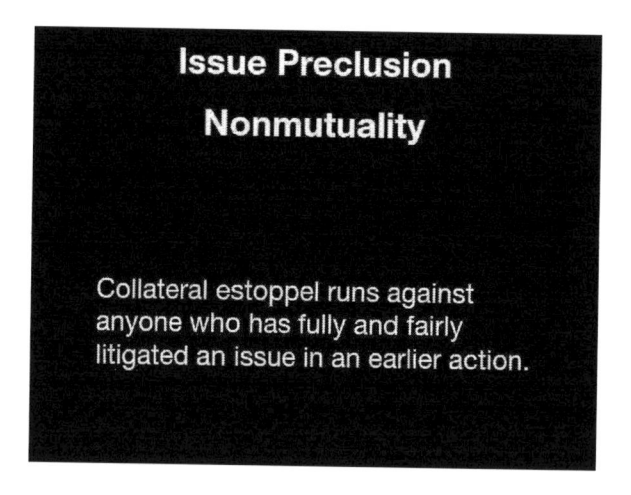

Parklane Hosiery Co. v. Shore
439 U.S. 322 (1979)

Mr. Justice STEWART delivered the opinion of the Court.

This case presents the question whether a party who has had issues of fact adjudicated adversely to it in an equitable action may be collaterally estopped from relitigating the same issues before a jury in a subsequent legal action brought against it by a new party.

The respondent brought this stockholder's class action against the petitioners in a Federal District Court. The complaint alleged that the petitioners, Parklane Hosiery Co., Inc. (Parklane), and 13 of its officers, directors, and stockholders, had issued a materially false and misleading proxy statement in connection with a merger.[1] The proxy statement, according to the complaint, had violated §§14(a), 10(b), and 20(a) of the Securities Exchange Act of 1934, as well as various rules and regulations promulgated by the Securities and Exchange Commission (SEC). The complaint sought damages, rescission of the merger, and recovery of costs.

Before this action came to trial, the SEC filed suit against the same defendants in the Federal District Court, alleging that the proxy statement that had been issued by Parklane was materially false and misleading in essentially the same respects as those that had been alleged in the respondent's complaint. Injunctive relief was requested. After a four-day trial, the District Court found that the proxy statement was materially false and misleading in the respects alleged, and entered a declaratory judgment to that effect. The Court of Appeals for the Second Circuit affirmed this judgment.

The respondent in the present case then moved for partial summary judgment against the petitioners, asserting that the petitioners were collaterally estopped from litigating the issues that had been resolved against them in the action brought by the SEC.[2] The

District Court denied the motion on the ground that such an application of collateral estoppel would deny the petitioners their Seventh Amendment right to a jury trial. The Court of Appeals for the Second Circuit reversed, holding that a party who has had issues of fact determined against him after a full and fair opportunity to litigate in a nonjury trial is collaterally estopped from obtaining a subsequent jury trial of these same issues of fact. The appellate court concluded that "the Seventh Amendment preserves the right to jury trial only with respect to issues of fact, [and] once those issues have been fully and fairly adjudicated in a prior proceeding, nothing remains for trial, either with or without a jury." Because of an inter-Circuit conflict, we granted certiorari.

I

The threshold question to be considered is whether quite apart from the right to a jury trial under the Seventh Amendment, the petitioners can be precluded from litigating facts resolved adversely to them in a prior equitable proceeding with another party under the general law of collateral estoppel. Specifically, we must determine whether a litigant who was not a party to a prior judgment may nevertheless use that judgment "offensively" to prevent a defendant from relitigating issues resolved in the earlier proceeding.4

A

Collateral estoppel, like the related doctrine of res judicata, has the dual purpose of protecting litigants from the burden of relitigating an identical issue with the same party or his privy and of promoting judicial economy by preventing needless litigation. Until relatively recently, however, the scope of collateral estoppel was limited by the doctrine of mutuality of parties. Under this mutuality doctrine, neither party could use a prior judgment as an estoppel against the other unless both parties were bound by the judgment. Based on the premise that it is somehow unfair to allow a party to use a prior judgment when he himself would not be so bound,7 the mutuality requirement provided a party who had litigated and lost in a previous action an opportunity to relitigate identical issues with new parties.

By failing to recognize the obvious difference in position between a party who has never litigated an issue and one who has fully litigated and lost, the mutuality requirement was criticized almost from its inception.8 Recognizing the validity of this criticism, the Court in Blonder-Tongue Laboratories, Inc. v. University of Illinois Foundation, supra, abandoned the mutuality requirement....The "broader question" before the Court, however, was "whether it is any longer tenable to afford a litigant more than one full and fair opportunity for judicial resolution of the same issue."...

B

The Blonder-Tongue case involved defensive use of collateral estoppel—a plaintiff was estopped from asserting a claim that the plaintiff had previously litigated and lost against another defendant. The present case, by contrast, involves offensive use of collateral estoppel—a plaintiff is seeking to estop a defendant from relitigating the issues which the defendant previously litigated and lost against another plaintiff. In both the offensive and defensive use situations, the party against whom estoppel is asserted has litigated and lost in an earlier action. Nevertheless, several reasons have been advanced why the two situations should be treated differently.

First, offensive use of collateral estoppel does not promote judicial economy in the same manner as defensive use does. Defensive use of collateral estoppel precludes a plaintiff from relitigating identical issues by merely "switching adversaries." Bernhard v. Bank of America Natl. Trust & Savings Assn. Thus defensive collateral estoppel gives a plaintiff a strong incentive to join all potential defendants in the first action if possible. Offensive use of collateral estoppel, on the other hand, creates precisely the opposite incentive. Since a plaintiff will be able to rely on a previous judgment against a defendant but will not be bound by that judgment if the defendant wins, the plaintiff has every incentive to adopt a "wait and see" attitude, in the hope that the first action by another plaintiff will result in a favorable judgment. Thus offensive use of collateral estoppel will likely increase rather than decrease the total amount of litigation, since potential plaintiffs will have everything to gain and nothing to lose by not intervening in the first action.13 A second argument against offensive use of collateral estoppel is that it may be unfair to a defendant. If a defendant in the first action is sued for small or nominal damages, he may have little incentive to defend vigorously, particularly if future suits are not foreseeable. The Evergreens v. Nunan; cf. Berner v. British Commonwealth Pac. Airlines (application of offensive collateral estoppel denied where defendant did not appeal an adverse judgment awarding damages of $35,000 and defendant was later sued for over $7 million). Allowing offensive collateral estoppel may also be unfair to a defendant if the judgment relied upon as a basis for the estoppel is itself inconsistent with one or more previous judgments in favor of the defendant. Still another situation where it might be unfair to apply offensive estoppel is where the second action affords the defendant procedural opportunities unavailable in the first action that could readily cause a different result.

C

We have concluded that the preferable approach for dealing with these problems in the federal courts is not to preclude the use of offensive collateral estoppel, but to grant trial courts broad discretion to determine when it should be applied.

The general rule should be that in cases where a plaintiff could easily have joined in the earlier action or where, either for the reasons discussed above or for other reasons, the application of offensive estoppel would be unfair to a defendant, a trial judge should not allow the use of offensive collateral estoppel.

In the present case, however, none of the circumstances that might justify reluctance to allow the offensive use of collateral estoppel is present. The application of offensive collateral estoppel will not here reward a private plaintiff who could have joined in the previous action, since the respondent probably could not have joined in the injunctive action brought by the SEC even had he so desired.17 Similarly, there is no unfairness to the petitioners in applying offensive collateral estoppel in this case. First, in light of the serious allegations made in the SEC's complaint against the petitioners, as well as the foreseeability of subsequent private suits that typically follow a successful Government judgment, the petitioners had every incentive to litigate the SEC lawsuit fully and vigorously.18 Second, the judgment in the SEC action was not inconsistent with any previous decision. Finally, there will in the respondent's action be no procedural opportunities available to the petitioners that were unavailable in the first action of a kind that might be likely to cause a different result.19 We conclude, therefore, that none of the considerations that would justify a refusal to allow the use of offensive collateral estoppel is present in this case. Since the petitioners received a "full and fair" opportunity to litigate their claims in the SEC action, the contemporary law of collateral estoppel leads inescapably to the conclusion that the petitioners are collaterally estopped from relitigating the question of whether the proxy statement was materially false and misleading.

II

The question that remains is whether, notwithstanding the law of collateral estoppel, the use of offensive collateral estoppel in this case would violate the petitioners' Seventh Amendment right to a jury trial....The Seventh Amendment has never been interpreted in the rigid manner advocated by the petitioners. On the contrary, many procedural devices developed since 1791 that have diminished the civil jury's historic domain have been found not to be inconsistent with the Seventh Amendment....

The law of collateral estoppel, like the law in other procedural areas defining the scope of the jury's function, has evolved since 1791. Under the rationale of [an earlier] case, these developments are not repugnant to the Seventh Amendment simply for the reason that they did not exist in 1791. Thus if, as we have held, the law of collateral estoppel forecloses the petitioners from relitigating the factual issues determined against them in the SEC action, nothing in the Seventh Amendment dictates a different result, even though because of lack of mutuality there would have been no collateral estoppel in 1791....

[The Court went on to hold that the Seventh Amendment was not a bar to successful assertion of issue preclusion.

NOTES Parklane introduces us to the concept of "offensive" use of issue preclusion. "Offensive" use of issue preclusion involves a plaintiff who is seeking to prevent a defendant from relitigating issues that the defendant had previously litigated and lost against another plaintiff.

IDENTITY OF ISSUES

Teitelbaum Furs, Inc. v. The Dominion Insurance Company, Ltd.
58 Cal.2d 601 (1962)

TRAYNOR, J.

Alleging losses by robbery, plaintiff corporations brought this action to recover $244,510.90 under contracts of insurance with defendant insurers. The jury returned a verdict for plaintiffs, and the trial court granted defendants' motion for new trial on the ground that the evidence was insufficient to support the verdict. The trial court denied defendants' motion for judgment notwithstanding the verdict. Plaintiffs appeal from the order granting a new trial. Defendants appeal from the judgment.

We agree with defendants' contention that their plea of collateral estoppel defeats plaintiffs' action. In a criminal action that became final before the present action was commenced, Albert Teitelbaum, president of plaintiff corporations, was convicted of conspiracy to commit grand theft, attempted grand theft, and the filing of a false and fraudulent insurance claim. The conviction was affirmed on appeal. Plaintiff corporations concede that the claim in this case is for the same loss involved in the criminal conviction and that they are mere alter egos of Teitelbaum. The issue adjudicated adversely to plaintiffs in the criminal action is identical with the issue in this action: whether the alleged robbery occurred as plaintiffs contend or whether it was staged by Teitelbaum as defendants contend. By its verdict, the previous jury necessarily found against plaintiffs on this issue.

The doctrine of res judicata has a double aspect: (1) it "precludes parties or their privies from relitigating a cause of action that has been finally determined by a court of competent jurisdiction." (2) "Any issue necessarily decided in such litigation is conclusively determined as to the parties or their privies if it is involved in a subsequent lawsuit on a different cause of action." (Bernhard v. Bank of America, 19 Cal.2d 807, 810 [122 P.2d 892]; In the present case, since plaintiffs' cause of action is different from that of the state in the criminal proceeding, we are concerned with the latter aspect, often termed collateral estoppel.

In the Bernhard case, supra, this court rejected the doctrine of mutuality of estoppel that had been applied to limit the scope of collateral estoppel, and held three questions to be pertinent in determining the validity of the plea. "Was the issue decided in the prior adjudication identical with the one presented in the action in question? Was there a final judgment on the merits? Was the party against whom the plea is asserted a party or in privity with a party to the prior adjudication?" The record in the present case provides affirmative answers to each of these questions.

Notwithstanding the apparent applicability of collateral estoppel, it is contended that the cases in this state do not indicate that a criminal conviction is conclusive in a subsequent civil action. Additionally, plaintiffs urge that the plea be rejected on the ground that since plaintiffs did not have the initiative in the criminal action and since Teitelbaum chose not to testify and was unable to utilize an important witness in the criminal proceeding, they did not have a full and complete day in court on the issue now sought to be foreclosed against them.

The cases do not preclude the application of collateral estoppel in a civil case to issues determined in a previous criminal prosecution. Those relied upon for the contrary proposition are either based upon the doctrine of mutuality of estoppel or involve a prior acquittal or involve the admissibility as an admission in a civil suit of a plea of guilty in a previous criminal action

* * *

In re Anderson, supra, rejected the plea as applied to a former acquittal on the ground that " 'the difference in degree in the burden of proof in criminal and civil cases precludes application of the doctrine of res judicata. The acquittal was merely ... an adjudication that the proof was not sufficient to overcome all reasonable doubt of the guilt of the accused.' " (107 Cal.App.2d 670, 672;)

A plea of guilty is admissible in a subsequent civil action on the independent ground that it is an admission. It would not serve the policy underlying collateral estoppel, however, to make such a plea conclusive. ["The rule is based upon the sound public policy of limiting litigation by preventing a party who has had one fair trial on an issue from again drawing it into controversy." (Bernhard v. Bank of America, 19 Cal.2d 807, 811 [122 P.2d 892].) "This policy must be considered together with the policy that a party shall not be deprived of a fair adversary proceeding in which fully to present his case." When a plea of guilty has been entered in the prior action, no issues have been "drawn into controversy" by a "full presentation" of the case. It may reflect only a compromise or a belief that paying a fine is more advantageous than litigation. Considerations of fairness to civil litigants and regard for the expeditious administration of criminal justice combine to prohibit the application of collateral estoppel against a party who, having pleaded guilty to a criminal charge, seeks for the first time to litigate his cause in a civil action.

Collateral estoppel applies to successive criminal trials and, although not widely adopted, has been applied in the better reasoned cases that have dealt with the problem here presented. Thus it is significant that this court found support in Eagle etc. Ins. Co. v. Heller, supra, in reaching its decision to abandon the requirement of mutuality of estoppel in the Bernhard case. To preclude a civil litigant from relitigating an issue previously found against him in a criminal prosecution is less severe than to preclude him from relitigating such an issue in successive civil trials, for there are rigorous safeguards against unjust conviction, including the requirements of proof beyond a reasonable doubt and of a unanimous verdict, the right to counsel, and a record paid for by the state on appeal Stability of judgments and expeditious trials are served and no injustice done, when criminal defendants are estopped from relitigating issues determined in conformity with these safeguards.

Plaintiffs contend, however, that in the absence of mutuality, collateral estoppel ought not be applied against a party who did not have the initiative in the previous action. Although plaintiffs' president did not have the initiative in his criminal trial, he was afforded a full opportunity to litigate the issue of his guilt with all the safeguards afforded the criminal defendant, and since he was charged with felonies punishable in the state prison, he had every motive to make as vigorous and effective a defense as possible. Under these circumstances, we hold that any issue necessarily decided in a prior criminal proceeding is conclusively determined as to the parties if it is involved in a subsequent civil action.

It should be noted, however, that a criminal judgment that is subject to collateral attack on the ground, for example, that it was obtained through the knowing use of perjured testimony or that has in effect been set aside by a pardon based on the defendant's innocence (see Pen. Code, 4900), is not res judicata in a subsequent action. (See Rest., Judgments, 11.) Plaintiffs have advanced no grounds that would sustain a collateral attack on the judgment, but they contend that there are special reasons why collateral estoppel should not apply in this case. They point out that Teitelbaum chose not to take the stand in the criminal prosecution except for the limited purpose of denying an alleged admission, and contend that he was unable to secure the testimony of an alleged co-conspirator.

Teitelbaum's election not to testify in his own behalf in the criminal case was presumably made on the assumption that he would benefit thereby. His error, if any, in trial strategy would no more defeat the plea of collateral estoppel than the failure of a litigant to introduce relevant available evidence in any other situation.

Teitelbaum urged his inability to compel the testimony of the alleged co-conspirator on his appeal from the judgment in the criminal case, and it was determined that it did not warrant a reversal. A fortiori, it will not sustain a collateral attack upon the criminal judgment.

The order denying defendants' motion for judgment notwithstanding the verdict and the order granting a new trial are reversed and the trial court is directed to enter judgment for defendants. Defendants shall recover their costs on these appeals.

ACTUALLY LITIGATED AND DECIDED

Illinois Central Gulf Railroad v. Parks
181 Ind. App. 141, 390 N.E.2d 1078 (1979)

LYBROOK, J.

[Jessie and Bertha Parks were injured when a car driven by Jessie in which Bertha was a passenger collided with an Illinois Central train. Bertha and Jessie sued Illinois Central; Bertha sought compensation for her injuries, and Jessie sought damages for loss of Bertha's services and consortium. Bertha recovered a $30,000 judgment on her claim, and judgment was rendered for Illinois Central on Jessie's claim.

Jessie then sued Illinois Central for his own injuries. On Illinois Central's motion for summary judgment, the trial court held that Jessie's claim was not barred by claim preclusion and that the prior action did not preclude Jessie on the issue of contributory negligence. Illinois Central took an interlocutory appeal.]

...Illinois Central Gulf's first allegation of error is an attempt to apply estoppel by judgment [the court's term for claim preclusion] in the case at bar, but the railroad concedes its own argument by admitting that Jessie's cause of action for loss of services and consortium as a derivative of Bertha's personal injuries is a distinct cause of action from Jessie's claim for damages for his own personal injuries.

Estoppel by judgment precludes the relitigation of a cause of action finally determined between the parties, and decrees that a judgment rendered is a complete bar to any subsequent action on the same claim or cause of action. Jessie's cause of action in the case at bar is a different cause of action from the one he litigated in the companion case; therefore, estoppel by judgment does not apply.

Estoppel by verdict [the court's term for issue preclusion], however, does apply. Using Judge Shake's terminology, the causes of action are not the same but, if the case at bar were to go to trial on all the issues raised in the pleadings and answer, some facts or questions determined and adjudicated in the companion case would again be put in issue in this subsequent action between the same parties.

To protect the integrity of the prior judgment by precluding the possibility of opposite results by two different juries on the same set of facts, the doctrine of estoppel by verdict allows the judgment in the prior action to operate as an estoppel as to those facts or questions actually litigated and determined in the prior action. The problem at hand, then, is to determine what facts or questions were actually litigated and determined in the companion case.

We agree with three concessions made by Illinois Central Gulf as to the effect of the verdict in the prior case: (1) that the verdict in favor of Bertha established, among other things, that the railroad was negligent and that its negligence was a proximate cause of the accident and Bertha's injuries; (2) that, inasmuch as Jessie's action for loss of services and consortium was derivative, if Jessie sustained any such loss it was proximately caused by the railroad's negligence; and (3) that, in order for the jury to have returned a verdict against Jessie, it had to have decided that he either sustained no damages or that his own negligence was a proximate cause of his damages.

This third proposition places upon the railroad the heavy burden outlined by Judge Shake in [Flora v. Indiana Service Co., 222 Ind. App. 253, 256-257 (1944)]:

…[W]here a judgment may have been based upon either or any of two or more distinct facts, a party desiring to plead the judgment as an estoppel by verdict or finding upon the particular fact involved in a subsequent suit must show that it went upon that fact, or else the question will be open to a new contention. The estoppel of a judgment is only presumptively conclusive, when it appears that the judgment could not have been rendered without deciding the particular matter brought in question. It is necessary to look to the complete record to ascertain what was the question in issue.

The railroad argues that, because Jessie's evidence as to his loss of services and consortium was uncontroverted, the jury's verdict had to be based upon a finding of contributory negligence. Illinois Central Gulf made this same argument in the companion case in relation to a related issue and Jessie countered, as he does here, with his contention that, although the evidence was uncontroverted, it was minimal and, thus, could have caused the jury to find no compensable damages. We reviewed the complete record in the companion case and held that the jury verdict against Jessie in that cause could mean that he had failed his burden of proving compensable damages....

We hold that Illinois Central Gulf has failed its burden of showing that the judgment against Jessie in the prior action could not have been rendered without deciding that Jessie was contributorily negligent in the accident which precipitated the two lawsuits. Consequently, the trial court was correct in granting partial summary judgment estopping the railroad from denying its negligence and in limiting the issues at trial to whether Jessie was contributorily negligent, whether any such contributory negligence was a proximate cause of the accident, and whether Jessie sustained personal injuries and compensable damages....

FULL FAITH AND CREDIT

Full faith and credit requires that judicial proceedings shall have the same full faith and credit in every court within the U.S. as they have by law or usage in the courts of such state from which they are taken. It requires every state to give a judgment at least the res judicata effect which the judgment would be accorded in the state which rendered it.

Durfee v. Duke
375 U.S. 106 (1963)

Mr. Justice STEWART delivered the opinion of the Court.

The United States Constitution requires that "Full Faith and Credit shall be given in each State to the...judicial Proceedings of every other State." The case before us presents questions arising under this constitutional provision and under the federal statute enacted to implement it.

In 1956 the petitioners brought an action against the respondent in a Nebraska court to quiet title to certain bottom land situated on the Missouri River. The main channel of that river forms the boundary between the States of Nebraska and Missouri. The Nebraska court had jurisdiction over the subject matter of the controversy only if the land in question was in Nebraska. Whether the land was Nebraska land depended entirely upon a factual question—whether a shift in the river's course had been caused by avulsion or accretion.3 The respondent appeared in the Nebraska court and through counsel fully litigated the issues, explicitly contesting the court's jurisdiction over the subject matter of the controversy.4 After a hearing the court found the issues in favor of the petitioners and ordered that title to the land be quieted in them. The respondent appealed, and the Supreme Court of Nebraska affirmed the judgment after a trial de novo on the record made in the lower court. The State Supreme Court specifically found that the rule of avulsion was applicable, that the land in question was in Nebraska, that the Nebraska courts therefore had jurisdiction of the subject matter of the litigation, and that title to the land was in the petitioners. The respondent did not petition this Court for a writ of certiorari to review that judgment.

Two months later the respondent filed a suit against the petitioners in a Missouri court to quiet title to the same land. Her complaint alleged that the land was in Missouri. The suit was removed to a Federal District Court by reason of diversity of citizenship. The District Court after hearing evidence expressed the view that the land was in Missouri but held that all the issues had been adjudicated and determined in the Nebraska litigation, and that the judgment of the Nebraska Supreme Court was res judicata and "is now binding upon this court." The Court of Appeals reversed, holding that the District Court was not required to give full faith and credit to the Nebraska judgment, and that normal res judicata principles were not applicable because the controversy involved land and a court in Missouri was therefore free to retry the question of the Nebraska court's jurisdiction over the subject matter. We granted certiorari to consider a question important to the administration of justice in our federal system. For the reasons that follow, we reverse the judgment before us.

The constitutional command of full faith and credit, as implemented by Congress, requires that "judicial proceedings...shall have the same full faith and credit in every court within the United States...as they have by law or usage in the courts of such State...from which they are taken." Full faith and credit thus generally requires every State to give to a judgment at least the res judicata effect which the judgment would be accorded in the State which rendered it. "By the Constitutional provision for full faith and credit, the local doctrines of res judicata, speaking generally, become part of national jurisprudence, and therefore federal questions cognizable here." It is not questioned that the Nebraska courts would give full res judicata effect to the Nebraska judgment quieting title in the petitioners. It is the respondent's position, however, that whatever effect the Nebraska courts might give to the Nebraska judgment, the federal court in Missouri was free independently to determine whether the Nebraska court in fact had jurisdiction over the subject matter, i.e., whether the land in question was actually in Nebraska.

In support of this position the respondent relies upon the many decisions of this Court which have held that a judgment of a court in one State is conclusive upon the merits in a court in another State only if the court in the first State had power to pass on the merits—had jurisdiction, that is, to render the judgment.

As Mr. Justice Bradley stated the doctrine in the leading case of Thompson v. Whitman, 18 Wall. 457 [(1873)], "we think it clear that the jurisdiction of the court by which a judgment is rendered in any State may be questioned in a collateral proceeding in another State, notwithstanding the provision of the fourth article of the Constitution and the law of 1790, and notwithstanding the averments contained in the record of the judgment itself." The principle has been restated and applied in a variety of contexts.

However, while it is established that a court in one State, when asked to give effect to the judgment of a court in another State, may constitutionally inquire into the foreign court's jurisdiction to render that judgment, the modern decisions of this Court have carefully delineated the permissible scope of such an inquiry. From these decisions there emerges the general rule that a judgment is entitled to full faith and credit—even as to questions of jurisdiction—when the second court's inquiry disclosed that those questions have been fully and fairly litigated and finally decided in the court which rendered the original judgment.

With respect to questions of jurisdiction over the person,[8] this principle was unambiguously established in Baldwin v. Iowa State Traveling Men's Assn., 283 U.S.

522 [(1931)]. There it was held that a federal court in Iowa must give binding effect to the judgment of a federal court in Missouri despite the claim that the original court did not have jurisdiction over the defendant's person, once it was shown to the court in Iowa that that question had been fully litigated in the Missouri forum. "Public policy," said the Court, "dictates that there be an end of litigation; that those who have contested an issue shall be bound by the result of the contest, and that matters once tried shall be considered forever settled as between the parties. We see no reason why this doctrine should not apply in every case where one voluntarily appears, presents his case and is fully heard, and why he should not, in the absence of fraud, be thereafter concluded by the judgment of the tribunal to which he has submitted his cause." Following the Baldwin case, this Court soon made clear in a series of decisions that the general rule is no different when the claim is made that the original forum did not have jurisdiction over the subject matter. In each of these cases the claim was made that a court, when asked to enforce the judgment of another forum, was free to retry the question of that forum's jurisdiction over the subject matter. In each case this Court held that since the question of subject-matter jurisdiction had been fully litigated in the original forum, the issue could not be retried in a subsequent action between the parties....

In Treinies [v. Sunshine Mining Co., 308 U.S. 66 (1939)], the rule was succinctly stated: "One trial of an issue is enough. 'The principles of res judicata apply to questions of jurisdiction as well as to other issues,' as well to jurisdiction of the subject matter as of the parties."...

To be sure, the general rule of finality or jurisdictional determinations is not without exceptions. Doctrines of federal pre-emption or sovereign immunity may in some contexts be controlling. Kalb v. Feuerstein, 308 U.S. 433 [(1940)]; United States v. United States Fidelity Co., 309 U.S. 506 [(1940)].12 But no such overriding considerations are present here....

It is to be emphasized that all that was ultimately determined in the Nebraska litigation was title to the land in question as between the parties to the litigation there. Nothing there decided, and nothing that could be decided in litigation between the same parties or their privies in Missouri, could bind either Missouri or Nebraska with respect to any controversy they might have, now or in the future, as to the location of the boundary between them, or as to their respective sovereignty over the land in question. Either State may at any time protect its interest by initiating independent judicial proceedings here.

For the reasons stated, we hold in this case that the federal court in Missouri had the power and, upon proper averments, the duty to inquire into the jurisdiction of the Nebraska courts to render the decree quieting title to the land in the petitioners. We further hold that when that inquiry disclosed, as it did, that the jurisdictional issues had been fully and fairly litigated by the parties and finally determined in the Nebraska courts, the federal court in Missouri was correct in ruling that further inquiry was precluded. Accordingly the judgment of the Court of Appeals is reversed, and that of the District Court is affirmed.

It is so ordered.

> **4 Lessons from *Durfee* vs. *Duke***
>
> An unnotified party over whom the court lacks personal jurisdiction may collaterally challenge the resulting judgment.
>
> A litigant who contests jurisdiction (whether SMJ or PJ) is bound by the court's decision on jurisdiction.
>
> A defendant who does not appear may collaterally challenge personal jurisdiction.
>
> A defendant who appears but does not challenge PJ thereby waives her objection.

OBTAINING RELIEF FROM A JUDGMENT

United States v. Beggerly
524 U.S. 38 (1998)

Chief Justice REHNQUIST delivered the opinion of the Court.

[In assembling the lands for a National Seashore, the federal government in 1979 brought a quiet title action (the Adams litigation) in the Southern District of Mississippi against respondents. Adams turned on whether, before the date of the Louisiana Purchase in 1803, the land had been deeded to a private individual. If so, it would belong to Beggerly, and the United States would have to purchase it; if not, the U.S. government would already own it. That case settled on the eve of trial for a relatively modest sum, reflecting the uncertainty of Beggerly's title.] Judgment was entered based on this settlement agreement. In 1994, some 12 years after that judgment, respondents sued in the District Court to set aside the settlement agreement and obtain a damage award for the disputed land....

During discovery in the Adams litigation, respondents sought proof of their title to the land. Government officials searched public land records and told respondents that they had found nothing proving that any part of Horn Island had ever been granted to a private landowner. Even after the settlement in the Adams litigation, however, respondents continued to search for evidence of a land patent that supported their claim of title. In 1991 they hired a genealogical record specialist to conduct research in the National Archives in Washington. The specialist found materials that, according to her, showed that on August 1, 1781, Bernardo de Galvez, then the Governor General of Spanish Louisiana, granted Horn Island to [a private party].

Armed with this new information, respondents filed a complaint in the District Court on June 1, 1994. They asked the court to set aside the 1982 settlement agreement and award them damages....The District Court concluded that it was without jurisdiction to hear respondents' suit and dismissed the complaint.

The Court of Appeals reversed. It concluded that there were two jurisdictional bases for the suit. First, the suit satisfied the elements of an "independent action," as the term is used in Federal Rule of Civil Procedure 60(b)....

The Government's primary contention is that the Court of Appeals erred in concluding that it had jurisdiction over respondents' 1994 suit. It first attacks the lower court's conclusion that jurisdiction was established because the suit was an "independent action" within the meaning of Rule 60(b)....[The Government argued that although] the District Court had jurisdiction over the original Adams litigation because the United States was the plaintiff, 28 U.S.C. §1345, there was no statutory basis for the Beggerlys' 1994 action, and the District Court was therefore correct to have dismissed it.

We think the Government's position is inconsistent with the history and language of Rule 60(b). Prior to the 1937 adoption of the Federal Rules of Civil Procedure, the availability of relief from a judgment or order turned on whether the court was still in the same "term" in which the challenged judgment was entered....If the term had expired, resort had to be made to a handful of writs, the precise contours of which were "shrouded in ancient lore and mystery."...

The 1946 Amendment [to Rule 60]...made clear that nearly all of the old forms of obtaining relief from a judgment, i.e., coram nobis, coram vobis, audita querela, bills of review, and bills in the nature of review, had been abolished. The revision made equally clear, however, that one of the old forms, i.e., the "independent action,"[2] still survived. The Advisory Committee notes confirmed this, indicating that "if the right to make a motion is lost by the expiration of the time limits fixed in these rules, the only other procedural remedy is by a new or independent action to set aside a judgment upon those principles which have heretofore been applied in such an action."...

The Government is therefore wrong to suggest that an independent action brought in the same court as the original lawsuit requires an independent basis for jurisdiction. This is not to say, however, that the requirements for a meritorious independent action have been met here. If relief may be obtained through an independent action in a case such as this, where the most that may be charged against the Government is a failure to furnish relevant information that would at best form the basis for a Rule 60(b)(3) motion, the strict 1-year time limit on such motions would be set at naught. Independent actions must, if Rule 60(b) is to be interpreted as a coherent whole, be reserved for those cases of "injustices which, in certain instances, are deemed sufficiently gross to demand a departure" from rigid adherence to the doctrine of res judicata. Hazel-Atlas Glass Co. v. Hartford-Empire Co., 322 U.S. 238 (1944).

Such a case was Marshall v. Holmes, 141 U.S. 589 (1891), in which the plaintiff alleged that judgment had been taken against her in the underlying action as a result of a forged document. The Court said:

According to the averments of the original petition for injunction…the judgments in question would not have been rendered against Mrs. Marshall but for the use in evidence of the letter alleged to be forged. The case evidently intended to be presented by the petition is one where, without negligence, laches or other fault upon the part of petitioner, [respondent] has fraudulently obtained judgments which he seeks, against conscience, to enforce by execution.

The sense of these expressions is that, under the Rule, an independent action should be available only to prevent a grave miscarriage of justice. In this case, it should be obvious that respondents' allegations do not nearly approach this demanding standard. Respondents allege only that the United States failed to "thoroughly search its records and make full disclosure to the Court" regarding the Boudreau grant. Whether such a claim might succeed under Rule 60(b)(3) we need not now decide; it surely would work no "grave miscarriage of justice," and perhaps no miscarriage of justice at all, to allow the judgment to stand. We therefore hold that the Court of Appeals erred in concluding that this was a sufficient basis to justify the reopening of the judgment in the Adams litigation.

The judgment of the Court of Appeals is therefore reversed, and the case is remanded for further proceedings consistent with this opinion.

NOTES Two types of procedure to obtain relief from judgments are specified in FRCP 60. One procedure is by motion in the court and in the action in which the judgment was rendered. The other procedure is by a new or independent action to obtain relief from a judgment, which action may or may not be begun in the court which rendered the judgment. In each case there is a limit upon the time within which resort to a motion is permitted, and this time limit may not be enlarged under Rule 6(b). If the right to make a motion is lost by the expiration of the time limits fixed in these rules, the only other procedural remedy is by a new or independent action to set aside a judgment upon those principles which have heretofore been applied in such an action. Where the independent action is resorted to, the limitations of time are those of laches or statutes of limitations.

Fraud, whether intrinsic or extrinsic, misrepresentation, or other misconduct of an adverse party are express grounds for relief by motion under FRCP 60(b).

Made in the USA
San Bernardino, CA
05 August 2019